Chapter	Learning from Success	Learning from Mistakes	Learning from the Global Market
Chapter 11 *Conducting Market Research in a Global Environment*	Darlene Mann: Lessons from a Technology Entrepreneur	Bibbentuckers: How One Company's Mistake Lead to This Grand Success	Researching the Effect of China on Entrepreneurship
Chapter 12 *Distribution Channels and Pricing*	Starbucks: Charging More Can Make Sense	Hibco Plastics: When Exporting Saves a Company	Ermenegildo Zegna Group: Recognizing the Importance of Brand
Chapter 13 *Designing a Marketing Plan from Start-up Through Growth*	SwordsOnline: Give-Aways Drive Business Tips for Getting Your Company Noticed	Strategy Involves Trial and Error	
Chapter 14 *Designing the Business*	The Trapeze School: A High-Flying Start-up New Pig Corp.: Industrial Cleaning Products with a Sense of Humor	Jewel Jet: No to a Patent	
Chapter 15 *Managing Operations*	Mercedes Electric Supply: Suppliers Are Partners Baldridge Quality for Small Business	BeansWax: Home Based Business Keeps You Busy – Very Busy	
Chapter 16 *Cash Planning and Start-Up Financing*	The Klapmeier Brothers: Flying High	Knowing the Critical Factor	
Chapter 17 *Managing and Evaluating Financial Performance*	Advice from the Big Guys – and Gals	PTP Industries: Quick Rise, Faster Fall	
Chapter 18 *Financing Growth*	WiDeFi: Tapping a New Breed of Venture Capitalists	Navigating "No Man's Land"	
Chapter 19 *Risk Management*	Ciena: Rebounding from Disaster When Disaster Strikes	The Lessons of Hurricane Katrina	
Chapter 20 *Harvesting the Wealth*	Schlotzsky's: When Your Franchisor Files for Bankruptcy	eToys: Taking Success for Granted	Selling the Business to a Foreign Buyer

Growing and Managing a Small Business

AN ENTREPRENEURIAL PERSPECTIVE

Second Edition

Growing and Managing a Small Business

AN ENTREPRENEURIAL PERSPECTIVE

SECOND EDITION

Growing and Managing a Small Business

AN ENTREPRENEURIAL PERSPECTIVE

Kathleen R. Allen

University of Southern California
Marshall School of Business

Houghton Mifflin Company   Boston • New York

Dedication

This book is dedicated to educators who believe in the positive influence of small business in communities around the world and to small business owners who understand the transforming power of entrepreneurship for wealth creation.

Publisher: George Hoffman
Senior Sponsoring Editor: Lisé Johnson
Senior Development Editor: Amy Whitaker
Editorial Assistant/Associate: Amy Galvin
Associate Project Editor: Eric Moore
Composition Buyer: Chuck Dutton
Associate Manufacturing Buyer: Brian Pieragostini
Executive Marketing Manager: Steven W. Mikels
Marketing Specialist: Lisa E. Boden

Cover image: © ArtZone and Photodisc

Printed in the U.S.A.

Library of Congress Control Number: 2006922363

Instructor's examination copy
  ISBN-10: 0-618-73098-2
  ISBN-13: 978-0-618-73098-8
For orders, use student text ISBNs
  ISBN-10: 0-618-70509-0
  ISBN-13: 978-0-618-70509-2

1 2 3 4 5 6 7 8 9—EB—10 09 08 07 06

Brief Contents

v

Contents

Preface

Business owners today are bombarded with a bewildering array of management theories and practices all claiming to be the solution to whatever ails a business. For established companies, implementing these theories and practices is a challenge because it may mean radically changing the way that a company operates and go against a firmly engrained culture. But in a small company, particularly in a start-up, the task is much easier because a small business is not encumbered by existing policies and practices. Therefore, small business owners have a distinct advantage when it comes to adopting the latest proven management strategies and employing them effectively to grow their businesses.

The theme that is threaded throughout this book emerged from the convergence of information technology, globalization, and a dynamic marketplace. It recognizes that the marketplace has dramatically changed, making many traditional business approaches and strategies obsolete or at best ineffective. To compete and grow in this challenging environment, small businesses must do more than just give lip service to putting the customer at the center of the business and integrating total quality. Small business owners must become entrepreneurial in their view of the business; that is, they must be opportunistic, or constantly on the lookout for new ways to grow, compete, and serve the customer. They must innovate in all aspects of the business and boldly consider strategies that will take their businesses in new directions to make them sustainable over time.

The principles espoused in this book are the result of the international research of many experts; they are proven philosophies that add value to the company and to the customer. The key issues discussed in this book revolve around the customer, the product or service, the process, the organization, and leadership and are considered as interdependent components of an integrated organization. The topics presented have value for small business owners and entrepreneurs alike who need to be proactive and flexible to meet the demands of rapidly changing customer needs in a global marketplace. As an educator, I firmly believe that we must prepare our students to deal successfully with the changes occurring in business and organizational management today. That can happen only if we are willing to discard old thought in favor of new approaches that more accurately reflect this dynamic new environment and are proven to build successful and enduring companies.

Content and Organization

The book opens with Part I: Entrepreneurship and Small Business Management, which in two chapters provides an overview of the nature of entrepreneurship and small business and their roles in the economy, the entrepreneurial mindset, and the environment in which entrepreneurship occurs. Chapter 2 looks at entrepreneurial strategies for how to take a business from the first customer through multiple customers and multiple products and how this growth process affects structure and strategy. It also considers how ethics and social responsibility play an important role in business strategy.

Part II: Paths to Business Ownership focuses on the various ways to approach business ownership: starting a business from scratch, acquiring an existing business, stepping into a family business, and launching a high-technology venture. In addition, Chapter 7 looks at the legal structure of a business and how to choose a legal form.

Part III: Planning and Organizing the Business looks at the preparations required to start and grow a company, from developing an effective business plan to creating a management team that can execute the business plan to developing the right human resources plan.

Part IV: Marketing for Growth focuses on a customer-centered strategy for growing and marketing the company and addresses such topics as market research to study the customer and the competitive market, the marketing plan, distribution channels, and pricing.

Part V: Designing and Managing the Business begins with what must be considered when planning the location of the business and the development of the business's products, which is a unique part of the book that is typically not found in other texts. In conjunction with product development, this part also considers how to protect products and services through intellectual property strategies.

Part VI: Financial Planning addresses all the issues related to financial statement creation and analysis, managing cash flow, and accounts receivable and payable management. It also deals with strategies for financing for growth, including the venture capital market, private placement, the initial public offering, and strategic alliances.

The final part, Part VII: Planning for Change, discusses the critical issues of risk management and preparing for and enjoying harvesting the wealth created by the business through a variety of mechanisms that include selling the business, doing an employee stock ownership plan, going public, and merging with another company. This part also deals with business failure.

Special Features of the Text

Growing and Managing a Small Business includes several pedagogical features of value to instructors and students.

- *Learning Outcomes* list key topics at the beginning of each of the twenty chapters.
- *Chapter Opening Case* at the start of each chapter explores real entrepreneurs' experiences with growing businesses. Each reflects the content of the chapter with which it is associated.
- *Chapter Closing Case* at the end of each chapter provides a look at yet another entrepreneur and how he or she managed the topic featured in that chapter. These cases are designed to provoke discussion and consideration of what to do next.

- *Learning from Success* is a boxed feature that provides concrete examples of successful entrepreneurs with key lessons learned at the end of many examples.

- *Learning from Mistakes* is a boxed feature that highlights the experiences of entrepreneurs who have come through challenges that relate to the topics in the chapter. The lessons learned by the entrepreneur are presented at the end of many of these features.

- *Learning from the Global Market* is a boxed feature that provides glimpses into topics surrounding international entrepreneurship.

- *Issues for Review and Discussion* at the end of each chapter offers questions that provoke discussion on topics in the chapter.

- *Experiencing Entrepreneurship* activities at the end of each chapter give students a chance to experience entrepreneurship firsthand by getting them out in the marketplace to find information and interact with entrepreneurs.

The Teaching/Learning Package

In addition to the pedagogical aids in the text itself, supplemental materials are provided for instructors and students.

- An *Instructor's Resource Manual* features suggestions for planning the course, learning objectives, lecture outlines, instructor's notes for the case studies, suggested answers to end-of-chapter questions, and supplementary lecture material that goes beyond what is presented in the text.

- A *Test Bank* contains over eighty questions per chapter, including true/false, multiple-choice, and essay questions that assess basic understanding as well as application of the concepts. A computerized version of the Test Bank is also available.

- *Videos* that explore various aspects of entrepreneurship provide additional real-world examples. An accompanying guide provides tips for using the videos in the classroom.

- *An Interactive Website* that will be expanded and updated as we receive feedback from our customers includes materials for both students and instructors. The student area of the site contains updates of resources and text materials, links to other useful sites on the web, video minicases, and examples of feasibility studies and business plans that can be used as models. The instructor's area contains the downloadable PowerPoint slides, updates, suggested answers to the materials on the student site, and additional teaching tips and information to enhance the learning experience. We look forward to receiving your feedback so that this website will evolve into a truly useful tool. Visit the site by clicking on *Business* at Houghton Mifflin's College Division Home at http://www.hmco.com/college.

Acknowledgments

Over the course of several drafts of manuscript, I had the assistance of many fine reviewers. I am indebted to those people who teach the entrepreneurship course and were willing to share their ideas and provide constructive feedback:

Edmund Clark, Northeastern University

Judy Dietert, Texas State University – San Marcos

Jason Duan, Midwestern State University

Connie Marie Gaglio, San Francisco State University

Charles Toftoy, George Washington University

Eugene Muscat, University of San Francisco

No author has ever worked with a finer publishing staff than the one I have at Houghton Mifflin. My gratitude for a very pleasant and rewarding experience goes to Amy Whitaker, Senior Development Editor; Lisé Johnson, Senior Sponsoring Editor; and Eric Moore, Associate Project Editor.

A book of this size cannot be completed alone. In addition to the tireless work of the staff at Houghton Mifflin, I appreciate the excellent case studies contributed by my Case Western colleague Edward Caner and to all the entrepreneurs featured in the minicases who inspired me with their courage, energy, and creativity. Thank you, too, to Mari Florence, for all of her fine work on the supplementary material.

My family keeps me going and striving to be better. Thank you, Rob, Jaime, and Greg. And as always, thanks to my husband, John, who makes my world go 'round.

Kathleen R. Allen

PART I

Entrepreneurship and Small Business Management

CHAPTER 1

Entrepreneurship and Small Business

Only those who will risk going too far
can possibly find out how far one can go.

T. S. Eliot

LEARNING OUTCOMES

- Discuss the roles of entrepreneurship and small business in the economy.
- Describe the global opportunity for entrepreneurs.
- Explain the entrepreneurial mindset and how entrepreneurs approach business ownership.
- List the various types of entrepreneurs.
- Discuss what must be considered before deciding to become a business owner.

Moosejaw Mountaineering

Robert Wolfe never thought that he would be heading a company that produced over $10 million in annual revenues. In the early 1990s, Wolfe graduated from college with a political science degree. What can you do with a political science degree? Well, you can become a backpacking guide. Wolfe and his close friend were avid mountain people, so deciding to support their passion by serving as guides made sense. It wasn't long before they discovered that they consistently recommended one particular store to people looking for backpacking and climbing equipment. It occurred to them that they knew as much about the business as anyone. One day in 1992, the pair decided that instead of giving business to someone else, it was time to get some of that business for themselves.

The two friends began with a 2,200–square foot store in tiny Keego Harbor, Michigan, where they hoped to provide high-end equipment and supplies for serious mountaineers. This concept was not about a trend or fad; it was about serving the die-hard hiker with the best equipment. They named the company Moosejaw Mountaineering and used suppliers for the initial funding. Then they staffed the store with wilderness experts, something no one else was doing. Soon, however, Wolfe's partner and longtime backpacking friend found that he was not passionate about the retail business and sold his interest to Wolfe.

Growing the Business

Undaunted by the departure of his friend, Wolfe quickly opened a second store in East Lansing, Michigan, and six additional stores soon after. It is often the case that when an entrepreneur attempts to grow quickly, especially in a high-overhead business like retail, he or she runs into serious cash-flow problems, and Moosejaw was no exception. The company had seasonal cash-flow needs that required a significant line of credit, particularly because they had to build up their inventory to meet end-of-year demand. Because Wolfe's family had a long-standing relationship with Merrill Lynch, he leveraged that relationship and was able to secure an increased line of credit to better manage the company's working capital.

Wolfe had three goals for his enterprise: (1) to expand the stores, (2) to boost the mail-order business, and (3) to build the brand. What he didn't expect was that Moosejaw's biggest expansion would come in the mid-1990s when the World Wide Web began providing a way for people to buy online. Wolfe didn't know anything about the Internet, but he did see the potential for the Web to overtake their mail-order business. In 1997 Wolfe's brother, Jeffrey, joined the company to make Moosejaw a serious player in the e-commerce business. Their online operating profit was becoming substantially greater than the retail store profit, and they were reaching a global market as well, so they wanted to take advantage of this portion of their business. They spent a lot of time working on the relationships with their suppliers who in turn made sure that Moosejaw appeared on the suppliers' sites 90 percent of the time when a customer searched on where to buy. In addition, because their retail stores hold large quantities of inventory, they were able to fill about 30 percent of their online orders from the retail inventory in their six stores. Today, the online portion of the business accounts for two-thirds of annual sales. As an added bonus, Wolfe sees the Internet as a great way to have fun with his business at low cost. For example, one Christmas he had an "All Pink Sale," and that theme and message was splattered over the website. To learn more about Moosejaw, visit www.moosejaw.com.

Advising the Entrepreneur

1. Would Wolfe's concept work as a start-up today? Given the increased competition in this market, what would be your entry strategy?

2. Wolfe seemed to be lucky in 1992, starting the business with very little planning. Would anything have changed had he done some planning?

3. As he positions the company to face increased global competition, what does Wolfe need to consider?

Sources: "Robert Wolfe's Key Move: Putting the Web to Work," *Startup Nation* (2005), www.startupnation.com; Merrill Lynch, "Moosejaw Mountaineering—Reinventing the Outdoors" (March 2004), http://askmerrill.ml.com; www.moosejaw.com.

If you dream about spending every day working on something about which you are passionate, small business ownership may provide the fulfillment of that dream. If you imagine taking charge of your life so that you have as much control over the work you do as you have over the other parts of your life, entrepreneurship may be the means to do just that. Every day in the United States and around the world, thousands of people are discovering that entrepreneurship is the best path to wealth creation and independence. Entrepreneurship benefits not only the individuals who follow that path but also the communities in which they do business and the economy in general. Entrepreneurs are the driving force behind the technological change that produces economic growth. They are able to recognize new customer segments, new customer needs, and new ways to manufacture and distribute, and they have the courage to create new companies to bring new products and services to market. These companies generate new jobs for the communities in which they operate and new products and services for the global community that they serve.

Today, even the smallest business is part of a rapidly growing global marketplace whether it wants to be or not. Its customers enjoy unprecedented choice in where they can do business and in the variety of products and services available to them. The smallest community likely has Internet access that brings the world to its doorstep. Local agricultural areas in Florida and California that once dominated the fresh-produce market are competing today with fresh fruit and vegetables from Chile, New Zealand, and other parts of the world. Even service companies cannot escape competition from the global community. The Internet has fostered the development of low-cost service companies in India, for example, that offer their programming services economically over the Internet to all parts of the globe.

Entrepreneurs are the primary mechanism by which demand is turned into supply. Entrepreneurs are also the principal source of venture capital to fuel high-growth companies and private investors who provide seed capital to emerging companies. The most successful and innovative entrepreneurs change society as we know it. In the early 1990s, when Marc Andreesen developed the graphical interface Mosaic (which later become Netscape Communications) to make the emerging World Wide Web user friendly and Sky Dayton created Earthlink to make it easy for the average user to connect to the Internet, they had a profound impact on business and on people's daily lives.

All these economic and societal benefits start with a small business. Small business has been an integral part of American history and is serving as an economic stimulus in developing nations around the world. In the past, it was relatively easy to start and grow a small business and simply focus on a local niche. But the world has changed, and small business owners must change with it. Today, small business owners need to think like entrepreneurs if they are going to successfully maneuver the minefields of a dynamic marketplace. This is an exciting time for small business, an opportunity to share in the wealth that is being created as a result of change. This book takes an entrepreneurial approach to small business creation and management in the firm belief that, for small business to not only survive but also thrive, small business entrepreneurs must innovate, create new value for their customers, and discover creative ways to grow.

This chapter provides an overview of the role of entrepreneurship and small business in the economy, the nature of small business, the global opportunity, and what needs to be considered before deciding to become an entrepreneur.

ENTREPRENEURIAL VENTURES AND SMALL BUSINESSES

In this book, we make a clear distinction between small businesses and entrepreneurial ventures. Generally, small businesses and entrepreneurial ventures are two different types of businesses whose owners have different intentions. **Small businesses typically start small and stay relatively small, providing a lifestyle, a job, and a modest level of income for their owners and having little impact in their industries.** They are often referred to as "mom-and-pop" businesses, suggesting family-owned businesses. (However, many mom-and-pop businesses have grown to become substantial firms with significant impact in their industries. Marriott Corporation and Wal-Mart are notable examples.) **Entrepreneurial ventures,** on the other hand, have founders with different motives and goals. These founders are innovative and growth oriented. Their purpose is not to create a job or an occupation for themselves but to create value and wealth that they can harvest at some future date. Sylvan Learning Systems, Inc., is an outstanding example of an entrepreneurial venture. Douglas Becker and R. Christopher Hoehn-Saric acquired this company and, in just five years with their drive and vision, turned it into one of the fastest-growing and most innovative educational companies in the United States.

Although throughout this text we distinguish between small businesses and entrepreneurial ventures whenever that distinction is important, we use the terms *small-business owner* and *entrepreneur* interchangeably because this book emphasizes the importance of small business owners thinking like entrepreneurs.

Entrepreneurship and Small Business in the Economy

Virtually every company starts out relatively small, but not every company stays small. Unfortunately, most of the research on entrepreneurship does not distinguish between those businesses that remain small and those that grow to become substantial companies. In fact, there is considerable disagreement about what actually constitutes a small business. The Small Business Administration (SBA) traditionally has defined a small business as one employing fewer than 500 employees. However, more than 90 percent of all businesses employ fewer than 500 workers, and most people find it difficult to think of a 400-person firm or even a 200-person firm as "small." In contrast, the Organization for Economic Cooperation and Development (OECD) and the U.S. Chamber of Commerce prefer to designate as a small business any firm employing fewer than 100 people. In the minds of many business owners, however, even a firm with 100 employees does not seem small. Given the current trend toward downsizing, outsourcing, and **virtual companies,** the relevance of using the number of employees as a defining factor for small business has been called into question. How does one measure the size of a company by number of employees when the company **outsources** (uses contract workers rather than permanent employees) for most of its primary functions such as manufacturing, distribution, and possibly marketing? In this book, we employ the definition of the OECD and designate small businesses as those with fewer than 100 employees.

Figure 1.1 depicts the range of categories of small business from the many microbusinesses to the relatively small number of high-growth ventures, or **gazelles.** The term *gazelles* was coined by David Birch of the research company Cognetics to explain young firms with at least $100,000 in revenues that grow at a rate of 20 percent a year for four years. Many of these firms, which number about 350,000 at any

FIGURE 1.1 Categories of Small Businesses

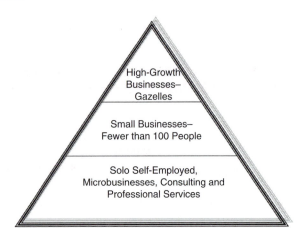

TABLE 1.1 Number of U.S. Firms by Size

	Number of Firms	Payroll (in thousands of dollars)
Firms with no employees (as of March 12, 2001)	703,837	34,289,996
1 to 99 employees	4,851,266	1,193,871,732
100 to 499 employees	85,304	539,384,914
500 employees or more	17,367	2,221,539,681

Source: *2002 County Business Patterns and 2002 Economic Census*, U.S. Census Bureau, http://www.census.gov/csd/susb/susb02.htm.

time, are highly visible technology firms, but about 30 percent of all gazelles operate in the wholesale and retail trades as well.[1] This category is generally where the most entrepreneurial-type firms are found.

The United States is unique for its entrepreneurial culture that supports the development of small businesses. It is estimated that about 52 percent of the adult population in the United States is involved in business ownership through owning a full- or part-time business, taking steps to start a business, or investing in another's business.[2] About 11 percent of working Americans over the age of 18 report business ownership as their primary economic activity, and about 18 percent report that they have made an investment in a business.

Table 1.1 breaks out the number of firms in the United States by size. It is interesting to note that the number of firms with fewer than 100 employees is fifty-four times greater than the number of firms with more than 100 employees. Looking at which industries attract small business provides a picture of diversity in

FIGURE 1.2 Small Business by Industry

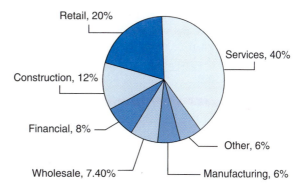

Source: "Major Industries by NAICS Codes," SBA's Office of Advocacy, 1997–2002, http://www.sba.gov/advo/research/data.html. Based on data provided by the U.S. Census Bureau, Statistics of U.S. Business. Percentages do not add to 100% because of rounding.

types of small businesses. Figure 1.2 presents the distribution of industries in which there are businesses with fewer than 500 employees. As expected, services and retail dominate. Delving deeper into the services category provides a picture of the types of services that small business owners typically offer. In order of size, they are as follows:

- Health services (physicians, nursing facilities, at-home care, and the like)
- Business services (advertising, programming, personnel, and so forth)
- Engineering, accounting, research management, and related services
- Membership organizations (trade associations, unions)
- Personal services (janitorial, hair salons)

Although small businesses comprise the largest proportion of businesses globally, it is those small business owners *with intentions to grow* that actually provide the majority of net new jobs to the economy (see the gazelles in Figure 1.1). Pro-growth business owners are driven to overcome the challenges in the marketplace and to interpret their economic world in ways that allow them to grow.[3]

There has been a lot of argument about the degree to which small businesses affect job creation. The SBA claims that from 1996 to 1997 (the most recent figures available) small businesses created 75.8 percent of net new jobs. Yet, many people caution that it is difficult to say that small business in general creates a certain percentage of new jobs. For one thing, recall that the SBA counts any business under 500 employees as a small business. For another, it is really just the fast-growth segment of small businesses that actually produces most of the new jobs. Birch's research reports that from 1995 to 1999 gazelles "generated practically as many jobs (10.7 million) as the entire U.S. Economy (11.1 million)."[4] About half of those gazelles have more than 1,000 employees. So what can be concluded from this debate? It appears that most new jobs come from new companies and new divisions of larger companies. New companies, for the most part, start small, so it is logical to assert that small business does in fact have an impact on the economy through new job creation.

Benefits of Small Business Ownership

In general, research has discovered that small business owners are a happy lot. Overwhelmingly, the public perception is that small business owners work harder than other people and that owning a small business is the best way to get ahead.[5] Although they work long hours and endure more stress, the benefits seem to outweigh the negatives. Some of the benefits of small business ownership include the following:

1. *Control of One's Destiny* Working for someone else leaves an individual at the mercy of the needs of that person, which is not compatible with the personalities of most small business owners. People who start their own business tend to be "control freaks." They want to be in charge of their destiny and take responsibility for what happens to them. Small business ownership provides the opportunity to do that because the owner of a business determines the destiny of that business, who is employed by the business, and how the business operates, among many other tasks.

2. *Wealth Creation* As discussed at the beginning of this chapter, entrepreneurship is the primary vehicle for wealth creation. Business owners not only create well-paying jobs for themselves, but they also amass wealth in the value of the businesses they create that can be harvested through a sale, initial public offering, or other liquidity event. In 2004 a record 8.2 million households in the U.S. had a net worth over $1 million (excluding their primary home). The groundbreaking work of Thomas Stanley and William Danko presented in their best-selling book *The Millionaire Next Door* revealed that the average American millionaire earned his or her wealth through small businesses such as auctioneer services, mobile home–park ownership, or paving contractor enterprises. It is notable that self-employed people comprise less than 20 percent of all the workers in America, but they account for two-thirds of the millionaires.[6] Entrepreneurs typically do not start businesses for the money, but they do know that, if they are passionate about what they are doing and become the best at it, their business will provide a supernormal return on investment.

3. *Fun while Working* One of the biggest advantages of business ownership is that owners create the organizational culture of their businesses; that is, they get to choose the people they work with and design the way the organization operates. This means that the entrepreneur's values are reflected in the organizational culture, so work blends smoothly with the entrepreneur's personal life. In other words, work doesn't feel like work. Entrepreneurs generally wake up every day eager to get to work because the work is so satisfying.

4. *Doing Good while Doing Well* Small business owners as a group are some of the most respected people in any community because they are generally very involved in their communities. It's a highly symbiotic relationship. The more a business owner gives back to the community through such activities as sponsoring sports leagues, being active in the local Chamber of Commerce, and creating new jobs, the more the business benefits from the patronage of the community.

Small Business Challenges

For all the benefits of small business ownership, owners face a number of challenges. Some of these challenges are similar to those faced by their larger counterparts, but others are uniquely their own and the result of size and limited resources. Listed from most critical to least, the top-ten problems that small business owners face as reported by the National Federation of Independent Businesses (NFIB) are the following:

1. Cost of health insurance
2. Cost and availability of liability insurance
3. Workers' compensation
4. Cost of natural gas, propane, gasoline, diesel, fuel oil
5. Federal taxes on business income
6. Property taxes (real, personal, or inventory)
7. Cash flow
8. State taxes on business income
9. Unreasonable government regulations
10. Electricity costs (rates)

It is interesting to note that health insurance costs are a "critical" issue for 65.6 percent of small business owners, which is the highest percentage reported for any problem in the NFIB survey's twenty-two-year history.[7]

If we consider the least severe problems for small businesses, beginning with the least severe, they are the following:

1. Exporting products/services
2. Competing with government or nonprofit organizations
3. Competing with Internet businesses
4. Dealing with increased national security procedures (a new problem in the 2004 survey)
5. Competing with imported products
6. Obtaining short-term (less than twelve months or revolving) business loans
7. Winning contracts from federal/state/local governments
8. Obtaining long-term (five years or more) business loans
9. Protecting intellectual property
10. Finding cost-effective mail service

Clearly, rising costs and taxes are the two biggest areas of concern for small-business owners. But despite these challenges, small business owners seem to be an optimistic group. The NFIB releases its Optimism Index monthly. This index records how confident small business owners are about the economy and its effect on their business prospects. The base year for the index (100) is 1986 when the real gross domestic product grew 3.5 percent and inflation stood at 3 percent. In June 2005 after a five-month decline, the Optimism Index rose to 100.8 from a base of 100. Hiring by small business owners was strong, with 53 percent of owners in a hiring mode, suggesting that businesses were looking to grow.[8]

Small Business Failure

Small business owners cannot always meet the challenges they face, which sometimes lead to business failure. Any aspiring business owner would be well advised to consider

LEARNING FROM MISTAKES

The Case of Streamline, Inc.

Tim DeMello's business concept was a variation on a theme. The theme was home delivery of groceries and services that would allow customers to place orders by midnight and receive their goods in a supplied refrigerator in their garages or basements by 6:00 p.m. on their designated day. The business model of DeMello's company, Streamline, Inc., called for 70 percent of sales to come from groceries and the rest from higher-margin products and services such as dry cleaning, shoe repair, and so forth. In addition, Streamline would enjoy the advantage of not having the high overhead costs of retail space. For the business model to work, however, customers needed to order regularly once a week. One of the initial concerns going into this business was whether customers would be satisfied with once-a-week delivery and not being home when the groceries were delivered.

By June 1999, Web shopping had exploded, and Streamline bought into the dot-com frenzy, changing its name to Streamline.com just before doing an initial public offering. Streamline raised $45 million in that offering, but in the first six months of 2000, it lost $23 million and its stock price plummeted from its $10 initial offering price to $3 per share. In September of that year, Streamline's primary

competitor Peapod acquired its assets and in November of that same year, Streamline closed its doors. Peapod's acquisition of Streamline does not mean that Peapod is out of the woods when it comes to long-term success. Peapod benefited from the enormous amount of capital available during the dot-com era, but it still needs to prove that online grocers can make a profit while operating warehouses around the country and in the face of major chains like Safeway entering the game.

The reason for Streamline's failure? DeMello forgot a cardinal rule of entrepreneurship: knowing that the customer is everything. People tend to be very particular about the vegetables, fruits, and meats that they purchase. Not many people are comfortable letting a stranger pick their food items. Furthermore, the margins in the grocery business are miniscule at best, which means that high volumes are essential. It is far more difficult to achieve those volumes in a new type of home-delivery service.

Lesson Learned: *Know your customer*.

Sources: J. A. Redmond, "Is Your Company at Risk?" *Inc.* (November 2000), www.inc.com; J. D. Macht, "Errand Boy," *Inc.* (November 1996), www.inc.com.

---

the risk of failing before making the decision to start or acquire a business. Some of the major risks for the small business owner include the following:

1. *Incorrect Estimation of the Market* A business is not a business without customers. It is one thing to come up with a great business idea that is validated by the enthusiasm of friends and family. It is quite another to make sure that there are enough other people interested in the business so that it has a chance to thrive. Lack of sufficient market research is often the major contributor to business failure in the first couple years, but market research is a manageable risk. If entrepreneurs conduct independent market research on their customers, they can eliminate much of this risk. (Chapter 11 focuses on helping entrepreneurs understand how to conduct effective market research to increase their chances of success.)

2. *Uncertainty* Even entrepreneurs who do thorough market research are lucky if their forecasts about market demand are correct 50 percent of the time. Today's global marketplace is constantly changing, and entrepreneurs must be prepared to accept uncertainty as a way of life. Successful entrepreneurs always have a plan B and keep their eyes open for the opportunities that always come with change.

3. *No Salary for the Owner* It is not uncommon in new businesses for the owner to pour all the early revenues back into the business to grow it. The owner is always the last to be paid, so it is important to prepare for business ownership by building up savings to cover the owner's personal expenses until the business can afford to pay the owner a salary.

4. *Loss of Investment* If starting or acquiring a business carries with it significant risk, the prospective business owner must be prepared for the possibility that the business might fail. Therefore, it is prudent to protect personal assets so that if the business does fail the owner will not be completely devastated. If the owner has received outside investment capital for the business, it is important to take money only from people who can afford to lose it. Unfortunately, friends' and family's money is the most expensive money that entrepreneurs can take because if the business fails, they pay for it for the rest of their lives.

5. *Long Hours and High Stress* Although there have been cases of successful entrepreneurs starting their businesses part time, the vast majority of business owners work approximately sixty to eighty hours a week in the beginning to get their businesses into survival mode. Stress in the early days of the business comes principally from uncertainty about demand for the product or service being offered. If the business has employees, there is stress when revenues do not materialize and employees must be paid. More than one entrepreneur has used a personal credit card to make sure that payroll was met until revenues were collected.

6. *Disillusionment* If this is the first business, it is likely that the entrepreneur will go through a period of disillusionment as unforeseen obstacles begin to appear. The best-laid plans may not pan out, and the entrepreneur may wonder if the right decision was made in starting or acquiring the business. Understanding that becoming discouraged is a normal part of the process helps the entrepreneur be patient and realize that all the planning and forethought will eventually pay off. Perseverance is a strong suit with entrepreneurs, and it helps them get through the inevitable downtimes.

Businesses that fold usually do so in one of two ways. **Failures** are firms that go out of business or reorganize through Chapter 11 bankruptcy, resulting in losses to creditors. **Discontinuances** are firms that cease operations with no outstanding debts. Failures include (1) ceasing to exist (discontinuance for any reason), (2) closing or a change in ownership, (3) filing for bankruptcy, (4) closing to limit losses, and (5) failing to reach financial goals. In 2000, the SBA reported that about 550,000 small businesses closed and that the business failure rate for one-person businesses was about 38.2 percent. These figures are not very encouraging unless some additional factors are considered. In general, if a small business makes it through the first two years of operation, its chance of succeeding increases with each passing year. This is generally because many business failures are casual businesses, or businesses on paper, in which either no significant effort was expended or it was determined that the concept was not feasible. An enormous number of these casual businesses are reported to the IRS on tax returns, so they also end up in the business-failure statistics. The Business Information Tracking Series (BITS) reports that about half of new employer firms survive beyond four years and about a third of closed businesses were successful at closure.[9]

For reasons explained earlier, out of the businesses that fail, only about one in seven closed with unpaid debts. So if a business doesn't close due to bankruptcy, what other factors would precipitate a closure? Business owners often close their businesses because they want to do something else, including starting a different business or retiring. In other cases, the owner has died without providing for succession. But, according to Dun & Bradstreet statistics, 88.7 percent of all business failures are due to management mistakes. Here are some of those mistakes:

- Owning a business for the wrong reasons
- Relying on advice from family and friends
- Underestimating how long it will take to be successful
- The entrepreneur's ego
- Poor market research
- Falling in love with the product or service
- Lack of experience with financial issues
- No clear focus
- Irrational exuberance
- Too much money

One might question how "too much money" could hurt a business. When entrepreneurs start with a lot of money, they tend to be less careful about how they make decisions because they know if they make a bad decision they have the money to recover. There is a fine balance between having too much money and not having enough.

The flip side of failure is survival. The SBA conducted a ten-year longitudinal study of companies of all sizes (including sole proprietorships) that were founded in 1976 and revealed some interesting outcomes. The survival rates for companies of all sizes, including sole proprietors, were dismal, from 76 percent after two years of business to 21 percent after ten years. On the bright side, if those companies survived long enough to hire employees, their survival rates went up significantly, from 94 percent after two years to 62 percent after ten years.[10] The most recent SBA findings from BITS show that 66 percent of new employers survive two years or more; 50 percent survive four years or more; and 40 percent survive six years or more.

So, what can an entrepreneur do to improve the chances of succeeding? The SBA research finds that the likelihood of small businesses surviving goes up if they are employer firms, they have starting capital greater than $50,000, the owner has a college degree, and the business is being started for personal reasons. Survivability is also increased by previous experience owning a business, starting with a team, and starting from home. The goal of this text is to give business owners the information and skills required to increase the probability of success. In addition, going through the process of writing a business plan prepares the entrepreneur as much as possible for all contingencies. (The business plan is discussed in detail in Chapter 5.)

THE ENTREPRENEURIAL PORTRAIT

Much has been written about entrepreneurs, what makes them tick, and what makes them different from everyone else. In recent times, a celebrity status has accrued to the likes of Microsoft cofounder Bill Gates, domestic diva Martha Stewart, and Internet innovator Meg Whitman of eBay. This notoriety is evident in the proliferation of magazines, books, and television documentaries that examine every detail of the entrepreneur's business and personal life. Entrepreneurship has become the new breeding ground for legends, superstars, and heroes.

Over the years, academic researchers have tried to identify the characteristics, personalities, and behaviors of entrepreneurs in a vain attempt to categorize, define, and analyze them. It has been an impossible task largely because entrepreneurs seem to defy categorization. They come in all shapes, sizes, and colors, with a diverse range of motivations and intentions. However, these researchers have found that entrepreneurs all have one fundamental characteristic: variously called "fire in the belly," "intense desire," or "the burning gut"; it is essentially passion. Passion drives entrepreneurs to seek opportunity, take risk, and keep going forward when all around them are saying, "It'll never work."

Along with passion, entrepreneurs commonly display several other characteristics. For example, research has generally concluded that entrepreneurs are not high-risk takers; they are, in fact, moderate-risk takers.[11] They don't leave their future to chance; on the contrary, entrepreneurs tend to identify the risks inherent in their ventures and then look for ways to minimize those risks. At the same time, however, security is not something they consciously seek to achieve because most entrepreneurs understand that opportunity lies in a changing environment. In that sense, they see change and the risks associated with it as a positive. Research has identified two major sources of uncertainty that entrepreneurs attempt to minimize: (1) uncertainty about market demand and (2) uncertainty regarding their own capabilities.[12] They tend to be risk averse when it comes to market demand but very confident about their own abilities.

Entrepreneurs seem to have a tremendous drive to succeed. They enjoy problem solving and setting goals for themselves and their businesses. Consequently, they also have a strong desire to be their own bosses, to have total control of their lives and the work they do. This need for independence, however, often makes it difficult for entrepreneurs to delegate authority to others. In most businesses, the ability of an entrepreneur to give up the reins of the business to those who have the management skills needed to take it beyond the start-up and growth phases is a crisis point that must be recognized. Failure to do so has often led to the downfall of the company.

Parallel to the need for independence is the entrepreneur's typically high internal locus of control. **Locus of control** refers to the degree to which people believe events in their lives are within their control as opposed to being under the control of external forces. Many studies have found a strong internal locus of control among entrepreneurs.[13] This leads to more proactive behavior in comparison to the reactive behavior of people with an external locus.

Finally, because of the inherent nature of the entrepreneurial environment, entrepreneurs tend to have a higher tolerance for ambiguity and change. They seem to prefer environments that offer more challenge and opportunity.

It is important to note that these characteristics are based on average tendencies. For every entrepreneur who has one or more of them, there is one who doesn't yet is successful. This is the dilemma faced by those trying to characterize the entrepreneur.

Researchers have also looked at the entrepreneur's experience prior to starting the new venture and have found that entrepreneurs tend to start businesses in industries with which they are familiar or in which they have some knowledge about the product, service, or market.[14] But experience in and of itself has not been shown definitively to increase the chances of success in starting and growing the business.

Of all the behaviors considered as particular to the entrepreneur, the entrepreneur as decision maker or problem solver has pervaded the research literature. Contributing much to the understanding of the relationship between decision making and environmental uncertainty, the seminal work of G. L. S. Shackle rejected mainstream economic theory and determinism for their failure to recognize the importance of time and uncertainty as a factor in entrepreneurial decision making.[15] In other words, what induces someone to be enterprising is essentially different from what induces someone to avoid uncertainty. Decision making under conditions of uncertainty is a way of life for most entrepreneurs.

Entrepreneurs as resource acquirers and creators of value are another behavior often found in the definition of entrepreneur.[16] And, of course, the opportunistic nature of entrepreneurs can't be denied. According to Stanley Kaish and Benjamin Gilad, "Opportunity, by definition, is unknown until discovered or created."[17] I. M. Kirzner calls this ability "entrepreneurial alertness."[18] In their study, Kaish and Gilad found that "entrepreneurs do seem to expose themselves to more information, and their alertness takes them to the less obvious places."[19]

Today, entrepreneurship is not just an art practiced solely by people who intuitively understand the nature of it. On the contrary, potential entrepreneurs can learn and practice a great many of the skills and practices needed to succeed in an entrepreneurial venture. More people are studying the "art" and systematizing it so that everyone can understand what it takes to be an entrepreneur. "Professional entrepreneurs don't just do, they understand what they're doing."[20] However, the one characteristic of entrepreneurs that can't be taught is the passion, the desire to accomplish something at all costs. That is an inherent characteristic that reveals itself when an individual discovers a business concept that he or she cannot let go of. Entrepreneurs who find themselves thinking, plotting, and planning day and night how to make a particular business concept happen have probably found their passion. That passion will carry them through the tough times ahead.

Assembling what is known about the entrepreneur reveals someone who recognizes an opportunity and has the passion and perseverance to put together the necessary resources to develop that opportunity into a concept, test its feasibility, and turn that feasible concept into a business. We also see someone who knows how to create value, value that can be measured and converted to wealth. This ability to create value provides a variety of exit strategies that enable the entrepreneur to realize the wealth that the business has created by selling a portion of his or her stock, selling the business outright, doing an initial public offering of stock, or merging with another company.

The Many Faces of Entrepreneurs

Today, much is known about the diversity of individuals who choose to become entrepreneurs. In this section, we explore what is currently known about women and minority entrepreneurs as well as the various types of entrepreneurs.

Women-Owned Businesses The rate at which women are starting businesses is increasing. In general, this growth stems from women's dissatisfaction with corporate life and the desire to have more control over how they balance work and family. The Center for Women's Business Research estimates that as of 2004:

> *nearly half (48%) of all privately-held businesses in the U.S. are owned 50% or more by women, for a total of 10.6 million enterprises. This includes 6.7 million majority (51% or more) women-owned firms, and another 4.0 million equally (50-50) women- and men-owned firms.*[21]

A World-Class Venture in the Recording Industry

You may not think of a rock group as a world-class business. But world-class entrepreneurship is almost a necessity to succeed in the intensely competitive recording industry.

From 1965 until the death of lead singer Jerry Garcia thirty years later in 1995, the Grateful Dead proved to be much more than a traveling 1960s retro show. In fact, the Grateful Dead is recognized as being responsible for many innovations that are now widely accepted practices in the music industry:

1. In the 1970s, they pioneered the use of a floor pedal on the microphone on stage, allowing the singers to turn off their microphones with their feet when they weren't singing. This prevented unwanted sounds, such as talking between songs or during instrumentals, from being carried to the audience.

2. They were the first to set up their own mail-order system to sell tickets to hard-core fans. About 50 percent of their tickets were sold in this manner.

3. Their extensive merchandising operation involving promotional items has been emulated throughout the music industry.

4. Against tradition, they initiated the notion of touring even when they weren't bringing out a new album. They learned from their customers, the fans, that more important than the music was the event of being at the concert.

5. They pioneered the "cool opener" at stadium concerts, using such name performers as Bob Dylan, Traffic, and Sting and turning the show into a mega-event. This practice is standard procedure today.

6. They created a telephone hotline that provided tour and recording information to their mailing list of more than 160,000 loyal fans.

Clearly, the Grateful Dead took the notion of "customer driven" to the max. They built an innovative, worldwide organization that lived for the customer. That is the essence of "world class." Today, the band, without its leader, can still be found touring the country and spreading the word.

On average, women-owned businesses are smaller than their male-owned counterparts, and this difference is often explained by the motivations of women to start businesses and by how they define success.[22] Women's goals relative to the companies that they start are more about changing the way business is done than making a huge impact on the economy. It is also noteworthy that approximately 55 percent of all women-owned businesses are in services, and these businesses are smaller and younger by nature.[23] In 1994, chai, the milky tea that has been a staple in India, had not yet penetrated the U.S. market. Oregon environmentalist Heather Howitt saw an opportunity to offer coffee drinkers an interesting alternative and left her job to start Oregon Chai. To attract the American palette, she spiced up the traditional chai. With superhigh-profit margins and Howitt pouring all profits back into growing the business, she achieved number 18 on the 1999 Inc. 500 list of the fastest-growing private companies in the United States. Her products are found in natural-food stores, chic cafes, and even supermarkets like Safeway.

Minority-Owned Businesses In 2000, 15 percent of all businesses in the United States were owned by ethnic minorities. Within the minority-owned sector, Asian

Americans earned more than 51 percent of all business revenues, with Hispanics following at 31 percent, African Americans at 12 percent, and Native Americans at 6 percent.[24]

Despite their minority status, Asian Americans have been extraordinarily successful as entrepreneurs, owning about one-third of the high-technology firms in Silicon Valley.[25] The Korean American community displays the highest rate of self-employment, with more than one in ten Koreans owning businesses.

Older Entrepreneurs When it comes to starting a business, research has found that people over the age of 50 years are more likely than their younger counterparts to assume the risk of starting a new business. Self-employment among people over 50 years of age is about 16 percent compared to 10 percent for all workers.[26] They tend to start businesses, not only because it is difficult to find another job but also because they want to supplement retirement income, experience a new challenge, or simply take control of their lives. At age 50, Janice Taylor left her investor relations position at a New York City media company to pursue her dream. While trying to lose weight, Taylor developed an approach to dieting that worked. It consisted of making art about food instead of eating it. She was then able to sell the art at art fairs and through her website. The line is called "Our Lady of Weight Loss." Although she is making less money than she did at her former job, she is far happier.[27]

Entrepreneurial Types

There are many types of entrepreneurs, and although they have many characteristics in common, they differ in their approach to entrepreneurship.

The Home-Based Entrepreneur Ned Berkowitz reached burnout and left the world of the road warrior as a regional sales manager with a six-figure salary to purchase a franchise that let him work from home. Today, he feels in charge of his life and can spend more time with his family because he no longer has to travel farther than from his office to the kitchen.[28] Today more than ever before, people are choosing to work from home for a variety of reasons: to avoid commuting, to get away from corporate bureaucracy, to spend more time with family, and to work in a pleasant and relaxed environment. The types of businesses that they operate include consulting, financial services, real estate development, e-commerce, independent film production, and even manufacturing. The home-based entrepreneur's ability to avoid the traditional office results from designing a company in which the founders and employees usually collaborate virtually via technology and meet in person when they need to. It is estimated that there are 34–36 million home-based businesses comprising 52 percent of all small businesses and contributing about $314 billion to the economy.

The Traditional Entrepreneur The traditional entrepreneur is an individual or team of individuals who identify an opportunity and launch a company to execute the opportunity. Generally the business concept is one that the entrepreneur is passionate about, and the start-up route is chosen because the venture is either completely unique and therefore there are no existing businesses to acquire or the entrepreneur simply has the desire to build the company from the ground up. These entrepreneurs may build bricks-and-mortar businesses, delve into e-commerce, or operate a virtual company in which most of the activities of the business are outsourced. Robert Criscuolo believes that there is nothing better than owning a business. In 1997, he started a skilled labor–staffing company with money that he had saved from the various jobs that he had taken on, everything from being a house painter and gas station attendant to a deejay. His last job had been a customer-service position with a New Jersey–based Macy's department store. When that company wanted to transfer him to New York City, he left to take a sales position with a job-placement firm. That is where the idea for his business was born. With a partner to take over the administrative side of the business, Criscuolo was free to focus on sales and marketing, his strength. Not taking a paycheck for the first year motivated him to work hard to make the business a success. In 2004, Criscuolo's business was doing about $2.5 million in sales.[29] (We will explore in detail the activities of this type of entrepreneur in Chapter 3.)

The Serial Entrepreneur Some entrepreneurs enjoy the chase; that is, they like identifying opportunities, gathering resources, and building a company. What they don't like is running the company, so once things are operating fairly smoothly, this type of entrepreneur tends to move on to the next adventure. They may sell the business, but more often than not, they hand the management of the business to a partner and they take a secondary role that leaves them time to explore other opportunities. Consummate serial entrepreneur Wayne Huizenga started with one garbage truck and soon built the biggest waste-management company in the world. Then he took on the video rental business with Blockbuster and the used-car business with Auto Nation. In addition, he owns several sports teams, a very different type of business.

The Corporate Venturer With the recognition by large corporations that they were losing ground to scrappy entrepreneurial companies, a new type of entrepreneur was born: the corporate venturer. Not an entrepreneur in the traditional sense, this individual is one who typically works in a large company and acts in an entrepreneurial way to develop new products, new divisions, or spinoff companies. Corporate venturers do not risk their own capital, but they do risk their reputation. Corporate venturers proliferate when the capital markets make it difficult to start ventures that require a lot of funding and when the incentives within the organization make it worthwhile to do so. Bruce Griffing was the corporate venturer behind General Electric's digital x-ray project that ultimately became a huge division of the company.

The Opportunistic Entrepreneur Whereas the traditional entrepreneur conceives and builds a sustainable business out of something that he or she is passionate about and then stays with it for some time, the opportunistic entrepreneur is looking for a way to make something happen quickly and then exit, having made a lot of money. That something may be a fad product, a marketing play with an existing product that has a short window of opportunity, or an arbitrage opportunity in which the entrepreneur can acquire a product at a low price and then turn around and sell it at a higher price, thereby making money on the spread. One entrepreneur had quite a successful business for a time by purchasing the goods off damaged railway cars and trucks at a fraction of their cost and then selling the products into discount stores like the highly successful 99 Cent Stores chain.

MAKING THE DECISION TO OWN A BUSINESS

World extreme-snowboarding champion Steve Klassen wanted a career that supported his lifestyle and his love of snowboarding and the outdoor life. So after graduation from college, he opened a snowboard shop in Mammoth, California, one of his favorite skiing destinations. By hiring knowledgeable snowboarders to staff it and building a loyal customer base, Klassen built Wave Rave Snowboard Shop into a successful venture. Because Klassen understood that to survive in a competitive industry he continually had to innovate and find new markets, what began as a lifestyle small business has grown to include products, guided global snowboard safaris, and product representation.

Before deciding to become an entrepreneur or a small business owner, it's important to examine personal values, beliefs, and goals and to look for business opportunities that are compatible with them. Before launching his business, Klassen considered an exciting opportunity for an extreme-sports theme park in the Los Angeles area. However, the more Klassen got into the planning and the search for capital, the more he found it was taking him away from what he wanted most—to live and work in an area where he could do his favorite sport, snowboarding. Ultimately, he decided not to pursue the venture and is happily growing his business in Mammoth Lakes in new directions. To see what Klassen has to offer, visit www.waveravesnowboardshop.com.

Before beginning to search for opportunities, prospective entrepreneurs should address a number of issues so that they are in a better position to judge whether or not a venture opportunity is the right one for them.

Reasons to Own a Business

This is an important issue. Most entrepreneurs would say they start businesses for reasons other than money: independence, freedom, creativity, power, and fun. Individuals who want to start a business just to make money should step back and examine their reasoning. There are easier, less risky, less time-consuming ways to make money than starting a business. The NFIB reports that the median earning for a small business owner is just $30,000, the same as for wage and salaried workers. Therefore, it is important to understand the personal reasons behind wanting to start a business. Starting a business takes a huge commitment of time, money, energy, and devotion.

Some types of ventures are more demanding than others in terms of time, level of stress, and level of physical exhaustion. Some ventures take several years to develop and are far riskier than others. At 22 years of age, an entrepreneur can afford to fail many times and recover to start another venture. At age 38 or 45, the picture may look quite different. Obligations in the form of family, mortgage, and other responsibilities need to be managed while needed resources are diverted to the new business.

Feelings About Security and Ambiguity

Some new ventures can take up to two years or more to show a profit or at least be in a cash position that allows the entrepreneur to receive a salary. Prospective entrepreneurs who currently enjoy a regular paycheck and a certain lifestyle may have to make serious changes to enable them to launch or acquire a business. And if they are undertaking entrepreneurship with responsibilities such as a spouse and children, they need to have the family's support as well.

Lifestyle Needs

The decision to start or purchase a business directly affects the kind of lifestyle a person will lead. Moreover, where a person wants to live has an equal impact on the type of business that person can own. Two approaches can be used. Decide where to live first and then investigate a business opportunity that could be run from that location or come up with a business concept and then find the best place to implement that business. The route chosen depends on how important lifestyle is. For example, if the best place to locate a new manufacturing venture is near a port of entry for shipping, choices of areas to live are somewhat limited if involvement in the day-to-day operations of the company is essential, as it typically is. On the other hand, if living in a major city is not important, the operations of the manufacturing venture can be outsourced to an existing company in the port of entry, thus freeing the entrepreneur to live in an outlying, smaller community some distance away and operate the company as a virtual company.

Feelings About the Business Environment

Entrepreneurs find that a lot of feelings and beliefs that they didn't know they had often surface when they begin to think about starting and owning a business. Prospective business owners should ask themselves how they stand on the following issues:

- The use of debt or having a business that is highly leveraged
- Unions and the use of union workers
- Employees and the entrepreneur's ability to manage them
- Religious beliefs and how they might affect the people in the organization and the kind of business the entrepreneur chooses
- Government regulation and paperwork (some industries are much more highly regulated than others)
- Dealing with people from other parts of the world or even other parts of the United States
- Getting involved in the community
- Travel, if the business requires that the entrepreneur be "on the road" a lot
- Ownership and the entrepreneur's willingness to share ownership of the business with an investor or other person or persons

The entrepreneurial journey is an exciting and rewarding one. Every day brings new opportunities and new challenges, but for most entrepreneurs, the biggest reward is being in charge of their life. This book will help aspiring business owners and entrepreneurs decide if they want to take the journey to business ownership and independence.

ISSUES FOR REVIEW AND DISCUSSION

1. What is an entrepreneur?
2. What is the difference between an entrepreneurial company and a small business?
3. What are the benefits and challenges of business ownership?
4. Give three reasons why small businesses fail.
5. Discuss three reasons for expanding globally.
6. What are three typical characteristics of entrepreneurs?
7. Describe three different types of entrepreneurs.
8. What three questions do you need to ask yourself before you decide on a business to start or purchase?

EXPERIENCING ENTREPRENEURSHIP

1. Interview an entrepreneur with a business less than five years old. How did this entrepreneur come up with the idea for the business? What other issues related to start-up did she or he face? What qualities made this person more likely to become an entrepreneur than the "average" person? Present your analysis in a report.
2. Interview a small business owner and compare his or her mindset, goals, and business to those of the entrepreneur in question 1. How are they the same? How are they different? What conclusions can you draw?

LEARNING FROM ENTREPRENEURS, CASE 1.2

Flying High for a Living

On a clear day, Curt Westergard parked his trailer on an industrial street in Washington, DC, the site of the new Washington Nationals ballpark, which was scheduled to be completed in 2008. Using a map of the development, he quickly located home plate, a lamppost on the corner nearby. Satisfied that he was positioned well for what he was about to do, he jumped back into his trailer—his "mobile launch vehicle"—and from the "command and control" center, he activated the cargo doors on the roof of the trailer and released Momma Doc, a brain-shaped balloon with a long tail. Unwinding the cord to which Momma Doc was attached, Westergard and his assistant let the balloon rise to 110 feet. Then, they remotely snapped the shutters of the cameras that hung from the belly of the balloon. Within a matter of minutes, Westergard had downloaded the pictures that Momma Doc took to a laptop. These pictures would prove critical to the success of the ballpark project because they revealed that the future development slated to surround the new ballpark would actually block the sweeping view of the Capitol for fans. Changes had to be made.

Westergard, who hails from northern Virginia, is the founder and owner of Digital Design & Imaging Service Inc., which owns a fleet of unmanned helium aerostats, which are small blimplike vehicles, the largest of which is 12 feet long. He invested $400,000 in the business to launch it. It is a niche business with only a few dozen companies around the country. But as cities become denser and buildings grow taller, residents and tenants often want to know before a building is built what they will see from their windows. Aerostats are not new technology. In fact, they date back to the French Revolution when they were used to spy on Dutch and Austrian troops. They were also used during the Civil War to spy on the Confederate army. In the late 1970s, aerostats were replaced for a time by airplanes and manned forms of blimps, but these smaller, unmanned vehicles are now enjoying a renaissance for two reasons. First, you cannot bring an airplane or a larger manned blimp into a city at lower altitudes up to about 500 feet. Second, they make excellent surveillance vehicles in war zones. In Iraq, the U.S. Army maintains a fleet of 100-foot-long aerostats that serve as stationary platforms for surveillance cameras and lightweight radar.

There is also another market emerging for these miniblimps—surveillance for antiterrorism. Westergard is betting his money on this market. Larger high-altitude balloons have long been deployed effectively for surveillance, but they are extremely expensive to maintain and they can't be moved as quickly as targets shift. Today, terrorist threats are geographically dispersed and therefore require widespread surveillance over longer periods of time. The smaller aerostats take about four minutes to deploy and can remain aloft for three to four days or more. Westergard is proposing that a fleet of much smaller aerostats could be used in conjunction with a larger "mother ship" to more effectively and quickly gather data from numerous sites. These aerostats can carry payloads of 1 to 18 pounds depending on their size and can be deployed for longer periods of time at less cost.

To keep revenues coming in until he can get a government contract, Westergard does work like the ballpark project. His biggest city project may be capturing the views and wind measurements for the proposed 1776-foot Freedom Tower on the site of the World Trade Center in New York. It is not an easy business, but Westergard loves what he does and believes that he can beat the odds.

Advising the Entrepreneur

1. What are some of the unique issues that Westergard faces with a business like this?

2. Are there any other markets suitable for his aerostats?

Sources: A. Frangos, "Business Is Booming for High-Altitude Photos," *Wall Street Journal Startup Journal, Wall Street Journal* (April 20, 2005), www.startupjournal.com; C. Westergard, "Letter to the Editor," *Intelligence, Surveillance & Reconnaissance Journal* 3(3) (April 2004); M. Hewish, "Small Aerostats Provide Inexpensive Surveillance Platforms," *Jane's International Defense Review,* Jane's Information Group; Digital Design & Imaging Service (June 1, 2004). http://www.balloontest.com/.

CHAPTER 2

Entrepreneurial Strategies and Business Ethics

It is critical vision alone which can mitigate the unimpeded operation of the automatic.

Marshall McLuhan, Canadian communications theorist (1911–1980)
"Magic That Changes Mood," *The Mechanical Bride* (1951)

LEARNING OUTCOMES

- Discuss the role of vision and core values in the development of a business strategy.
- Explain how ethics and social responsibility are important aspects of business strategy.
- Discuss how industry serves as a context for strategy.
- Compare strategy and structure in a growing business.

A Research Firm Builds on Values

Chesapeake Research Review, Inc. (CRRI), is a Columbia, Maryland, company that supports clinical research by reviewing, assessing, and protecting the rights and welfare of human subjects. Because subjects volunteer for clinical trials for medical and behavioral experiments, CRRI's business must be conducted with the highest degree of integrity and ethics. This type of research is highly regulated by the U.S. Food and Drug Administration (FDA) as well as other federal and international authorities as to the safety and efficacy of new drugs and medical devices. It is considered a thought leader in a field where many other companies have not survived.

Felix Khin-Maung-Gyi had worked for a number of years as manager and consultant in clinical practice and research. With a doctorate in pharmacy, he understood well the ethics of clinical research. Matt Whalen was an expert in science and social issues, and throughout his career, he had learned much about how businesses function. When the two longtime friends lost their full-time jobs, they decided to start a business together to take advantage of what they had learned. They borrowed $2,000 from Khin-Maung-Gyi's aunt and launched their venture in the basement of Khin-Maung-Gyi's house. For two years, they took no salary and reinvested everything they made into the company to grow it.

Khin-Maung-Gyi and Whalen started the business with a set of core values that still serve the business: (1) transparent leadership with major business decisions made in open forums, (2) ethics and integrity, (3) clear and respectful communications, (4) customer care, (5) continuous learning, and (6) an intentional community. CRRI decided on transparent leadership because the work that they do is in the spotlight and under intense scrutiny. Sharing goals, challenges, and strategies with the entire team engendered trust and built a sense of community with a shared vision, but it also meant that sometimes decisions took longer than they would in a more command and control leadership style.

Ethics and integrity are part of everything the company does; in fact, it is essential to CRRI's business success. CRRI developed four principles (its 4Cs) to hardwire ethics into its operations.

1. *Compliance* In a highly regulated environment, compliance with FDA and other regulations is critical.

2. *Control* Rather than simply meeting minimum requirements, CRRI has chosen to control the compliance process by obtaining certifications and by benchmarking best practices.

3. *Conscience* CRRI relies on the judgment and conscience of its employees by giving them a broad level of structure and then allowing them the creativity and responsibility for decisions related to their work.

4. *Courage* CRRI employees are encouraged to speak out, especially when they see something that might compromise their research.

Communication is open and encouraged at CRRI. Problems are dealt with as they arise, and e-mail is used extensively throughout the organization. Communication skills are developed through workshops and "brown bag" lunches.

CRRI has three primary constituents: the drug companies that fund research, the human subject population, and the government regulatory agencies. Although they are not all customers in the traditional sense, they are all treated like customers and are the responsibility of the entire team. Full disclosure is one of the key tenets of CRRI's customer philosophy. Although it costs more in business processes, training, and time, CRRI believes that it is perhaps the key differentiating factor with their competitors.

Because their work is primarily knowledge based, Whalen and Khin-Maung-Gyi must be constantly in a learning mode, developing new skills and honing existing ones as well as training and coaching new hires. As in most industries, speed to market is critical, so CRRI must work to ensure that new knowledge and skills are quickly transferred to its customers in the form of more effective business processes and services.

Sometimes that means having to make a decision quickly to benefit the customer rather than take the time to coach a junior researcher through the process as a learning experience. In this sense, Khin-Maung-Gyi sees running a business as a balancing act. He says, "As leaders of a small business, we can also find ourselves stretched thin. . . . Whether you're dealing with revenue projections or cost calculations, every minute counts."

CRRI is dedicated to creating a community within the workplace that values each person's contribution and his or her wealth of experience. Each person brings something unique to the company, and together they form a strong bond with a common purpose.

Advising the Entrepreneur

1. CRRI operates in a highly competitive industry. Does its labor-intensive strategy make sense in a dynamic and highly regulated environment? Why or why not?

2. As the hiring person for CRRI, what would be your strategy for finding people who would fit into the company culture?

Sources: M. Whalen, F. Khin-Maung-Gyi, and D. Smithwick, "Leadership Style and Values Chart the Course for an Entrepreneurial Journey," *Journal of Organizational Excellence* 23(2) (2004): 43; Chesapeake Research Review, Inc., http://www.chesapeakeirb.com/; J. Bachenheimer and B. Brescia, "Good Recruitment Practice," *Pharmaceutical Executive* 23(6) (2003): 64.

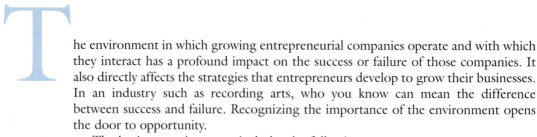

The environment in which growing entrepreneurial companies operate and with which they interact has a profound impact on the success or failure of those companies. It also directly affects the strategies that entrepreneurs develop to grow their businesses. In an industry such as recording arts, who you know can mean the difference between success and failure. Recognizing the importance of the environment opens the door to opportunity.

The business environment includes the following:

1. The industry of which the business is a part
2. The market on which it focuses its efforts
3. The economy in general
4. All the various people and organizations with which it interacts: suppliers, distributors, retailers, customers, and so on

One of the most important things aspiring entrepreneurs must do is take the time to learn about and understand their industries so that they know where the opportunities lie and how distribution channels work. A second important task is monitoring economic trends that may signal opportunities or threats to the business in the future. Yet another vital component of entrepreneurial success is getting to know the customers: who the customers are and what they want.

Businesses don't operate in a vacuum. They affect and are affected by everything that goes on around them. This chapter focuses on the environmental context for small businesses, the strategies that small businesses undertake to start and grow, and the social context—including ethics and social responsibility—that may spell the difference between success and failure. (Chapter 11 deals with the market, another important aspect of the small business environment.) We begin where all great businesses begin, with a vision.

A GREAT COMPANY BEGINS WITH A VISION

Perhaps the most important function of an entrepreneur or leader is to be the catalyst for a clear and shared **vision** that the company will pursue.[1] It is possible for a company to be profitable without a vision, but research indicates that vision is essential to an enduring company. Vision is a bold view of what the company can become. It's the glue that binds everyone in the company to a common purpose. Vision is what makes a company independent of any individual person—in other words, enduring. It also provides a context within which decisions are made.

Contrary to some beliefs, vision is *not* an esoteric pronouncement by a charismatic leader or the ability to see the future. Rather, it is what makes the difference between a company that achieves superior long-term performance and one that is simply successful. But vision is even more than this. Companies with vision have etched themselves into society's very foundations and changed the way we all carry out our lives. 3M's scotch tape and Post-it® Notes, GE's light bulbs and appliances, and Motorola's cellular phones and paging systems are but a few examples of enduring companies with a vision that translated into products that changed our lives. The answer to what makes these companies special, why they are a cut above their competition, and why they have survived lies in the vision that endures through decades of change in management, through economic ups and downs, and through changing technology and customer requirements.

James Collins and Jerry Porras, in their groundbreaking book *Built to Last: Successful Habits of Visionary Companies,* present the results of six years of research on what they called "visionary companies."[2] These companies were the number one and two in their industries and had endured more than fifty years. What distinguished these companies is the important lesson for entrepreneurs to learn about vision. Entrepreneurs tend to focus all their efforts and energies on "the great idea," often to the exclusion of the notion of building a company. It's no wonder, then, that they can't answer the fundamental questions, "What business are we in, and why?" "The great idea" was one myth Collins and Porras buried as a result of their research. They found that very few of the visionary companies started with a great idea; in fact, most did not find entrepreneurial success early on at all.[3] The driving force for these companies was instead adherence to their purpose and core values, which was the company's unique ideology. They were companies that were not afraid to take risk and were led by CEOs who had worked their way up through the ranks.

Entrepreneurial Leadership and Vision

Those who study leadership are increasingly seeing a shift from traditional command and control leadership styles to a more entrepreneurial style. Great entrepreneurial leaders today tend to display a number of important characteristics.

■ *They inspire trust.* To inspire trust, leaders must be trustworthy themselves, and they must create an environment that signals trust. This means making it easy for employees and other stakeholders to share information, to take risks, and even to fail without fear of recourse.

■ *They inspire passion.* A leader is not a leader unless there are followers. Passionate leaders help their employees understand what they contribute to the success of the organization and ensure open lines of communication. Their enthusiasm for the company mission is palpable and it inspires employees and stakeholders to invest themselves in the success of the company.

■ *They inspire innovation.* Great leaders understand that a small business is only as successful as its ability to innovate in a fast-changing environment. Entrepreneurial leaders encourage creativity and reward "out-of-the-box" thinking.

■ *They inspire optimism.* No small business ever becomes successful without first going through a number of hardships and disappointments. Entrepreneurial leaders are unfailingly optimistic that even if the worst happens, they can recover and rebuild, and that optimism inspires faith in their employees and stakeholders.

Research has distinguished leaders from managers and others in a number of important ways: (1) drive, or their motivation, ambition, energy and tenacity; (2) honesty and integrity, (3) self-confidence; (4) cognitive ability; and (5) knowledge of the business.[4] The leader may not have the formal authority in the organization, but the leader can influence others to act.[5]

Great entrepreneurial leaders have vision, which is their guidepost for developing and growing a business. In the next section, the components of vision are considered.

The Components of Vision

The Collins–Porras vision framework proposes that the company's core values, purpose, and mission comprise the vision.[6]

Core Values Core values are the fundamental beliefs that the business holds about what is important in business and in life in general—in other words, a "philosophy of life." (See Table 2.1 for the core values of three highly successful companies.) Core values derive from the personal values of the entrepreneur. They can't be "set" or created but are actually a reflection of what already exists. The core values of any company are "a set of basic precepts that plant a fixed stake in the ground: 'This is who we are; this is what we stand for, this is what we're all about.'"[7] Core values are so fundamental to the existence of the company that they rarely change over time. Johnson & Johnson, for example, articulated the following principle in 1943, which is still in force today:

> *We believe that our first responsibility is to the doctors, nurses, hospitals, mothers, and all others who use our products. Our products must always be of the highest quality. We must constantly strive to reduce the cost of these products. Our orders must be promptly and accurately filled. Our dealers must make a fair profit.*[8]

It could be argued that entrepreneurs are too occupied managing cash flow and meeting customer demands to concern themselves with anything as esoteric as visions and core values. Yet a visionary company's ideals are set down in the earliest stages of its development, certainly long before it is ever profitable, and those ideals guide the company's evolution. This is not to say that providing a quality product or service is not equally important in the early stages of a company, but in today's competitive environment, the company vision is critical to long-term success.

When deciding on the core values for the company, it's important to limit the number to no more than five or six so that they truly are core values that will endure

TABLE 2.1	Core Values of Three Very Successful Companies
American Express	Heroic customer service Worldwide reliability of services Encouragement of individual initiative
Chesapeake Research Review	Transparent leadership Ethics and integrity Clear and respectful communications Customer care An intentional community Profit, but profit from work that benefits humanity
Nordstrom	Service to the customer above all else Hard work and productivity Continuous improvement, never being satisfied Excellence in reputation, being part of something special

Sources: J. C. Collins and J. I. Porras, *Built to Last: Successful Habits of Visionary Companies* (New York: HarperBusiness, 1994); M. Whalen, F. Khin-Maung-Gyi, and D. Smithwick, "Leadership Style and Values Chart the Course for an Entrepreneurial Journey," *Journal of Organizational Excellence.* 23(2) (2004): 43.

over time. One way to measure whether a core value will stand the test of time is to determine whether the company would give the value up in the face of being penalized for holding that value. For example, if a company's core value is "the customer is always right," could the entrepreneur ever see a situation where the customer would not be right or where the company would not treat the customer as if he or she were right? If it would, it's not a core value.

Purpose Purpose is the fundamental reason for the existence of the business, and it emerges directly from the core values and beliefs. A purpose is analogous to trying to reach the end of a rainbow. A company is always making its way toward it, but it never actually reaches it.

For example, founder of Consumer Fire Products (CFP), Irene Rhodes's business purpose is to save people and property from fire:

> CFP will never reach the day when it has completely saved everyone and every building endangered by fire, but it will always have a firm purpose toward which it strives.

Mission Mission is a statement of a clear and compelling but broad goal that serves to focus effort. In contrast to purpose, a mission is always achievable, and once it is achieved, the purpose is used to define a new mission. The mission is a way of translating the broad purpose of the organization into a defined goal. A goal must have an end point; therefore, the mission should clearly state by which date it will be achieved. It's also important that the mission be exciting, something people can grab hold of and feel and have an intense desire to accomplish.

In 1977 Sam Walton, founder of Wal-Mart Stores, Inc., set the following mission:

To become a $1 billion company by 1980

In practical terms, this meant doubling company size in three years. Wal-Mart achieved $1.2 billion in that time period.

Company Culture

Researchers disagree about exactly what **culture** is. Some believe it is the reflection of the core values of the company, which stem from the firm's history.[9] Others believe culture is changeable, that it really reflects the behaviors and attitudes of those in the company at the time.[10] In their 1982 book *Corporate Cultures: The Rites and Rituals of Corporate Life,* Terrence Deal and Allan Kennedy coined the term *corporate culture* to describe the organization's tendency to develop its own characteristic way of doing things.[11] In very simplistic terms, organizational culture is the personality of the company, that intangible set of values that determines how and why the people in the organization respond to their business environment as they do.[12] A description of the company culture may be spelled out in the company handbook, but the real culture is found in the attitudes and actions of the organization's people as they interact on a daily basis. For example, if a business claims that it values customers above everything else, yet there is no evidence of the customer experience anywhere in the business, one wonders if this is really the company culture or simply a wish expressed through the company's vision.[13]

It is often said that entrepreneurial companies—start-ups in particular—have a distinct culture, one much different from that of large, established corporations. This is misleading because not all start-ups are alike. If the founders come from the big corporate environment or from a traditional business school education, they are very

LEARNING FROM SUCCESS

A Winning Golf Concept

No one thought that Roger Maxwell had much of a chance trying to compete in the golf industry with a museum-like retail concept, no retail experience, and no interest from investors. Undaunted, Maxwell poured $1 million of his own money into the concept and opened his store, In Celebration of Golf, in a mall in Scottsdale, Arizona, in 1996. He had good reason to believe he was in the right place at the right time. Every year over 2.2 million people bring their golf clubs to the Phoenix–Scottsdale area, and Maxwell caters to those who consider golf a religion. He has long been a collector of golf memorabilia and it is displayed everywhere in his 13,000–square foot store. The critics said that his inventory was too broad to be sold at good margins and he needed to computerize his back office so that he could better track what was going on.

Furthermore, there was concern that there was no good way to expand to another store and create the same kind of atmosphere. But Maxwell proved them all wrong. As of 2001, his Scottsdale store was pulling in over $5 million annually. Then in 1999, he opened his second store at the Venetian resort complex in Las Vegas with the potential of doing upwards of $10 million a year in sales. Maxwell probably won't be able to expand rapidly, given the museum quality of some of the products he carries, but he is enjoying success in something he is very passionate about. And he definitely knows his customers.

Sources: A. M. Borrego, "In Celebration of Golf," *Inc.* (January 2001), www.inc.com; E. O. Welles, "Going for the Green," *Inc.* (July 1996), www.inc.com.

likely to think in terms of elaborate organization charts and multiple levels of management. Often it is founders who don't have these experiences who tend to organize in ways that facilitate communication and that make the business happen and who end up with the maverick, "just do it" culture generally associated with start-ups. A significant part of company culture is ethics and, increasingly, social responsibility, both of which are discussed next.

THE STRATEGIC VALUE OF ETHICS AND SOCIAL RESPONSIBILITY

Although for the past several years the media have been disclosing the fraud and deception of several large corporations, small business has not escaped with a clean record. Often desperate to raise funding to compensate for revenues that have not yet materialized, small business owners are tempted to push the limits of ethical business practices in the name of survival. The root of most ethical dilemmas lies in placing self-interest and personal gain ahead of the interests of others. In business, the interesting irony of that is that, from an economic perspective, ethical behavior actually reduces transactions costs, generates trust, and thereby improves efficiency. In other words, it pays to be ethical.

Simply put, **ethics** is the moral code by which we live and it derives from the cultural, social, political, and ethnic norms by which we were raised as children. People's ethics are reflected in the way that they conduct themselves in their personal lives and in their business lives. As small businesses take advantage of strategic alliances and outsourcing functions to other companies, mutual trust and ethical behavior become essential components of business strategy. Traditionally, entrepreneurs have attempted to hire people who share their values, but as the need to partner and create complex networks to achieve company goals becomes more prevalent, it is difficult to ensure that the companies with which entrepreneurs partner share the same ethical values.

Broadly speaking, ethical dilemmas can be found in four major areas: conflicts of interest, survival tactics, stakeholder pressure, and pushing the legal limit.

1. *Conflicts of Interest* Conflicts of interest occur when an individual's personal interests collide with professional obligations. Unfortunately, for small business owners, this happens quite frequently. For example, an entrepreneur may want to maintain his or her manufacturing facility to ensure profits and provide jobs for the community, but the community claims that the manufacturing plant is not good for the environment. The entrepreneur now has to balance competing interests in the face of the company potentially losing money.

2. *Survival Tactics* The toughest test for most business owners is in the area of survival. Maintaining high ethical standards is easy when things are going well, but when revenues are not coming in and it is unclear how the next payroll will be met, some entrepreneurs face the quandary of how to maintain their ethical standards while making sure that the business survives. Problems like the loss of a major customer that would not derail a large corporation could be devastating to a small business.

3. *Stakeholder Pressure* Small businesses have many stakeholders—customers, employees, suppliers, distributors, and investors—and they all exert pressure on the business to succeed. Rarely do stakeholders have the long-term vision of the entrepreneur, so their short-term needs often conflict with the realities of the business as the entrepreneur has defined them. Under these circumstances, research has concluded that it is best for the entrepreneur to hold to his or her ethical code and base decisions on what is best for the company.

4. *Pushing the Legal Limit* There is a temptation on the part of some entrepreneurs to play so close to the edge of legality that they eventually get caught. The price is very high—often the loss of their business and their reputation. Ethical entrepreneurs do not risk their businesses or their reputations, and they are vigilant in avoiding dealing with companies that might use quasi-legal practices against them to gain an advantage in the market. For example, some unscrupulous companies make claims in the media about their competitors that are not accurate. They know that customers often believe what they see on television or in print and rarely verify its accuracy. When this type of attack happens to a small business, however, it has no choice but to defend its reputation, and that costs money.

Here are two examples of ethical dilemmas. How might they be resolved?

■ A struggling online retail store is not producing revenues at the rate that the owner originally projected. At the same time, the company is spending money faster than expected to acquire new customers. The owner promises visitors to the site that their private information will be protected. One of the quickest ways for Internet companies to bring in cash is to sell customer information lists to companies looking for them. Furthermore, if this owner begins tracking where her customers go on the Web, she can also sell that information to advertising firms who will pay top dollar for it. Of course, these solutions will violate customer privacy, but if the owner doesn't generate cash quickly, she may have to go out of business. What should she do?

■ The owner of a popular coffee house in a mid-sized New England community is approached by one of his employees who confides to him that another employee is planning to leave the company and start a competing one only a block away. The entrepreneur now faces a dilemma. The employee about to leave is currently involved in an important advertising campaign for the coffee house and it will be completed in a couple weeks. If the entrepreneur fires her immediately, it will delay completion of the campaign, and the employee might use the ideas that she was developing for the campaign to launch her own business and compete. What should he do?

Codes of Ethics

Codes of ethics have long been used to formally state a business's standing on a variety of ethical issues both for its internal (employees) and external stakeholders. Creating a code of ethics that honestly reflects the values of the organization is no easy task. Research has identified several dilemmas that businesses must deal with in the development of their codes of ethics.[14] In general, these dilemmas speak to challenges in developing and managing a code of ethics in the face of competitive pressures and dynamic environments. One of the goals of a code of ethics is to increase the moral resistance of the company—that is, the degree to which the company can resist situations that would exert downward pressure on the moral values of the organization. One of the critical factors that influences moral resistance is the competitive environment, which can often tempt an entrepreneur to choose a short-term solution for a quick gain and to deviate from his or her ethical values. The competitive environment can also affect employees who are accountable for results but who have not been given sufficient authority to carry out their tasks without resorting to questionable tactics. Other challenges stem from decisions regarding the specificity of the code (detailed versus concise or concrete versus general). The code must be detailed and concrete enough to provide clarity, but it must also be concise enough to be useful.

It is important that a code of ethics be written down so that stakeholders in the organization take it seriously. The code then provides a mechanism for avoiding ethical dilemmas and dealing with them when they occur. When considering some of the potential ethical dilemmas that a business could face, several questions should be asked:

1. Will the actions taken result in the greatest good for all parties involved?

2. Will the actions respect the rights of all parties?

3. Are the actions just? Will anyone be hurt by the actions?

4. Would the company be proud if its actions were announced in the local newspaper?

Gaining employee and stakeholder buy-in to the ethical codes that the company intends to adopt is important. Workshops and other sources of education should be made available so that everyone understands how to deal with a variety of situations that the business might encounter.

The Socially Responsible Small Business

Today, an increasing number of companies are doing much more than simply earning profits in an ethical manner. They are also concerned about giving something back to their communities and demonstrating their interconnectedness with society as a whole. This community awareness may take the form of pollution controls, sponsoring community activities, recycling campaigns, and grants to community organizations. An organization's ability to operate in an ethically and socially responsible manner has been shown to contribute to both its competitive advantage and its legitimacy, and it directly relates to the firm's ability to factor social issues into strategic business decisions.[15] In fact, it can be argued that social responsibility is no longer discretionary but rather an integral part of small business strategy. As an example, James Blackman, founder of the award-winning Civic Light Opera of South Bay Cities in southern California, dedicates several nights of every production to give free admission to underprivileged and physically challenged children so that they will have an opportunity to see and enjoy an aspect of culture previously unknown to them.

Social entrepreneurs are distinct from other types of entrepreneurs because they start their businesses with a social mission and they face different challenges than their for-profit counterparts.[16] Their rewards come principally from the social value they create by being change agents for the betterment of society. However, entrepreneurs who seek to start socially responsible businesses should be forewarned of the importance of choosing an achievable mission for their company. Ben & Jerry's cofounder Ben Cohen launched Community Products Inc. to help save the rainforest by donating 60 percent of its profits to that effort and by purchasing his raw materials from developing countries. But that level of commitment strained the organization's ability to provide excellent working conditions and pay workers market rates. The company ended up in bankruptcy because it did not consider that one company could not do what whole nations had not been able to do.

Recent research has identified five abilities that socially responsible businesses possess in common:[17]

1. *Value-Based Public Relations* The most socially responsible businesses do an effective job of gathering intelligence about stakeholders and disseminating that information throughout the organization.

2. *Stakeholder Involvement* Integrating stakeholder management processes into the business's strategy and identifying the company as stakeholder focused is another factor that contributes to social responsibility.

3. *Ethics* The business is committed to the reinforcement of ethical behavior and regard for others.

4. *Communication with Stakeholders* For the most socially responsible small businesses, communication with stakeholders is substantive and goes beyond mere symbolism.

5. *Accountability* The business has a reporting system to track its social efforts, and employees genuinely believe that their company is responsible to stakeholders.

Becoming Socially Responsible

Any small business has the potential to do something positive for the community in which it does business. A good place to start is by selecting a single cause that is compatible with the company's core values. Then, the company can focus its efforts and

LEARNING FROM THE GLOBAL MARKET

"Rock-Paper-Scissors" to Determine Strategy?

Small business strategies are plans for moving ahead in an unpredictable world. They are the entrepreneur's best guess as to what the company can achieve given the information in hand. Sometimes choosing among possible strategies when the choices are equal becomes a matter of flipping a coin.

In January 2005, Taskashi Hashiyama, president of Maspro Denkoh Corp, a Japanese electronics company, was debating who should have the honor of selling his company's multimillion-dollar art collection. The choices were Christie's or Sotheby's, and he was struggling with the decision. Ultimately, he made the decision using a time-honored game called Rock-Paper-Scissors (RPS, or *jankenpo* in Japanese). The rules are simple: Paper covers rock, rock blunts scis-

sors, and scissors cuts paper. On the count of three, each player changes his or her fist into one of the three weapons and the winner is determined. In this case, Christie's scissors beat Sotheby's paper, and the decision was made. Actually, RPS, which is believed to have migrated to Europe from the Far East during the mid-1700s, requires more mental skill because a strategic player must predict the moves of his opponent. Chicago-based Thought-Works Inc. uses RPS regularly to settle disputes, break ties, and make strategic decisions.

Source: "This Just In: Hand Jive, Even Corporations Are Making Decisions with Rock Paper Scissors" by Jennifer Crick from *Fortune Magazine*, June 1, 2005. Copyright © 2005 Time Inc. All rights reserved. Reprinted by permission.

partner with a nonprofit in that area to fill in the knowledge gaps. Getting the entire organization involved is very important to the success of the effort. The company can contribute in a number of ways:

1. Donate the company's products or services.
2. Join with other businesses in the community to enable larger projects—for example, adopting a school and focusing all the companies' charitable giving and donations of time to that school specifically.
3. Offer the company's expertise free of charge.

It doesn't cost much or take much time to give back to the community, and the rewards are great to the company that does so. Community members are more likely to purchase from companies that give back, and local newspapers are eager to report on the company's community activities, providing the company with a wealth of free publicity and positive public relations.

A FRAMEWORK FOR UNDERSTANDING THE SMALL BUSINESS ENVIRONMENT

The easiest way to look at the small business environment is to start with the industry in which the business operates. Research has identified three dimensions of the industry: carrying capacity, dynamism, and complexity.[18]

Carrying Capacity

Carrying capacity is the extent to which the industry can support growth of new firms. In other words, does this industry provide a favorable environment for a new business to enter and become profitable? Entrepreneurs naturally seek out an environment that allows the business to grow and obtain the resources it needs. Two signs indicate that an industry may be approaching its carrying capacity:

1. It is becoming increasingly difficult for new companies to enter the market.
2. The rate of sales growth in the market has slowed.

When this occurs, a new venture must enter with the plan to reshape the industry by creating demand for a product that didn't exist previously.

Dynamism

Dynamism, the second dimension of the environment, is the degree of certainty or uncertainty in the environment, as well as the stability or instability of the industry. Dynamic industries in volatile environments produce higher degrees of uncertainty; that is, things are changing so fast that it is virtually impossible to guess what might happen next. One example occurs in technology industries such as software and telecommunications. The speed at which technology changes and becomes obsolete creates high degrees of uncertainty and unpredictability in the environment of these industries. Uncertainty affects the structure of the business. As uncertainty goes up, the amount of information increases and creates demand for more information to

TABLE 2.2 Characteristics of High-Complexity and Low-Complexity Environments	
High-Complexity Environment: Software Industry	**Low-Complexity Environment: Agriculture Industry**
Very volatile	Stable and predictable
Hostile competitors	Collaborative competitors
Heterogeneous producers	Homogeneous producers
Restrictive—many controls	Unrestricted—few controls
High level of technical sophistication	Low level of technical sophistication

process decisions to maintain a particular level of performance.[19] So the more uncertain the environment is, the more information the entrepreneur needs to make decisions and attempt to predict the future.

In contrast, relatively stable industries such as the mechanical tool industry have low information requirements; consequently, they move more slowly and are more predictable.

Complexity

Complexity, the third dimension, is the degree to which the number of inputs and outputs in the environment in which the business operates causes interdependence.[20] In other words, the greater the number of suppliers, customers, competitors, and government agencies the entrepreneur depends on, the more complex is the industry. A global marketplace and changing technology have created more complex environments for most industries today. Growing businesses that operate in a network-type environment where outsourcing to other companies is common usually have to deal with more suppliers and customers. It has been argued that when a firm faces a more complex environment, it perceives a higher degree of complexity and therefore requires more information to make decisions.[21] For example, the greater the number of competitors in the firm's environment, the information load will be higher, and the environment will be more complex, requiring the entrepreneur to obtain more information to make decisions.

Complexity can be measured by

- The degree of turbulence or volatility (how quickly things change).
- The degree of hostility among competitors.
- The degree of heterogeneity among producers (how different they are).
- The degree of restrictiveness through the regulatory environment.
- The degree of technical sophistication.

Table 2.2 compares a highly complex environment with one of low complexity for two industries.

INDUSTRY STRUCTURE AND COMPETITIVE STRATEGY

As stated previously, it is vital that the owner of a small, growing business understand the nature of the industry so that strategies can be developed that give the business the highest probability of success. The industry in which a firm operates is a significant portion of the total business environment and has an enormous effect on the competitive strategy of the firm.

The classic books written by Michael Porter set forth a framework for understanding the fundamental realities of the industry environment. Porter's five-forces model analyzes the relationship between industry structure and strategic opportunities and threats, considering various strategic groups such as suppliers and buyers. This model is used to demonstrate how a firm's strategy is influenced by opportunities and threats in the environment. According to Porter, five forces drive competition and affect the long-run profitability of a firm (as well as other firms in the industry):

- Barriers to entry in the industry
- Threat from substitute products
- Threat from buyers' bargaining power
- Threat from suppliers' bargaining power
- Rivalry among existing industry firms

Short-run profitability, in contrast, is affected by such things as economic forces, changes in demand, material shortages, and so forth. Let's look at these five forces within the business's competitive environment in more depth in the context of a small, growing business.

Barriers to Entry in the Industry

In some industries, barriers to entry are high and discourage new entrants. These barriers may include the following.

- *Economies of Scale* Many industries have over time achieved economies of scale in marketing, production, and distribution; consequently, the established firms in that industry have attained production costs that have declined relative to the prices of their goods and services. It is therefore difficult for a new entrant to achieve these same economies. In terms of competitive strategy, this means that if a new business enters the industry on a large scale, it risks retaliation from established firms. In contrast, if it enters on a small scale, it may be unable to compete because of high costs relative to rival firms. In this instance, a niche strategy whereby the entrepreneur creates a market that he or she controls may allow entry. Domino's Pizza entered the saturated pizza market through a new channel of distribution—home delivery—that it controlled for a time to give it a chance to compete and gain strength before competitors copied the strategy.

- *Brand Loyalty* Overcoming customers' loyalty to established products and services in the industry can require an extensive advertising campaign to create brand awareness. This can be a very costly strategy and a significant barrier to entry for new businesses.

- *Capital Requirements* Capital requirements are a daunting barrier in many industries. New entrants may incur enormous costs for plant, equipment, research and development (R&D), and marketing just to compete on a par with established firms. New businesses often have resorted to outsourcing expensive manufacturing to companies with excess capacity.

- *Switching Costs* It is difficult to get buyers to switch from one supplier to another. This is due to switching costs, the costs the buyer incurs in time and money to retrain staff and potentially learn a new technology or to build a new relationship with a supplier.

- *Access to Distribution Channels* It is often difficult to get distribution channel members to accept the new business's products or services without costly persuasion techniques. This is particularly true in the grocery industry in which shelf space is at a premium. A new venture may look to other types of outlets, such as specialty retailer Trader Joe's, to enter this difficult industry.

- *Proprietary Factors* Barriers to entry also include proprietary technology, products, and processes. When established firms hold patents on products and processes that the new business requires, they have the ability to keep that company out of the industry or make it very expensive to enter. Most favorable location is another form of proprietary barrier. Existing firms in the industry may own the most advantageous business sites, forcing the new business to locate in a less competitive site.

- *Government Regulations* By imposing strict licensing requirements and limiting access to raw materials through laws or high taxes, the government can effectively prevent a firm from entering the industry.

In most cases, the aforementioned barriers can be overcome by creatively exploring new avenues that may include a niche market, a new distribution channel, a new advertising technique, or a new process, to name a few.

Threat from Substitute Products

A company must compete not only with products and services in its own industry but with those that are logical substitutes in other industries as well. Generally, these substitute products and services accomplish the same basic function in a different way or at a different price. For example, a video arcade that is competing for consumers' entertainment dollars also competes against movie theaters, bowling alleys, laser tag venues, and other establishments.

Threat from Buyers' Bargaining Power

Large buyers of products and services, such as Wal-Mart and Price/Costco, can force down prices in the industry through volume purchases. This is particularly true where an industry's products comprise a significant portion of the buyers' requirements. The largest buyers also pose a threat of backward integration, whereby they actually purchase their suppliers, thus better controlling costs and affecting price throughout the industry. A young, growing business that wants to deal with the discounters must be prepared to keep its costs low to meet the price demands of these major distributors. Marcel Ford, founder of Botanical Science, whose first product was a silk plant cleaner, used the major discounters as his distribution channel. One reason his company is successful today is that he kept his costs, both production and overhead, as low as possible so that he could take advantage of the volume sales these discounters produced.

Threat from Suppliers' Bargaining Power

In some industries, suppliers exert enormous power by threatening to raise prices or change the quality of the products that they supply to manufacturers and distributors. If the number of these suppliers is small relative to the size of the industry or the industry is not the primary customer of the suppliers, that power is magnified. A further threat from suppliers is forward integration—that is, that they will purchase the outlets for their goods and services, thus controlling the prices at which the products are ultimately sold and competing against others who must purchase their products at wholesale. An example is Intel Corporation, the principal supplier of computer processing chips to the personal computer (PC) industry. Intel is able not only to affect costs for PC makers but also to affect the product life cycle.

Rivalry Among Existing Industry Firms

In general, it can be said that a highly competitive industry drives down profits and ultimately the rate of return on investment. To position themselves in a competitive market, companies resort to price wars, advertising skirmishes, and enhanced service. These tactics are often seen in the airline, computer, and some food products industries, to name just a few. Once one firm decides to make such a strategic move in the industry, others follow. To compete in this type of industry requires that the new entrant create a niche that has not been served by the established firms and enter without causing movement on the part of the major players. It also requires convincing the customer that the value you provide is worth your higher price.

HOW DO SMALL BUSINESSES COMPETE?

Studying the industry via the five-forces model is a valuable exercise that provides a clearer picture of this aspect of the environment. However, examples abound of firms that have achieved a competitive advantage in industry environments that were less than inviting.

Four important questions need to be asked about the capabilities of any small business to compete:

1. Does the business have the resources and capabilities necessary to take advantage of opportunities in the environment and neutralize threats? The extent to which a company's resources and capabilities match the opportunities and threats in the environment can change over time. What may have originally been strength for the company can suddenly become weakness. Hunter Fan is a good example. Its market leader technology was created to cool large manufacturing plants; but with the invention of air conditioning, it lost its competitive advantage and was forced to change its strategy. When energy conservation became an issue in the 1970s, Hunter saw an opportunity to exploit a new market—homeowners—and began creating fans with a decorative flair.

2. How many competing firms already own the same valuable resources and competencies? If several companies possess the same valuable resources or competencies, none are likely to have a competitive advantage. A resource or competency must be rare to offer an advantage in that sense. The advantage a common resource has is that

it is a requirement for survival in the industry and therefore a barrier to entry to potential competition. Companies introducing rare resources or competencies gain a significant temporary advantage over a period of time before others can acquire them.

3. Do firms without a resource or capability face a cost disadvantage in obtaining it? Competing firms often incur significant costs in acquiring the "rare" resources and competencies of companies that possess them. If this is the case, the firms that possess the resources and capabilities are able to maintain a competitive advantage over a longer period of time. On the other hand, if a new competing business can find suitable substitutes for these resources, it may be able to achieve competitive parity over the long term.

4. Is the firm organized to take full advantage of its resources and capabilities? To exploit resources and capabilities, companies must have supporting resources such as management control systems, a formal reporting structure, compensation policies, and technology that helps them acquire and process information as well as or better than their competitors. As a new company begins to prepare for rapid growth, this infrastructure and these systems must be in place, or strategies will quickly fall apart.

To sustain a competitive advantage, a rapidly growing entrepreneurial company must consider not only the opportunities and threats presented by the environment but also the strengths and weaknesses of its own resources and capabilities. A company with strong resources and competencies can successfully compete even in an environment that appears to have few opportunities and many threats.

LEARNING FROM MISTAKES

The Ten-Minute Manicure

When Vivian Jimenez decides to do something, nothing can get in her way. The daughter of Cuban immigrants, she was the vice president of interactive media services at one of the largest public relations firms in Florida when she decided that she would rather be an entrepreneur. An airline industry conference inspired the idea for ten-minute manicures. Jimenez and her friend Karen Janson were hooked; the idea was so simple. So in April of 1999, Janson decided to quit her job to devote herself full time to the venture, and Jimenez and another friend, Lorriane Brennan O'Neil, came on board to help. They planned to install kiosks next to high-traffic areas in the airport and hire $7-an-hour nail technicians; with just five customers an hour and three to four kiosks per airport, they could pull in a projected $3.2 million in annual revenues. By August

2000, they had still not raised any money to launch the venture. Most investors wanted to see proof of concept before they would risk their capital, and they wanted returns far in excess of what businesses like this could produce. The mistake that the team made was focusing only on the airport-kiosk business because those contracts are increasingly hard to get. They also needed to have sufficient financial backing from friends and family to prove the concept so that investors would feel that the risk had been reduced somewhat.

Sources: K. Dillon, "The Start-Up Diaries: Three Women and a Kiosk," *Inc.* (January 2000), www.inc.com (accessed July 8, 2005); *Inc.* staff, "Start-Up Diaries: A Vexing Catch-22," *Inc.* (August 2000), www.inc.com (accessed July 8, 2005).

STRATEGY AND STRUCTURE IN A GROWING BUSINESS

The competitive strategy focus that has long received so much attention was due principally to the work of Michael Porter,[22] although it actually had its origins in the work of A. P. Chandler, J. Bain, and I. Ansoff.[23] Chandler referred to strategy as "the statement of the firm's goals and its policies and practices for achieving those goals." The issue of management practice itself did not arise until later, when researchers began to look at the stakeholders of an organization and to view employees as one among several constituencies, which also included founders, stockholders, and others with a vested interest in the company.[24] U.S. management practices prior to the 1980s did not hold employees in high esteem as stakeholders. It was not until the globalization of the marketplace in the 1980s when firms began studying Japanese management philosophy that U.S. firms began to rethink the role of employees in the company's strategy. Japanese firms, even those operating in the United States, regularly ranked their employees higher as stakeholders; in fact, Japanese companies attained superior performance through the careful nurturing of what they considered their greatest asset: their human resources.[25] Therefore, much of current management practice is based on the original Japanese model.

Organizational Structure

Organization theory has also produced many models of organizational structure designed to match a particular business strategy, beginning with the very early bureaucratic and hierarchical models. During the 1960s and 1970s, the work of P. R. Lawrence, J. W. Lorsch, and others taught us that environmental differentiation affects organizational structure.[26] In other words, the way a business is structured depends on the environment in which it operates. This theory was followed by the matrix model, which supported dual reporting relationships, and the contingency model, which said that the organizational structure is a function of critical elements in the firm's environment and customers. In the early 1980s, the concept of the strategic business unit (SBU) became popular and was shaped by the merger and acquisition fever of that period. Still, the basic concept of the hierarchy pervaded all these models, whether the company was organized based on function or on geographic location.

Beginning in the mid-1980s, however, total quality management (TQM) began to make inroads in the thinking of many business leaders as they sought ways to improve performance beyond mere strategy and structure. The goal of TQM was to respond more efficiently and effectively to the needs of the customer through the use of continuous improvement and just-in-time delivery. The important element in this new approach was that it was the first to move away from hierarchical modes of organization to a flatter, more decentralized structure. This required empowering employees at all levels to make decisions, as well as to self-inspect at every point of the process to ensure a quality outcome. The result was employees who worked in self-directed teams and were now significantly more important as stakeholders in the company. The timing of the entry of TQM is certainly critical because it coincides with the emergence of the information/technology revolution, which made decentralization possible by linking all organizational functions via a local area network. Most recently, organizational structure and strategy have taken yet another leap to virtual organizations and agile webs, which create a very loose organizational structure that is flexible and easily changed as needed, and to the cellular structure modeled after a living cell. A cell can exist on its own, but it can do things that are more complex if it acts with other older cells in alliances and networks. These newest organizational structures are well suited to entrepreneurial ventures that need to be able to respond quickly to environmental changes.

Strategy for Sustainability and Long-Term Profitability

Entrepreneurial small businesses suffer from the liability of newness. Without a track record of success in the industry and market that they have chosen, it is difficult for potential partners and stakeholders to believe that the business can do what it says it can do and for the business to prove that it can execute its mission; that is, it is difficult for the small business to gain legitimacy so that it can acquire the resources it needs to succeed. Therefore, its early strategy must include the establishment of a positive reputation as quickly as possible. Reputation is the company's identity as seen by its stakeholders—customers, suppliers, distributors, investors, employees, and so forth.[27] A positive reputation can signal to others that this business has the ability to obtain customers, top employees, resources, and the partnerships it needs to fulfill its mission. Although reputation building would seem like a critical component of any business strategy, few small business owners consider it directly. They tend to assume that it follows from the success of the business's operational strategies, which is not always the case. In fact, research points to the fact that small businesses can improve their chances of success by developing a comprehensive strategy focused on building the positive reputation of the company.[28] How does a small business undertake such a strategy? The strategic reference point (SRP) framework provides a useful jumping-off point for evaluating important organizational factors that influence the company's performance.[29] Based on SRP, Figure 2.1 presents a typical strategy matrix depicting the options, which are explained further below, available to the small business entrepreneur.

1. *Exploitation of Existing Assets* In this strategy, the entrepreneur uses the business's internal assets to solve immediate problems in the market, gain quick profits, and grow quickly.

2. *Core Competency Development* This is a long-term approach involving significant investment in internal capabilities to produce innovative products with superior service support.

3. *Image Creation* This again is a short-term strategy to quickly create a company image through marketing and associating the company with partners of significant reputation. This is known as "renting" the reputation of another firm.[30]

4. *Strategic Alliances* The entrepreneur gains a good reputation by joint venturing with an established company whereby it can supply its core competency and receive missing resources in return.

Choosing a Strategy to Build Reputation

The strategy that a small business chooses depends on the stakeholders in the business. For example, if the entrepreneur has taken investor capital, those investors likely have a short-term view of the business and want to see returns on their investment in the near future. Buyers also often seek a short-term return if they need a particular product or service immediately. When it comes to attracting top employees in management positions, those candidates may be looking to associate with a company that has a strong reputation, even if its association with more established companies garners

FIGURE 2.1   Strategies for Building a Positive Reputation

		Time Frame	
		Short-Term Objective	**Long-Term Objective**
Focus	**Internal Context**	Exploit Existing Assets	Develop Core Competency
	External Context	Develop Image	Build Strategic Alliances

that reputation. If the entrepreneur is looking to grow the company quickly, she may choose the route of producing products and services that are not innovatively ambitious but allow the company to secure a significant portion of the market quickly. The problem with this approach is that it only survives in the short term and does not give the company a sustainable position for the future.

The core competency strategy is generally highly touted by the strategy literature as the most effective way to gain long-term sustainability. At the same time, many investors don't have the patience to stay with the investment for the long term and so do not welcome this strategy. There is a possibility that the company may run out of cash before it achieves its long-term goal.

The image-building strategy is one of smoke and mirrors. If the small business does not deliver on its promises, it will find itself in a worse position than if it had taken a longer-term strategy. There is also the problem that the small business may not be able to maintain its image long enough to produce the level of quality products and services that customers expect.

Strategic alliances with established, name-brand customers are an excellent way to gain a positive reputation by association. This is particularly important when dealing internationally, and research has found that gaining these international partnerships is very difficult.[31] The problem with alliances is that often the small business becomes dependent on the larger company and ends up losing its identity. Small businesses are advised to consider some combination of the four approaches, depending on their situation. Strategic alliances are discussed in more detail in the next section.

Strategic Alliances

A small business can choose to focus on a single product or service, but today to create new value for customers, it must leverage its limited resources across a number of different products and services.[32] This strategy can often result in bureaucracy and organizational complexity that then leads to inefficiencies. It is critical that small-business owners balance the need to vertically integrate (acquire suppliers or distributors) or diversify with the need to manage costs and share risks. This balance can be accomplished effectively through the use of strategic alliances in which the small business focuses on its area of competence and lets its partner carry the load of functions or activities that are outside its core competencies.

A **strategic alliance** or partnership with another company is distinguished from the independent contractor relationship in that it is a more formal and typically closer relationship. Moreover, *independent contractor* is a designation for tax purposes, whereas *strategic alliance* is not. Through strategic alliances, growing companies can structure deals with suppliers, manufacturers, or customers that help reduce expenditures for marketing, raw materials, or R&D. Strategic partners are considered stakeholders in the company because they have an investment of time and money in its products or services. Moreover, in many cases, their investment is irreversible; that is, if the new venture fails, liquidation of its assets will not make the stakeholder whole. This puts the stakeholder at significant risk and underscores the importance of minimizing stakeholder exposure and selecting partners who can bear the risk. An effective strategic alliance should benefit both companies, particularly when one company is much larger than the other. This type of relationship works best when the following is true:[33]

- *Diversification* Partners who have diverse investment interests generally are better able to bear the risk of investment in a new venture that is focused rather than diversified.

- *Experience in Bearing This Form of Risk* Partners such as 3M that are used to dealing with new ventures have a greater understanding of the nature of these small companies. Certainly, such an association gives the new company more clout in the marketplace.

- *Excess Capacity* Firms that do not have to make additional investments in plant and equipment can provide their existing excess capacity to the start-up and thus benefit both partners.

Strategic alliances have many advantages; among them is the opportunity for the small business to learn from its larger and more experienced partner.[34] However, this benefit can quickly turn into an asymmetrical opportunity or a form of competition called *coopetition* in which the partnering companies also compete with each other.[35] These situations require a great deal of coordination and communication. They also require trust and ethical responsibility, which was discussed earlier in the chapter.

Three theoretical frameworks have played a role in describing the issues related to strategic alliances: transaction cost economics, agency theory, and team production theory. **Transaction cost economics,** sometimes called cost–benefit analysis has been employed to attempt to explain the choice that business owners have between doing the work in-house and creating a more hierarchical organization structure or contracting externally, suggesting a more flat structure.[36] This theory asserts that contracts with strategic partners (and contracts in general) are subject to opportunism whereby one party has more information than the other, and "hold-up," or the reluctance to invest in the partnership in the belief that the partner might renege on the contract.[37]

Agency theory considers the situation in which one party (the agent) acts on behalf of the other (the principal) and the two have conflicting goals and interests. This type of partnership can become costly because the principal must spend valuable time monitoring the effort of the agent and ensuring that the work is being done in a way that benefits the principal.

Team production theory addresses situations in which it is not possible to precisely measure the contribution of each partner, so the rewards benefit the entire team. As a result, the alliance may experience the "free-rider" problem when some team members contribute less than others.[38] This form of cheating has been the basis for the argument that in business ethical behavior is valuable and more profitable than unethical behavior.[39] It is also the basis for a positive company reputation, which reduces the costs and problems associated with strategic alliances as discussed earlier.

Strategic partners should be selected carefully for their compatibility with the entrepreneur's goals and values as well as their capabilities relative to business success.

The R&D Limited Partnership One specific type of alliance is the **R&D limited partnership,** a vehicle whereby growing high-technology ventures that carry significant risk due to R&D expense can share that risk with a more established company. The limited partnership (usually formed by private investors or venture capitalists) contracts with the new venture to provide the funding for the R&D to develop a market technology that will ultimately be profitable for both companies. Limited partners are able to deduct their investment in the R&D contract and enjoy the tax advantages of losses in the early years on their personal tax returns; they also share in any future profits. In this form of partnership, the new venture acts as a general partner to develop the technology and then structures a license agreement with the R&D partner whereby the new venture can use the technology to develop other products. Often the limited partnership's interest becomes stock in a new corporation formed to commercialize the new technology. An alternative to this arrangement is an agreement to pay royalties to the partnership.

CHOOSING AN ENTRY STRATEGY

For new businesses, there are basically three strategies for entering a market: (1) niche, (2) differentiation, and (3) cost superiority. *Niche strategy* involves recognizing or creating a niche, or small space, in the market that no one else is serving. *Differentiation strategy* is finding a way to make a product/service different from what is currently in the market. *Cost superiority strategy* is based on providing a product or service at the lowest price to the customer. Let's consider each for its strategic value to the entrepreneur.

Of the three strategies, niche is perhaps the most advantageous because it allows entrepreneurs to control a segment of the market that they define and where they can potentially control 100 percent of the niche. If no one else is serving that niche, then for a short period of time, the entrepreneur does not face direct competition and therefore has the opportunity to establish a foothold and grow. The niche business also enjoys the opportunity to establish a reputation and standards that others will need to follow. Once the small business owner has captured one niche, another niche can be defined. This pattern is then repeated, enabling the business to grow without immediately facing stiff competition from large, established companies in the broader market. This strategy is sometimes called "finding a niche," but that suggests that the entrepreneur is not in control of the situation but rather is at the mercy of serendipity. Entrepreneurs do not go seeking niches; they create them by understanding their customers' needs. An excellent example of this is the business that Karen Adams started. Adams was passionate about children. After becoming a first-time mom, she left the world of technology in which she had successfully built two companies to start an Internet business that sold $50,000 Cinderella pumpkin-coach beds for girls. Now, that is a niche! Once the niche in children's furnishings was doing well, she began looking at other rooms in the home and providing goods that customers could not find anywhere else.

Starting the entrepreneurial journey with a clear understanding of the environment and a strategy to guide decision making puts what otherwise would be a very unpredictable journey more in the control of the entrepreneur. The most effective strategy is based on the vision and values of the founding team and takes ethics and social responsibility into consideration in all of the company's actions.

ISSUES FOR REVIEW AND DISCUSSION

1. Describe the nature of the environment for growing entrepreneurial companies today.
2. What is the role of technology in today's business environment?
3. What kinds of barriers to entry can an industry erect?
4. Discuss three significant trends in the business environment today.
5. Which continuing trends offer opportunities for entrepreneurs?

EXPERIENCING ENTREPRENEURSHIP

1. Choose an industry and apply Porter's five-forces model to it. What conclusions about the nature of the industry can you draw based on the findings?
2. Interview two people in the industry that you chose in question 1 to determine if your conclusions are correct.

Netflix® Delivers

Every day thousands of people open their mailboxes to find the DVDs that they rented online from Netflix, the leader in its niche market. From a subscriber base of 857,000 after its initial public offering in 2002 to over 3 million in 2005, this upstart challenger to video stores has managed to outdistance its competitors to claim 80 percent of the U.S. online movie rental business, with projected 2005 revenues of over $700 million and net income in 2004 of $21.6 million. Netflix carries 45,000 films at each of its warehouses around the country and makes it easy for customers to find the best movies for them through its recommendation engine. Against such mammoth competitors as Blockbuster and Wal-Mart, how can this small company prevail?

The Birth of Netflix

Reed Hastings was no stranger to entrepreneurship. He sold his first company, Pure Atria Software, in 1997 for $750 million. Following the sale, he spent a year as CEO of TechNet, which is a technology-lobbying group out of the Silicon Valley. One day he rented a video, *Apollo 13,* from Blockbuster but forgot to return it. To his surprise, Blockbuster charged him $40 in late fees. Instead of getting mad, he got even. He figured that he could deliver next day to anywhere in the San Francisco Bay area from a distribution center in San Jose. In 1998, DVD players were selling for $700, so not as many people had DVD players as VCRs. However, DVDs would be less costly to mail. Hastings set up a business model that charged $4 per rental plus $2 postage, and customers hated it. He quickly learned that consumers were interested in the idea of paying one flat monthly fee for as many movies as they wanted to rent. The new business model was based on prepaid subscriptions, which provided significant cash-flow advantages to the company. Hastings launched the service in 1999, and within three months he had 100,000 subscribers.

During the next year, former MGM executive and CEO of the Screen Actors Guild Bob Pisano joined Netflix's board of directors and helped Hastings sign revenue-sharing agreements with most of the film studios in Hollywood. Netflix would buy the DVDs at cost and then give a percentage of the subscription fee back to the studio.

Hastings saw his company as the Starbucks of the video industry and Blockbuster as the Dunkin Donuts of the industry. Recognizing that he had entered a commodity business, Hastings wanted to find Netflix's differentiation, so from the beginning Netflix not only delivered DVDs but also suggested DVD titles to subscribers through its recommendation engine and the CineMatch database. About 70 percent of Netflix's customers rent from the recommended list.

Netflix employs several marketing channels to attract subscribers. Using paid search listings, banner ads, and permission-based e-mails, it is able to acquire new customers online. In addition to cooperative advertising with the film studios and others, Netflix pays for online marketing on a placement, per-impression basis, or per-click basis, and pays "bounties" for referrals.

Netflix has been willing to make hard choices to maintain its market leadership in the face of shareholders looking for profits. It maintains the highest gross margins in the industry and the lowest operating costs in the business.

The Online Movie Rental Market

A variety of distribution channels exist for filmed entertainment: movie theaters, airlines, hotels, home video rental, cable and satellite television, pay-per-view (PPV), video-on-demand (VOD), and broadcast television. Studios typically release their filmed entertainment content to the home video market three to six months after theatrical release, to PPV and VOD seven to nine months after theatrical release, and to cable and satellite one year after theatrical release. These time frames are gradually being shortened with some films being produced for direct-to-home video distribution.

The online move rental market has become a booming business, taking away millions of dollars from theater box offices. In 2004, about 71 million U.S. television households had DVD players (64 percent of households), and rental volume doubled to about $600 million, making it one of the fastest-growing consumer markets. It is projected that online subscribers will reach 8 million by the end of 2006 (Adams Media Research), which is a rate of 60 percent per year, and sales are projected to grow to $931 million by the end of 2005 and to $2.9 billion by 2011. The entry of major competitors with huge marketing budgets like Blockbuster and Wal-Mart has served to create more customer awareness for the online rental business.

The efficiency of online/postal service distribution can easily be seen when one calculates that it would take 500 video stores to serve the entire Los Angeles area, while an online service can serve it with only one warehouse. However, it is essentially a commodity product, and the price of DVDs keeps coming down.

Those film studios that have revenue-sharing agreements with market leader Netflix are seeing the benefits to their off-center movie assets (below "A" category films). Studios do not put a lot of marketing dollars into low-budget and independent films, so when a company like Netflix tracks customer preference and manages to target a large group that enjoys these types of films, it sends a strong message to the film studios about where to spend their money.

Video-on-demand over the Internet has been the "Holy Grail" for most consumers, but for most online rental businesses, the broadband penetration will need to increase and delivery costs will have to come down before it makes financial sense. Right now it can cost more than $30 to distribute DVD-quality film over the Internet and take several hours for customers to download. That will change in five to ten years. It is expected that the Internet movie-delivery business will be very large some day, but studios will still want to maximize revenues from DVD sales and rentals on new releases before licensing rights for electronic distribution over the Internet. For the next few years, Internet downloads will mostly be composed of back-catalog titles.

The Competitive Challenge

In 2003, Walmart.com went national with a service designed to crush Netflix. It offered 12,000 titles delivered by mail three at a time with no late fees and for $1 less than Netflix on the subscription fee. The market watchers could see Netflix going down for the count. But Netflix proved that David could still best Goliath. Wal-Mart did not bring out the big marketing guns to announce their new service, most probably because it was a very small piece of the big picture for them. Wal-Mart had spent more than $100 million

and only achieved 1 million subscribers against Netflix's far smaller budget and 6 million subscribers. The barriers to profitability in this business are huge but difficult to see because the business seems deceptively simple. By May 2005, Wal-Mart had given up the online rental business in exchange for Netflix agreeing to promote buying DVDs on Walmart.com.

Meanwhile, Blockbuster is still in the battle, and the result is that subscriber fees for both companies are trending down. As of this writing, Blockbuster charges $3.15 less a month for the same three-movies-at-a-time service, but it also throws in two free in-store rentals. Netflix carries more titles immediately available, and it delivers somewhat faster than Blockbuster. Web surveyor ForeSee has rated Netflix number one in customer satisfaction among the top forty Internet retailers. However, Blockbuster is not the only concern for Hastings. There is some buzz that Amazon.com will enter the fray!

The Future

Netflix found a match made in heaven when it decided to join forces with TiVo, another media upstart. Their agreement lets subscribers of both services download Netflix DVDs over the Internet directly into their TiVo boxes. TiVo, who has been battling giant media companies like Comcast and EchoStar, acquired Strangeberry in 2004. Strangeberry enables users to plug a DSL or cable modem into the back of the TiVo box and pull digital media off the Internet. The two companies now have a powerful connection that is drawing some concern from media companies who see the potential for high-quality movies being released freely onto the Internet. Moreover, the cable companies, through whose pipes downloads will occur, are not going to stand by quietly and let this happen. Cable firms are not obligated to allow their competitors' traffic on their networks, and if they choose to shut down Netflix, their customers may be forced to migrate to DSL, which is controlled by the common carrier phone companies.

Netflix is potentially an acquisition target. With over $175 million in cash on its balance sheet, no debt, and high growth, it presents an interesting opportunity. Hastings believes that the best chance for acquisition will come when they move strongly into downloading. The future is a moving target in the entertainment industry, however, and Netflix still has to maintain its leadership position long enough to get there.

Advising the Entrepreneur

1. What is the Netflix business model? Do you see it changing in the near future? How and for what reason?

2. In your estimation, what is Netflix's primary competitive advantage and why?

3. What impact will Netflix have on the video-distribution industry?

4. What must Netflix do to succeed in the face of direct competition from established distributors such as the nationwide chain Blockbuster?

Sources: J. M. O'Brien, "The Netflix Effect," *Wired* 10(12) (2002), www.wired.com; B. Stone, "I Want a Movie! Now!" *Newsweek* (September 13, 2005), www.msnbc.msn.com; "Netflix Makes It Big in Hollywood," *Fortune* (June 13, 2005): 34; Netflix 2004 Annual Report; B. Mohl, "Customers Win Big in Netflix–Blockbuster War," *Miami Herald* (July 5, 2005), www.MiamiHerald.com.

Paths to Business Ownership

CHAPTER 3

Starting a Business

The first rule of entrepreneurship has to be that you do something you really love—you can't make it otherwise.

David Birch, economist, 1987

LEARNING OUTCOMES

- Describe the new venture creation process.
- Compare and contrast business life cycles with industry life cycles.
- Explain how opportunity recognition occurs.
- Discuss the critical components of a business concept.
- Describe the feasibility analysis process.
- Explain bootstrapping as an entrepreneurial strategy.

What It Means to Be Overstocked

If you started a company in 1999, it is likely that it was an Internet company, and it is likely that it did not survive the dot-com implosion of April 2000—that is, unless it was Overstock.com, the highly successful closeout retailer. Overstock.com offers discount, brand-name merchandise for sale over the Internet. Customers have the opportunity to shop for bargains conveniently from their home twenty-four hours a day, and Overstock's suppliers now have an alternative inventory liquidation distribution channel. In 2002 the company completed an initial public offering on the NASDAQ exchange. Then a $20 million branding campaign in 2004 produced over $221 million in revenues as of the end of the fourth quarter of 2004. Not bad for an entrepreneur who self-funded his business. The secret to CEO Patrick Byrne's success? Knowing his customer—a confident 40-something woman who loves the notion of an online treasure hunt.

Overstock's brand is about low cost and volume sales, and Byrne wants his company to be the lowest-cost retailer online, beating Amazon. That branding campaign was designed to promote Overstock's newest offering, Club O for avid bargain shoppers. For $29.95 per year, customers would receive 5 percent off Overstock's listed price on all purchases (except for travel packages), in addition to a flat shipping fee of $1 per order (instead of the standard $2.95). Shoppers who placed one to two orders a month would recoup the membership fee through the reduced shipping rate.

Customer service is a critical component to any online retailing business, and if it is not handled well, the business will lose customers. However, it does not have to be the core competency of the business to be successful. Byrne decided in 2004 that he would outsource customer service to a specialist. Because Overstock's business cycle is heaviest during the holiday season, it made sense not to have to add to its core staff every year for a few weeks. With an outside call center, Overstock can offer 24/7 service in any time zone, something that would have cost the company a lot in labor to achieve. Moreover, Overstock stays in contact with Sento Corp., the Utah-based customer-service operation it uses, particularly in regards to the hiring of sales representatives for order processing. Overstock insists on background checks for fraud protection, and it regularly inspects for quality.

Although Overstock outsources most of its customer service, it does not completely divest itself of contact with the customer. It maintains a corporate call center with about forty people who handle escalated calls—those calls forwarded from the outsourced call center for treatment at a higher level. Here, many of the common logistics and merchandising problems that customers experience are taken care of.

Overstock's record is astounding. In the first quarter of 2005, revenue was up 102 percent compared with the same period in 2004. Gross profit grew 194 percent over the previous year, and at 15 percent, the gross margin was up from more than 4 percent from 2004. Although the stock price has been down, the company is on the verge of profitability, and its revenue growth numbers are better than both Amazon's and eBay's.

In addition to its quantifiable successes, Overstock has this to boast about: During the company's quarterly conference call with the analysts, nearly 500 shareholders typically phone in to listen. The reason for the high number of attendees may be that everyone wants to find out what unpredictable CEO Byrne will say next. He has no fear of censuring those who he believes are targeting his company with unfair criticism. At the same time, he provides unparalleled disclosure to shareholders and refuses to accept analysts' often-aggressive expectations of the firm's performance.

In 2005 Byrne diversified his rapidly growing company by acquiring a privately held travel company, Ski West Inc., in a $25 million deal. Ski West was started in 2001 and serves a niche area of hard-to-find lodging in popular ski resorts in the United States and Canada. Overstock is also providing compensation based on future performance to Ski West employees who stay on board. For Ski West, being acquired by Overstock means that the company's services will be exposed to a much broader audience. For Overstock, the compatibility is obvious. Overstock already sells ski apparel and luggage. Now it can offer travelers a complete package including travel arrangements. The online travel industry has stabilized somewhat with major players like Sabre's Travelocity and InterActiveCorp's Expedia now producing dependable results.

Byrne believes that some day Overstock will overtake Amazon. The trajectory is in place, and if Byrne can maintain effective operations as the company grows, it may have a chance.

Advising the Entrepreneur

1. What is the vital component of Byrne's business? Why?

2. Analyze Overstock's growth strategy. What would you recommend to the CEO?

3. What are the biggest challenges facing Overstock in the next few years?

Sources: "Patrick's Key Move: Targeting Women," *Startup Nation,* www.startupnation.com (accessed June 24, 2005); "Overstock.com to Buy Travel Web Site," *Yahoo Finance* (June 24, 2005); R. A. Munarriz, "Overstock: All about the Snow," *The Motley Fool* (July 27, 2005), www.fool.com; W. D. Crotty, "Overstock.com Misunderstood," *The Motley Fool* (April 22, 2005), www.fool.com/news.

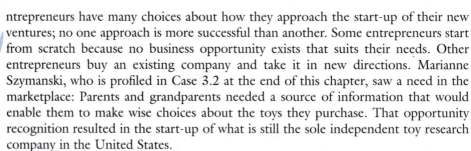

Entrepreneurs have many choices about how they approach the start-up of their new ventures; no one approach is more successful than another. Some entrepreneurs start from scratch because no business opportunity exists that suits their needs. Other entrepreneurs buy an existing company and take it in new directions. Marianne Szymanski, who is profiled in Case 3.2 at the end of this chapter, saw a need in the marketplace: Parents and grandparents needed a source of information that would enable them to make wise choices about the toys they purchase. That opportunity recognition resulted in the start-up of what is still the sole independent toy research company in the United States.

This chapter examines the journey entrepreneurs make when they recognize opportunity and conceive the idea for a new business. It begins with an overview of the entire path, looking at the various stages in the life of a business. The chapter then takes a closer look at opportunity recognition, the testing of a business concept through feasibility analysis, and lastly, provides an overview of some very early start-up funding strategies.

THE NEW VENTURE CREATION PROCESS

Ambiguity is the ubiquitous companion of any new venture. Born into an uncertain environment, start-ups by nature must be flexible, able to adjust quickly in response to rapidly changing needs and requirements. It is important to note that this process takes place within a context that includes the environment in which the new venture operates and the entrepreneur, who acts as the catalyst for new venture creation within that environment.

Every entrepreneur brings to a new venture a unique set of characteristics and behaviors that spring from the entrepreneur's cultural background, education, socioeconomic status, experience, and the family setting in which he or she was raised. All these factors give the entrepreneur a set of values that affect everything that she or he does, from intentions to management style.

The environment is the most comprehensive component in the venture-creation process. It includes all factors that affect the decision to start a business—for example, government regulation, competitiveness, and life-cycle stage. Within specific industries and in specific geographic regions, environmental variables and the degree of their impact will differ. The new venture process begins with an idea for a product, service, or business. The entrepreneur develops that idea into a business opportunity or business concept that is then tested in the market through a process of feasibility analysis. **Feasibility analysis** is used to inform the entrepreneur about the conditions required to move forward and develop the business. Once the entrepreneur has determined that the concept is feasible, a business plan is developed to detail how the company will be structured and to describe its operations. Some time between doing a feasibility analysis and creating the business plan, entrepreneurs begin to gather the resources—human resources, capital, facilities, and equipment—that are required to launch the business. All of this activity defines the pre-start-up stage.

No real agreement exists on when the actual start-up stage begins. Some argue that a company is in "start-up" from the moment that the idea for the business is conceived, whereas others see start-up as the early period in a company's life when it first begins to deal with its customers. This book considers start-up as that point where the new venture has gathered all the necessary resources and is ready to begin doing business with its customers.

An entrepreneur starts a business because the concept appears to be feasible. But testing the concept in the real world is what actually determines if the business has viability—in other words, whether it has a life beyond the business plan. **Viability** is the point at which the company is generating internal cash flows sufficient to allow the business to survive on its own without cash infusions from outside sources such as the entrepreneur's own resources, investors, or a bank loan. The type of business and the capital requirements for launching the business affect the point of viability. If viability does not occur for two or more years due to substantial start-up costs, as in the case of many high-technology start-ups, it is important to consider ways to reduce those costs. One way may be through the use of a virtual corporation and subcontracting many of the more capital-intensive activities to a firm that has achieved greater efficiency in terms of cost (Chapter 15 discusses this option).

LEARNING FROM SUCCESS

Still Flying After All These Years?

Two entrepreneurs want to make it possible for the average executive to be able to fly in private jets. With any luck, Pogo Jet is set to launch in 2006 with tiny jets flying between small airports and targeting executives. This venture is a grand comeback for People Express founder Donald Burr and his partner, former American Airlines CEO Robert Crandall. Burr's business model for People Express was timely in 1980 when he pioneered low fares and employee loyalty. However, encroaching competition and overexpansion in the airline industry eventually dealt a final blow to the company in 1987. Time will tell if this former entrepreneur can make a comeback.

Source: "Where Are They Now?" *Fortune* (April 19, 2005): 162.

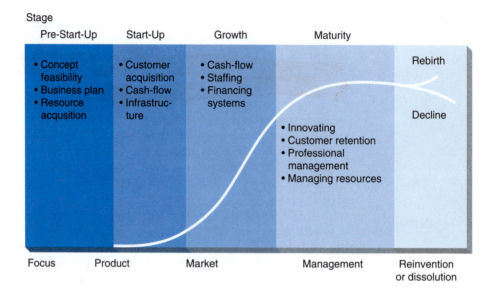

FIGURE 3.1   The Life Cycle of the Company

Business Life Cycles

Companies have life cycles that parallel those of human beings. They begin at conception, go through the labor of start-up, are born, endure adolescence, become mature adults (though sometimes rather immature adults), and ultimately die or are reborn in another form. For some companies, the life cycle is brief, a rocket burst that lasts only a short time. For others, life spans decades as is the case with companies such as GE, IBM, and Merck.

The five stages of a business's life cycle are the following:

1. Pre-start-up
2. Start-up
3. Growth
4. Maturity
5. Rebirth or decline

At each stage of the life cycle, the needs and goals of the company differ. Researchers Terpstra and Olson reviewed the myriad theories and models of organizational life cycles and stages of development and concluded that, in general, organizations tend to move sequentially through major stages of development, each with its own set of management issues.[1] Figure 3.1 illustrates this concept. For example, start-ups tend to be associated with marketing and financial problems, whereas strategic and management issues plague the growing company. As a company moves from young to mature, it typically grows larger in size, becomes less focused and more diverse, and attains a greater degree of complexity.

The focus of the entrepreneur changes at each stage in the cycle. During the period from pre-start-up through early growth, the company tends to be very product focused, looking inward to the concept that forms the basis of the business opportunity. This introverted period is the reason why entrepreneurs are often accused of being "in love" with their products—the great idea.

At start-up, product focus continues as the new venture tests its operations plan and puts an infrastructure in place to respond effectively to the demands of early growth. As the firm moves into the growth stage, if its operations are well honed, it begins to focus outward to the marketplace and the potential customers with whom it needs to build lasting relationships. If the company successfully traverses the growth stage and establishes a loyal customer base, it becomes a mature company with relatively more predictable revenue flows. It now faces a new set of challenges, however: how to manage the resources it has accumulated over time and how to remain competitive. If at maturity the company becomes complacent and continues to operate the way it always has, it will ultimately decline. If instead the company looks for ways to reinvent itself through new technology, new products, and new processes, it can experience a rebirth and go through another growth cycle. This is of course a very simplified rendition of a company's life cycle.

In reality, the length of time from conception to maturity varies with the industry, the type of business, and environmental factors present during the growth process; the life cycle of a business is by no means a sure path. Some companies fail before the growth stage; others can't gather sufficient resources or don't have the infrastructure in place to permit them to successfully pass through the rapid-growth stage, and they fail at this point. Still others manage to survive the trials of start-up and growth to reach a mature stage, only to succumb to competitive pressures or dramatic changes in the market to which they are ill equipped to respond. However, a company can reach a mature stage and then—through the introduction of new technology, for example—be "reborn" and go through a new growth stage. Certainly, technology has been the catalyst for many a rebirth. It has also been responsible for the death of many businesses, particularly when companies fail to recognize the substantial changes that it brings about. It is therefore important to understand the nature of companies at the five basic stages so that the growing company can adjust its strategies to effectively prepare itself for the next phase in its life cycle.

LAUNCHING A NEW BUSINESS

Before examining the details of starting a new business, it is important to distinguish among four concepts that are fundamental to understanding start-ups: (1) idea, (2) business opportunity, (3) opportunity recognition, and (4) opportunity creation. A new business typically begins when an entrepreneur recognizes or creates an opportunity in the marketplace and has an idea for a business that will make the most of that opportunity.

Ideas are a dime a dozen; everyone has them countless times throughout each day. They are the inspiration to make decisions. Business opportunities are ideas that involve products or services with commercial potential and have a business model or way to make money from the opportunity. **Opportunity creation** is developing a product, service, process, or niche that has not existed before; it requires high levels of creativity. Typically, opportunity creation involves an invention process that is characterized by four activities: connection, discovery, invention, and application.

- **Connection** occurs when two ideas are brought together that normally are not juxtaposed, such as nature and machines which produced the field of nanotechnology or microscopic machines that copy nature in the way that they operate.

- **Discovery** happens once a connection has been made. It is actually the result of the connection in the form of an idea.

- **Inventions** are the product of turning an idea into a product or service.

- **Application** comes about when the inventor can apply the invention to a number of different uses or applications in a variety of industries and situations.

    Opportunity recognition is the process of using creative skills to identify an innovation—product, service, process, or marketing method—based on something already existing in the marketplace. In the next section, opportunity recognition is explored more fully.

Opportunity Recognition

Entrepreneurs can recognize an opportunity in the marketplace when they are acutely aware of their environment and the problems, needs, and gaps within it. Successful entrepreneurs see the world through an opportunistic lens; that is, they see not only problems but also solutions and ways to create businesses that can provide those solutions. Opportunity recognition is the idea-generation stage in which creativity and an open, accepting mind take precedence over evaluation.

The environment in which a person typically works can either stimulate or discourage creativity.[2] To create an environment that encourages creative thought, choose a place where distractions are minimized. In the fast-paced electronic world where people are constantly interrupted by cell phones and e-mail, it is vital to creativity to spend some time each day in quiet contemplation with no distractions and no interruptions. It is difficult to develop a consistent train of thought otherwise.

An environment that mixes people up is also more conducive to creative thought, so it's important for entrepreneurs to take themselves out of their typical surroundings and put themselves in a new setting that might enable them to make new connections. Whether the idea is brand new or an improvement on an existing product or service, it will benefit from an environment that stimulates creativity.

Most business ideas come from something that already exists in the market, and most entrepreneurs improve on those ideas or find underserved niches. The classic example is Starbucks Coffee. A cup of coffee was a commodity available everywhere before Howard Schultz raised it to the level of an event. He improved on what was standard fare and created new value for customers, who are now willing to pay around $4 to have their own customized coffee experience.

New ideas can spring from anywhere. The most common source of new ideas is the entrepreneur's experience followed by business associates, friends and relatives, hobbies, and market research. Doug Hall, master of creativity and inventor of the Eureka Stimulus Response™ Method, gives some unusual tips for freeing up the ability to generate ideas:[3]

- Look at paint chips. Paint chips are an almost limitless source of stimulation, particularly such exotic hues as Glidden's chocolate kiss or smoked pearl. They stimulate images, moods, and emotions.

- Go to video rental stores. Movies offer a wealth of images and ideas. Hall talks of the scene from *Rocky* where Rocky wakes up, heads into the kitchen, pulls a carton of eggs out of the refrigerator, cracks a half-dozen raw eggs into a glass, and chugs the liquid down. This image resulted in Hall's development of beverages in which his client's product is mixed with fruits and juices—easier to sell than raw eggs!

- Play with Play-Doh. The smell of Play-Doh reminds most people of their child-hood. Play with it. Mold it into sculptures. Build prototypes from it.
- Listen to music. Music is a great idea generator. Individuals should experiment to find the type of music that works for them. Yoshiro Naka Mats, the prolific Japanese inventor, prefers jazz or Beethoven's *Fifth Symphony*.

It is helpful to keep a notebook handy at all times. Ideas may strike at the most in-opportune time, and too often if they are not written down that instant, they will vanish.

Potential business owners who successfully put themselves into an opportunistic mode find no lack of ideas for potential products or services. After several ideas have been generated, the question now becomes which to choose. So many ideas, so little time! A process that is usually effective is as follows:

1. List all the ideas in no particular order.
2. Eliminate those that do not offer an immediate value proposition and business model that make sense—in other words, those for which there doesn't appear to be a way to make money.
3. Review the remaining ideas and choose the one that inspires the most passion and enthusiasm.

Choosing an idea that inspires passion is vital. If the idea then proves feasible and the entrepreneur attempts to start the business, that business will take a tremendous amount of time, energy, and devotion to make it happen, so it's certainly better if the entrepreneur loves what he or she is doing.

The next step in the entrepreneurial process of starting a business is to turn the idea into a business concept that can be tested.

Developing a Business Concept

A business concept describes the four essential elements required to test whether a potential business idea is feasible. This is true for both a new business and a new growth strategy for an existing business. The four components of the business concept are the business (product or service), the customer, the benefit to the customer, and distribution.

Suppose the idea for a new business involves providing international location sites to film studios over the Internet. The concept for this new business can be defined more concretely by answering the following questions:

- What is the product and/or service that is the basis for the business? In other words, what is the business, and what is it offering? For example, this entrepre-neur is in the information business, providing movie location sites internationally.
- Who is the customer? That is, who will pay for the product or service (distribu-tor, retailer, end user, and so on)? The customer in this case is the film produc-tion company.
- What is the benefit to the customer? What is the company providing that the cus-tomer needs? The business provides the customer with the ability to visually check

sites, explore possibilities, and make decisions without having to leave the office. In other words, the company is providing convenience and saving the customer time and money.

- **How will the benefit be delivered?** The benefit will be delivered via a website that will provide stills and full-motion video of movie location sites and the ability to interact with the company to secure a location.

Once the business concept is developed, the next step in the process is testing the concept.

Developing a Business Model

One of the essential components of any business concept is the business model, which is how the business will make money from its product or service offerings. Entrepreneurs must determine how to create value that customers will pay for and secure a competitive advantage for the business.

A poorly conceived business model in which customers cannot see the value can precipitate business failure. For example, Funerals.com was built on the belief that when someone died, their family would want a convenient online shop for taking care of all the funeral needs. What the entrepreneur did not understand was that grieving families wanted to talk with another human being; the last place they wanted to go was their computer. Business models also fail when the financials don't make sense; for example, recall the story of Streamline.com, an online grocery-delivery service that could not generate the volume needed to survive in the slim-margin world of a commodity business. Customers were not willing to pay enough more than they usually paid for groceries to let the company survive. Developing a business model is a four-step process:

1. *Position the company in the value chain.* The **value chain** is the distribution channel from supplier to customer or end user. It includes every business that contributes to the production and distribution of a product or service to a customer. Where a business is located in the value chain determines the type of business it is and many aspects of the business model including level of risk and potential gross margins. A retail business demands substantial capital and carries a higher level of risk than, for example, a distributorship because the retail business deals with the consumer or end user directly. (The value chain is discussed in more detail in Chapter 12.)

2. *Figure out who pays whom.* The position in the value chain establishes the identity of the entrepreneur's actual customer. If the entrepreneur's business is manufacturing, then the direct customer is likely to be a distributor or retailer and the end user is the consumer or another business. It is important to understand the costs, pricing, and markups along the value chain to enable every member of the chain to make a reasonable profit as they add value and then sell to the next person in the chain.

3. *Calculate customer impact.* The entrepreneur must consider how a chosen business model affects customers' buying habits, perceptions of the product or service, or their willingness to purchase. If customers must make a major change in the way they typically purchase these types of goods or if they need to make a major investment of time to learn how to use the new product, it may affect their willingness to purchase.

4. *Identify multiple revenue streams.* It is never a wise idea to rely on one source of revenue from a product or service because that leaves the business vulnerable to shifts

in customers' tastes and preferences. Marianne Szymanski (see Case 3.2) has moved from providing education about toy products to selling licensed products related to children. She can place her brand and the credibility that she has created with her independent toy research firm onto these products. Szymanski now has revenue streams from online magazine subscriptions, magazines sold quarterly through large book chains, and nontoy children's products.

Entrepreneurs need to think creatively about their business models. Often times, by studying business models in other industries, an entrepreneur can find new ways of doing business that provide a competitive advantage. This process is called **disintermediation.** For example, many entrepreneurs have found a way to reduce the size of the value chain by going direct to the customer via the Internet. Disintermediation sometimes works in industries where customers do not perceive the value of intermediaries.

Entrepreneurs can also redefine value. Instead of simply designing a product or service and then trying to find customers with whom there might be a fit, entrepreneurs can sometimes take a more proactive approach with the customer. This can result in a new business model. One team of entrepreneurs, for example, who provided information technology assistance to small business owners, would study the operations of a typical small business in a particular industry—such as real estate appraisal—to determine how that company might modify its processes to become more efficient and effective. They would then approach the small business owner with the solution and a plan for implementation. Typically, the owner was so pleased to have a technical person who actually understood his business that the team was hired to implement the solution.

LEARNING FROM MISTAKES

Test the Concept First!

Bruce Judson is certain that his Internet business, For Speed Anywhere, failed because he spent too much money on the product before he knew what customers wanted. He developed software that compared prices for cable and DSL services and with it provided a service that enabled customers to evaluate which connection would be right for them. Judson responded to customers' inquiries by sending them an e-mail the next day. What he did not learn until after he spent money on software development was that the customers wanted answers in real time.

Judson's mistake was that he failed to consider customer behavior. Today, Judson is a big proponent of microbusinesses that allow an entrepreneur to maintain his or her day job until the business can sustain itself and the entrepreneur's salary.

Lesson Learned: Do not spend a lot of money before you test the business concept.

Source: A. Cuozick, "Avoiding the Pitfalls Common to Startups," *Wall Street Journal Startup Journal* (June 24, 2005), www.startupjournal.com.

FEASIBILITY ANALYSIS

The business concept is tested through a process of feasibility analysis that answers three fundamental questions:

1. Are there customers and a market of sufficient size to make the concept feasible?
2. Do the capital requirements to start, based on estimates of sales and expenses, make sense?
3. Can an appropriate start-up team be put together to make it happen?

The feasibility study helps the entrepreneur decide if the conditions are right to go forward. If the conditions are not favorable, it is necessary to review the results of the various tests to see whether another approach might make the concept feasible. Many concepts can achieve feasibility if the right conditions are in place and the entrepreneur is willing to put the time, money, and effort into its execution.

Generally, the information available when the feasibility study is conducted is not as complete or detailed as it is in the business plan because entrepreneurs need to gather just enough information to make a go/no-go decision. Nevertheless, a well-done feasibility study can prevent a company from throwing money at a new product or service for which there is no market, a market of insufficient size, or no efficient way to produce the product and make a profit. Of course, in a growing company, feasibility studies may not be necessary for every new product or service introduced. Typically, derivative products and services, incremental or small improvements on existing products and services, will not require a full-blown feasibility study, particularly if the customer has been giving feedback on the core product all along. However, a new family of products, platform products, will benefit from a more formalized approach because they typically require substantial expenditures in product development and market research.

Components of Feasibility Analysis

Feasibility analysis includes testing four aspects of the business concept: product or service, industry/market/customer, founding team, and finances. Table 3.1 provides some in-depth questions that guide the process. Summaries of these four aspects are given next.

Industry/Market/Customer. The analysis of the industry is an important part of a feasibility study because it provides the context for the development of a new business and can actually serve as the source of the new business opportunity. Furthermore, designing a strategic position in a growing and healthy industry helps to ensure a successful venture.

The makeup of an industry and the way it works are fundamental to shaping how the new venture enters the industry and grows. Like businesses, industries experience a life cycle. Figure 3.2 depicts this life cycle and its associated activities. In general, when a new industry emerges, it is often due to the introduction of a technology that creates opportunities that could not have existed previously. The industry then moves into a rapid-growth period wherein new companies jockey for position and the right to determine industry standards. As more and more firms enter the industry and compete, intense product differentiation occurs that ultimately forces some companies out of the industry. By the time the industry has reached maturity, several major

TABLE 3.1 Feasibility Analysis: Key Questions

Area to Be Analyzed	Key Questions to Ask
Industry	1. What are the demographics, trends, and life-cycle stage of the industry?
	2. Are there any barriers to entry? If so, what are they?
	3. What is the status of technology and R&D expenditures?
	4. What are typical profit margins in the industry?
	5. What are distributors, manufacturers, and suppliers saying about the industry?
	6. Who are the major players in the industry?
Market/Customer	7. What potential markets are available to the business?
	8. What are the demographics and psychographics of the target market?
	9. What is the profile of the first customer? What is the "pain" that is being cured with the business's product or service?
	10. What is the customer demand for the product or service? How will you triangulate that demand figure to arrive at the best estimate of demand?
Product or Service	11. What are the features and benefits of the product or service?
	12. What product development tasks must be undertaken, and what is the timeline for completion?
	13. Which intellectual property rights can be acquired?
	14. How are these products or services differentiated from others in the market?
	15. Who are your competitors, and how are you differentiated from them?
	16. What are your competitors' core competencies? Do they have the ability to move into your competitive space?
	17. Which distribution channel alternatives are available to your business, and which customers will they serve?
Founding Team	18. What experience and expertise does the founding team bring to the business?
	19. What gaps do you have in experience or expertise?
	20. How will you fill those gaps?
Financials	21. What are your start-up capital requirements?
	22. What are your working capital requirements?
	23. What are your fixed-cost requirements?
	24. How long will it take to achieve a positive cash flow?
	25. What is the break-even point for the business?
	26. What are the detailed assumptions or explanation for the numbers you are projecting?
	27. What are the major milestones in the business for the next two years, and how will those milestones trigger changes in your business?
	28. What is the timeline for completion of all the tasks to start the business?

players dominate and set the standards for everyone else. At this point, if new research and development (R&D) does not produce innovation that results in another surge of growth, the industry could face decline and eventual death.

However, every industry is different, and the speed and duration of the life-cycle stages varies. For example, in 2004 the declining recorded music segment of the media and entertainment industry began to grow again, driven primarily by spending on cellular phone ring tone downloads and expanded digital distribution.[4]

Table 3.2 displays the fastest-growing industries in terms of employment as reported by the U.S. Department of Labor. Some of these industries include software publishers, management consultants, and employment services.

FIGURE 3.2 Industry Growth Cycle

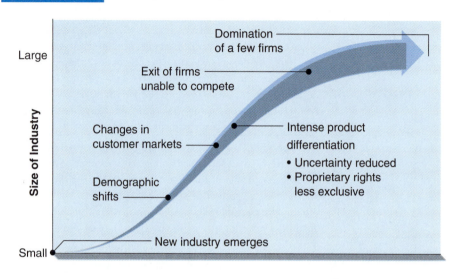

TABLE 3.2 Fastest-Growing Industries in the United States

| Industry Description | 2002 NAICS* | Thousands of Jobs | | Change | Average Annual Rate of Change |
		2002	2012	2002–2012	2002–2012
Software publishers	5112	256	429.7	173.7	5.3
Management, scientific, and technical consulting services	5416	731.8	1137.40	405.6	4.5
Community care facilities for the elderly and residential care facilities	6233, 6239	695.3	1077.60	382.3	4.5
Computer systems design and related services	5415	1162.70	1797.70	635	4.5
Employment services	5613	3248.80	5012.30	1763.50	4.4
Individual, family, community, and vocational rehabilitation services	6241–6243	1269.30	1866.60	597.3	3.9
Ambulatory healthcare services except offices of health practitioners	6214–6219	1443.60	2113.40	669.8	3.9
Water, sewage, and other systems	2213	48.5	71	22.5	3.9
Internet services, data processing, and other information services	516, 518, 519	528.8	773.1	244.3	3.9
Child day-care services	6244	734.2	1050.30	316.1	3.6

Source: U.S. Department of Labor (November 2004).

*North American Industry Classification System.

FIGURE 3.3 Five-Forces Analysis

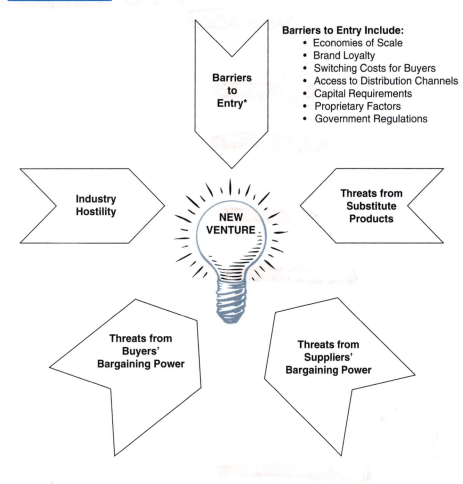

Many frameworks exist for organizing the analysis of an industry to expose patterns and trends. A few of them are discussed here.

■ *Five-Forces Analysis* This analysis is based on the work of Michael Porter and has been perhaps the most frequently used framework (Figure 3.3). The five forces are

1. Barriers to entry.
2. Industry hostility.
3. Threats from substitute products.
4. Threats from buyers' bargaining power.
5. Threats from suppliers' bargaining power.

The framework is based on the premise that to sustain high-performance levels in any industry, the entrepreneur must develop a strategy that reflects the way the industry actually works.[5] Porter asserts that the five forces drive competition and affect long-run profitability, whereas economic forces, shifts in demand, material shortages, and technology shifts tend to affect short-run profitability.

- *Starbuck Framework* This framework is based on three concepts introduced by researcher William Starbuck: carrying capacity, uncertainty, and complexity.[6]

  1. **Carrying capacity** reflects the ability of the industry to support growth through new firm entry as well as growth of existing firms. A large number of competitors that control the supply chain may make it difficult for a new venture to enter and survive.
  2. **Uncertainty** is the degree of ambiguity and volatility in the industry. Dynamic industries that are in a constant state of flux present more risk and more opportunity for the new ventures that enter them.
  3. **Complexity** is the number and diversity of inputs and outputs that affect the company, such as suppliers, customers, and competitors. In highly complex industries, new ventures must learn to manage a number of different relationships well.

- *SWOT Analysis* This framework is in the form of a matrix, and its name is an acronym for strengths, weaknesses, opportunities, and threats. It relates to the firm's capabilities—or lack of them—and how they may be leveraged to create potential for growth (opportunities) and factors that could negatively affect the firm (threats).

- *STEP Analysis* This is another matrix that focuses on specific aspects of the macroenvironment. Its name is derived from four factors:

  1. Social, which is the demographic and cultural aspects of the industry
  2. Technological, which includes such things as R&D activity and rate of technological change
  3. Economic, which is the firm's cost of capital and industry purchasing power
  4. Political factors such as government regulation that might affect the business's operations

Figure 3.4 depicts STEP analysis.

Market/Customer If an industry is a grouping of businesses that are related to particular products and services, a market is a grouping of customers. Within that grouping of customers, the entrepreneur finds the segment of the market that is most likely to purchase the product or service being offered—the first customer. Primary customers are typically identified by a need, often called a "pain" in the market. For example, when Patrick Byrne founded Overstock.com, he believed that women who like to shop for bargains at stores like Marshall's and TJ Maxx would appreciate the convenience of being able to do just that any time of day or night from their home.

Identifying the pain is the first step. Understanding the customer and the potential demand for the product or service requires in-depth market analysis employing primary and secondary research methods. (Market research techniques for entrepreneurs are the subject of Chapter 11.)

Market research of the customer has two objectives. First, it provides a detailed description of the primary customer that includes demographics, buying preferences, and feedback on the product or service that the entrepreneur is offering. The following questions are addressed by the research:

- Who is most likely to purchase the product or service at market introduction?
- What do these customers typically buy, how do they buy it, and how do they hear about it?

FIGURE 3.4 STEP Analysis

Social and Cultural Factors (e.g., changing demographics)	**Opportunities:** Increasing demand for assisted-living facilities
	Threats: Increasing market will attract more new ventures
Technological Advances (e.g., more information available more rapidly)	**Opportunities:** Can meet specific needs of customers
	Threats: Mass marketing is no longer effective
Economic Trends (e.g., the economy is pulling out of a recession)	**Opportunities:** Customer spending is increasing
	Threats: Government may act to curtail spending and associated inflation
Political and Regulatory (e.g., government is seeking to reduce its costs)	**Opportunities:** Provide new products and services
	Threats: Business must take more responsibility and incur increased costs

■ What is their buying pattern? How often do they buy?

■ How can the new venture meet the customers' needs?

Creating a customer matrix from the information gathered makes it easier to look at different customer segments and determine which one is most likely to contain the first customer. Figure 3.5 provides an example of a customer matrix for a new venture. Notice that the entrepreneurs in this example have identified three potential types of customers for their product—a software estimation tool that helps companies determine how long and how much it will cost to produce a software program that the company is developing. The primary customer is the first customer on which the company will focus. Secondary and tertiary customers are markets that the company will explore after it has made significant inroads with the primary customer. In this example, the entrepreneurs have identified the product or service, benefits, distribution, primary competitor, market size, and purchasing pattern for each customer type. Note that other variables may be added to the matrix to compare potential customers on more factors such as price, switching costs, and so forth. The most important information to derive from the matrix and any other data collected from customers is the answer to the questions, "Who is the first customer?" That is, "Whose problem is being solved by this product?"

Determining which customer to target first is primarily a function of finding out which customer has the greatest need for the product. The purpose of the first customer is to get a stream of revenues flowing into the new company. The other customer segments can be targeted once the company has secured a base with the first customer.

FIGURE 3.5   Customer Matrix of a New Venture

Customer Matrix[1]

Customer	Primary Customer	Secondary Customer	Tertiary Customer
Product / Service	Main cost estimation product: • Sell complete package • Interface engine • Knowledge database Educational service: • Training events	Cost estimation service: • Work with in-house cost estimation team • Build customized software package Educational service: • Training events	Main cost estimation modules: • License modules • Interface engine • Knowledge database
Benefit	More accurate cost results provide: • Cost savings • Feeling of accomplishment • Feeling of ownership Ease of use: • No frustration • Time savings Improved communication between parties: • Relaxed work environment		Bundling software package: • Increased sales • Competitive advantage • Value added
Distribution	• Sales associates • Website	• On-site service • Sales associates • Website	• Sales associates • Website
Primary Competitor	• Other software supplier, operating in the same market segment		• Other cost estimation package suppliers
Market Size	• 42% of total software suppliers	• 42% of total software suppliers	• To be determined
Purchasing Pattern	• Annual license agreement	• Initial customized product development • Annual license agreement	• One-time contract

[1] Customer grid provided by SWEst (Software Cost Estimation Interface) team consisting of Bruno Bachinger, Justin Jessee, Thomas Obkircher, and Gregory Wood, MBAs, Marshall School of Business, University of Southern California.

The second objective of market research is to estimate demand for the product or service by providing the entrepreneur a sense of how many customers are actually interested in purchasing. It is critical that the entrepreneur understand that demand figures are only estimates; therefore, gathering various perspectives on demand through a process called triangulation is important. (Forecasting demand is covered in Chapter 16.)

Another objective of market research is competitive intelligence. Unfortunately, gathering competitive intelligence is not often well executed. Typically, entrepreneurs merely scratch the surface of understanding their competitors by looking only at demographics and market share. Although these are important data to collect, perhaps more important is the understanding of the competitors' strengths, or their core competencies and weaknesses, and how those might translate into opportunities, threats, and strategies that could negatively affect the entrepreneur's business.

Another mistake that entrepreneurs make is to benchmark their businesses against competitors. Instead of trying to match competitors' strength for strength, it would be more advantageous to create new value for customers, value not being addressed by competitors. In other words, it would be wiser to raise the bar for competitors rather than trying to equal them.

Entrepreneurs generally encounter three types of competitors: direct, those competing in the same market for the same customer; indirect, or competitors who offer substitute products; and emerging competitors, those who are about to change direction and compete directly. For example, suppose an entrepreneur has launched a new business to provide the first online employee leasing services to the restaurant industry in the Cleveland, Ohio, area. The entrepreneur finds direct competition from offline leasing services that have a foothold in that city and have built long-standing relationships. There is indirect competition from state jobs programs and online bulletin board services like Craigslist or monster.com. The entrepreneur encounters potential emerging competition from large companies such as Marriott Corporation that have a core competency in training people for skilled jobs in the food industry. Competition does not always come from obvious sources, so entrepreneurs must think very creatively about who their competition might be. It is essential that the entrepreneur determine how a potential competitor could compete and how a competitor's core competencies could transfer to the entrepreneur's business.

Product or Service Despite the best efforts of entrepreneurs and product developers, the probability of a successful launch of a new product is only about 60 percent.[7] The primary reason for failure is a lack of sufficient quality market analysis. (Chapter 14 examines effective entrepreneurial strategies for product or service development as well as methods for protecting intellectual assets.)

Every business eventually develops products and services, and every business goes through a design and development phase before launching a product or service. Products and services create assets for the business; therefore, every business also has intellectual property of one sort or another. The product or service analysis portion of the feasibility study looks at what products and services the business will offer, how they will be developed, and how they will be protected.

Founding Team It used to be common for solo entrepreneurs to launch businesses, retain sole ownership, and make all the decisions for the company. In a rapidly changing global marketplace, being a solo entrepreneur is becoming less and less viable. In fact, a growing body of research supports the idea that launching a venture with a team produces a greater chance for success.[8] With a team, all the work and risk of starting a business is shared, and there appears to be more commitment when team members know that they cannot let the rest of the team down. Moreover, if team members bring different expertise and experience to the mix, the new venture can operate longer before having to hire additional people. Finally, an excellent founding team with some start-up experience lends a lot of credibility to the business when it needs to seek investment capital or a bank loan.

However, even with businesses started by teams, much evidence supports the idea of a lead entrepreneur—that is, the team member who has the vision and self-efficacy to ensure that the venture proceeds.[9] In general, the best founding teams have some characteristics in common:

- The team shares a common vision for where the business will go.
- Everyone is passionate about the concept and willing to dedicate themselves to it.
- At least one member of the team has experience in the industry.

Courage and Persistence Save the Day

You have to take advantage of opportunity when it strikes. In 1995, Janie Tsao, who with her husband cofounded Linksys, the major wireless router company, was determined to get the Best Buy account. At that time, it was rare that a company the size of Linksys would win a national account, but Janie was resolute. In April 1996, she attended the RetailVision trade show but could not secure an appointment with the buyer for Best Buy. Determined not to go home without a sale, she boldly tracked him to his hotel room and there presented their product line. The result was a $2 million order. Janie's company recently sold to Cisco for $500 million.

Lesson Learned: *Entrepreneurship takes courage and persistence*.

- The team members all have excellent contacts for sources of capital.
- Members of the founding team have the basic business functions covered: finance, marketing, and operations.
- All founding team members have excellent credit ratings.

These characteristics are also important to investors, so demonstrating in the feasibility analysis that they are present and accounting for gaps in the team's capabilities is important. Often those gaps can be filled outside the founding team through advisors, directors, and independent contractors. (These extended team members are discussed in more detail in Chapters 9 and 10.)

Financials The primary purpose of the financials in the feasibility analysis is to calculate the start-up capital requirements based on projections of sales and expenses. This is no easy task because the new venture has no track record and any projections are only as good as the quality of research that the entrepreneur conducts. The financial projections need to inspire confidence in those that use them to decide if the venture is a good investment. The best way to accomplish this is by providing detailed assumptions to explain how the numbers were derived. The entrepreneur also wants to create a timeline that depicts major milestones in the first couple of years of the business. These milestones signal a change in revenues and expenses that might trigger the need to hire more people, build up inventory, or reduce capacity. (A detailed discussion of the financial calculations can be found in Chapter 16.)

START-UP RESOURCES

Resource gathering is an important aspect of entrepreneurship, and fortunately, it is one of the skills for which entrepreneurs are known. Putting together sufficient resources to start a business requires enormous creativity and persistence, with the ultimate reward being a company that is able to reach critical mass and take advantage of significantly more choices for growth capital.

Bootstrappers are start-up entrepreneurs who have no financial resources beyond their own savings. They realize that to get what they need to start their businesses— location, equipment, money, and perhaps employees—they must possess a double dose of creative ingenuity and supreme self-assuredness. Bootstrapping is begging, borrowing, or leasing everything required to start the venture, and bootstrapping entrepreneurs generate money for the business any way they can. John Schnatter founded Papa John's International, the $164+ million pizza restaurant franchise, with $1600 in personal savings. Schnatter started the company in a broom closet in the back of his bar, at first surviving on profits from selling cheap beer.[10]

Most entrepreneurs start their ventures with their own resources. Bill Gates and Paul Allen started Microsoft in a cheap apartment in Albuquerque with virtually no overhead, a borrowed computer, and very little capital. Ross Perot, one of the great bootstrapping success stories, started EDS with $1000. There are many reasons why most new ventures are initially funded solely through the resources of the entrepreneur:

1. New ventures by definition have no track record, so all the estimates of sales and profits are pure speculation. Therefore, investors see new ventures as very risky.

2. An enormous number of new ventures fail, so the risk for an outside investor is usually too high to consider.

3. Many new ventures have no intellectual property rights or licenses that would give them a competitive advantage.

4. The founders often lack a significant track record of success.

5. Too many new ventures are "me too" versions of something that already exists; the owners have not identified or created a competitive advantage, which makes investment risky.

For these and other reasons, it is not unusual that the only people willing to take the risk on a new venture are the entrepreneur and perhaps his or her friends and family. Entrepreneur resources include savings, credit cards, friends and family, retirement funds, a part-time job, sales of assets, and home equity loans. Credit cards are an expensive choice for entrepreneurs, but when weighed against missing an opportunity to start a business, most entrepreneurs end up using them at start-up. At the extreme for this alternative were the three founders of Encore Productions, who predicted a boom in audiovisual shows for conventions and meetings. Every time the three founders received a credit card application in the mail, they sent it in. At one point, the three of them had accumulated 100 cards and $500,000 in credit. They used the cards like credit lines, paid them off quickly, and used them again. Started in 1988, Encore Productions today is a multimillion-dollar company with over 200 associates.[11]

The Bootstrap Business Location

Many entrepreneurs stay close to home when they start their businesses; many begin their venture in their home. Businesses that don't require a storefront location can easily begin their development in a spare room or a garage. Other entrepreneurs have managed to negotiate free rent and lower lease rates in buildings where a lessor is having difficulty releasing the space. Still others have negotiated with larger companies to lease a portion of its space and take advantage of its reception area and conference room.

Hiring as Few Employees as Possible

Normally, the greatest single expense a business has is its payroll (including taxes and benefits). Subcontracting work to other firms, using temporary help, or hiring

independent contractors can help keep the number of employees and their consequent costs down. Marianne Szymanski founded Toy Tips Inc., a nationally recognized, independent product-testing and research firm in Milwaukee, using student interns from Marquette University and bartering for office space. The interns received university credit for working with her, and she didn't have to deal with payroll. Toy Tips Inc. is featured in Case 3.2 at the end of this chapter. (The issue of raising capital is discussed in more detail in Chapters 16 and 18.)

Starting a business from scratch is both an exciting and stressful experience. With a blank slate on which to paint the vision of a successful business, the entrepreneur is faced with many choices and even more decisions. A thoroughly researched and carefully prepared feasibility study can help any entrepreneur increase the chances for success. In the next chapter, we look at an alternative to starting from scratch: acquiring an existing business.

ISSUES FOR REVIEW AND DISCUSSION

1. How can entrepreneurs use bootstrapping to help them start their businesses?
2. Distinguish among the four stages in the life cycle of a company and the focus that management takes at each point.
3. Explain the purpose of a business model and how it is developed.
4. Discuss the reasons for conducting a feasibility study to test a business concept.

EXPERIENCING ENTREPRENEURSHIP

1. Find a start-up company in your community. Interview the entrepreneur about how he or she gathered the resources necessary to start the business. Evaluate the effectiveness of the entrepreneur's strategy in a report.
2. Spend some time in your local airport or shopping mall observing activities and people. Uncover a pain in the market. In one paragraph, describe a business concept that will fill that need.

Toy Tips® Inc.

Sometimes businesses grow and evolve into something quite different than what they were at the start. Toy Tips is a national marketing and research firm that has made its founder, Marianne Szymanski, a sought-after media guest. She has appeared regularly on *Good Morning America,* the Fox News Channel, CNN, *USA Today, CNBC Power Lunch,* and many others. But in 1991 Toy Tips was just the dream of the 23-year-old with degrees in marketing and psychology from Marquette University in Milwaukee.

Like many entrepreneurs, Szymanski was opportunistic and saw a problem that needed to be solved. She had some experience in the toy industry, through which she realized that there was no source of unbiased and independent information about toy safety, age appropriateness, or educational quality. In fact, Szymanski found that the magazines touting top-ten lists of toys were really paid by the toy manufacturers—hardly impartial recommendations. Szymanksi decided to make her yet-to-be company a reliable, independent source of information about toys.

Using her savings, Szymanski began the business as a 900 number, the National Toy Information Hotline, where people could call to receive the latest information on toy safety, product recalls, and tips on age-appropriate toys. They would pay $2 a minute for each call. Fortunately, the media picked up an appearance on a local talk show, and the business took off faster than she expected. A letter to the Toy Manufacturers of America, the voice of the toy industry, resulted in information and hundreds of samples from toy companies. Working out of her home and testing toys on the living room floor with neighbor children, Szymanski soon realized that she needed another location. She worked out a barter arrangement with a pediatrician, and ultimately was given the opportunity to work out of the childcare center at Marquette University. By the end of 1991, she was working with 50 manufacturers. By the end of 1992, the number had swelled to 140, and her revenues had doubled. To date she has tested more than 10,000 toys from more than 600 manufacturers.

Even though the business was growing, Szymanski couldn't afford to hire employees, so she asked the university to offer an internship program for students with her company. Engineering students tested the toys, journalism students helped her do fact checking and gather information for articles, public relations students helped her with her media tour, psychology and education majors participated in focus groups and testing, and marketing students developed questionnaires and researched the needs of parents. Media contacts gave Szymanski the publicity that she needed to attract the attention of companies such as Toys 'R Us, McDonald's, and Rayovac.

Today, Szymanski combs the toy world to provide research that enables parents and companies to choose toys that are safe and fun. Toy Tips has tested more than 34,000 toys and juvenile products at the Toy Research Institute and at over 500 Toy Tips test sites worldwide. Toy Tips is unique in that it accepts no payments from manufacturers. Szymanski publishes Toy Tips Magazine Online with a distribution of 6.6 million copies. She writes the research articles and uses freelancers for graphic design and the web site. More than 20 million copies have been distributed through Toys 'R Us, Target, Jiffy Lube, Hilton Hotels, and Children's Hospitals in the United States and Canada. So successful is the magazine that in the fall of 2005 she began distributing a quarterly glossy print version through Barnes and Noble.

Szymanski recently expanded her business to include KidTips®—recommendations and advice on nontoy products for kids, such as backpacks. Products are tested for durability, ease of use, sensibility, and value to the consumer. This has led to considering licensable products on which she can put her KidTips brand. The first product is a toy cleaner spray. Most parents do not regularly clean their children's toys, so germs collect on them causing illnesses that could potentially be avoided if the toys were clean. She is working with a manufacturer in Sacramento, California to create a custom product.

Social responsibility has always been a critical aspect of Szymanski's business. Once toys have been tested, they are donated to children's hospitals and to charities in the United States and in Africa to be distributed to children in need. The company hosts the Toy

Tips Annual Executive Toy Test, a fundraiser to raise money for children's charities. Szymanski also created the first toy-lending library in her hometown of Franklin, Wisconsin. She recently received a grant to create a Toy Tips museum exhibit that will travel around the country.

In a business where credibility is everything, Szymanski wonders whether her business could ever be a candidate for sale or acquisition. How could she be certain that the new owner would carry on the values for which the business is known?

Advising the Entrepreneur

1. In what ways was Szymanski able to bootstrap her way to entrepreneurial success?

2. What are the competitive advantages Szymanski created for the business?

3. In which direction should Szymanski take the company now?

4. Is Toy Tips a good candidate for acquisition or sale? Why or why not?

CHAPTER 4

Acquiring a Business and Franchising

In the business world, the rearview mirror is always clearer than the windshield.

Warren Buffett, U.S. financier and investment businessman (1930–)

▶ LEARNING OUTCOMES

- List the reasons why entrepreneurs choose to purchase existing businesses.
- Discuss the criteria for finding the right business.
- Explain how to research a potential business acquisition.
- Compare and contrast franchising with buying an existing independent business.
- Discuss the various techniques for valuing a small business.
- Explain how to negotiate a small business acquisition.

Franchising in the Rent-to-Own Sector

It was October 1996, and Charles Smithgall III was running out of patience, not to mention cash. The previous November he had invested $400,000 of his own money in a franchise, Aaron's Sales & Lease Ownership in Louisville, Kentucky. Then in May, he had opened a second store in Kentucky after borrowing $200,000. In about two months, he would be out of money because the stores were simply not generating sufficient cash flow. But just before he was about to sell his businesses to another franchisee, things turned around, and his stores started making money; all they had needed was time.

Aaron's leases and sells furniture, consumer electronics, appliances, and other accessories. The franchise was founded in 1955 by Charles Loudermilk, who started with an inventory of 300 chairs that he rented for 10 cents a day. He built the company into the leader in the furniture rental and lease-ownership industry focusing on customers who would appreciate his value proposition: guaranteed lowest price, automatic preapprovals with no credit required, and ownership within twelve months. The Aaron's franchise system has over 1000 company and franchise stores with plans to open two new stores per week. Aaron's is also known as a company that gives back to the community through a variety of nonprofit groups such as Habitat for Humanity, Toys for Tots, and Samaritan House.

Before Smithgall opened his first Aaron's, he had no experience in the furniture business. His previous endeavors had been in construction, cable television, and radio. It was a college friend who suggested to Smithgall that he consider the Aaron's franchise because, his friend joked, it was a "great business for someone who's not very smart and has a lot of energy." After opening his first store, Smithgall was intrigued with the idea of becoming a multi-unit franchisee, so in 1997 and 1998 he added four stores, and then in 1999, he added six more, all through internal cash flows. It was then time to expand outside of the South, but he needed to find a location with the right demographics. Providence, Rhode Island, seemed like a good choice because it had a large blue-collar popu-

lation, which was the mainstay of the business. He also decided that it was time to bring in some professional management because the business was becoming increasingly more complex and he wanted to grow it more quickly.

Smithgall found the perfect partner in David Edwards who co-owned a business called SEI that ran seven Aaron's stores. Edwards would run the business from Connecticut, while Smithgall would deal with the financial, corporate, and real estate issues from his base in Atlanta. They called the new company SEI/Aaron's Inc., and in 2002 it acquired fourteen additional stores, eleven in upstate New York that were considered turnaround opportunities. The Aaron's stores' sales were not on par with the company's other holdings, but Smithgall saw this as an opportunity to make fundamental changes in management and, in some cases, in the store location. He succeeded in making the new stores profitable and then began looking for his next location.

Ruth Raines, another Aaron's multi-unit franchisee with eight successful stores in Arkansas, agrees with Smithgall about the importance of planning for growth and using internal cash flows whenever possible. According to Raines, the owner has to pay attention to the length of time it takes for a store to become profitable and to generate positive cash flow. Opening another store before the first one has reached profitability is a recipe for disaster. Furthermore, all the ingredients for successful growth need to be in place before moving ahead. Those ingredients include people, lenders, builders, and the franchisor.

Today, Smithgall believes that he has all of the ingredients for success in place, and his plan is to grow his business to 100 stores and $100 million in annual revenues by 2008. His long-term goal is to create a business that lives on when he wants to retire so that he can pass it to a successor.

Advising the Entrepreneur

1. Smithgall wants to build an empire. How would you advise him to grow the business for the next

few years? In what areas of the country should be
begin looking?

2. What do you think of the strategy of Smithgall
working out of Georgia and Edwards out of
Connecticut? What are the challenges and
opportunities in this type of arrangement?

Sources: "Aaron's History," www.sciaarons.com (accessed
July 21, 2005); G. F. Caron, "Small Business: Empire
Builders: A Look at Three Entrepreneurs Who Each Started
with One Franchise," *Wall Street Journal* (December 15,
2003): R8; R. Raines, "Staying Conservative, Focused and In-
the-Loop," *Franchising World* 37(3) (March 2005): 62.

ot all entrepreneurs prefer to start a business from scratch. Starting with a blank slate is intimidating to some, and generally, there is more risk and more work for those who do so. These entrepreneurs prefer to purchase an existing business or franchise for a variety of important reasons:

- It is less risky than starting from scratch because facilities, employees, and customers are likely to be in place.
- It is an easier route to owning a business if the entrepreneur has limited business experience, especially if the owner stays on for a time to help with the transition.
- The chances for success are increased, particularly if the business has a good reputation, because of established contacts in the industry and a loyal customer base.
- The business may have established trade credit, which is crucial because relationships with suppliers and others take a long time to develop.

With an existing business, the new owner at least knows that the business has had a successful track record. Of course, that does not ensure success in the future, but the possibility for success is more predictable than with a start-up that has no history of success.

Despite the benefits of existing businesses, they rarely come without problems. In the first place, the business may have been put up for sale because it has not been successful and the owner is tired of dealing with it. It may have developed a negative reputation, its inventory may be outdated, and its location may no longer be appropriate. On top of all this, chances are the owner has priced the business at more than it is worth in the marketplace because he or she has put so much effort into it and it is painful to see the company sold for less than what the owner thinks it is worth. To further compound the risk, an owner is not likely to confess the real reason the business is being sold, which may be one or more of the following:

1. Larger companies are squeezing the company out of the market.
2. Key employees have been leaving.
3. The company faces the threat of a major legal action.
4. Competitors' products are better.
5. The owner has a better opportunity elsewhere.

The owner is more likely to say the business is being sold because he or she wants to retire or is suffering from some illness. Therefore, the potential buyer must do considerable investigation to uncover the real reasons for the sale.

FINDING THE RIGHT BUSINESS

Knowing that he wanted to avoid any business that was high risk and had low margins, Larry Broderick, CEO of Denver-based SteelWorks Corp., developed a set of criteria to decide what kind of business to start. Some of the criteria were related to his personal needs, but most were about finding the right business model and were based on his previous experience.[1] Here are a few of them:

1. A business that had a broad scope that would insulate it from market downturns
2. A business with existing customers and vendors
3. A low-tech business but with high growth
4. A market that was not so large so as to encourage major players but not so small that the company couldn't grow
5. Available float from suppliers; in other words, leeway in having to pay vendors
6. Manageable seasonality
7. Cost cutting potential

Every entrepreneur's criteria are different because everyone has unique reasons for wanting to purchase a business and unique experience that gives them a sense of the type of business that is likely to be successful. Starting the search with a set of criteria enables an entrepreneur to quickly eliminate businesses that do not make sense or are not aligned with the entrepreneur's goals.

Sources of Business Opportunities

Perhaps the best sources of information about business opportunities are attorneys, accountants, or bankers because the businesses that they recommend are generally

LEARNING FROM SUCCESS

The Brady Bunch Succeeds at Franchising

In 1999 the Brady family was named the Mail Boxes Etc. franchisee of the year. Since that time, their business has grown to $3.1 million in 2004, helped by the acquisition of the Mail Boxes Etc. franchise by United Parcel Service (UPS).

Dan Brady and his family built their success not by opening one new franchise after another but by taking over foundering franchises that already existed and breathing new life into them. Brady has this to say about his family's accomplishments: "We've learned over time: If you buy an existing location with an existing customer base and cash flow and infuse it with

operational smarts and great execution, the rate at which you can grow positive cash flow and your odds of success go way up as compared to starting the whole thing from scratch." An existing business has another advantage. It is much easier to perform due diligence on the business and make better decisions.

Lesson Learned: *Great management can turn a failing business into a success.*

Source: "Dan Brady's Key Move: Reducing Risk by Buying Existing Franchise Locations," *Startup Nation,* www.startupnation.com (accessed June 24, 2005).

those with which they have had experience. In addition, a long-standing relationship with an attorney, accountant, or banker means that they know a buyer's financial status and needs and can better make a match between a buyer and a potential business opportunity.

There are several other sources of information on business acquisitions, such as the business opportunities section of newspapers like the *Wall Street Journal* and trade publications. It is also possible to find businesses at liquidation auctions, but unless the entrepreneur is a turnaround specialist, taking on a business that has experienced severe problems may be riskier than starting from scratch.

Business Brokers Of the approximately 240,000 small and mid-sized businesses that are sold each year, about 3300 brokers handle half of those sales.[2] Brokers work for business sellers who pay a commission of one to 10 percent of the transaction price. The average sale price of a brokered transaction is $275,000, but it can run into multiple millions. Business brokers vet their clients carefully because their reputations are on the line. They want to make certain that anyone they bring to their client is a serious buyer who will follow through. Some of the things that a potential business owner can do to attract the attention of a business broker are

- Give more information about themselves and the business than the broker requires to indicate a sincere interest.
- Demonstrate strong financial qualifications.
- Be willing to move to a new location to take advantage of a business opportunity.
- Keep an open mind about the type of business; consider a wide range of opportunities.
- Be persistent and follow up with the broker.
- Be in a position to respond quickly when an opportunity becomes available. This means having financial records in order and money available.

Evaluating the Business

Kenny Industrial Services LLC is a Chicago-based cleaning, painting, and maintenance company that was created through a series of strategic acquisitions.[3] CEO Michael Rothman has a set of criteria for acquisition that works for him. First, he buys only companies in which he has a high degree of confidence because he plans for growth of 12 percent in the first year moving to 20 percent by the third year. He always pays for the acquisition with a combination of cash and a note from the seller. Second, he looks for the best practices in the new company and adopts them. His goal is always to ensure that the acquired company fits well with his core company. This formula for success serves as a tough measure for evaluating a potential opportunity.

Buying a business and starting a business require the same kind of research. In either case, the entrepreneur will need to

- Develop a set of criteria for judging the business based on the entrepreneur's needs and goals.
- Understand the industry and the market niche in which the business will operate.
- Examine the records of the business.
- Talk to employees, suppliers, and customers.

- Examine equipment and facilities to make certain they are current and in good working order.
- Examine all contracts.
- Verify the value of the business based on industry statistics and perhaps the advice of a professional business appraiser.

Prior to purchasing the business, the entrepreneur needs answers to many questions to understand the business's profitability and potential for further growth. Does the business generate enough cash to support growth, or will outside capital or perhaps a loan be required? If capital is required, does the business have valuable assets that could serve as collateral for a loan? What is the business's reputation? Is the business free of legal problems? Is the location of the business optimal?

Also, it is imperative that a professional conduct a thorough examination of the financial records for the previous five years or more, keeping an eye out for ways that the seller may have manipulated the numbers to make the business appear more profitable than it may actually be. If the seller does not permit the entrepreneur to examine the company's books, this should serve as a red flag, and the entrepreneur should probably pass on the purchase of this business.

In addition, a number of factors often go without investigation even though they can negatively affect the business, often without any warning. One such factor is a change in the direction of the industry in which the business operates. For example, in the early 1990s, James Carney started Workgroup Technology Corp. (WTC), an $8 million software developer based in Lexington, Massachusetts. Like many entrepreneurs, he got caught up in the day-to-day activities of the business and neglected to notice that the industry around him was changing. By 1997 the software industry was migrating to Web-based software, but WTC was too busy with its current customers to react. After an initial public offering in 1996, the company's stock dropped to just over $1 a share until 2002 when Softech Inc. acquired it. Carney's advice to entrepreneurs is not to rely on initial success to predict where success will come from in the future. It is important to spend time regularly looking to the future to see how things might change.

Another factor that must be considered when evaluating a business opportunity is the direction of community development. Many a business has lost a substantial amount of its customer base when a freeway bypassed the street on which the business was located or the business was not strategically located in the path of future growth. Yet another item to consider in some types of businesses is the status of union contracts. If a union contract renegotiation lies in the immediate future, the entrepreneur may want to consider if he or she is prepared to deal with the negotiation and the possibility of a strike if things do not work out.

In short, a thorough evaluation of the business is essential. A business acquisition or start-up is an important investment of time, money, and reputation for the entrepreneur; it should never be undertaken in haste or without due diligence.

FRANCHISING

A **franchise** is a form of business in which the franchisor sells to a franchisee (the buyer) the following:

- The right to do business under a particular trade name or brand
- The right to a proprietary product, process, or service in a proven market

TABLE 4.1 Fastest-Growing and Most Successful Franchises	
Fastest-Growing Franchises	**Most Successful Franchises**
Subway	McDonald's
Curves (women's fitness)	Subway
7-Eleven	Burger King
Kumon Math & Reading Centers (supplemental education)	7-Eleven
Jan-Pro Franchising Int'l. Inc. (commercial cleaning)	Domino's Pizza
Quizno's	Hardee's
Jani-King (commercial cleaning)	The UPS Store
Coverall Cleaning Concepts (commercial cleaning)	KFC
Liberty Tax Service	Jani-King (commercial cleaning)
Jazzercise, Inc.	Baskin-Robbins

Source: Annual Franchise 500 Listings, *Entrepreneur* (February 2004).

- Training and assistance in setting up the business
- Ongoing marketing and quality control once the business is established
- A financial system
- A marketing plan
- Economies of scale for purchasing and marketing

The franchisee in turn pays an upfront fee and a running royalty on gross sales, typically in the 3 to 8 percent range.

Franchising is experiencing a period of renewed expansion spurred by globalization and the movement of more traditional franchises into nontraditional locations such as airports, universities, and hospitals.[4] Franchising is responsible for more than $1 trillion in annual U.S. sales and about 40 percent of all retail sales. Franchises employ one in every fourteen workers, and a new franchised outlet opens every eight minutes.[5] (See Table 4.1 for a list of the fastest-growing franchises and the most successful franchises.)

Although franchising is a mature concept in the United States, Europe, and Australia, it is experiencing rapid growth as well in Asia, South America, Central America, and Mexico.[6] About half of all franchises opened by U.S. franchisors in the past decade were opened in other countries. Moreover, there is an increase in the number of multi-unit franchisees, with some franchisees owning hundreds of outlets across many states.[7]

Multi-unit ownership is particularly popular in the fast-food arena. Researchers have observed two types of multi-unit franchising: area development franchising and sequential multi-unit franchising.[8] In an area development agreement, the franchisee is obligated to open a specified number of units within a defined period. In a sequen-

| FIGURE 4.1 | Three Types of Franchise Opportunities and Their Associated Risks and Benefits |

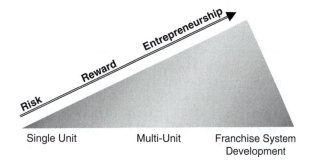

tial agreement, which is the most common type, the franchisee has the right to open additional outlets, but each outlet must go through a separate franchise agreement.

The Nature of Franchises

One of the more prolific bodies of research used to explain the theory behind franchising is agency theory, which proposes that the risk of growth is placed in the hands of the franchisees who pay the upfront fees and ongoing royalties on sales.[9] Agency theory also explains the relationship of the franchisor to franchisee. Franchising is a way to avoid adverse selection (not knowing if the party hired was actually capable of doing the work) and moral hazard (not being sure that the agent was putting forth the maximum effort).[10]

In general, franchises come in two broad types: business format franchises and dealerships or distribution franchises. The most popular type of business format franchise offers a product, an established brand, and an operating system, such as Great Harvest Bread Company and Jiffy Lube or a service like tax preparation, employee leasing, payroll preparation, and real estate services. Dealerships provide a way for manufacturers, such as automobile manufacturers, to distribute their products without having to deal directly with the customer. Those who purchase dealerships are generally required to meet quotas, but like other types of franchises, they also benefit from combined marketing strength.

A body of research has explored what differentiates those who seek small business ownership through the purchase of a single franchise unit versus those who own multiple units as investments and those who develop franchise chains as entrepreneurs. As depicted in Figure 4.1, the level of risk and reward as well as the degree of entrepreneurial skills involved increase as one moves from single-unit ownership through area development to franchise system development. In general, those who choose the single-unit ownership approach have a desire to be their own boss and to do that in the more secure and proven format of a franchise.[11] Those who go into area development franchise agreements are required to act more entrepreneurally because, as they decide to add more franchises to their collection, they must analyze the situation, conduct feasibility analysis, and invest more of their own capital and other resources into the development. At the farthest end of the spectrum is franchise system development, which carries with it the highest levels of risk and reward and requires the highest level of entrepreneurial attitude and skill set.

Benefits of Franchising for the Franchisor and the Franchisee Franchising has experienced tremendous interest because there are significant benefits for both the franchisor and the franchisee. For the franchisor, franchising is a relatively easily accessible source of capital for retail expansion, which is important when a chain needs to grow rapidly to effectively compete.[12] Because franchisees earn profits based on the performance of their units, franchisors are relieved of the responsibility of continually monitoring each unit, as they would need to do if all the stores were company owned.

One reason why franchisees are attracted to the franchise system is that they become part of an established system with an almost turnkey business that provides some degree of independence and a lot of support. In a good franchising partnership, there is trust and mutual respect that works to the benefit of both parties. Franchisees have the benefit of getting into business ownership more quickly than they would with an independent business, and often they see their business achieve the break-even point faster. What contributes to that speed is the ability of the franchise to purchase with quantity discounts from the franchise system that a typical independent business owner would not have. Franchisees benefit from national advertising programs in which they invest and which would be beyond the reach of most small independent businesses.

Perhaps the biggest benefit to the franchisee is tapping the experience of the franchisor. First-time business owners often make many costly mistakes because of lack of real-world experience. The franchisee, by contrast, can avoid many of those mistakes through training and support from the franchisor.

Risks for the Franchisee and the Franchisor Although there are many advantages to franchising, it is not without risk. Even if a business is designed well but not executed well, it will fail. Despite the benefit of associating with an established brand, the franchisee is still opening a new business with all the related challenges. If the franchisee does not have excellent management skills (the fundamental reason why businesses of all types fail), the business will be at risk. This is particularly true because the franchisee pays the franchisor up to 10 percent of gross sales monthly, so it is a huge challenge to control costs and make a profit. A number of studies have determined that failure rates among franchisees range from 38.1 percent to 71.4 percent.[13] Another risk for franchisees is the bankruptcy of the franchisor. Several well-known franchises have experienced reorganization through Chapter 11 bankruptcy, including Days Inns, Nutri-System, and 7-Eleven. During the process, the brand's image is tarnished and that may affect the revenues to the franchisee. Because it is likely that the franchise agreement had an arbitration clause in it, the franchisee will not have the option of going to court to seek restitution of lost revenues. Some franchises are very slanted in favor of the franchisor and should be avoided. Still others are scams that require the franchisee to pay multiple times the actual value of the concept, equipment or supplies. Doing effective research on potential franchises will help avoid these types of businesses.

Franchisees should understand that the wealth and goodwill from a successful franchise are largely controlled by the franchisor through contract, which is very different from an entrepreneurial business where all the control is in the hands of the entrepreneur. Those who are looking for the opportunity to be their own boss will not find complete independence in a franchise situation because the franchisor makes the major systemwide decisions. Franchisees will be required to strictly adhere to the operations standards set by the franchisor or risk termination of the franchise agreement. Periodic inspections by the franchise corporate office will ensure that the franchisee is not deviating from the system standards. Franchisees may also be required to purchase all their supplies, equipment, and materials from the franchisor, sometimes at prices that exceed what they might pay somewhere else. Potential franchisees need to weigh these risks against the benefits discussed in the previous section.

For the franchisor, building a franchise chain carries with it the ultimate risk of creating something for which there is little demand on the part of franchisees or from potential consumers for its product or service. Franchisors will need to carefully investigate potential franchisees to ensure that they are qualified to manage and grow a business and will represent the brand well. This is not easily accomplished, and many franchisors complain of the high cost of attracting qualified, high-quality franchisees.[14] In addition, the franchisor must invest significant time and capital into preparing the business to franchise; expenses include legal, accounting, consulting, and training. Furthermore, franchisors must be prepared to operate for several years without a profit.

The choice of whether to permit franchisees to own multiple units is also of concern to a franchisor. Although the benefits for growth of the system are great, there is also a risk that a franchisee who owns a substantial number of units in a given geographic area could leverage that control to the detriment of the franchisor. Therefore, as in any business relationship, franchisors and franchisees must have an incentive to work together for the success of the franchise system as a whole.

Evaluating a Franchise Opportunity

Entrepreneurs seeking to use franchising as a way to rapidly grow their companies or potential franchisees looking to purchase a business need to do their homework. The evaluation issues for each are different, but the importance of conducting the evaluation is the same for both. Here we discuss the critical factors that entrepreneurs and potential franchisees must consider before moving forward with their opportunities.

The Franchisor's Evaluation Looking at franchising from the perspective of the franchisor, it is important to recognize that not every type of business is appropriate for a franchise concept. Some of the business characteristics that should be present in an excellent franchise concept include the following:

- Registered trademarks
- Successful prototype stores with a track record of profitability and a positive reputation
- A business that can be systematized so that it can be easily replicated
- A product or service that can be successful in many different geographic regions
- A detailed prospectus that spells out the franchisee's rights, responsibilities, and risks
- An operations manual that specifies all the functions of the business and their associated policies
- A training and support system
- Site-selection criteria and architectural standards

Furthermore, the franchisor must be prepared with adequate funding because preparing the business to offer franchises can cost several hundred thousand dollars.

One of the critical documents to be developed during the preparation of the franchise for sale is the franchise agreement. This should be undertaken with the guidance of a qualified attorney and an accountant. The franchise agreement can be compared to a lease agreement in which the franchisee is renting the use of the business for a specified period. It will detail the rules by which the franchisor and franchisee will abide during the term of the agreement, including ways to terminate the agreement, how to deal with disagreements, potential for renewal of the agreement, first right of refusal or option to take on additional franchises, costs associated with the purchase of the franchise, intellectual property rights, requirements to open the business (stock of goods and materials), and whether the franchisee has the right to sublease or sell the franchise to someone else.

One very important item in the agreement is whether the franchisee has exclusivity in a specific geographic region. Research has found that territorial exclusivity decreases the chance for failure in a franchise chain and that it makes franchise acquisition more attractive for franchisees because it reduces the risk of encroachment by other franchisees and attracts more franchisees to the system.[15] On the negative side, because franchisors alone determine the terms of the franchise agreement and control the right to terminate the agreement, the franchisor has the opportunity to withhold information from the franchisee about plans for geographic density—that is, how many franchises can locate in a particular geographic area. Franchisors earn their profits based on royalties derived from the entire franchise system, so they have a real incentive to create densities within geographic regions. If they leave growth in the hands of franchisees in a particular territory, it will generally occur much more slowly.

Franchisees, by contrast, earn their income on profits net of royalties paid from the outlets that they own, and therefore they want control over geographic regions. So franchisees typically look for exclusivity in their agreements, and franchisors must balance being able to attract sufficient franchisees to make the system work against not providing exclusivity and being able to add new franchises where necessary to thwart competition. The Subway chain chose the route of offering nonexclusive franchise territories and, as a result, it faces frequent litigation from franchisees who believe that the franchisor is making it difficult for them to be profitable.

The Franchisee's Evaluation In many respects, deciding to purchase a franchise is very much like deciding to purchase an independent business, except that because potential franchisees tend to look at a franchise as a proven concept with a turnkey operating system, they often fail to do enough due diligence before making the decision to purchase. They simply rely on what is conveyed to them in the franchisor's Uniform Franchise Offering Circular, the disclosure document required by the regulators. However, it is vital that potential franchisees know that no one ensures that the circular is completely truthful and that additional research on the franchisor should be conducted. The circular is essentially a prospectus that discloses the risk, required fees and investment, bankruptcy information, litigation issues, time in business, and financial statements of the franchise. The circular also provides a list of the expenses associated with purchasing the franchise. These expenses include the following:

- Location acquisition
- Lease deposits if renting or the cost of the land if buying
- Architectural designs
- Zoning if the property is not appropriately zoned for this use
- Equipment, supplies, and fixtures, and freight costs if they are delivered
- Improvements on the site—for example, building and landscaping
- Signage

- Start-up inventory
- Insurance on the property, liability, worker's compensation, casualty, and automobile
- Employee training and set up for opening day
- Legal and accounting fees
- Working capital to cover revenue gaps

In addition to studying the circular, potential franchisees should answer a number of very important questions prior to entering a franchise agreement:

1. Does the franchisor have an excellent reputation in the industry?

2. Is the franchisor in partnership or any other legal relationship with another franchisor? If so, how will the franchisee be protected should that relationship fail?

3. Is the franchisee required to do anything that appears questionable from a legal or ethical perspective?

4. Under what circumstances can the franchisee or franchisor terminate the franchise agreement, and what are the consequences to either party?

5. Will the franchisor grant an exclusive territory? Is that area subject to reduction or modification? If so, under what conditions?

6. Will the franchisor reveal the certified financial figures for one of its franchises, and can those figures be verified with the franchisee?

7. Will the franchisor provide a management-training program, an employee-training program, public relations and advertising support, or credit?

LEARNING FROM THE GLOBAL MARKET

Lifestyle Versus Entrepreneurship: New Zealand's Dilemma

Many New Zealand business owners have found the perfect life–work balance. In fact, those who own lifestyle businesses in New Zealand probably spend more time on their lives than on their businesses. Sandra and Rory Burke, for example, run a textbook publishing company from their 35-foot sailboat in the waters off New Zealand. Often they are far enough out from the shore that they can't get e-mail or cell phone messages. They like their business just the way it is and figure that to grow it they would have to dock, find office space on solid ground, and hire some employees. And that prospect is not very appealing to them.

New Zealand's adult population is highly enterprising with about 14.7 percent of adults involved in launching a business, a rate higher than that in the United States. But despite that level of entrepreneurship, New Zealand's standard of living is declining because most of that country's business owners only want to earn enough money to support their lifestyle; they don't long to achieve overwhelming success—or riches. Their goals are more modest than those of their American counterparts, a stance that is negatively affecting the country's economy. "We despise the growth mania that we hear Americans talk about, the compulsion to get more customers," says Howard Frederick, who tracks the country's small businesses at Unitec New Zealand, an Auckland university. "Here it's "More customers? That's a bother.'"

Source: D. McGinn, "The Trouble with Lifestyle Entrepreneurs," *Inc.* (July 2005), www.inc.com.

8. Does the franchisor assist in finding a suitable location?

9. What is the financial health of the franchisor? Can financial statements be verified?

10. What is the track record of the franchise?

11. Has the franchisor conducted an in-depth investigation of the franchisee to ensure that he or she has the necessary skills and financial requirements to operate the business successfully?

12. How much capital will be required to start and operate the business to a positive cash flow? Does the initial fee include an opening inventory of products and supplies? What do royalties pay for and how are they calculated?

In addition to answering these questions and many more that are not included here, it is imperative to consult with an attorney familiar with franchises to ensure that nothing has been missed and that everything is in order.

VALUING A SMALL BUSINESS

Businesses are given a valuation for a variety of reasons: to determine a price for buying or selling, for estate and tax purposes, in divorce settlements, and for raising capital to grow a business. What is clear about business valuation is that it is more art than science. A wealth of tools is available to predict value, including complex software tools that promise to reduce valuation to a simple formula. However, all of valuation comes down to this simple truth: A business is worth what a buyer is willing to pay. Value is a subjective term with myriad meanings. In fact, at least six different definitions of value are in common usage:

- **Fair market value** is the price at which a willing seller would sell and a willing buyer would buy in an arm's-length transaction. By this definition, every sale would ultimately constitute a fair market value sale.

- **Intrinsic value** is the perceived value arrived at by interpreting balance sheet and income statements through the use of ratios, discounting cash-flow projections, and calculating liquidated asset value.

- **Investment value** is the worth of the business to an investor and is based on the individual requirements of the investor as to risk, return, tax benefits, and so forth.

- **Going-concern value** is the current status of the business as measured by financial statements, debt load, and economic environmental factors, such as government regulation, that may affect the long-term continuation of the business.

- **Liquidation value** assumes the selling off of all assets and calculating the amount that could be recovered from doing so.

- **Book value** is an accounting measure of value and refers to the difference between total assets and total liability. It is essentially equivalent to shareholders' or owners' equity.

A number of factors affect the valuation of a business. Small business owners typically attempt to pay the fewest taxes possible by using legitimate deductions such as high salaries for owners, above-market rent for buildings leased to the business from a family trust, and company automobiles and other expenses. Therefore, financial statements have to be adjusted, or recast, to understand the full earning potential of the business. As a result, it will take some investigation to determine the real earnings of the business.

Precisely what is being sold will have an effect on the value of the business to the buyer. In an asset sale, which historically has been the most common type of sale, the seller is taxed at the corporate level and again when the proceeds of the sale are transferred out of the corporation. The liabilities remain with the seller. This type of sale might trigger a higher valuation for the buyer. Of course, buyers are not required to purchase all the assets of a business, especially if those assets are not producing income.

Owners typically prefer to sell stock because then the sale results in a single capital gains tax. However, a stock sale is only available to incorporated businesses and is not necessarily advantageous to a buyer if the business has depreciable assets on its balance sheet because the buyer cannot "step up," or increase, the value of those assets and increase depreciation charges, which would reduce taxable income. In addition, the buyer assumes all the liabilities of the company. Consequently, a stock purchase would likely trigger a lower valuation from the buyer's perspective. However, a stock purchase is preferable to some buyers if the corporation has a good credit rating and if certain important contracts have been made between the corporation and suppliers, lessors, or employees.

Methods for Valuing a Business

There are numerous ways to value a business. Here we focus on four methods that are in common use: adjusted book value, multiple of earning, discounted cash flow, capitalization of earnings.

Adjusted Book Value The book value of a going concern is simply the owner's equity—that is, the value of the assets less the outstanding debts. Adjusted book value is based on balance sheet items. The difficulty with this method lies in how assets are valued—as realizable value or as liquidation value. Cash and near-cash items are easily valued, but in the case of accounts receivable, not all are readily collectible. The buyer will need to learn what the bad-debt rate for the business is so that it can be deducted and thereby provide a better estimate. But there will also be costs associated with collection that have to be taken into account. Land and facilities have real estate market value that an appraiser would have to estimate. In short, both inflation and depreciation affect the value of all assets to some degree. Therefore, balance sheet items are adjusted upward or downward to reflect their fair market value. Because many entrepreneurial companies in the early stages tend to have few assets relative to firms at later stages of development, this approach may not reflect the true value of the company.

Multiple of Earning Using a price/earnings (P/E) ratio to value a business is a common method among publicly owned companies because it's simple and direct. This ratio is determined by dividing the market price of the common stock by the earnings per share. For example, if a company has 200,000 shares of common stock and its earnings before interest and taxes (EBIT) is $250,000, the earnings per share will be 200,000/$250,000, or $.80 per share. If the price per share rose to $3, the price/earnings ratio would be $3/$.80, or $3.75. The business would then be valued at $750,000 (200,000 shares × 3.75). This method is also preferred for middle market manufacturers.

Another method that typically results in a higher valuation uses a year's worth of after-tax earnings and multiplies it by the industry average multiple based on the P/E ratios of public companies in the industry. This method must be considered with care. To say that a young, private company with earnings of $250,000 in an industry where the average P/E is 12 should be valued at $3 million probably is overstating the case. It has been suggested that public firms have a premium value of about 25 to 35 percent over a closely held company, and so any P/E multiple used should be discounted to reflect that premium.[16] That would mean that the private company in the example now has a value of $2,250,000 ($250,000 × 9). Even with discounting, the variation in the ways a company can calculate earnings and the difficulty in finding a public company that is comparable often make this a dubious measure at best for purposes of valuation.

The EBIT multiple is not really an arbitrary number; it is, instead, associated with rules of thumb in the industry. For example, one rule of thumb is that if a company purchases a new machine for its factory, the company should be able to recoup the cost within five years based on the savings in labor costs. Similarly, in buying a business, the business should be able to pay for itself in three to five years if earnings remained the same. Therefore, a conservative buyer might want a 20 percent return on investment in this type of company, which is five times earnings. Paying ten times earnings will produce a 10 percent return.

Discounted Cash Flow If valuing the business by its potential earning power is the goal, the most common measure and the one that gives more accurate results is future cash flows because only cash or cash equivalents are used in the calculations. The method is called **discounted cash flow analysis,** or capitalization of future cash flows to the present value. This simply means calculating how much an investor would pay today to have a cash-flow stream of x dollars for x number of years into the future.

For this analysis, the entrepreneur uses pro forma cash-flow statements for the business and determines a forecast period. (Refer to Chapters 16 and 17 for discussions of pro forma cash flows and methods for forecasting sales and expenses.) The length and nature of business cycles in the industry must also be understood so that a forecast period that goes either from trough to trough or peak to peak in a cycle is chosen. In other words, there needs to be at least one complete business cycle within the forecast period to give a fair representation of the effect on cash flow (see Figure 4.2).

Once the forecast period has been defined and the cash-flow projections prepared, a discount rate must be chosen. This is not a purely arbitrary exercise. The buyer or investor's point of view must be considered, and that viewpoint will often involve the opportunity cost to the investor/buyer of investing in or buying the business. In general, the discount rate is based on the level of risk of the business and the opportunity cost of capital. More specifically, the rate should be based on three factors:

1. The rate achievable in a risk-free investment such as U.S. Treasury notes over a comparable time period. For example, for a five-year forecast, the current rate on a five-year note is appropriate.

2. A risk factor based on the type of business and the industry should be added to the interest rate in item 1. Several precedents for determining what these factors are have been established over years of study. One accepted standard is that offered by James Schilt[17] in the form of five categories of business. Note that even within each category there is room for degrees of risk.

FIGURE 4.2 Business Cycles and the Forecast Period

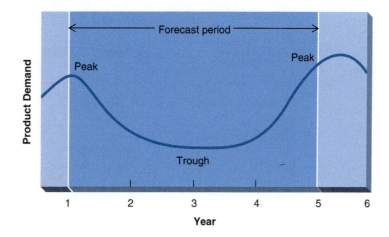

- Category 1: Established businesses with good market share, excellent management, and a stable history of earnings: 6 to 10 percent
- Category 2: Established businesses in more competitive industries, still with good market share, excellent management, and a stable earnings history: 11 to 15 percent
- Category 3: Growing businesses in very competitive industries, little capital investment, an average management team, and a stable earnings history: 16 to 20 percent
- Category 4: Small businesses dependent on the entrepreneur or larger businesses in very volatile industries and the lack of a predictable earnings picture: 21 to 25 percent
- Category 5: Small service businesses operating as sole proprietorships: 26 to 30 percent

3. The life expectancy of the business because typically discounting is based on this factor.

The example in Table 4.2 illustrates this valuation method. Assuming the current rate on a ten-year Treasury Note is 6 percent and the business is a category 2 business at a 14 percent risk factor, the adjusted discount rate becomes 20 percent. Using a calculator or a present value table, the present value of the five-year cash-flow stream can be calculated. This example shows that this hypothetical business will throw off $1,575,000 of positive cash flow over five years. Hence, a buyer would be willing to pay $875,000 today for that business, given the discount rate.

If three scenarios have been created—best-, worst-, and most-likely cases or success, survival, and liquidation—there will be three values for the business. The entrepreneur then assigns a probability of occurrence to each scenario and multiplies the discounted cash flow by that probability to arrive at an adjusted present value. A variation of this method is the **excess earnings method,** which combines the estimate of future earnings with the value of the business's existing assets minus liabilities. The advantage of this approach is that it accounts for goodwill, which is an

TABLE 4.2 One Method for Discounting Cash Flows

Assume: 6% risk-free rate plus 14% risk factor (category 2 business).
Discount the cash flow: 20% discount rate.

End of Year	Cash Flow ($1000s)	Factor (20%)	Present Value ($1000s)
1	200	.8333	166.7
2	250	.6944	173.6
3	300	.5787	173.6
4	375	.4823	180.9
5	450	.4019	180.9
Totals	1575		874.7

intangible asset that represents the difference between an unproven business and an established, successful one. Prior to using this approach, it is important to recast historical earnings to depict how the business would have looked without the owner's excess salary and other perks. In brief, this method has the following steps:

1. Compute the adjusted tangible net worth of the business. Tangible assets are adjusted up or down for market value; then liabilities are subtracted.

2. Compute the opportunity cost of this investment. How much would the investor/buyer earn by investing the same amount in another, comparable investment?

3. Forecast net earnings. Earnings from previous income statements can provide a basis for the forecast, which is made before subtracting the owner's salary.

4. Calculate the extra earning power, which is the difference between forecasted earnings and opportunity costs.

5. Estimate the value of intangible assets or goodwill. If the business has extra earning power (some small businesses and family businesses do not), that figure can be multiplied by what is known as a years-of-profit (YOP) figure. An average business will have a YOP of 3 to 4; a high-risk business may have a YOP of 1; and an established business may have a YOP of 7 to 10.

6. Calculate the value of the business by adding up the figures.

Once a mathematical estimate of value has been achieved, other factors will come into play that are difficult to put into the equation and are more rightly points of negotiation. All the projections used in the valuation of the business are based on assumptions, and the buyer/investor will likely question them and perhaps discount the value of the business even further. Another factor affecting the final valuation is the degree of legitimate control that the owner has in the business. This is typically measured by the amount of stock that the owner holds. Buying out an owner who holds the majority of the stock is more valuable than buying out one who does not. Finally, intangibles such as a loyal-customer list, intellectual property, and the like will also create additional value for the business. The "real" value, or market value, of the business will be ultimately determined through negotiation with investors, lenders, or underwriters. However, doing the calculations just discussed provides an excellent jumping-off point for the negotiations.

Capitalization of Earnings With this method, it is important to be able to determine the historical annual earnings of the company, which is represented by EBIT (earnings before interest and taxes) or EBITDA (earnings before interest, taxes, depreciation, and amortization). Whichever figure is chosen, it is then divided by a capitalization rate, which is the return that the buyer requires on the investment. For example, if the company's EBITDA was $500,000 and the buyer needed a 20 percent return on investment, the price the buyer would be willing to pay would be $2,500,000.

Placing a Value on a Service Business Service companies are a bit different from product companies when it comes to valuation. The biggest asset of a service company is employees, including senior management and followed by customers and the business system. What is difficult about placing a value on a service company is that much of its value depends on personal relationships between management and customers. Without those relationships, there is no business. Therefore, when considering the purchase of a service business, it would be critically important for the buyer to place some conditions on the deal and pay out the purchase price in stages to protect against significant changes in the business after closing. Some important conditions might be the following:

LEARNING FROM MISTAKES

When the Weather Rains on a Franchise's Parade

Smoothie franchises began in the late 1980s in southern California and quickly spread through the West and Southwest. People loved the taste of a cool, sweet smoothie on a warm day, and there were plenty of those days in the West. In March 1998, David Van Meter purchased a franchise from Juice Stop Branding Corp. and located it in Boulder, Colorado. His grand opening was a hit—customers lined up down the street. However, Van Meter soon noticed that any time the weather got cloudy or windy, people stayed away; in December and January, sales fell by 60 percent, much more than the 25 percent that he had predicted. He had significantly underestimated the effect of weather on smoothie sales. The weather, however, did not deter competitors from leaping into the smoothie craze and that cut further into Van Meter's meager profits.

As he attempted to find ways to increase sales year-round, the Atkins diet suddenly reemerged, creating yet another obstacle: Many people now viewed smoothies and their high-carbohydrate count in the same category as desserts, rather than a healthy, nutritious snack. Unable to turn around four years of net losses, Van Meter sold his business to a former employee in October 2002. Those who stayed in the smoothie business have begun to locate in indoor malls and airports where weather is not as much a factor. They have also begun to diversify their offerings to attract new customers, helping to "smooth out" their earnings throughout the year.

Lesson Learned: *Location matters and so does the ability to adjust to changes in the marketplace.*

Source: "Small Business (A Special Report); Not-So-Smooth Sailing: The Smoothie Franchise Seemed Like an Idea Poised for Limitless Growth; But Then it Ran into a Little Problem: The Weather" by Daniel Nasaw from *The Wall Street Journal*, December 15, 2003, p. R9. Copyright © 2003 Dow Jones & Co. Reprinted by permission of Dow Jones & Co. via Copyright Clearance Center.

- The owner must stay on as an employee for two years or perhaps as an employee for one year and as a consultant for two more years.
- Any loss of an account that was in place at the closing of the sale will reduce the payout by some defined amount.
- One-third of the total purchase price will be paid at closing. The remainder will be paid in equal payments over three years.

As careful as evaluation procedures are, they still have a significant "crystal ball" aspect because at several critical points in the process the entrepreneur makes subjective decisions. There is really no way to completely avoid this dilemma. It has been estimated that new ventures encounter more than 300 significant unexpected events that will substantially affect the business in the first three years of its life alone, and it is impossible to factor all those variables into the equation. The bottom line is that there is no best way to value a business, particularly because each situation is different. The most prudent approach is probably to use several techniques and, through negotiation with the investor/buyer, determine the one that makes the most sense for the situation and is a win–win solution for both parties.

NEGOTIATING THE ACQUISITION

Once general agreement on terms has been reached between a buyer and a seller, it is time to negotiate the specific terms of the agreement and the price. The valuation tools that the buyer used to estimate the value of the business may get set aside by a seller who has a fixed price in mind. This is when negotiation takes over. *Negotiation* is the process of coming to agreement on terms and price in a way that provides a win for both parties. The buyer typically drafts and signs a nonbinding letter of intent that spells out the terms of the deal as they are understood at that point. If the seller also signs the letter, it signals their mutual intent to move forward with the agreement.

The buyer will put up a refundable deposit as earnest money, or good-faith money. These actions trigger a new round of due diligence that is more in-depth because the buyer now has permission to contact the seller's attorneys, vendors, bankers, and so forth. However, throughout the due diligence, the buyer will probably be under a confidentiality clause and will be prohibited from disclosing any information relative to the negotiation. This is done to protect the business in the event the sale does not go through for whatever reason. In general, the seller will keep the most sensitive information about the business—for example, trade secrets and customer lists—secret until the buyer actually signs the contract for purchase.

In some cases in which the seller is working with a business broker, the broker may solicit bids from a number of interested parties in the form of letters of intent. In this instance, it is wise for the buyer to put forward his or her best offer. One way to avoid having to deal with a controlled auction as described is to put up a larger deposit and have the seller agree to not shop the business during the negotiations.

Negotiating the Price

In general, it is always wise to let the other party make the first offer of price. However, this is a commonly known negotiating tactic, so if both parties are waiting for the other to make the offer, the deal will go nowhere. The reality is that the seller typically sets an asking price or gives a range of prices to attract buyers with the right financial requirements. Moreover, if the seller is using a business broker, the broker will require a listing price.

If the seller's asking price is based on a formal and independent appraisal, the buyer is more likely to offer something closer to the asking price and less likely to waste the seller's time with a low-ball offer, generally about 50 percent of the asking price or lower. Where a seller is firm on a price and the buyer really wants the business, the buyer can attempt to modify the terms of the deal to make up for having to pay more than expected.

Negotiating the Terms

As important as the price of the company are the terms of the purchase agreement. Terms can mean the difference between a win–win for the buyer and seller and a difficult transition that puts stress on everyone. In this section, we discuss some of the key terms in a purchase agreement.

Seller Financing Buyers will often want to know if the seller is willing to finance at least a portion of the deal. It is estimated that seller financing is a factor in more than half of all business sales. It is beneficial to the buyer and the seller because the buyer does not have to invest as much cash and the seller can defer some capital gains tax on the sale. To do this, however, both parties will need to comply with the IRS rules on installment sales. It is important to note that franchises are not generally seller financed.

Earnouts and Indemnifications Sometimes there is disagreement about what the business is worth. To resolve the conflict and still close the deal, the terms will include an earnout clause in which the purchase price is stated as a minimum price subject to an increased price if the business achieves specified financial goals at some designated point in the future. Typically, the goals are expressed in terms of percentages of gross sales or revenues because net sales are easily altered through the manipulation of expenses. An example of an earnout clause might be that the seller will receive 2 percent of gross sales collected over $2 million for three years and payable annually.

If there are major unknown liabilities for the buyer, the buyer may request an indemnification clause in the sales contract, specifying that if the buyer becomes the subject of a lawsuit from a customer, employee, or supplier during a specified period, the seller will pay the costs of defending the lawsuit. The problem with indemnification clauses is enforcement if the seller is no longer associated with the business and cannot be found. An alternative that is safer for the buyer is to require that some portion of the purchase price be placed in an escrow account for a defined period against the possibility of a lawsuit.

Seller and Key Management Issues As a rule, a buyer wants the seller to maintain a relationship with the business for some time after the sale. This relationship can be in the form of an employment contract or a consulting agreement. The reason for keeping the seller and perhaps key management is that the buyer wants to ensure that the business will continue as is, but more importantly, that the buyer can capture the tacit knowledge (knowledge not codified in business documents) that was built up over time. If the seller and key management leave immediately, that knowledge is lost to the new owner.

Another critical issue related to the seller and key management is avoiding a situation in which the seller leaves the company and starts another one to compete against the buyer. This can be accomplished through a noncompete agreement that specifies where the seller cannot compete or use certain trade secrets, business processes, customer lists, and so forth that now belong to the buyer. For a noncompete agreement to be enforceable, it can only restrict the seller from owning a business similar to the one that was sold, in the same geographic area, for a specific period of time. However, potential buyers should be aware that noncompetes are very difficult to enforce.

Closing the Deal

Officially, *closing* occurs when all the necessary documents have been signed, expenses to date have been apportioned between the buyer and the seller, and the accounts and keys to the business have been transferred to the new owner. The closing can occur when all the parties meet with their respective attorneys or an escrow can be used, which is a third party who acts as the agent to ensure that everything is completed. It is a good idea to do a final walk-through the business just before closing to make sure that nothing has changed since the terms of the deal were drawn up.

Buying an existing business or franchise may be the perfect way for someone to become an entrepreneur without incurring the risk involved in starting from scratch. With sufficient research and due diligence, the right business can be found and a successful deal negotiated.

ISSUES FOR REVIEW AND DISCUSSION

1. What are some of the key factors that need to be taken into consideration when choosing a business to purchase?

2. What are the primary differences between an independent business and a franchise?

3. From an entrepreneur's perspective, what is the difference between a franchisor and a franchisee?

4. What are some key points that entrepreneurs should think about when negotiating a deal with the seller of a business or a franchise?

EXPERIENCING ENTREPRENEURSHIP

1. Interview an entrepreneur in your community who acquired a business. Write a report that details how that entrepreneur found the opportunity and what type of research that he or she did prior to purchasing it.

2. Identify a franchise opportunity that interests you. Determine if you meet the requirements to become a franchisee. Then talk with a franchisee in that business about the pros and cons of owning a franchise. Would you go forward with this opportunity? Why or why not?

When the Little Things Count

In the fall of 2000, the restaurant industry in Chicago was collapsing under the weight of the longest slump in thirty years. It did not seem like an opportune time to start a fast-food restaurant, but that didn't deter Mike Roper from opening his first Quizno's Sub franchise in Olympia Fields, a suburb south of Chicago. By the second year, sales in that store had skyrocketed 40 percent, far exceeding his predicted 4 percent increase. Moreover, in 2003, a year in which fast-food giants McDonald's and Burger King were cutting back on locations, Roper added two more stores.

The Fast-Food Industry

The International Franchise Association reports that every eight minutes a new franchise unit is added to the more than 320,000 already operating in the United States. These franchises cover 75 industries and generate more than $1 trillion in sales annually. The sub sandwich industry can trace its U.S. origins to Philadelphia's Hog Island shipyards during World War I and to New Orleans and the po'boys created by the Italian immigrants who later moved to New York, bringing their popular sandwich with them. Today, the sub sandwich has become a regular feature of the American diet. Some consider it the antiburger. In fact, it has been calculated that sales of the sub sandwich category in 2001 grew 12 percent over the prior year, while sales of hamburgers grew at only 2.7 percent.

The major players in the industry are unquestionably Subway, with more than 23,128 units worldwide and sales of over $468 million, and Quizno's with more than 3600 units and sales at $130 million and growing at 30 percent annually. The nearest competitor to Quizno's is Blimpie with 1750 stores and $28 million in 2003 sales. Other smaller players include Potbelly's Sandwich Works, Jimmy John's, Pickerman's, Panera, Togo's Great Sandwiches, and Einstein's Bagels (see Figure 4.3).

Chicago was an early location for many of the chains in this industry. Subway has had stores in Chicago since the late 1970s and now claims 500 locations in the Chicago area. But Quizno's, which began in Denver in 1981, is coming on strong. In 1998 it had only 4 stores in the Chicago area, by 2003 there

were 102, and today there are more than 200. One primary difference between Subway and Quizno's is that Quizno's toasts it subs, which is currently very popular. Quizno's also offers three sizes of sandwiches, whereas Subway offers two. Still, nationwide, Quizno's has a long way to go to catch up with Subway.

Many believe that dominating a local market is the key to success. Once one market has been penetrated, the company can move to another. Spreading restaurants all over the country makes no sense because the company never achieves dominance in a particular market quickly enough. Also, the reality of the food services business is that customers, in general, are not loyal and if they have a bad experience somewhere, they are not likely to return. Therefore, to be successful in this business, one has to focus on quality, give the customer a good experience, and be convenient.

Roper's Foray into Franchising

Mike Roper had no experience in the food services industry. His background consisted of small information technology and data-processing companies. In 2000 when the technology boom ended, he began to think about what he wanted to do next. He believed that his previous work had given him some skills that he could leverage to run his own business, but he had no idea of the type of business he should own.

One day Roper stopped by a Quizno's to grab a sandwich. As he enjoyed the taste of his chicken mesquite sandwich, he realized that he had never tasted anything quite like it—a real competitive advantage in the market as far as he could tell. Locating an 800 number for the company that he discovered on the wall at the restaurant, he called the Denver-based chain to inquire about what it would take to become a Quizno's franchisee. He found out that he would need about $190,000 in capital of which $70,000 had to be cash. He qualified financially as a franchisee and then proceeded to go through several months of training and finding a location that met Quizno's requirements. Quizno's has very strict location requirements; it typically starts in the outskirts of a large city and works its way in.

FIGURE 4.3 The Sandwich Segment of the Fast-Food Industry

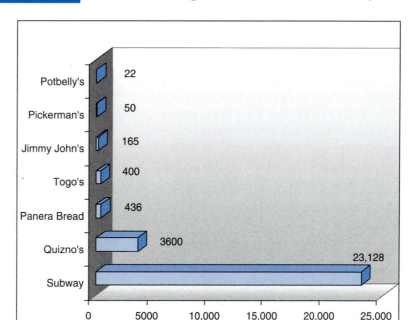

For several weeks before the store opened, Roper and his family had a promotional campaign that included handing out menus tucked inside bags of chocolate-chip cookies. Then Roper went door-to-door to all the businesses within a three-mile radius, dropping off coupons for free sandwiches and menus. On the first day, he faxed all the businesses that he had visited to let them know that the store was now open. Then he opened the store at 11:00 a.m. and waited. It was not until 11:40 that the first customer entered the store, but just a few minutes later he had a line of customers that went out the door.

His opening-day strategy has been used time and time again whenever business slows. In fact, when sales really dropped after September 11, 2001, Roper began using direct-mail packs to offer free sandwiches. That strategy may not seem a good way to make money, but people always buy other things like chips and drinks when they redeem their coupons. Roper has calculated that if he spends $400 on coupons, he generally doubles his profit. It is important to find ways to get customers to taste his products, and Roper believes that it is the little things you do that count.

Roper also collaborates with local schools to grow his business, often placing ads in the high school newspapers offering bagged lunches with small sandwiches, chips, and cookies. Social responsibility plays a role in his growth strategy as well. Roper supports local churches and schools by setting aside days on which he donates $1 from every sandwich he sells to that church or school. Although he barely breaks even on that deal, the publicity he gets is priceless.

Roper attributes much of his success to the fact that he treats his employees well. If employees are happy, then customers are happy, he believes. The fast-food industry is known for its high turnover rates, so Roper decided that he would give his employees a reason to consider a career with the company. He offered them medical, dental, and retirement benefits. As a result, he now has sixty employees, a third of which work full time.

Roper is now faced with encroaching competition from Subway and Panera Bread Co., although interestingly enough he counts a Subway manager and two Subway owners among his customers. He plans to use his grand-opening strategy—giving out cookies and coupons—whenever a competitor's store opens, but he wonders if there is anything else he can do to ensure that his customers remain loyal.

Advising the Entrepreneur

1. How would you advise Roper about dealing with competition, both the major competition, which is Subway, and those trying to catch up to Quizno's?

2. What are some ways Quizno's can diversify without losing what differentiates it from the competition?

3. What is the biggest challenge you see for Quizno's in the coming decade, and what should they do about it?

Sources: S. Leung, "Small Business: Secrets of My Success: What Separates the Profitable from the Unprofitable Franchisee? It's Often the Small Stuff," *Wall Street Journal* (December 15, 2003): R4; W. Hageman, "On One Corner Stands Reigning Champ Subway. On the Other, the Challenger, Quizno's," *Quizno's Sub Public Relations* (January 12, 2003), http://quiznos.internetarchives.com.

CHAPTER 5

Stepping into a Family Business

What distinguishes man . . . is that man perceives the good and the evil, the fair and the unfair, and all sentiments of a similar nature, and whose communication precisely form the family and the state.

Aristotle, *Politics*

LEARNING OUTCOMES

- Describe the unique dynamics of the family firm.
- Distinguish between family and nonfamily businesses.
- Compare and contrast the advantages and challenges of a family business.
- Explain the management scheme of the family business.
- Discuss the role of succession and its impact on the business.

Can Furniture Shopping Be Fun?

Furniture shopping and fun are not often associated, but for Barry and Eliot Tatelman, fun is the foundation of their enormously successful family business, Boston-based Jordan's Furniture. What makes this furniture store unique is that its owners break all the traditional rules of business. In an industry where "one-day only" sales to drive customers to the store are the norm, the Tatelmans don't have sales; instead, they hold to a single-price policy. In fact, they never advertise price. Rather, they use tongue-in-cheek advertising to promote the store and themselves in ways that generate a laugh and make people curious to visit. They are most famous for turning furniture shopping into entertainment. Here's an example.

The Natick, Massachusetts, store is 130,000 square feet and contains a central hall designed to look like Bourbon Street, New Orleans. Every few minutes, animatronic versions of Elvis Presley, the Village People, the Beatles, and the Supremes jump out onto balconies to serenade the shoppers as they stroll through the hall to find the furniture, which is displayed with great care in decorated display rooms. The Tatelmans believe that the key to sales lies in driving traffic to the store, and they are determined to discover the most unusual and innovative ways to do that.

Jordan's is a family business incorporated in 1928 by the Tatelmans' grandfather, Samuel, who opened the first store in the Boston suburb of Waltham. In the 1960s, Samuel's grandson, Eliot Tatelman, quit Boston University before graduating to join Jordan's full time. Then in 1972, Eliot's brother, Barry, graduated from college and took the position of head of advertising for Jordan's. Eliot and Barry, who were now in charge of the family business, drew inspiration from Walt Disney—an expert at target marketing. They decided, for very practical reasons, to focus on the 18- to 34-year-old age range because this group needed to buy a lot of furniture, not just a few replacement pieces. Furthermore, this group would probably appreciate the entertainment aspect of their business most because they were young and just starting families.

Their first successful product was waterbeds at a time when waterbeds were all the rage. One of the unsolved problems with waterbeds was that they never matched the rest of the furniture in a bedroom. The Tatelmans decided to solve this problem by enclosing the mattresses in wooden frames that matched other bedroom items, such as chests and chairs. They were the only store in the country doing this at the time, and it became a huge success. On average, Jordan's sold twenty-five mattress sets a day at $600 each. It was then that they decided to buck a trend in the furniture industry with the concept of "underpricing"— that is, charging one price and holding no sales. Customers loved it.

In 1987 the Tatelmans decided to take their Walt Disney–style entertainment to the maximum and combine furniture shopping with entertainment in their third store in yet another Boston suburb, Avon. In 1992 they added a $2.5 million laser-enhanced thrill ride that they christened MOM (Motion Odyssey Movie), which took customers through motion picture images. The lines to get into the store were an hour and a half long, and it put the brothers on the map.

The Tatelman brothers are celebrities in the Boston area, mainly due to their radio and television ads in which they "Jordanize" popular commercials. They've created unique spots by spinning trendy advertisements such as the milk industry's "Got Milk?" and GAP's dancer-filled chino commercials. Often they don't even mention a product; instead, they try to entertain and make customers want to come to their stores to see the latest changes.

In the 1990s, the Tatelmans, for all their good fortune with this business, now had to face the issue of succession. Each brother had two children, but only Eliot's older son was interested in working for the company. What would be fair to all the children? The two were pondering this question when an opportunity came along—a very prominent investor who was interested in purchasing their business. The Tatelmans had never considered selling the business to a strategic buyer or doing an initial public offering because they did not want to risk a change in the direction of their company. However, when they learned that the interested investor was Warren Buffet and that Jordan's would be part of his enormously successful umbrella company Berkshire Hathaway, the picture changed. In October 1999, in true Barry and Eliot style, the Tatelmans hosted a Dr. Seuss "green eggs and ham breakfast" and announced to their employees that they had sold the company, assuring them that nothing would change. Then, as a show of support, they paid each employee 50 cents for every hour they had worked to date; some employees received as much as $20,000. Although this gift cost the brothers $10 million, the return in goodwill was invaluable. As of 2003, when numbers were last made available, the company was doing over $270 million in annual sales and employed 1162 people.

Today, Eliot and Barry—as well as their unique vision—remain with the company. They recently opened IMAX theatres at two store locations, producing tremendous customer draw and providing an additional source of revenue.

In their effort to be the best, not the biggest, the brothers have always carefully considered how to grow the business. With the retailing style that they have chosen, it might be difficult to grow the business nationwide, and it wouldn't be as much fun. The Tatelmans want to be close enough to the stores to be able to walk into each of them, and they want each store to be unique—Jordanized, so to speak.

Advising the Entrepreneur

1. Given the Tatelmans' growth strategy so far, what would you advise them to do to achieve further growth?

2. What other forms of entertainment might draw customers to a furniture store?

Sources: A. Lubow, "Wowing Warren," *Inc.* (March, 2000), www.inc.com; *Hoover's Fact Sheet,* http://premium.hoovers.com (accessed June 5, 2005); B. Tatelman, "Corporate Culture at Jordan's Furniture," *Furniture World* (2002), www.furninfo.com.

Family firms come in all shapes and sizes, ranging from the very large Anheuser-Busch and Ford Motor Company to microbusinesses operated out of the family home, and they play a vital role in the U.S. economy. Estimates of the number of family businesses approach 3 million. This estimate includes businesses that employ two or more family members as owners or two or more family members who help manage the business that one of them owns.[1] If a relatively broad definition of *family firm* is used, one in which family members participate in and have major control over the strategic direction of the business, research shows that family businesses employ 62 percent of the workforce and contribute approximately 64 percent of the GDP (gross domestic product). With a more moderate definition of family business—in which the intent of the founder is to keep the business in the family—research concludes that family businesses employ 58 percent of the workforce and contribute 59 percent of the GDP.[2] It is estimated that 39 percent of all small businesses are family owned with two or more family members managing a business that one member owns. However, when firm size reaches twenty employees or more, the proportion of family businesses rises to 54 percent.[3] The most likely joint owner of a family business is the spouse, followed by sons, brothers, and fathers. In fact, about 85 percent of small-business owners are currently married.[4]

Family businesses are also highly valuable to the communities in which they operate because they tend to focus on building customer loyalty, they participate more actively in the community than other types of businesses, and they generally display a culture of shared values with the community.[5] Moreover, they take a long-term perspective on their businesses, which helps ensure a more stable community. All these factors come together to make for a positive environment for entrepreneurial activities.[6]

UNDERSTANDING THE FAMILY BUSINESS

Family businesses have many things in common with other types of businesses, but it is the dynamics of the family itself that give these businesses their unique advantages and also present some serious challenges.

Early research depicted the family business as three connected subsystems consisting of ownership, management, and the family.[7] The interaction of these three subsystems is what gives the family firm its unique personality; however, this framework does not reflect the impact of entrepreneurship on the family firm. More recent research views the family business as an "ideological triangle," or combination of entrepreneurialism, managerialism, and paternalism, in which ideology is composed of cognition, or awareness, and emotion.[8] **Entrepreneurialism** is about recognizing, seizing, and exploiting opportunities. At one extreme, entrepreneurship is viewed as inspiring and visionary; at the other extreme, it can threaten those who are uncomfortable with the ambiguity and risk. Not all family businesses operate from an entrepreneurial perspective. On the contrary, many family businesses choose to maintain the status quo out of fear of changing what has worked for generations. Unfortunately, however, these businesses leave themselves vulnerable to a shifting marketplace. Family businesses that do choose to take an entrepreneurial approach to the management of their businesses are comfortable with taking risk. Because they seek opportunities to take the business in new directions, these businesses are more likely to be sustainable in the long term.

Managerialism is related to administrative procedures and organizational structures. At one extreme, managerialism often leads to a bureaucratic structure; at the other extreme, it results in a laissez-faire approach in which everyone does whatever he or she wants and central control is absent. Whether the family firm takes an entrepreneurial approach to doing business will also affect its managerial choices. An entrepreneurial leader is unlikely to choose to create a bureaucratic structure because it stifles creativity and makes it difficult for the company to be flexible and quick to respond to environmental changes. However, an entrepreneurial approach can result in a laissez-faire approach if the entrepreneur has no management skills whatsoever and assumes that everyone knows what they are supposed to do. In this case, the entrepreneur needs to designate a chief operations officer or manager who can provide the skills that he or she lacks.

Paternalism is about the protection and guardianship of the family business, and it carries both positive and negative connotations. On the positive side, paternalism is concern for the safety of the business and its sustainability into future generations. The founder encourages and supports the development of the members of the next generation to prepare them to take over the business. On the negative side, paternalism can result in an owner-manager making all the business decisions for employees and thereby taking away their responsibility and freedom to choose. In a highly paternalistic family business (or maternalistic if the owner-manager is the mother), the objective is to keep the business solely within the family. Consequently, the founder will have a dominating presence in the business and will take great pains both legally and financially to ensure that the business is never influenced by people from outside the family. The other negative aspect to extreme paternalism is that it tends to close off the business from fresh ideas and approaches that could only come from outsiders. Groups, like families, that work together all the time are frequently subject to groupthink, or predictable ideas based on previous experience. Today when most industries are in a state of flux, it is more important than ever that family businesses be open to new ideas from new sources.

Family Versus Nonfamily Businesses

Agency theory provides one framework for understanding the differences between family-owned businesses and nonfamily-owned businesses, or agent-managed businesses. **Agent-managers,** as contrasted with owners in this context, are the managers who run a business without having an ownership stake. In businesses where the owner is not the manager and may even be at a distance from the business in a more entrepreneurial capacity, the business incurs higher agency costs due to the need to monitor the agent, from misaligned interests or goal incongruence, and from the potential for agent management to take advantage of its day-to-day controlling position.[9] For example, agent-managers may utilize profits for their own gain by increasing their salaries, reducing their workload, and adding more perks to their compensation mix. **Owner-managers,** by contrast, are predisposed to create business value because their motivations are different; their wealth is generated from the successful growth of the business, not a salary paid to them by the business.

Agent-managers are less likely to be loyal to their company because they generally do not have an ownership stake; therefore, the failure of the family business is not as devastating for the agent-manager as it is for the owner. On the other hand, agent-managers do bring more objectivity to decision making than an owner-manager, who

LEARNING FROM SUCCESS

When Succession from the Outside Makes Sense

In 1990 Norm Jalbert—who had been with J. Royal, a family-owned specialty sealing distributorship for thirty-one years—assumed leadership of the small company. Knowing that none of his three children were interested in coming into the business, he immediately began planning for a succession at some point in the future. The company was continuing to grow, so Jalbert considered every option including a merger, an acquisition of another firm, or a buyout by a larger company. Along the way, he met Russell Vroom, who worked in the same kind of business. The two realized that together they could significantly grow J. Royal; in fact, just three years after Vroom joined the company, it doubled in size. Jalbert knew that he had found his rightful successor, and together they met with attorneys and bankers to craft a succession plan. He then stepped into the role of president and focused on developing a new territory while Vroom assumed the role of chief executive officer. It has been a smooth transition because as Jalbert said, "I think succession planning begins the moment that you gain ownership." This plan worked out well.

Source: R. Trombly, "Passing the Torch," *Industrial Distribution* 90(4) (2001): 69–74.

may find it impossible to separate him- or herself entirely from the business when making decisions.

There is another way in that owner-managed companies differ from professionally managed companies. Owner-managed companies tend to be more centralized and sometimes secretive in their decision making so that the owner does not risk losing control. They also use fewer formal procedures for monitoring and control and rely instead on personal methods of control. This need for control may explain in part why professionally managed firms are generally larger than owner-managed firms. The professional manager has more incentive to grow the business because his or her compensation is directly tied to the performance of the business, while the owner has less incentive to grow the business beyond his or her capabilities to control it.[10]

Advantages of a Family Business

Some agency theorists believe that family businesses may actually be an ideal form of organization because the goals of the owner are aligned with the goals of the business.[11] Moreover, they believe that the owners will generally make wise decisions for the long-term success of the business because their ultimate goal is to leave a legacy to future generations. Therefore, they will also be more likely to manage resources in a way that creates wealth for the family.[12]

Research shows that family businesses pay higher wages to their employees than other types of businesses[13] and that they provide a more flexible work environment that brings out the finest in their employees.[14] Family members employed by the business have been found to be more productive than nonfamily members, and they communicate more effectively, especially information of a confidential nature, through efficient informal communication and decision-making channels.[15] Combine this with the fact that employee acquisition and transaction costs are less for family businesses and the picture for these businesses is very positive. This recent optimistic attitude toward family businesses has encouraged more people to pursue this route to entrepreneurship.

The concentration of ownership in family management can provide a strong commitment to the company's mission while allowing for self-examination and the ability to change course without losing forward movement.[16] The cohesiveness of the family unit may explain why most family businesses do not have formal codes of ethics. Rather, they use role modeling to demonstrate appropriate conduct and commitment to relationships. Family businesses can also be less susceptible to changes in the macroeconomic environment because they take a long-term view of business and therefore are less reactive when making decisions in response to short-term changes in the business environment.[17]

Family Business Resources

In the field of strategy, long-run differences in firm performance that are not attributed to industry or economic conditions are often explained by the firm's internal idiosyncrasies in the form of resources (see Figure 5.1). Resources include physical assets such as capital, plant, and equipment; intangible assets such as patents and relationships; individual and company-wide skill sets; and proprietary or highly efficient organizational processes, information, policies, and tacit knowledge. For example, a firm's relationships with suppliers and control and monitoring mechanisms for

FIGURE 5.1 The Unique Family Resource Base

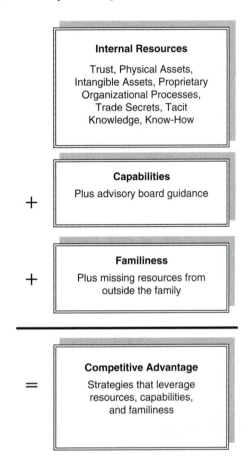

Internal Resources

Trust, Physical Assets, Intangible Assets, Proprietary Organizational Processes, Trade Secrets, Tacit Knowledge, Know-How

+

Capabilities

Plus advisory board guidance

+

Familiness

Plus missing resources from outside the family

=

Competitive Advantage

Strategies that leverage resources, capabilities, and familiness

production may be sources of competitive advantage that are unique to that firm. In the family firm, trust is a resource that provides a competitive advantage by reducing transaction costs. These resources are idiosyncratic because no two firms possess the same mix of experiences, knowledge, relationships, or assets. Having a mix of resources does not suggest that all resources create competitive advantages for the business. In fact, to possess value, a resource must have four attributes:[18]

1. It must be valuable in that it contributes to the exploitation of opportunities or it protects the firm against threats from the environment.

2. It must be rare in the sense that not all competitors have this resource.

3. It must be imperfectly imitable; in other words, a competitor cannot put together all the components to produce an exact copy of the resource.

4. There cannot be strategically equivalent substitutes.

Resources are valuable under certain conditions and not under others. It is important to determine not only when and how a resource is valuable but also what capabilities the business derives from the resource, what potential there is for a sustainable competitive advantage and return on investment from the resource, what strategies will allow for the exploitation of these resources, and what measures can be developed to assess the performance that the firm derives from exploitation of the resource. For a family firm to achieve high levels of performance, it needs to apply tacit knowledge gained from its activities to coordinate and mobilize the unique resources it controls.[19] Tacit knowledge is distinguished from explicit knowledge in that it is not articulated or codified in any form such as a manual or product description. Instead, it consists of beliefs, mental schemes, insights, and know-how that are rare and difficult to imitate; for these reasons alone, tacit knowledge is generally associated with higher levels of performance.[20] Tacit knowledge is embedded in the context in which it was created, so it is very difficult to transfer this knowledge. As a result, it can be very useful as a competitive advantage in a family firm, but it can also cause problems during management succession when the transfer of vital information to the next generation is critical. Unless the owner-manager makes a concerted effort to pass along the tacit knowledge gained in his or her role as family head of the business, that valuable learning will be lost forever.

Researchers are attempting to understand one other element to the resource bundle that a family business develops, and that is "familiness." **Familiness** is the "unique bundle of resources a particular family business possesses because of the systems interaction between the family, its individual members, and the business."[21] It is analogous to *goodwill* in the valuation of a business because it is an intangible asset, such as trust, that creates unique value for the business. Familiness as a management resource can range from consolidated family ownership and daily involvement from multiple generations to controlling family ownership with input only at the strategic level from the board.

For all the benefits that accrue to family-owned businesses, there are also a number of important challenges that should be understood.

Challenges of a Family Business

Assumptions, expectations, role ambiguity, and a myriad of other problems plague family businesses in ways that they do not affect nonfamily businesses. For example, at times severe conflicts may arise that can cause family members to stop talking to one another or to exclude certain members from the business entirely. In extreme cases, one family member may sue the other, which is what happened with the Pritzker family, owners of the $15 billion empire that includes the Hyatt Hotel chain.[22] Due to numerous disputes and disagreements over money, the family decided to liquidate its holdings and divide them among eleven family members. Meanwhile, Liesel Pritzker sued her father, Robert, and the rest of the eleven family members, claiming that he had shifted at least $1 billion out of her trust fund. That suit was settled in the young heir's favor in January 2005, but the family's problems continue.

One of the biggest challenges in family businesses is the degree to which the business depends on one individual, namely, the owner-manager. Although it can be argued that reliance on the owner-manager brings more control and focus to the organization, it can also be argued that heavy dependence on the owner-manager is risky for the business when the owner does not delegate decisions based on expertise. Research shows, however, that reliance on the owner-manager does change with age and time; that is, as owners grow older and as the company increases in size, owners typically reduce the number of decisions that they make and delegate more to the

How Dividing Responsibility Equally Can Lead to Disaster

County Linen is an industrial laundry business in England that has been serving such august institutions as the House of Parliament and the Savoy Hotel for more than 150 years. When Dudley Moore, the current head of the company, decided to retire, he handed the reins of the business to his sons, Tim and Anthony, to run the business together with equal managerial responsibility. As is often the case with a poor succession choice, the business began to lose money and the morale of the employees under the two sons was in a freefall. Instead of a peaceful retirement, Moore is working full time to get his family's business back on track. The mistake was in not choosing just one person to lead the company. It's vital to choose the single best person with the right skills and choose from the outside if the right person is not in the family.

Source: "Don't Let Family Ties Lead to Family Business Failure," *Business Advice from the Business Experts, Enterprise North East Trust* (September 16, 2004), www.enetrust.com.

next generation.[23] However, family firm founders by and large don't think about who their successors will be, and when they do, they often favor passing the business on to family members over recruiting people from outside the family who may have more experience and better skills. (The issue of succession in a family business is discussed in a later section.)

Family businesses tend to rank short-term issues as their primary concern, such as taxes, finances, marketing, and operational issues. This makes sense because, from what we know about small business owners in general, they are often operating in survival mode and focused solely on the day-to-day activities of the business. Family businesses are commonly at a disadvantage when it comes to acquiring resources, largely because their owners are predisposed to being more risk averse.[24] Seeking new resources for the business involves going outside the business for investors, management talent, or other resources that the business does not currently possess. Many owner-managers attempt to avoid bringing in outsiders as resources because they believe that it threatens the security of the family. Today, however, businesses of all types need to seek assistance and resources from third parties unrelated to the business just to remain competitive. The family that avoids resources outside the family will find itself at a competitive disadvantage.

MANAGEMENT IN THE FAMILY FIRM

In general, family firms are organized around hierarchies that are based on familial relationships, particularly the parent–child relationships. There is often much overlap between the family and the business system, between personal autonomy and parental control, and between short-term and long-term goals, each having distinct guiding principles.[25] The conflict that frequently arises from trying to balance these dualities can cause difficulty in making decisions, in implementing those decisions, and, most important, in committing to them. A case in point is the example of one family firm that held strictly to a rule of not allowing female descendants and their children to hold management positions in the family business. This rigid rule prevented the business from benefiting from some of the best talent in the family, who happened to be the male son of a female descendant. Eventually, the family business was sold, which was the only way to infuse the radical change that was required to move the business forward.[26]

The owner-manager is at the root of many of the conflicts that arise in family businesses. The next section considers the role of the owner-manager.

The Role of the Owner-Manager

In approximately 75 percent of all family businesses, the company is highly dependent on the owner-manager to make all the major decisions in at least three out of five major functional areas of the business: finance, marketing, sales, operations, and management. Furthermore, about 57 percent of all family businesses have fewer than two key managers in addition to the owner, which validates the commonly held notion of the dominant owner-manager.[27]

A stream of research focused on family businesses uncovered a number of interesting facts about the management of family firms that deserve some attention. Family businesses tend to be highly dependent on the owner-manager, but with each succeeding generation, there is a change in focus, management style, and objectives.[28] With each generation, strategy benefits from and builds on core competencies developed in the previous generation; consequently, later generations become increasingly more qualified to lead the company.[29] At the same time, however, inertia may set in; traditions may become rigid, and the firm may begin to rely heavily on the way things have always been done. Consequently, management becomes unwilling to take risk that might jeopardize the business even when there is a high probability of reward. The degree to which a family firm is willing to take risk has been found to depend on four factors: (1) the owner's service as chief executive officer (CEO), (2) length of time as owner, (3) family stakeholders, and (4) family involvement in the business.

Serving as the CEO provides owners the power and authority to allocate resources in ways that are calculated to grow the business. It is the role that allows for the natural independence and action orientation of the founder to be satisfied, but it can also lead to making decisions on behalf of the business without considering the input of others in the organization. Some family firm owners have centralized decision making so much that is impossible for employees to think creatively about the company. Some CEO/founders, as a direct result of the length of their tenure, create an inertia in their companies that makes them less willing to take the risk of innovation.[30] Moreover, the more time that the founder spends in office, the more sources of information become "increasingly narrow and restricted, and the information is more finely filtered and distilled."[31] This suggests that when founders are actively involved in the family business over a long period, the business is shielded from the influence of other family members and from those on the outside. However, some founders with long tenures in the leadership position feel enough confidence about their tenure in the position to begin to think more creatively and to encourage innovation among their employees.

Where many family members own a large percentage of the stock in the family business, as opposed to the situation in which the founder owns the majority of the shares, they may work in concert to prevent radical change that might affect the wealth that they have invested in the company. Rather than take the risk of a new strategy that has no guarantees of producing a large return for the company, they often prefer to maintain the status quo and protect their current assets. As more and more of the family wealth is tied to the success of the company, it is less likely that family shareholders will support major changes in any aspect of the organization. However, in businesses where multiple generations of the family are involved in the day-to-day activities of the business, the firm is more likely to benefit from fresh ideas and experiences that bring new knowledge to the firm.[32]

Bringing Children into the Business

By the time Earl G. Graves and his wife, Barbara, had grown *Black Enterprise* magazine to its twenty-fifth year, they had all three of their sons working in the business in distinct roles. Earl Jr. (Butch) was heading advertising and sales and was being positioned to take over the main business. Johnny, who began his career as a lawyer, launched Black Enterprise Unlimited, which would take the company's products beyond just the magazine. And Michael, the youngest, was on his way to overseeing the Pepsi franchise that the family owned in 2000. Although each has his own goals and responsibilities, the brothers are extremely close and share the values given to them by their parents. Whatever their career choices, they were always expected to get an education, start a family, and be productive citizens in the community.[33]

Many founders of family firms like Earl Graves have supported the importance of bringing family members into the business at the earliest age possible so that they have the opportunity to learn about the business and grow into the positions for which their education and interests make them best suited. Depending on the age of the child, the initial tasks assigned to them may be quite simple, but tasks serve to instill in the child a sense of pride and accomplishment. As children reach their teens and twenties, however, they may decide to take a different path for a while. Dick and Nancy Ponzi built their dream business, Ponzi Vineyards, near Portland, Oregon, in 1968 when Dick left a job as an engineer for the Walt Disney Company. They decided to use a "soft sell" with their children, allowing them to begin careers outside the family business to make sure that if they did return to the vineyards, it was for the right reasons. As it worked out, one by one, all three children returned and found roles in the business that best suited their talents. In fact, each one had acquired experience in his or her career that helped determine where they could add the most value in their parents' business. Daughter Luisa, who was a pre-med student, had taken a trip to France where she became enthralled with the making of wines. Today, she is the chief winemaker for the family business. Maria, another daughter, had been an ad executive for *Inc.* magazine; she is now leading their marketing effort.[34]

Siblings in Business

Brothers Barry and Eliot Tatelman (see Case 5.1) went into the family business together because they liked each other and worked well together, two critical factors for any family business. Mirzett Evans and his sister, Glenda Heldris, have never found partners more satisfying than each other, which is surprising in one respect: They are sixteen years apart in age. In their company, Innovative Installers, an office furniture installation and facility management company based in Silicon Valley, they both display a strong work ethic and intense drive that they hope sets a standard for their employees.[35] Another sister and brother team, Alan and Lisa Thompson, have found that differences are valuable as well. Alan is more a pioneer and risk taker, whereas Lisa is the practical one who can manage new ideas and make them happen. These differences have helped their company, MailSort, a direct-mail and mail-processing company, succeed in a tough industry.[36]

All of these sibling teams agree that what matters most are the family relationships. To ensure that the family relationship outlasts the business and that going into business with a family member will be successful, it is important to consider whether[37]

- There is any lingering sibling rivalry from childhood.
- The siblings can separate business from family.
- One of the siblings is better prepared to lead the organization.
- There are others in the family who should be involved in the business.
- Agreement can be reached on fair compensation without regard to who is older.
- Spouses and children will have an impact on the business and, if so, in what ways.

Working as a sibling team can be very rewarding if these few potential problems are addressed in advance.

Advisory Boards

Increasingly, family firms are tapping into the value of advisory boards in which guidance on strategy and decision making are needed. Leaving governance to a more formal board of directors, the advisory board is designed to guide the company's decision making on issues such as financing, launching a new product, acquiring another company, succession planning, or selling the company. The advisory board is not meant to be an arbiter of family disputes and is not generally effective at dealing with personal family issues. Its role is strictly to advise management on business matters.

For owner-managers, the most critical factor in choosing an advisory board is trust. This distinguishes the family firm advisory board from other types of advisory boards.[38] Most nonfamily businesses seek independent board members, even on their advisory boards, so that they can reap the benefits of objective thought and a little distance from the business. Family firms, by contrast, seek individuals whom they trust enough to guide their children after they have left the company. That is not to say that family firms never select outsiders or independent board members. In fact, those family firms that understand the value of objective opinions are eager to include these types of people on their advisory boards.

Although some advisory boards will serve pro bono, especially if the company is new, it is wise to plan on paying by the meeting in a range of about $500 to $2000, depending on the size of the company. Advisory boards typically meet quarterly in half-day meetings with perhaps an annual full-day meeting. The CEO of the company usually chairs the meeting and customarily plans some time to meet alone with the board to seek advice on a more personal level. In many respects, the role of CEO is a lonely position because he or she represents the company to the outside world and to the employees. If the CEO is troubled about a decision or needs guidance in how to effectively deal with a situation, he or she cannot easily go to employees without risking engendering a lack of confidence in the CEO's ability to do the job. Therefore, every CEO needs a trusted advisor to use as a sounding board. Many

LEARNING FROM THE GLOBAL MARKET

Management Succession in Chinese Family-Owned Businesses

In addition to dealing with a fast-changing global economy, Hong Kong–based family businesses are coming to grips with the need to pave the way for a successful transition when the founder eventually leaves the organization. Today, an effective transition involves not only the transfer of control and ownership but also major changes in the business model and the way business is conducted in order to bring the small business into the information age.

The second-generation owners (2GOs) of family businesses in Hong Kong are typically educated overseas, so they have learned management styles and strategies that differ substantially from those traditionally held by first-generation owners (1GOs), who relied on personal influence and trust instead of formal business transactions. In general, the 1GO selects the 2GO based on competence. For a time, the 1GO will main-

tain a paternalistic management style but then gradually move to a more participatory style as the 2GO gains more skills and confidence. For the 2GO, coming into the family business where the 1GO holds onto power even as the succession transition is taking place is not easy, but the skills they have typically learned in their overseas educational programs have helped them to display a more collaborative style. This ability to work cooperatively helps smooth the transition to the point where they can prove their competence and take over the reins of the company completely.

Source: "Management Succession: A Case for Chinese Family-Owned Business" by Walter W. C. Chung and Karina P. K. Yuen from *Management Decision*, 41/7 (2003) 643–655. Reprinted by permission of Emerald Group Publishing Limited.

times this trusted advisor is the CEO's attorney, but just as frequently it could be a board member or fellow CEO in a noncompeting business.

SUCCESSION

The Family Firm Institute predicts that within the next five years 39 percent of all family-owned firms will experience a transition in leadership due to retirement. It is an unfortunate fact that fewer than 30 percent of those family businesses will survive into the second generation and even fewer will make it to the third generation.[39] Most business owners have put in place procedures to ensure that employees are paid on time, that payroll taxes are paid by the deadline, and that the company's bills reach their vendors in a timely fashion. However, if something unexpected happened to the owner-manager of a family business, how prepared would that business be?

John Esposito began planning for succession on the day that his three sons became old enough to join his mortgage brokerage business, Bentley Mortgage Corp. of Danbury, Connecticut. While they were growing up, the topic around the dinner table was often the mortgage business, so it was no surprise that in 1986, his oldest son joined the firm, followed closely by the younger two. Each one eventually found his passion in one particular area of the business: One son took over sales, one son headed up processing and scheduling, and one acted as the company underwriter. The eldest son serves as president, but each son holds a one-third interest in the company, and, therefore, major decisions are made by consensus.[40] This family's succession plan went smoothly, and the children grew into their respective roles, but few successions are this simple. Nearly a third of all family businesses have no designated successor, and for that reason alone, it is important to plan for succession. The next major section addresses the important task of developing an effective succession plan.

Common Conflicts in Succession Planning

The most difficult aspects of succession planning always involve people and deep-seated emotional issues. In this section, we look at the classic conflicts of parent–child, mother–son, and sibling rivalry to understand how they affect decisions about a succession plan.

Parent–Child Conflict Because the parent–child bond is generally considered the strongest emotional bond, it is also true that this relationship can result in high levels of conflict. If parents suspect that the children will not be able to work together for the good of the business, they may decide to divide the business among the children using separate revocable trusts with trustees chosen by the children. This means that if the parents later found that the children were not acting in the best interests of the business, the trusts could be revoked and the assets taken back. Under this scenario, the parents would also want to withhold enough assets to provide for themselves for the remainder of their lives, perhaps putting those assets into a revocable trust as well. However, most estate planners advise that the parent appoint an independent person or institution as trustee to avoid conflicts among the children should one be singled out to act as trustee.

Mother–Son Conflict Although the mother–son relationship has usually been heralded as a positive one, conflicts can arise if the father has died and the mother has remarried. An effective succession plan would protect the inheritance of any children and allow the mother use of the assets while she is alive. If the children are not yet capable of taking over the management of the company, a professional manager could be hired and overseen by the board of directors or a specially appointed management committee that would protect the interests of the family.

Sibling Conflict It is a sad fact that sibling rivalry and conflict plague many family businesses, particularly when it comes to succession planning. Issues such as a favored child, different talents, competition, and the need for fairness all come into play. Where there are multiple issues that make a simple succession impossible, the parents can consider creating a private trust company of which one parent is the CEO during his or her lifetime and each of the children has a specific role. Then family assets could be placed in a separate trust over which the private trust company is the trustee. In this way, the siblings could work together even after the death of the parents and keep the family business intact for future generations.[41]

Creating a Successful Succession Plan

The topic of succession arouses many feelings that reveal the complexities of family dynamics. Succession reminds founders of their mortality, and it also brings up some difficult discussions, such as who in the family is most competent to lead the organization. Research has proposed nine criteria for successful successions:[42]

1. Business property divided equitably and separated from family property
2. Interdependent parent–successor relationship
3. Parent trust of the successor
4. Parent withdrawing from the management of the business
5. Successor joining the business of his or her own free will
6. Formal succession plan
7. Good relationship between successor and employees
8. Successor bringing experience from outside the family business
9. Successor having experience in a number of roles within the family business

Some research concludes that succession planning comes to the attention of the family business once operational and financial issues are satisfied and that this is true no matter what the age or size of firm.[43] Succession is an evolutionary process, not an event that can occur quickly. The owner gradually reduces his or her participation in the business while the successor slowly takes on more responsibility. The successful transfer of a business to a successor depends on a variety of factors and on satisfying the needs of diverse stakeholders, among them the founder and other owners, the successor, other family members, any professional managers, and any other business partners who might be affected by the change in management.[44]

A succession plan begins with a vision for the future of the company. What will the company look like in ten years? Fifteen years? It is also a matter of deciding what the family wants for its future. When does the founder want to retire? What does the founder plan to do after leaving the business? At what point will another family member be ready to take the lead? In addition, founders have many choices for their exit that will need to be investigated. They can

- Keep all ownership and control within the family and stay involved.
- Retain ownership but hire an outside CEO.
- Sell to employees or a third party.
- Transfer a portion of the business annually to family members to take advantage of gift tax laws.
- Do an installment sales whereby the founder receives future interest and principal payments and the business is sold over a defined period.
- Set up an employee stock ownership plan to transfer ownership to employees over time.

These options are discussed in detail in Chapter 20. Here it is important to recognize that founders have these options that they can match to their specific needs, and each should be considered on its merits.

In some cases, owner-managers have created a succession plan but have not revised it to keep pace with changing laws regarding taxes and inheritance. Moreover, sometimes the goals of the founder and the goals for the business have changed, and these changes need to be reflected in the succession plan as well.

Culture and Succession

The culture of the family firm affects the outcome of a succession plan. Culture can be defined as "a pattern of basic assumptions invented, discovered, or developed by

TABLE 5.1   Types of Culture in a Family Firm

Organizational	Familial	Governance
Paternalistic or maternalistic: Founder acts as father or mother figure who protects the employees.	Patriarchal or matriarchal: One family member, usually the founder, makes all decisions and defines all goals.	Board of directors: Made up of insiders, the primary shareholders in the business.
Laissez faire: Founder does not take an active role in controlling the organization.	Collaborative: Family members share information and decision making while adhering to common goals.	Advisory board: Made up of people who the family trusts to provide objective advice.
Participative: Founder encourages employees to take an active role in the decision making.	Conflicted: No common goals exist.	"Paper" board: Set up to "rubber-stamp" the decisions of the founder.
Professional: Decision making occurs as a result of rules and impersonal codes.		

a group and taught to new members of that group as the correct way to behave."[45] A family firm will normally be comprised of three types of cultures: (1) organizational, (2) familial, or (3) governance (see Table 5.1).

The organizational culture within a family firm generally takes on one of four distinct forms:

1. Paternalistic/maternalistic: The founder essentially acts as a father/mother figure protecting the employees through a hierarchical structure.

2. Laissez faire: The founder does not take an active role in controlling the organization.

3. Participative: The founder encourages employees to take an active role in the decision making.

4. Professional: Decision making occurs as a result of rules and impersonal procedures.

In the same way that the business may be described by several different cultures, the family may also be differentiated along cultural lines—that is, being patriarchal (or matriarchal), collaborative, or conflicted. In the patriarchal culture, one family member, generally the founder, makes all the major decisions and defines the goals relative to the family. In the collaborative culture, the family members share information and decision making while adhering to common goals that they decided on. In a conflicted culture, there are no common goals, and it is essentially everyone for him- or herself. This type of familial culture makes it difficult to grow a business to any substantial size.

The third type of culture affecting the family business is the governing board, which may consist of a formal board of directors, an advisory board, or, in some cases, a "paper" board. The formal board of directors in a family business normally consists of insiders, the primary shareholders of the business, whereas the advisory board consists of people whom the family trusts to provide objective advice on the direction of the business. The paper board is essentially a board that rarely meets, and when it does, it is to "rubber-stamp" the decisions of the founder. Sometimes outside members of the board of directors act in this capacity as well. In fact, research has found that in about 54 percent of cases the dominant configuration with regard to the board of directors prior to succession is a "rubber-stamp" board. After the succession, the dominant form is the advisory board.[46] Whatever the cultural configuration of the family business, it must provide for an easy transition. Some research has found that a configuration that consists of a collaborative family and a participative business will be more effective at supporting long-term survival and growth.[47]

Choosing the Successor

Selecting a successor is not an easy task. Even if candidates from within the family are available and qualified, choosing someone from within the family is not always the best move for the company. The skills required of a competent successor will be related to the stage of the business, so chances are that the founder's successor will have a different set of skills than the founder had. For example, the entrepreneurial skills that were required to recognize the business opportunity, gather the resources necessary to launch the business, and take the business to a point of survival were probably within the mix of skills that the founder of the family business possessed. If the business has grown substantially by the time the owner-manager decides to transition out of the leadership position, it is likely that it is time for a CEO with professional management skills to ensure that the now more complex operations and human resource capabilities of the company are well managed. If no one in the second generation has an interest in the business or no one is qualified to assume the mantle of leadership, the company will need to look outside. This is not necessarily bad for the company; the most important thing is to find the right talent for the position and to secure someone who has a passion for the business.

It is wise to begin a series of family meetings several years before succession is imminent to make sure that family members' goals are understood, especially the goals of those members who are not active in the business on a daily basis, and that these goals are in alignment with the business's goals. Generally, from these meetings it is clear who is interested in assuming the role of CEO at some future date. Each family member should write a job description for the position and a list of the skills, experience, and attributes they would bring to the position. Family members should also demonstrate their understanding of the business, its operations, and its financials.

Bringing in outsiders with professional expertise to help in the crafting of a succession plan is extremely useful because qualified outsiders provide an objective point of view that considers what is best for the business. They will also help in placing a value on the business. Those outsiders may actually come from the company's board of advisors, or they may be hired from a pool of consultants that focus on family business issues and attorneys who specialize in estate and succession planning. Marc Beerman, president and second-generation owner of a New Orleans–based distributor of hydraulic, pneumatic, and electric tools and parts, began his succession planning in

1992.[48] His siblings had never been involved in the business but had an equal claim on the business's wealth. Beerman's goal for the succession plan was to gain voting control of the company's stock so that he would not lose the value he had created in the company. He was responsible for the growth of the company, and he believed that he should benefit from that growth. When the family began planning for succession, they brought in an independent appraiser to determine the value of the company at the 1992 level and include an amount for goodwill. The amount of that valuation would be divided among the siblings, and the payout of that value would occur over twenty years so that it would not unduly disrupt the business's cash flow.

Whether the successor can successfully achieve credibility and legitimacy as the new company leader largely depends on the quality of the training the successor receives, which is composed of knowledge acquisition and leadership abilities. The successor must internalize the mission, values, and goals of the company as well as acquire knowledge about the company's business environment and the players in it. This knowledge is essential to being able to predict and solve problems that might face the business in the future.[49] That is why it is valuable for successors to have come up through ranks of the business over several years before assuming the leadership position. Family businesses are known for their mentoring of successor relationships, and this type of learning facilitates the absorption of invaluable tacit knowledge.

Planning for a Transition

The founder needs to give some thought to his or her future financials needs, so that the transition between being the full-time CEO and being fully retired will be relatively short. For the sake of the new CEO in a family business, it is important that the founder not be lingering around providing color commentary on the decisions of the new CEO. Founders can transition out of their company in a number of ways that will benefit both the business and the founder. They can serve on the board of directors as chairperson, step back into an area of the business that they enjoy on a part-time basis (such as working in new-product development), or can take on a public relations role for the company in the community, promoting it and making important connections on behalf of the company. Knowing in advance which route best suits the founder and the business will ease the transition significantly.

Not all founders leave the business through retirement. It is an unfortunate fact that some leave without warning as was the case when Kansas City–based Data Center Inc., a nationwide bank information processing and technology company, lost its CEO to an airplane accident in November 2004. To ensure that the company doesn't falter after such a loss, redundancies must be in place. These could include having a CEO in training, encouraging employees to learn multiple positions in the company, or identifying someone on the board of directors with the experience to step in as interim CEO. In any case, having key-person insurance on critical management will at least provide some funds to acquire the help that the company will likely require.

Succession by Merger or Acquisition

It is not surprising that sale of the family business is rarely considered an option because the family may not want someone outside the family to own the business. However, some family businesses reach the point where the family decides that it is no longer feasible to keep the business solely within the family. Perhaps there are no children suitable to lead the company, or perhaps the founder has died and the family no longer wants to run the business. Whatever the case, for the business to survive and grow, it must either be sold to a third party or merge with another company.

For family businesses, mergers and acquisitions (M&As) can be either a proactive or reactive strategy. On the offensive, M&As can provide opportunities for growth and make the company more competitive. On the defensive side, they can be an excellent exit strategy for the business owner who wants to exit and, at the same time, ensure that employees can continue to work for the company.[50] A merger, if handled well, can provide a way for the founder to harvest the wealth that he or she has created. (The subject of mergers and acquisitions is treated in Chapter 20.)

The family business has the potential to be the most successful and satisfying form of business ownership available if the family makes an effort to understand and prepare for the rewards and challenges of this type of venture. Some of the most successful businesses in the world today are family businesses that learned how to grow and yet maintain their family values.

ISSUES FOR REVIEW AND DISCUSSION

1. Are there any circumstances in which a family business might not be the appropriate form of business?
2. How does the role of the owner-manager affect the success or failure of the family firm?
3. Do the advantages of a family business outweigh the disadvantages? Why? Why not?
4. What are five key things that owners need to remember when considering succession?
5. Under what circumstances is succession outside the family a good idea?

EXPERIENCING ENTREPRENEURSHIP

1. Interview the owner and a nonfamily employee of a family business. Compare and contrast their views of the business, goals, strategies, and potential for growth in a three-page report.
2. Choose either Case 5.1 or Case 5.2. Using phone or onsite interviews and additional secondary research, compare and contrast the two businesses in terms of how family and business are integrated, the management style, and their succession plans.

From a Mom-and-Pop Business to a Megabusiness

Don Zacharia's big dream was to become a screenwriter. The last thing he thought he would wind up doing is managing his father's liquor store, Zachys, which his father opened in Scarsdale, New York, in 1944. After a stint in the army, from which he was discharged in 1956, Zacharia and his new wife trekked to Hollywood to find their fortune. However, Zacharia did not have the patience to wait for the success that often takes years in Hollywood and, in many cases, is never achieved. He eventually gave up and returned home to work for his father in the liquor business. Zacharia and his father did not get along well, and by 1961, it was clear that Zacharia had to either buy his father out or leave the business. Because he now had a growing family, he decided to buy the business and grow it.

The Retail Liquor Industry

Due to outdated laws and government corruption, the 1960s was not an easy time to be in the liquor business in New York State. Fair-trade wine and liquor laws dating back to the Prohibition era called for fixed prices. If a retailer sold a bottle of liquor for even a couple pennies less than the competition, he would lose his liquor license. Finally, after a particularly high-profile corruption case, then-Governor Nelson Rockefeller appointed a commission to explore ending the fair-trade laws. Zacharia, who didn't wait for the commission to make a final decision, began lowering his prices, which produced lines of people at Zachys' door eager to purchase liquor at bargain prices. His competitors became angry and sued, and Zacharia found himself embroiled in court battles. However, by 1964, the federal courts struck down the laws calling them unconstitutional restraints of trade. As a result, Zachys' revenues exploded from $400,000 to over $1 million.

Diversifying the Product Line

Zacharia was good at spotting trends, and by the late 1960s he saw that Americans were beginning to drink more white wine instead of cocktails. At the time he bought out his father, wine comprised only about 10 percent of the inventory. Not knowing much about wine, Zacharia went to New York City to learn how the very successful Sherry-Lehmann shop operated. It was there that he learned about selling futures, which means that, for example, the retailer would buy a particular wine while it was still in cask, several years before it was ready to be bottled and shipped, and sell it to the customer. The belief was that during the time between when the retailer purchased the wine and sold it to the customer, the wine would appreciate. The customer would save money, and the retailer would have immediate cash.

The futures business is risky, particularly in wine because very few vintages appreciate in a short period of time. There are additional risks for customers. For example, if the wine merchant's business fails, there is no way customers can recoup the money that they paid in advance. Zacharia gave his customers more peace of mind with futures because Zachys bought futures before the customer had given them a check. One of the most successful purchases that Zachys ever made was the futures on 1982 Bordeaux, which was incredibly inexpensive because at the time $1 bought an astounding 10 French francs. A case of Chateau Gruaud-Larose, for example, cost $110 a case in 1984; in 2005, it sold for $250 a bottle. With this success under its belt, Zachys became one of the top leading American players in the Bordeaux futures market. These futures now made up 20 percent of Zachys' total business.

When 2000 was declared the most important year for Bordeaux ever, sales at Zachys went from 2000 cases to 16,000 cases, which caused some serious warehousing problems for the company. It became vitally important that customers pick up their orders instead of storing them at Zachys.

The Third Generation's Push for the Internet

In 1995 the Internet was in the early stages of commercial use when Don's son, Jeff, and son-in-law, Andrew, realized that it would be an important part of Zachys' future. Don wanted to wait before jumping in, figuring that they could learn from others' mistakes. In 1996 they registered the URL zachys.com but did not build a site until 1998. After a few months of reworking the site to make it faster and more user friendly, they began to see surprising growth of about 25 to 35 percent a year. Today, 25 percent of sales are on the Internet, 50 percent in phone calls, and 25 percent at the retail site.

Planning for the Future

So far, Zachys is a family business in which the family still works well together. In many family businesses, problems begin when the second generation brings in the lawyers to work out ownership and succession issues. Zacharia wisely brought in a trusted attorney very early to act as an intermediary in the semiannual meetings between Zacharia and Jeff and Andrew. He also pulled in trust and estate attorneys to make sure that his wife and two daughters, who are not involved in the business, were taken care of; but they would not receive company stock. His son, Jeff, and daughter, Jennifer (married to Andrew), would receive grantor retained annuity trusts (GRATs). With GRATs, Zacharia would give away his stock over six years and retain fixed annual annuity payments. At the end of the six years, the business would be owned completely by the grantees, and the annuity payments would stop.

Another reason for the family's success is that each family member has a specific responsibility. This is a consistent theme in most success stories of family businesses. Jeff is the principal buyer of Bordeaux and focuses on operations, while Andrew specializes in Italian wines and focuses on bringing in money. At one point while Don was still in charge, Jeff and Andrew wanted to invest in more warehouse space; Don said no. So, Jeff and Andrew formed a new company called

New York Fine Wine Storage in 1997. Its primary customer is Zachys, but it rents out its excess climate-controlled space to private customers. In the warehouse are some of the finest wines in the world, many being stored for their celebrity owners.

Don is not out of the business entirely; in fact, his division of Zachys is the wine-auction business, which he owns completely. Sales from the auction drive traffic to the Zachys online store as well as to the retail outlet, and it achieved its first profit in 2005. Prior to Don starting the auction, Zachys had partnered with highly regarded Christie's auction house, but eventually the partnership unraveled. Christie's is a huge company that moves much more slowly than the nimble family business. Today, Jeff Zacharia is the president of Zachys. He is absolutely passionate about the business, but he knows that this continues to be a highly competitive business where fortunes can take a turn for the worse if he is not diligent.

Advising the Entrepreneur

1. What are the biggest challenges facing Zachys, and how should Jeff Zacharia deal with them?

2. Are there any other diversification strategies that Zachys ought to consider?

3. How would you rate this family business and why?

Sources: J. Anderson, "Wine Sellers," *Inc.* (April 2005), www.inc.com; P. D. Meltzer, "Christie's Auction House Splits with Zachys," *Wine Spectator* (January 31, 2002), www.winespectator.com; "Jeff Zacharia '83," *Kenyon College*, www.kenyon.edu (accessed July 31, 2005).

CHAPTER 6

Launching a High-Technology Venture

For a successful technology, reality must take precedence over public relations, for Nature cannot be fooled.

Richard Feynman (1918–1988)

LEARNING OUTCOMES

- Differentiate between disruptive and sustaining technologies.
- Discuss the innovation and commercialization.
- Explain the distinct characteristics of biotechnology and biomedical ventures.
- Describe the technology adoption and diffusion cycle.
- Explain the purpose and method for licensing technology.

Launching *SpaceShipOne:* Commercializing Private Space Flight

Until October 4, 2004, no one thought that a jet-engine aircraft could penetrate the 100,000 feet invisible barrier that separated sky from space. But on that day, Burt Rutan's pudgy little aircraft lifted off the runway in the Mojave Desert of California with a pilot on board who steered the groundbreaking aircraft out of the atmosphere and into space. Less than a week later, the journey was repeated—a feat that earned the company the Ansari X-Prize and heralded the age of commercial space travel.

For Burt Rutan, a dentist's son who grew up in the 1940s in Dinuba, a farming town in the central valley of California, the mission was the achievement of a lifelong dream. Airplanes had always consumed Rutan—he actually soloed in a plane before he obtained his driver's license. After earning an aeronautical engineering degree from California Polytechnic, he became a test engineer at Edwards Air Force Base and remained there for seven years. With that experience under his belt, he launched his first company, RAF (Rutan Aircraft Factory), to sell plans for two-seater aircraft to pilots who wanted to build their own planes as a hobby. Over time, he figured out a method for hand-building the exterior components of the plane out of strips of fiberglass that were soaked in glue and placed over foam, which was stronger and lighter than either wood or aluminum. Because he could not afford a real wind tunnel to test the structural integrity of his designs, he would strap the parts to the roof of his station wagon and speed down the road with them at 80 miles per hour.

By 1982 Rutan was ready to begin designing, building, and testing prototype aircraft for large customers like the U.S. Air Force and the National Aeronautics and Space Administration (NASA). He called his new company Scaled Composites; it grew rapidly and employed 100 people by the mid-1990s. This was a remarkable achievement by any measure because the company is located in a remote area of the Mojave Desert with nothing to motivate families to move there besides the fun of working with Rutan. In 1986, after his brother flew the first flight to circumnavigate the world without refueling, Rutan became a

celebrity, but by the mid-1990s, he was ready to do something more challenging. The big question that he was playing with was how to transport people into space in a less costly and less complex manner. No one seemed to be interested until 1996 when his friend Vern Raburn managed to talk Paul Allen, Microsoft cofounder and a space travel enthusiast, into coming to Mojave to talk with Rutan. Allen was fascinated by what Rutan showed him but at the time did not see how it would ever come about. Meanwhile the X-Prize for the first manned, nongovernment-funded flight to reach an altitude of 62 miles and repeat the trip with the same vehicle within two weeks would win $10 million. After further discussions with Rutan, Allen decided to invest $25 million in the effort, with the agreement that he would own the technology developed by Rutan through a new company called Mojave Aerospace Ventures.

Rutan was not highly confident that he could achieve a supersonic aircraft that would head into space at Mach 3, or three times the speed of sound. To do so, he would need to build a special flight simulator, build a thruster system to turn the spacecraft once in space, design and build an electronic navigation system, and build a rocket motor, all of which he had never done before. However, one by one, Rutan's team found solutions to each engineering challenge. But testing presented new challenges that shook the confidence of everyone for a time, and even Allen questioned if he had funded the right project.

In April 2003, Rutan began flight-testing the *White Knight,* the name for the aircraft that could carry *SpaceShipOne* to 46,000 feet and let it loose. Six months after that, *SpaceShipOne* surpassed its first record by breaking the sound barrier in its first manned flight. Then in June 2004, it shot through the 62-mile mark and became an official spacecraft.

Richard Branson, Virgin Atlantic's adventurous founder, immediately flew to Seattle to meet with Allen after the success of the test flight. Branson wanted to fund the development of commercial space-liners based on this success. The deal he and Allen agreed on includes Virgin paying up to $21.5 million over fifteen years to Mojave Aerospace, which has planned its first flights for 2008 on what Branson calls Virgin Galactic. Ticket prices are set at $210,000; more than 7000 people are waiting to fly.

With all this support and enthusiasm, there are still many questions to be answered. Rutan has never commercialized any of his prototype aircraft, and to date no spacecraft exists that can carry five passengers. Furthermore, Rutan has competition from Elon Musk, the founder of PayPal, who operates SpaceX in El Segundo, California, where he is working on an orbital space vehicle. In the meantime, revenues are coming in from booking orders to launch satellites.

Rutan is considered by many to be a national treasure, and *SpaceShipOne* with its mothership, *White Knight,* are "widely considered to be the most promising, recyclable, and efficient uses of advanced aerospace tech-

nology seen in recent years." Rutan may have found the business model that will make space tourism a reality, but there are still many hurdles to clear.

Advising the Entrepreneur

1. What do you believe is the biggest challenge facing *SpaceShipOne,* and how would you deal with it?

2. Has Rutan put the right business partnerships in place to be able to commercialize his technology? What does he still need?

Sources: D. H. Freedman, "Entrepreneur of the Year," *Inc.* (January 2005), www.inc.com; C. Palmeri, "A Giant Leap for Burt Rutan," *BusinessWeek Online* (October 5, 2004), www.businessweek.com; J. Twist, "Burt Rutan: Aviation Pioneer," *BBC News,* http://newsvote.bbc.co.uk (accessed August 20, 2005).

Entrepreneurs who seek to launch technology businesses today face an ever-changing set of challenges, customers, and values. The demand to produce better, faster, cheaper technology places a nearly impossible burden on companies attempting to successfully compete in this environment. Moreover, the need to acquire intellectual property protections such as patents and turn those into revenue-generating assets has never been greater. Arguably, the ultimate challenge is to produce a continuous stream of incremental innovation and punctuate that with periodic introductions of radical innovation to ensure long-term sustainability.[1] Every year, thousands of new technology products are introduced to the market, but the majority of these technologies are simply incremental innovations—improvements on existing technology. Most incremental innovations fail to make a profit for their companies. By contrast, companies like 3M and Hewlett-Packard have survived longer than most because from time to time they bring out a radical or disruptive innovation that changes the game and displaces everything that preceded it, thus creating a new platform for further incremental innovation.

Where an incremental innovation addresses current needs in the market, a disruptive technology supersedes existing standards and addresses future customer needs. Disruptive technologies come about when customers' needs can no longer be satisfied within the current technological parameters; consequently, disruptive technologies produce far-reaching effects. When disruptive technologies are successful, they bring about significant improvements in features, benefits, and costs, but they are rarely successful or profitable in the early stages of product launch.[2] The lack of profitability until they reach mass-market acceptance is caused by their generally poor performance. For example, in the late 1950s Sony launched its battery-powered transistor radio. The sound quality was poor by any standards, and so the product did not at first succeed in the mass market. However, once teenage fans of rock-and-roll music realized that the radio would enable them to listen to their music wherever they went, they became the early adopters. For them it solved a problem: They could listen to their favorite music away from their parents, who did not want to hear it.

Once a disruptive technology improves in performance and achieves mass-market acceptance, it has an enormous impact on the economy because it produces new categories of products and services as well as new companies and jobs. Some examples include Edison's light bulb, eyeglasses, moveable type, the birth control pill, and lasers. Three current disruptive technologies that will have an enormous impact on every industry in terms of innovation and opportunity are the genome, nanotechnology, and wireless technology. The mapping of the human genome, announced in June 2000, is leading to genetic therapies targeted at an individual's specific genetic makeup and potentially the ability to cure the worst diseases. It has opened the door to hundreds of business opportunities such as equipment to perform genetic testing. Some prognosticators claim that by 2040 every physician will have a black bag of genetic tools for dealing with patients' unique needs.

Nanotechnology came from a need to develop a nonsilicon chip used in computers that would replace the silicon chip with less expensive molecular computing components. Nanotechnologies are molecular machines based on nature, and they comprise technologies that operate in the nanometer (1 billionth of a metric unit) area of scale.[3] Today, nanotechnologies are found in almost every area of technology development. Nanosphere is one company that has stepped up to the challenge of turning the promise of nanotechnology in medicine to reality. The Illinois-based company is using nanotechnology to transform the medical-testing industry. It is commercializing a technology developed by two Northwestern University scientists that can detect minute particles of protein that serve as markers for Alzheimer's disease in spinal fluid. The company is in talks with a large pharmaceutical partner that can use this diagnostic tool to develop an associated drug.[4]

Wireless technology has made it possible for anyone to send and receive e-mail, buy and sell stock, check inventory levels, and monitor shipping progress, all with the help of a Web-enabled cell phone or personal digital assistant (PDA). Engineers have only begun to penetrate the surface of all the possibilities for wireless technology. Alex Lightman, who founded Charmed Technology, is calculating that people will eventually become walking Internet portals by wearing wireless technology embedded in clothing.[5]

Most disruptive technologies come from small entrepreneurial companies because large corporations suffer from what has been called "the incumbent's curse." The theory is that large corporations, which have significant investments in their current technology, often suffer from technology inertia or the fear of drifting too far from their successes.[6] Therefore, most radically new technology comes from smaller firms with no sunk costs in existing technology and no shareholders with short-term goals to protect. Smaller firms are in a better position to take on the risk of new technology development.

Technology presents an enormous opportunity for entrepreneurs to create new ventures that have the potential to grow large and change the way things are done. Starting a technology company is not an easy undertaking. The next section explores the process of bringing a new technology to market.

LEARNING FROM SUCCESS

Play Ball!

When the Boston Red Sox defended its World Championship title in the fall of 2005, it did so with a team that consisted of some well-known superstars, some new pitchers, and an off-field team of technology consultants. This is the new face of Major League Baseball.

CEO Richard Nicholas founded E Solutions in 1998 and was designing intranets for major corporations when a life-changing opportunity came along. Yankees' owner George Steinbrenner needed to upgrade his scouting system. The Yankees had been doing manual data entry and faxing scouting reports back to the home office; it was a very archaic system. Today, baseball is burdened with enormous payroll costs and anything a team can do to ensure that they get what they pay for is critical. Nicholas saw an opportunity to address a real pain in the market. E Solutions and its ScoutAdvisor program were not the first to market. In fact, IBM's PROS software was the dominant player in the market at the time, but it was far more expensive and IBM charged for every modification. E Solutions is competing by customizing at no charge, which is a real benefit to teams who want to avoid having any other team learn how they do things. Nicholas asserts, "We've customized this software for one client 30 times." By 2003 E Solutions had six clubs on its roster of clients, and by 2005 it owned 30 percent of the market with teams like the Red Sox, the St. Louis Cardinals, and the Anaheim Angels.

Lesson Learned: *If you keep the customer happy, you can compete against even large companies.*

Sources: ScoutAdvisor, http://www.scoutadvisor.com/; M. Overfelt, "Numbers Game: An Upstart Technology Company Is Helping Baseball Teams Manage Their Most Valuable Resource: Talent," *Fortune Small Business* (May 1, 2005), www.fortune.com.

THE INNOVATION AND COMMERCIALIZATION PROCESS

Bringing a technology to market is not a straightforward process starting with innovation and ending with a product that customers purchase. It is in fact a rather iterative process with many feedback loops and changes of direction as new information is acquired and the entrepreneur/inventor learns from mistakes. Figure 6.1 depicts the commercialization process as a flowchart of activities organized into major categories or milestones. This particular chart depicts the most complicated form of the process entailing regulatory elements required for biotechnology and biomedical products. That aspect of the commercialization process will be discussed in its own section. Each of the other major categories is discussed in the following sections.

Phase 1: Research and Invention

The discovery of something completely new generally consists of four activities: (1) connection, (2) discovery, (3) invention, and (4) application. Connection is the recognition of a relationship that no one has seen before—the eureka moment that leads to the discovery of something new. That something new is developed into an invention, which, in the case of a technology venture, is a new technology that has potential application or utility in the market. Technologies that are brand new with no precedent and that fundamentally change the way things are done are called disruptive technologies. Often they become a platform for the development of multiple applications for very different markets.

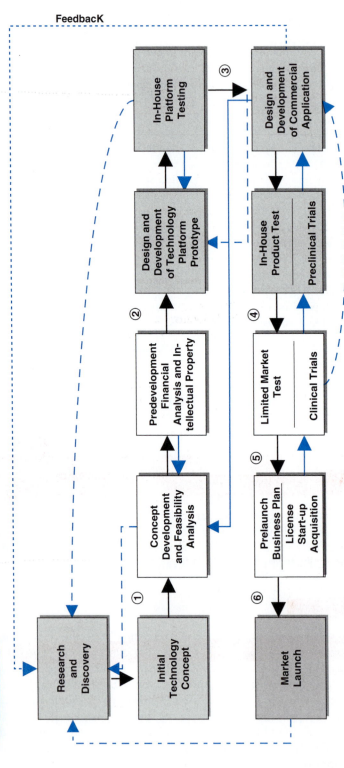

FIGURE 6.1   The Technology Innovation and Commercialization Process

Roadblocks and Speed Bumps

1. Fear of the unknown: Is there something novel and patentable?
2. No market knowledge: Is there a customer and a need?
3. Is there funding for prototyping and identifying applications?
4. What is the level of acceptance and demand?
5. License? Start a company? Be acquired?
6. Transition from R&D to operations

The majority of all new technology products are actually incremental innovations. With the pace of technological change escalating and product cycle-times shrinking, there is a great deal of pressure on technology companies to concentrate on quick wins in the form of incremental innovation.[7] The problem with this strategy is that a company cannot sustain long-term growth on incremental technology; it must continually introduce radically new technologies that will disrupt the market and may even create new industries.

Inventing a new technology product is only the beginning, and it is certainly not enough to guarantee that a sustainable business can be derived from that product. An **opportunity** is the intersection of an idea and a market need.[8] There must be a value proposition or benefit that can be supplied to a customer through an identified distribution channel and a business model that allows the entrepreneur to make money.[9] At the end of this first major phase, a technology opportunity has been identified and now must be tested both from a technical or engineering perspective and from a market perspective.

Phase 2: Initial Technical and Market Feasibility Analysis

The space between discovery and identification of a market has been referred to as the "valley of death" because it is the area where most new-product ideas fail due to a disconnection between the laboratory and the market. To turn an exciting technology from an engineering perspective into a useful product that customers will pay, entrepreneurs must meet many challenges and overcome many uncertainties. These challenges and uncertainties often relate to the technology itself at this very early stage. Also, because investors cannot quantify the risks associated with the technology and the market has yet to be identified, they wait until the business case has been made before taking time to do thorough due diligence on a technology business. It is not surprising then that most funding for the first two stages of the innovation and commercialization process comes from public sources like government and foundation grants.

Many inventor/entrepreneurs skip phase 2 and move directly from the initial concept to physical prototype development (phase 3). This is a mistake because phase 3 is a point at which the developer incurs significant costs, which dramatically increase his or her risk. To reduce the risk of phase 3 as much as possible, an initial feasibility analysis that looks at both the technology and the potential market for it must be conducted in phase 2. If first customers or early adopters have been identified, they should provide feedback at this point. One word of caution here: If the technology being developed is disruptive, it is very difficult to identify the potential market precisely because by definition a disruptive technology addresses a need that does not yet exist. Nevertheless, understanding early in the process what it will take to generate interest in the technology is important so that the company can prepare financially to support the costs of customer acquisition. (Feasibility analysis was discussed in Chapter 3.)

During the development of a new technology, the first critical decision is whether to apply for a patent to protect the asset that is being created. Three important questions need to be answered in order to make this decision:

1. Does the technology have a useful purpose?

2. Is a patent required for the successful commercialization of the product?

3. Does the technology meet the U.S. Patent and Trademark Office's (PTO) requirements for patenting? There are four basic requirements:

   a. It must have utility; that is, it must be useful, not whimsical. However, the PTO did issue a patent in 1995 for a laser-beam invention to motivate cats to exercise (Patent No. 5,443,036).

   b. There must be no prior art or knowledge publicly available or published about the invention prior to one year before the date of patent application. This means that the invention must be new or novel in some important aspect.

   c. The invention cannot be obvious to someone with ordinary skills in the field of invention. The invention must contain new and unexpected results and cannot be the next logical step in a process.

   d. The invention must fit into one of five categories established by the U.S. Congress: (i) machine or something with moving parts or circuitry (for example, fax, rocket, photocopier, laser, electronic circuit); (ii) process or method for producing a useful and tangible result (for example, chemical reaction, method for producing products, business model); (iii) article of manufacture (for example, furniture, transistor, diskette, toy); (iv) composition of matter (for example, gasoline, food additive, drug, genetically altered life form); (v) a new use or improvement of something from the first four categories.

For some technology products, the window of opportunity is too narrow to allow for the time it takes to receive a patent, which may be as much as two years or more from the date of application. Understanding the nature of the industry and market with which the entrepreneur is dealing helps in making a wise decision. When considering whether to patent, it is always a good idea to consult with an attorney who specializes in intellectual property because an attorney knows how to craft the patent application in a way that provides the best chance of getting it through the PTO process.

Phase 3: Platform Prototyping, Production Process, and Testing

To fully determine that a technology meets a real need in the market and to ensure that it can actually be manufactured, a working prototype is necessary. This is perhaps the most expensive stage of the commercialization process because, as a general rule, prototypes cost about ten times as much as the final production product costs. Furthermore, as the technology is tested, it faces redesign of components to reflect new information, and redesign is one of the most costly aspects of product development. Working in parallel with the other activities of the commercialization process, the prototype is built and field-tested with potential customers to assess its utility, determine which features are important, and, in some cases, establish ergonomics requirements. The prototype also assists the entrepreneur in calculating future manufacturing costs and a possible price. Another obstacle that challenges the developer at this stage is the need to build the infrastructure requirement to produce the final product for the marketplace. Large-scale infrastructure needs like a manufacturing plant or assembly facility and small-scale infrastructure like materials suppliers and distributors must be designed, costs must be estimated, and sources for the infrastructure must be found.

Phase 4: Testing the Business Opportunity

Testing the business opportunity is the stage of the commercialization process that links innovation with the market. If developers have determined in phase 3 that the technology has value for customers, they still need to calculate how much of that value the company can actually capture.[10] Research points to the benefits of considering technology and market factors simultaneously.[11] It is at this stage that the actual feasibility of a business is determined from information gathered during industry and market research. This research employs both primary data, or data gathered by the entrepreneur directly from the customer or others in the industry, and secondary data, or data gathered from sources such as the Internet and research conducted by third parties such as research firms and industry analysts. Research leads to the development of a business model, which is critical to a successful business opportunity because value creation happens only when the entrepreneur attaches a business model to an invention. Therefore, it makes sense to identify a first customer who understands the technology, who has a problem that the technology solves, and who is ready, willing, and able to buy. Finding a first customer is perhaps more important than trying to capture a large market where the mechanisms for value capture are not as well established.[12]

Effective market testing leads to the second major decision point in the process where the entrepreneur must determine whether to license the rights to manufacture and market the technology to another company, sell the technology outright to another company, or create a company to produce and sell the technology. There are no hard-and-fast rules as to which avenue to choose under specific conditions; however, in general, technologies that take significant additional development beyond the capabilities and resources of the entrepreneur are licensed to a larger company so that the entrepreneur can reap the rewards of discovery through a royalty stream from the licensee. This is often the case with pharmaceuticals and other medical devices, which are too costly for a small business to commercialize effectively. (Licensing is discussed in more detail in a later section.) Disruptive technologies are often launched via new technology companies that grow rapidly once the technology has passed the early adopter stage or are acquired by a larger company as a way to diversify that company's product line. In the latter case, the small technology company serves as the outsourced research and development (R&D) lab for the larger company.

Phase 5: Business Development

If the decision has been made to launch a company, it will be necessary to prepare a comprehensive business plan that details the operations, policies, marketing and growth strategies, and financial plan for the business. A legal structure for the business must be chosen with the help of an attorney (see Chapter 7) and the search for outside capital, if it is needed, will begin. (The business plan is discussed in detail in Chapter 8.)

The transition from R&D to business operations is often a difficult one because the required skill sets for each activity are so different. Frequently, the technology inventor is a scientist or engineer with no business experience; consequently, the need to think about hiring staff, raising money, finding facilities, managing inventory, and so forth is daunting at best. Typically, scientists and engineers partner with businesspeople to launch a new venture. Before venture capitalists or private investors provide capital, they often demand the hiring of professional management to run the business. They want the assurance that the technical founders are free to devote themselves to the further R&D that will be required to sustain competitiveness over time.

The transition from R&D to operations is also never a smooth one because the team is always encountering technical issues that pull it away from its new market focus. The R&D team enjoyed the luxury of experimentation, the ability to fail, and the time to improve continually on what it developed. The operations team works in a completely different environment.[13] If the team does not design its manufacturing processes in parallel with the product development, the launch of the company may be held up until that problem can be worked out. The operations team is charged with generating cash flow for the business after a protracted period in which the company existed solely on the personal investment of the founders or on research grants. This is no easy task for several reasons. A brand new technology takes a long time to gain market acceptance because customers need to understand the benefits and learn how to use it. Moreover, it is not uncommon for the original assumptions about product design and markets to change once the product is in the market. For example, when PDAs were introduced in 1995, they were loaded with communications functions that the engineers thought were essential for customers to have. However, what they discovered as they observed customer usage was that the most important function on the PDA from a customer perspective was the scheduling function. Therefore, they had wasted a lot of time and money including features that customers did not need.

The technology commercialization process for biotechnology and biomedical ventures is different in many respects from other technology ventures, and these differences are addressed in the next section.

LEARNING FROM MISTAKES

When an Idea Backfires

In 2005 Paul Purdue's e-commerce shipping company based in Maumee, Ohio, was disintegrating. In February of that year, he had installed a new wireless inventory system in this iFulfill.com fulfillment business. Instead of making things more efficient, however, it actually caused confusion and missed orders. As things progressively worsened, employee morale sank, customers fled, and the company's debt soared. On July 25, Purdue closed the door on his seven-year-old business and terminated the employees. During all this negative activity, his marketing consultant, an avid blogger, had advised Purdue to "do something controversial." So Purdue had started a blog on the Internet to try to attract readers, and he was highly successful but not in the way that he intended. People used the blog to post complaints about the company and to warn vendors to reclaim their products. Moreover, some of these customers

thought that the blog was simply about satisfying his ego. On August 4, 2005, he posted the following regarding what went wrong:

> Looking back now I realize that I'm not a manager, I'm a nerd. In the early days, it was easy. There was only me and it was a long time before we grew to be the size we ended up. But as we grew, I got pulled in all different directions and found myself micromanaging all areas—not a good way to manage. I tried to be a Jack of all trades, but the end of that saying is "master of none."

Lesson Learned: *Focus on the critical success drivers for the business.*

Source: "Blogging as You Go Belly Up," *BusinessWeek Online* (August 15, 2005), http://www.ifulfill.com/weblog/ www.businessweek.com.

UNDERSTANDING BIOTECHNOLOGY AND BIOMEDICAL VENTURES

Biotechnology product development is a source of both opportunity and risk. Whether the company is a large pharmaceutical (pharma) or a small entrepreneurial venture, the process and the risks are essentially the same. The advantage that the large pharma has over the small technology businesses is a continuing stream of revenues from other products that it has developed and that can offset losses on a failed new product.[14] Nevertheless, it takes fifteen years on average to take a drug from the test tube to market at a cost of over $500 million, and the risk along the way is high. The Pharmaceutical Research and Manufacturers of America reports that for every 5000 compounds that make it through animal testing, or preclinical trials, only about 5 move to human trials, and only 1 of those makes it to the pharmacy shelves. Even when a drug makes it to market, there exists the possibility that it carries unforeseen toxic side effects, which will result in the product being recalled. American Home Products Corp. had to pull its successful obesity drug Redux off the market when it was reported that it caused heart valve problems. It had been tested in more than 4000 patients and had been sold in Europe for many years.[15]

The Clinical Trial Process

The biotechnology industry faces many risks that do not challenge developers in other industries. The biggest risk factors in terms of the delays they cause in product development are clinical trials and Food and Drug Administration (FDA) approval. More specifically, researchers report that writing and proposals, management duties, and testing compounds that would never be used to produce drugs as the tasks that produce the most delays.[16] Table 6.1 depicts the drug development process. Each phase is considered in more detail in the following sections.

Preclinical Testing Discovery is a critical component of the development process, so much so that large pharmas often financially support their small business counterparts with the expectation that they will bring a promising new drug into the pharma's portfolio. In preclinical testing, the company studies how a promising lab compound works in whole animals, which add a substantially greater level of complexity. The goal of this phase is to generate data that will convince the FDA that it will be safe and worthwhile to test the compound in humans. Animal trials provide information on such things as toxicity, effectiveness, and how quickly the drug disappears from the bloodstream, among others. This phase typically takes about three to four years to complete.

Clinical Trials Clinical trials are studies done with humans who have the target disease. They are used to determine whether a drug works well enough to give to patients, whether the side effects outweigh the benefits, what the correct dosage regimen is, and whether the drug is better than current treatment methods. In addition, clinical trials offer a way to calculate the cost-benefit for a new treatment, which is important in a managed-healthcare environment. Clinical trials consist of three phases. Phase I focuses on the best way to use the drug and whether it is safe. Phase II provides information about how the drug behaves in people and how effective it

TABLE 6.1   The Drug Development Process

		Clinical Trials					
	Preclinical Tests	**Phase I**	**Phase II**	**Phase III**	**FDA Review/ Approval**	**In Market**	**Phase IV**
Years	6.5	1.5	2	3.5	1.5	Total: 15	
Test Popula- tion	Test tube and animal studies	20–80 healthy volunteers	100–300 patients	1000–3000 patients			Patients
Purpose	Safety and effective- ness	Safety and dosage	Effective- ness and potential side effects	Confirm effective- ness and long-term side effects			Post- marketing monitoring
Success Rate	5000 evaluated	5 com- pounds enter clinicals			1 com- pound approved		

Source: Pharmaceutical Research and Manufacturing Association, http://www.phrma.org/newmedicines/resources// 2000-09-18.74.cfm.

is. Phase III trials are often called *pivotal trials,* and their purpose is to generate data that will lead to FDA approval. Some drugs that are focused on life-threatening diseases in which no effective treatment currently exists are fast-tracked through phase III. An example is Amgen's Epogen, an agent for the anemia associated with end-stage renal disease.

Medical Devices

Medical device development is one of most fundable areas of new-product development. Medical devices can be found in fields ranging from cardiovascular to orthopedic and even sleep disturbance. Whether a medical device has commercial value is commonly assessed through finite element analysis, which looks at design, economic life, FDA requirements, and the ability to shorten the design cycle and get the device to market quickly. For medical devices, the challenges lie in reducing development time, increasing the confidence of success, and avoiding surprises and delays. One of the key factors in reducing the time to market is minimizing the number of design iterations that are prototyped. This can be accomplished through computer-aided design in which elements of the design can be tested virtually. Testing of a medical device design is essential for refining the design, to test for fatigue, and to validate that the device does what it is supposed to do.

Most new devices are launched by start-up companies whose physician and/or engineer founder discovers a solution to an unmet clinical challenge. Personal funding typically supports bench and animal testing for a period of two to three years and may consume $10 million to $20 million before clinical trials begin. First clinical use is considered the target milestone that a company must achieve for viability. Because of the time factor in obtaining FDA approval to initiate clinical studies in the United States, approximately 75 percent of first clinical use device testing occurs outside the country.[17] In the United States, the Center for Devices and Radiological Health of the FDA regulates medical devices. Devices are classified according to their risk, using a three-tiered system. Class I devices do not require formal FDA review before market introduction because general controls are sufficient to ensure safety and effectiveness. Class II devices require FDA clearance of a premarket notification application (PMA or 510(k)) before the device can be marketed. Class III devices include such things as heart values and coronary stents, which are life sustaining. They require FDA approval of a PMA with clinical data before they can be marketed.

The healthcare industry will be of great interest to investors and entrepreneurs for the foreseeable future, and it affords many opportunities for new ventures that can make money and solve critical health problems. To successfully bring any technology to market requires an in-depth understanding of the patterns of adoption and diffusion that all technologies experience. These patterns are reviewed in the next section.

THE TECHNOLOGY ADOPTION AND DIFFUSION CYCLE

The manner in which new technologies achieve market acceptance is quite distinct from other types of products, especially those that are improvements on existing technologies. Figure 6.2 depicts the technology adoption–diffusion cycle, which was first developed by the U.S. Department of Agriculture (DOA) in the 1930s as it was attempting to understand why farmers were resistant to adopt new strains of seed potatoes.[18] The DOA found that it had placed too much confidence on the feedback from innovators and early adopters who seek out new technologies long before the mass market is willing to tackle the learning curve and incur the switching costs of moving to a brand new technology. The innovators provide proof of concept, in other words, that the technology actually works as claimed. The early adopters, a relatively small group of customers, generate excitement on the part of the entrepreneurs because early adopters actually pay for the technology. However, entrepreneurs must understand that between the early adopters and the mainstream market lies the valley of death—the chasm—where many new technologies fade away until they die or until they can create enough critical mass eventually to cross the chasm and be adopted by the mainstream market.

New technologies must find a way to cross the chasm so that they have the opportunity to become the industry standard. Accomplishment of this difficult task requires that the entrepreneur seek out niche markets and encourage early adopters, who are typically original equipment manufacturers, to modify the technology to meet the specific needs of a niche customer. By getting the technology into multiple niche markets, more people become aware of its benefits, and the company has a better chance of making it across the chasm. With multiple niches conquered, the company will reach critical mass and be propelled into a tornado, which means that the mass market switches to the entrepreneur's technology and the company experiences a flood of demand. If the company survives the tornado (and many do not because they lack the

FIGURE 6.2 The Technology Adoption–Diffusion Cycle

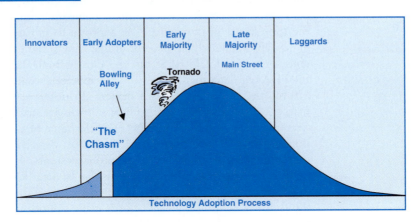

manufacturing and distribution systems to deal with demand), it arrives at "Main Street" where growth slows and no longer comes from selling to new customers but from selling more to existing customers. It is clear that to be successful, a company must have its infrastructure in place before being carried into the tornado, or it will simply make customers angry because it cannot deliver on its promises. In the tornado, the only thing that matters is getting product to customers. Demand is there; in many cases, more demand than the company can reasonably handle. The company that successfully negotiates the tornado will find itself in the dominant position in its industry. One of the common strategies used to cross the chasm and create a tornado is licensing the technology to multiple developers who can get the technology into several markets simultaneously.

LEARNING FROM SUCCESS

Design Is the Key to Innovation Success

Bob Marchant is adamant about blending aesthetics and utility into everything he designs, and according to Marchant, "Design is in everything we do." Modo is an Oregon-based manufacturer of carts that hold medical equipment and supplies. Operating in a highly competitive market in which products are viewed as commodities, Modo has grown 20 percent per year since 1997 by integrating design and management. The entire field of design has changed, according to Richard Buchanan, a professor at Carnegie Mellon's School of Design in Pittsburgh. Today, design is about "how people relate to other people and the products that mediate that

relationship." Whether a company is designing a high-technology product or a medical cart, it is important to understand thoroughly how customers will use the product and to make that usage an experience. Marchant follows that philosophy at Modo where designers, engineers, and business types work side by side and the culture clash has meant more creative ideas being generated. With customers like Medtronic, Philips, and General Electric, he seems to have found the key to innovation success.

Source: T. Raz, "Driven by Design," *Inc.* (October 2002), www.inc.com; http://www.modo1.com/index.php.

LICENSING TECHNOLOGY

Licensing is more than a $110 billion a year industry in the United States and over $170 billion worldwide.[19] Although it is a fact that the greatest dollar volume of licenses belongs to large corporations, the majority of licensors and licensees are small companies.[20] Licensing is often more advantageous to the inventor because it speeds up the time to market and it is easier for the inventor than attempting to identify, develop, and market all the possible applications of the technology.[21] Some inventors choose to license the distribution rights to their technology to benefit from reaching multiple markets simultaneously without the enormous expense of developing distribution channels and an effective sales force.

Noninventor entrepreneurs frequently use licensing as a mechanism to acquire a technology with which to launch a new business. Licensing a proven technology is a quick way to get to market without incurring the heavy costs of research and product development. Entrepreneurs seeking to start a technology venture should investigate technologies available for licensing from universities and independent laboratories as well as government agencies such as NASA and NOAA (National Oceanic and Atmospheric Administration). Because licensing a technology carries with it significant responsibility, entrepreneurs should make certain that the following elements are in place:

- The technology works the way the licensor claims.
- The licensor can provide performance data from a working prototype, which typically is superior to laboratory performance.
- The licensor can guarantee some appropriate level of performance.
- The licensor completely owns the technology.

In technology businesses, the challenge is not simply to get a new product to market; it is to find a way to effectively convert valuable know-how in the form of patents, copyrights, trademarks, or trade secrets into multiple revenue streams. Figure 6.3 presents a variety of options for accomplishing this goal, but nearly all require some form of licensing. From the inventor's perspective, selling or licensing the technology to a company that can develop it further and build applications in various markets is the least costly and least risky route to commercialization. This strategy would enable the inventor to focus his or her resources on new inventions that could also be licensed. In this way, the inventor remains in the invention business. As the inventor's company moves down the pyramid, it faces increasing liability and costs because it must build a working prototype, test it, meet regulatory requirements, design and build market applications, and develop facilities and distribution channels. Likewise, as the licensee moves up the pyramid, the costs and risk go up because a licensee who simply purchases know-how must be able to develop a useful application, engineer a prototype, and test it—all of which carry with it a great deal of risk.

For the licensor and the licensee, the decision whether to do the work in-house or sublicense it to another firm is an important one. If the work is done in-house, the new company will need to complete all the tasks required to work its way through the pyramid.

Determining What Can Be Licensed

From the inventor/entrepreneur's perspective, what is being licensed to someone is a bundle of rights that may include a number of patents, know-how, and distribution

FIGURE 6.3 Technology Value Pyramid

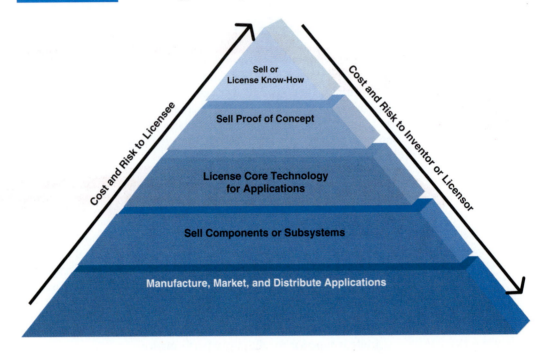

rights to specific markets or geographic areas. In every case, these rights may either be exclusive—that is, no one else possesses those rights—or nonexclusive, meaning that someone else might have distribution rights but not in the same market, for example. The goal for the licensor is to create a bundle of rights that achieves the highest value for the technology and allows the licensee to also obtain a high value for what he or she adds to the technology. To accomplish this, the licensor needs to understand the licensee's needs as well as the needs of the market. In other words, the licensor must conduct in-depth market research to present a compelling case to the licensee. The licensing process is depicted in Figure 6.4 from both the licensor's and the licensee's perspectives.

The licensor also needs to investigate potential licensees to ensure that they possess the required knowledge, skills, and resources to successfully commercialize the technology and fulfill the conditions of the license agreement.

The License Agreement

A **license agreement** is the contract between the licensor and the licensee that defines the terms and conditions under which the two parties will operate. The following are some of the clauses commonly found in a license agreement; however, entrepreneurs should always consult with a qualified attorney so that the final agreement contains the appropriate clauses for the entrepreneur's particular situation.

■ *Grant Clause* This clause describes what is being delivered to the licensee by means of the agreement whether it is to manufacture, distribute, use, and so forth. It also

FIGURE 6.4 The Licensing Process

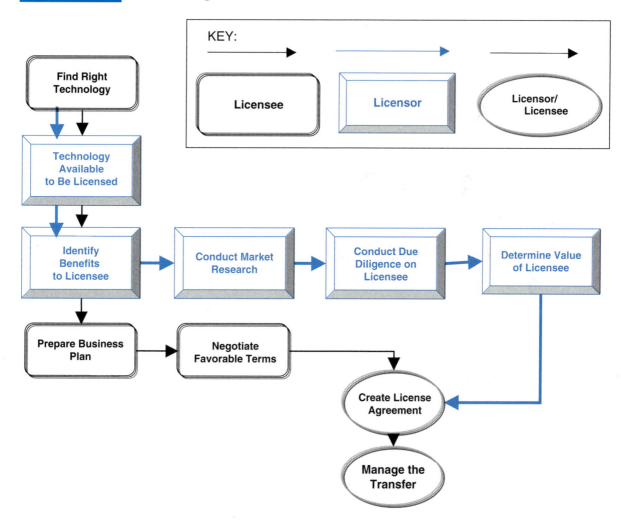

states whether the license is exclusive or nonexclusive, states whether the licensee has the right to sublicense, and may also contain an immunity-from-infringement clause to protect the licensee from potential patent infringement by the original inventor.

■ *Performance Clause* This clause identifies agreed-upon dates by which the licensee should have achieved certain goals. These goals may include completing the development of the technology application, obtaining a first purchase order, or identifying sales targets. For the licensor, performance targets are critical because they ensure against licensing the technology to someone who then does not perform.

■ *Secrecy Clause* This clause is also known as a confidentiality clause, and it restricts disclosure of proprietary information for a specified time. It also details which information can be disclosed and to whom.

■ *Payment Clause* The method of payment for the license is discussed in this clause. Typically, there are several types of payment including an upfront fee, a lump sum paid in installments based on performance, or a running royalty based on a percentage of the net sales price. If the license agreement involves a foreign licensee, this clause also specifies the currency in which the payments are made. A U.S. licensor generally wants payment made in U.S. dollars, but sometimes a combination of currencies is agreed upon. The important thing to remember is that foreign currency fluctuates and, over the life of the agreement, that may amount to a big variation in payments.

- *Grantback Clause* This clause is often referred to as an "improvement" clause. It allows the licensee to make improvements on the invention, but any rights to the improvement must be granted back to the licensor. Similarly, there may also be a grantforward clause that gives the licensee the right to use improvements that the licensor makes on the technology.

- *Agreement Term* Every contract must have a termination date, and license agreements are no different. This clause may also allow for extensions of the agreement by mutual consent.

Valuing the Agreement The licensor needs to place a value on the license agreement. There are many factors that affect the value of a technology and its associated license agreement:

- The economic life of the technology or how long it can provide revenues to the company
- The probability of competitors designing around a patent, if there is one
- The potential for government regulation that might adversely affect the marketability of the technology
- The probability of changes in market conditions that might render the technology useless or obsolete

Whether the agreement is exclusive or nonexclusive also affects the value of the license agreement. In general, licensors only grant exclusive licenses to established companies with demonstrated capabilities in the field who can afford higher royalty rates and who needs to do further development to prepare an application of the technology for market. An exclusive license agreement is valuable because it gives the licensee a temporary monopoly and time to establish itself in the market. By contrast, nonexclusive licenses are the typical choice where a technology platform has broad applications in many markets such that no one company would have all the necessary capabilities to effectively commercialize the technology. Gene therapy is but one example of a broad field with many possible applications, many of which are still unknown. Here, nonexclusive licensing or exclusive licensing to a very narrow market makes sense.

More entrepreneurs than ever before are launching high-technology businesses because they recognize the important position that technology will hold in the economic future of any country. To successfully start, grow, and manage a technology business requires a clear understanding of the nature of these ventures, their differences from other types of businesses, and the strategies that complement their unique characteristics.

ISSUES FOR REVIEW AND DISCUSSION

1. How can technology companies improve their chances of long-term sustainability?

2. Why do disruptive technologies not make sense economically for large firms?

3. How can technology ventures improve their chances of making it through the valley of death in the commercialization process?

4. What is the significance of intellectual property to a technology venture?

5. In what ways are biotechnology ventures different from other technology ventures?

6. What is the importance of understanding the technology adoption and diffusion cycle?

7. Why do entrepreneurs choose to license technology?

EXPERIENCING ENTREPRENEURSHIP

1. Interview an entrepreneur with a biomedical venture to learn about the commercialization process. What aspects of that process proved the most difficult to overcome?

2. Pick a disruptive technology that interests you. Develop a report that traces the history of the technology, including as many elements of the commercialization process as possible.

When Innovation Is the Purpose of the Business

Inventor Scott Augustine knows that invention is the easiest part of the innovation process; turning an invention into a product that has commercial value is the difficult part. Augustine is no stranger to successful products. His first product, the Bair Hugger, a surgical warming blanket, holds over 85 percent of the market and actually started a new industry. His company, Augustine Medical, now a subsidiary of Arizant Inc., is a new-product development company that has been profitable since its third year in 1990. As of 2002, the company owned 108 patents, all of which decorate the walls of its Eden Prairie, Minnesota, offices. Augustine's goal is to produce at least one disruptive technology per year, in addition to many other incremental innovations.

Augustine also thinks creatively about how he hires people. The company employs its share of engineers, but it also hires prop builders from regional theater and opera companies to ensure that everyone is building something as early as possible in the creative process. Every department in the company is required to experiment, even if it only means eliminating a step in a manufacturing process. Augustine's mantra is, "Think it, build it, test it."

Starting the Company

Augustine grew up in the Tanzanian jungles as the son of missionaries. Because they lived more than 200 miles from a city, his family was forced to be creative about supplying their needs. Their only power came from a diesel engine hooked to a generator, and every year it had to be taken apart and refurbished. Augustine even made his own toys, so trying new things was second nature to him.

Augustine spent time in the navy, acquired a medical degree, and then moved to Kansas City to begin work as an anesthesiologist. It wasn't long before his frustration with the operating room led to the idea for his first medical device. He was disturbed that he wasn't able to control a patient's temperature during surgery, so he began to envision a cocoon of warm air moving around the patient—a kind of "personal little room." On a workbench in his garage, Augustine fashioned an inflatable blanket with holes. Next he needed a mechanism for commercializing this technology.

With the help of his father, he launched Augustine Medical from his garage in 1987. "I'm a huge believer in garages," he proudly proclaims. In fact, even today, his business is housed in a huge garagelike building where he has space to separate new-product teams from the rest of the employees, allowing them a distraction-free space for creativity to flow. Because innovation doesn't occur on a time clock, Augustine lets employs determine their hours. Augustine's own best ideas have come to him while running.

Augustine and his partner, Randy Arnold, have been friends since the seventh grade when they worked together at a small boat company. Augustine is the inventor, and Arnold is the builder. After dropping out of college, Arnold took a job at the Guthrie Theater in Minneapolis where he constructed props and scenery. When Augustine started his company, the first person he knew he wanted to hire was Arnold. It took a while before Arnold made the connection between medical devices and the theater and was willing to take the risk of joining a start-up. It didn't take long, however, before he discovered that medical devices face the same kinds of problems that theaters do. "It's all mechanical," he claims. It's all about getting something to work.

Developing and Protecting Products

Research and development at Augustine Medical costs about 8 percent of annual revenues, which is on par with other medical device companies. If a device requires clinical trials, or regulatory work, and intellectual property, then that figure jumps to 11 percent.

Prototyping is one of the core strengths of Augustine Medical; in fact, computer models do not enter the picture until a working prototype has been constructed and manipulated. The engineers and prop builders have become experts in better, faster, cheaper product development. Augustine did not want to rely on the Bair Hugger and its derivatives as the company's sole product, so after 1994, Augustine began developing new-product lines. In a period of just seven years, he applied for 129 patents. Because intellectual property was a key element in the company's competitive strategy, Augustine hired John Rock to manage their patents and ensure that they did not file duplicate claims or create any vulnerabilities in the patent line. Rock set out to graphically map the company's patents and the result was a genealogy of the company that tracks all its patents, patent applications, and their antecedents and dependents. In this way, when a researcher comes to Rock with a new idea, he can check to make sure they have not disclosed an idea like it in a previous application. Rock also reads hundreds of patents every week to look for technologies that they need to avoid or those that might be worth licensing.

A Change of Plans

For all its efforts to effectively manage its intellectual property, Augustine Medical did not prepare for an intellectual-succession plan. Because Augustine was the only person in the company who had both a medical background and R&D experience and because he was the primary source of new ideas, this oversight proved fatal.

In July 2002, Augustine announced that he would be stepping down from his role as CEO of Augustine Medical in favor of John Thomas who had served as president for eleven years. In January 2003, Arizant Inc. was formed out of a reorganization of Augustine Medical. Arizant became the parent company and consisted of two subsidiaries: Arizant Healthcare Inc., which would sell temperature-management products, and Augustine Medical, Inc., which would market wound-care products. Each entity would operate independently.

What caused all of these changes? Why would a company reorganize when it was experiencing such success? In early 2003, after an extensive FBI investigation, it was found that Augustine Medical had misled medical providers into submitting false reimbursement claims for its Warm-Up Active Wound Therapy, a product that was enjoying tremendous sales. Augustine Medical had encouraged its healthcare providers to list the wound therapy under a generic code for medical-supplies category without specifically identifying it.

Augustine Medical and its officers pled guilty to Medicare fraud and were ordered to pay more than $7.5 million in fines. Augustine was personally fined $2 million and placed on probation for three years. Augustine Medical's former Medicare reimbursement consultant was fined and sentenced to five months in prison, and the U.S. government recovered $2.2 million in Medicare overpayments.

In June 2004, Arizant was acquired by Citigroup Venture Capital Equity Partners, L.P., to fulfill one of three commitments by Arizant President and CEO John Thomas: liquidity. Two other commitments included focusing the company on the Arizant Healthcare subsidiary, which was seeing record levels of sales, and resolving the U.S. Department of Justice investigation over Medicare reimbursement in the Augustine Medical subsidiary.

Advising the Entrepreneur

1. What type of intellectual-succession strategy would you recommend that Augustine Medical put in place, and why?

2. How can a company avoid the kind of fraudulent practice that it faced under the guidance of a medical reimbursement consultant?

Sources: L. Buchanan, "The Innovation Factor: Inside the Idea Mill," *Inc.* (August 2002), http://pf.inc.com; "Wound Care Manufacturer and Former Officers Fined $7.5 Million," *HomeCare Monday* (September 20, 2004); "Citigroup Venture Capital Equity Partners, L.P. to Buy Medical Device Company Arizant Inc.," Press Release, www.arizanthealthcare.com; "John Thomas Named CEO of Arizant Inc.," Press Release (January 30, 2003), www.bairpaws.com/arizanthealthcare/index.shtml; "Arizant Inc. Is Formed," Press Release (January 27, 2003), www.bairpaws.com/arizant/012703.shtml.

CHAPTER 7

Choosing a Legal Form of Business

Corporation, An ingenious device for obtaining individual profit without individual responsibility.

Ambrose Bierce, U.S. author and satirist (1842–1914),
The Devil's Dictionary

LEARNING OUTCOMES

- Understand the various legal entities available for new businesses, including sole proprietorship, partnership, corporation, and limited liability company.

- Explain the criteria used to decide the best legal form for a particular type of business.

A Different Kind of Partnership

Jennifer Overholt, a former product marketing manager at Sun Microsystems, was looking for the ultimate business for a soloist at heart: a business with no overhead and no assets to manage. A business with no central office, secretarial pool, or accounting services. Overholt wanted a business that would bring together the right people to attack a problem and get paid for the solution, at the same time that it had no overhead, no slack time, and no waste.

It was in 1994 that Overholt realized that she wanted to have more control of her time and to work on the projects that interested her, so she left Sun and became a consultant. Utilizing her well-developed network of contacts, she soon began to receive a number of interesting offers for work. Although she enjoyed the work she was doing, it was unpredictable. She also wanted someone to bounce off her ideas as well as to cover for her if she needed to take time off.

Overholt had frequent dinners with her longtime friend from Sun, A. C. Ross, who had also gone the consultant route. It didn't take long before their conversations worked their way around to the idea of a partnership. A partnership would be a way to give them more legitimacy, balance workloads, increase their talent base, and generally make things more fun. But they knew they didn't want a traditional partnership. One evening they pulled one of Overholt's old classmates from Wharton into their dinner conversations, and the three began to plot a strategy to create a new kind of consulting business with a very loose structure that would give each partner a great deal of freedom.

The trio all agreed that they were only going to take engagements in the San Francisco Bay Area so that they would not have to travel. Next, they wanted to focus on technology marketing, and there were specific kinds of projects, such as white papers, they were not willing to do. Choosing a name for the company was an exercise in creative thinking. After discarding names of stars, planets, and gods from Greek mythology, they selected Indigo because it sounded good and because their marketing materials could be designed in that color, which would make it easier for people to remember. In September 1996, they began sending brochures and business cards to their network of contacts. They also created a website and a company phone number that routed calls to each partner's home office. Soon the jobs began arriving in such volume that they had to turn down assignments, something they would have never done as soloists. To increase their skill sets and help manage the volume of work, they maintained a list of freelancers who they could tap for specific tasks that needed to get accomplished quickly.

It wasn't long before the trio quickly realized that if they wanted to be able to take time off and keep the company engine chugging along, they needed to grow Indigo to six partners. Tapping into their contact lists once again, they found three solo contractors who had impressive lists of contacts and experience in qualitative analysis, consumer marketing, and computer hardware. Moreover, these three women all shared Indigo's values, which is essential when running a business that is based on trust. The new partners signed the partnership agreement and contributed a small amount of capital to cover new marketing materials and changes in the website. The company was now at six principals, and that is where they wanted to keep it. Any more partners would reduce their flexibility too much.

When a client calls Indigo's company line, those partners interested in the project meet with the client to determine needs. Depending on the specific requirements of the project, one partner is the lead, and others support that partner. Most of the collaboration among the partners is accomplished through e-mail and instant messaging.

In recent years, many companies have begun cutting back on consulting expenses, but Indigo remains optimistic. "Small companies have less money than ever to hire a permanent team," says Michelle Lee, one of Indigo's partners, "So I think we're still going to be needed."

Advising the Entrepreneur

1. Was the group wise in electing a loose form of partnership? Is there any reason they should consider another legal structure?

2. How would you compensate partners and grow the business?

Sources: Indigo Partners http://www.indigohq.com/; S. Shellenbarger, "Telework Is on the Rise, but It Isn't Just Done from Home Anymore," *Wall Street Journal* (January 23, 2002): B1; J. Bick, "The New Face of Self-Employment," *Inc.* (January 2001), www.inc.com.

O f all the environmental factors that influence a growing company in significant ways, none is more pervasive than the law. From the moment an idea for a business is conceived to the moment it is dissolved, the law plays a powerful role in everything that the company does and in every aspect of its organization. Choosing the legal form of organization is one of the most important decisions an entrepreneur will make about the business because the choice of legal structure will affect start-up costs, tax planning, entrepreneur liability, and the entrepreneur's ability to secure outside capital, among many other things. Which form to choose is determined by the type of business and the entrepreneur's goals for that business and should always be made under the guidance of a qualified attorney. This chapter looks at the various forms of legal structure, their advantages, disadvantages, and best uses.

THE LEGAL FORM OF THE COMPANY

All companies operate under one of four broad legal classifications: sole proprietorship, partnership, corporation, and limited liability company. Choosing the form that is most appropriate for a company at a particular time is a function of (1) the level of liability protection required, (2) the operating requirements, and (3) the effect on the company's tax strategy. It is possible to change forms during the life of the company, and each form has its own requirements. Some entrepreneurs choose to start their ventures as sole proprietors or partnerships because these are the easiest and least expensive forms to create. Later, as the venture takes off or it needs investment capital, it may switch to the preferred corporate form or limited liability company. Entrepreneurs with complex businesses and more potential to incur liability generally start with these forms. It is also likely that a business may change its legal form for financial, tax, or liability reasons. Table 7.1 presents a summary comparison chart of all the legal forms of organization.

Sole Proprietorship

The **sole proprietorship** is the most common and oldest legal form. More than 76 percent of all businesses in the United States are sole proprietorships.[1] It is the most popular form because it is flexible, easy and inexpensive to start, and has few government regulations. Operating as a sole proprietor requires nothing more than a DBA (Certificate of Doing Business Under an Assumed Name) if the entrepreneur does

TABLE 7.1 Comparison of Legal Forms

Issues	Business Form					
	Sole Proprietorship	Partnership	Limited Liability Company	C-Corporation	Subchapter S-Corporation
Number of Owners	One	No limit	No limit. Most states require a minimum of two members	No limit on shareholders	100 shareholders or fewer
Start-Up Costs	Filing fees for DBA and business license	Filing fees for DBA; attorney fees for partnership agreement	Attorney fees for organization, documents; filing fees	Attorney fees for incorporation documents; filing fees	Attorney fees for incorporation; filing fees
Liability	Owner liable for all claims against business, but with insurance can overcome liability	General partners liable for all claims; limited partners liable only to amount of investment	Members liable as in partnerships	Shareholders liable to amount invested; officers may be personally liable	Shareholders liable to amount invested
Taxation	Pass-through; taxed at individual level	Pass-through; taxed at individual level	Pass-through; taxed at individual level	Tax-paying entity; taxed on corporate income	Pass-through taxed at individual level
Continuity of Life of Business	Dissolution on the death of the owner	Dissolution on the death or separation of a partner, unless otherwise specified in the agreement; not so in the case of limited partners	Most states allow perpetual existence. Unless otherwise stated in the Articles of Organization, existence terminates on death or withdrawal of any member	Continuity of Life	Perpetual existence
Transferability of Interest	Owner free to sell; assets transferred to estate upon death with valid will	General partner requires consent of other generals to sell interest; limited partners' ability to transfer is subject to agreement	Permission of majority of members is required for any member to transfer interest	Shareholders free to sell unless restricted by agreement	Shareholders free to sell unless restricted by agreement
Distribution of Profits	Profits go to owner	Profits shared based on partnership agreement	Profits shared based on member agreement	Paid to shareholders as dividends according to agreement and shareholder status	Paid to shareholders as dividends according to agreement and shareholder status
Management Control	Owner has full control	Absent an agreement to the contrary, partners have equal voting rights	Rests with management committee	Rests with the board of directors appointed by the shareholders	Rests with the board of directors appointed by the shareholders

not use his or her name as the name for the business. This certificate can be obtained by filing an application with the appropriate local government agency. The fictitious business name statement ensures that the company is the only one in the area (usually a county) using the name it has chosen and provides a public record of business ownership for liability purposes.

From a legal or tax perspective, the sole proprietorship does not exist apart from its owner; therefore, it pays no tax. Consequently, a salary or draw taken by the owner is not considered an expense of the business and cannot be deducted as such. The owner (the sole proprietor) is the business and is the only person responsible for its activities, profits, and liabilities. All profits of the company, including the owner's salary, are taxed at the owner's personal income tax rate whether or not they are ultimately put back into the business. In other words, sole proprietorships do not have retained earnings.

Although the sole proprietorship is easy and inexpensive to start, it does have some drawbacks. Sole proprietors have unlimited liability for any claims against the business; as a result, they put at risk their homes, bank accounts, and other assets. To protect against this liability, sole proprietors often obtain business liability insurance and "errors and omissions coverage," which protects against unintentional acts of negligence, such as putting incorrect information in an advertisement. It is also more difficult for sole proprietors to raise capital because they typically rely solely on their own financial statements. Moreover, unless provisions have been made in the owner's will, the business survives only until the owner dies.

The Hobby Rule Sole proprietorships fall under the hobby rule of the Internal Revenue Code. If a company makes no profit in three out of five years, it is in danger of being judged a hobby, with the result that losses suffered cannot be deducted from gross income to reduce taxable income. One test of the hobby rule is whether affairs of the business are conducted in a businesslike manner, for example, maintaining separate personal and business bank accounts, keeping formal accounting records, and so forth. The hobby rule certainly points up the need for sole proprietors to keep their business and personal lives separate.

Partnership

Section 6 of the Uniform Partnership Act refers to a **partnership** as "an association of two or more persons to carry on as co-owners a business for profit." In this context, the term *persons* also includes companies and corporations, with the exception of charities and other nonprofit organizations because they do not expect to earn a profit. A partnership is essentially a sole proprietorship involving more than one person in terms of its advantages and its treatment of income, expenses, and taxes. However, where liability is concerned, there is a significant difference. In a general partnership, each partner is held liable for the acts of another partner in the course of doing business for the partnership. This is called the **doctrine of ostensible authority,** or apparent authority. For example, if a partner enters into a contract on behalf of the partnership, all the partners are bound by the terms of the contract. The ability of a single partner to bind the company and the rest of the partners to an agreement they may not like points to the need for choosing partners carefully and drawing up a partnership agreement. (Partnership agreements are discussed in the next section.) One exception to the doctrine of ostensible authority is that personal creditors of a partner—that is, for debt the partner has incurred in his or her personal

Business Forms in Russia

Since 1991 the former Soviet Union has undergone radical changes with respect to business. However, business forms in Russia have a history that is hundreds of years old, interrupted only during the communist era when no private business activities were permitted for about seventy-five years. Without large amounts of available investment capital, the vast majority of new businesses are small and, like in the United States, sole proprietorships. It costs about $3.17, or 3 percent of a month's income, to establish a proprietorship in Russia as contrasted with about $25 in New York. Russia has two types of partnerships, simple and full. Simple partnerships do not need to be registered and pay no tax at the firm level, whereas full partnerships pay tax as a firm. Entrepreneurs also have the opportunity to become involved in cooperatives as a business form. Cooperatives have some of the advantages of partnerships, such as the right of participants to manage the business, and lack some of the disadvantages, such as limited liability for founders.

Many Russian businesses must conduct business under the name of the owner; they are not allowed to use assumed names; Russia does not have the DBA option. This is a problem when the owner wants to sell the business. Goodwill, the intangible asset that is built up in the name of the business, accrues to the owner's name, which cannot be transferred in a sale, so effectively there is no way to realize the value of goodwill. The way that Russian business owners overcome this challenge is to use assumed names in their signage.

Russian law is in transition. Although their business development was interrupted, Russians have been in touch with the commercial world, and they are working quickly to reach a point of greater stability in their business forms.

Source: "Comparative Forms of Doing Business in Russia and New York State—Proprietorships, Partnerships, and Limited Partnerships" by Robert Rothenberg and Tatyana V. Melnikova from *American Business Law Journal*, Spring 2003, Vol. 40, Issue 3. Reprinted by permission of the authors.

life—can attach only personal assets of the partner who defaulted, including the partner's interest in the business.

Partners also have specific property rights. For example, each partner owns and has use of the property acquired by the partnership unless otherwise stated in the partnership agreement. In addition, each partner has the right to share in the profits and losses, each may participate in the management of the general partnership, and all elections, such as depreciation and accounting methods, are made at the partnership level and apply to all partners.

Entrepreneurs sometimes form partnerships with cofounders during the development stages of a new product or in the early start-up stages of a new business because it's easy, quick, and inexpensive to do. However, like the sole proprietorship, the partnership generally is not recommended as an appropriate legal form for a growing business, principally because it does not afford any liability protection. Nevertheless, because many companies form strategic partnerships with other companies as they grow for the purpose of sharing resources, competencies, and risk, it is important to discuss some key issues related to partnerships.

How a Partnership Is Formed A partnership can be formed with a simple oral agreement or can even be implied from the conduct and activities of the parties. In the latter case, the Uniform Partnership Act (UPA) says that the receipt by a person of a share of the profits of the business is prima facie evidence that he or she is a partner in the business. This is an important point because if an individual receives a share of the profits of a business with which he or she is associated, that individual may also become liable for its debts.

To this point, all references to partners have meant general partners. In a general partnership, each partner assumes unlimited liability for the dealings of the partnership. By contrast, a limited partner's liability is limited to the size of the investment so that if a limited partner invests $50,000 in the business, the most that partner can lose is $50,000. It is important to recognize that limited partners cannot be active in the management of the business. The penalty for doing so is the loss of their limited liability status.

Several other types of partners can be used in this form of business ownership; among them are the following:

- **Secret partners** are active but unknown to the public.
- **Silent partners** are usually inactive but have a financial interest in the partnership.
- **Dormant partners** are not generally known publicly to be a partner.

The Partnership Agreement Although the law does not require it, it is critical that partnerships draw up a written agreement based on the UPA. It should spell out the business responsibilities, profit distribution, and transfer of interest should a partner die or leave the partnership. Too many partnerships fail to plan for these situations.

LEARNING FROM SUCCESS

When Target Is Your First Customer

Joe Heron is CEO of Minneapolis-based Ardea Beverage Co., which he founded in 2003. Looking for his first customer, he set his sights on Target, the mega–discount retailer. To get an entrée to Target, he worked with a highly respected food broker, FMN Moscoe, which helped start negotiations in May 2003. The negotiations were a painful combination of paperwork, product insurance, and upgrading his company's infrastructure so that if Target said yes, he would be ready. Those negotiations lasted until April 2004 when Target decided that it would undertake a slow roll-out of Heron's NutriSoda—a healthy soda containing amino acids and B vitamins and no sugar, aspartame, sodium, and caffeine—in 100 stores around the country. The rollout was successful, and Target agreed to put the soda in 365 stores. By 2005 Ardea Beverage was set to realize over $3 million in sales. "There's nothing more exciting than watching somebody go to a shelf and buy your product," claims Heron. So far, Heron has

handled his success well, something that not every entrepreneur can claim. Some of the actions that he took before landing his big client ensured that Ardea would be ready for success. He did not rush out and spend the money before receiving it because he knew he would need it to grow the business. He mapped out a strategy and attempted to predict the challenges that his company would face partnering with such a large customer. He made sure that his supply line partnerships were in place and ready to deal with Ardea's increasing needs, and he leveraged the brand of his first customer to put his sodas in specialty stores and in twenty-one airports.

Lesson Learned: *Prepare for success.*

Sources: A. Y. Pennington, N. L. Torres, G. Williams, and S. Wilson, "The Real Deal," *Inc.* (September 2005): 74–80; R. Resnick, "How to Cope with Overnight Success," *Entrepreneur.com* (October 11, 2004), www.entrepreneur.com.

For example, in 2000 Dr. Richard Irons and his wife, Kirsten Judd, founded a for-profit professional association, Professional Renewal Center, which helps professionals overcome work-related challenges such as substance abuse and career burnout.[2] Irons managed the medical side of the business, but after his sudden death in 2002 at the age of 52, Judd found herself with no succession plan in place and ten employees to think about. Judd was forced to immediately begin searching for a new medical director in the midst of great sorrow. It took over a year to get the company back on track financially, but as of September 2005, it had finally reached the level of revenues the company earned the year that Irons died.

Because partnerships are inherently fraught with problems arising from the different personalities and goals of the people involved, a written document executed at the beginning of the partnership will reduce the number of disagreements and provide for an orderly dissolution if irreconcilable differences arise. A good partnership agreement, whether among individuals or companies, formal or informal, should address the following issues:

- The legal name of the partnership
- The nature of the business
- The duration of the partnership
- Contributions of the partners
- Sales, loans, and leases to the partnership
- Withdrawals and salaries
- Responsibility and authority of the partners
- Dissolution of the partnership
- Arbitration

In the absence of a partnership agreement, all partners are considered equal. At the end of the tax year, the partnership files a tax return, and each individual partner files an information return, Form 1065.

Many partnerships incorporate buy–sell agreements and key-person life insurance into their partnership agreements to guard against the loss of one of the partners through death or voluntary departure. A buy–sell agreement is a binding contract that governs[3] who is entitled to purchase the departing partner's interest in the business, what events can trigger a buyout, and the price to be paid for the partner's interest. Having an agreement in place before such events occur will avoid disagreements and legal battles with the departing partner or his or her family. Absent a buy–sell agreement, when one partner dies, the other may be forced to work with the spouse or family member of the deceased who may not know anything about the business. Without a partnership agreement, one partner could actually sell his or her interest in the business without the consent of the other partner. Consider the following scenario. A company has three owners who have equal shares in the business. They have a buy–sell agreement stating that the remaining two owners will buy out the third owner's shares at market value. This is typically done with insurance on the owners. Now suppose the owner, who subsequently dies, has a son who is working in the business. Because the buy–sell agreement did not address this situation specifically, the son will get cash from the insurance but have no ownership interest in his father's company. This situation could have been avoided with an estate-planning agreement. In the agreement, the shareholder purchases the life insurance and puts it in an irrevocable life insurance trust for the child. The insurance can be purchased using personal savings. If the subject owner lives three years beyond the transfer, the proceeds of the trust become free of estate taxes. When the owner dies, the trust pays for the stock with the proceeds from the insurance. The agreement will also provide that the child's stock carries no voting rights during the lives of the remaining owners.

Key-person life insurance has saved many companies from financial problems when the founder or other key executive dies. This type of insurance can be used to take care of the expenses to buy out the deceased partner's interest.

Corporation

About 17 percent of U.S. businesses are **corporations,** but they account for 87 percent of all sales transactions, probably because they are the favored legal form for growing entrepreneurial companies.[4] There are two types of corporations, C- and subchapter S-corporations. (The specific differences of the S-corporation will be treated after a general discussion of corporations.) The **C-corporation** is the only form that is a legal entity in and of itself. The U.S. Supreme Court defines the corporation as "an artificial being, invisible, intangible, and existing only in contemplation of the law." It is chartered or registered by a state and can survive the death or separation of its owners from the company. Therefore, a corporation can sue, be sued, acquire and sell real property, maintain perpetual succession, have a corporate seal, lend money, and make and alter its bylaws. The owners of the corporation are its stockholders, who typically invest capital in the corporation in exchange for shares of stock. Like limited partners, stockholders are liable only for the money they have invested in the corporation.

There are several types of C-corporations:

- A *domestic corporation* is organized under the laws of the state in which it incorporates.

- A *foreign corporation* is chartered in a state other than the one in which it will do business. A California corporation doing business in New York, for example, is considered a foreign corporation.

- A *public corporation* is one whose shares are traded on one of the stock exchanges. Growing companies often choose an initial public offering (IPO) as a way to secure the capital for further growth. (IPOs are discussed in Chapter 20.)

- A *closely held corporation* is one whose stock is held privately by a few individuals, often family members such as husband and wife.

How a Corporation Is Created A corporation is created by filing a certificate of incorporation with the state in which the company will do business. It also requires the establishment of a board of directors that will make strategic policy decisions for the company and hire the officers who will run the business on a day-to-day basis. Another necessity to maintain the corporation's limited liability status is the formal documentation of board of directors' meetings. Many entrepreneurs with growing companies have failed to have the required board of directors' meetings and take minutes, which can cause them countless problems if they are ever questioned by a government agency. In addition, the state will also require articles of incorporation, which are generally standardized for each state.

Where to Incorporate Where to incorporate is a decision that must be made carefully. For the most part, incorporating in the state in which the company intends to do the principal share of its business makes sense and is less costly in time and money in the long run, particularly if the company intends to conduct business on a national or international basis. In comparing states as sites for incorporation, the company should consider the following:

- Capitalization requirements, powers of directors, and flexibility of operations
- Incorporation fees and related taxes
- Cost of qualifying a foreign corporation in areas where the company will do business as compared with the cost of incorporating there
- Rules dealing with tender offers, if the stock will be widely held
- Annual fees and taxes
- State stamp taxes applicable to the original issue of the stock and any later transfers

In general, a corporation will not have to qualify as a foreign corporation doing business in another state if it is simply holding directors' and shareholders' meetings in the state, holding a bank account, hiring independent contractors, or marketing to potential customers where the transaction will be completed in the company's home state.

Advantages of Corporations Corporations enjoy many advantages over sole proprietorships and partnerships. Limited liability is one important advantage of the corporate form. The owners (shareholders) are liable for the debts and obligations of the corporation only to the limit of their investment. The only exception is payroll taxes withheld from employees' paychecks but not deposited for the Internal Revenue Service. This means that, with rare exceptions, the owners' personal assets cannot be seized as a result of something the corporation does. The corporation can raise capital through the sale of stock, and it can issue different classes of stock to meet the various needs of its investors. For example, it may issue nonvoting preferred stock to conservative investors, who will be first to recoup their investment in the event that the corporation must liquidate its assets. It may issue common stock, which has voting rights, and common stockholders may share the profits remaining after the preferred holders are paid their dividends, assuming that the corporation does not retain those profits to fund growth. Common stock is more risky than preferred because its shareholders are paid after the preferred. Nevertheless, the common shareholders are entitled to vote at shareholders' meetings and to divide the profits remaining after the preferred are paid their dividends.

Corporations often enjoy more status and deference than do other legal forms, largely because they are a legal entity that cannot be destroyed by the death of one or all of the principal shareholders. This is very advantageous to entrepreneurs dealing in a global market because they are viewed as more serious contenders in the market. There is also the perception that corporations keep better records than other forms of ownership because they receive greater scrutiny from government agencies.

Owners of corporations can benefit from retirement funds, Keogh and defined-contribution plans, profit-sharing plans, and stock option plans. These fringe benefits are deductible to the corporation as an expense and are not taxable to the employee. Moreover, owners can hold certain assets, such as real estate, in their own names and lease the use of the assets to the corporation, thus giving them another income stream that is an expense to the corporation.

Disadvantages of Corporations Like other legal forms, corporations suffer from disadvantages as well. The corporation is a more complex form that costs more to create. Although it is possible to incorporate without the aid of an attorney, it's not recommended. A more serious disadvantage derives from the fact that the corporation is a separate entity for tax purposes. As such, if it makes a profit, it must pay a tax whether or not the profit was distributed as dividends to shareholders. And unlike the partnership or sole proprietorship, shareholders do not receive the benefit of writing off losses to reduce taxable income (the S-corporation does enjoy this benefit). In a C-corporation, if those losses can't be applied in the year they were incurred, they must be saved to be applied against future profits. Accordingly, C-corporations pay taxes on the profits that they earn, and their owners (shareholders) pay taxes on the dividends that they receive (already taxed as profit at the corporate level)—hence, the drawback of "double taxation."

By creating a corporation and issuing stock, an owner gives up a measure of control and privacy to the shareholders and board of directors; consequently, unlike in the sole proprietorship or the partnership, corporate owners are accountable first to the shareholders and second to anyone else. For a young entrepreneurial company or closely held corporation, however, the reality is that the board of directors serves at the pleasure of the entrepreneur. Only if and when the company becomes a public corporation does the entrepreneur potentially lose some control. Nevertheless, in a private corporation, where several investors hold the stock, the entrepreneur will have to consider the input of those stakeholders (those who have a vested interest in the company).

Corporations must act as an entity separate from its owners. Personal finances must be kept completely separate from corporate finances. In addition, the corporation must hold directors' meetings, maintain minutes, and not take on any financial liability without having the resources to back it up. If a corporation fails to do any of these things, it can become the victim of what is called "piercing the corporate veil," which leaves the directors and officers of the corporation vulnerable to personal liability.

Professional Corporations Under state law, certain professionals—such as health-care professionals, engineers, accountants, and lawyers—are permitted to form corporations called professional service corporations. Those who hold shares in this type of corporation must be licensed to provide the services it offers. In addition to the professional corporation, professionals can access a special form of limited liability company called the professional limited liability company (PLLC). With this form, the member (shareholder) is liable only for his or her own malpractice, not that of other members as would be the case in a general partnership. Many professional firms are moving away from the general partnership because of high cost of liability insurance to the limited liability partnership, which is much closer to the corporate structure in terms of limited liability.

S-Corporation

The subchapter S-corporation, or simply **S-corporation,** has been a popular legal form for many years. Unlike the C-corporation, it is not a taxpaying entity. Instead, it is a financial vehicle that passes the profits and losses of the corporation to the shareholders, much as a partnership does, to be taxed at the individual partners' rate. It differs from the C-corporation in several ways:

- As in a partnership, owners are taxed on corporate earnings whether earnings are distributed as dividends or retained in the corporation.

- Unlike in a C-corporation, any losses that the S-corporation incurs can be used as a deduction on the owner's personal income tax up to the amount invested in the corporation. If there is more than one shareholder, the loss is shared according to the percentage of ownership, as in a partnership.

- If the owner sells the assets of the business, a tax on the amount of appreciation on those assets is levied. With a C-corporation, in contrast, the gain is taxable to the corporation, and the balance paid to the stockholder is also taxed.

If a C-corporation elects to become an S-corporation and then reverts back to a C-corporation at some later date, it will not be able to elect S-corporation status again for five years.

There are very specific requirements for S-corporations. For example, the S-corporation may have only 100 shareholders or fewer, and these shareholders must be U.S. citizens or residents. The profits and losses from the business must be allocated in proportion to each shareholder's interest. An S-corporation shareholder may not deduct losses in excess of the original investment.

Businesses that don't have a need to retain earnings are suited to the S-corporation structure. For example, if an S-corporation decides to retain $500,000 of profit to invest in growth, the shareholders must pay taxes on that profit as though it had been distributed. Some banks may not want to lend to S-corporations that distribute all their earnings because this practice makes it more difficult for the company to grow. This negative aspect of the S-corporation is similar to the problem that sole proprietors and partnerships face. Consequently, growing entrepreneurial companies with global intentions may prefer the C-corporation form. Furthermore, though most deductions and expenses are allowed, S-corporations

LEARNING FROM MISTAKES

Sole Proprietorship Can Be Expensive

Leslie Jones was certain that she had chosen the correct legal form for her wedding and event planning company, SBO Weddings, based in Washington, DC. She had decided to operate as a sole proprietor because it was easy and inexpensive to set up. Furthermore, she didn't consider it to be a highly risky venture, so she avoided the more costly and complex corporate forms. What she did not do was talk to a tax accountant before making her choice. If she had, she would have learned that as a sole proprietor, she would have to pay self-employment tax, which is the employee's and the employer's

portion of FICA, or Medicare and Social Security. As of 2005, the self-employment tax rate amounts to 15.3 percent. Jones has since shifted her company to an S-corporation. Now the company pays 7.6 percent, and she pays 7.6 percent on her income as an employee of the company.

Lesson Learned: *Always check the tax implications of any legal structure.*

Source: T. Holmes, "Big Mistake," *NFIB Business Toolbox* (February 3, 2003), www.nfib.com.

cannot take advantage of deductions based on medical reimbursements or health insurance plans. Another consideration is that unless the business has regular positive cash flow, it could face a situation where it makes a profit, which is passed through to the owners to be taxed at their personal rates, but generates insufficient cash to pay those taxes. Also, S-corporations that operate in several states may experience problems with varying state regulations. If a company elects S-corporation status and later decides to do an IPO, it will need to convert to a C-corporation form first.

Companies that typically benefit from election of the S-corporation status include service businesses with low capital asset requirements, real estate investment firms during times when property values are increasing, and start-ups that are projecting a loss in the early years. Companies that want to retain earnings for expansion or diversification or those that incur significant passive losses from investments such as real estate may want to choose another form of business.

Limited Liability Company

The **limited liability company** (LLC), when formed correctly, often offers a better alternative to corporations, partnerships, and joint ventures because it combines the limited liability of a corporation with the pass-through tax advantages of a partnership or an S-corporation, in addition to the flexibility of a more informal structure. Many growing entrepreneurial companies are taking advantage of this form. Most LLCs will be organized like partnerships for tax purposes so that income tax benefits and liabilities will pass through to the members. In New York and California, however, the LLC will be subject to state franchise taxes or fees.

Only privately held companies can become LLCs, and they must be formed in accordance with very strict guidelines that vary from state to state. The next section discusses the formation of an LLC.

Guidelines for Forming an LLC LLCs are formed by filing articles of organization, similar to articles of incorporation, but their shareholders are called members and their shares of ownership are known as interests. The members can manage the company, or they can hire professionals to manage it. Like a corporation, the managers, officers, and members are not personally liable for the actions of the company except where they have personally guaranteed these activities. The members create an operating agreement, which is very much like a partnership agreement that details the rights and obligations of the members. Unlike the S-corporation, there is no limitation on the number of members or their status, and the LLC can issue more than one class of stock and allow foreign members. The LLC may be dissolved involuntarily by nonpayment of franchise or other taxes, by failure to maintain a registered agent and address within the state, or by order of the court. It may be dissolved voluntarily by vote of the members. If at some time in the future, the entrepreneur decides to do a public offering, the LLC must be converted to a C-corporation by transferring the LLC assets to the new corporation. It is not as easy to go in the other direction because capital gains tax must be paid on the appreciation in the value of the company.

LLCs are popular vehicles for companies with global investors, family-owned businesses, and professional service organizations. It is important, however, to check the special requirements of each state because they vary in some aspects.

The Nonprofit Corporation

Many entrepreneurs are finding opportunities that are well suited to a nonprofit corporate form and are even growing world-class nonprofit companies. A **nonprofit corporation** is one established for charitable and public benefit (for example, scientific, literary, educational), religious benefit, or mutual benefit (for example, trade associations, tennis clubs)—all purposes recognized by federal and state laws. Additional examples of nonprofits are schools, religious organizations, research institutes, hospitals, museums, and childcare centers. Like the C-corporation, the nonprofit (or not-for-profit) corporation is a legal entity and offers its shareholders and officers the benefit of limited liability.

The common misconception about nonprofits is that they are not allowed to make a profit. Nothing could be further from the truth. As long as the business is not organized to benefit a single person and is created for a recognized nonprofit purpose, it can earn a tax-exempt profit if it has also met the IRS test for tax-exempt status. However, any income it derives from for-profit activities is subject to income tax.

For entrepreneurs who seek to be socially responsible or simply to help others, the nonprofit form has many advantages. It enables corporate donors to deduct their donations as a business expense, so the nonprofit can pursue cash and in-kind contributions of equipment, supplies, and personnel. It can also apply for grants from government agencies and private foundations. However, like any corporation, the nonprofit has a number of disadvantages. When entrepreneurs form a nonprofit corporation, they give up any proprietary interest in the corporation and dedicate all the assets and resources of the corporation to tax-exempt activities. If the entrepreneur ever dissolves the corporation, its assets must be distributed to another tax-exempt organization.

Furthermore, setting up a nonprofit that has tax-exempt status is time-consuming. To qualify to operate as a nonprofit corporation, a company must pass two distinct hurdles:

1. Meet the state requirements for designation as a nonprofit corporation.

2. Meet the federal and state requirements for exemption from paying taxes by forming a corporation that falls within the IRS's narrowly defined categories. Under IRS 501(c)(3), a nonprofit may not engage in substantial activity that is not for tax-exempt purposes.

My Own Business, Inc. was started as a nonprofit entity to help new businesses succeed in every community. It is an educational nonprofit that offers free online courses and training to people wanting to start businesses. They are supported by a number of major companies that want to sponsor economic development.

DECIDING ON A LEGAL FORM

With an understanding of all the legal forms available to the entrepreneur (see Table 7.2), it is important to have some criteria in place to assist in making a wise decision about which legal form to choose. Clearly, getting the advice of a qualified attorney is also essential. The answers to the following questions will guide the entrepreneur in the decision-making process.

- How many people will own the business? If two or more owners hold the business, it is classified for federal tax purposes as either a corporation or a partnership. If the

TABLE 7.2   Summary of Legal Forms of Business

Sole Proprietorship	Partnership	Bridge Forms	Full Corporate
	General partnership	S-corporation	C-corporation
	Limited partnership	Limited liability company	Nonprofit

business entity has only one owner, it is classified as a corporation or a sole proprietorship.[5] That means that if the owner wanted the limited liability of an LLC but to be taxed as a partnership, he or she would need to take on a partner. A solo owner of an LLC will be treated like a sole proprietorship for tax purposes.

- Does the founding team possess all the skills required to operate this type of business? If the team must bring in outside partners or hire employees, they will be starting the business with more liability.

- Do the founders have the ability to cover their living expenses during the first year with funds outside the business? If they can, they can avoid taking on outside capital that would require a more expensive form of organization.

- Are the founders willing and able to assume personal liability for claims against the business? If so, they may not need to form a corporation.

- Do the founders need to have complete control over the company? Acquiring outside investment capital could take some of the control away from the founder.

- Do the founders expect to experience losses in the early stage of the venture, or will it be profitable from the beginning? Early losses can be passed through to the owners in forms such as the partnership, S-corporation, and the LLC.

- Do the founders expect to do an initial public offering at some point? A C-corporation will be needed before undertaking the IPO.

Small business owners who are seeking limited liability will generally form either an S-corporation or an LLC and elect to be taxed as a partnership. Although both the S-corporation and the LLC are flow-through entities for federal income tax purposes, there are differences with regard to many issues related to taxation.[6] In general, partnerships are the more favorable tax entity over S-corporations, and this is the primary reason why most LLCs elect to be taxed as partnerships. Partnerships provide broader flexibility with respect to allocating tax attributes so that a specific gain, loss, income, or deduction can be allocated to certain owners in a manner that may not match their original proportionate contribution to the partnership. In an S-corporation; however, changing the pro rata ownership interests could potentially result in the termination of the S-corporation. A general partner's earnings from self-employment would include his or her share of partnership operating income. By contrast, income distributed from an S-corporation, in which the owners receive reasonable wages, is not subject to self-employment tax, which consists of the employee's and the employers' share of FICA, or Social Security and Medicare taxes. Furthermore, if the business anticipates going public, the transition to a C-corporation from an S-corporation is significantly easier than from a partnership.

Milestone Planning

Most businesses go through several stages that present more or less risk and associated liability and therefore are best suited to a particular legal form. Figure 7.1 illustrates the various stages that a company might experience and the relevant choices in the legal form. Consider this example. Entrepreneur Chong Lee is married to a highly paid marketing executive for a major hospitality company that provides significant benefits. His wife's financial security enables Lee to devote himself full time to developing a new product that he has been working on for some time out of the garage at his home. The product is nearly ready to test in the market, so he decides to rent a small warehouse office and hire two workers to help him produce the initial inventory of products. At this point, he believes that he must limit his liability because he and his wife have acquired some valuable assets and they don't want to risk them in the event that the business fails. He also realizes that in any product business issues of product liability can arise. He expects to continue to experience business losses for about two years until he can recoup his development costs and initial marketing costs with sales of the product. Lee sees this product taking off eventually, and he knows that he will need investor capital to grow the business as fast as he predicts the market will demand.

FIGURE 7.1   Sample Evolution of Legal Forms

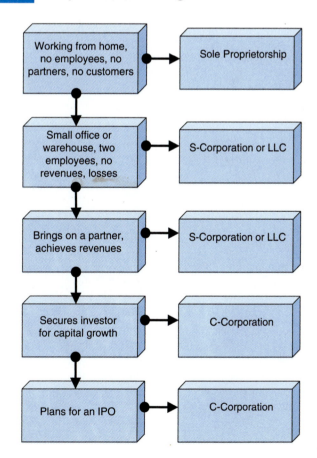

Many entrepreneurs start their businesses from home, and if they are in product development, it is not likely that they are incurring any liability, so forming a corporation is probably not necessary. In addition, at this point Lee's company is burning through cash and not earning any profits, so it would be important that he be able to deduct those losses against any other personal income. This would not be possible with a C-corporation. Once Lee's business grows out of the home and he begins to hire employees, he must consider either being heavily insured or moving the business to a legal form that provides him and his assets limited liability. If the business were still incurring losses, an S-corporation or an LLC would provide him with limited liability status and allow profits and losses to pass through to him and be taxed at his personal rate. Prior to acquiring investment capital, however, he will probably need to convert to a C-corporation.

Deciding on a legal form of organization is not a static decision but instead is based on the changing needs of the company and the entrepreneur. It is important that entrepreneurs think about the ultimate goal for their business so that they can prepare and put in place the most effective legal structure.

ISSUES FOR REVIEW AND DISCUSSION

1. Compare and contrast the sole proprietorship, partnership, and corporate forms of organizational structure in terms of liability, life of the business, transfer of interest, and distribution of profits.

2. A manufacturing venture in the medical device industry with twenty-five employees and a plan to go public in three years will probably consider which legal form? Justify your response.

3. Describe a business that would benefit from nonprofit status. Be specific and justify.

EXPERIENCING ENTREPRENEURSHIP

1. Pick a business that you could potentially consider starting. Trace the evolution of the business in terms of legal structure, explaining at each point why a particular structure was chosen.

2. Prepare a two-page report on current thought about where to incorporate. Use both primary and secondary resources to justify your conclusion.

LEARNING FROM ENTREPRENEURS, CASE 7.2

Black Letter Discovery

John Sanchez knew that he had the solution to a real problem facing law firms. The Internet had made the data creation process easier; however, so much data was now available that law firms were inundated with documents to review and often lacked sufficient qualified personnel to review those documents at a low hourly rate. Costs were skyrocketing and firms had to find a way to reduce them because their clients were rebelling. Sanchez had the answer, but could he compete in a market that included some huge companies with enormous resources?

The Launch of JDpost

John Sanchez and George Mandella were close friends at high school in Temple City near Pasadena, California. After a brief separation during college, they reconnected in the late 1990s when Sanchez was attending law school at the University of California, Hastings College of Law, and Mandella was working on a technology project in the San Francisco Bay Area. Sanchez saw an opportunity to solve a problem that law students were experiencing: There was no central place where law students could go to find jobs, scholarships, and housing. Sanchez and Mandella decided to combine their talents in law and technology to create an Internet community for law students, calling it JDpost. Their plan was for users to pay to post their housing needs and employers to post their job opportunities, and they accepted some advertising related to law students. In no time, their site became the number one message board for people preparing for the bar.

After graduation, Sanchez went on to work in the in-house counsel department for a Silicon Valley venture fund where he stayed until the fund folded. He then joined a large plaintiff's firm as a litigation attorney where he was exposed to complex and voluminous discovery matters, including managing a heavy caseload and teams of paralegals. Meanwhile, Mandella became the chief technology officer of an Internet communications company that serviced large life sciences companies. He oversaw the company's project management, engineering, strategic and technical consulting, and RandD. The duo knew that they were destined to work together. The key was to find an opportunity that would leverage Sanchez's legal experience and Mandella's technical experience.

For Sanchez, JDpost was never about making money. His strategy was to form the basis for other businesses that *would* make money. By the time Sanchez and Mandella had launched their next venture, they had a loyal community of practicing attorneys from the law classes of 1998–2005 and current students from 229 law schools throughout North America and around the world.

The Legal Industry

It appeared that there were two forces converging on the practice of law that provided an opportunity for Sanchez: (1) the explosion of electronic data that had to be produced in litigation and other legal intensive transactions and (2) the budget constraints on corporate law departments. Either force alone was a formidable challenge, but the combined effect was undisputedly significant and was threatening to change the way law is practiced. It was becoming increasingly costly for law firms to review all this information as part of the discovery process. Discovery is the pretrial phase in a lawsuit in which each party can request documents and other evidence from other parties or can compel the production of evidence by using a subpoena or requesting depositions. In the United States, discovery can involve any material that is relevant to the case, with the exception of privileged information or information that originates from the work of attorneys on the other side. Discovery often produces a settlement because the strength of each side's case is revealed.

Corporate law departments were faced with the need to reduce costs and operate more efficiently. Some of the ways that they addressed the challenge included seeking alternative fee arrangements, developing internal capabilities, and outsourcing routine tasks that were easily converted to an efficient process. According to Sanchez, "making budget is the new mantra for corporate law departments and will remain so for the foreseeable future."

A 1999 University of California study, cited by the U.S. District Court for New Jersey in the Bristol-Myers Squibb Securities Litigation, found that 93 percent of all information created was digital; only 7 percent was in paper form and other media. As a result, the discovery of evidence in the courtroom has undergone a profound change in terms of the enormous volume of data that may be required of either side in litigation, government review, or a sophisticated business transaction. The process of discovering, producing, and presenting electronic information is also undergoing critical change, and that includes the scope of lawyer review necessitated by the volume of materials slated for review and the challenge of managing that process in an economically efficient fashion.

Document review by attorneys is potentially a multibillion-dollar industry due to the risk/reward potential of facing sanctions for failure to produce documents or strategically producing or failing to produce certain information. Corporate clients need an intellectually competent, subjective, and accurate review of all key data. Many firms in the industry have focused on providing objective coding, intelligent software, and other analytics, but a legal review will not be certified complete without the subjective analysis performed by a skilled legal team.

The focus of the competition has been on electronic discovery, which is processing electronic data into searchable litigation databases. The Socha-Gelbmann Electronic Discovery Survey for 2005, as reported in *Law Technology News,* found that in 2004 domestic commercial electronic discovery revenues were about $821 million, which was a 94 percent increase from 2003. The value proposition of firms like KrollOnTrack, FIOS, Concordance, Applied Discovery, Summation, CaseMap, and many others is that their technology can sort data faster than human labor can. If you place that into the context of law with billable hours, the cost savings are immense. With so many companies competing in this space, there is no market leader in a market predicted to reach $3 billion.

In 2005 companies were beginning to focus on document review as a discreet product or service. These companies were geographically diverse with various value propositions, and no one company dominated or was the recognized leader. In general, the major players were staffing/manpower companies, such as Robert Half International, Hudson Global, Ajilon, and Kelly Law Registry, who saw document review as a logical extension of their product and service offerings.

Black Letter Discovery

Black Letter Discovery (BLD), so named for the legal term that means "no dispute as to meaning," was the business concept that Sanchez and Mandella had in mind to solve the problem of the increasing cost of discovery. Its purpose would be to provide a fully integrated and outsourced solution at a 70 percent reduction in cost. BLD hired temporary attorneys specialized in document review who would be called in as needed on a particular case. Confident that they had a winner, Sanchez and Mandella, who came on board part time in October 2003 and then full time in July 2004, put together $3000 and started the business. With limited resources, they knew that they had to bootstrap this venture, which meant controlling costs and keeping their egos in check.

BLD was competing against large publicly traded staffing companies, and it faced some reluctance on the part of law firms to give up a source of revenue. Sanchez knew that he needed to find a way to ensure the law firms that this service was in their best interests. BLD planned to specialize in projects with large volumes of documents that required a fast turnaround. BLD's point of differentiation was that they would focus exclusively on providing experienced document review professionals and overflow office space and review facilities to house large-scale document review projects. Without any money for marketing materials, business cards, a website, or the like, they had to rely on their only possessions: an office in the financial district of San Francisco and a phone. Sanchez cold-called 200 law firms and corporations and let everyone he knew know about BLD. Their first client was a small law firm in San Francisco where Sanchez knew the office manager, and she called with a $10,000 job two weeks after they opened for business.

The second client came about as a result of a legal newspaper article, which Sanchez read, in which a doctor was quoted about managing litigation. He called her, met with her, and had their second client by November 2003 with a deal worth over $100,000. Sanchez was then referred to a company based in Washington, DC. After three intense months of proposals and phone meetings, BLD landed a global pharmaceutical company that was involved in international class-action litigation and faced with reviewing over 5 million pages of electronic data. BLD bid for the job against a publicly traded staffing company and won the bid by convincing the company that BLD could save it $500,000 per month and by guaranteeing that it would deliver on time. Although the pharmaceutical company had in-house counsel and a lead outside law firm, the cost of wading through so many documents was prohibitively expensive, particularly given that it was low-level legal work. Nevertheless, Sanchez immediately faced a problem with the lead law firm who was reluctant to give up the income from the document review work. Sanchez took the lead counsel to dinner and succeeded in making him feel more comfortable about the arrangement, particularly because the law firm, given their high overhead, could not compete with BLD's prices.

To meet the tough requirements of this new client, BLD set out to identify, interview, and then select a team of qualified attorneys. Then they set up their facility to provide workstations for the attorneys as well as space for the pharmaceutical company's lead law firm's supervisory and quality-control personnel. BLD also provided a site project manager to work with the law firm and external vendors to ensure productivity, accuracy, and quality control. The review process took about eighteen months and succeeded in saving the company millions of dollars in billable time. In addition, BLD refined its process from the knowledge that it gained with this customer and prepared to seek additional large customers.

The business model for BLD was based on a renewable stream of revenues from customers, high margins, low overhead, and a novel idea with a first-mover advantage. JDpost provided a built-in marketing channel and gave the team credibility. BLD now had infrastructure and clients, but Sanchez believed that they were still not connecting on the sales side because of a lack of capital and resources to advertise. "We wanted to believe that we could succeed with a good idea, but we needed capital." Sanchez soon learned that managing sales was a critical success driver for the business. "You have to be honest with yourself and with salespeople if it's not working out. Management process is important. The failure and success of our sales team is a reflection of our management process." After a couple of poor decisions and consulting a sales coach, Sanchez put in place a sales process that included goals, clear metrics, and milestones. He also defined success and failure for his salespeople and created a culture that encouraged sales. "There is a fatal naiveté in assuming that someone will be motivated by compensation, commission,

integrity, etc., and will succeed without any nurturing, guidance, or prodding." This new strategy began to work, and in 2004, only a year after launch, BLD had revenues of $2 million.

The Birth of BarGraders

Sanchez and Mandella are classic serial entrepreneurs, always scanning the horizon for new opportunities that are synergistic with JDpost. Monitoring the posts on their website and Sanchez's own experience with preparing for the California bar exam inspired another chance to offer a service to their legal community. Law students generally focus on the multiple-choice part of the bar exam in the belief that it is the most difficult when in fact most people fail their state bar exams because of the essay portion. Sanchez knew that more states were allowing test takers to do their essays on laptops. He saw the opportunity to provide a communication platform that would link former state bar exam graders with those preparing to take the exam. Law students would complete practice essays, and the bar graders would grade them exactly as they would be graded for the real bar exam and return the results within twenty-four hours. The concept seemed feasible, and in June 2005, Sanchez and Mandella launched the beta site for BarGraders Inc. to prove the concept.

Quality was important, so Sanchez found graders who had graded no less than eight administrations of the bar exam—in other words, thousands of exams. To create a barrier to entry for others who might want to compete with BarGraders, Mandella developed a patent-pending technology that tracked a test taker's performance based on bar exam questions. Every answer could be evaluated against an objective matrix to derive a distinct and accurate numerical score as well as identify the element that got the test taker to that score. As students took more tests, they were able to improve on certain areas in which they were weak. Sanchez also envisioned tracking a law student from law school through the bar exam and having customers learn from the experiences that he shared through a blog on the BarGraders Inc. website.

Sanchez and Mandella started with the California bar exam and one experienced grader, using no advertising except banner ads that they placed on JDpost. After the first seven customers were secured, they realized that their concept was feasible, and they began to prepare to add New York, Florida, New Jersey, and

Texas for the February 2006 multistate exam, which accounted for 77 percent of all the people taking the bar. Again, they had captured a first-mover advantage.

The Future

Juggling three businesses is not easy even if those businesses serve a common customer base. Although Sanchez is a qualified attorney, he and Mandella consulted with another law firm when it came to deciding the legal structure of their businesses. BLD, Inc. is a wholly owned subsidiary of Gotsearch, Inc. whose DBA is JDpost. BarGraders, Inc. is a completely separate company. The duo originally started with one LLC, Gotsearch, but then converted it to a C-corporation because they were advised that the tax issues with LLCs are complex, especially regarding maintenance of capital accounts and accounting for foreign partners. They found the C-corporation to be "a more appropriate structure to accommodate investors and acquisition, which has become more possible now that BLD is posting some meaningful numbers."

Because there doesn't seem to be enough time in the day, Sanchez and Mandella focus on two companies: BarGraders, Inc. and BLD, Inc. JDpost practically runs itself. As they look to the future, they wonder which company should get the most attention, where the opportunity costs are the highest, where the red herrings are and how they can find them before they materialize. Hiring and correctly compensating the right salespeople will always be a challenge, but at least they're heading down the right path.

Advising the Entrepreneur

1. Evaluate the three-company strategy that Sanchez and Mandella have implemented. Do you agree with it? Why or why not?

2. Where are the potential red herrings in these businesses, and how can Sanchez and Mandella overcome them?

Planning and Organizing the Business

CHAPTER 8

Developing the Business Plan

Prediction is very difficult, especially about the future.

Neils Bohr, Nobel laureate in physics

LEARNING OUTCOMES

- Describe the business planning process.
- Explain the structure of the business plan.
- Discuss how to prepare a persuasive business plan.
- Organize and structure a business plan to effectively present your business.

Betting on Innovation

Dr. Henry Fabian is one of a growing number of physicians going back to school to earn a business degree. With HMOs and Medicare determined to keep the cost of healthcare down, physicians are finding it difficult to operate a private practice and make money. As a result, many are returning to the university in an effort to learn how to more effectively manage their practices, to change career direction, or to seize an opportunity. Fabian falls into the last category. A surgeon with a successful practice in Cleveland, Ohio, Fabian enrolled in Ohio State's Fisher College of Business in 2002 to earn an MBA. However, for Fabian, the MBA was simply a means to an end because his real objective was to develop a product and business that would provide surgeons with a better solution to current methods for relieving pain in spinal arthritis patients.

Fabian's medical practice involved inserting an implant to fuse two vertebrae in the spine. It was an excruciatingly long and stressful surgical procedure that he likened to "fitting a sailboat through the mouth of a bottle." If the doctor makes one mistake, the patient could be paralyzed. His invention is a titanium-alloy spinal implant, which he calls the Columna. It goes into the tube compressed to one-third its full size and then expands once it is inside the body. The chief advantage of Fabian's approach is that it is minimally invasive and therefore less risky. With an increasing market for lumbar fusion surgery (it grew from 50,000 procedures in 1999 to 200,000 in 2003), and with baby boomers reaching the age where they may have to undergo fusion surgery to relieve severe back pain, Fabian believes that the demand for safer back surgery will increase as well.

While at Ohio State, Fabian teamed with four other students to write a business plan for a company they were calling Vertebration. The team consisted of Thomas Abbas who had twenty years of manufacturing and operations management experience, Rick Karr who had fifteen years experience in marketing and technology sales, Lisa Paley who had eighteen years of experience in the healthcare sector, and Jason Smith who had ten years of experience in systems design and

manufacturing automation. In June 2004, they entered the annual Fisher business plan competition and won $89,000 for first place. (Business plan competitions have become very popular around the country as a way to give students a chance to gain experience in raising capital.) Their win at the Ohio State competition meant they were entered in *Fortune Magazine*'s second annual Student Showdown—where they also won first place. In September the company inked a deal to distribute products with EBI Biomet, a New Jersey–based orthopedic implant company, provided they could raise $2.8 million for research and development. The business plan was projecting sales of 4320 units in 2007.

FDA requirements are always a concern with medical devices, but Vertebration was counting on receiving an exemption because its product was similar enough to existing ones. However, this similarity could present another problem, that of differentiating itself from the competition. Yet another challenge facing Vertebration came from established physicians who saw this type of minimally invasive surgery as a passing fad and who preferred a larger incision for better visibility. Fabian wondered how he might address these challenges so that his solution would go beyond his own practice.

Advising the Entrepreneur

1. How would you advise Fabian on the best approach to achieving acceptance for his procedure from the medical community?

2. What challenge do you see that is facing Vertebration that has not been addressed in this case? How would you advise that Fabian deal with that challenge?

Sources: "Vertebration Wins $100,000 Business Plan Competition," Fisher College of Business, Ohio State University (June 2, 2004), http://fisher.osu.edu/news-cob/index.php?folder=65&news=231; M. Overfelt, "Student Showdown: Ready to Operate," *Fortune Small Business* (November 2004): 70.

t the start-up stage, a business plan is like a fast-moving storm, changing from minute to minute and never looking quite the same way twice. This is because a new venture is continuously seeking information that will help refine its goals, activities, and financial picture as it struggles to become an established company. Consequently, business plans for new companies are modified frequently until the right fit is achieved. Because of the dynamic nature of the business plan in the earliest stages of a new venture, it not always wise for entrepreneurs to devote hundreds of valuable hours to perfecting their business plan if they do not need outside capital. The majority of the research on business planning finds that entrepreneurs are better served by engaging in organizing actions like leasing facilities and equipment, seeking investment capital, and initiating promotion of the company's products and services.[1]

Even when an investor is required, chances are that investor is most interested in the track record of the founding team and in whether the business has achieved traction. One survey of forty-two venture capitalists found that 43 percent of them had invested in a venture in the previous three years without the benefit of a business plan.[2] Moreover, only 36 percent reported that the business plan was "very important" in their evaluation. Virtually all of the venture capitalists preferred to discover a potential investment through referral from a trusted friend.

If the entrepreneur has tested the business concept in the market through feasibility analysis and found it viable, it may be possible to launch the business before a business plan is prepared. This enables the start up to gather real-world responses to the company's product and service offerings, modify them, and then prepare a business plan that is more likely to be accurate than the entrepreneur's best guess at how the market will respond to the business. Today, it is less important to submit a professionally crafted business plan than it is to convey to an investor what the business has accomplished and to prove that it has its first customer in hand.[3] Investors want to be assured that the proposed business model works. A first customer goes a long way toward demonstrating that.

After start up, the business plan becomes an integral part of the company's strategic planning process. It is a blueprint for the growth and development of the company. The plan also conveys the vision, purpose, core values, and strategies the company will use to grow and serves as a benchmark against which the founders make decisions and measure the company's progress toward its goals. Unfortunately, most small businesses do not regularly update their business plans, and when they do, it is on an as-needed basis.[4] Small business owners typically prepare plans to seek investment capital or a line of credit, and when they do, according to recent research, about 75 percent of them achieve their objective.[5] This chapter explores how to effectively *plan* for a successful business while actually *doing* the business.

THE ROAD TO THE BUSINESS PLAN

Business planning means the entrepreneur gathers information to understand the business opportunity that she wants to exploit, to identify the potential risks, to develop strategies to deal with those risks, and to project financial success. The business plan documents how that information will be used to create a new business or to grow an existing business.[6] Organization theory consistently supports the notion that planning before taking action improves the outcome.[7] However, a study of 2,994 new businesses by Arnold Cooper and colleagues found that 28 percent of entrepreneurs seized an opportunity because it existed without any formal planning and another 13 percent did it because they had no better alternative; so not all new ventures start with a plan.[8] Nevertheless, planning has three advantages for entrepreneurs: (1) It enables them to make faster decisions once they are in business; they do not lose time in trial-and-error efforts;[9] (2) it helps them manage the supply and demand of resources more efficiently; and (3) it enables them to achieve their goals in a timely fashion by defining steps to that achievement.[10] A recent study of Swedish firm founders over their first thirty months found that entrepreneurs who engaged in planning activities prior to launching their business were less likely to disband and that business planning increased the level of organizing activity, which means that more entrepreneurs with completed business plans actually start their ventures.[11]

Who should write a business plan? Those who benefit most from a formal business plan are new business owners, those seeking a strategic partner, those seeking outside capital for expansion, and those seeking bank financing.[12] As a document for internal use, the business plan helps the company stay on course, and it serves as a benchmark against which to compare actual business performance.

The Value of the Business Plan

Remember that creating a business plan is no guarantee of success. Companies have succeeded despite poorly written business plans and have failed even when the plan was carefully crafted. Some companies, such as Pizza Hut and Crate and Barrel, were successful in the beginning without business plans, although Pizza Hut wrote one later, before PepsiCo acquired it. Today, the business plan is a tool that business owners use to enhance their chances of successful growth in a more complex global marketplace. As such, it is important that all key management be involved in developing the business plan.

LEARNING FROM SUCCESS

Waste Not, Want Not

Tom J. Fatjo Jr. loves the trash business. For over thirty-five years, he has stuck with a very simple business model: buy small mom-and-pop operations, roll them up and do a public offering, and use the proceeds to purchase more small companies. He has started four trash-handling companies in this fashion. "It's an industry I know and understand," he asserts. "I know almost everybody." Of course Fatjo's business model is not new; it is in fact the very business model that took Waste Management Inc. and Allied Waste Industries Inc., the $40 billion industry leaders, to their current success. Despite a checkered history, the waste industry has been good to Fatjo who has always been able to raise money and sell his operation when it gets too big. In the

1960s, he started his first company with a single truck and built it into Browning-Ferris Industries Inc., the first publicly traded trash company. In 1992 he founded Republic Waste Industries Inc., then TransAmerican Waste Industries Inc., and his most recent, Waste Corp. of America.

Lesson Learned: *Know an industry well, and you will find many opportunities.*

Source: "Finding a Business Plan That Works and Sticking with It—Tom Fatjo Applies Simple Financial Formula to Industry He Knows and Likes: Garbage" by Jeff Bailey from *The Wall Street Journal*, October 9, 2001, p. B2. Copyright © 2001 Dow Jones & Co. Reprinted by permission of Dow Jones & Co. via Copyright Clearance Center.

Some entrepreneurs choose to write several different versions of their plans, tailored to the needs of different interested parties. Others may decide to give only relevant sections of the plan to third parties. For example, it may not be prudent or necessary to give a deal structure section to a potential management employee or a detailed operations section to a banker.

In the first year, the company typically reevaluates and updates the plan several times to refine it and bring the activities of the company in closer alignment with the goals as stated in the business plan. If significant differences in estimates are observed, for example, the company will attempt to learn what may have caused the differences and adjust projections for the next period to account for any changes. In this way, the business plan always reflects what the company is actually doing and is always current when the company needs to approach an investor/banker or attract key personnel.

Relating the Feasibility Study to the Business Plan

The feasibility study (see Chapter 3) is about testing a business concept in the market to identify the conditions under which the entrepreneur is willing to go forward and start the business. By contrast, the business plan is about an execution strategy to implement the business concept. Generally, the information available when the feasibility study is conducted is not as complete or detailed as it is in the business plan because, during feasibility analysis, entrepreneurs need to gather just enough information to make a go/no-go decision.

Once the entrepreneur has determined that a new business concept is feasible, it's time to turn the feasibility study into a business plan, which is a statement of a plan for the creation of a new company or the growth of an existing company in a new direction. Whether it is written for a start-up or a growing company, one critical purpose of the business plan is to persuade others—those third parties who may be potential investors, lenders, or key management personnel. This contrasts with the feasibility study, which normally is done for the entrepreneur or the founding team as a decision tool. Each of these groups interested in the business plan is looking for different things, and it's important that the entrepreneur understand what those needs are.

Meeting the Needs of Interested Third Parties

The business plan generally serves three purposes: (1) It is a reality check for the entrepreneur, ensuring that the entrepreneur is aware of all aspects of the business; (2) it is a complete and comprehensive picture of the business at a specific point in time; (3) it is a statement of intent for third parties who may be interested in becoming involved with the business. These third parties can be grouped into four categories: investors, lenders, key management, and strategic partners.

Investors Investors focus heavily on the qualifications of the management team as well as on those factors that predict growth, usually found in the market analysis. They want to be assured that their investment will increase in value over the time they are involved with the company and that it's in good hands. Investors typically look for market-driven companies as opposed to product- or technology-driven companies because they are interested in such things as short payback periods.[13] In other words, if customers recoup the initial investment in the product quickly, they are more likely to buy; therefore, the market holds more potential. Investors want to know that customers perceive a value in the user benefits through documented evidence of customer contact and research and that the entrepreneur's predictions are based on solid evidence and thorough knowledge of the target market.[14] They are interested in the amount of return expected relative to the amount of risk incurred. The farther along in the evolution a new product is, for example, the lower the risk and, consequently, the lower the expected rate of return on the investment. Investors also look at the deal structure—that is, what their investment buys them in terms of an equity interest and subsequent ownership rights in the company. In addition, they want to know how they can liquidate their investment at some future date. Because most new ventures don't distribute dividends, investors often set up harvest strategies—ways to collect the benefit of their investment—such as an initial public offering (IPO) of stock, a sale, or a buyout (these methods are discussed in Chapter 9). The primary flaws that investors find in most business plans include overly optimistic financial projections, over-the-top claims, a poor explanation of the business model, and no demonstrable customer demand.

Lenders Bankers and other lenders are interested primarily in the company's margins (the difference between sales and cost of goods sold) and cash-flow projections because they are concerned about how their loans or credit lines to the business will be repaid. *Margins* indicate how much room there is for error between the cost to produce the product or deliver the service and the selling price. If the margins are tight and the business finds itself having to lower prices to compete, it may not be able to pay off its loans as consistently and quickly as the bank would like. Similarly, bankers look at *cash flow projections* to see if the business can pay all its expenses and still have sufficient money left over at the end of each month to grow the business. Clearly, bankers are also interested in the management team's qualifications and track record, but there are other items of concern as well:

■ The amount of money that the entrepreneur wishes to borrow. It is important for the entrepreneur to justify this figure.

■ What the loan will accomplish; that is, the lender wants to know how the money will be used to improve the company's financial position.

■ The type of collateral the company can offer. Only certain assets of the business have value to a banker, things such as industry-standard equipment and facilities that can relatively easily be converted to a new use.

■ How the business will repay the loan. The banker will want to understand the earning potential of the business over the life of the loan and, more important, how much cash the business will generate.

■ How the bank will protect itself should the business not meet its projections. Bankers want to be assured that the entrepreneur has a backup plan to meet its obligations to the bank.

■ How much of a stake in the business the entrepreneur controls. Bankers want to know that entrepreneurs have "skin in the game;" that is, the entrepreneur should have invested capital in the business so that they are less likely to walk away should the business run into problems.

Key Management Potential key management is interested in the business plan to get a complete picture of the business and the role that they might play in its growth. (Key management issues are discussed in Chapters 6 and 7.)

LEARNING FROM MISTAKES

Everyone Makes Mistakes

On April Fools day 2005, the editors at *Inc.* magazine decided to have some fun and feature the many and varied mistakes that entrepreneurs had made. Here are a few of them.

The CEO of Bramble Berry, a make-your-own-soap company based in Washington, was forced to take a sudden ten-day buying trip. She decided to leave the company in the hands of a part-time employee who had actually been fired, assuming that she would do her best to impress her former boss. Instead, the employee had to be fired—again.

Barry Becher and Ed Valenti, who founded the company that sold the infamous Ginsu knives on late-night infomercials, made two huge mistakes that cost them millions of dollars. First, they priced their knives (and everything that went with them) at $19.95 for no particular reason; they could have easily charged more and customers would have paid. Second, when Ted Turner offered them the opportunity to advertise on CNN, they turned him down because they couldn't understand how people would actually watch television twenty-four hours a day.

Finally, Mike Michalowicz, founder of a data forensics company in New Jersey, was trying to find some salespeople who would do anything to make a sale. He decided to test the candidates by scheduling interviews at 4 a.m. Much to his chagrin, only two desperate people, hardly the best of the lot, responded. No one else took him seriously.

Lesson Learned: *Don't price a product at less than it is worth*.

Source: "Hey, We All Make Mistakes!" by P. J. Sauer in *Inc Magazine*, April 2005, p. 21. Copyright © 2005. Reprinted by permission of Inc Magazine via Copyright Clearance Center.

Strategic Partners Vendors, manufacturers, and suppliers are really strategic partners of the business. They have a vested interest in the business succeeding because it is a source of income for their business. Entrepreneurs often form alliances with larger companies to provide capabilities that they don't have, such as raw materials, manufacturing and assembly capability, warehousing and distribution, and so forth. Entrepreneurs many enter into an agreement with the other company to receive materials, investment capital, or services in exchange for an equity interest in the entrepreneur's venture. Because strategic partners are investing resources in the start-up venture, they need to know that the management team can execute on its promises and that the marketing and growth strategies of the new venture make sense. Strategic partners will want to review the company's growth plans and market strategy because these sections of the business plan indicate how much business the strategic partners may get—in other words, what the value of the strategic alliance is to them. They are also interested in the company's ability to pay them for the work that they do.

Understanding in advance what investors, lenders, key management, and strategic partners need to know to work with the entrepreneur helps structure a business plan to meet those needs.

THE BUSINESS PLAN STRUCTURE

The first reason to undertake a business plan is to translate a feasible business concept into a company that can implement the concept. Recall that when the concept was being tested through feasibility, we were attempting to determine (1) if there were

Is Small Business the Solution in Iraq?

Sadik Hamra, whose fifteen-year-old Baghdad-based company, Hamra Cookies, employs 160 people, believes that he represents the future of Iraq. With plans to acquire a neighboring dairy and hire another 100 unemployed Iraqis, he is confident that the way to jumpstart the economy and create new jobs is through small business. Apparently the U.S. government agrees with him because the Department of Commerce is now trying to help Iraqi companies get launched and grow by establishing chambers of commerce. The U.S. Army's "Operation Adam Smith" is also working to revitalize Baghdad's commercial districts in addition to eventually building a business incubator at Baghdad University. Several non-government organizations are also offering their services to mentor entrepreneurs and distribute loans and grants that are more palatable than what local banks are offering. Hamra needs $4 million to acquire and refurbish his dairy, and the banks are requiring collateral of 200 to 800 percent of the total amount he needs. "My company needs America," he asserts, and he hopes to get help from the U.S. Agency for International Development (USAID), which in July 2005 supported training events for thirty-one Iraqi small- and medium-sized businesses and also approved fourteen small business grants. USAID also trained 13 consultants who will provide business planning services to Iraqi companies so that they are better able to access credit.

Sources: A. T. Gajilan, "Entrepreneurs in Iraq Tangle in U.S. Red Tape," *Fortune Small Business* (November 2004):18; "Small- and Medium-Sized Iraqi Businesses Receive Grants, Training," *PortalIraq* (July 7, 2005), http://www.portaliraq.com/index.php.

customers and a market of sufficient size to make the concept doable, (2) if the capital requirements to start based on estimates of sales and expenses made sense, and (3) if the entrepreneur could put together an appropriate team to make the concept happen. With the business plan, by contrast, the focus shifts to creating a company and issues such as process, marketing plan, and management enter the picture.

Begin with a Presentation

Once all the data about the business have been gathered and before spending hours writing a comprehensive business plan, it makes sense for entrepreneurs to put together an elevator pitch—a short, compelling statement of the business concept that includes why this concept is relevant right now, why there is demand to support the business, and why the founding team is the right team to execute the plan. Working through the process of putting together a PowerPoint presentation of the business forces the team to focus on the critical success factors for the business; that is, what must be in place for the business to succeed? Then when the founding team sits down to write the full business plan, it will be easier to maintain focus and avoid deviating from those critical success factors. (Later in this chapter, the matter of how to present the business plan will be addressed.)

The Components of the Business Plan

Table 8.1 presents a suggested outline of the business plan; however, any plan should reflect the personality and goals of the company, so there is no one format that works

TABLE 8.1   Business Plan Outline

Executive Summary

Include the most important points from all sections of the business plan.

Keep the summary to two or three pages maximum.

Make sure that the first sentence captures the reader's attention and the first paragraph presents the business concept in a compelling way.

Table of Contents

Business Concept

What is the business?

Who is the customer?

What is the value proposition or benefit(s) being delivered to the customer?

How will the benefit be delivered (distribution)?

What is the differentiation strategy?

What is the business model?

What are the spinoffs from your original products/services, and what is the company's potential for growth?

Founding or Management Team

Qualifications of founding team

How critical tasks will be covered

Gap analysis, or what's missing (professional advisors, board of directors, independent contractors)

Industry/Market Analysis

Industry analysis
- Demographics, major players, trends, etc.

Target market analysis
- Demographics, customer grid or market segmentation, etc.
- Customer profile (based on primary research)
- Competitor analysis and competitive advantages (competitive grid)
- Distribution channels (alternatives and risk/benefit)
- Entry strategy (initial market penetration, first customer)

Product or Service Plan

Detailed description and unique features of product or service

Technology assessment (if applicable)

Plan for prototyping and testing (all businesses require this)

Tasks and timeline to completion of product or service prototype (all businesses)

Acquisition of intellectual property

Operations Plan

Facilities

Business processes

Plan for outsourcing

Manufacturing and distribution

Organization Plan

Philosophy of management and company culture

Legal structure of the company

Table 8.1 Business Plan Outline *(continued)*

Organization chart
Key management
Duties and responsibilities

Marketing Plan

Purpose of marketing plan
Target market
Unique market niche
Business identity
Plan to reach first customer

Financial Plan

Summary of key points and capital requirements
Detailed business model
Risk factors and mediation
Break-even analysis and payback period
Narrative assumptions for financial statements
Full set of pro forma financial statements (cash flow, income, balance sheet) for three
     years
Plan for funding

Growth Plan

Strategy for growth
Resources required
Infrastructure changes

Contingency Plan and Harvest Strategy

Strategies for dealing with deviations from the plan
Strategies for harvesting the wealth created from the business

Timeline to Launch

Tasks that will need to be accomplished up to the date of launch of the business in the
     order of their completion. Also includes milestones of first customer, multiple
     customers, and multiple products. This is effectively accomplished with a graph.

Bibliography or Endnotes (footnotes may be substituted)

Appendices (A, B, C, etc.)

Questionnaires, maps, forms, résumés, and the like

for every business. The following sections of the plan are those considered crucial in persuading the owners and others that the company has a healthy future. They are discussed in brief in this chapter, and references to other chapters where the topics are discussed in more detail are given.

Executive Summary Every business needs a great story, a reason that people say, "What a great idea!" That compelling story is told in a two-page **executive summary** that also presents the critical success drivers from all the sections of the plan. Readers of the business plan often look first at the executive summary to see whether they are interested in reading the entire plan. Consequently, it is vital that the executive summary grab the reader's attention in the first sentence. The summary should open with the key selling point or benefit of the business. This may mean, for example, introducing a problem and countering with the products and services that the company will offer to alleviate that problem. Alternately, the executive summary may open with a provocative statistic or statements that entice the reader to go further to learn more about the business concept. In any case, the first paragraph should contain a clear and concise statement of the business concept: customer, benefit, product or service, and distribution. In addition, the profitability of the company and potential for growth should be emphasized. Remember that the entrepreneur has only about thirty seconds to capture the attention of an investor, banker, or venture capitalist who probably sees many business plans each month.

Using the following business plan checklist as a guide, the remainder of the executive summary can be structured to present the most important points from every section of the business plan.

Business Plan Checklist

✓ Did the executive summary grab the reader's attention and highlight the major points of the business plan?

✓ Did the business product or service plan clearly describe the purpose of the business, the customer, the benefit to the customer, and the distribution channel?

✓ Did the management team section persuade the reader that the team can successfully implement the business concept?

✓ Did the market analysis support acceptance for the business concept in the marketplace?

✓ Did the process plan prove that the product or service could be produced and distributed efficiently and effectively?

✓ Did the management and organization section assure the reader that an effective infrastructure was in place to facilitate the goals and operations of the company?

✓ Did the marketing plan successfully demonstrate how the company will effectively create customer awareness in the target market?

✓ Did the financial plan convince the reader that the company has long-term growth potential and will provide a superior return on investment for the investor and sufficient cash flow to repay loans to potential lenders?

✓ Did the growth plan convey a sense of direction for the company and demonstrate the potential to make money for investors?

Business Concept   The first section, the **business concept,** gives the reader a clear understanding of the business: the purpose, mission, and product or service concept. Recall that the business concept has four components: the business (what business the company is in), the customer, the benefit to the customer, and the distribution channel. A well-constructed business concept usually can be stated concisely in two to three sentences. For example:

> *Sunshine Learning Products is in the business of helping children learn through computer technology. It will design and manufacture hardware and software for young children that will be sold through computer and toy retail outlets.*

Creating a concept statement forces the company to focus on the most important aspects of its business. After reading a well-constructed concept statement, the reader should know exactly what the business is all about.

Founding or Management Team This section of the business plan provides evidence that the founding or management team has the skills to execute the business plan. It also includes an analysis of any expertise that may be missing from the team and how the company intends to fill the gap. The management team section is arguably the most important section of the business plan. It is often said that a great concept can fail because of a poor management team, but a great team can take a mediocre concept and make it a success. If the growing company is seeking capital to feed the avaricious demands of growth—and few companies are not—investors, lenders, and other financial resources are likely to look first to the people running the company. Just as the management team is the principal influence in the success of the company, it is also the chief reason companies fail. (Building a successful management team is the subject of Chapter 9.)

Industry/Market Analysis It is important to place the business in a context. The industry is the context, or environment, in which the business operates, so this section presents a detailed analysis of the state of the industry: where it is in the life cycle, the defining characteristics, opinion leaders, and much more. (A comprehensive discussion of industry analysis can be found in Chapter 3.) The market, by contrast, is defined by a set of customers. This section is significant because it presents support for the contention that a market and demand for the company's products and services exist. An in-depth analysis of the customer includes the size, location, buying habits, and needs of the customer base. An effective market analysis also demonstrates that the company has talked to the customer and that there is market acceptance for the business concept. A complete customer profile based on interviews or focus groups ensures that the company is on the right track.

In addition, a comprehensive analysis of both direct and indirect competitors and a description of emerging competitors and substitute products demonstrate that the company has considered all possible competition. (More details on market analysis can be found in Chapters 3 and 11.)

Product or Service Plan This section of the business plan presents a detailed description of the products and services. It addresses the status of product development as well as additional steps, such as intellectual property acquisition, that must be taken before having a product that is ready to sell to the public. It also includes the time and cost requirements for completing the development tasks. The business plan, however, is not the place to provide copious pages of technical specifications and details in an effort to describe how the product or process works. Most outside readers of the plan are more interested in the benefits than in the mechanics of the product or process. The benchmark question to be asked is, Does the reader need to know this piece of information to understand the product or service?

If the company is introducing a new product, one that needs to be designed and built, this section summarizes the product development process, leaving the more technical description for the process section of the plan. (A more complete discussion of product development appears in Chapter 14.) It is important to include tasks to be completed and time to completion. Zenas Block and Ian Macmillan suggest milestone planning.[15] This process includes ten milestones, or performance points, at which the entrepreneur must make choices that will either enhance his or her chance of success or potentially result in failure:

1. Completion of concept and product testing
2. Completion of prototype
3. First financing
4. Completion of initial plant tests (pilot or beta test)
5. Market testing
6. Production start-up
7. Bellwether sale (first substantial sale)
8. First competitive action
9. First redesign or redirection
10. First significant price change

In addition, any perceived or actual environmental impact from the business and how the company intends to mitigate that impact should be noted.

Operations Plan This section contains a discussion of the distribution channels that will be used to move the product or service from the producer to the end user. A major portion of this section is devoted to a description of how the business will operate, where it will get its raw materials, how they will be manufactured and/or assembled, and what type and quantity of labor are required to operate the business.

It is useful for nonmanufacturing businesses, such as retail and service businesses, to think in production terms, to see that every company produces something. Every company has a process and systems that need to be designed and prototyped. It is certainly not wise, for example, for a new restaurant to open the first day without having "walked through" the coordination of all the activities that will take place, from timing the preparation of the menus to ringing up the cash register. This is a process that can be laid out and monitored. (For more on issues related to the product or service plan, see Chapters 12, 14, and 15.)

Organization Plan The organization section of the business plan deals with the design of the business and describes the company culture and management style (for example, team based, flat structure) that stems from the core values articulated in the business concept. It also discusses the legal structure and distribution of ownership in the company. In a growing company, a formal organization chart is often used to depict key management personnel with their duties and responsibilities, compensation, and incentives packages. It may also depict outsourced capabilities and future personnel additions, as well as major policies regarding employees and benefits. (Chapters 8 and 14 present a more complete discussion of organization issues.)

Marketing Plan The marketing plan consists of the philosophy, strategies, and tactics that the company will use to build its customer base. It begins with a statement of the purpose of the plan; in other words, it describes what the company is attempting to accomplish. It follows with the plan for achieving that purpose and the benefits that will accrue to the customer as a result. Likewise, the plan will identify the target market—the unique market niche the company intends to occupy—and the distribution channels it will use to reach the customer.

An important part of the marketing plan is establishing the company's identity—the way it will be perceived by the customer. The company's identity in the marketplace springs directly from the purpose it established for itself. For example, Starbucks Coffee places enormous importance on its employees. In an industry that regularly experiences high employee turnover and low wages, Starbucks views its employees as a competitive advantage and offers them a comprehensive compensation package, healthcare, and stock options to give them a vested interest in the company. This value is communicated to the customer in a very personal manner by the way Starbucks' employees treat their customers.

The marketing plan will also discuss the marketing tools (advertising, direct mail, trade shows, and so on) that will be used to create customer awareness and build customer relationships, the media plan with the schedule of uses and costs of each, and the total marketing budget as a percentage of sales. (Chapter 13 discusses the marketing plan in more detail.)

Financial Plan The financial plan presents the company's forecasts for the future of the business and the capital requirements for growth. Generally, these forecasts are in the form of pro forma financial statements broken out by month in the first year or two and then annually for the next two to five years, in addition to a break-even analysis and other relevant ratios. The goal of this section is to demonstrate the financial health of the company and present the assumptions that the company made in doing the forecasts. It is designed to reveal that all the claims about the product, sales, marketing strategy, and operational strategy come together in an effective business model that has the potential to allow the business to survive and grow over the long term.

In a start-up venture, pro forma income and cash-flow statements for three years are fairly standard. Balance sheets may also be included but are more relevant to an existing business. An important part of a start-up financial plan is a cash-needs assessment, which details how much capital in terms of fixed costs, working capital, and start-up funding is required to launch the business.

An existing business will have the advantage of a track record on which to base its projections. Therefore, it will present a full set of historical and current financial statements as well as pro forma statements for the future. (A discussion of financial analysis with sample financial statements appears in Chapters 16 and 17.)

Growth Plan The growth plan presents the company strategy for growing beyond its current status and the methods by which it will obtain the resources it needs to successfully grow. The growth plan may call for an IPO, which may require some form of mezzanine (intermediate) financing in the short term to get the company through the IPO process. Or the company may be looking to franchise as a growth strategy and will need to look at the costs and payback period that this strategy entails. (These and other growth strategies are discussed fully in Chapter 9. Harvest strategies are the subject of Chapter 20.)

Contingency Plan and Harvest Strategy The **contingency plan** is simply a way to recognize that sometimes the best-laid plans don't work the way the company intended. It presents potential scenarios, usually dealing with situations such as unexpected high or low growth, or changing economic conditions, and then suggests a plan to minimize the impact on the company. This section is particularly helpful when a company is launching a new product, testing a new service, or going into a new market. Entrepreneurs should be careful, however, not to get too carried away building relatively rare pessimistic scenarios. Only those that have a high probability of occurring should be presented.

Timeline to Launch This section addresses the tasks that will need to be accomplished up to the date of launch of the business in the order of their completion. The section also deals with the milestones of first customer, multiple customers, and multiple products. This is effectively accomplished with a graph.

Appendix The appendix is the place to put supporting documents and items that can be easily pulled out if they are not appropriate for a particular reader. Such is the case of the contingency plan and the deal structure. It is also a good idea to include résumés of key management members.

PREPARING THE PERSUASIVE BUSINESS PLAN

An effective business plan will answer a number of fundamental questions that anyone interested in the business will want to know.

- *What need is being served?* In-depth market research with potential customers will provide proof of need and also demonstrate the level of demand for the product/ service. In addition, market research helps the entrepreneur develop a thorough profile of the first customer.

- *Can the founding team successfully execute the plan?* The plan should demonstrate that the founding team has the expertise and experience to carry out the business strategy. It should also prove that the founding team has capital invested in the business, not just "sweat equity," and that they have the passion, motivation, and persistence to make this business a success.

- *Why is this the right time to launch this business?* Timing is critical. Every business has a window of opportunity for success, and the business plan needs to convey the rationale and evidence that this is the best time to start this business. If others have failed with this type of business in the past, what environmental forces have changed to allow the founding team to succeed now?

- *What is the venture's bundle of competitive advantages?* Every sustainable business has several competitive advantages in various aspects of the business. The business plan must address how the business will use those competitive advantages to create a unique unserved niche in the market and how it will sustain those competitive advantages over time.

- *How will the business make money?* Most business plans lack sufficient thought about the business model and how value will be created at various points in the business's life. In the early stages of a new venture, value is created by adequate capitalization, highly regarded investors, an experienced management team, a unique product or service, and the ability to continually innovate in a rapidly expanding market.[16] During growth, value is created by market positioning, customer volume, effective operating systems, large gross margins, positive cash flow, and a superior return on equity.

- *What kind of start-up capital is required?* How much money is needed to launch the business and operate it until it achieves a positive cash flow from the revenues of the business? How will capital be allocated among increasing sales, boosting profits, or enhancing the value of the company? How will the business model provide a superior return on investment and a liquidity event for the exit of the investors?

Common Mistakes

In their eagerness to present the business in a positive light, entrepreneurs may err on the side of hyperbole; that is, they claim high goals and outcomes for which there is no support. Entrepreneurs should be careful not to commit the following mistakes:

- Projecting a level of growth for the business that exceeds the capabilities of the team and the business. In an effort to attract investment capital, entrepreneurs want to show that the business will double or triple its sales over the next few years, but for investors to feel comfortable with this prediction, it is necessary to provide evidence that market demand will produce this level of growth and that the business will have systems and controls in place to manage rapid growth. Too many businesses falter and even fail under the pressure that rapid growth brings.

- Entrepreneurs pride themselves on their ability to do many things, and in the early stages of a new venture, this talent is important. However, as the business grows and becomes more complex, the need to delegate the responsibility for certain aspects of the business becomes essential. That is why investors prefer to see management teams.[17]

- Projecting operational performance that exceeds industry averages. Although it is possible that a small business might have a competitive advantage that enables it to perform at a level above average in its industry, it is not likely. Superior levels of operational performance in areas such as inventory and receivables turnover, bad debt, and productivity result from economies of scale and experience, which a new or small business is not likely to achieve for some time. Understanding the typical performance metrics for the industry will help the entrepreneur to project more realistic levels for the business.

- Underestimating the need for capital to either begin the business or to grow the business. After launch, every business needs enough capital to sustain itself until revenues to the business produce cash flows to cover expenses and to grow the business to the next level. This capital must cover increased financing for marketing, hiring additional personnel, and expanding equipment and facilities. When calculating capital needs, allowing for the unexpected is also important.

- Using price as a competitive strategy. It is not often that a new or small business can compete on price. Offering the lowest price on a product or service means that company is in the commodity business, like Wal-Mart, which suggests that it has lower operating costs than its competitors. Entrepreneurs usually avoid commodity businesses unless there is a way to add new value and exact a premium on the price.

Writing the Plan

Make no mistake about it, writing a business plan is a time-consuming process that should involve the entire founding team. If the business has been launched between the feasibility analysis and the writing of the business plan, this process will need to be positioned among all the day-to-day activities of operating a business. It is important to identify who is responsible for what aspect of the plan because updated data on the industry, market, customer, and costs will need to be gathered. The data that were gathered for the feasibility study may now be outdated. Furthermore, instituting a deadline for completion of the plan ensures that it gets finished.

Regarding the length of the plan, the general rule of thumb is fewer than thirty pages. However, there is no correlation between length and either quality or persuasiveness of a business plan. Clarity, conciseness, and directness will do a better job of selling the business than a plan that incorporates a lot of superfluous information. It is also important that the entrepreneur/team write the plan themselves rather than pay someone who doesn't have a vested interest in the vision to do it. The personality of the team, the enthusiasm for the concept, and the excitement about the potential for the new venture should be conveyed in the business plan, and outsiders will have a difficult time doing this. A good plan will take up to about six months of concentrated effort to compose. Once it is completed, however, updates are easy to incorporate.

The business plan should not be considered the final word on a company's goals and strategies. It is a picture of the company at a specific point in time. Wise business owners know that their business plan is a living document that must reflect an ever-changing environment. Although the company values and overriding purpose will not change, over time, everything else probably will.

ISSUES FOR REVIEW AND DISCUSSION

1. What is the role of the business plan, and how does it differ from a feasibility study?
2. What are the key mistakes to avoid when developing a business plan?
3. Who are the principal outside readers of the business plan, and what are they looking for?
4. In your opinion, which is the most important section of the business plan, and why?

EXPERIENCING ENTREPRENEURSHIP

1. Interview an entrepreneur about his or her growing company to determine the purpose of the business and its core values and mission. Does this entrepreneur have a business plan? Why or why not?
2. Do some primary and secondary research on what people are saying about the value of business plans. Make sure to get the perspective of investors, entrepreneurs, and lenders. What conclusions can you draw?

LEARNING FROM ENTREPRENEURS, CASE 8.2

A Fire in Her Belly

In October 2003, wildfires consumed 3640 homes in southern California. This tragedy inspired Irene Rhodes to finally fulfill a lifelong dream. As a firefighter in rural Oregon, she was interested in the properties of fire-retardant foam and was curious about the ways that it might prevent wildfire disasters. Leveraging her firefighting experience and the lessons learned from owning a landscape business, she started Consumer Fire Products in 2005 with a patent-pending technology that could mean the difference between life and death for people living in rural areas.

The Birth of an Opportunity

Back in the 1980s, Rhodes was fighting fires in rural Oregon. She married and had two daughters; then, with her husband, Ralph (also a firefighter), she started a commercial landscaping and irrigation company while graduating with honors from a community college in Eugene. She and her husband began to discuss the possibilities for the use of fire-retardant foam to protect dwellings in rural areas. Their knowledge of irrigation systems led them to the idea for a system that would automatically dispense environmentally safe foam when sensors detected that a home was threatened by fire. They knew, however, that if they were to be successful at this emerging venture, they would have to attach some "book smarts" to their "street smarts." The family decided that Irene would take their two young daughters and move to Los Angeles where she had been accepted into the undergraduate business program at the University of Southern California for the fall of 2004. Moving from the country to a huge city and entering a university program where the students were young enough to be her children were two of Rhodes's major challenges. A third was helping her husband with the business—from a distance. Rhodes wondered how she would get through it all.

The Business Concept

Many homeowners face the possibility of losing their home and belongings to fire. Most homes are not constructed of the proper materials to prevent them from burning when a fire strikes. To add fuel to the situa-tion, firefighting agencies do not have the human resources to adequately handle the problem. In 2003 alone, there was more than $12 trillion in fire damage in the United States, up 19 percent from the previous year.[18]

To address this problem, Rhodes's company, Consumer Fire Products, Inc. (CFPI) developed the FOAMSAFE™ system, "a patent pending exterior fire protection system that automatically activates whenever a property is threatened by fire and releases an environmentally safe foam solution that covers the property and prevents it from burning." The first customer is the forestry services, which will benefit from a convenient, safe, and low-cost method of fire protection. The system consists of a base unit about the size of an air conditioner that is installed near the dwelling. The base feeds specially designed emitters placed throughout the property with the EPA-approved foaming solution, which is safe to humans, animals, and the environment. The system can be activated manually or remotely and is automatically activated by heat-sensor technology. Using very little water, the FOAMSAFE system can cover and protect both horizontal and vertical surfaces and can be applied hours before a wildfire actually reaches the property. After the threat has passed, the foam gradually disappears, or the homeowner can simply rinse it off.

CFPI assembles the system at its Oregon facility and distributes it throughout the western United States via direct sales offices in southern California. It also sells to certified home builders and developers to install at the time of construction.

The Industry and Market

CFPI operates in the fire protection industry, which has four primary categories of businesses: (1) fire protection sprinkler systems, (2) compressed air foam units generally mounted on fire trucks and other similar vehicles, (3) airport fire protection to foam runways, and (4) residential fire protection systems.

The sprinkler system sector benefits from new requirements for their installation in all new buildings. Depending on the type of material to be protected, the system will emit either water or chemicals. The biggest negative of these systems is that once activated, they destroy any contents within the building, and they only protect the interior of the building. Compressed air foam systems, generally used by fire and rescue agencies, are mounted on trucks and trailers. They are commonly used where water is scarce. Residential fire protection systems typically consist of a small backpack or dolly-mounted pump. They are simple and easy to use but are ineffective against a wildfire.

Rhodes conducted primary market research to learn who her first customers might be and what their needs were. She laid out a grid of all possible customers and compared them on a number of relevant variables: demographics, psychographics, location, current buying habits, purchase process, price sensitivity, and benefits sought. (A portion of the grid appears in Table 8.2.) Although she expected that her first customer would be the homeowner, she found that those most willing to buy a new product like this were the public fire agencies. Rhodes held focus groups with fire officials in the expectation of receiving feedback on what could be done to drive sales to homeowners. To her surprise, the fire officials were keenly interested in how they might use the FOAMSAFE system to protect national monuments, parks, and structures within national parks. If she could sell one unit to the Forest Service to test, they might be willing to purchase twenty-five more for the Los Padres National Forest where most of the fires in southern California in 2003 occurred.

In addition, Rhodes surveyed homeowners in wildfire areas and found that 90 percent of those at risk were concerned about losing their home to wildfires and that 89 percent would purchase an exterior fire protection system. Moreover, in the age bracket of 46–60 years old with an income over $60,000, virtually all stated that they would spend $10,000 or more on a system. Only some of these potential customers were protecting themselves by clearing away 30 feet of brush and vegetation from their homes—a precaution that was not fully guaranteed to work even if taken.

Competition for FOAMSAFE could potentially come from the compressed air foam system manufacturers; however, they would be infringing on a system patent that Rhodes has filed for. The second source of competition would be companies currently selling small portable systems, but they use aspirating nozzles, not compressed air foam, and they are not as effective.

The Team

Irene Rhodes's company has five team members who fill a variety of positions in the company. Rhodes, cofounder/CEO, has more than fifteen years of experience in landscape and irrigation. She also has ten years of experience in electromechanical design working on NASA projects, and three years as a firefighter. Her husband, Ralph, is cofounder/COO of CFPI and brings thirty years of fire industry and fire personnel management experience to the team. Prior to his work in the fire industry, he was a detective and police officer. Gerald Foxwell had fifteen years of experience as a senior project engineer for Delco/General Motors and additional experience in sales to government and private customers. Ward Weiman is an industrial engineer with experience at Kodak and Texas Instruments and will lead the development of the final product. Rick Citron is an attorney advising the company. The company intends to hire a CFO and an information technology consultant when revenues reach a level that allows the company to do so.

Financials

In her business plan, Rhodes outlined an aggressive plan for growing the company based on the results of her market research.

> The management team has compiled an aggressive but realistic plan for the company's growth. The break-even analysis shows that once eighteen units are sold, the break-even point will have been reached. This translates to approximately 1-1/2 units per month. In the first year, 50 units are anticipated to be sold, and the sales projections increase as the years increase. The team has put CFPI on a track to create a business worth in excess of $100,000,000 within a period of seven years. Built upon estimates of the preceding revenue streams, and the implementation of the aforementioned sales and marketing programs, this company is poised to be a significant presence in the consumer fire protection industry. Projected financial summary results for years 4–7 can be found in Table 8.3.

Launching the Business

In March 2005, Rhodes won the First Annual USC University-wide Business Plan Competition. Winning

TABLE 8.2   Customer Definition Grid

Customer/ Prospect	Who Are They?	Demographics	Psychographics	Location/ Range	What Do They Currently Buy?	Purchase Process	Price Sensitivity	Benefits Source
Homeowner of urban or rural property	Families and couples who do not like city living	30–65 years old; annual income: $70K and up/year	Want freedom of country living; this is their escape	Urban rural/ interface and rural living in the United States	Small, portable systems are all that are available	Direct mail; *Home and Fire* magazine	Initially it seems like a lot until they put it in perspective	Lower fire insurance; protection of homes where wildfire is a risk
Ranches in the urban/ rural areas	Cattle ranches and businesses in the rural areas that are high risk for fires	Family businesses; 36–70 years old; annual income: $40K and up	Very independent; take care of themselves	Rural living and urban/rural interface across the United States	Fire extinguishers; water pumps in their wells; no serious systems	Word of mouth; someone they can trust	If they think it will work, they will spend the money	Protection of the animals/ranch without having to move the animals or lose the ranch
Resort owners; businesses in urban/ rural areas	People who want to work but not in a conventional way; like resort life	Age: 40 and up; mom-and-pop operations; country/fancy; annual income: $40K and up	Independent resort living or country living; avoid city life and business	Lakes, rivers, campgrounds, mountains, etc.; across the United States	Only interior fire sprinklers have been purchased; a few have portable pumps, etc.	Word of mouth, magazines, direct mail, advertising	It is a mixed demographic; some are affected by price, and some are not	Lower fire insurance; protection of vegetation and structures; less fear of fire

Table 8.2 Customer Definition Grid (continued)

Vacation home-owners located in urban/rural areas	People who just want to get away.... *when they want to* get away	Families or couples, singles and time sharers; annual income: $60K and up	Vacation is status; want to protect it; worry about it when away	Same as above	See above. Most have no protections except water, hose, and fire extinguishers	Word of mouth, magazines, direct mail, advertising	Price is not an issue because they typically like to have what is in style	Less fear of fire when they aren't present; knowing their belongings are safe
Government fire agencies: forest services and county and rural agencies	Our own firefighters who protect us from fires	25–60 yrs old; income via grants/taxes; each agency different	Don't want to risk manpower on protecting structures or fire stations	Urban/rural fire stations, national parks, monuments; any structures	They use their own man-power, fire trucks, and water sprinklers	Through sales staff procurement office and San Dimas office	Know what this should cost and sharp on pricing, but it is not their money	Reduction of need for personnel to protect their own structures

TABLE 8.3 Projected Financial Summary Results for Years 4–7			
	2008	**2009**	**2010**
Net Sales ($)	10,500,000	31,500,000	95,500,000
Cost of Goods Sold ($)	3,675,000	11,025,000	28,350,000
Gross Profit ($)	6,825,000	20,475,000	66,150,000
Operating Expenses ($)	4,200,000	11,025,000	33,075,000

gave her a $25,000 cash prize and six months of free rent in the Business Technology Center in Altadena, a high-technology incubator located north of Pasadena, California. Rhodes calculated a timeline for moving from production to market:

■ April 2006: Marketing/Sales set-up, preparation for production and unit sales.

■ May 2006: Provide UL Laboratories with a prototype unit that they can test for rating.

■ June 2006: Anticipate delivery of first unit to Los Padres National Forest. Marketing blitz begins with brochures sent to residents of potential fire-threatened areas locally in southern California and Oregon.

■ June 2006: First FOAMSAFE systems available for public purchase.

■ August 2006: Anticipate more orders from government fire agencies as word spreads. Units are being installed in residential homes and properties around southern California area. Additional systems are being sold and delivered in Oregon.

In 2005 the patent process was proceeding. Rhodes was using the provisional patent that she had written as the basis for the patent application that her attorney would complete. The company built a truck and trailer unit to use for demonstrations and bought a large delivery truck. Rhodes also placed an ad in *Home and Fire* magazine, and the magazine was also writing an article about the company. CFPI moved into the offices at the technology center in Altadena in the summer of 2005 and were benefiting from the networking opportunities with the thirty other companies in the incubator. CFPI was also building the second-generation system with some new features. Rhodes found a company in San Diego that was producing a patented automatic scanning device with a sensing range of 6 miles. She was considering deploying this sensor on the FOAMSAFE system. CFPI secured a contractor's license for California to allow the company to install the systems and obtain liability insurance.

Advising the Entrepreneur

1. What are the critical challenges that you see facing this business, and what should Rhodes do to overcome them?

2. Evaluate the team for this venture. Is it the appropriate team to execute the business plan?

3. What would you need to know to feel comfortable with Rhodes's financial projections?

CHAPTER 9

Creating a Management Team

Management is nothing more than motivating other people.

Lee Iacocca (1924–)

LEARNING OUTCOMES

- Discuss how to build an effective management team.
- Describe the benefits of using professional advisers.
- Explain the role of the board of directors.
- Discuss how to effectively use advisory boards.
- Explain the various management agreements that a small business needs to have in place.

The Real Purpose of an Advisory Board

In 1995 when David Gumpert and Paul Baudisch incorporated their online direct marketing company, NetMarquee, with $10,000, one of their first tasks was to build an effective advisory board. With little money to hire top-management talent, they decided to tap their networks for people who would serve on one of their advisory boards. The roles they needed to fill were diverse. They were looking for a financial expert, someone who was proficient at strategy, and someone who knew family businesses, their first customers.

Their second task was to write a comprehensive business plan so that they could raise money. When the plan was completed, Gumpert and Baudisch sent it around to the venture capital community in Boston. They received absolutely no response. As they were about to throw in the towel on the venture, their board of advisors stepped up and suggested that they stop raising money, spend less time perfecting the business plan, and spend more time making sales. After the first sales were achieved, the duo worked with public relations professionals to get some of the most successful clients written up in industry journals. Finally, the telephone at NetMarquee began to ring.

The advisory board also insisted that the duo bootstrap wherever possible, and that included collecting quickly on receivables. The result was that revenues doubled every year, and they achieved their first profit in 1997. They also learned the counterintuitive lesson that if a product or service has value for the customer, it is important to raise prices so that the customer values the product. One of their advisors quipped, "Within just a few years, you'll be charging hundreds of thousands of dollars to build Web sites," and, in fact, by 1999 NetMarquee had several clients who were paying several hundred thousand dollars a year for their services. It was at that point that Gumpert and Baudisch realized that not taking investor capital had actually been a benefit. Once again the advice of the advisory board had paid off.

In 1999 the two founders realized that if they were to take the company to the next level—the big leagues—they either had to seek that outside investment capital that they had been avoiding or they would need to

merge with a larger company, which really amounts to selling the company. Furthermore, the job of finding the right financial partner takes a lot of time and effort. The partners knew that they couldn't dedicate time to the search and still manage the business, so Baudisch ran the business and Gumpert focused on the search. They hired a facilitator, or intermediary, who helped them through the negotiation process, but they also learned that the "best decisions are the ones that first come from your head, then sit well in your gut." Once again pulling out their contact list, they managed to snag several potential suitors by the summer of 1999; however, the candidate that stood out from the crowd was Circle.com, a company with which NetMarquee had worked in the past. The two companies had the same vision for Internet marketing, which was a positive, so Gumpert and Baudisch took this company to the board of advisors for their approval, which they quickly received. They also had the deal reviewed by their lawyer and accountant who gave their consent. At the time of the sale, the advisory board cashed out of their stock and options. They had joined the company to be part of a new company in an emerging industry, and they had played an important role in the company's success by sharing their expertise and guiding the company in becoming an attractive acquisition target. Having a great board enables a start-up company to do more, do it faster, and do it a whole lot better.

Advising the Entrepreneur

1. Besides selling the company, in what other ways could Gumpert and Baudisch have grown the business to the next level?

2. What did you learn about partnerships and advisory boards from this example?

Sources: P. R. Baudisch, "Looking for RightCo. Inc.," *Entreworld.org* (accessed September 15, 2005); D. E. Gumpert, "Burn Your Business Plan," *AT&T Business Resources,* www.att.sbresources.com (accessed September 15, 2005); D. E. Gumpert, "Tough Love: What You Really Want from Your Advisory Board," *Inc.* (November 2000), www.inc.com (accessed October 1, 2005).

Entrepreneurship today is a collective activity rather than a solo endeavor by an intrepid lone entrepreneur.[1] Research is focused on issues of the team's effect on firm performance, how teams relate to venture capitalists, and team composition.[2] Much research argues for the existence of the lead entrepreneur, speculating that if such a person truly exists, he or she exhibits different characteristics from the rest of the team.[3] One important study found that successful lead entrepreneurs tend to come from entrepreneurial families and have higher levels of education. They typically have previous entrepreneurial or management experience, stronger communications skills, more self-confidence, and more resourcefulness than their counterparts in unsuccessful firms.[4] By contrast, more recent research has not supported this claim, finding that at least the skills of planning, recognizing opportunities, and evaluating opportunities are generally possessed by all members of an entrepreneurial team although significant differences have been found in the areas of vision and self-efficacy.[5]

The 1990s saw the rise of a now popular form of organization: the virtual organization, or networked company, which allows a small company to look and act larger than it really is. The virtual organization is an opportunity-based form with the ability to create resources to develop and market complex products more rapidly and frequently than one company could do alone. The underlying philosophy behind the virtual organization is a focus on the firm's core competencies and the forming of alliances with other firms that can add their core competencies to the mix. The aggregation of many core competencies gives the virtual organization a critical mass that is unrealizable in any other organizational form. It makes it easier for a company to take earlier advantage of a window of opportunity by having in place a mechanism that coordinates all of the competencies needed to undertake the project.

BUILDING AN EFFECTIVE MANAGEMENT TEAM

The management team is a critical part of any organizational design, but the entrepreneurial leader is responsible for and significantly affects the performance of the organization[6] as well as the organization's effort, cohesion, goal selection, performance norms, and goal attainment.[7] Entrepreneurial leaders who do not accept their formal role increase the probability of business failure.[8] An effective entrepreneurial team leader can guide the team toward consensus decision making, which means that the team arrives at "substantial but not necessarily unanimous agreement."[9] Recognizing that teams with defined goals perform at a higher level than teams without goals, the entrepreneurial leader also ensures that the team has meaningful and challenging goals that are measurable so that the team knows when goals have been achieved.

In their quest for independence, entrepreneurs often attempt a new venture as a soloist so that they can retain sole ownership, make all the key decisions, and not have to share the profits; however, this strategy may be a mistake. Although the autocratic approach to starting a business is still the most common one in small businesses and in the craft or artisan areas, in today's volatile, global market it is becoming increasingly difficult to succeed alone, particularly if the goal is to create a world-class company. With more new ventures operating in complex, dynamic environments and requiring more capital to start and grow, it is highly unlikely that any one person has all the knowledge and resources to start a potentially great company as a soloist. It is also highly unlikely that any one start-up company has all the competencies it needs to be competitive.[10] Therefore, at start-up and during initial growth, entrepreneurs tend to pull together a team but often in a rather haphazard fashion and for reasons that frequently have nothing to do with what the team members can contribute to the organization. This, unfortunately, is a mistake. Putting together a genesis, or founding, team is one of the most important tasks facing an entrepreneur with a new business concept or a business owner seeking to grow the business and should be undertaken with the greatest of care. This chapter looks at how to create an effective management team and how to link a company to others in a virtual organization or network.

Collaboration is an essential ingredient in any world-class start-up. Studies of high-technology start-ups demonstrate that a team effort provides a better chance for success than a solo effort.[11] There are several other important reasons for using a team effort:

- The intense effort required for start-up can be shared; thus, the load on any one person is lessened.

- Should any one member leave the team, the start-up is less likely to be abandoned.

- With a founding team that includes expertise and experience in major functional areas (marketing, finance, and operations), the new venture can proceed farther on the growth path before it needs to hire additional personnel.

- A quality founding team lends credibility to the new venture in the eyes of lenders, investors, and others.

- The ability to analyze information and make decisions is improved because the lead entrepreneur has the benefit of the varied expertise of his or her team members; in this way, ideas may be viewed from several perspectives.

Starting as a team doesn't always mean having to give up ownership. Team members can be people and companies to which the entrepreneur outsources certain functions or from which the entrepreneur receives needed advice. Figure 9.1 provides an illustration of the various resources available to form the entrepreneur's business team.

Characteristics of Small Business Management

Many of the challenges that small business owners and entrepreneurs face stem directly from the nature of their management style. Figure 9.2 depicts the spectrum of management types across the life of a new business. In the earliest stages of a new venture, the entrepreneur may be a soloist, creating the business out of a room in his or her home with no people-management needs. As the company grows, it becomes clear that founders often are not the best managers of their companies because they tend to be promoters and resource gatherers who are not focused on the details of the business operations.

Small companies face a number of risks that must be effectively managed:[12]

- **Market risk,** which may consist of adverse market price movement such as exchange rates and interest rates

- **Credit risk,** which is the possibility that a customer may fail to honor contractual obligations

FIGURE 9.1 The Entrepreneur's Team

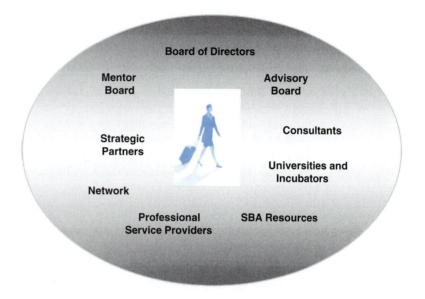

FIGURE 9.2 Small Business Management Stages

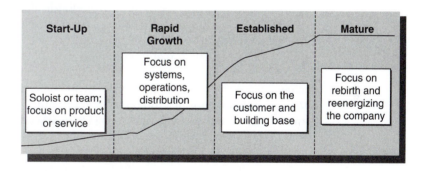

- **Operational risk,** which consists of poor internal systems and controls as well as external events
- **Business volume risk,** which results from changes in supply and demand

If the entrepreneur does not have all the skills required to manage these various forms of risk (and few do), he or she needs to find these skills outside the company and incorporate them into the management team.

What to Look For in a Team

When an entrepreneur decides to use a team to create the new venture, he or she generally looks for people who have complementary skills. In other words, if the entrepreneur is an engineer, finding a market expert and someone who knows how to raise capital would be advantageous to the new venture. Clearly, because the start-up of a new venture is a multifunctional process, the entrepreneur and the venture benefits greatly from a team comprising a variety of strengths and disciplines. Another advantage to forming a quality team is the fact that this founding team has a vested interest in the new venture. Team members invest not only their time but also usually their money. Thus, the burden of raising the resources necessary to start the venture is distributed among the team members, giving the lead entrepreneur access to the network of contacts of the other members in addition to his or her own. This approach vastly increases the information and resources available to the new venture and allows the venture to grow more rapidly.

Regardless of the legal form a business takes, the management or founding team is for all intents and purposes a partnership—with all the attendant benefits and problems (Chapter 7 discusses some of these problems). Any time that individuals decide to work with a partner or with several partners, they must choose that partner for the right reasons. Reasons for an entrepreneur to choose a particular person as a partner include knowing that the person shares the same values and vision for the company, has complementary skills that bring something needed to the mix, and has integrity.

All three of these qualities must be present if the partnership is to succeed. In addition, research has found that team heterogeneity in functional expertise and educational background is a significant predictor of long-term success[13] and innovation.[14] Moreover, teams with diverse skills seem to handle the complexities of new ventures better than homogenous teams.[15]

It is essential to divide responsibility in a way that makes each partner accountable for some aspect of the business. For example, when two or three people comprise the team, ownership in the company is typically divided equally among the partners, especially if they originated the concept together. Nevertheless, it is important that one partner have the role of lead entrepreneur—CEO—and that duties and responsibilities are divided such that if a disagreement arises on a particular issue, one person can ultimately make the decision. For example, in a two-person partnership, one member might be the product development, or creative end, of the team and the other the business end. In a three-person team, duties may be split based on the three basic functions of the organization: finance, marketing, and operations. All partners should share the vision for the company, but individual partners have responsibility for particular functions of the business.

A carefully chosen management team can carry the company through pre-start-up and start-up and usually well into the growth phase, at which time it often becomes necessary to bring in professional management if the original team doesn't have management expertise in mid-sized companies.

Common Errors in Team Building

Putting together the extended management team is a serious undertaking that, if unsuccessful, could have severe ramifications for the future of the company. Several common mistakes in forming the team should be avoided:

- Forming the team without careful consideration of the experience and qualifications each member brings to the team.
- Putting together a team whose members have different goals.
- Using only insiders—that is, friends and family—on the board of directors instead of the people most qualified to advise the business.

LEARNING FROM SUCCESS

How Entrepreneurial Leadership Helped One Baseball Team

Baseball is big business and teams face the same challenges as any other type of business: finding and training top people, differentiating themselves from the competition, building a solid corporate culture, and managing cash flow. When Omar Minaya agreed to manage the Montreal Expos in 2001, these activities were not being managed well, and the organization was floundering. The Expos had averaged ninety-five losses per season for the previous four years, and the fans had fled. The team had lost its TV contract, the owner had moved to Florida, there were dozens of vacancies to fill, and to top it all off, Major League Baseball had chosen the team for extinction.

For Minaya, the first Latin American general manager in baseball, this would be a makeover in the extreme, but he was up to the challenge and he wasted no time getting started. In his first month with the team, Minaya hired approximately 100 new staff members. Then he set out to find a partner,

someone who had the management skills that he lacked. He successfully persuaded Tony Siegle, a 61-year-old veteran who had served as assistant general manager of many teams over his long career, to be part of his team. Each day the partners would prioritize what had to be accomplished, and each evening they would review what had been accomplished and set priorities for the next day. Just six months later, the team exploded to the top of the baseball world on the strength of Minaya's determination and passion for the sport. They ended the 2002 season in second place to the Atlanta Braves on a payroll of only $39 million. Quite a feat when you consider that the Braves payroll was $93 million!

Lesson Learned: *Go for small wins.*

Source: J. Anderson, "Managing the Impossible," *Inc.* (April 2003), www.inc.com (accessed September 20, 2005).

- Using family members or friends as attorney and accountant for the business.
- Giving the management team all stock in lieu of salary. The lead entrepreneur does not want significant shares of stock in the hands of people who may leave the company later. Furthermore, loose stock can land in the hands of the firm's competitors.

A well-chosen team can make the difference between a company that is successful and one that is mired in conflicts and disputes. Both the internal and external teams must be committed to the vision for the company.

PROFESSIONAL ADVISERS

When a new venture is in the infancy stage, it generally doesn't have the resources to hire in-house professional advisers, such as an attorney or accountant. Instead, it must rely on building relationships with professionals on an as-needed basis. These professionals provide information and services that are not normally within the scope of expertise of most entrepreneurs, and they can play devil's advocate for the entrepreneur, pointing out potential flaws in the original business concept and the growth strategies. Growing companies that are putting all their resources into growth often aren't able to hire in-house professional advice. This is not a problem because continuing to use these advisers on an as-needed basis is probably a more effective allocation of resources. Because they are essentially independent contractors, it is important to understand what they do and how to choose them.

Attorneys

Many businesspeople attempt to avoid using lawyers until they get into trouble. This can be a costly error for a company because a good attorney can often help a business avoid expensive litigation and protect its rights. In fact, today stricter laws in the areas of antitrust, banking, the environment, and securities may affect a company's strategies and ability to do business as planned, even in the early stages of its life.

Attorneys generally specialize in one area of the law, such as tax, real estate, business, or intellectual property. Therefore, it is critical to select an attorney who specializes in the particular area of law the small business owners need. Attorneys can provide a wealth of support for a new and growing venture. Within their particular area of expertise, attorneys can

- Advise the entrepreneur in the selection of the correct legal organizational structure (sole proprietorship, partnership, or corporation).
- Advise and prepare documents for intellectual property rights acquisition.
- Negotiate and prepare contracts for the entrepreneur, who may be buying, selling, contracting, or leasing.
- Advise the entrepreneur on compliance with regulations related to financing and credit.
- Keep the entrepreneur apprised of the latest tax-reform legislation and help minimize the venture's tax burden.
- Assist the entrepreneur in complying with federal, state, or local laws.
- Represent the entrepreneur as an advocate in any legal actions.

Understanding Legal Fees Many attorneys bill in quarter-hour increments based on an hourly rate ranging from $150 to more than $500. That means that a five-minute phone call to an attorney who bills at $250 per hour in quarter-hour increments costs the client about $60. It's important to question how various attorneys in the firm bill and also how time for paralegals and staff is billed. There are several ways to pay an attorney:

- *Retainers* Many companies put a firm "on retainer," meaning they typically pay a periodic fee (often monthly) to the firm for specified types of work such as reviewing contracts and phone calls.
- *Contingency Fees* Contingency fees are fees that the law firm collects if it wins a case in litigation. In other words, the firm typically receives nothing until the case is resolved. Under this scenario, the entrepreneur should make sure that he or she is in charge of the case and determines whether the case settles or is appealed.
- *Stock* In the case of young, growing firms that don't have the cash for attorney fees, law firms sometimes accept stock. Obviously, to agree to this type of compensation, the law firm must believe the value of the entrepreneurial company will grow substantially. Giving up equity in the company probably should not be considered as the first choice.
- *Billable Hours* This is the method by which attorneys calculate the amount of work that they do for a client. It may even include the time spent by a senior partner explaining the case to a junior partner or associate. The entrepreneur should request statements that detail the amount of time billed by each person in the firm on the client's work.

Choosing an Attorney Choosing a good attorney is a time-consuming but vital task that should occur prior to start-up. Decisions made at the inception of the business may affect the venture for years to come; hence, good legal advice is critical. Accountants, bankers, and other businesspeople are excellent sources of recommendations for attorneys. This strategy is more likely to produce a good attorney who is also ethical in his or her professional or personal dealings. It is important to retain an experienced attorney who can competently do what the company needs and who is willing to listen, has time to work with the management team, and is flexible about fees while the business is in the start-up phase.

The management team also needs to determine whether to retain a large or a small law firm. Both have advantages and disadvantages. Large firms can often cover all the specific legal needs of a company—a one-stop shop of sorts—but are typically more expensive, and often a young company finds itself relegated to the youngest, most inexperienced attorneys. Large firms don't usually seek out small businesses as clients because the amount of legal business they may bring to the firm is not enough to cover the law firm's overhead; consequently, small, growing companies are often intimidated by the attorneys who represent them. Smaller law firms, in contrast, are less expensive but may have to refer clients to outside experts for specialties such as patent law. Nevertheless, they may be able to do the bulk of legal work required by the typical company in the early years.

To help keep legal fees in line, standardized documents should be developed based on the advice of an attorney that can be used in a variety of situations with minor modifications so that the attorney doesn't have to be involved each time. Above all, entrepreneurs need to practice preventive care by consulting an attorney before an issue becomes a real problem and need to realize that legal fees, like anything else, are negotiable.

Accountants

A lawyer is the company's advocate, but an accountant is bound by rules and ethics that do not permit advocacy. Therefore, where an attorney is bound to represent the company no matter what it does, the accountant, who is bound by the generally accepted accounting principles (GAAP), cannot defend the company if it chooses to do something that violates the GAAP.

Accounting is a fairly complex form of communication that entrepreneurs must understand. In the beginning of the business, the accountant may set up the company's books and maintain them on a periodic basis. Or, as is often the case, the entrepreneur may hire a bookkeeper to do the day-to-day recording of transactions and go to the accountant only at tax time. The accountant also sets up control systems for operations as well as payroll. A growing business is involved in a number of tasks related to accounting, which include the following:

- Verifying and posting bills
- Filing yearly tax returns
- Writing checks
- Preparing budgets
- Issuing invoices
- Making payroll tax deposits

- Making collections
- Securing insurance benefits
- Balancing the checkbook
- Keeping employee records
- Preparing financial statements
- Preparing stockholder reports if the company is a corporation
- Establishing inventory controls

An accountant can assist in all these areas. Once the new venture is beyond the start-up phase and growing consistently, it needs an annual audit to determine if the accounting and control procedures are adequate. In addition, the auditors may require a physical inventory. If everything is in order, they issue a certified statement, which is important should the entrepreneur ever decide to take the company public on one of the stock exchanges. At that time, the investment banking firm handling the IPO (initial public offering) will probably want three years of audited financial statements.

Finding an Accountant Like attorneys, accountants tend to specialize, so finding one who has experience working with young, growing businesses is an advantage. It is highly likely that the accountant who takes the company through start-up and early growth may not be the same person who takes care of its needs when it reaches the next level of growth as a mid-sized company. As the financial and record-keeping needs of the business increase and become more complex, the entrepreneur may need to consider a larger firm with expertise in several areas.

Bankers

Having a qualified banker on the company's professional advisory team is an issue not only when the company needs a line of credit for operating capital or to purchase equipment but also from the moment the business account is opened. Small business owners should think of bankers as business partners who are capable of providing expertise in several areas. Bankers are a source of information and networking contacts; they help the company make decisions regarding capital needs, assist in preparing pro forma operations and cash-flow analyses, and evaluate projections the entrepreneur has made. In addition, bankers are a rich source of assistance in all facets of procuring financing.

Entrepreneurs often have problems with bankers because the two view the world in fundamentally different ways; for example, bankers tend to focus on the loss potential, whereas entrepreneurs focus on the profit potential. To ensure that a banker understands the business, the market, and the customer, a thorough business plan should be provided. It should explain exactly how much capital is required, what the justification is for the amount, and how the funds will be used. Bankers must feel confident that the business will generate the funds to repay the loan and that it has enough collateral to protect the bank in the event that the entrepreneur defaults on the loan. Because banks do not value a company's assets dollar for dollar, they often look outside the company to the entrepreneur's personal assets, which can strengthen the collateral status.

Choosing a Banker Selecting a banker should be as careful a process as that for choosing an attorney or accountant. A list of criteria that defines the needs of the company with respect to the banking relationship helps narrow the search. Other business owners, as well as attorneys and accountants, are also excellent sources of relevant information on how well a particular bank works with companies in a specific industry.

When choosing a banker, it is beneficial to seek out an officer with a rank of assistant vice president or higher because these officers are trained to work with new and growing businesses and have a sufficient level of authority to quickly make decisions that affect the new venture. The problem today is that banks, like other businesses, are consolidating and downsizing, so bank officers are frequently moved around. Therefore, it is useful to have more than one person of authority in the bank who knows the company.

When interviewing a prospective banker, be sure to ask the following:

1. Does the bank regularly work with small business owners?

2. What are the costs related to the kinds of transactions that the small business will do with the bank? Fees vary and too many small business owners pay fees that are unwarranted for the value an account generates.

3. What kinds of services will the banker provide?

Working with a Banker A good banker wants to see the company before extending a line of credit or a loan. The company should be prepared to show itself in the best possible light by introducing the banker to the management team and key employees. Any attempts to restrict access to certain parts of the business or to certain people will probably not be looked on favorably. It is also important to thoroughly know and understand the company's financials, including assets. Demonstrating products give the banker a clearer understanding of the value of what the business is doing. It's always wise to anticipate any concerns that the banker may have and discuss contingency plans in a positive way. Finally, the management team should demonstrate its awareness of safety and environmental issues and how the company is successfully dealing with them.

Insurance Agents

Many entrepreneurs overlook the value of a relationship with a competent insurance agent. A growing venture requires several types of insurance, including the following:

- Medical
- Unemployment insurance
- Errors and omissions
- Workers' compensation insurance
- Auto on company vehicles
- Liability (product and personal)
- Life on key management
- Bonding
- Property and casualty

Major insurance firms can often handle all types of insurance vehicles, but many times the company needs to seek specialists for protection such as bonding (a common vehicle in the construction industry to protect against failure of a contractor to complete a project), product liability insurance, and errors and omissions (which protects the business against liability from unintentional mistakes in advertising). A company's insurance needs change over its life, and a good insurance agent helps it determine the needed coverage at the appropriate times.

In many small companies, what will happen to the company should the founder die is a real concern. Sonya Pasa, the owner of Reno, Nevada-based Joseph's Vienna Bakery and Café, believes that the most important thing a small business owner must do to be prepared for loss of the founder is to know the business inside and out. It is too easy to simply rely on a partner or spouse. Pasa's husband, Joseph, died of a heart attack suddenly, and she was left with a business that she was not sure she could operate alone. It took conversations with business counselors and assistance from the Service Corps of Retired Executives (SCORE) to help her decide that she could and should continue the business, one step at a time. As it was, the only day that she closed the store was the day of her husband's funeral.[16]

Whenever there is a situation in which a single person is responsible for a key component of the business—research and development, securing capital—key-person insurance is needed, and a company should plan to purchase as much as it can afford.

LEARNING FROM MISTAKES

Firing the Board

After the founding of his energy company, World Energy Solutions Inc. in 2000, Richard Domaleski formed what he thought was an excellent board that would guide him in the operations of his company, an auction house for electricity and gas credits based in Worcester, Massachusetts. The board was comprised of nine friends and investors who Domaleski expected would help his company succeed. Instead, eight months later, Domaleski told the board sadly, "We haven't been effective." With the exception of one director who became the company's COO, the rest resigned their positions. It was clear that change was essential.

Actually, Domaleski was ahead of the curve because his bold move came one year before the Enron scandal hit the news and precipitated a new look at boards of directors. Today, it is not as easy to find qualified board members due to higher workloads, limits on the number of boards on which a director can serve, and increased overall liability. Furthermore, with the advent of the Sarbanes Oxley Act, the Public

Company Accounting Oversight Board's stiff new requirements for disclosure and documentation, the profile of the in-demand director has become the CFO of another company rather than the CEO. In an effort to avoid another debacle, Domaleski reduced the size of his board to five people, and he looked for members who could assist in raising capital, advise on start-up operations, and guide new customer acquisition. He also instituted a probationary period so that he could determine if a board member actually added value to the team. This time Domaleski got it right. Within the first two months, one finance expert helped secure $1 million in funding. By 2002 the company's revenues were up tenfold. Out of a market of sixty competitors, including Enron, World Energy Solutions is one of only three or four companies left standing.

Lesson Learned: *Don't be afraid to reinvent your board of directors.*

Source: T. Raz, "Governing: Boardroom Makeover," *Inc.* (March 2003), www.inc.com (accessed September 14, 2005).

BOARDS OF DIRECTORS

The **board of directors** is part of the corporate governance structure, which was created to provide a form of checks and balances in companies where ownership was absent from the day-to-day operations of the business.[17] The board of directors oversees the managers and ensures that their actions are in the best interests of the company and its owners. The board focuses "on guidance and strategic oversight. . . . The ultimate responsibility for directing the company, however, lies with the board."[18]

The decision to have a board of directors is influenced by the legal form of the business; consequently, if the new venture is a corporation, a board of directors is legally required. Furthermore, if the company at some point requires venture capital, the venture capital firm will probably demand a seat on the board. This is because directors are empowered. They can make decisions that affect the company, and they can hire and fire the CEO. Beyond this, boards of directors serve a valuable purpose because, if chosen properly, they provide expertise that will benefit the company, and in that capacity they act much like members of a board of advisors. They also assist in establishing corporate strategy and philosophy, as well as goals and objectives.

It's important to distinguish between boards of privately owned corporations and those of publicly owned corporations. In a privately owned corporation, the genesis team typically owns all or the majority of the stock, so directors serve at the pleasure of the owners or entrepreneur who has effective control of the company. On the other hand, directors of publicly traded companies have legitimate power to control the activities of the company and, in many cases, have been able to fire the lead entrepreneur if they felt that he or she was preventing the company from achieving its goals.

Inside Versus Outside Boards

Boards can be composed of inside or outside members or a combination of the two. An inside board member is a founder, an employee, a family member, or a retired manager of the firm, whereas an outside member has no direct connection to the business. Which type of board member is better is a matter of opinion and circumstance because research provides no clear results on this issue. In fact, research reports that only 5 percent of closely held companies allow their boards to be dominated by outsiders and about 80 percent of private companies tend to put outsiders on a board of advisors instead. In general, however, outside directors are beneficial for succession planning and capital acquisition because they often bring a fresh point of view to the strategic planning process and expertise that the founders may not possess.

Insiders, by contrast, have the advantage of complete knowledge about the business; they are generally more available to meet and have demonstrated their effectiveness in the organization. They usually have the necessary technical expertise as well. On the other hand, there are often political ramifications stemming from the fact that board members report to the CEO and for that reason may not always be objective and independent in their thought processes. Insiders may also lack the broad expertise necessary to effectively guide the growth of the business beyond its current state.

Whether or not the new venture requires a working board of directors must be carefully considered. Most working boards are used for their expertise, strategic planning, auditing the actions of the firm, and arbitrating differences. Although these activities are not as crucial in the start-up phase, a board of directors can network with key people who can help the new venture and assist in gathering resources and raising capital. Some investors ask to be included on the board so that they can monitor their investment in the company, whether that investment is money or time. This is common with large, private investors, bankers, and even accountants. To ensure that the company ends ups with the best people on the board, standards should be set in advance and strictly adhered to.

During the growth period of the company, the management team is normally burdened with operational details, the need to generate sales, and the problem of maintaining a positive cash flow. Dealing with a board of directors is not something they want to do. But the board can offer the struggling team an objective point of view and the benefit of their considerable experience.

Choosing a Board

An effective board has people who represent the various stages of a growing business—that is, people who have managed businesses from start-up through growth and, in particular, someone who has managed a business larger than the entrepreneur's business.[19] When the management team evaluates people to serve on the board of directors, it should ascertain the answer to these questions for each candidate:

- Does this person have the necessary technical skill related to the business?
- Does she have significant, successful experience in the industry?
- Does he have important contacts in the industry?
- Does she have expertise in finance, capital acquisition, and possibly IPOs?
- Is his personality compatible with the rest of the board?
- Does she have good problem-solving skills?
- Is he honest and ethical?

When considering a board appointment, a time period should be specified; otherwise, a director appointed by the team may believe the position is an appointment for life, much like being appointed to the Supreme Court. To maintain the inflow of fresh ideas to the company, board members should serve on a rotating basis.

The chairperson, who in a new venture is typically the lead entrepreneur, heads the board. The entrepreneur is also, most probably, the president and CEO. A single person, often another member of the founding team, may hold the additional positions of secretary and treasurer.

Boards normally meet an average of five times a year, depending on the type of business. How often the board meets is largely a function of how active it is at any point in time. Directors typically spend about nine to ten days a year on duties related to the business and are usually paid a retainer plus a per-meeting fee; their expenses are also reimbursed. The compensation can take the form of cash, stock, or other perquisites. Additional expenses related to the development of a board of directors include meeting rooms, travel, and food.

Today, getting people to serve as directors is difficult. Because of the fiduciary responsibility they hold, in some cases they can be held personally liable for the actions of the firm, and the frequency with which boards are being sued is increasing. For this reason, potential directors may require that the business carry directors' and officers' liability insurance on them; however, the expense of this insurance is often prohibitive for a growing company. Some states—for example, Texas and Wisconsin—have passed statutes that protect directors of public and private companies from lawsuits.

Advisory Board

The use of advisory boards by entrepreneurs is a growing phenomenon in part because today's entrepreneurs often have educational backgrounds and corporate work experience that has taught them that boards are a valuable asset for a growing company. In contrast to the board of directors, the **advisory board** is an informal panel of experts and others interested in seeing the company succeed. They may meet once or twice a year to advise the entrepreneur; however, more and more boards of advisors are looking like boards of directors. They are being paid for meetings, especially those where they are asked to contribute significant time and effort on the company's behalf. This has often resulted in the loss of liability protection, which is one of the principal reasons that boards of advisors have been chosen over boards of directors in the first place. Recent court rulings have led many to suggest that there is no difference, for liability purposes, between a board of directors and a board of advisors. A rule of thumb about paying advisory board members is to pay about a $1000 a meeting plus expenses as well as offering stock. Some would argue that advisory board members should be on retainer so that company management can call on them as needed rather than waiting for a formal meeting.

Advisory boards are often used when a board of directors is not required or in the start-up phase when the board of directors consists of the founders only. An advisory board can provide a new venture with the needed expertise and an objective viewpoint without the significant costs and loss of control associated with a board of directors. It is a good compromise when the company cannot afford to hire such advice on an in-house basis. The board's focus on strategic issues, for which most entrepreneurs don't seem to have time, can often save a company from potentially fatal mistakes. Its access to networks of potential sources of capital, technology, strategic partners, and favorable publicity are invaluable to a growing firm on a limited budget.

Effective board members have a broad spectrum of experience in business that gives them a perspective that the entrepreneur lacks. Often, entrepreneurs also want a lawyer, an accountant, and other business professionals who can advise the company on particular issues. It is important to attract "heavyweights," or people who are known in an industry, to the board. Clearly, one of the best ways to attract name talent is through stock that gives the advisor a potential for benefiting from the advice that he or she provides. Being associated with the entrepreneur's company must add value to the advisor's résumé. Some entrepreneurs have employed very creative ways to attract great advisors. One Florida-based construction company used charitable donations to attract high-income executives. The executives received expense reimbursement and then a large donation was made to their favorite charity in their name.[20]

Mentor Board

Being the CEO or owner of a company can be a lonely position. There are times when owner/managers need advice, guidance, and assurance that they are making the right decisions. When an owner/manager needs help, he or she cannot easily go to management and employees in the company because it might cause concern or

Creative Thinking Saves the Day

When things are going well, the skills that an entrepreneur lacks are not so apparent. Effective leadership is tested in the trenches, when the going gets tough. Diana Pohly, CEO of Pohly & Partners, a Boston-based producer of custom publications, knows what tough times feel like. In 2001 with the economy in a slump, she was faced with having to cut $400,000 from her budget. Any CEO knows that the quickest way to reduce the budget is to lay off employees. Resisting that strategy, Pohly decided to be more creative and instead convinced six senior managers to take pay cuts of 15 percent and staffers to take cuts of 10 percent. The plan worked and by 2003 the company saw a profit of $400,000 on sales of $10 million.[21]

suggest problems with the company. In this case, owner/managers need a personal board, or **mentor board,** of trusted people outside the company that they can turn to for advice. Often an entrepreneur's mentor is someone who is living the type of life that the entrepreneur wants to live and therefore serves as a role model.

THIRD-PARTY MANAGEMENT ASSISTANCE

In the early stages of a small business, the resources to hire top management are limited, so small business owners look to outside assistance that they can tap on an as-needed basis. This type of assistance comes in many forms, and several of them are reviewed here.

Management Consultants

There is no more ubiquitous type of professional service provider than the management consultant, or CEO coach. Typically, these consultants are people who have gained a wealth of experience in a particular area of business and are now sharing what they have learned with the small business community. To effectively employ consultants, it is imperative that a business owner have a clear picture of type of help required so that the right consultant is hired. Goals and objectives should be agreed upon up front with the consultant as should the fee and method of payment. Often it is better for the owner's budget to settle on a fixed price for the project with a defined percentage of deviation from that figure. Alternatively, consultants often quote hourly and daily rates that can range from $150 to $500 or more per hour and $1000 to $5000 a day. The best way to find a consultant is through recommendations from other business owners in the industry or through the owner's attorney or accountant.

Universities

Universities are an excellent source of faculty consultants and student interns. Entrepreneurs can tap into the expertise of graduate students who generally also have industry experience in business, science, engineering, communications, and many other fields. A good place to start at a university is an entrepreneur program because entrepreneurship is a field that integrates all business functions as well as the product or service development functions.

Small Business Administration Services

The Small Business Administration (SBA) provides a wealth of information to small-business owners and some affiliated services that entrepreneurs should definitely access. For example, Small Business Development Centers are typically affiliated with universities or colleges and their mission is to provide education, research assistance, consulting services, and export services to small businesses. SCORE provides free management advice and consulting from retired business executives. They have been very successful in using their years of expertise to help small business owners with the myriad problems that they face.

Business Incubators

Incubators offer space, services, education, and mentoring to start-up businesses. However, many also have affiliate programs that small businesses can join to access the education and mentoring without locating in the incubator. The Technology Business Center in Altadena, California, has one such program that has been a rich source of advice and networking for small businesses in the area. Its executive director, Mark Lieberman, claims over dozens of affiliate businesses in addition to the thirty companies that reside in the incubator.

Networks

More and more, entrepreneurial networks are forming in communities to link businesses and people with common interests. The Southern California Biomedical Council, the Northwest Entrepreneur Network, and The Young and Successful Network are examples of such networks. For entrepreneurs, tapping into networks like these is one of the most essential things an entrepreneur can do to ensure a successful business. The contacts made through these organizations are invaluable when it comes time to raise money, seek a strategic partner, or find key management talent.

Strategic Partners

It is rare today that a small business has all the capabilities that it needs within the management team. More often than not, the business needs to outsource to strategic partners certain functions that are not within its core competency. These partners become a critical part of the entrepreneur's network. (Strategic partners are addressed in Chapter 2.)

MANAGEMENT AGREEMENTS

Several legal agreements are useful to have in place to prevent problems from arising in the management team. Three of the most common of these agreements are non-compete, shareholder, and buy–sell agreements.

Noncompete Agreements

Employers protect themselves against the loss of their trade secrets and their top employees with noncompete agreements. By signing a noncompete agreement, employees promise not to seek employment from a direct competitor for a specified period of time after leaving the company and not to disclose to others any company trade secrets. Trade secrets are a source of competitive advantage for a company and include such things as processes, customer lists, vendor lists, techniques, and formulas.

For a noncompete agreement to stand up in court, there must be a good business reason for it to exist—for example, to protect a trade secret or a customer list that the company has built over time. It should be used only with employees who actually have access to the "insider" information and must offer a benefit to the employee to be valid. That benefit is usually a job offer that is contingent on the candidate signing the agreement. For an existing employee, providing a promotion or raise would also serve as the required benefit for signing. The requirements of the noncompete agreement must be "reasonable" in terms of the length of time involved, geographic scope, and the scope of employment in which the former employee can engage. In general, an agreement whose duration is six months to two years is deemed reasonable. It should also be noted that noncompete agreements are not enforceable against employees in California. In that state, a nondisclosure or confidentiality agreement can be used.

Shareholder Agreements

Shareholder agreements are valuable instruments for avoiding many of the challenges facing a small business when it secures outside investment capital or provides stock to key management; however, they are no substitute for making certain that shareholders are satisfied with the way that management is running the company.

In general, two forms of stock purchase agreements are used. One is the *stock redemption agreement* that states that the corporation must redeem a shareholder's stock when a defined event occurs—for example, the death of a shareholder. This obligation to repurchase is used to avoid having the shares fall into the hands of the shareholders beneficiaries who may not have had an involvement in the company. The second type is a *cross purchase agreement,* which obligates the other shareholders in the company to purchase the stock to keep it from being passed on to beneficiaries. In practice, a combination of the two is employed so as to avoid having any shareholder be obligated unconditionally to purchase the stock.[22]

One of the most contentious areas of a shareholder agreement is the method for establishing the purchase price of the shares, which should always be decided at the time the agreement is put together rather than at the time that shares are being transferred. Determining a date for valuation purposes, such as the date of a shareholder's death or the date of the previous year's end-of-year financial statements, is a critical aspect of assessing the purchase price. One simple method for assessing value is a fixed-price method that sets the price per share in the agreement, regardless of the market. Another involves calculating the book value of the assets; however, caution should be exercised when using this approach because book value is not a reliable measure of the value of the business. Yet another option is for the directors of the corporation (assuming a corporate form) to set the value of the shares at the annual board meeting. Perhaps the best approach, however, is to use the expertise of professional appraisers.

Buy–Sell Agreements

Every business should make use of buy—sell, or buyout, agreements, which are binding contracts between partners or co-owners that dictate when and how an owner may sell his or her interest in the company and who and for how much it can be purchased. Typically, these agreements are exercised when an owner retires, dies, or divorces a spouse. But they are also important in the event that an owner faces personal bankruptcy, which could force the liquidation of the company to satisfy that owner's debts. To avoid that situation, the buy–sell agreement should require an owner to disclose the intent to file bankruptcy and then sell his or her interests back to the company. That buyout money then goes to the bankruptcy trustee, and the business is not affected.

This chapter emphasizes the importance of the management team to the success of the business. That team is composed of founders, key management employed by the company, trusted third parties who advise the management team, and strategic partners who undertake some of the functions of the business. Forming an effective team is one of the most critical tasks that a business owner undertakes because it affects everything the business does.

ISSUES FOR REVIEW AND DISCUSSION

1. What kinds of businesses might be started effectively as a soloist? As a team? Justify your response.

2. What must be in place for a partnership to succeed? Why?

3. At what point in the growth of a company should the entrepreneur consider creating a board of directors or an advisory board?

4. Describe the advantages and disadvantages of inside versus outside board members.

5. Why is it necessary to create shareholder agreements with owners and non-compete agreements with employees?

EXPERIENCING ENTREPRENEURSHIP

1. Interview a professional—lawyer, accountant, or banker—about his or her experience with and ability to work with small, growing companies. What benefits can this professional provide you as an entrepreneur?

2. Identify a successful entrepreneurial company in your community. Through background research of news articles and primary research with members of the management team, identify the key success factors that this management team brings to the business.

KIYONNA Klothing: From Virtual Business to the Internet

In January 1996, Kim Camarella was about to begin her final semester in the entrepreneur program at the University of Southern California and was searching for a great concept on which to build her business plan. At the time, she was interning at a local computer software company. One day she and a coworker, Donna Maldonado, were having a conversation, and Maldonado observed that there was no fashionable clothing for plus-size young women. From her entrepreneur courses, Camarella knew the value of finding a need in the market that wasn't being met. Maybe Maldonado had just given her the business concept she was looking for.

Camarella decided to do further research and gain some hands-on experience with a popular plus-size clothing designer. She conducted focus groups and extensively evaluated the market and discovered that indeed there was an untapped niche market of full-figured young women who wanted contemporary and stylish clothing. This realization marked the first step toward creating a company that would change industry perceptions of plus-size women's clothing.

The Birth of KIYONNA Klothing

Camarella, a petite woman herself, began discussions with Maldonado and another acquaintance, Yvonne Buonauro, who had a degree from the Los Angeles Institute of Design and Merchandising. With a firm vision of what this company could become, the three young founders developed a business plan and named the company after themselves—Kim, Yvonne, and Donna—KIYONNA Klothing. Kim would serve as president, Yvonne as vice president of design, and Donna as vice president of sales and marketing.

The three immediately set to work to create a thirty-piece line of clothing, using the ideas generated in their focus groups and based on industry predictions about what would be fashionable in the upcoming spring. The next step was to find a pattern maker and a sample sewer to bring their ideas to life. In October 1996, the company showed its first line of clothing for spring 1997 at the Big and Tall Women's Show in Las Vegas and got an overwhelming response. "KIYONNA Klothing walked away from the show with

its first four customers," Camarella boasted. As orders continued to come in, the company employed independent contractors to begin the first production run.

Although the partners had made personal investments to start the company, their money was quickly depleted. They managed to secure two short-term loans totaling $20,000 from Camarella's and Buonouro's fathers to cover production, marketing, and other operational costs. In January 1997, they hired an independent sales representative at the Los Angeles CaliforniaMart to promote the line, and in June 1997, they brought a Dallas representative on board.

Problems with Early Growth

As a growing, small company, they faced many challenges. Their volume had not yet reached the level of other apparel manufacturers, so it was difficult to find companies that would do the work for them. They also had quality-control issues. Because they didn't have a quality-control person to inspect the goods on site, they often received damaged or substandard goods. Another problem, typical of the fashion industry, was returns from retailers. A major department store, for example, would place a $1500 order, pay in thirty days to get an 8 percent discount, and then return $500 worth of the clothing to KIYONNA while retaining the 8 percent on the full amount.

Yet another challenge was cash flow. As a small, unknown apparel company, KIYONNA lacked the clout to negotiate terms with vendors; yet its own customers, the retailers, demanded net thirty days. The three partners enrolled in the SBA's prequalification program for women business owners so that they would have more clout when they applied for a bank loan. Around this same time, the partners had a disagreement that resulted in Camarella and Buonauro buying out Maldonado.

Having overcome all these challenges, by the summer of 1997, KIYONNA Klothing appeared in seventeen boutiques around California and New York, as well as in the upscale Nordstrom department stores in southern California and Alaska. It had been featured in leading magazines such as *Big Beautiful Woman* and

Seventeen. This free publicity resulted in more than 1000 calls from plus-size women in less than one week. Women loved the stylish clothing; the challenge for KIYONNA was to find ways to convince retail buyers, who were typically reluctant to take a risk on a new line, to purchase it for their stores. KIYONNA was beginning to consider mail order to reach the growing number of customers who didn't have access to retail outlets that carried the line, when the Internet took the company in a different direction.

The Internet's Impact on the Business

In March 1999, KIYONNA launched a website that was intended as an additional marketing vehicle to the fashion magazines to drive customers to the boutiques where their clothing line was carried. The company built out an e-commerce site on the off chance that customers might want to buy online, although in 1999 purchasing apparel online had not really caught on yet. To Camarella's surprise, they began receiving orders from the very first day. Quickly they learned that customers expected the website to operate much like a retail store; that is, customers expected to come back to the site each week and find new merchandise displayed. That meant that Camarella had to find a way to keep the site fresh so that customers would keep coming back. In the apparel industry, collections come out at certain times of the year and generally the entire collection is presented. Camarella decided to stagger the introduction of a new collection over a three-month period so that customers would always find something new. In fact, that is the principal method that the company uses to keep customers coming back. Unlike some stores that offer incentives and condition their customers to require incentives to get them into the store (whether in-store or online), Camarella did not want to go that route; she wanted her customers to come back for the possibility of seeing something new that they just had to have. She also used e-mail to announce new items, and today the company boasts of over 100,000 loyal customers who receive her e-mail campaigns. "Sometimes, you don't have new product but just want to contact people once a week," notes Camarella. E-mail is an effective way to do that.

Having an online showcase for her collections meant that the company now had to do a more professional job of marketing. Camarella began by setting up photo shoots about four times a year with professional photographers and models around a theme. Those photos helped attract women seeking sexy and stylish clothing. Camarella also hired an Internet marketing firm to help them better target their advertising and to undertake website personalization. Now, if a woman goes onto the Internet and finds KIYONNA, the company can identify where she is coming from and launch a specific campaign to reach her needs. For example, if she clicks on dresses and spends some time there and then moves to information about buying, KIYONNA might offer her a coupon for free shipping. This firm is helping Camarella convert "hits" to customers, a difficult challenge in e-commerce. Although KIYONNA Klothing is featured in over 100 boutiques domestically and in Scotland, Germany, and Bermuda, online sales overtook in-store sales in 2002.

It was at that time that Camarella parted ways with the last of her two partners, Yvonne Buonauro, the designer, who had grown tired of the plus-size industry and wanted to move on. She was bought out of the business, and Camarella was finally able to run the business precisely as she wanted. She put one employee in charge of boutique sales and another on online sales. Other employees focused on marketing and production. The business is seasonal with the biggest season being May through September, the wedding season, when growth averages 25 percent a month. Sales in 2004 were $2.5 million with five employees. Camarella still outsources to a patternmaker, sewer, and cutter located near her offices in Huntington Beach, California. Since she moved her company there in 2004, the neighboring city of Westminster has become a mini-apparel district.

One big challenge in the apparel industry is returns, "that horrible thing that happens in my industry," quips Camarella. In the plus-size market in particular, there is a problem with fit, so returns can range from 6 to 20 percent, depending on the item. Until all returns are in, it is difficult to know how much profit that the company will make. Camarella has attempted to reduce the return rate by keeping her sizing in line with the largest producer of plus-size clothing, Lane Bryant.

Looking to the Future

In December 2004, Camarella gave birth to her first child and took four months off from the company to be with the baby. Unfortunately, the apparel industry suffered a downturn in March–May 2005, which severely affected KIYONNA's revenues, so Camarella had to get back to the office to make sure that things would turn around.

There are a lot of details in the apparel business. Camarella advises aspiring entrepreneurs to keep accurate records and get automated from the start. "You have to stay on top of it every day," Camarella says. "Listen to the customer, and listen to yourself." She believes strongly in her vision of a company that will give plus-size women the confidence that they look as stylish and attractive as smaller-size women.

As Camarella looks to the future, she believes that the company has reached the point where it needs to grow more rapidly. To diversify her product line, she added a lingerie website and a swimwear line. She is now considering a plus-size maternity line and a line of clothing that is trendier and less expensive to appeal to her younger customers. It is a tough industry. She has created a niche that has been very successful, but now it is time to grow quickly to the next level.

Advising the Entrepreneur

1. Given her experience with partners, would you advise Camarella to take on a new partner to grow the business? Why or why not?

2. How would you advise Camarella to grow the business more rapidly?

CHAPTER 10

Preparing a Human Resources Plan

Effective leadership is putting first things first. Effective management is discipline, carrying it out.

Stephen Covey

What's Not to Like!

Dov Charney is perhaps one of the most unusual CEOs in the world. Not because he prefers to be known as the senior partner of his company rather than the CEO. Not because he has no assistant. And not because he rarely checks voicemail or e-mail and carries no PDA. Charney is unusual because he is bucking the trend of outsourcing to China and India. He has taken his intense passion for T-shirts, a passion that began while he was still living in Canada, and built an empire called American Apparel, the largest apparel manufacturer in America, a company that was expected to top $250 million in sales in 2005 with 10,000 SKUs (stock keeping unit) in production.

Early on, Charney was frustrated by the fact that Canadians couldn't buy the high-quality, better-fitting T-shirts that were available in the United States. He began his business by taking trips to towns along the U.S.–Canadian border, buying up stacks of T-shirts and taking them back to Canada to sell at a profit. Later, when he attended Tufts University in Boston, he brought his business with him. Ultimately, he dropped out of school to join with a friend to plan for a business that would create the "ultimate T-shirt" and sell wholesale to retailers. Charney figured that he could easily differentiate himself because of his obsession with quality and fit. In fact, he conducted market research at strip clubs to understand how to fit T-shirts to the many shapes of women.

In 1997 American Apparel began selling to bands, museums, artists, and anyone who wanted to screenprint on high-quality T-shirts. From the beginning, the goal was to build a company that manufactured in the United States so that it had a shorter supply chain, which would allow it to be flexible and fast. A competitor like Gap, with layers of management and factories in China, does not have that flexibility. "I could have that shirt made and in my stores by Friday. Design it on Monday, cut it on Tuesday, sew it on Wednesday, ship it on Thursday, it is in New York on Friday. They can't do that," Charney asserts.

The company grew but it did not realize its potential until Charney hired Marty Bailey as his vice presi-

dent of operations in 2002. Bailey then brought all the activities of the value chain in-house, from design to distribution. He grew the factory to 2000 workers producing a million garments a week by organizing the workers into teams that could be pulled in to create any type of garment in the American Apparel line. He paid them based on performance but never below $8 an hour. Because the factory was so efficient, he could afford to pay higher wages and not join the union. Some workers earn as much as $27 an hour. Employees receive medical, dental, and education benefits and even massages. Their lunches are also subsidized. As a result, the company has a list of over 1000 people waiting to apply for jobs. Today, the factory consists of three huge pink buildings in an industrial area of downtown Los Angeles with the capability of supporting $400 million in sales and 200 stores before the company will need to expand. In 2003 the company opened 13 retail outlets: big, white boxes with young employees who seem to have come out of Central Casting. From there, its retail stores grew to all parts of the United States and Canada as well as eight other countries.

The 36-year-old Charney is an easy target for critics who complain that he is irreverent and leads a prurient and bizarre life that plays out in his company's provocative ads, which feature employees and people whom he has met on the street in various stages of undress wearing American Apparel clothing. But there is another side to this radical company leader who can't carry on a conversation for more than a few seconds without answering his cell phone. He is passionately socially responsible. American Apparel doesn't follow the apparel industry's love of logos, plastering the company name all over everything it produces. It puts no logos on its garments and prefers that customers see it as the company that pays fair wages and provides great working conditions—no sweatshops here. American Apparel has been called a "beacon of hope" in a garment district that still is known for its horrific working conditions. Charney believes that if you give workers a better life, they will "work ten times harder."

Advising the Entrepreneur

1. How can Charney maintain the culture that he has built in his company as the company expands rapidly to all parts of the globe?

2. Can Charney's human resource strategy work for other types of companies that are currently outsourcing?

Sources: J. Collard, "Too Sexy for His Shirt," *The Times Magazine* (February 12, 2005); www.americanapparel.net (accessed September 17, 2005); J. Dean, "Dov Charney, Like It or Not," *Inc.* (September 2005), www.inc.com; R. Walker, "Conscience Undercover," *New York Times Magazine* (August 1, 2004).

People are arguably the most important asset of any company, but few entrepreneurs spend enough time and effort to effectively prepare for, hire, and train this vital resource. One reason for this neglect is that during start-up the founding team has typically filled all the functions of the organization and, assuming everything has gone well, the team has worked closely and well together. Hiring new people into the organization is much like bringing a stranger home to live with the family; he or she doesn't always fit into the culture that has developed through start-up and early growth, and it takes time to teach the newcomer how everything is done. If employees are a company's most important asset, the development of a human resources plan should be a primary function of the management team. This chapter explores how to find and keep good employees, as well as how to protect a company against unnecessary employee-related litigation.

RECRUITING AND HIRING

There are two approaches to determining when it is appropriate to bring in new employees. The first could be called the "when we have to" approach: Owners bring in new people when they are ready to delegate authority and the company needs some professional management and structure. The second is the "start with a big management team" approach: Based on its initial resources, the company hires the best management that it can and continually adds to the team as profits grow. This allows the entrepreneur to focus on the aspect of the business that interests him or her most and delegate other functional responsibilities to the rest of the team.

Determining which approach is better for the company is generally a function of the type of company and the resources the company possesses. For example, a software company that has spent two years in product development with a team of designers and programmers probably finds it critical to hire a professional management team to launch the product because the founding team's expertise is in product development, not business development. On the other hand, a service company may be able to develop its business to its fullest before adding management personnel to help it expand to other geographic locations. In either case, when to hire additional management is determined by

- The founding team's ability to delegate.
- The resources available for hiring.
- The need to create more structure.

Recruiting the Best Employees

Recruiting is the process by which a company locates individuals to fill employment positions. The recruiting function is perhaps the most critical and least attended-to facet of the employee hiring process. This is surprising because it is the recruiting process that determines whether potential employees are in fact appropriate for particular positions. Small, growing businesses that lack experienced human resource management (HRM) personnel tend to hire a person for a particular job rather than take an in-depth look at how well that individual would fit into the culture of the organization and whether or not she or he has the potential to grow with the company.

A targeted and focused approach to employee recruitment best suits a small company. It enables an entrepreneur to look for more qualified candidates and for candidates who can fill more than a single role. While posting a job opportunity on a jobs site like Monster.com brings in a flood of résumés, unless the company has a full-time recruiting staff, and most small businesses do not, it may not be the best route to take. Matt Lewis, cofounder of Baked, a bakery in Brooklyn, New York, was trying to find a baker and a finisher who decorates the baked goods. He first tried the city's culinary school, but those applicants typically wanted to work in restaurants and create very fancy desserts. He finally tried Craigslist, a no-frills community site and found someone right in the neighborhood who was perfect for the job.[1]

Hiring a human resource consultant to help set up a recruiting and hiring process may be a wise investment. An alternative is to find a human resource expert to serve on the advisory board, particularly in businesses that are highly labor intensive and experience industry-wide high turnover, such as the restaurant industry.

Employees can be found through a number of proven methods, including the following:

- Advertising in the classifieds
- Recruiting at high schools, vocational schools, colleges, and universities
- Public employment offices
- Private employment agencies ("headhunters")
- Referrals from current employees and others in the industry
- Networking with local organizations
- Temporary help services

Competition for good job candidates is great, so small business owners must be prepared to sell the unique benefits of working for a growing firm. Some of these benefits include the ability to make decisions that directly affect the company, to move quickly into positions of responsibility, and to work in a more flexible work environment.

The Job Description

The best way to ensure a chance of interviewing the appropriate people for a position is to use a job description. A good job description includes the following:

- The educational and work experience required. This is an important initial screening device, but should be stated as "desired levels" rather than "required" because often the best person for the position does not have the exact educational or work experience stated in the job description but is bright and capable of being trained quickly.

- The duties and responsibilities of the position outlined in sufficient detail that the potential candidate understands what is expected, but generally enough to allow for some flexibility of tasks.

- The person to whom the candidate is responsible.

- The personal characteristics needed for the position, such as good communication skills, self-motivation, creativity, and so forth.

- A clause stating that the company can make some relatively minor changes in the job description without rewriting it.

In designing a job description, specifications, and an application for employment, it is important to recognize that the equal employment opportunity laws prohibit a company from discriminating based on age, sex, color, race, national origin, religion, and other factors during the recruiting and hiring process. For example, a job description cannot require a photograph of the applicant unless the position is one for which appearance is the primary attribute, as in modeling. This is to avoid discrimination based on race or physical size.

Holding to the letter of the law is critical. In a time of increasing regulation and litigation, it is important that employers maintain excellent records during the hiring process as well as during employment, particularly because the burden of proof is on the employer to provide evidence that the company is innocent of discrimination.

The Selection Process

Once the criteria for the position and the candidate have been determined, it becomes necessary to find the most effective way to gather information on potential candidates and choose among them. There are two major sources of information—self-report and observation or empirical research—and these can be further subdivided into measures that tell the company something about the candidate's past experience, present character, and potential for advancement.[2] See Figure 10.1 for an overview of the recruitment and selection process.

Self-Report Sources and Research Two of the most common self-report measures to look at the past experience of the candidate are the résumé and the job application form. Both are good for screening applicants before the interview process; however, caution must be exercised because, particularly in the case of the résumé, applicants tend to embellish their achievements. Caution should also be exercised when using standardized job application forms because they often contain questions that could lead to accusations of discrimination. Here are some important clues to look for in a résumé:

- Did the applicant stay in previous positions for a reasonable length of time?

- Is the applicant's prior work experience relevant to the position being applied for?

FIGURE 10.1 The Recruitment and Selection Process

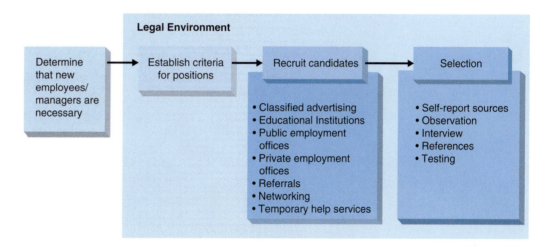

- Does the overall appearance and quality of the résumé suggest a candidate who is serious about his or her career?
- Was the candidate successful in emphasizing skills, experience, and education needed in the position being applied for?

To learn more about the candidate's character and how he or she might fit into the culture of the organization, many companies give personality tests and integrity tests. These tests provide an insight into the candidate's values, interests, and needs. To learn about the candidate's potential for advancement, employers often use situational interviews. These are discussed in a later section.

A candidate's past experience is studied by using references from previous supervisors or coworkers, performance appraisals, and drug tests,[3] and current abilities can be assessed by observing work samples or the results of aptitude tests. Future potential is often measured through interviews that involve hypothetical, or what-if, situations to which the candidate must respond.

Interviews

It is often said that the résumé is merely a tool to allow a candidate to get a foot in the door of the company. People are not normally hired based solely on the résumé but based on how well they present themselves in an interview situation. It is during interviews, however, that many employers cross the line, asking questions that are illegal to ask prior to the point of hire. Table 10.1 displays some questions that should not be asked and their acceptable alternatives. Failing to exercise due care in the questions asked of candidates can result in a lawsuit for discrimination.

Another mistake many young (and some mature!) companies make in their hiring practices is failing to prepare for the interview process. Often this difficult but essential task is left to someone with little experience and an inability to convey the company's vision. Consequently, it is no surprise when the best people for the position are not identified or hired. Because today it is more difficult than ever to discharge someone from a position and costly to retrain someone new, a young, growing company

TABLE 10.1   Interview Questions: What's Allowed and What's Not

In October 1995, the EEOC (Equal Employment Opportunity Commission) released guidelines that allow for some prehiring discussion that previously had been disallowed. For example, if an applicant has an obvious disability (for example, uses a wheelchair), it is permissible to talk about what accommodations might be necessary if the applicant were hired. Otherwise, the following questions may not be asked prior to the point of hire.

1. What is your age?	Only in the case of a young applicant can the employer ask if the person can prove he or she is of legal age after hiring. In other cases, age questions such as "When did you graduate from high school?" are not permitted.
2. What church do you attend?	No questions regarding the religion of the applicant or the applicant's family are allowed.
3. Do you have children, or do you plan to get pregnant?	Questions regarding personal family plans or living arrangements are not permitted.
4. Have you ever been arrested?	"Have you ever been convicted of a crime?" is permissible.
5. How is your health?	"Do you have any condition that would prevent you from doing your job?" is permissible.
6. You have beautiful skin; where are your ancestors from?	Questions about ancestry, heritage, culture, etc., are not permitted.

would be wise to spend more effort investigating and learning about the people it hires. Following are some suggestions for achieving a successful interview:

- Choose a suitable place for the interview that puts the candidate at ease and permits a period of time without interruptions.

- If more than one person from the company is to participate in the interview process, all should be present at the start of the interview with plans in place as to how the interview will be conducted.

- A brief opening welcome and statement about the company by the interviewer gives the candidate a chance to get adjusted to the interview environment.

- Open-ended questions provide more information than those that require short one- or two-word responses.

- Because experience, education, and basic skills are represented on the résumé, the interview should focus on clarifying any issues the résumé raised and getting at the character of the candidate. The goal is to answer the question "Can this person provide the company with the skills it needs and work well with others?"

- Sometimes the most innocent-appearing questions ("Do you like to travel?" "What do you like to do in your spare time?") really seek valuable information. In this case, will the person travel for the company? And does this person have demanding interests that will keep him or her from working long hours when needed?

- Questions such as "What is your definition of success?" or "What are your strengths and weaknesses?" tell the interviewer a lot about the character of the candidate and what is important to him or her.

- The interviewer should talk no more than 15 percent of the time and should take notes either during the interview or immediately after. The notes should refer to answers given by the candidate as well as feelings the interviewer had while listening and observing the nonverbal communication (body language) of the interviewee.

Checking References and Testing

Another area where young companies fall short in the hiring process is checking references. Often they assume that because a candidate listed someone as a reference, that person will necessarily give a good recommendation. That is not always the case! The fact is that well over half of fired employees who file a defamation claim recover damages. Wrongful-discharge claims can result in very costly verdicts. Consequently, many former employers will be reluctant to give more than factual information, such as how long the candidate was on the job. To overcome this, employers might consider hiring an independent firm to do background checks on potential employees, especially where the position is critical. In either case, it is important to check references.

Testing the applicant is another commonly used technique for screening. These tests may consist of psychological tests, performance tests, drug tests, and physical examinations. The benefit of doing these tests up front far outweighs their cost. Having to fire an employee and risk retaliatory litigation is far more costly, in both time and money; however, any test used to screen an applicant must be related to the job and must also come from a reliable source.

Using Temporary Employees

Today, many small businesses are wary about hiring employees without a way to get out of the arrangement if it does not work out. Particularly in businesses in which the need for employees varies seasonally, growing companies are looking for a way to have skilled employees when and where they need them but not have to carry them on the payroll when they are not needed.

One solution to this dilemma is to use temporary workers from an employment agency on an as-needed basis. Temporary help agencies have begun to specialize in providing specially trained workers for specific industries. This approach also works when a company wants to "try out" an employee before hiring him or her permanently. The National Association of Temporary and Staffing Services reports that 16 percent of former temporary workers took permanent jobs with the firms that hired them on a temporary basis.

TRAINING AND EVALUATING EMPLOYEES

Every employee, including new management, will require orientation, some degree of training, feedback, and eventually evaluation. Orienting the new employees to the workplace and introducing them to the people with whom they will be working is an important start. They will also need to understand the policies and procedures of the company including work hours, benefits, and performance criteria. New employees should be encouraged to ask questions, and a follow-up orientation should be held a couple weeks into their employment to review the information and make sure that the employees have assimilated everything.

Formal training on such things as machinery, equipment, safety, and company-specific software needs to take place immediately after the orientation period so that new employees can begin to perform the functions for which they were hired. Many companies assign a new employee, as an apprentice, to someone in the same position. For example, a new retail clerk may work alongside the company's best clerk so that they can practice procedures and learn how they should treat customers. The experienced clerk gives feedback and encouragement and over time becomes the mentor to whom the new employee can turn if there is a problem.

At the end of the first three months of employment, the new hire will typically experience his or her first performance evaluation with a supervisor. This is an opportunity to review the employee's on-the-job performance and to set goals for the next evaluation period. Some companies consider the first three to six months as a probationary period. If the new hire successfully completes that period, he or she is a full-fledged employee and begins to receive benefits.

There are many effective models for training and evaluating employees. Consulting with an experienced human resources expert will help the small business owner choose the one that is right for his or her company.

LEARNING FROM SUCCESS

Think Small and Hire Slowly

Konstantin Guericke's competitive advantage is that he knows exactly the kind of person to hire for his entrepreneurial company, LinkedIn Corp., based in Palo Alto, California. LinkedIn is a Web networking firm that he cofounded in 2003; it was his fifth start-up. While most entrepreneurs struggle with how to find the right people for their start-ups, Guericke has a profile of the ideal employee and a way to find that employee. He avoids the candidates with big-business experience because they don't know how to deal with a start-up company. They need rules and processes to be happy. Guericke wants people who are linked into current trends, who can respond quickly, and change course on a dime. He wants people who are passionately committed to the company's vision so

that they are willing to work long hours on their own and stand up to the "naysayers." Where does he find these people? He goes to his colleagues and friends as well as the networks of his current employees.

Moving slowly to hire and hiring people who can fit in with the start-up culture is essential to success. Having to fire an employee is costly in terms of severance pay, time, and resources to find a replacement, and perhaps litigation.

Lesson Learned: *Think small and hire slowly.*

Source: J. Mintz, "Don't Think Big, and Other Hiring Tips," *Wall Street Journal Startup Journal*, www.startupjournal.com (accessed June 24, 2005).

INDEPENDENT CONTRACTORS AND EMPLOYEE LEASING

Independent Contractors

Independent contractors own their own businesses and provide products and services to other companies under contract. They work under the control of the person who hires them only as to the result of the work they do and not as to the means by which that result is accomplished. When Marcel Ford of Botanical Science created his now successful silk plant cleaner, he hired an independent chemist and a packager to handle the design and manufacturing of the product. This helped him to get to market faster and at a lower cost.

Independent contractors are usually specialists in their fields; in other words, they focus on their core competency. Because the independent contractor pays his or her own withholding taxes, Social Security, Medicare, unemployment, and workers' compensation insurance, the cost of hiring an independent contractor is often less than that of hiring an employee. These benefits can amount to as much as 32 percent or more of the base salary or wage. Thus, an employee might cost the entrepreneur $52,800, including the above-mentioned benefits, whereas an independent contractor might cost only $40,000 to $45,000.

Business owners do need to be careful when employing independent contractors. If the IRS rules regulating classification of workers as independent contractors are not followed, an employer can be held liable for all back taxes plus penalties and interest, which can result in a substantial sum, as much as 12 to 35 percent of the total tax bill. Therefore, employers using independent contractors should always consult an attorney, draw up a contract with each independent contractor that specifies that the contractor will not be treated as an employee for state and federal tax purposes, and verify that the independent contractor carries his or her own workers' compensation insurance and the necessary licenses to conduct business.

There are, however, some protections for business owners who use independent contractors. Under the Safe Harbor law of the Revenue Act of 1978, companies cannot be held liable for employment taxes arising from an employment relationship if they

- Had a reasonable basis for treating the person as an independent contractor. A reasonable basis is normally a judicial precedent, such as an IRS audit or letter stating that this person is an independent contractor, or a long-standing industry precedent, as in the case of real estate salespeople.
- Has filed required returns with the federal government.
- Has not classified an employee with the same duties the independent contractor performs.

If the company does not pass these requirements, the IRS can choose to apply the more specific 20-point test for classifying workers as employees (see Table 10.2). Even if all the IRS rules are followed, however, there is no guarantee that the IRS won't challenge the company's position. The 20-point test is not part of the tax code, so the IRS is not required to use it in making its assessments. Therefore, it is important to document the relationship with an independent contractor through a legal agreement that explicitly demonstrates that the independent contractor owns his or her own business.

TABLE 10.2   The IRS 20-Point Test for Independent Contractors

An individual is considered an employee if he or she
1. Must follow company instructions about where, when, and how to carry out the work.
2. Is trained by the company.
3. Provides services that are integrated into the business.
4. Provides services that must be rendered personally.
5. Cannot hire, supervise, and pay his or her own assistants.
6. Has a continuing relationship with the company.
7. Must follow set hours of work.
8. Works full time for a company.
9. Does the work on the company's premises.
10. Must do the work in a sequence set by the company.
11. Must submit regular reports to the company.
12. Is paid regularly for time worked, by the hour, week, or month.
13. Receives reimbursements for job-related expenses.
14. Relies on the tools and materials of the company.
15. Has no major investment in facilities and resources to perform the service.
16. Cannot make a profit or suffer a loss through the provision of these services.
17. Works for one company at a time.
18. Does not offer his or her services to the general public on a regular basis.
19. Can be fired at will by the company for reasons other than failure to produce specified results.
20. May quit work at any time without incurring liability.

Employee Leasing

Leasing employees is a growing trend among companies that are trying to better manage the most expensive item in their budgets. It is quite different from using temporary services in that employee-management firms actually hire the company's staff and lease them back to the company. So the entrepreneur in effect hires the employees and then leases those same people back from the management company. The management company then handles payroll, files taxes, deals with insurance, and takes care of other human resource issues for a percentage of the total payroll. This saves the growing company time and money and usually provides the employees with broader benefits and less expensive healthcare premiums.

Several issues should be considered before signing a contract with an employee-leasing company:

- The firm should be licensed if that is required by the state in which it does business.

- Some firms are fully indemnified by large insurance companies to fund their benefits programs, whereas others are self-funded. The latter should maintain 15 percent of total premiums in reserve.

- It is important to check the banking track record of the firm to ensure that employees will receive their pay on time.

- Current and former clients should be contacted to determine how successfully the employee-management firm conducted business and fulfilled the requirements of the contract.
- The management firm should have a broad range of insurance options.
- The leasing firm should supply the company with regular reports.

In contrast to leasing firms, temporary agencies send their own employees into the company on a temporary basis. Temporary agencies are another excellent source of personnel, particularly in instances where they are only needed for a season or a specific event.

COMPENSATION FOR EXECUTIVES

In companies large and small, the issue of executive compensation is receiving a lot of attention from politicians—who see it as a way to use an "us against them" tactic to their political benefit—and the press, which seems to like to portray business as the enemy. But for growing entrepreneurial companies, deciding how to compensate the founding team and any hired management is a dilemma with no guidelines. An *Inc.* magazine poll of its list of the 500 fastest-growing private companies found that the needs of the company were a significant factor in determining how much the CEO got paid and that 39 percent of respondents believed their pay was below market average. It also found that 71 percent of the CEOs used a pay-for-performance link and 66 percent noted that bonuses made up a significant portion of their pay.

Executive compensation packages can consist of a varied combination of salary, stock, and bonus components. Consequently, the mix of these elements can have a critical impact on both the executive's accumulation of wealth and the company's profitability. Following are examples of some of these components.

Base Salary

Base salary is that part of the compensation package that is relatively "fixed"; that is, it does not vary with the performance of the company. Two trends are occurring with regard to base salaries. First, companies are starting to flatten their salary structures to permit broader ranges of base salary at every level to account for differences in performance. Second, the time between salary adjustments is increasing and the amount of change is decreasing relative to nonfixed or variable salary components. In start-up companies, the CEO/entrepreneur typically takes almost 80 percent of his or her total compensation in base salary. This is because the company can't afford the benefits and perquisites much larger companies offer.

Short-Term Incentives

Short-term incentives are given for a period of one year or less, usually on an annual basis, and are paid in cash although they may include stock. Deciding who receives these incentives may depend on the company's reaching a target level of performance toward a goal, be based on a formula-driven share of a bonus pool based on financial results, or be determined purely at the discretion of the owners. This last approach is not uncommon in young entrepreneurial firms whose performance has not yet achieved any level of predictability.

Long-Term Incentives

Long-term incentives are based on performance for a period longer than a year and usually consist of stock appreciation grants, restricted stock or cash grants, and performance grants. Of these, the most common is stock options because they are an unbiased method of linking executive rewards and shareholder returns.

Stock Appreciation Grants Stock appreciation grants are based on future appreciation of the company's stock. They consist of stock options, the right to purchase shares of the company's stock at a fixed price for a specified period of time; stock appreciation rights, the right to receive direct payment for the option's appreciation during the term without actually exercising the option; and stock purchases, which permit the purchase of stock at a discount under either fair market value or full value and sometimes with financial aid from the company.

Restricted Stock or Cash Grants With new laws requiring that stock options will now have to show up on the books as an expense, more companies are looking at restricted stock. Unlike stock options, which give employees the right to purchase the stock at a set price after it has potentially appreciated, restricted stock gives the employees the stock outright, but puts performance or tenure with the company as a restriction on the right to sell the stock and risk of forfeiture until the required employment tenure has been reached. It is estimated that as of 2004, about 61 percent of public companies were still using stock options.[4]

Performance Grants Performance grants are grants or rights to receive stock, whose value is based on the company's long-term performance or a specified formula, or the right to receive dividend equivalents paid on a specified number of company shares. An attorney and an accountant conversant in these types of incentives should be consulted for advice on the best plan for a particular type of business and its stage in the life cycle.

Benefits and Perquisites

Typically, benefits such as a health plan and an IRA and perquisites such as a car or a club membership amount to approximately one-third of the compensation package. In addition, many executives are seeking such things as "change-in-control severance agreements," often called "golden parachutes," and SERPs, special executive retirement plans whose pensions use a more generous formula than that used for other employees. These "perks" are generally prone to much scrutiny by people within the organization as well as by the government and are difficult to justify. Again, seeking expert counsel before implementing any of these highly scrutinized benefit plans is encouraged.

Paying the Owner/Manager

In a new venture, the owner/manager often does not take a salary until the company is producing a positive cash flow. The reality is that they need to ensure that employees are paid first as well as other fixed expenses. When it does come time to pay themselves, most owner/managers cite "company needs" as very important in their decisions about how much to pay themselves. But there are other resources that can help entrepreneurs make this crucial decision:

- Published industry surveys by agencies and trade associations
- Executive search firms
- CEO roundtables—these are peer groups usually in companies of about the same size
- Trade magazines and the popular press
- Public company annual reports
- Industry consultants
- Compensation specialists
- Classified ads
- The American Compensation Association

COMPENSATION FOR EMPLOYEES

It has always been the fate of growing entrepreneurial companies to have to do what large, established companies do but with better quality and far fewer resources. Despite limited resources, if they want to continue to grow, companies need to hire the best people they can get and offer them a competitive wage and benefits package. Today, employees are no longer simply an expense for the company; they are an asset that must be cultivated and maintained. The statistics today tell a challenging story. In the 1970s, the labor force grew at about 2.6 percent annually. In 2005 it slipped to 1.1 percent, and the future does not look bright. The Bureau of Labor Statistics predicts that this growth rate will shrink to 0.2 percent by 2015 when the baby boomers retire and fewer young workers are available to take their place.[5] As a result, the emphasis today is on employee retention and loyalty, and employers are looking at more than bonuses and incentives; they are offering lifestyle benefits such as flex-time, career development, and training.

The issue of compensation is central to the concerns of the employee in choosing to work for a particular company; likewise, for the employer, employee wages directly affect the cost of doing business. Before making microdecisions such as how much to pay for a particular position, it is important to gather some key information that will help create an overall compensation strategy for the company. Some key questions to answer include the following:

1. What are others in the industry paying for the same position? To accurately assess this issue, you should compare total compensation costs per individual employee (including taxes and benefits) and per total number of employees, as well as the return on profit and sales for each dollar spent on labor.

2. What is the supply and demand for employees in the industry, in particular those with the specific skills that the company needs?

3. What responses or outcomes are being rewarded? What is the employee expected to achieve for this compensation?

4. What is the company's cost and profit structure? How much is available for compensation packages?

5. What is the typical turnover rate for employees in this industry? (High turnover means higher costs for training.)

6. What type of training can the company provide? Can training be done on the job? Do we have to hire someone to do it?

7. What is the potential for growth and promotion within the company's structure? Are there opportunities for employees to move up and expand their skill base?

8. What is the value of the pay level to employees? What do employees perceive their pay should be for a particular position?

9. To what types of rewards do employees in these positions respond? Besides money, what other types of rewards do employees expect?

By answering these questions, the company is more likely to formulate a compensation policy that is realistic for the industry and the employees who work in it.

In general, pay comes in two types: cash and benefits. It has been reported that in the United States, 70 percent of pay comes in the form of cash, with the rest in deferred cash benefits such as healthcare, IRAs, and paid vacation.[6] Total labor costs will usually determine whether a company can afford to locate in a particular country or in a particular region of the United States. As productivity increases and more companies learn to work smart, however, labor costs as a percentage of total costs will decline.

Timing of pay and promotion is also part of the compensation strategy. Some companies prefer to bring employees in at a fairly low wage but allow for significant growth over a period of time, whereas other companies hire people at an above-average rate but take much longer to promote and raise pay. The mix of compensation is also an important consideration. Many companies offer a base salary plus a portion of the compensation that is "at risk"—that is, based on team or organization performance.

Compensation and Company Life Cycle

The work of L. R. Gomez-Mejia and D. B. Balkin provides some of the first evidence that choosing pay systems that match corporate strategies and objectives translates into better performance.[7] If companies go through a fairly predictable process of birth, growth, maturity, and decline, it makes sense that each of these stages calls for a different compensation strategy. For example, pay based on outcome (performance) is very suitable for the growth period when the upside potential is high, but a stable salary might better reflect a more mature company where gains are small. It has also been suggested that companies with unrelated products or a single product pose more risk than a company with a platform of related products.[8] Consequently, the riskier scenario with the higher upside potential calls for outcome-based pay and a more decentralized approach to management.

Research has also found that money incentives are associated with the largest average increase in productivity. Greater emphasis on short-term bonuses and long-term incentives based on base pay for middle- and upper-level management is correlated with higher profitability. Profit sharing has also been shown to be associated with higher productivity, but this should not be construed as a cause-and-effect relationship.[9] Similarly, employee stock ownership plans (ESOPs) appear to give positive results, but again no causal relationship has been established.[10]

Much attention has been paid to gainsharing and the positive results obtained from its use. This is generally attributed to the fact that employees can clearly see a relationship between what they do and what they receive. With a global economy now affecting virtually every business, it will be important for entrepreneurial companies to understand how compensation strategies in the United States may have to be modified to achieve the same results in another country. One example is the high need for risk avoidance in countries such as Japan, South Korea, and Taiwan, which may preclude the use of outcome-based pay that has been so successful in the United States.

Noncash Benefits

Many growing entrepreneurial companies cannot offer complex compensation packages that require a lot of cash outlay, but they can offer other benefits. One of those benefits is stock, which was discussed in the section "Compensation for Executives." Equity compensation gives employees a stake in the company, and the philosophy is that they will work harder and with higher quality if they know that what they do affects the stock value.

People stay with organizations primarily because of the nonfinancial aspects of the business, such as culture and work environment. Consequently, more companies are turning to nonmonetary recognition awards. Mercer HR consulting found that 72 percent of companies responding to one of their surveys employ nonmonetary recognition awards.[11] For example, Mary Naylor's company, VIPdesk, actually creates "experience-driven" rewards for its clients to use with their employees. Clients treat their employees to personal chef services, makeovers, and even surfing lessons. The explanation is that cash bonuses tend to engender a sense of entitlement. The bonus becomes part of the expected pay instead of being a reward for performance as it was originally intended to be.

One noncash benefit that fits this category is flextime, which is a popular approach for employees who don't need to work full time and want more control over their time. One employee may work from 8:00 a.m. to 12:00 p.m., and another comes in from 12:00 p.m. to 4:00 p.m. Flextime also allows employees to take work home and communicate with the company via fax and Internet. The benefits of flextime to the company are several. It tends to create a more positive work environment, one that meets the employee's individual needs. It increases employee productivity and empowerment, which also results in lower turnover. To successfully implement a flextime program, it is important to develop a detailed policy that spells out the company's expectations and reflects input from the employees.

Entrepreneurs with small, growing companies and limited resources need to think creatively about how to provide noncash incentives until the business is in a position to add cash incentives to the mix. See Table 10.3 for examples of noncash benefits.

Noncash benefits include intrinsic rewards, which are those rewards that come from the work itself such as job satisfaction or the fulfillment that comes with knowing that everyone is committed to a single cause—in this case, the success of the business. The problem is that once the business experiences success, entrepreneurs tend to forget that the people who they hire need to feel that entrepreneurial spirit. It is important that entrepreneurs remember that extrinsic rewards lose their motivational effect fairly quickly. When employees are asked about what makes them happy on the job, the responses usually focus on intrinsic values, the desire to be a significant contributor to the company's success.

It is also vital that small business owners make sure that employees *understand* the incentive system. One way to do that is to get employees involved in designing the plan, which will result in more meaningful incentives. Incentive goals should be changed annually to keep the momentum going, but they should not be changed without warning.[12]

TABLE 10.3   Some Typical Employee Noncash Benefits

- Employee discounts
- Paid vacations and legal holidays
- Automobile or a specified allotment for an automobile
- Travel expenses
- Retention by employee of frequent-flyer mileage
- Housing support
- Moving expenses
- Reduced-cost food service at work
- Recreation facilities or memberships
- Education for employees and employees' children
- Workshops and seminars for employee development

Health Plans

The average total benefit costs per active employee for all industries in 2004 was $6,679, a 7.5 percent increase over the previous year but the smallest increase since 1999.[13] Still, the trend is for companies to offer health maintenance organizations and preferred provider organizations as a cost-containment measure, as well as increasing deductibles that employees pay out of pocket.

Some firms have chosen a self-funded health plan in an effort to reduce healthcare costs. Mark Brier of Boar's Head Meats, a Virginia-based company, saw his costs soaring but the benefits remaining the same or declining. "We weren't happy with the way the provider was paying the claims . . . We were paying more and getting less. We had to do something."[14] In fact, the federal Pension and Welfare Benefits Administration estimates that four of every ten U.S. companies that offer health insurance self-fund, and the Society of Professional Benefit Administrators found that 65 percent of employers with fewer than 100 employees are self-funding. Most self-insurers set aside an amount in their budgets based on past claims and then they purchase indemnity insurance to limit exposure above that amount. These indemnity policies, called stop-loss or reinsurance, protect against higher-than-predicted individual claims and catastrophic group expenses. Companies considering self-funding should have at least fifty employees and be comfortable with the volatility of this type of plan.

Many small businesses are using their combined strength through trade associations to provide health coverage at a lower cost. This is an effective way to increase a company's clout when negotiating for healthcare premiums.

Pension Plan Options

In the United States, retirement income traditionally has been viewed as a three-part system consisting of Social Security, pension plans, and retirement savings. One of the many reasons this system has failed is that so many employees have no pension plans from their employers. Only a small percentage of small companies provide such plans because the options are limited and the administrative costs are high. Following are some examples of the options.

Help *Others* Learn from Your Mistakes

John Osher is that rare combination of inventor and entrepreneur. The creator of hundreds of consumer products and several companies, he also founded Cap Toys, which he built to $125 million in annual sales and then sold to Hasbro Inc. in 1997. After selling the business, he decided to list all the mistakes that he had made along the way so that he could avoid them the next time; he came up with seventeen of them, which he often shares with students when he gets the opportunity to speak. Three of the less obvious mistakes are

1. Hiring too many people and spending too much on office space. Don't spend money on things that don't generate revenue and hire as few people as possible.

2. Neglecting to manage the entire company as a whole. Too many entrepreneurs focus on 5 percent of the business and never see the big picture.

3. Seeking confirmation of your actions rather than seeking the truth. Look beyond family and friends for feedback.

Osher learned from his mistakes and went on to create Dr. John's SpinBrush, a $5 electric toothbrush that became the best-selling toothbrush in America and enticed Procter & Gamble to purchase that company for $475 million.

Lesson Learned: *Learn from your mistakes!*

Source: M. Henricks, "What Not to Do," *Entrepreneur.com* (February 2004), www.entrepreneur.com.

401(K) Plans These are very beneficial to employees because they not only allow employees to contribute tax-free dollars to the plan but also allow the employer to contribute as well. Small companies have avoided this benefit because of the high administrative costs, approximately $73 per employee; however, because the tax benefits go to the employee, the employer can choose to pass this administrative cost on to the employee.

Simplified Employee Pension Plans Simplified employee pension plans (SEPs) benefit small business owners with twenty-five or fewer employees who can't afford the more traditional plans. The small business owner sets up the plan through a financial institution and makes tax-deductible contributions to the employee's annuity account. As of 2005, these contributions may amount to as much as 25 percent of the employee's compensation or $42,000, whichever is less. The employer can then deduct these contributions as expenses. Eligible employees must have worked for the company for at least three of the previous five years.

THE LEGAL CONTEXT OF HUMAN RESOURCE MANAGEMENT

A significant portion of the already skyrocketing cost of employees is the result of legislation and regulation by the government. In addition to the cost of compliance, there is the confusion of multiple sources of regulation. Laws related to employment originate in the U.S. Supreme Court, Congress, the Immigration and Naturalization Service, the Department of Labor, and the National Labor Relations Board, in addition to state and local agencies and courts. Often both federal and state laws will apply to a given situation. The remainder of this section discusses some of the various laws that affect the management of workers in a company setting, including laws affecting compensation, safety, and liability.

Laws Affecting Compensation

The laws pertaining to the recruiting and hiring of employees were discussed in the first section of the chapter. Every company should be aware of the major laws that affect how employees are paid. They include the fact that employees have the right to bargain collectively for wages, benefits, and working conditions (National Labor Relations Act of 1935); employees must receive time-and-a-half for all hours worked in excess of forty per week (Walsh-Healy Act of 1936); and all employers must pay men and women the same wage for the same work (that is, skill, responsibility, and effort) (Equal Pay Act of 1963).

Laws Affecting Safety

No one would disagree that safety in the workplace is an important issue, and recently the trend has been toward more and more costly regulation. Two major areas of safety regulation are the rules under OSHA and workers' compensation.

LEARNING FROM THE IRS

The IRS and Executive Pay

It is not unheard of for companies today to receive a notice from the IRS under Section 162(a)(1) of the Internal Revenue Code claiming that an executive's salary is unreasonably high and demanding the company pay back taxes on the amount that the IRS claims should have been declared as taxable profit. The IRS has no authority to dictate what a company can pay its employees, but it can state what it believes to be reasonable as a business expense. Generally, the IRS targets smaller companies that can more easily manipulate income, often by using family members as employees. Reasonableness of pay is subject to several criteria:

1. Qualifications in terms of education and experience in the industry.

2. Nature and scope of work.

3. Size and complexity of the business.

4. Economic conditions: If the company is successful despite a weak economy, this is attributable to the leadership of the entrepreneur and can reasonably call for greater compensation.

5. Salaries versus payments to stockholders: If the company does not pay dividends, it sends up a red flag to the IRS that perhaps a portion of the tax-deductible salary is really dividends.

6. Financial condition: The company needs to show that it grew substantially while the highly paid management team was leading it.

7. Comparable pay: The pay should be similar to that of other companies at the same level in the industry.

8. Arm's-length dealings: Would an independent investor approve the pay?

TABLE 10.4	Staying on the Right Side of OSHA and Workers' Compensation

- Develop a safety program with the input and commitment of everyone.
- Get employees back to work as soon as possible after an injury.
- Increase job satisfaction and commitment to the company. Happy employees translate into fewer claims.
- Pay premiums only on straight time (not overtime or vacation time).
- Check the rate categories for all employees carefully.
- Have the company pay the smaller claims itself.
- If the company has a higher-than-average safety record, ask for a discount in premium.
- Check insurance records carefully, especially for claims from people who don't currently work for the company or haven't for a long period of time.
- Shop around for the best rates and don't be afraid to change agents midstream.
- Take care of injuries quickly.
- Help employees understand that high premiums mean lower profits and less money in their pockets.

OSHA The issue of a safe and healthy work environment is the purview of the **Occupational Safety and Health Act** (OSHA) of 1970 and its administrative unit. OSHA requires that employers eliminate hazardous areas in the workplace and maintain health and safety records on all employees. OSHA inspectors regularly target companies in which certain hazards are inherent in the nature of the business, such as asbestos. They conduct rigorous inspections, liberally dispensing fines and penalties where violations have occurred. Table 10.4 offers several tips to help a company avoid high premiums and the stress of OSHA audits.

Workers' Compensation Workers' compensation is another significant safety-related expense, so much so that some companies have made location decisions based on the cost of workers' compensation in a particular state. Workers' compensation insurance is a no-fault system under which workers receive guaranteed compensation for injury at work and employers are protected from unlimited liability by covering the cost of the premiums. The insurance has three components: The first covers medical bills and lost wages for the employee; the second covers the owner should the spouse or children of a permanently disabled worker decide to sue; and the third is employment practices liability, which insures against lawsuits arising from claims for such things as sexual harassment and discrimination. The cost of worker accidents and false claims has threatened the life of many a business. To further exacerbate the situation, premium rates, which are based on the type of business that the company is and its accident history, vary from state to state, resulting in some states having a competitive advantage over others in certain industries. Among the fastest-growing and most vexing claims are those for repetitive-motion injury, such as carpal tunnel syndrome, and stress-related disabilities, although the most popular claim is for back injury.

Laws Related to Liability

Another rapidly growing area of legislation and consequent cost to growing companies is liability for violating employee rights. Today, a company may be held liable and be sued for damages for a long list of acts that range from race and sex discrimination (Civil Rights Act, 1993) and age discrimination (ADEA, 1993) to record-keeping violations (Immigration Reform and Control Act, 1993).[15] Not only are these suits expensive to defend, but if the company is found in violation, it also potentially faces catastrophic damage awards.

Family and Medical Leave Act

The Family and Medical Leave Act, which applies to companies with fifty or more employees, allows workers to take up to twelve weeks of unpaid leave each year to care for family members or to deal with serious medical problems. Physicians, chiropractors, podiatrists, midwives, clinical social workers, and many other caregivers may certify serious medical problems. To qualify for this benefit, an employee must have worked for the employer for twelve months for at least 1250 hours. Payment of health insurance premiums continues during the leave. If an employer believes medical certification is suspect, it can ask for a second opinion.

Religious Bias

Companies that require a worker to be on the job on a religious holiday can be found to be in violation of Title VII of the Civil Rights Act of 1964, which prohibits discrimination based on religion. The regulations regarding this issue come under the purview of the EEOC, which requires that employers reasonably accommodate their workers' religious practices as long as doing so doesn't pose an undue hardship on the company. Unfortunately, there is no clear definition of "reasonable accommodation," and because of the wide variety of religious practices, the issue of accommodation is handled on a case-by-case basis.

Sexual Harassment

The rulings regarding unwanted sexual advances and harassment on the job began to get very tough in the 1980s. The courts have expanded the definition of sexual harassment, and businesses are now developing policies in an effort to ward off embarrassing and expensive lawsuits. The EEOC reports that sexual harassment complaints grew from 4400 in 1986 to 5600 in 1990. In its first ruling on the subject, the Supreme Court held that sexual harassment violates Title VII of the 1964 Civil Rights Act when the act is unwelcome and represents an abuse of power in the workplace. Generally, harassment can be divided into two categories: quid pro quo, where advancement on the job or a raise is conditional on certain sexual favors, and hostile working environment cases, where the employee is subjected to a sexually offensive environment against his or her will. Harassment includes but is not limited to verbal and nonverbal assaults of a sexual nature and physical harassment. As a result, business owners should establish policies that educate and make clear to employees what conduct is not acceptable in the workplace. In doing so, entrepreneurs can solicit guidance from the EEOC.

Protecting the Company Against Lawsuits

Fighting a lawsuit by an angry employee is a costly expense for any company but especially for a growing, small business with limited resources. The problem is that employees can sue without putting up any money because they typically seek out attorneys who work on a contingency basis and may collect more than 50 percent of the award if they win. If they lose, there is no cost to the client. Consequently, it is a win–win situation for the employee. Also, unaware entrepreneurs, who are focusing on acquiring customers and meeting market demands, often forget to carefully document issues related to employment and are shocked at how seriously a disgruntled employee can hurt their already struggling business. A little effort on the front end can prevent costly litigation on the back end. Small business owners can do several things to at least minimize the chances of being sued:

1. *Be very careful about who is hired.* All expectations should be spelled out before the person is hired and documented for future reference. Every effort should be made to accurately assess the person's character and trustworthiness, and references should be carefully checked.

2. *Keep a file on each employee.* The file should contain documentation of all events of importance in terms of promotion, raises, training, performance evaluations, and potential for termination, written in a style that is factual and suitable as evidence in a court of law. It is also wise to have more than one person contribute to this file.

3. *Always put in writing any communications with an employee regarding performance.* The dates on which any violations of expectations occurred and the specific nature of those violations should be stated very clearly. It is important to obtain written confirmation of receipt from the employee.

4. *Before terminating any employee, seek counsel from an attorney.* An attorney experienced in labor law can check the company's documentation for potential problems or openings for the employee to sue.

INTERNATIONAL HUMAN RESOURCE MANAGEMENT

The global marketplace has increased the possibility that a growing company will ultimately have facilities and do significant business on a worldwide basis. This presents new dilemmas for companies whose only experience has been managing employees within the borders of the United States. It is widely believed that international human resource management (IHRM) is more difficult than domestic HRM because of macro-environmental factors such as cultural, socioeconomic, institutional, and political elements, which differ in nearly every country.

Research on IHRM is flourishing as more and more companies report their experiences in terms of (1) issues that employees face when transferring overseas, (2) the IHRM function and activities, (3) the many factors that influence IHRM, and (4) IHRM in individual countries. It is believed that firms intending to operate internationally need to understand and diagnose the contexts in which they will function so that they can integrate their domestic and international operations. When it comes to finding employees for overseas operations, companies seem to take three approaches:[16]

1. Find potential employees based on who is available or who volunteers.

2. Use local professionals knowledgeable about the market to locate the appropriate personnel.

3. Use transferees—that is, those from the domestic side of the company who have cross-cultural skills.

Using locals for the bulk of personnel needs is usually a wise decision, particularly in marketing, as it is difficult for someone who has not lived in a culture for a long time to truly understand the nuances of communication in that culture. Unfortunately, many firms do not pay attention to that advice.

Some firms are making the effort to develop their employees for careers in the international arena by providing training and skills needed to function effectively in a particular cultural environment. However, attempts to transplant in whole or in part U.S.-type HRM programs such as employee empowerment and performance evaluation based on merit will often meet with failure because of tremendous cultural differences. Where the goals of the firm may remain intact on a global level, implementation of those goals will probably see variation country by country. Check the resources at the end of this chapter for more information on global HRM.

The issue of how to maintain some sense of company vision and goals when operating in diverse environments will be a challenge for a long time to come. Perhaps it will be in the global arena that HRM, the management of the human assets of the company, will finally become a significant partner in the company's strategic planning.

ISSUES FOR REVIEW AND DISCUSSION

1. List three key items that should be part of any job description.

2. What are some questions that should never be asked of interviewees?

3. What are the various possible components of an executive compensation package? How does the IRS view executive pay?

4. Describe three noncash benefits used as employee incentives.

5. Discuss three of the many regulations affecting workers and employers in the workplace.

EXPERIENCING ENTREPRENEURSHIP

1. You are starting a restaurant business and need to create a compensation policy. List and gather the information that you will need to do this. Then arrange to talk to a restaurant owner about his or her compensation policy to compare the results.

2. Find a company that is doing business internationally and ask how its HRM policy has changed to accommodate the cultural differences in other countries.

3. Interview the CEO of a growing company about how she or he handles executive compensation. In particular, how did the founder(s) decide to pay himself or herself?

LEARNING FROM ENTREPRENEURS, CASE 10.2

Management Is the Name of the Game

Ann Deters is not your typical entrepreneur. In fact, she is not your typical woman. As the 47-year-old CEO of Vantage Technology (an *Inc.* magazine 500 company that markets mobile cataract-surgery equipment), the founder of SevenD & Associates (a chain of outpatient-surgery centers), and the mother of five children (the youngest is 3 years old), she is the epitome of effective management. "I was always determined to be a hard-driven career woman," she claims. But successfully managing her life was not always easy.

Down on the Farm

Born in a rural community in Illinois, Deters seemed destined to embrace entrepreneurship. Her grandfather had started a seed company, which her father and his brothers successfully grew. Then her father took some of the profits from that company and put them into an investment firm that would provide venture capital for family members who wanted to start businesses. As a teenager, Deters sat on several boards of her family's companies, but then in her twenties, she left the farm to take a position as a CPA with PricewaterhouseCoopers in St. Louis, determined never to move back to her tiny home town. However, her high school sweetheart, a hog and grain farmer turned businessman, had other plans for Deters and eventually managed to entice her to come back to Effingham and marry him. Then her father, who now felt comfortable that she understood business, offered her a job at his company, J. M. Schultz Investment Co., which oversaw four companies.

Meanwhile, Deter's husband, Dennis, was working at another of the four companies, Vantage, where three years later Deter was to become the CEO. The husband-and-wife team was working day and night while trying to fit the business into their children's schedules. Soon it became clear that it wasn't working—there was no balance.

The Companies

Vantage Technology is a cataract-surgery outsourcing firm that now services over 100 healthcare facilities in 16 states. For many years, hospitals had been looking for ways to make money on cataract surgery, and

Vantage saw that as an opportunity to help them provide this capability without a huge capital investment. Hospitals pick the day(s) each month on which they wish to perform cataract surgery; then the Vantage surgical coordinator arrives at the hospital with the equipment, sets it up, oversees the equipment during surgery, and assists in operating room cleanup. In this way, the hospital enjoys a revenue stream of several hundred dollars per procedure without incurring the ongoing expense of equipment and upgrades.

Vantage was launched in 1990 as a way to provide a cost-effective surgery option to rural hospitals and to help seniors access community hospital services. Over more than a decade it evolved into a turnkey service for cataract surgery in rural and metropolitan hospitals and included training on how to launch an ophthalmic surgery unit, upgrade existing equipment, and improve operating room efficiency. The company works with ophthalmologists and optometrists to help them improve their programs by giving them the advantage of volume purchasing power and targeted marketing programs.

SevenD & Associates, the second of Deter's companies, provides surgical management to closely held ambulatory surgery centers. Its services extend from feasibility analysis of a surgical center, to potential location assessment, to business planning of the financial aspects of the center, to designing and building the center and then handling licensing and certification, procurement, and staffing. In other words, they provide the physician/owner with a turnkey operation. Deters is uniquely qualified to offer this range of services because as a CPA she gained years of experience in doing feasibility analysis to determine if the concept for a surgery center made market and financial sense. Her experience as a construction executive prepared her to manage the design, planning, and building phases of a surgical center. As a bank director, she made important contacts that would smooth the path for the development. Finally, she had extensive management experience. The turnkey approach was very attractive to physicians who wanted to focus on their patients and not worry about running the business. Furthermore, history has shown that successfully building and operating a surgery center is a very risky endeavor, so Vantage removes much of that risk for the physician.

Managing Chaos

By 1993 Deter knew that it was time to hire a management team to cover all the critical areas of the business including the role of president. She also hired an operations manager and a sales manager. Then she began delegating to others many of the responsibilities that she had previously insisted on doing herself. Her husband stopped traveling and settled into a position overseeing the company's sales representatives, and Deter even dropped off of several community boards so that she was home in the evenings with her children. Accomplishing these changes did not happen quickly because the company was growing rapidly and the couple found that they needed to devote eight hours a day to the business to ensure its success. In fact, achieving balance took about eight years and a lot of trial and error. The key for Deter was hiring peo-

ple whom she could trust. Moreover, she needed to have help with the children and her home. Although she would be letting go of many activities to lead a more balanced life, she wondered if she was merely trading one task for another because now she had to manage the people who were replacing her. How to do that effectively was a real concern.

Advising the Entrepreneur

1. How would you advise Deters to effectively take care of two businesses and a family while attempting to lead a more balanced life?

2. Are there synergies between the two businesses that could be leveraged?

Sources: SevenD & Associates, http://www.7d.bz/; "Focus on SevenD & Associates," *Outlook* (Summer 2003), www.ooss.org. http://www.vantage-technology.com/our_company.html; D. Fenn, "The Fully Managed Family," *Inc.* (October 2002), www.inc.com.

Marketing for Growth

CHAPTER 11

Conducting Market Research in a Global Environment

It is the new and different that is always most vulnerable to market research.

Malcolm Gladwell, *Blink: The Power of Thinking without Thinking* (2005)

▶ LEARNING OUTCOMES

- Characterize the target market.
- Describe the entrepreneurial market research process.
- Discuss the nature of a customer profile.
- Explain how to gather competitive intelligence.

Cleaning Up!

Sometimes the best opportunities are born when astute entrepreneurs take a fresh look at a commodity product. Howard Schultz, the founder of Starbucks, did just that with coffee. Adam Lowry and Eric Ryan took an out-of-the-box look at the household cleaners market and launched Method products, which manufactures and distributes uniquely packaged, naturally derived, biodegradable cleaning products. After only five years in business, Method products is generating annual revenues of $40 million on 100 products.

Lowry and Ryan were best friends in high school in Detroit and reconnected several years later when they shared an apartment in San Francisco. One day they challenged themselves to identify the most commonplace products in the market and then figure out a way to give them new appeal. Lowry had graduated with a chemical engineering degree and had worked as a researcher at a "green" plastics company in Michigan, then as a climate-change researcher, and finally as a member of the U.S. sailing training team for the 2000 Summer Olympics. Ryan had experience in style and branding. The combination of the partners' backgrounds served to inspire an entrepreneurial venture. "I knew as a chemical engineer that there was no reason we couldn't design products that were non-toxic and used natural ingredients," says Lowry. He also knew that the product would be more expensive, so they would need to also create a high-premium brand to warrant the increase in price.

Product research helped the duo come up with cleaning products for each room of the house that were very different from their more toxic and less exciting competitors' products. Starting with a line of five spray cleaners, they delivered their goods to stores in a pickup truck. From there they added dish soap packaged in a revolutionary design and delivery system, and in 2003, they added hand soap, dilutable floor cleaners, and wipes. In 2004 they included a complete laundry line and two lines of premium candles. Through their market research, they were able to reason that because the major players in domestic cleaning products such as Unilever and Procter & Gamble focused on price to be competitive they were not able to invest in additional active ingredients like fragrance and design. Lowry and Ryan, by contrast, wanted Method products to appeal to the emotions of the customer and make their products more like accessories instead of things to be hidden in a cabinet. That was their niche in the market. Method products sold in stores like Linen 'n Things and Target, and then in August 2005, Lowry and Ryan opened a retail "pop-up shop" near Union Square in San Francisco. (A pop-up shop is a temporary retail space that is used to get people to try the products in a fun environment.) With this shop, they have taken the idea of fashionable cleaning products to one of the most fashionable areas of San Francisco. They even hold weekly happy hours to attract the younger crowd. Everyone is wondering what is next for Method, whose tagline is "People against dirty."

Advising the Entrepreneur

1. How would you advise the Method team about their growth strategy going forward?

2. Are there other commodity products that would be synergistic with their line that they could give the same fashionable treatment?

Sources: "Selling Cool in a Bottle—of Dish Soap," *Business 2.0* (December 2003): 75; "Adam Lowry's Key Move: Taking a Fresh Look at an Old Product Category," *Startup Nation*, www.startupnation.com (accessed June 24, 2005); Method Products, http://www.methodhome.com/ (accessed June 24, 2005); N. Nadaraja, "Method to the Madness," *Home & Garden Articles, SFStation*, www.sfstation.com (accessed June 24, 2005).

arket research is a vital part of any business owner's effort to gain insights into whether there is a need in the market that the company can serve, whether the right product or service is being offered, and whether the correct business model has been chosen. Market research answers several critical questions:[1]

1. Is the business concept viable from a market perspective?
2. What are the major risks and information gaps in this venture, and what information is needed to characterize and minimize these risks?
3. Are the business model and entry strategy likely to succeed?

For example, market research helped Adam Lowry and Eric Ryan find a niche in a market of huge competitors (see Case 11.1). Their research also made them aware of the risks that they faced and the information that they still needed to acquire. Before opening a business, entrepreneurs must know whether there is interest from the market, and if there is, how *much* interest. In other words, is there enough demand to make the venture worth the effort? Do the customers recognize and appreciate the value proposition? Can the product be sold at a price that allows the company to make a reasonable profit?

There is a lot of uncertainty in starting a new business or growing an existing business. Research has identified areas where entrepreneurial information is typically incomplete:

- Risk in the form of financial return to investors[2]
- Complexity, or the number of inputs with which a business must deal[3]
- Ignorance, or that which the entrepreneur doesn't know that he doesn't know[4]
- Indeterminism, or not knowing how an entrepreneur's actions will affect outcomes[5]

One way that entrepreneurs manage this uncertainty is by a systematic process of experimentation and the development of prototype business designs.[6] Analogous to the prototypes that product developers create to perfect their product designs, these prototype business designs help an entrepreneur more effectively test the market and determine which design is most feasible. For example, suppose an entrepreneur was looking to start a business based on a new line of trendy clothing. Instead of conducting broad-based research to determine the best way to launch this business, the entrepreneur could begin by looking at several business designs that might be suitable for this product, including manufacturing and using distributors, selling the clothing via an online retail store, or opening a bricks-and-mortar store. The position on the value chain, asset requirements, labor requirements, critical success factors, potential risks, and key issues are different for each design and therefore provide important information to help the entrepreneur decide the most appropriate design. Each design requires unique sets of information that need to be collected during market research. This chapter looks at how entrepreneurs can conduct effective and efficient market research when deciding to launch a new business or grow an existing business.

Lessons from a Technology Entrepreneur

As a technology entrepreneur and venture capitalist, Darlene Mann can see the mistakes that entrepreneurs make from both perspectives, and she can also identify what it takes to be successful. First and foremost, Mann believes that entrepreneurs need to understand that just because they can conceive and build a product doesn't mean that they can cure a pain in the market. She suggests answering three important questions:

1. Who needs what the entrepreneur wants to sell, and how much of it do they need?

2. How much do customers spend to meet that need today?

3. Will the entrepreneur's product meet the need and save or make the customer a lot of money?

Answering these questions requires a thorough understanding of the customer. Mann recalls when she was director of product marketing at Verity Inc., which produced complex software for search and retrieval. Verity believed that the technicians at their customer companies were highly experienced. As a result, Verity was unconcerned with the level of intricacy of their software. In fact, however, the companies that they served had scarce resources and did not have the people with the required skills to install the software. In the end, Verity had to reengineer its product to make it less complex, which cost Verity a year in entering the market. Mann's success strategies come from real experience and will help any entrepreneur successfully interpret the various needs of customers.

Lesson Learned: *Get the customer involved in the product early.*

Source: D. Mann, "Hitting the Market," *Entreworld.org* (March 2000).

CHARACTERIZING THE TARGET MARKET

The customer, or target market, is that segment of the marketplace that will most likely purchase the product or service. The target customer is not always the end user of the product or service. Consider the simplified example in Figure 11.1. It depicts a manufacturer producing a product that is sold to a distributor, who in turn sells to the end user—the consumer, perhaps, or another business. The manufacturer's customer is the distributor who pays for the goods. The distributor's customer is the consumer, or end user. Even though the manufacturer is not selling directly to the end-user customer, it must know that customer well because that is the customer who is actually using the product and ultimately determines its success or failure. The distributor, on the other hand, is also an important customer of the manufacturer because unless the manufacturer can convince the distributor of the value of the product, the manufacturer does not have an outlet to sell it other than to go direct, which would then put the manufacturer in the retail business. So both the intermediary (the distributor) and the end user are customers of the manufacturer. Throughout this book, we use the term *customer* without differentiating the two types because the strategies and tactics discussed generally apply to both, and it is necessary for any company to establish lifelong, learning relationships with both.

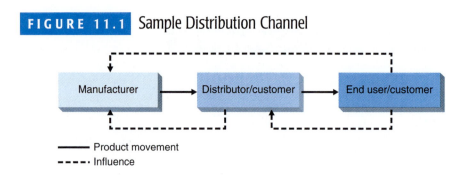

FIGURE 11.1 Sample Distribution Channel

Defining the Customer

Knowing as much as possible about the customer is critical to all of the activities of the business. Mary Naylor of VIPdesk—which offers concierge services, reward programs, and customer-care solutions to brand leaders in the travel, auto, financial services, and retail industries—found that the more she knew about her customers—their habits, likes, and dislikes—the better she was able to meet their needs without expensive mass-marketing techniques that may not have reached the specific customers that she was targeting.

Traditionally, companies have relied on demographic and psychographic studies done by such companies as Mediamark Research, Inc., and the Simmons Market Research Bureau. Demographics include such factors as age, income level, education, and race, whereas psychographics deal with attitudes and intentions, values, and lifestyles. These firms conduct random samples of the population to segment the consumer market in a way that make it easier for companies to determine the size and characteristics of their markets. Market segmentation is a way to divide the target market into groups of customers with similar needs. Markets may be segmented in four basic ways: product or service, geography, psychographics, and demographics.

In some cases, markets are segmented by the bundle of benefits that the product or service provides the customer. Some customers may be looking for the highest quality and convenience and will pay for it, whereas others seek average quality and don't want to pay too much. The category can be further segmented based on how much of the product is purchased—that is, high-volume versus low-volume purchasers—and on how the product will be used.

Entrepreneurs often segment based on the geographic area in which customers are located. This is because customers in different regions have different purchasing habits or desire different features and benefits. Segmentation by geographic area is also used to plan for more efficient distribution, warehousing, and servicing.

Segmenting by psychographics means looking at personality traits, motives, and lifestyles or values. Knowing a common personality trait in a target market, such as propensity to take risks, provides a lot of clues that can be used to develop a marketing plan. Segmenting by demographics is another way to look at the target market. Market research firms can report down to the precise neighborhood what people typically buy, how much they spend, how much they earn, how they live, and what they say they do. Researchers use many demographic factors that affect buying behavior, including ethnicity, region, social class, age, and gender. Some demographic data help identify the likelihood that a person will choose to buy a product.[7] Demographic data also make it possible to segment the target market into subgroups that are different from one another. For example, if the target market is retired people over age 60, their buying habits (such as product requirements and quantity or frequency of purchase) may vary by geographic region or by income level. Finally, census data can be used to arrive at an estimate of how many target customers live within the geographic boundaries of the target market. Then, within any geographic area, those who meet the particular demographic requirements of the product or service can be segmented out.

It is not only consumer markets that are described by demographic data. Business markets can also be described in terms of their size, revenue levels, number of employees, and so forth. Information about business demographics is found at such sites as Economy.com's "The Dismal Scientist" at http://www.economy.com/dismal/ and the Census Bureau at http://www.census.gov.

Entrepreneurial companies know that the first customer is found during the conceptual development of the product or service. In other words, customer acquisition begins before the company even has a product to sell or a service to offer. In this way, when the company is ready to launch the product or service, it benefits from the collaboration of a pool of customers who, having a vested interest in the company because of their participation in the product development, are likely to "spread the word."

ENTREPRENEURIAL MARKET RESEARCH

Had Debra Fine judged the potential for her proposed upscale-toy concept solely by what she was seeing in the newspapers at the time, she would have decided that starting a toy business when major retailers were filing for bankruptcy was not a good idea. Instead, she spent a year researching the market, talking to board members of the American Specialty Toy Retailing Association in Chicago and to parents and discovered that sales at upscale stores were actually trending upward. Had Fine never done comprehensive market research, she may have never decided to purchase an established company that she could improve on. She purchased Small World Toys Inc. and made it a division of her company Small World Kids Inc. As of 2005, the company was valued at $27 million.[8]

Many entrepreneurs figure that they can't afford to do market research, but there are many ways to conduct effective market research without breaking the budget of the new venture. For example, secondary research—research that others have done—is readily available on the Internet and through university libraries. If the entrepreneur's customer is typically online, then using one of the many online survey sites like Zoomerang.com and Surveymonkey.com provides an inexpensive way to conduct surveys and tabulate the results.[9] If customers are not online, then finding a freelance market research consultant can run from $75 to $100 an hour and is much less expensive than hiring a market research firm.

Before conducting any type of market research, however, it is important to prepare for it. There are reasons why this research is being undertaken, and those reasons form the basis for the type of data that will need to be collected. The following questions help bring to surface the underlying rationale for the research.

1. What is the entrepreneur trying to achieve?

2. Whom is the entrepreneur attempting to convince?

3. What does the entrepreneur need to know to make a compelling case for market need?

In the beginning stages of market analysis, companies typically have a fairly loose description of the target market. This description is refined as discussions with potential customers take place during the field research. The key questions that need to be answered are the following:

- Who is the customer?
- What do they typically buy, and how do they hear about it?
- How do they like to buy this type of product or service?
- How often do they buy?
- How can the company best meet the customer's needs?

Most young companies lack the resources for professional marketing services; therefore, entrepreneurs must "pound the pavement" to gather the required data. The research conducted on the target market provides some of the most important data that the entrepreneur needs to decide if he or she is producing a product or service that customers want. The market research process for entrepreneurs differs in four fundamental ways from the research undertaken by large companies: (1) Entrepreneurs' questions about the market are generally broader and more exploratory in nature; (2) entrepreneurs have fewer resources to work with; (3) they are usually on a short timeframe; and (4) they typically have limited experience with their customer.[10] To ensure that useful and correct conclusions are drawn, the research methods that entrepreneurs employ must be sound. In general, a six-step process ensures that the information needed to make the crucial decision to start a business or launch a new product is gathered efficiently and effectively:

1. Develop the business concept and design so as to identify customer, benefit, product/service, distribution, and business model.
2. Assess and prioritize information needs, key assumptions, and unknowns based on the prototype designs.
3. Conduct interviews with opinion leaders and experts in the industry and market.
4. Prepare for market research.
5. Conduct field analysis or primary research with the customer.
6. Organize, analyze, modify, and conduct further research.

Step 1: Design Some Business Prototypes

Entrepreneurs design and prototype a potential business by developing a business concept and a business model. The concept describes the customer, value proposition, product or service being offered, and the channel through which the benefit will be delivered. The business model describes how the business will make money. The business design (concept and business model) is really a hypothesis for how the entrepreneur thinks that the business will be successful. To serve its purpose of reducing the uncertainty associated with a new business, the hypothesis will need to be tested through experimentation and market research.

During the development of the business design, it is important to identify "deal killers" and critical success factors (CSFs). Deal killers are aspects of the business design that could prove fatal to the business—for example, discovering that another company has intellectual property covering a key component in the entrepreneur's product or learning that the property location critical to a restaurant under development has been sold. Unfortunately, deal killers do not always surface until market research reveals them, but it is essential to consider what could make the business design infeasible.

CSFs, by contrast, are the rewards for designing a successful business, and they come in the form of investors, a buyout by a larger company, a big revenue stream, multiple revenue streams, and enhanced business valuation. Understanding what the entrepreneur is betting on is important to defining the success factors that must be in place to achieve the big win.

Step 2: Assess and Prioritize Information Needs

The prototype designs generate information needs that must be prioritized based on their importance to business success. Before collecting market data, determining exactly what must be known about the market is necessary. Will the data demonstrate demand for the product or service? Will they describe the customer? Will they give a sense of trends in the market? Good researchers first decide what they are attempting to accomplish with the research in order to gather the correct type of data. Nothing is more discouraging to a researcher than collecting all the data only to find that a crucial piece of information is missing.

Some of the data collected will help describe the market structure, which includes such things as the number of sellers and their size, whether the market is fragmented or mature, whether it displays sensitivity of demand to change in price, and how many potential buyers there are. An ideal market that investors would like to see might have the following characteristics:

- Over $100 million and growing
- 30 to 35 percent growth rates
- High and durable gross margins of 40 to 50 percent or more
- Relatively low start-up requirements
- Allows for break even in two years or less

The previous points serve as a benchmark against which to judge a market. Not all markets for small businesses have these advantages, but if a proposed business concept falls very short of most or all of them, the entrepreneur may want to reconsider or revise the concept to position it better for success.

Step 3: Conduct Interviews with Opinion Leaders and Industry/Market Experts

The most important information that entrepreneurs gather comes from actually talking with people in the industry who understand the value chain, the markets and the customers. These experts can provide a quick test of feasibility, suggest ways to refine the business concept, and provide guidance on areas of market research that the entrepreneur may not have considered. In addition, they can save the entrepreneur time.

Step 4: Prepare for Market Research

Before conducting market research based on the prioritized information needs that the entrepreneur has developed, it is important to have a plan for market research. This entails first knowing what kind of information can be collected from secondary

TABLE 11.1   Sources of Data on Customers

- **U.S. Bureau of the Census** Provides the ten-year U.S. population census, monthly "Current Population Survey," and "Survey of Income and Program Participation." Census data can be used to look at group demographic data within specific geographic regions and to estimate how many potential customers are within the geographic boundaries of the target market.
- **Community economic development departments** Provide statistics on local population trends and other economic issues, as well as businesses locating in the community.
- **Chambers of Commerce** Offer information on the community in general as well as businesses.
- **Small Business Administration** Provides broad-based information and services for small businesses.
- **Small Business Development Centers** Branches of the Small Business Administration, contain a wealth of information and services for small businesses.
- **Trade associations** Typically keep statistics on their members and their industries; some of this information may be available to the public.
- **Trade journals** Give information on what is happening in an industry: trends, problems, opportunities, and sources of information.
- **Government Printing Office** Provides free-of-charge pamphlets and documents on just about anything that a business owner might want to know.
- **Trade shows** Attending trade shows in your industry is an excellent way to learn who the competition is and to see what the latest trends in the industry and your specific market are.
- **Competitors** Competitors can be a great source of information. Become their customers and study their strategies and how they deal with their customers. Who are their customers and why? What can you provide the customer that they are not providing?

sources and understanding how this will be accomplished. Secondary data should be examined first because they may reveal reasons to either go ahead with or kill a particular product or service concept before primary research is begun. Secondary research may also provide the entrepreneur with the background information necessary to ask more focused questions of experts and customers. The Internet is a good place to start the hunt for secondary research because it contains a wealth of information on industries and specific markets from both government and private sources. Table 11.1 lists some sources on customers in various markets.

Online sources are not the only sources of secondary market data. Most communities have economic development departments or a Chamber of Commerce that keeps statistics on local population trends and other economic issues. Some communities have Small Business Development Centers, branches of the Small Business Administration that offer a wealth of useful information, as well as services, for small and growing businesses. Other sources available in the library include reference books and trade journals on all types of industries (many of these are also available online). Apart from the library, useful information can be obtained from trade associations such as the National Association of Manufacturers, commercial research firms, and financial institutions.

Step 5: Conduct Field Analysis or Primary Research with the Customer

For an entrepreneurial company, no data are more important than those the company itself collects through observation and talking to people. This is called primary data. There is no substitute for talking to customers because information collected from them will be accurate and more current than anything in print. There are two broad types of primary data collection methods: exploratory and confirmatory. Exploratory methods, which include interviews and focus groups, are used to gather a broad understanding of and general insights into the market and customer. Confirmatory methods are used once a comprehensive understanding of the market is achieved and the entrepreneur wants to more precisely validate the findings. They also include interviews and focus groups as well as surveys, choice modeling, and concept testing. Some methods are more effective and less costly than others, and a decision to use one or more of them is usually based on time and money.

Structured Interviews Although more costly and time-consuming than mail or phone surveys, structured interviews have many advantages. Because they are conducted in person, the response rate is high, and they provide more opportunity for clarification and discussion. Furthermore, interviews permit open-ended questions that can lead to more in-depth information, and expert interviews provide an opportunity to network and develop valuable contacts in the market. It is possible to use a combination of surveys, phone calls, and interviews. For example, the company may start with phone surveys to obtain basic information and follow up with interviews with the most useful sources.

Focus Groups One more efficient way to gain valuable information before investing substantial capital in production and marketing is to conduct a focus group. The company brings together a representative sample of potential customers for a presentation and discussion session. If the company is introducing a consumer product, it may choose to present the new product in concert with other products to test the unsolicited response to the product when presented with its competition. For example, if the product is a new type of nonalcoholic beverage, it might be served along with several competitors' beverages in glasses labeled with numbers. Feedback on taste, aftertaste, and so on can then be solicited.

Some products and services do not easily lend themselves to blind studies such as this, especially where there are no direct competitors. In those instances, the product can simply be presented to the focus group and their opinions and feedback solicited. It's important that the person leading the focus group understands group dynamics and can keep the group on track. Often, focus group sessions are videotaped so that the management team can spend more time analyzing the nuances of what occurred. Thus, in many ways, focus groups can often prevent the company from making the costly error of offering a product or service for which little or no interest exists.

Surveys Conducting a phone, mail, or online survey entails designing a survey instrument, usually a questionnaire that provides the desired information. Questionnaire design is not a simple matter of putting some questions on a piece of paper. There are in fact proven methods of constructing questionnaires to help ensure unbiased responses. It is beyond the scope of this book to present all the techniques for questionnaire construction; however, several key points should be remembered:

1. Keep the questionnaire short with lots of white space so that the respondent is not intimidated at the outset.

2. Be careful not to ask leading, biased questions.

3. Ask easy questions first, leading up to the more complex ones.

4. Ask demographic questions (age, sex, income) last, when the respondent's attention span has waned. These questions can be answered very quickly.

5. For questions that people generally hesitate to answer (age, income), group possible responses in ranges (for example, 25 to 35 for age, $35,000 to $45,000 for income) so that the respondent doesn't feel that he or she is giving away very private information.

6. Keep in mind that people generally increase their income classification one class and decrease their age one class.

Mail and online surveys are a relatively easy way to reach a lot of people in the target market and take less time than many other methods. However, mail surveys suffer from a very low response rate, often less than 10 percent, which makes the data gathered from the survey suspect in its ability to accurately represent the beliefs of potential customers. Moreover, entrepreneurs who use mail surveys (or online surveys) do not have the benefit of nonverbal communication, which is a significant loss considering that at least 85 percent of all communication is nonverbal. In general, a follow-up mailing is necessary to achieve the desired response rate. Phone surveys have two advantages over online or mail surveys: They allow for explanation and clarification of questions and responses, and the response rate is higher, but they also are prone to surveyor bias.

Choice Modeling and Concept Testing These methods are generally employed later in the development of the business and are used to confirm the results related to a specific issue like buying patterns. In general, entrepreneurs use these methods to understand what drives a customer to make a purchase decision.[11] Choice modeling is a method for identifying the variables that influence customers' choices from among a set of alternatives (for example, brands). Conjoint analysis, another form of choice modeling, helps the entrepreneur determine the optimal combination of features in a product or service, whereas direct attribute weighting involves weighting features to figure out those that might influence a customer's decision process.

Choosing the Sample All these techniques to gather primary data require the selection of a representative sample from the target market. This step in measuring the market should be taken with great care because it determines the validity of the results. In general, a random sample of potential customers should be chosen—that is, one over which the company has as little control as possible over who is selected to participate in the sample. Most companies, for reasons of cost and time, choose to use a convenience sample. This means that not everyone in the defined target market has a chance of being chosen to participate. Instead, for example, a sample may be selected from people who happen to be at a particular shopping mall on a particular day. Clearly, it is possible to reach all potential customers at that mall, but if the prospective customer typically shops at malls, there is a good chance of achieving at least a representative sample from which fairly reliable results can be derived.

Even if a convenience sample is used, there are ways to ensure that participants are selected randomly. Using the mall example, the selection system may be to select

FIGURE 11.2 The Market Research Process

Data when organized → Becomes information that when analyzed → Becomes intelligence

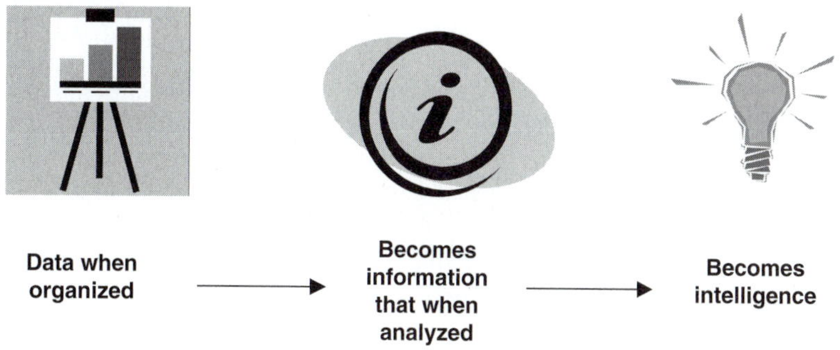

and survey every fifth person who walks by. In this way, the person is not chosen based on his or her attractiveness (or lack of it) or any other reason, for that matter. Alternatively, using a random number generator on a computer, names can be selected from a telephone book. Whichever system is employed, the key point is that the selection of the sample must not be biased.

Sometimes entrepreneurs claim they took a sample of friends and relatives who loved the new-product idea. Friends and relatives may be able to provide some initial feedback, but they are not the best source of unbiased information. The market research that a company does results in a go/no-go decision, so it is critical that it be done correctly. The credibility of the market research results is directly affected by the quality of the sample selected.

Step 6: Organize, Analyze, Modify, and Conduct Further Research

Although a critical task, effective data collection is only part of the market research process. Equally essential is the ability to examine the data, organize it, look for significant connections, and present the data in a meaningful way. Only when data are turned into competitive intelligence does it serve to help the entrepreneur position the business correctly (see Figure 11.2). Market research produces a segmentation of the market, a number of potential customer groups, a profile of the likely first customer and potential competitors, and a sense of market demand. One useful way to look at various customer segments to determine which should be the primary customer is to construct a customer grid that lays out the benefits, distribution, and product or service for each customer segment. (See the customer matrix in Chapter 3 that highlights three potential customers for SWEst, a software developer.) Once the customer segments are identified, the entrepreneur has to make a choice. Which of these three customers should the entrepreneur go after first? The decision where to go first is affected by size of the market, customer demand, and resources, but the most important consideration is which customer is most likely to buy. Note also that the different benefits and distribution strategies for each customer may actually produce different businesses—for example, a retail outlet, a wholesale distributorship, or an Internet business. The type of business that the entrepreneur wants to own influences the decision on first customer.

LEARNING FROM MISTAKES

When Someone Else's Mistake Is Your Opportunity

Robert Byerley was upset. His new $100 dress shirt was ruined by his local dry cleaner, and the Dallas-based company refused to replace the damaged shirt with a new one. But Byerley took that bad experience and turned it into a business opportunity. Byerley believed that most people would pay premium prices for high-quality dry-cleaning and laundry services, and with this goal in mind, his business was born.

Fortunately, Byerley did not only consider his own anecdotal experience; he launched into a week of in-depth market research looking at government reports and trade publications to learn that dry cleaning was a $16 billion-a-year industry. He also talked to experts in the industry to understand how the dry-cleaning business worked and what the best practices were. He knew that he would be entering a very fragmented market with more than its share of mom-and-pop businesses on nearly every street corner with loyal customers. These businesses typically attracted customers through discount coupons, a practice that Byerley determined was not compatible with his notion of premium service

and quality. By contacting the Better Business Bureau, he also learned that dry cleaners consistently received the highest number of complaints of all business types, the biggest complaint being that they do not stand behind their work. This would work to his advantage.

To get customer feedback on the store's name and look, he worked with a marketing firm to hold focus groups. He also used focus groups to critique the dry-cleaning work of his fifteen closest competitors. All that research paid off when Byerley opened his first store in Plano, Texas, which became profitable in its fourth month. He followed quickly with two more stores in Dallas.

Lesson Learned: *Effective market research can overcome stiff competition*.

Sources: A. Zimmerman, "To Really Know a Market, Dig beyond the Obvious," *Street Journal Startup Journal*, www.startupjournal.com (accessed June 24, 2005); Bibbentuckers, http://www.bibbentuckers.com/locations/lemmon.asp.

The Customer Profile

Entrepreneurs need to be able to describe the primary customer, be it a consumer or a business, in great detail. This complete customer profile emerges from primary research. The profile is critically important to the marketing strategy because it provides information vital to everything from product or service design to distribution channels and the marketing plan. Some of the information that goes into the customer profile of a consumer or a business includes age, income level, education, buying habits (when, where, how much), where customers typically find these types of products and services, and how they would like to purchase. The list contains other data as well, depending on whether the customer is a consumer or a business. Sandy Gooch is one of the leaders in the health-food industry. When she was preparing to open her first store, she had a complete picture of her target customer: a 45- to 50-year-old professional woman who was well educated, was a lifelong learner, valued physical fitness, and read labels when she shopped. She would also be a regular shopper who stopped into the store several times a week on her way home from work. Certainly, not everyone who shopped at Mrs. Gooch's is a 45- to 50-year-old professional woman, but that is her primary customer, the customer most likely to purchase when Gooch started the business. Knowing that much about her customer enabled Gooch to tailor her advertising. Mrs. Gooch's ads always contained a lot of information, for instance, because she knew her customers wanted to learn something from each ad.[12]

If the customer is a business, it can be described essentially in the same way—for example, as a small- to mid-sized construction company with annual revenues of $5 million that makes purchases quarterly, buys primarily over the Internet, and pays within sixty days. The customer profile is also an important piece in the marketing plan, which is discussed in Chapter 13.

GATHERING COMPETITIVE INTELLIGENCE

One of the weakest areas of most feasibility studies or business plans is the competitive analysis because the entrepreneur typically looks only at what can easily be seen on the surface rather than digging for facts that are not as obvious. Entrepreneurs should examine their competitors' strengths, weaknesses, opportunities, and threats as thoroughly as they study their own. In this way, the entrepreneur can find ways to create new value for customers rather than simply benchmark against competitors.

LEARNING FROM THE GLOBAL MARKET

Researching the Effect of China

China is an increasing presence in the world economy, and it is connected to businesses in every other country in the world through the Internet. It is important that small business owners be aware of these critical facts:

1. China's economy is far larger than the $1.4 trillion (2003) that official reports indicate. This research reports only legal businesses, but China also has an enormous underground economy. Furthermore, a dollar spent in China will buy five times more goods than a dollar spent in an average American city. Consequently, the economy of China looks more like one with a gross domestic product of $6.6 trillion, or about two-thirds the size of the U.S. economy.

2. In 2003 foreigners invested more in launching and building businesses in China than in anywhere else in the world including the United States.

3. The Chinese economy is very entrepreneurial with new businesses that develop fast and lean in ways that make money quickly. They can also quickly cut their prices and put U.S. businesses out of

business—this occurred in the U.S. sock-maker industry. U.S. companies are now asking their suppliers to meet the best price out of China—the China price has become the global standard for the lowest price.

4. Raw materials are becoming more expensive because China is purchasing huge quantities of things like copper, aluminum, oil, and nearly 40 percent of the world's cement.

5. There are hidden costs in doing business with China, which uses its enormous market to obtain concessions from foreign firms that can help China build its industrial strength.

6. China does not police its intellectual property, so foreign companies cannot easily fight the taking of their technologies and other proprietary goods.

There is no way for small business owners to avoid the impact of China on their businesses, so a portion of any market research undertaken should focus on that issue.

Source: T. C. Fishman, "How China Will Change Your Business," *Inc.* (March 2005): 70.

Identifying the Competition

There are generally three types of competitors for a product or service: direct, indirect or substitute, and emerging. Identifying exactly who these companies are and uncovering their strengths, weaknesses, market share, and business strategy will put the new venture in a better position to be a contender in the target market.

Direct competitors are those businesses that supply the same or similar products or services. Indirect competitors do not supply the same product; in fact, they may not even be in the same market as the new venture, but they do compete alongside it for customer dollars. For example, consumers may choose to spend their limited dollars at the movies rather than on an expensive restaurant. Or a business looking for videoconferencing capability may choose an Internet-based system delivered through an application service provided rather than purchasing and maintaining equipment. Therefore, it is important to look outside the immediate industry and market to learn about all possible competitors.

An entrepreneur also needs to look beyond existing competition to emerging competitors. In many industries today, technology and information are changing at such a rapid pace that the window of opportunity for successfully starting a new venture closes early and fast. Consequently, entrepreneurs must be vigilant in observing new trends and new technology, both in the industry in general and in the specific target market.

Finding Information About Competitors

Collecting information on competitors is one of the most difficult parts of researching the market. It is easy to gain superficial information from the competitor's advertising, website, or facility. However, amassing the less obvious types of information, such as revenues and long-term strategies, are another matter. Information on publicly held competitors can be found in annual reports and other filings required by the U.S. Securities and Exchange Commission (SEC). Unfortunately, however, most start-up companies are competing against other private companies that are not willing to divulge these sensitive data.

Although it is helpful to gather as much "hard data" as possible about competing companies, it is also important to collect information on their current market strategies, management style and culture, pricing strategy, customer mix, and promotional mix. Competitive intelligence can be found by visiting competitors' websites or the outlets where their products are sold and evaluating appearance, number of customers coming and going, what they buy, how much, and how often in addition to talking to customers and employees. Buying competitors' products to understand the differences in features and benefits and to learn much about how they treat their customers is also valuable. Public companies can be investigated through Hoover's Online (www.hoovers.com), the SEC (www.sec.gov), and One Source (www.onesource.com).

Looking for the Less Obvious

Competitors can threaten a new or existing business by possessing a core competency that is not readily visible in the typical facts that are reported, especially if those competitors come from outside the entrepreneur's industry and market. For example, suppose that the entrepreneur's business concept is a company that trains unskilled workers for well-paying jobs in industry. The entrepreneur looks at all the competitors in the training market and decides that he or she can compete because a unique niche has been created in the market. What the entrepreneur has failed to do is look outside the market to companies that might have the same core competency and might have the resources to shift to the entrepreneur's niche very rapidly. Those companies are not always obvious. For example, one of Marriott's core competencies is training unskilled workers in the language and work skills that they need to perform the various jobs in Marriott's hotel chain. It certainly has the resources to take this competency into any niche it desires. To make sure that they are not missing a potential threat, entrepreneurs should determine

- What the competitor has to do to be successful in its own core business. Are there any core competencies that it must acquire?
- Which of the competitor's core competencies are transferable to the entrepreneur's business.
- Whether the competitor has a competency in the same area as the entrepreneur.[13]

If the competitor is a large company, the entrepreneur may strategically position his or her company to be acquired because most large companies acquire core competencies rather than develop them.

Market Fit

Designing an effective market entry strategy is a function of market fit. Figure 11.3 presents a matrix of market fit that shows how newness of the product or service to the company and newness of the product or service to the market affect market strategy. A product or service that is new to the company but not to the market means that the company will have difficulty catching up with competitors in terms of economies of scale and experience in the market. A product or service that is familiar to the company and familiar to the market is essentially a commodity and will typically require a price-driven market strategy unless the entrepreneur can discover a way to take the product out of the commodity status as Starbucks' Howard Schultz did with coffee. A product or service that is new to the company and new to the market generally involves a brand new or disruptive technology. It requires a market strategy that reflects the need for building customer awareness, customer education, and the resources to sustain a long marketing campaign to ensure mass adoption. It also requires a long learning curve in terms of production capability and refining of the product as it gets out into the market. Finally, a product or service that is not new to the company but is new to the market requires a strategy of customer education and consequently an enormous marketing budget; but because the product or service is familiar to the company, it should be very efficient in producing and distributing the product.

Employing a Niche Strategy to Compete

Entrepreneurs typically use a niche strategy to compete in a market. What this means is that the new venture focuses on a particular customer group, an unserved need, or a specific geographic region not currently served effectively by other players in the market. By selecting a segment of a market, niche entrepreneurs attempt to insulate themselves from market forces such as competitors and the barriers to entry in an industry. Focusing on any of the key elements of the business—customer,

FIGURE 11.3 Market Fit

		Newness to Market	
		Low	High
Newness to Firm	**High**	Product–company fit issue	Maximum uncertainty and risk
	Low	Cannibalization: Size of incremental impact	Product–market fit issue

product design, price, service, packaging, geographic focus, and distribution—can create niches.

Many a new venture has entered an established market via a niche by finding a gap in the market that enables the company to compete without going head-to-head with major companies. Where there is a need that has not been served, the niche strategy offers a safer route to establishing a foothold in the market. For example, Counter Assault specializes in bear products that discourage bears from approaching humans. It serves a niche in a market of people who live and play in bear country in the West.[14]

The important thing to remember about niche creation is that it gives a new venture time to define and "own" a segment of the market. Working in a niche gives the company time to develop, to become stronger and better able to compete against companies in the mainstream market. However, niche strategies can fail when the costs to serve the niche exceed the size of the market, so it is important to choose an appropriate niche. Niches, by their very nature, are small and usually serve to provide only an entry strategy, not a sustainable strategy for long-term viability.

The market plan is a critical component of a business's ability to create awareness among potential customers and enter a market in a way that allows the business to be successful.

ISSUES FOR REVIEW AND DISCUSSION

1. How do entrepreneurs go about defining a first customer?
2. Why is it important to develop a research strategy for investigating the market that a new venture or existing business might enter?
3. What is the most effective method for gathering primary customer data, and why?
4. What would be an effective strategy for gathering competitive intelligence? Justify your strategy.
5. What is the role of market fit in developing a niche strategy?

EXPERIENCING ENTREPRENEURSHIP

1. Choose a business concept that interests you. Using the six-step market research process, demonstrate how you used that process to determine who the first customer might be.
2. Pick a business in your community and analyze the competitive market for this business. Are there any companies that appear to have the core competency to move into the company's competitive space? How can they do that?

Finding the Right Customer

On July 28, 2005, Alien Technology Corporation, the leading provider of radio frequency identification (RFID) products, announced the completion of a $66 million round of financing led by SunBridge Partners. The financing provided the company with capital to continue its expansion and drive new market opportunities in the face of accelerating global demand for RFID. Then on September 13, 2005, Alien announced that it would produce its most widely used RFID labels at 12.9 cents, a 44 percent decrease in the price over the previous twelve months, moving the company toward the goal of "widely available, economic RFID labels." William Joseph smiled as he thought of how far the company had come. Although no longer a part of the company on a daily basis, he was a shareholder, and the potential to benefit from the work he had done at the company was just around the corner.

Background

As an undergraduate student in finance and marketing, Joseph listened to his favorite professor as he tried to influence Joseph to go into marketing. Joseph and his student team had completed a couple of research projects for Ford Motor Co. and Cadillac Catera and had actually won a prize for their strategy for how to take two new products to market. Both companies had applied the team's research to product launches, but the team had been pushed to the side when it came time for Ford and Cadillac to implement their ideas. The members had to accept that; for them, this would be simply an educational experience.

Undaunted, Joseph graduated with degrees in finance and marketing in 1996 and was heading off to take a job in Corporate America when his father called to tell him that there was a start-up in the state of Washington, Isothermal Systems Research, that needed a business plan. Intrigued, Joseph investigated the opportunity and ended up turning down a big salary at Sun Microsystems to work in a town of 300 people and with a new company. He lived in the attic of a bed-and-breakfast inn, and because he would not be paid until the company received its funding, he did consulting on the side. This was Joseph's first chance to write a real business plan, and he took the task very seriously as he positioned the company for funding

and explored markets for early adoption of the company's technology. He raised $8 million in DARPA research funding, and when it came time to raise venture money with the business plan to take the technology to market, Joseph found himself negotiating with top venture capitalists like Brad Jones of Redpoint Ventures. It was a year before the company paid Joseph for his work and gave him stock in the company, but today that company does about $30 million to $50 million in revenue and is on the way to doubling in size.

During the time that Joseph was working in Washington, he met a person with a doctorate in materials science from Stanford University who had invented a neuroradiological device. Joseph helped him win funding from NIST (National Institute of Standards and Technology) and then in 1998 took a position with Beckmen Display in 1998. Beckmen was a Berkeley, California-based manufacturer of television displays. In 1997 Beckmen had hired Jeffrey Jacobson as CEO of the company, and he quickly changed the name of the company to Alien Technology to reflect his interest in things extraterrestrial. He also changed the original mission of the company from television displays to producing little plastic displays for credit cards—smart cards—what he thought at the time was an innovative marketing product that would allow bank customers to conveniently check their balances on their smart cards.

Once again, Joseph was tasked with writing a business plan and raising money to further develop the technology needed for the smart card displays. Joseph wrote the plan and won $8 million from DARPA, which funded R&D and overhead. Jacobson was then able to leverage that funding to get approximately $80 million from venture capitalists to produce smart cards employing Alien's core technology, fluidic self-assembly (FSA), a process that uses water to place chips on plastic. With this proprietary process, Alien was able to shape the chips like ice cubes, dump the chips into water, then float the chips using gravity across the surface. FSA enabled them to place a million chips an hour.

In 2000 Jacobson moved the company to a 20,000–square-foot facility in Morgan Hill, California, to be closer to his home. In 2001 Alien had begun building an 80,000–square-foot facility to produce smart cards for financial institutions when those institutions suddenly backed out of $30 million in purchase orders. The banks had come to the conclusion that smart cards were more of a want than a need with their customers; in other words, there was no business case and no pain in the market. With no prospects of a market for smart cards and running dangerously low on cash, Alien began laying off people and quickly went from 160 employees to 60. Because he had always focused on engineering talent, Jacobson did not have enough expertise in business development and marketing to know how to handle the loss of the market for smart cards. He needed a new customer base or a new product, or both, and fast.

Joseph was never one to shy away from a challenge. He quickly began looking for new ways to use the FSA technology and discovered that RFID might be a possible new direction for the business because Alien could leverage its FSA technology to make RFID tags in higher volumes and at lower cost than those that were currently being produced. RFID is the "premier technology for automating the identification and tracking of commodities and collecting valuable information on their whereabouts, contents, physical state and more." With RFID, every item can have a unique identifier, and the system can identify many items at once. As a result "RFID can collect huge volumes of actionable data each second from immense numbers of RFID-tagged items as they move across conveyors, through dock doors and even off of store shelves." When RFID is part of a network, the data collected can be analyzed and used to trigger company decisions. In 2001–2002, RFID was an infant industry going nowhere and primarily found in the government and military sectors.

Moving into RFID

Talking to industry experts, Joseph discovered current RFID customers were asking for lower-cost tags, but it was when he researched the consumer-packaging industry that he came upon the inspiration for Alien's new direction. Consumer-packaging customers required billions of tags to track their products. The semiconductor industry could not handle that kind of volume, and its integrated circuit chips were larger and cost more to make. With the FSA technology, Joseph calculated that Alien could place 1 million chips per hour at less than 30 microns on a side as compared to

just under a millimeter in size for integrated chips. This meant that Alien could produce smaller chips at a significantly lower cost. Armed with the results of his research, Joseph went back to Jacobson with a plan to gradually transition Alien to the wireless RFID industry where it could specialize in markets that involved high volumes of low-cost RFID tags, such as supply chain, logistics, baggage handling, and retail tagging, especially in the pharmaceuticals segment.

Convinced that RFID was Alien's future and with Jacobson's blessing, Joseph started building a company within a company. He raised $500,000 to pay for engineers that he brought on board to support the new technology. Then he secured a $70 million position as a Department of Defense line item and raised another $20 million in venture funding. Alien then acquired Wave ID to secure the wireless technology that it needed to manufacture a complete package of tags and readers. Joseph then set out to prove the technology in the consumer products industry. Figuring that the first customer would be critical, he started with Wal-Mart, the largest consumer products retailer in the world, and managed to convince them of the value of RFID to their business and how it would solve a huge problem for Wal-Mart. In 2003 alone, Wal-Mart had lost $8 billion to shrinkage and from not being able to find products when it needed them. RFID was the answer.

"This was the purchase order heard around the world," says Joseph. It was for 500 million units, and it effectively launched the RFID consumer products industry. Quickly Wal-Mart required all of its top suppliers to switch to RFID from bar codes. Within six months, the new RFID division overtook Alien's display business. RFID had a business case and a value proposition for the end user that was quantifiable whereas smart cards had not.

By the end of 2001, nearly all the people involved in the display business were gone. It was at that point that Jacobson stepped in and informed Joseph that he would not let him lead the RFID division as promised, even though Joseph had taken the company in a direction that allowed it to be successful, in fact, to survive. Joseph decided that it was time to go back to school and get his MBA.

Working Outside Alien

Joseph left Alien but remained a consultant to the company while he pursued his MBA at the University of Southern California. He also continued to consult to the company on work that he had begun with Department of Defense. This work eventually caught the attention of Senator Dorgan of North Dakota (chairman of the Senate Defense Appropriations Committee) who thought that RFID was important for his state's economic growth as well as for national security. In 2002 Dorgan, along with Senator Stevens of Alaska, awarded $70 million from the defense appropriation budget, and they asked Joseph to comanage the Microsensor Systems (MSS) Program through DARPA to make super low-cost sensors for the military as well as help North Dakota State University (NDSU) set up businesses. Today, the MSS program is regarded as the military's top research program for battlefield sensors as well as homeland security applications.

Market research has always played a critical role in Joseph's ability to exploit an opportunity, and he approached the process very strategically. He believes that market research should be quantitative and start with the customer, then work back from the customer to the numbers and the justification for those numbers. "The justification for the business case must include adoption costs and benefits as well as switching costs for the customer." Another opportunity to use these skills emerged when an NDSU professor approached Joseph to see if he was interested in starting a business. Joseph agreed to conduct a feasibility analysis to develop a business model for the proposed company that would provide innovative low-power solutions for customers in the areas of wireless systems and embedded computing. With the business concept judged feasible, in the late summer of 2003, the professor left the university and with Joseph

started Packet Digital. The company's proprietary technology lay in the area of power management enabling electronics that use batteries to enable power on demand. In 2005 the company became profitable on approximately $2 million of sales, and it was expecting sales of between $5 and $7 million in 2006. Once again, Joseph chose to remain in a consulting role to Packet Digital as he began to think about his next venture. Meanwhile, in 2005 Alien Technology had brought on a new management team that wanted to make things right with Joseph because they attributed their now 25 percent compounded monthly revenue growth to his efforts. They had an impending initial public offering with eight investment banks involved and a market valuation of over $1 billion. Joseph was about to reap the rewards of his work with Alien Technology.

Advising the Entrepreneur

1. How can Joseph use his talent for spotting important markets as he thinks about his next venture?

2. Describe the type of entrepreneur that Joseph is. What must he put in place to allow him to act in the role of a serial entrepreneur?

Sources: "Alien Technology Corporation Achieves Another Step toward Pervasive, Economic RFID with Announcement of 12.9 Cent RFID Labels," Alien Press Release (September 13, 2005), http://www.alientechnology.com/newsevents/2005/press091305a.php; "AlienTechnology Selects Fargo, North Dakota for Manufacturing Site," NDSU Research Technology Park Inc. (2002), www.ndsuresearchpark.com; interview with William Joseph (September 15, 2005); Alien Technology, www.alientechnology.com.

CHAPTER 12

Distribution and Pricing

People want economy and they will pay any price to get it.

Lee Iacocca

LEARNING OUTCOMES

- Explain how distribution can be a competitive strategy for a small business.
- Discuss the role of intermediaries in the distribution channel.
- Identify the issues involved in exporting and importing products
- Discuss the roles of pricing objectives, strategy, and structure in determining the best pricing for an entrepreneur's product or service.

A New Way to Grow in an Old Industry

The healthcare industry is not the easiest industry in which to do business, and if you're in the distribution business, it is likely that you may be caught between large manufacturers and customers who want to save money. In the wholesale drug business, Cardinal Health is one of dozens of companies that buy products from pharmaceutical giants and stock the shelves of local drugstores. In this industry, demand is not the issue—the issue is saving money. Hospital administrators are under great pressure to contain costs. Patients, faced with the rising costs of drugs, are looking for creative ways to find prescription drugs at a lower cost. Few companies are able to see the opportunity in this type of environment, but Cardinal did. In fact, Cardinal's goal was to focus on finding every opportunity it could so that it could be more than just an intermediary in a very tough industry.

One of the opportunities it found was to provide services to hospital pharmacies by delivering medications right to the patient rather than merely to the hospital's pharmacy. Another opportunity was to provide services to pharmaceutical manufacturers. From its position in the middle of the value chain, it could add value by offering services in drug formulation, testing, manufacturing, and packaging. This would free up the pharmas (pharmaceutical manufacturers) to focus on drug discovery.

Cardinal spied yet another opportunity in a problem facing commercial pharmacies—drugstores, one of its customers. Drugstores depended on third-party reimbursement to get paid, and the paper trail in this area was difficult at best to navigate. Cardinal developed a software system called ScriptLINE, which automated the reimbursement process and made it easier and faster for commercial pharmacies to get paid.

It is rare for a distribution company to innovate in so many areas, but when a company like Cardinal does, it produces enormous growth. In Cardinal's case, from 1991 to 2001, the company grew at a compounded annual growth rate of 40 percent, double the rate of its nearest competitor. Cardinal's strategy was to look for customer pain and develop a product/service to cure that pain. The sale of a product to a customer was only the beginning. Customers acquired the product, learned how to use it, maintained it, stored it, and even disposed of it. Each of these activities had the potential to produce a problem for the customer; consequently, each of these problems became an opportunity for Cardinal to solve it and in doing so generate more loyalty from the customer. It is no wonder then that the offspring of the original product reaped even more revenues for the company than the original product did.

Growing rapidly the way Cardinal did is expensive, so to make money while growing Cardinal focused on operational excellence by consolidating its distribution centers, moving from forty to twenty-four centers. To its surprise, it found that these twenty-four distribution centers actually generated ten times more revenues than all forty did; in other words, the money saved in distribution was available to grow the company. Cardinal is no longer a small company, but it has proven that larger companies can grow at the rate of smaller businesses if they take advantage of their hidden assets—those intangible assets that take a long time to accumulate and those that most small businesses do not yet enjoy.

Small businesses have a lot to learn from Cardinal's strategy. By creating and leveraging hidden assets early in the life of the business, small distribution businesses can discover niches that may be too small for a large company but that will allow the small business to grow rapidly.

Advising the Entrepreneur

1. What were Cardinal's hidden assets, and how did it use them to grow its distribution business?

2. Based on Cardinal's strategy, what advice would you give a small distribution business in the office products industry that was looking to grow?

Source: A. D. Slywotzky and R. Wise, "Double-Digit Growth in No-Growth Times," *FastCompany* 69 (April 2003): 66.

Companies that are experiencing spectacular growth today have discovered new ways to grow, not through new or improved products but through "hidden assets" like expertise, unique customer access, and by focusing on an unserved need in a niche market.[1] Today, distribution offers as many opportunities for growth, innovation, and competitive advantage as any of the other marketing functions. In fact, many successful companies, such as PriceCostco, a wholesaler to the public, and Ferguson Enterprises, a distributor of plumbing and heating equipment, have built their businesses on effective distribution of products. In marketing terms, the distribution decision involves finding the most effective way to get products to customers. But that is only part of the story. Where the company lies in the distribution channel determines what kind of business it is in and who its primary customer is. For example, in Figure 12.1, the manufacturer is the producer of the product and also the customer of the supplier that supplies the raw materials or parts to produce the product. The manufacturer's primary customer is the distributor, which buys product and sells it to its primary customer, the retailer. The retailer, in turn, has the consumer as the primary customer. This is known as an **indirect channel of distribution** in that there are intermediaries between the producer (the manufacturer) and the consumer. Notice that independent representatives (reps) and agents may also enter the channel in addition to the other members or to replace the distributor. A manufacturer can choose to sell direct to the industrial user, using no intermediaries, or it can use distributors or manufacturer's reps, who market to end users. Another alternative is to work with agents, who act as a sales force for the manufacturer and either go through a distributor or directly to the industrial user.

In an industrial channel of distribution, businesses sell to other businesses. For example, a manufacturer may be targeting another manufacturer for the sale of its products. The options for industrial markets are similar to those in the consumer market, with the exception that the ultimate customer or end user is another business. In a **direct channel of distribution,** by contrast, the manufacturer cuts out the intermediaries and sells direct to the consumer. (Figure 12.2)

Depicting the distribution channel graphically has great value. Apart from the obvious benefit of showing the various options available to get the product or service to the customer, graphing the channel assists in

- Judging the time from manufacture to purchase by the end-user customer.
- Determining the ultimate retail price (or wholesale price in the case of industrial channels) based on the markups required by the intermediaries.
- Figuring the marketing responsibilities and costs. Manufacturers may help distributors and retailers with promotion, but the heaviest responsibility and cost fall on the channel member that deals with the ultimate customer: the end customer or end user.

The graph of the distribution channel can also be depicted as a **value chain** indicating the markups along the channel, as in Figure 12.3. At each stage, the channel member adds value to the product by performing a service that increases the chances the product will reach its intended customer. For example, the manufacturer charges the distributor a price that covers the costs of producing the product plus an amount for overhead and profit. The distributor, in turn, adds an amount to cover the cost of the goods purchased and his or her overhead and profit. The retailer does the same

FIGURE 12.1 Indirect Channel of Distribution

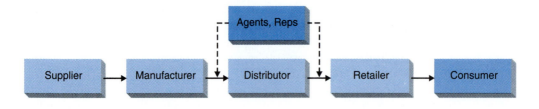

FIGURE 12.2 Direct Channel of Distribution

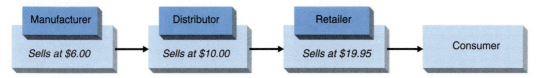

FIGURE 12.3 The Value Chain

Difference = Overhead + Profit

and charges the final price to the customer/end user. The amount of markup at each point is a function of the industry and the demand for the product. A wholesaler, for example, will generally have an established markup or gross profit margin for a particular product line. Price is critical to the wholesalers because most retailers purchase based on price. Wholesalers offer discounts and terms based on quantity ordered.

On the surface, it appears that the final retail price could be substantially lower, perhaps even priced at the rate the distributor sold to the retailer in the example in Figure 12.3. However, that reasoning is flawed. The distributor performed a valuable service. He or she made it possible for the manufacturer to focus on producing the product and not incur the cost of warehouses, a larger marketing department, a sales force, and a more complex shipping department. All these activities now become a cost to the manufacturer of doing business with retailers and must be factored into the decision to choose a direct distribution channel.

This chapter looks at distribution and pricing as strategic components of a company's marketing plan. Distribution strategy affects marketing tactics (discussed in Chapter 13) and pricing strategies, and it must be closely aligned with customer needs to be effective.

DISTRIBUTION STRATEGY

In general, the classic topology of distribution channels is that the functions that are performed throughout the channel seem to fall into three broad categories: transaction activities, service activities, and physical distribution, or logistics. The channel members are those companies that perform the actual functions of the channel. Two critical decision areas must be addressed in any business's distribution strategy: (1) forward integration decisions and (2) optimal channel assignments.[2] A **forward integration decision** generally has to do with whether the business owner should hire others to do its distribution or own the distribution. Small businesses often do not have the capabilities to manage their own distribution, and with limited resources, they tend to focus those resources on core competencies while outsourcing distribution. However, as the company grows, it may choose to own its distribution so that it can exert more control and be more profitable. By owning its own distribution channels, the business can create a competitive advantage and set up barriers to entry for others.[3] **Optimal channel assignment** is about choosing the various channel members that may handle distribution for the small business. (These channel members are discussed in more detail in the section "Intermediaries.")

Distribution is also a physical element in the process strategy of a product company. The infrastructures of traditional distribution systems were designed with the expressed purpose of expediting marketing strategies that served mass markets of customers that all looked alike. Today, distribution has become a significant competitive strategy in two major arenas. First, the new paradigm of mass customization calls for a different distribution strategy, one that allows a company to successfully compete in a dynamic marketplace by offering customers exactly what they want when they want it. Some early examples of this type of strategy were direct marketing, cable TV shopping, and e-commerce. Second, low-cost distribution is a powerful tool for value creation in markets with sophisticated customers and products and services that are less differentiated. In such a situation, price becomes the defining factor. Wal-Mart's low-cost distribution strategy is probably the best example of a highly successful distribution strategy that can force manufacturers to lower prices or modify their operations to deliver on price and with a minimum level of quality. In commodity-type industries, such as food, manufacturers are often obligated to become their own low-cost distributors to survive. Even service industries are affected by these category killers. For example, information is rapidly becoming a commodity, with hundreds of companies positioning themselves as the low-cost provider of Internet content services.

Looking at Distribution Channel Partners like Customers

Distribution channel members are really the small business owner's customers because they are the ones who provide the revenues to the business. Therefore, it is useful to analyze distribution channels in a manner analogous to the way that customers are analyzed: segmentation, value proposition, and relationship management.[4] Channel members can be segmented into types—dealers, salespeople, resellers, and so forth. Each of these channel member types performs a different function and has different requirements. In addition, each has a different relationship with the small business in terms of contribution to profit. The reason to segment the channel members is that small business resources are typically limited, so it is important to

LEARNING FROM SUCCESS

Charging More Can Make Sense

Small business owners often believe they have to compete on price; that if their competitors lower their prices, they must do the same. But this is not always the way to go. Sometimes you have to have the courage to charge more for your product. When he launched Starbucks, Howard Schultz knew that he was creating a coffee experience that didn't exist in the way that he envisioned it. He also understood that many consumers today are tired of poor customer service, and that many would pay for better customer service and an experience they perceived as valuable. He knew that customers aren't loyal to companies that don't treat them as if they're important. So Schultz first ensured that customers received a quality product and a high degree of service, and then charged a premium. In doing so, he proved that you can win customers in a niche product or service by offering more and charging more.

Sharron Senter, a marketing consultant, also understands the importance of protecting your pricing. When clients balk at her consulting fee, instead of lowering the fee, she looks for ways to provide her services more efficiently for the client so that they pay less overall. In this way, she doesn't compromise her consulting rate and is able to build a long-term relationship with her client based on trust and respect for each other's needs.

Lesson Learned: *Resist the tendency to lower prices or compete based on price.*

Sources: Senter, Sharron, "Small Business Pricing Strategies," *Webpronews.com* www.webpronews.com/ebusiness/smallbusiness/wpn-2-20050406SmallBusinessPricing Strategies.html, April 4, 2005; Zahorsky, Darrell, "Super Charge Your Business with a Profit Pricing Strategy," *Small Business Information,* sbinformation.about.com/cs/marketresearch/a/pricing.htm, Accessed April 20, 2006; Hanft, Adam, "Courage to Charge More," *Inc Magazine Forum,* www.inc.com/resources/marketing/articles/ 20040901/pricing.html, Accessed April 20, 2006.

---

maximize the return from an investment in a particular distribution channel, and this is accomplished by optimizing the choice of channel partners.

Small business owners must demonstrate a value proposition, or benefit, to their channel partners so that the partners have a reason to do business with them and are motivated to push their products. Small businesses are competing for the attention of the channel partner against large companies with greater volumes of product to sell. To capture the channel partner's attention may require discounting the price and providing advertising and other types of support. It is also important to track the effectiveness of a particular distribution channel by assessing it against defined business outcomes, which could be sales from end customers or length of customer relationship, for example. The bottom line is that an effective distribution channel partner must be aligned with end-customer needs and enhance the profitability of the small business.

Multiple Channels of Distribution

The issue of using multiple channels for distribution has risen to the forefront of debate. In 2003, it was estimated that 63 percent of retailers employed three or more distribution channels in their marketing strategies.[5] The use of multiple channels arises from the need to meet more complex customer needs in a more competitive environment. For example, a very complex and technical product might require a highly skilled salesperson, whereas the entire purchase transaction for shoes can be conducted effectively online without the need for human intervention. Multiple channels enable many customer touch-points, or points where products and services can be purchased or serviced, and they enable the customer to take more control of the transaction.[6] Technology has made it possible for companies with multiple channels to gather important customer data across channels that identify new customer needs and provide feedback on current products and services.

Internet-Enabled Strategies

Despite the fact that the Internet has assumed a less dramatic role when it comes to distribution strategy, it is still a compelling way to connect and to communicate, and it has changed the way that many businesses do business. For small business distribution strategy, the Internet has been a significant asset in terms of reducing the costs of distribution. The Internet can easily reach any customer day or night and in any time zone automatically without involving expensive personnel. Customers can purchase twenty-four hours a day without needing to access a salesperson. Changes in products can occur quickly as can changes in the way that the website looks and feels. Online retailers do not need to be concerned with shelf space because they have unlimited free space to offer their products.

Research has identified four types of Internet distribution strategies, each with its advantages and disadvantages. They are functional decomposition, cloning, forward integration, and strategic industry alliance.[7]

Functional Decomposition In **functional decomposition,** the small business uses the Internet to provide the service component, but the customer still makes the final purchase transaction through a distributor. Customers may go to the website simply to view products, secure information, and compare products. This distribution strategy works well for products that are not easily purchased online because the customer must experience the product or test the product prior to final purchase. With complex transactions, however, the customer, by gathering information from the website first, can then go to the distributor better armed with the right questions. One industry that has used this approach successfully is the real estate brokerage industry. The National Association of Realtors created an official website (www.realtor.com) that provides up-to-date real estate information and data on listed properties. It does not replace the role of real estate agents but does allow them to work with a better-informed client and that saves them time.

The functional decomposition approach can be complementary to other approaches, and it also offers a relatively inexpensive alternative to a full e-commerce site. Because this channel does not replace the physical channel (distributors, sales agents), it will not cause channel conflict but can actually help increase sales to the channel members. However, with this model, the Internet site becomes a cost center for the business (it does not generate revenues directly), and it is not easy to measure the effectiveness of the channel because linking customer visits to the site to actual sales transactions is difficult unless the distributor is willing to cooperate in that regard by querying customers as to where they learned about the product.

Cloning Cloning is duplicating the small business's distribution strategy on the Internet. For example, a bed-and-breakfast inn might duplicate its reservation system online to capture and better serve customers who prefer to do business online. For the small business, this dual system lets the business transfer its experience offline to the online world relatively easily and in doing so creates economies of scale for the business. Furthermore, this strategy gets the company's brand out in front of customers in more locations and with a wider scope than would be possible with simply a bricks-and-mortar location, and this means the potential for reaching new markets. Nonetheless, cloning does present some challenges in terms of coordinating online and offline efforts, and it leads to a number of important questions such as

- Should the company charge the same prices online as offline?
- Do customers behave differently online from purchasing in a physical retail store?

Some research has suggested that these two sites might actually compete with each other for the same customers.[8] In general, the types of products that do not sell well in the Internet channel are those that have low differentiation and require frequent purchase, such as hair products and cosmetics.[9]

Forward Integration With a **forward integration** strategy, the small business disintermediates its channel; that is, it bypasses the intermediaries in the channel to sell direct to the customer. In this way, the business can have a stronger relationship with its customers and more quickly meet their needs. The biggest advantage of forward integration is the cost savings that comes from not having to pay fees to distributors. Another advantage is the ability to control distribution better and therefore sense and respond more quickly to market changes. However, the initial development costs for an e-commerce site, which includes logistics, inventory, and fulfillment, can be relatively high. Moreover, if the small business owner does not have experience in distribution, there will be a learning curve that will take time to scale, and marketing costs will rise to create brand awareness that was not needed when a known distributor was used.

LEARNING FROM MISTAKES

When Exporting Saves a Company

When a company faces setback after setback, the owners often wonder if it is time to close the business and move on. Mark Pavlansky, president of Hibco Plastics, must have considered such a move when Hibco experienced a series of blows that threatened to derail his business permanently. It began in 1993 when Hibco lost IBM, its biggest customer, which caused Hibco's sales to plummet almost 30 percent. Then before Hibco could recover, the recession of 2000 drove down prices and margins. Revenue declined by 25 percent, and the company had to lay off forty people, a cut of 40 percent. It was a desperate time.

Understanding that reducing costs are the quickest way to improve profits, Pavlansky looked to Mexico. Pavlansky worked with an inventor by the name of Wayne Castleberry who came up with the idea of converting the foam plastic that Hibco produced into synthetic soil and exporting it to Mexico. With his brothers, who also worked at Hibco, Pavlansky took some classes in exporting and launched the new strategy. That move completely transformed the business because it let Pavlanksy see that taking a risk could open up their market. From that point on, Hibco continued to seek out new niche markets.

Lesson Learned: *Taking risk is the essence of entrepreneurship.*

Source: J. Bailey, "The Exporting Advantage," *Inc.* (August 2005), www.inc.com.

Strategic Industry Alliance When it doesn't make sense for a small business to use one of the previously discussed strategies, a **strategic alliance** may be in order. With this strategy, several complementary businesses join forces to provide a common distribution channel to customers who demand a variety of choices and volume prices. One example in the film industry is MovieLink, which is a strategic alliance of five major film studios—MGM, Sony, Universal, Warner Bros., and Paramount—whose purpose is to bypass the online video rental giants like Blockbuster Entertainment and let customers download movies to their computers for the same price as the typical rental.

A strategic alliance offers the advantages of saving distribution costs and offering variety and volume to customers. This strategy works best in a market that consists of a few major players, an oligopoly, so that the alliance achieves enough power in the market. Alliances always require a lot of coordination, and this should be taken into account when considering this approach.

INTERMEDIARIES

Intermediaries are the channel members who provide services that help take a product from a producer to the end customer, the one who primarily benefits from those products and services.

Suppliers

Every business makes use of suppliers, or vendors, in some fashion to provide raw materials for production, products to resell, or supplies to run the business. But suppliers have an equally important role in providing information that helps the business owner make important decisions about new products, competitor strategy, and cutting costs. Therefore, choosing effective suppliers is a critically important task for any business owner who is seeking a fair price, reliability, stability, and a good location. Business owners are always looking for the best price on suppliers' products, but price is only part of the mix and sometimes not even the most important part. Reliability is equally important because a business owner could achieve the lowest price but then not receive the product, receive a portion of the shipment, or receive damaged goods. A great supplier has systems in place to ensure that the right products go out at the right time and in good condition. It is a wise idea to not rely completely on one supplier; that way one supplier can always back up a loss by the other. It is also important to use suppliers who have been in business for some time, particularly if they are supplying a critical raw material or product. Products that weigh a lot can rack up a lot of freight charges if they come from a supplier at a significant distance. It would be important to balance the lower price of the supplier against the added shipping costs. In the business-to-business market, discounts from suppliers are the norm, and they will vary depending on the quantity purchased. Suppliers will let the business owner know the volumes required to reach particular discount levels.

Most business owners find that it is better to have fewer vendors and have closer relationships with them.[10] A closer relationship allows the business owner to visit the supplier's plant, talk with workers, and even work with suppliers to develop new products. This is critical because the price on the invoice is not the only cost of doing business with a supplier. Before the first order, businesses will need to develop requests for proposal, detail specifications for the products they need, and qualify the supplier—all this before a deal is ever transacted. Then the business will need to place the order, negotiate the terms of the deal, inspect the products when they arrive, and deal with any problems in the order. All these tasks result in a cost to the business. Business owners need to track all costs associated with dealing with a specific supplier, and if the costs are significantly above average, they should consider switching to a more effective supplier.

Wholesalers/Distributors

Wholesalers, or distributors (the terms are interchangeable in common usage), buy products in bulk from manufacturers and then seek retail outlets to reach the consumer or other businesses in an industrial channel. The wholesaler removes from the manufacturer the responsibility of finding suitable retail outlets for the products. A distributor can mean the difference between success and failure for a business. When a company entrusts its most valuable assets—its customers—to the distributor, it becomes conspicuously clear that selecting a good distributor is a crucial part of the marketing plan. Good distributors not only will contribute to increased sales but also will help with product planning for the future. The specifics of what a distributor may do depend on the distributor. Some of the tasks performed by them include the following:

- Warehousing of products
- Advertising and promotion
- Packaging and displays
- Training of retail sales personnel
- Transportation to retailers
- Service backup
- Restocking of retailers' shelves

The key to finding a good distributor is knowing to whom to talk. Some sources of information on distributors are customers, suppliers, lawyers, business consultants, and bankers (they will have knowledge of a distributor's payment record). Business owners should look for a distributor who provides good service, prices competitively to retail outlets, and is trustworthy. When that distributor is chosen, the company should execute a written contract with the distributor and monitor performance on a regular basis by sampling retail customers to determine if they are satisfied with the product and the service that they are receiving from the distributor.

Consider a hypothetical situation in which a manufacturer called GoodPro sold its products to a number of retailers, including one very large retailer. It tended to analyze its sales data by lumping all smaller retailers into one group and looking at them together. But sales data are often not an effective way to assess channel partners.[11] It is more effective to look at individual stock-keeping units. When GoodPro did that, it found to its surprise that five of the largest of its retailers were actually not making a profit for the company and that a few of the smaller retailers had better prospects for growth. GoodPro also learned that the largest retailer did not have a good conversion ratio; that is, the retailer generated a lot of traffic through promotions but not enough of that traffic converted to actual sales of GoodPro's products. The cost of the promotions, which GoodPro had to share, cut into the profit significantly.

Another area that has a big impact on the profitability of a product is logistics, which includes inventory, freight, and returns. Large distributors offer a distinct advantage for small businesses owners because they can maintain a larger inventory, avoid stock-outs, and deliver quickly.

Logistics Firms

It takes a long time before a young, growing company can justify having its own distribution center. Consequently, many growing companies are outsourcing their packaging, warehousing, inventory control, and trucking requirements to third-party **logistics firms.** In distribution terminology, *logistics* is the timely movement of goods from the producer to the consumer. In addition to providing other services, logistics firms can negotiate the best deals and the most efficient carriers, potentially saving the growing venture thousands of dollars.

Agents/Manufacturer's Representatives

Often manufacturers/producers will retain agents, brokers, or manufacturer's reps to find suitable outlets for their products. Agents will arrange agreements with wholesalers and retailers for the manufacturer. Agents usually do not buy or hold an inventory of goods from the manufacturer; instead, they bring together manufacturers and distributors or retailers to establish the most efficient distribution channel. The manufacturer, or producer, shares the cost with other manufacturers represented by the agent and pays a commission only on what the agent sells.

LEARNING FROM THE GLOBAL MARKET

Recognizing the Importance of Brand

The Chinese market contains 22 percent of all the people in the world, so as that country begins to establish its own brands, it is quickly becoming the master of its market. Furthermore, at the same time as it builds it brands at home, it is also building economies of scale that will serve it well in the global marketplace. To take its place in the worldwide economy, however, China must first overcome its image as a country that pirates major company brands.

Paulo Zegna, the cochief of Ermenegildo Zegna Group, a Milan men's fashion house, was surprised to find that a Chinese company had copied his designs and put his company's name on the product. What was more surprising was learning that the Chinese company had bought their raw wool from Zegna's supplier in Australia and that it used the same machines and consultants to produce the product. But when the product sold, Zegna did not receive a penny from the sale. Why wouldn't the Chinese company put its own brand on the product and sell it? Because Chinese brands have traditionally been associated with sweatshop labor that takes jobs from Western countries, so it does not do as well in other countries or even in its own country. To succeed in the global market with its own brands, China will need to repair its image and create its own products. If it can accomplish that, it will be a significant market force indeed.

Source: G. Colvin, "From Knockoff Bags to Knockout Brands," *Fortune* (June 27, 2005): 52.

Manufacturer's representatives are essentially independent salespeople paid on commission who handle the manufacturer's business in specific territories. Unlike agents, who bring buyers and sellers together for individual transactions, manufacturer's reps work with a specific manufacturer on a continuing basis, receiving a commission per product sold. Reps may also provide warehousing in a territory and handle the shipping of the product to the retailer.

IMPORT/EXPORT STRATEGIES

The decision to do business in the global market involves dealing with a number of important issues: choosing the right global market, determining how to finance international transactions, finding strategic partners in the other country, and choosing intermediaries and logistics companies. The results of these decisions will greatly affect the success of the business. Typically, businesses will either export or import in the global market. Exporting is selling products to another country, and importing is buying products from another country to sell in the small business owner's home country.

Finding the Best Global Market

Finding the best market for a product or service can be a daunting task, but some sources and tactics will help make the job easier. The *International Trade Statistics Yearbook of the United States,* which is available in any major library, is an excellent place to start. Using the Standard Industrial Trade Classification (SITC) codes found in this reference book, information on international demand for a product or service in specific countries can be found. The SITC system is a method of classifying commodities used in international trade. It is also important to be familiar with the harmonized system (HS) of classification, a ten-digit system that puts the United States "in harmony" with most of the world in terms of commodity-tracking systems. If an international shipment exceeds $2,500, the company must know its HS number for documentation.

Demand for U.S. products is usually reflected in four areas:

1. The dollar value of worldwide imports of a specific type of product to a country.

2. The level of growth of these imports as determined by import demand records over time. Countries whose levels of import demand exceed worldwide averages for a product or service are good choices.

3. The share of total import demand to a country that U.S. products enjoy. This figure should exceed 5 percent. A lower figure could indicate that tariffs might be affecting growth.

4. Additional sources of information such as the district office or the Washington, DC, office of the International Trade Administration and the Department of Commerce (DOC). The Commerce Department's database links all the DOC International Trade Administration offices and provides a wealth of valuable research information.

The successful launch of a program of global growth includes a marketing plan and budget as well as someone on the team who has international management experience or export/import experience. Depending on the budget, a consultant with an expertise in this area could be hired. Attending foreign trade shows to learn how business is conducted in the countries in which the company is interested in doing business will be important and a good place to learn who the major players in the industry are and who the competition is.

Export Financing

To make a sale in the global market, a company must have the funds to purchase the raw materials or inventory to fill the order. Unfortunately, many entrepreneurs assume that if they have a large enough order, getting financing will be no problem. Nothing could be further from the truth. Export lenders, like traditional lending sources, want to know that the company has a sound business plan and the resources to fill the orders. Entrepreneurs who want to export can look for capital from several sources:

- Bank financing
- Internal cash flow from the business
- Venture capital or private investor capital
- Prepayment, down payment, or progress payments from the foreign company making the order

A commercial bank will be more interested in lending money to a small exporter if the company has secured a guarantee of payment from a government agency such as the Import-Export Bank, which will limit the risk undertaken by the bank. Asking buyers to pay an up-front deposit large enough to cover the purchase of raw materials is also an option for a young company with limited cash flow.

Letters of Credit

A letter of credit is a bank document that guarantees a customer's bank drafts up to a certain amount for a specific period of time. It is a firm agreement that must be met to the letter to remain valid. For example, if an export company cannot meet the ship date, the letter may lose its value.

The following are some suggestions for constructing letters of credit:

- Make sure that the advising bank is the supplier's (exporter's) own bank.
- Make sure that the company address on the letter of credit is exactly as it is on company stationery. Correcting an error here will result in a fee from the bank.
- Include an "at-sight" clause, which means that when the documents called for in the letter of credit are presented to the advising bank, the exporter will get paid within five days.
- Make sure that the shipping date meets the company's production schedule.
- Ensure that the payment of the letter of credit can be made through a U.S. bank to avoid delays.
- Make sure that the internal bank reference number is on all documents to avoid rejection.
- Include an expiration date for the letter of credit that is one month *after* the ship date to allow the exporter time to gather and present the documents to the advising bank.

- Ensure that the company has a "clean airway bill" or ocean bill of lading, meaning the wording is exactly as it is in the letter of credit, even down to spelling.

- Do not put the details of every item shipped in the letter of credit. Put them instead on the packing lists, invoices, and purchase orders to avoid the chance for discrepancies that would result in the rejection of the letter of credit.

- Do not allow for transshipments (taking goods from one aircraft or vessel and putting them on another), unless the customer allows it and takes responsibility for potential damage.

- Allow for partial shipments to speed up cash flow.

Foreign Agents, Distributors, and Trading Companies

Every country has a number of sales representatives, agents, and distributors who specialize in importing U.S. goods. It is possible to find one agent who can handle an entire country or region, but if a country has several economic centers, it may be more effective to have a different agent for each center. *Sales representatives* work on commission; they do not buy and hold products. Consequently, the exporting company is still left with the job of collection, which, when dealing with a foreign country, can be costly and time-consuming. *Agents* provide a way to circumvent this problem. Agents purchase the company's product at a discount (generally very large) off list and then sell it and handle collections themselves. They solve the issue of cultural differences and the ensuing problems inherent in these transactions. However, with an agent, the company loses control over what happens to the product once it leaves the company's control. The company has no say over what the agent actually charges customers in his or her own country. If the agent charges too much in an effort to make more money, the company may lose a customer. Companies that are just starting to export or are exporting to areas not large enough to warrant an agent should consider putting an ad in American trade journals that showcase U.S. products internationally. Companies producing technology products may be able to find a manufacturer in the international region they are targeting that will let them sell their products through its company, thus giving them instant recognition in the foreign country. They could also become a potential source of financing for the exporting company.

Another option is to use an export trading company (ETC) that specializes in certain countries or regions where it has established a network of sales representatives. ETCs may also specialize in certain types of products. What often happens is that a sales rep reports to the ETC that a particular country is interested in a certain product. The ETC then locates a manufacturer, buys the product, and then sells it in the foreign country. Trading companies are a particularly popular vehicle when dealing with Japan.

Choosing an Intermediary

Before deciding on an intermediary to handle the exporting of products, a company should

1. Check the intermediary's current listing of products to see if the company's products seem to fit in with the intermediary's expertise.

2. Understand with whom they will be competing (that is, does the intermediary also handle the company's competitors?).

3. Find out if the intermediary has enough representatives in the foreign country to adequately handle the market.

4. Look at the sales volume of the intermediary. It should show a relatively consistent level of growth.

5. Make sure that the intermediary has sufficient warehouse space and an up-to-date communication system.

6. Examine the intermediary's marketing plan.

7. If needed, make sure that the intermediary can handle the servicing of its products.

Once an intermediary has been selected, an agreement detailing the terms and conditions of the relationship should be drafted. An attorney specializing in overseas contracts should be consulted, and the contract should be based on performance. A one- or two-year contract, with an option to renew if performance goals are met, should be drafted. Many intermediaries want a five- to ten-year contract, but it is important to be firm; it is not in the company's best interests to do a longer contract until it knows that the person is loyal and can perform. Other issues the agreement should address include

- The company's ability to use another distributor. Negotiate for a nonexclusive contract to have some flexibility.

- The specific products the agent or distributor will represent. This is important because, as the company grows, it may add or develop additional products and not want this agent to sell those products.

- The specific geographic territories for which the agent or distributor will be responsible.

- The specific duties and responsibilities of the agent or distributor.

- A statement of agreed-upon sales quotas.

- A statement of the jurisdiction in which any dispute would be litigated. This will protect the company from having to go to a foreign country to handle a dispute.

Choosing a Freight Forwarder

The freight forwarder's job is to handle all aspects of delivering the product to the customer. The method by which a company ships a product will have a significant impact on the product's cost or the price to the customer, depending on how the deal is structured, so the choice of a freight forwarder must be carefully considered. The ability to fill a shipping container to capacity is crucial to reducing costs. Freight forwarders prepare the shipping documents, which include a bill of lading (the contract between the shipper and the carrier) and an exporter declaration form detailing the contents of the shipment, and they can present shipping documents to the company's bank for collection. The company, however, is responsible for knowing if any items being shipped require special licenses or certificates, as in the case of hazardous materials or certain food substances.

PRICING

When Glaxo introduced its anti-ulcer drug Zantac at a premium price as the follower to a market dominated by SmithKline's Tagamet, it went against conventional wisdom.

When Taco Bell announced in 1994 that it would hold all prices until 2000, it was betting that value for the customer at the lowest price would win the fast-food wars. And when Netscape gave away its browser to establish an installed base of customers for its technology and then went public at an extraordinarily high valuation never having sold a product, it proved that pricing at zero had value. Whether entrepreneurs decide to price at a premium, at the minimum, or at zero, price is one of the most visible decisions that entrepreneurs make.[12] Surprisingly, research has found that business owners rarely give price the attention it deserves. They either assume that as long as they cover costs and return a profit, the price must be correct, or they see that they are charging about the same as everyone else, so the price must be correct. However, price is an important strategic variable in any business model, particularly in the dynamic markets being seen today, and wise entrepreneurs develop complex pricing structures that better reflect customer needs. This means that business owners are faced with a fairly large number of decisions related to price that include price objectives, strategy, promotions and discounts, and pricing for various products and services. Each of these areas has a number of options associated with it. Pricing decisions tend to fall into three main categories: (1) cost-based versus market-based pricing; (2) reactive versus proactive pricing; and (3) standardization versus flexibility pricing.

1. **Cost-based versus market-based pricing** Rather than focusing on demand, competitors' strategies, and the company's marketing strategy, many business owners concentrate on covering their costs of doing business. They do this by charging cost plus some amount for profit; keystoning, or doubling the costs; or applying some formula to give them the return that they need.

2. **Reactive versus proactive pricing** Business owners who respond readily to competitor's pricing structures whether or not it is in the best interests of their company are called reactive in their pricing. When business owners modify their prices only when there is no other choice, they are considered conservative in their pricing strategy. These risk-averse owners also closely benchmark their competitors and stick to simple pricing schemes. By contrast, business owners who are willing to take some risk typically use more novel approaches to pricing and are more aggressive, even when there is the potential for loss. However, when their pioneering pricing strategy succeeds, the rewards are enormous.

3. **Standardization versus flexibility pricing** Business owners who follow a standardization pricing strategy charge the same price regardless of customer, the purchase context, or competitor's pricing. By contrast, business owners who follow a flexible pricing strategy will vary prices to meet the needs of specific customers or different contexts.

The marketplace today demands a more entrepreneurial approach to pricing that is market-based, flexible, proactive, and risk assumptive.[13] Most markets are dynamic, so products move quickly through them. Time to market has decreased substantially; therefore, decision windows close more rapidly. Moreover, the competitive environment is more hostile and more creative about undermining the efforts of another company serving the same market. It is more difficult to differentiate products and services, so most products and services eventually trend toward commodity status, which means that they must compete on price. Competing on price means lower profit margins and the need to sell in higher volumes to make money. All this leads to fragmented markets with niche opportunities. In this type of market, entrepreneurs cannot be conservative or risk averse, nor can they simply sit back and respond to competitor pricing. They need to aggressively capitalize on customers' perceptions of value and adjust their price to reflect those various perceptions.

Pricing Objectives

Before determining how to price the product or service, it is important that the company have a long-term pricing objective that takes into account both the level of sales the company wants to achieve and the profit margin it seeks. Companies often focus on price per unit of product produced, but total profit determines whether or not the company stays in business. Pricing presents problems when firms don't get enough information from customers, when they rely on comparing current orders with past orders, and when they have inadequate systems for calculating accurate costs. Therefore, having long-term goals in a pricing objective is critical to successful pricing, and customizing that pricing to reflect information from customers is essential. Long-term goals are typically statements of position in the market and give a marketing plan focus. Some examples of long-term pricing objectives include

- Becoming the lowest-priced supplier in the industry.
- Creating the widest price range.
- Maximizing penetration of a market.
- Creating price leadership in the industry.
- Positioning the company in a specific market segment.
- Obtaining a specific share of the market.
- Maximizing profit[14]

Many studies have found that firms generally have multiple pricing objectives and that these objectives change with time.[15] Once the pricing objectives are in place, it is necessary to establish strategies to achieve those objectives.

Pricing Strategy

Pricing strategy is the method by which the goals or objectives of the company are achieved, and it is determined by conditions existing within the company and in the industry in which the company operates. These environmental conditions affect the decisions that business owners make about their pricing strategies. In general, the work of Noble and Gruca found that there are four categories of conditions that suggest particular pricing strategies: new product, competitive product, product line, and cost-based pricing.[16] Table 12.1 presents the four categories of conditions, or determinants, and their related pricing strategies. New products are in the unique position of being able to price high relative to the market, at least for a time. This premium pricing, called price skimming, enables the company to recoup some of its development costs before competition enters the market and forces prices down. Skimming is typically used when a product is brand new—that is, when there are no other directly comparable products and where there are customers who are price insensitive. These customers tend to purchase without regard to price in order to be the first to own the new product or to meet some special need.[17] Firms launching new products that have economies of scale can take advantage of penetration pricing and experience curve pricing to set a low price for the new product in order to accelerate the adoption

TABLE 12.1   Business Conditions and Pricing Strategies

Conditions and Strategy	Strategy Definition
New-Product Pricing	
Price skimming	Entering the market at a high price until competition forces the price down. The initial higher price is used to recoup the development costs.
Penetration pricing	To gain quick acceptance and broad-based distribution in a highly competitive market with similar products, introducing the product at a much lower price with minimal profit. Once sufficient market share is obtained, the price is gradually raised to match the competitive market.
Experience curve pricing	Introducing the product at a high price; then, as technological improvements enable the company to reduce its costs, reducing the price. In this way, the company can maintain a price advantage over competitors.
Competitive Pricing	
Leader pricing	The company initiates price changes.
Parity pricing	Pricing based on competition; the company looks at competitor's pricing strategies and prices in line with theirs.
Low-price supplier	Pricing below cost to attract customers to other products in the company's line because the loss leader no longer has value.
Product Line Pricing	
Complementary product pricing	Pricing the core product very low when the product has associated accessories, services, or supplies that have high margins.
Price bundling	Bundling the product with several other products, the sum of which costs less than the total of the individual products.
Customer value pricing	Modifying the product to meet different customer needs and price accordingly.
Cost-Based Pricing	
Cost-plus pricing	Adding together the cost of producing the product, the related costs of running the business, and a profit margin to arrive at price. It may also be called markup pricing or rate-of-return pricing.

Source: Based on the work of P. M. Noble and T. S. Gruca, "Industrial Pricing: Theory and Managerial Practice," *Marketing Science* 18(3) (1999): 438.

process. This is important where the entrepreneur wants the product to become the de facto standard.[18]

By contrast, when a company introduces a product that is not highly differentiated from its competitors, it will be important to price at or near one or more of the competitors. Typically, competitive markets are more mature, so demand is easier to calculate, and depending on resources, switching costs, and economies of scale, the entrepreneur may choose to employ leader pricing, parity pricing, or be the low-cost leader. Price leaders typically enjoy the greatest market share, so they set the pricing levels for the rest of the industry. Others benchmark their prices against the market leader. Firms that have high costs and are not in a position to command a premium price for their product usually follow parity pricing.[19] Firms with superior process, economies of scale, and lower-cost structures can afford to take a low-cost leader position, but low costs also allow for a price leader position.

Pricing strategy for business owners who have a line of products is influenced not only by the competitive market but also by the products and services within their own company. Consequently, they will look at bundling, complementary product pricing, and customer value pricing. Bundling is an interesting way to use price to create a competitive advantage. Rather than sell the parts to a system independently, the entrepreneur sets a price on the entire system, which, if the entrepreneur produces all the parts, makes it possible to sell the system at a more competitive price than a competitor who had to outsource some of the parts. The best example of complementary product pricing is Gillette's strategy of selling razors very inexpensively and then selling the consumable blades at a premium. Hewlett-Packard uses a similar strategy with its printers and cartridges. Customer value pricing lets the company be creative about how to price its products and services to various customers and in various combinations. For example, in 1990, McDonald's reduced the price of its basic hamburger to 59 cents to attract new customers to a stagnating market.

Despite the fact that cost-based pricing is the most widely practiced strategy, it does have significant weaknesses, not the least of which is that it ignores the influence of the market and what customers are willing to pay. The following are some possible goals and pricing strategies to achieve them:

- *Increase sales.* This may entail lowering prices to increase the volume sold.
- *Increase market share.* Lowering prices may increase volume, thus increasing market share.
- *Maximize cash flow.* Cash flow can be increased through a number of methods, including raising prices and reducing direct costs and overhead.
- *Maximize profit.* Similar to maximizing cash flow, this can be accomplished through several methods, including raising prices, lowering prices and increasing volume, or decreasing overhead.
- *Set up entry barriers to competition.* Lowering prices based on using efficient production methods, achieving economies of scale, and keeping overhead low often can set up entry barriers to companies that can't compete on that scale.
- *Define an image.* Setting a higher price based on higher perceived quality will help enhance image.
- *Control demand.* A company that does not have the resources to meet demand can set prices higher to control demand.

Knowing what a pricing strategy is supposed to accomplish in advance of setting a price will ensure compatibility with the company's goals.

Pricing Structure

Pricing structure, or all the aspects of a product or service that have a price attached to them, is where business owners can exercise the greatest amount of creative thought and flexibility. Companies use several pricing strategies at various stages of the business life cycle as well as the product life cycle (see Figure 12.4). Whichever strategy is chosen, it is important to understand what customers are willing to pay based on the perceived value of the product.

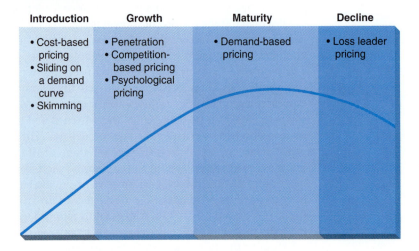

FIGURE 12.4 Pricing Strategies

Introduction	Growth	Maturity	Decline
• Cost-based pricing • Sliding on a demand curve • Skimming	• Penetration • Competition-based pricing • Psychological pricing	• Demand-based pricing	• Loss leader pricing

Price Tactics

Tactics have to do with the actual price that is assigned to a product or service. Price is often used to convey positioning as in $3.99 to suggest a bargain versus $5,000 to create a high-end image. Rebates, coupons, discounts, and promotions are all tactics to drive the customer to the product based on price.

Warning Signs of Pricing Problems

Price is not a static component of the business; it must change with customer needs and with changing conditions in the business environment. There are some warning signs that a company needs to revisit its pricing. Failing to modify or revise a pricing strategy in response to these warning signs can cost the company valuable customers and significant profits.

- Prices are always based on costs.
- Different people in the organization set prices with no agreement among them.
- Prices always follow the competition.
- New prices are generally a percentage increase over the previous year's prices.
- Prices to all customers are the same.
- Discounts are standardized.

Distribution and pricing are critical aspects of an effective marketing strategy for any small, growing business. If designed and managed well, they can strengthen the bundle of competitive advantages that the business has developed.

ISSUES FOR REVIEW AND DISCUSSION

1. How can distribution be a competitive strategy for a growing company?
2. What are some of the critical issues associated with multiple channels of distribution?
3. Compare and contrast wholesalers/distributors with agents/manufacturer's reps.
4. How does an entrepreneur determine the best global market to enter?
5. When determining pricing strategy, what factors should an entrepreneur consider?

EXPERIENCING ENTREPRENEURSHIP

1. Find two companies that are successfully making distribution strategy their competitive advantage and compare and contrast them.
2. Interview an entrepreneur who is exporting to a global market. What challenges has this entrepreneur faced, and how has he or she dealt with them?

The Challenge of Extending a Brand

Ward Setzer is known among the rich and famous for the powerboats that he manufactures, which cost a minimum of $6 million and include helicopter landing pads and saunas. It is very much a niche business—his company can deliver only two boats a year. Setzer, at age 45, decided that it was time to think about planning for an early retirement. Realizing that the company was not producing enough income to support the kind of retirement that he desired, he figured it was time to diversify and leverage what he saw as a valuable brand—Ward Setzer Design. The model for this new direction was Calvin Klein, who designs high-end apparel but also has a more modest line of clothing under his CK label. Setzer saw the possibility for a "bargain" line of boats, but he also calculated that he could perhaps attach his name to surfboards, wakeboards, all-weather gear, and marine hardware.

Background

A naval architect by trade, Setzer began his yacht construction career as the lead designer for Hattaras Yachts based in Palm Beach, Florida. When not designing, he spent his free time sitting on the seawall next to the Palm Beach Yacht Club, watching the boats sail by and dreaming of new designs. He was working for renowned designer Jack Hargrave, who was known for his superlarge yachts. In 1991, Setzer was ready to go out on his own. He started Setzer Design Group in Cary, North Carolina, with a goal to produce superyachts that were classic in design and therefore had longevity.

The Luxury Boat Industry

In 1997, after a prolonged economic downturn, the luxury-yacht construction industry began to grow rapidly. By 2006, it had nearly tripled, and the total value of boats 80 feet or longer was approaching $5.7 billion, according to *ShowBoats International*. Attendance at international boat shows was increasing, and sales at the boat shows in south Florida were breaking records. In 2004 alone, more than $600 million in boats were sold during a five-day period at just one boat show. With plenty of disposable income, today's

luxury yacht owners are looking for ways to store their jet skis, surfboards, and sea kayaks on their yachts, so the average size of these superyachts has grown dramatically to over 244 feet for expeditionary models.

Facing the Challenge

Although with three International Super-yacht Society Design Awards under his belt, Setzer is a "rock star" in his industry; there is a difference between the Ward Setzer name and Calvin Klein. The latter had gained name recognition among the broad mass of consumers when he began to diversify into other products and a low-end line, whereas Setzer's name is recognized only among an elite group of boating enthusiasts. Although confident that he could succeed, Setzer was nervous that by moving into the nonelitist market of surfboards, it might damage his core brand. "If you sit down with a dozen wealthy people, only four might have a yacht and the rest don't know what you are talking about," says Jill Bobrow, the editor-in-chief of *ShowBoats International* magazine. Setzer's customers made it clear to him that they were not interested in having him devalue the brand.

To attempt to address the challenge, Setzer created a separate company, Windswell Designs, and licensed his lifestyle and marine products using a cobranding technique with both Windswell Designs and the Setzer Signature label. He also designed a line of 32-foot and 38-foot boats to attract boating enthusiasts who couldn't afford a luxury yacht. He would distribute these boats through Windswell in hopes of not disturbing his luxury yacht brand.

In October 2005, Setzer successfully launched his Windswell Designs at the Fort Lauderdale International Boat Show, the largest and most important in the industry. The new Setzer line includes surfboards, windsurfers, water-sports toys, marine hardware, and furniture. Setzer, an avid surfer himself, modeled the boards on the computer but drew the actual lines of the surfboard by hand and gave them the same sweeping look of his luxury yachts.

Today, Setzer still constructs his own personal boats by hand. "I think it's sacrilegious for a designer

to draw something he doesn't know how to build."
He is confident that his new line under the Windswell
brand will do well and expand his company's reach.
Only time will tell if his new distribution and marketing strategy will work.

Advising the Entrepreneur

1. Evaluate Setzer's decision to move into the
   Windswell line. Do you believe that it will hurt his
   core brand? Why or why not?

2. The growth in the superyacht industry will not
   continue forever. How should Setzer prepare for a
   potential change in the economics of the
   industry?

Sources: G. Bounds, "Extending an Elite Brand to a New
Product Line," *Wall Street Journal Startup Journal* (October 13,
2005), www.startupjournal.com; S. Murphy, "Former PBer
to Compete, Launch Line at International Boat Show," *Palm
Beach Daily News* (October 2, 2005); G. R. Byrd, "The Spirit
of Yachting" (October 2005), www.trinityyachts.com.

CHAPTER 13

Designing a Marketing Plan from Start-Up Through Growth

Don't forget that [your product or service] is not differentiated until the customer understands the difference.

Tom Peters, *Thriving on Chaos* (1987)

▶ LEARNING OUTCOMES

- Discuss the purpose and uses of a marketing plan.
- Explain how to maintain successful, long-term customer relationships.
- Describe the impact of global marketing on a small business.
- Compare and contrast the marketing strategies for new technologies and other products.

Selling Shoes in Cyberspace

Nick Swinmurn is one of those people who, once he finds a great pair of shoes, just has to have more than one pair. One day while searching in vain for a new pair of his favorite Vans, he realized that others must face this problem. He thought that maybe his inability to find a new pair of his old shoes was the basis for a business opportunity.

Since his graduation from college in 1996, Swinmurn had served as a group-ticket salesman for the San Diego Padres baseball team, then as sales manager for an Internet automobile retailer, and he was ready for something new. As part of the Internet generation, Swinmurn naturally thought about an e-commerce business, so he decided to investigate the shoe business further.

What he found was that footwear is a $40-billion industry and that about 5 percent of the sales are conducted via mail order. He also learned that people have no idea how many different types of shoes are available to them because they are generally limited to what their local stores carry. In early 1999, Swinmurn began developing a concept and talking to people in the shoe business and at trade shows. By June of that year, he had raised seed funding of $150,000 from friends and family, and in July he convinced a shoe buyer from Nordstrom, the upscale department store, to come on board. This key person gave Swinmurn credibility in the eyes of the manufacturers.

Swinmurn knew that the only way he could successfully sell shoes online was by providing extraordinary customer service in three important areas. First, customers had to feel comfortable that they could return something that didn't work out. To do that he provided a 365-day return policy for defective or unworn shoes and quick response on customer calls. Second, Swinmurn had to make it easy for customers to find the right shoe. He put clear pictures on the site that could be enlarged and rotated to provide a view of the shoe from any angle, and he used a powerful search engine to speed up customers' ability to find exactly what they were looking for. Finally, he had to reduce the wait for customers to receive their shoes, so he guaranteed shipment of orders the same day that they are received and offered two- and three-day delivery services. He also provided standard shipping at no charge.

Zappos.com's high degree of service spread by word of mouth. Soon, 60 percent of his orders came from repeat customers and 20 percent from referrals. Zappos.com was projecting $300 million in sales for 2005 with almost 500 employees. In addition to relying on referrals, Swinmurn created a pay-for-performance advertising program in conjunction with Commission Junction, which provided a Web-based solution that would connect Zappos.com to Commission Junction's quality Web publishers. The way it works is that Zappos.com compensates publishers who put Zappos.com ads on their sites on a cost-per-sale basis—giving a 15 percent commission on each sale. After using this approach, Zappos.com grew substantially.

Swinmurn is not resting on success. Although he has erected excellent barriers for his competitors, he knows that there is always another Nick Swinmurn out there waiting to capitalize on an opportunity.

Advising the Entrepreneur

1. What other forms of advertising and promotion would be appropriate for Zappos.com?

2. Visit the Zappos.com website and critique it. Are there any improvements that you would advise Swinmurn to make?

Sources: Zappos, Inc., www.zappos.com; "Focusing on Service—Nick Swinmurn's Key Move," *Startup Nation* (June 24, 2005), www.startupnation.com; "Zappos.com Case Study," *Commission Junction,* www.cj.com (accessed October 7, 2005).

Marketing consists of everything a business owner does to make customers aware of the business so that they buy its products and services on a repeat basis. *Marketing* includes the name of the business, the features and benefits of the product or service that is sold, the process employed to manufacture or deliver products and services, the packaging, the location of the business, and the advertising, promotion, public relations, sales efforts, after-sale service, and follow-up needed to keep the customer. *Guerrilla marketing* is a bundle of tactics that entrepreneurs with limited resources use to reach their customers and build relationships as effectively as or more effectively than large companies with significant resources. This chapter focuses on fundamental marketing strategies and guerrilla tactics that small, growing companies can use to create awareness of the company and to build long-term customer relationships.

A new company faces the dual challenge of marketing a new product or service and promoting the company itself. A new, exciting product or service may attract initial customer attention, but customers also want to feel comfortable that a stable, healthy business is behind that product or service. Though company credibility is not always a prerequisite in the consumer products market (consumers often buy from companies in Chapter 11 bankruptcy), it is certainly vital in the industrial or business-to-business products markets and in the service industry. So for new companies, marketing strategy deals with two fronts: the product or service and the company.

An additional problem that both new companies and established companies sometimes face is that their founder or owners have learned about marketing from experience with large companies, so they only know one side of marketing: the kind of mass marketing strategies used by giants such as Procter & Gamble, Wal-Mart, and Intel. Small businesses, by contrast, have unique needs and face unique challenges,

LEARNING FROM SUCCESS

Give Away Your Product!

Can you build an entire business on swords? Titus Blair was convinced that it was possible. Starting with a fascination with swords, Blair decided to capitalize on a series of movies that featured exciting swordplay—*Gladiator, Lord of the Rings,* and *The Last Samurai.* In 1998, with $100 from his savings, he created an online retail store and then drove traffic to it by buying advertising placements on search-engine sites such as Google. But this approach only produced about 1000 visitors a month, and Blair needed to find a way to produce a significantly greater amount of growth in order to establish SwordsOnline as the premier location for those steel blades.

In 2002, the Florida resident began to experiment with contests in which he would give away a sword.

"We have swords, and we want to use swords to promote swords," he claimed. When a visitor came to the site, they were asked to register a "wish list" of swords, valued up to $500 each, that they would like to win. Once a month, Blair randomly selected a winner and a sword from the winner's wish list. The tactic was a huge success, doubling the user base every three months. On the days that Blair sends out a monthly e-mail to registrants, sales move up from 2 percent to 7 percent. As of 2004, revenues were at $3.25 million.

Lesson Learned: *Give away the product you're trying to sell.*

Source: "Titus Blair's Key Move: Promotions to Drive Traffic," from *Startup Nation,* www.startupnation.com (accessed June 24, 2005). Reprinted by permission.

principally because of resource deficiencies; thus, they require different strategies. The fact that entrepreneurs must look at marketing from a different point of view does not mean the strategies they come up with are "second class." Quite the contrary: some start-up marketing strategies, such as personalized customer service, have become so successful that large corporations are now adopting similar programs. The ability to deal with the customer on a more personal level is a distinct competitive advantage and certainly a way to compete successfully against established firms.

THE MARKETING PLAN

The marketing plan for an entrepreneurial company is a living guide to the ways that the company plans to build customer relationships over its life to fulfill its mission statement. The plan details the strategies and tactics that will create awareness on the part of the customer and build a loyal customer base over time. Marketing plans are written at many points in a business's life. Certainly, the original business plan contains a marketing plan for introducing the company and its products and services to the marketplace. Later the business owner may develop a marketing plan to create market awareness and positioning for the company, to introduce new products and services, and to grow the business, perhaps in a new direction.

A marketing plan takes time to implement, and the results take time to see. One of the biggest problems with most marketing plans is that they are not followed long enough to achieve the desired results. Changing the plan precipitously is precisely the wrong thing to do. It takes time to build customer relationships. It also takes time for a particular marketing strategy to build confidence in the customer. On average, a customer sees an ad fifteen or twenty times before actually purchasing the product. The marketing plan is therefore an investment in the future of the business, and any investment should be carefully prepared. Five steps put an entrepreneur in a position to prepare an effective marketing plan.

1. *Make a list of the options.* To know which marketing options to consider, talk to other business owners, customers, and suppliers. Reading books and articles on successful marketing strategies can also be a source of inspiration. This idea-generation process produces a list of possibilities that may range from sponsoring a business conference to advertising in a national trade publication. The nature of the possibilities generated reflects the needs of the company's particular customers. Determining which strategies are the most effective or even feasible can be left for later.

2. *Think like a customer.* The business must be imagined from the customer's point of view. What would entice a customer to enter a store, buy its products, and take advantage of its service? In other words, what is the value proposition for this customer? Richard Branson, founder of Virgin Airways, designed his planes and services based on how he felt as a passenger on an airplane. Scott Samet and Douglas Chu focused on what moviegoers wanted from the snacks they purchased when they designed Taste of Nature: to give them the ability to mix their own snacks from large plastic bins. The most effective way to learn what customers want is to talk to them, observe them, and, in the end, become one of them.

3. *Study the competition.* By studying competing companies, entrepreneurs can get a clear sense of what it takes to be successful and which marketing strategies the competition employs effectively. They can also determine what their company can do better than the competition.

4. *Analyze the options and rank them.* Marketing strategies that don't meet the needs of customers or are simply not feasible at this time (usually for budgetary reasons) should be eliminated. Then the top-ten choices can be rank ordered.

5. *Verify that the strategies chosen are compatible with the business model.* Once the top-ten choices have been made, they should be evaluated for how effectively they might produce a revenue stream for the company.

The Marketing Plan in One Paragraph

Many experienced marketers suggest that the first step in creating the marketing plan is to condense all the ideas about the marketing strategy into a single paragraph that says it all. Impossible? Not at all. A single, well-written paragraph forces the company to focus carefully on the central selling point of the overall marketing strategy—to determine what grabs customers' attention and entices them to buy. The paragraph should include the following elements:

- The purpose of the marketing plan: *What will the marketing plan accomplish?*
- The benefits of the product or service: *How will the product or service help the customer or satisfy a need?*
- The customer: *Who is the primary customer, and how will the company build a relationship with that customer?*
- The company's convictions—its identity: *How will the customer define the company?*
- The market niche: *Where does the company fit in the industry or market? How does it differentiate itself? How does it differentiate its customers?*
- The marketing tactics to be used: *What specific marketing tools will be employed to create awareness and build relationships?*
- The percentage of sales that the marketing budget represents: *How much money will be allocated to the marketing plan?*

The following is an example of a marketing plan in one paragraph that covers all these points:

> *The purpose of the marketing plan is to create awareness for GenPower Corporation, which will sell innovative, portable power equipment at the highest quality and the lowest possible cost by positioning itself as the leader providing reliable, dual power source products that reduce the number of pieces of equipment that the user must own. The target market is the construction industry and, more specifically, those who use power tools in areas where no source of power is available. The niche that GenPower will enter is that of construction companies that own or lease power equipment. Initial marketing tactics will include direct sales to equipment rental outlets, advertisements in trade publications, and trade shows. GenPower's customers will see the company as service oriented with a quick response to customer needs in both service and product design. Twelve percent of sales will be applied to the marketing strategy.*

With the focus derived from the "one-paragraph marketing plan," the full plan can be undertaken. A complete marketing plan covers issues related to the customer, the product or service, price, promotion, and distribution. (Pricing and distribution are addressed in Chapter 12.)

Understanding the Product or Service

For marketing purposes, the product or service should be thought of as a bundle of benefits to the customer. These benefits include a wide variety of features: attractiveness, distinctive characteristics, quality, options, warranties, service contracts, delivery, and so forth. Perhaps more important for the customer are the intangible benefits such as savings in time, convenience, money, or improved health. To feel comfortable about buying a product or service, customers must know about and understand these benefits.

In a customer-focused marketing plan, it is assumed that the customer has played a part in the design and development of the product or service. In other words, the product or service has been customized to meet the needs of the individual customer. Part of the marketing strategy as it relates to the product or service, then, is to involve customers in the product development phase so that the ultimate product or service meets their exact needs. (For more information about product development, see Chapter 14.) It is also important to focus on the intangible aspects of the product or service. Intangibles are those things that are difficult to measure: quality, innovative technology, service, and reliability. They are the key to differentiation in a market where products, services, and technology quickly become commodities in the eyes of the customer.

Product or Service Positioning Product or service positioning is the way that customers view the product or service in relation to competitors' offerings: Is the product of higher quality, less expensive, more attractive, and so forth? In short, **product positioning** defines the product by its benefits to the customer. Consequently, products are typically repositioned several times during the product life cycle as customer tastes and preferences change. Not only is the product or service positioned but also the company. Savvy customers today are concerned more and more about the reputations of the companies that they deal with. If, for example, a company associates with distributors whose level of service is not up to its standards, this reflects negatively on the entrepreneur's company. Precious marketing dollars are wasted if the company fails to respond to customers' perceptions. Using a one-to-one relationship marketing approach means that the company communicates with the customer enough to know how he or she perceives the product or service.

A statement of the product's position relative to competitors' products should be written from the customer's point of view. For example,

> *The customer will see EZ-Alert as a high-quality, state-of-the-art security device for parents who want to keep track of their children in public situations.*

The positioning of a product or service should be tested in the market prior to doing a full product launch. Several methods can be used; each varies in the time and cost involved:

- In a **peer review,** the entrepreneur or management team asks friends to give an opinion on the positioning statement for the product and on how the product performs in this position.

- In a **distribution channel review,** salespeople, distributors, and retailers are asked what they think of the position statement. Typically they have a good sense of where the company and its products might fit in the industry.

- With **focus groups,** the company brings together a group of potential customers to get their feedback and to undertake blind product reviews. Focus groups consist

Strategy Involves Trial and Error

In a fast-changing world, plans may be obsolete before they are implemented, but the key to ultimate success is quickly learning from mistakes and trying again. History provides some apt examples of entrepreneurs whose persistence carried them beyond their initial failures. Thomas Edison probably holds the record for a string of failures, 10,000, before finally finding a filament that would create light. Apparel giant Levi Strauss started out with hopes of being a gold miner during the California Gold Rush in the 1840s, but luck was not on his side when it came to mining. But instead of giving up and going back home, he took some time to look around and while doing that discovered an interesting opportunity. The hard-working miners needed sturdy pants in which to work, so Strauss began selling canvas pants out of the back of his wagon. Instead of striking yellow gold, he struck entrepreneurial gold with his Levi Strauss jeans.

Lesson Learned: *Mistakes often lead to success.*

---

of people who have not participated in the design and development of the product, so their opinions are unbiased.

■ **Test marketing** involves producing a limited amount of product and selling it in a defined geographic region to determine if the product positioning is correct. The cost of this approach must be weighed against getting the product into the market as quickly as possible, particularly where there is a first-mover advantage to be gained. Time to market is becoming more important in light of rapidly changing technology and markets. However, having the customer involved at every stage of product development shortens that time significantly and makes it more likely that the product does not experience problems after the launch. The final positioning statement should be communicated to everyone in the company so that all share a common philosophy and communicate a consistent message to the customer.

Branding Building brand loyalty in a time of rapid change, when technology has created new media markets, is challenging at best. Today, branding must represent the qualities and philosophy of the company as much as the product, but for many consumer product and service companies, building a brand name becomes a war of images. An ad featuring a young, slim, athletic-looking woman drinking a "light" beer seems to be an oxymoron, but subliminally it hits the mark. In such an ad, drinking light beer is touted as healthy and youthful. Whether or not it is true is irrelevant; the image remains.

For companies that participate in the war of the images, the battle is everything. In many television ads today, viewers don't even know which brand is being promoted; often the name appears only briefly at the end of the ad. Such is the case with some Calvin Klein and Nike ads. The strategy of these companies is not to sell product with these ads but to get people to pay attention to advertising once again. Today customers are so bombarded by advertising that they have almost become immune to its influences, so companies are taking drastic measures to regain their attention.

A countermovement, however, has begun to occur among some entrepreneurial companies. A number of very successful companies, such as Ben & Jerry's Homemade,

Smith and Hawkens, and Starbucks Coffee are resisting image positioning as the way to communicate their message. Instead of promoting brand names, they choose to communicate the philosophy of their company, which is at the core of all their products and by its very nature differentiates these companies from others in the market. They do not go head to head with their competitors in a war of images; they create their own niche in marketing strategy by seeking ways to increase pride and loyalty in not only their customers but also their employees. They break with tradition to make themselves stand out.

The differences in products that these new marketing strategists promote are real and measurable. These real distinctions not only separate them from the false reality of their competitors' images but also expose those images for what they are. Of course, developing a sound company philosophy or culture is not an overnight achievement. It takes time, and while the company is working at building that philosophy, the image builders probably receive the bulk of the attention. Nevertheless, persistence pays off when the company delivers precisely what it said it would deliver.

Brand-name recognition, when achieved, must be protected from inferior products that might attempt to secure a competitive advantage by trading on a name or slogan that is associated with a successful brand. For example, McWilliams Wines, an Australian company, used the slogan "Big Mac" to promote a 2-liter wine bottle. McDonald's, the famous American fast-food chain, took McWilliams to court, saying that its use of the Big Mac slogan would mislead the public into thinking a relationship existed. The court concluded that confusion might occur, but the slogan was not misleading because the term "Big Mac" is descriptive. Therefore, McWilliams had not infringed on McDonald's rights.[1]

In her book *Defending Your Brand against Imitation*, Judith Zaichowsky suggests several actions that a company can do to protect a brand name:[2]

1. Use the trademark as an adjective in the name of the product, for example, *Sanka Brand Decaffeinated Coffee*.

2. Make sure that the media use the trademark correctly. Check ads and articles written about the company and report any errors for immediate correction.

3. Use a specific typographical treatment. For example,

EZ - A l e r t

4. Be careful in the selection of a brand name. Test it thoroughly and look to avoid names already in use or covered by copyrights, names too similar to existing trade names and those already in use with unrelated products.

Packaging and Labeling The packaging and labeling of products should reflect the philosophy of the company and the type of business. For consumer products, packaging actually becomes another form of advertising and promotion. Packaging has to grab the consumer's attention as it sits among many competing products on crowded shelves. Industrial products generally require packaging that is more utilitarian. The design doesn't need to attract attention because the packaging merely makes it more convenient to transport the product. Consequently, industrial packaging typically consists of brown boxes with bold, colored lettering to identify the contents and the manufacturer.

With products that are marketed globally, packaging may be even more important, not for shipping purposes but because in some countries—notably Japan—a premium is placed on the artistic design of the package, and customers are even willing to pay more for a beautiful box.

Just like the product, the packaging must be designed and tested for consumer response and distribution channel response. It should serve the functions for which it was designed. In general, packaging should:

- Tell what the product is. This description can range from product features to directions for use, ingredients, remedies for misuse, level of quality, and warranty information.
- Describe its key benefits to the customer, such as convenience, price, quality, and features.
- Highlight the company philosophy. It could state, for example, "Our customers come first with us."
- Be distinctive and attractive enough that customers can recognize the company's products from the package design alone without having to read anything.
- Use safe and recyclable materials wherever possible.

Package design is something that requires the services of a professional, which is not an inexpensive undertaking. However, many business owners can testify to the fact that good packaging sells product. Good design is rewarded by increased sales and also by the industry. Likewise, poor design receives its share of attention in the press as well. A classic example is L'eggs pantyhose, which received much criticism of its nonenvironmentally friendly plastic egg container. Nevertheless, the manufacturer refused to change the package by which it was recognized everywhere. By contrast, the original packaging of audio CDs (the plastic jewel box in a cardboard container twice the size of the CD) was changed due to consumer and distributor protest over excessive packaging.

Building Relationships and Repeat Sales Through Promotion

The promotional plan establishes the identity and vision of the company that will be conveyed through all of its marketing efforts from advertising to public relations. *Identity* is how the company sees itself and how it wants customers to see the company. Recall that *vision* is the fundamental belief in what the company aspires to be and is composed of the company's core values, mission, and purpose. Identity and vision are quite different from image. An *image* is what the company wants the public to perceive it as being, whereas the company's identity and vision define what it is in reality. A company that hopes to build lifelong customer relationships will stay away from image-creating techniques and focus instead on vision-conveying techniques. With this in mind, the promotional plan for growing the business is one the company implements and uses consistently for the long term. It is the plan in which the company invests to build a strong and loyal customer base.

The promotion function of the marketing strategy is the creative one, for this is where guerrilla advertising, publicity, sales promotion, and personal selling tactics—in short, the promotional mix—is decided (see Figure 13.1). Not every company has the same promotional mix; it is a function of the type of business, the mission, the target market, and, of course, the budget. For entrepreneurs with new or growing ventures, the last item, the budget, dictates that they must be highly creative in their promotional mix and strategy because, normally, resources are very limited. Entrepreneurs have used

FIGURE 13.1   The Promotional Mix

several strategies to estimate how much money they need to set aside in their budgets for promoting their businesses. These include the following:

- *Use a percentage of sales.* If the companies in an industry typically spend about 5 percent of their sales on the promotion effort, that percentage becomes a benchmark figure for the entrepreneur's company.

- *Keep up with the competitors.* Entrepreneurs may decide to mimic the promotional mix of their competitors and spend what they spend. This is not necessary if the entrepreneur has defined a niche that is not being served.

- *Calculate what is needed to achieve the company's goals.* Some products and services require more promotion than others to create awareness. For example, a brand new product with which customers have no experience requires a lot more promotional effort to create awareness and educate customers.

Promotional creativity begins with a clear understanding of the customer, the economy, current trends, and even the daily news because a creative idea for promotion can come from anywhere, including a current event. Today, social responsibility is a big issue—hence the proliferation of ads, such as those of Mobil Oil, depicting a company that cares about people and natural resources. In fact, the ad may never mention the product it is trying to sell. Tying a marketing strategy to current trends such as social responsibility means that the company must remain flexible and willing to change the strategy if the current trend changes. Customers are fickle, and no matter how sound or beneficial a trend may be, they eventually tire of it, and a new strategy must be employed.

Promotion is also the way that entrepreneurs convey their dedication to total quality and the highest levels of customer satisfaction. A good promotional mix incorporates the input of everyone in the organization to create an integrated plan. It should convey the dedication to superior quality in the types of promotion that are chosen and in the way that they are carried out. And all promotion should focus on the benefit to the customer of doing business with the entrepreneur's company.

Advertising to Reach Customers Companies advertise to create product awareness or company awareness. It is impossible for a small business owner to escape advertising because it is present everywhere, from the sign announcing a store or office to the salesperson or receptionist who greets the customer. Good advertising attracts the right customers and builds an excellent company image. If done effectively, it also increases sales. But advertising alone cannot guarantee sales if the product/service doesn't provide value for the customer or create continued sales if the company doesn't follow up with customers to ensure that they are satisfied.

To be successful, advertising must accomplish four things:

1. Target the correct audience.
2. Present a positive picture.
3. Reflect the vision and culture of the company.
4. Ask for the sale.

There are three general choices of media for advertising: print media, broadcast media, and miscellaneous media. The choice of which to use depends on the type of business and what is typically done in the industry. Advertising should target where the customer expects to find it. The media comparison chart (Table 13.1) displays the options available to a small business.

This section has provided just a few of the hundreds of tips and techniques available to entrepreneurs who wish to advertise products or services in the most efficient and effective ways while the new venture is growing. The series of books on guerrilla marketing by Jay Conrad Levinson is highly recommended for its marketing suggestions geared specifically to young, growing companies.

Publicity and Public Relations *Publicity* is essentially free advertising for a product or business through newspaper articles and radio and television stories, and talk shows. *Public relations,* however, is the strategy for presenting the company and its philosophy to the public. Publicity is one of the best entrepreneurial marketing tools there is because it gets attention and it is free.

The key to successful publicity is having a product or business that is newsworthy. For example, the product may be environmentally friendly, or the way the company was founded may be unique. Companies such as Ben & Jerry's Homemade and Body Shop International have received millions of dollars' worth of free publicity because they have interesting stories and socially responsible messages. There are several ways to get some publicity. The business owner can get in touch with a reporter to test an idea, and, if the reporter is interested in writing a story, the owner should send along a press kit containing a press release, biographies and photos of key people, any necessary background information, and copies of any other articles written about the company. Whenever possible, the management team should get to know people in the media on a first-name basis. This gives the company instant clout when it needs free publicity. The media are always looking for news and appreciate the effort to give them something newsworthy.

A rich source of data for publicity and public relations are the customer stories that exist everywhere in an organization. These have the side benefit of attracting new customers who tend to place more credence on what other customers say.[3]

TABLE 13.1   Media Comparison Chart

Media	Advantages	Disadvantages	Hints
Print Media			
Newspapers	Broad coverage in a selected geographic area Flexibility and speed in bringing to print and modifying Generates sales quickly Costs relatively little	May reach more than target market Difficult to attract reader attention Short life	Look for specialized newspapers for better targeting. Include a coupon or 800 number. Locate ad on right-hand page above the fold.
Magazines	Can target special interests More credible than newspapers	Expensive to design, produce, and place	Look for regional editions. Use a media-buying service. Use color effectively. Check on "remnant space," leftover space that must be filled before magazine goes to print.
Direct marketing (direct mail, mail order, coupons, telemarketing)	Lets you close the sale when the advertising takes place Coverage of wide geographic area Targets specific customers More sales with fewer dollars More information provided Highest response rate	Not all products suitable Need consumable products for repeat orders Response rate on new catalogs is very low, about 2%.	Create a personalized mailing list and database from responses. Entice customers to open the envelope. Use several repeat mailings to increase the response rate.
Yellow Pages	Good in the early stages for awareness Good for retail/service	Relatively expensive Targets only local market	Create ad that stands out on the page.
Signs	Inexpensive Encourage impulse buying	Outlive their usefulness fairly quickly	Don't leave sale signs in windows too long; people will no longer see them.
Broadcast Media			
Radio	Good for local or regional advertising	Can't be a one-shot ad; must do several	Advertise on more than one station to saturate market. Sponsor a national radio program. Provide the station with finished recorded commercials. Stick to thirty-second ads with music.

Table 13.1 Media Comparison Chart *(continued)*

Media	Advantages	Disadvantages	Hints
Television	Second most popular form of advertising People can see and hear about product/service Can target at national, regional, or local level	Very expensive for both production and on-air time Must be repeated frequently	Time based on GRP (gross rating points). Range is $5–$500 per GRP. Use only if you can purchase 150 GRPs per month for three months. Seek help of media-buying service.
Cable TV shopping	Good for new customer products Targets the consumer Good products sell out in minutes	Not a long-term strategy Good only for products between $15 and $50 Product must be demonstrable	Call network for vendor information kit. Contact buyer for your product category. Be prepared to fill an initial order of between 1000 and 5000 units.
Infomercial	Good for consumer items that can't be explained quickly	Very expensive to produce Hit rate is about 10%	Most profitable times are late nights, mornings, and Saturday and Sunday during the day. Test time slots and markets to confirm effectiveness.
Miscellaneous			
Affinity items (T-shirts, caps, mugs) searchlights, couponing, in-store demonstrations, videotapes, free seminars	Good for grabbing consumer's attention Effective yet inexpensive way to showcase the company	Value varies significantly with type of business and product or service	Every company should make use of affinity items to create free publicity.

MAINTAINING CUSTOMER RELATIONSHIPS

Customer acquisition is one outcome of marketing, but **customer relationship management** (CRM) is essential to economic success. Basically, CRM is a database approach to maximizing shareholder value through winning, tracking, understanding, and keeping the right customers.[4] It also involves profiting from the customer life cycle, which is the behavior of customers over the time that they are with a company. Customer loyalty is the goal, but even more than customer loyalty, the goal is customer advocacy. Figure 13.2 depicts the traditional four-step marketing loyalty ladder with additional rungs indicating how customers become advocates. People who have come in contact with the entrepreneur's business through trade shows, advertising, or many other means are considered *suspects,* a pool of potential business *prospects,* those who have been further qualified to determine that they have

FIGURE 13.2 The Customer Loyalty Ladder

Evangelist

Loyal Buyer

Repeat Customer

First-time Customer

Prospect

Suspect

intentions of doing business with the company. Through the art of promotion and selling, prospects are turned into *first-time customers,* those customers who have engaged in a single transaction with the company. First-time customers then become part of the company's segmentation, targeting, and personalization process in an attempt to move them to the *repeat customer* rung. At this point, it is important to use stickiness tactics that increase switching costs for the customer and tie them exclusively to the entrepreneur's product or service. Examples of stickiness tactics are VIP clubs, frequency programs, and special discounts. Assuring that customers on this rung are completely satisfied is essential to edging them into the **evangelism** category where they become a real promotional arm of the company.

If the entrepreneur wants to successfully move more customers to the top rungs of the ladder, she or he must adhere to a number of principles. Table 13.2 presents nine principles for increasing customer value.

Tracking Customers

For relationship marketing to work, the company needs individual information from transaction data. Instead of mass surveys, entrepreneurial companies need to run experiments.[5] For example, an e-commerce company may be looking to find out:

1. Whether a $19.95 price point is more effective in terms of number of sales than a $29.95 price point.

2. What the "look" of the e-commerce site should be full color? A mix? A lot of information? A minimal amount of informaton?

3. Who responds best to online marketing: current customers? New customers? Women?

By testing several versions of the site on various types of customers and measuring the results, the company can learn a lot about who its long-term customers will be. The secret to success is long-term tracking of individual customer preferences and

TABLE 13.2 Principles for Increasing Customer Value

Reduce Buyer Remorse	Set realistic expectations and reinforce the decision to purchase.
Reinforce the Value Proposition	Add complementary services to ensure that the benefit is received.
Encourage Adoption	Check on customers' consumption status. It is important that they use the product or service.
Increase Satisfaction	Use customer feedback to make changes that increase customer satisfaction.
Develop Switching Costs	Make it difficult for customers to switch easily to another product.
Become a Trusted Advisor	Build trust by listening, being honest, and collaborating with customers.
Increase Understanding of Customer Needs	Needs change, so stay in touch with customers' needs and adjust the product or service offering accordingly, even anticipating a need.
Qualify for Repurchase Opportunities	Maintain contact with existing customers and follow up on leads.
Gain Customer Referrals	The best referrals happen in the absence of a request; they are earned through customer satisfaction.

Source: "Effective Relationship Marketing Part Two: Grow," *CRM Today,* http://www.crm2day.com (accessed September 30, 2005).

buying habits so that future promotional efforts can be better aligned to that customer's needs. This tracking is accomplished through segmentation (dividing customers into distinct groups with similar needs), targeting (delivering relevant messages to customers based on their needs), and personalization (tailoring messages to specific individuals). Amazon built an incredibly valuable online asset in its customer database that enabled the company to deliver targeted and personalized messages to its audience who appreciated it.[6] The expectation is to increase the value of the overall customer base because it is not realistic to expect that the value of each customer can be increased. To increase overall value, decisions must be made about which customer segments have the potential to become more valuable and which do not and should be avoided. Sometimes companies invest in future value—for example, credit card companies who set up booths the first week of classes in the fall at colleges and universities. They give away gifts and encourage students to sign up for their credit cards, not because the companies believe that these students are profitable customers in the short term, but because they have a long life expectancy and the credit card companies are looking to acquire customers for long-term relationships. The segmentation and targeting process is depicted in Figure 13.3.

Business owners should not rely solely on customer data and formal CRM systems to predict behavior. Instead, wise entrepreneurs know that they must spend a lot of time talking to customers. Paul Orfalea, founder of Kinko's, enjoyed spending his days wandering around the Kinko's stores talking with customers and employees to gauge the heartbeat of the business and to find ways to improve products and service. He always learned more about what made each Kinko's store tick and what was not working by walking around than he ever learned from management reports. But some companies become concerned when their customer-service people spend too much time handling customers or providing support. Their CRM tools help them decide that they could be

FIGURE 13.3 The Segmentation and Targeting Process

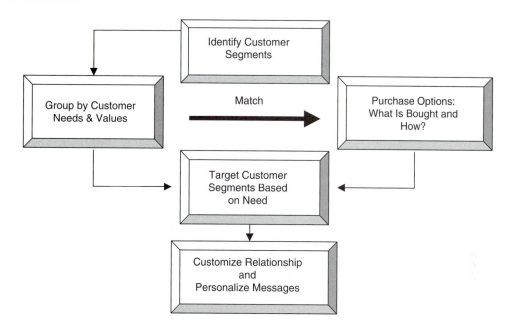

more efficient if the customer-service person spent x amount of time less with the customer; however, what the CRM tool does not tell them is whether that extra time spent results in additional sales or higher customer satisfaction—in other words, effectiveness.[7]

In traditional marketing, customer feedback is commonly obtained through warranty registration, service plans, and company questionnaires. But to successfully implement relationship marketing requires a dialogue with the customer over time. It cannot be a one-shot deal because customers basically see marketers as adversaries. Customers don't believe marketers have their best interests at heart—and they are probably right when it comes to traditional marketing. Furthermore, customers have endured this type of marketing for so long that they are typically resistant and suspicious of a company's initial efforts to establish a "relationship."

The Customer Scorecard

Businesses typically score customer relationships on three major factors:

1. Recency: When did the customer last make a purchase?
2. Frequency: How often does the customer purchase?
3. Monetary value: How much does the customer spend on average per purchase, and how much has she or he spent over the last six months or one year?

Of course, a company wants to collect other information that is particular to its business and that helps it segment its customers. For example, a company wants to know the number of new customers it adds each month, the percentage of customers who actually purchase, customer satisfaction, existing customer revenue, and average customer lifetime value (how to calculate this value is discussed in a later section).

Getting Feedback from Customers

Achieving a sale in durable goods—cars, appliances, major electronics—involves more time on the part of the customer and the salesperson, so there is more opportunity to gather valuable personal information on the customer's requirements during the sale and at the point of sale. In addition, these products normally carry a warranty and/or service agreement, a club membership, or an application, all of which set up another opportunity to get input from the customer. The important point to remember is that multiple chances for contact with the customer always produces better information because the customer is less suspicious of the company's motives and more likely to be agreeable to building a relationship with the company based on trust.

Consumer goods is the more difficult arena in which to capture customer information because buying decisions are often made quickly and without a lot of careful thought or attention. Some techniques that have worked well for growing companies are the following:

- Asking customers to put a name and address on a **coupon** that they are redeeming for a purchase discount gives the company a way to contact the customer in the future with additional offers and also starts a file of the customer's preferences and buying habits. It's important that the company use a coupon clearinghouse that validates the coupons and returns them to the company to be entered into the database.

- **Affinity merchandise** are items imprinted with the company's name, logo, and perhaps advertising, such as caps, T-shirts, pens, and so forth. These items serve as an endorsement of the product that the company is selling.

- **Contest applications** provide an opportunity to get more information from a willing customer who hopes that such cooperation increases his or her chances of winning the contest.

- **Store credit cards** and **membership clubs** provide an easy way to gather valuable customer information, again from a willing customer.

In collecting data from customers, it is important to identify the key points in the process where satisfaction of the customer is affected. These may be points of interaction with the customer or points where delays or problems could affect the quality of the outcome for the customer. Three such points are the following:

- How the company handled a failure in the system
- How the company handled a customer's special request
- How employees responded under a variety of conditions

Identifying and Rewarding the Best Customers

It is unrealistic to think that a company can build long-term relationships with all of its customers, especially if the number of those customers is into the thousands and beyond. It is realistic, however, to search the company's customer base for the most valuable customers, those that warrant in-depth relationships. Who are those customers? Simply stated, they are the customers who account for the biggest percentage of the company's revenues. It is not uncommon for a company to find that as few as 24 percent of its customers account for 95 percent of its revenues. These are the customers who the company needs to know well, and these are the customers who it needs to keep happy. By the same token, the company should also identify the worst customers and jettison them because they are wasting the company's time and money.

After a company has been in business awhile, it becomes easier to identify the most valuable customers. One way is to calculate the lifetime customer value based on viewing the customer as a series of transactions over the life of the relationship. A statistical method for doing this involves calculating the present value of projected future purchases using an appropriate discount rate and period of time for the relationship. Add to that the value of customer referrals and subtract the cost of maintaining the relationship (advertising, promotions, letters, questionnaires, 800 numbers.) The result is the customer's lifetime value. Another nonstatistical method is to simply talk with the customer and ask what his or her intentions are. The better the company knows the customer, the more valuable and reliable the information is.

Companies can do a variety of things to provide special programs, incentives, and rewards for their best customers. The following sections discuss some of these approaches.

Frequency Programs The airlines have used frequency programs with great success. Those who fly the most frequently with the airlines receive the most benefits in terms of free tickets, VIP service, and upgrades. Rewards increase with use; therefore, the customer has a vested interest in using that airline for all of his or her traveling. However, frequency programs have also been used successfully with all types of businesses. Cosmetic companies, for example, have issued cards to customers that give them a free product after a certain number of product purchases. Similarly, small entertainment centers such as miniature golf facilities and water parks often offer discounts for season passes to customers who use the service the most. Frequency programs derive their benefit from repeat purchases. The more a customer buys from a company (assuming satisfaction), the higher the probability they will buy repeatedly and the lower the cost to the company of each repeat purchase. In a one-to-one relationship approach, it is vital to single out the best customers for special treatment.

Just-in-Time Marketing Keeping track of important dates for customers gives the company an opportunity to contact the customer on a special occasion such as a birthday, to remind the customer of his or her need to repurchase something, or to notify a customer of an impending sale of an item that she or he typically buys. This approach is known as just-in-time marketing. Chris Zane of Zane's Cycles in New Haven, Connecticut, became the most successful bicycle shop in the area and one of the top ten in the United States by using one-to-one techniques. He availed himself of just-in-time marketing when he heard that another local shop was going out of business and the owner was leaving the area. He arranged with the phone company, for a small fee, to forward all calls going to the defunct business to his shop. In that way, the customers of the defunct business were directed to a new source for their cycling needs. He also bets on customer relationships by offering lifetime service on every bicycle that he sells.[8]

Complaint Marketing A dissatisfied customer typically tells at least nine other people about the problem he or she faced with the company. And, of course, those nine people tell their friends. It's easy to see how quickly one dissatisfied customer can destroy a company's reputation. Consequently, any company ought to think of complaints not as something to avoid dealing with but as opportunities for continual improvement. It should be easy for customers to make a complaint, and they should be able to carry on a dialogue with a human being who listens and attempts to under-stand. Nothing is more frustrating than having to leave a complaint on a voice mail message.

Some companies have used bulletin board services on the Internet to let cus-tomers communicate their complaints. Though effective, companies who do so should be prepared to handle more complaints by this method than by other methods because this system works almost too well. Customers communicating by computer feel freer to vent their frustrations more vociferously than when they are greeted with a soothing, caring voice on the other end of a phone line. And because anyone with access to the Internet can read these diatribes, a strong complaint can build momen-tum and create more problems than necessary for the company. One way to stem complaints at the source is to provide satisfaction surveys at every point of contact with the customer so that the company can find any problems quickly and early before the customer becomes so angry that resolution and satisfaction is nearly impossible.

Maintaining Customer Relationships for Life

Customers stop buying from a company for a variety of reasons, including (1) dis-satisfaction with aspects of the product or service, (2) ineffective complaint han-dling, (3) a more competitive offer from another company, or (4) changes in product, service, or personnel that the customer doesn't like. If a company that has an annual defection rate of 10 percent cuts that rate in half, the average lifetime of a customer relationship doubles from ten to twenty years, and profits on that cus-tomer increases from $300 to $525. In her classic book *Serving Them Right,* Laura Liswood calculated the cost of losing customers.[9] Below is a scenario based on her work.

The Cost of Losing Customers

Accounts lost	2,000	167 accounts every month
	× $1,200	Average revenue per account
	$2,400,000	Total lost revenue for the year
Profit lost	× .12	Profit margin
	$280,000	Total lost profit
Account closing costs	$20	Per account
	× 2,000	Number of closed accounts
	$40,000	Total costs to close accounts
Total costs	$280,000	Total profit lost
	+ 40,000	Closing costs
	$320,000	Annual cost of losing customers

Losing customers is serious business for a company. Retaining customers, by contrast, can be very profitable for two reasons. First, over time the operating costs related to that customer decline in relation to increased purchasing on the cus-tomer's part. Second, in addition to base profit, the company earns profit from refer-rals, larger and more frequent purchases, reduced servicing costs, and price premiums. Just as in production where the goal is zero defects, in marketing the goal is zero defections. Customers become more profitable over time, so it pays to work to retain them.

Customer Satisfaction Programs The success of any program to build lifelong customer relationships is totally dependent on the quality of communication between the customer and the company. The customer must feel that everyone from all levels of the organization is committed to customer satisfaction and quality. To achieve this, the company must establish company-wide quality goals and policies, develop plans to achieve those goals, establish controls to evaluate progress, and provide incentives to management and employees to meet the goals. Inputs about the level of quality and service that the company is providing comes from customer satisfaction surveys, management's perceptions of customer satisfaction, audits by mystery shoppers and customers, and observations during customer visits to the company. Frequently, observation is the only way to learn what the customer is really experiencing because typically the customer does not report the problem to the company.

Winning Back Lost Customers Customers stop purchasing from a company for a variety of reasons, but about 70 percent of them leave for no reason at all. Dealing with lost customers is a reality in today's volatile marketplace. Some companies deal with lost customers aggressively, and others merely retain the name of the customer in their files in case they want to contact the customer at some later date. Ending communication with the lost customer is a mistake, however. It is important, if possible, to get an exit interview with the customer, particularly if that customer has been a valuable one. During this brief discussion, the company learns specifically why the customer is leaving and what it can do to improve its products or services so that this doesn't happen again. Often a positive exit interview leaves the door open for the customer to come back later. In fact, a company is more likely to entice lost customers to return than it is to attract new customers.

Unique Marketing Situations

There are several categories of unique situations that business owners face with developing a marketing plan. These include trade shows and exhibits, marketing to industrial customers, selling to superstores, selling commodities.

Trade Shows and Exhibits For some entrepreneurs, trade shows, fairs, and exhibits are a primary way to expose their products to a large audience and to reach specialized audiences that might otherwise be difficult to find. Trade shows and the like are also a good way to find out who the competitors are and what marketing techniques they are using. It's the place to meet and negotiate with sales reps and get names for a mailing list. But the primary reason to display products at a trade show is to eventually make the industry aware of the company and its products and, ultimately, to sell more product. To accomplish this effectively, a company should visit a number of trade shows to note effective and ineffective presentation and consider partnering with a compatible company to share the expenses of a booth.

Marketing to Industrial Customers When the target market the company is trying to reach is other businesses, the marketing strategy differs somewhat in terms of advertising and promotion. Consumer products and services require a lot of high-profile advertising and promotion to entice customers away from the myriad other choices that they have. With industrial products and services, the focus is on letting the targeted businesses know that the product or service is available and what it can do for them. In general, industrial products and services do not use broadcast media or the most popular print media. Instead, they rely heavily on direct mail, personal selling, trade shows, and articles and advertisements in trade journals.

Because most industrial product manufacturers distribute their products through wholesalers, it becomes the wholesalers' job to market to and locate retail outlets. If the small business is dealing with industrial customers, it is important to investigate how products are promoted in that industry. This provides a good idea of where customers typically look when they are trying to find a product or service. Talking to customers about the marketing strategies in the industry and how effective or ineffective they are is also an important way to see if a new marketing strategy better serves the customers' needs.

Selling to the Superstores For many consumer product companies, a substantial portion of their revenues come from a few customers known as "superstores": discount outlets such as Target and Wal-Mart, category killers such as Home Depot and Toys 'R' Us, or warehouse clubs such as PriceCostco. These giant outlets have enabled small manufacturers and others to market on a national and international level, whereas without them, these same companies might have been forced to take a more conservative regional approach. It is estimated that mass merchandisers account for 40 percent of all U.S. retail sales.[10] Despite the fact that they comprise less than 3 percent of all retail outlets, the very top discount chains—those with fifty or more stores—account for 11 to 13 percent of all retail sales. It's no wonder, then, that attracting and keeping these valuable customers is important to the financial well-being of small manufacturers. It affects product development, brand visibility, factory efficiency, and the company's ability to retain quality sales reps, not to mention the ability to pay back lines of credit and maintain a positive cash flow.

If a company's marketing strategy includes marketing to the mega-retailers, it's important that the right person is approached and presented with the company's case; usually, this is a buyer. It typically takes several phone calls before the buyer calls back. As in everything else business owners do, the pitch is crucial, and a superstore should see that the company understands who the consumer is, who the competition is, and how the company's product will sell. A large chain should never be approached without being prepared to deliver when that first order materializes. Usually, if the chain likes the product, it will place an initial order to test it in a few of its stores before rolling it out nationally. It's important to remember that these chains, if they do take the product to all their stores, order tremendous quantities, and the small business must have the infrastructure in place to handle the volume. It may also be required to invest in enterprise software systems to manage supply levels for the superstore.

Selling a Commodity High quality and service have become the standard in many industries; therefore, the only differentiating factor among companies' products is price. The company sees its sales increase but profits decline along with margins; so essentially, the owners are working harder and making less money. The phenomenon is known as *commoditization,* and it is something that can happen almost overnight. Here are some signs that portend this problem:

1. Customers begin treating the company as just a bid, and face-to-face contact decreases. This is typical in the construction industry where a low bid often wins over quality because the product, a building, is perceived as a commodity.

Tips for Getting Your Company Noticed

Here are four low-cost ways to win the attention of potential customers and put a company in the limelight:

1. *Sponsor a special event.* Silverado Furniture Company in Napa, California, stages a "Business after Hours" event to help raise money for the local Chamber of Commerce. The benefit to Silverado is that it gets to showcase its latest products to the more than 300 professionals who attend the event. This creates leads for its salespeople.

2. *Become an expert.* Sandra Beckwith wanted to gain national recognition for her public relations firm in Rochester, New York. So she wrote a newsletter for women that took a "lighthearted" look at male behavior and called it "The Do(o)little Report." She sent the first issue to 400 media outlets and got mentions in *USA Today* and the *Wall Street Journal,* among others.

3. *Give products away, especially to celebrities.* Gregg Levin sent cases of his PerfectCurve® baseball cap device to professional baseball teams. He knew that the media do many interviews with cameras in the locker room where baseball players park their caps on the PerfectCurve to keep the bills curved.

4. *Offer free information.* It doesn't take much money to create and offer a free pamphlet giving tips to customers that will help them use the company's products and services better. Or go online with a free newsletter, as Azriela Jaffe did. In fact, she uses two newsletters to help her clients and gain attention for her business: "The Entrepreneurial Couples Success Letter" and "The Best Ideas in Business." She also created a website for her company, Anchored Dreams, at http://www.isquare.com/crlink.htm.

2. Unbundling of products and services: Where a company used to enhance its products and bundle them with services to sell more to the same customers, these bundles are being pulled apart by customers who are focusing on price and doing more of the service part of the bundle in-house.

3. The company's salespeople constantly have to deal with customer complaints about price. In this instance, the product has lost its inherent value.[11]

Where a product starts to become a commodity, it is vital to understand that the value the product once had has now shifted to the value of the relationship among the company, its sales reps, and the customer. The company must now look for that unique value that only it can deliver. Unfortunately, many companies become reactive rather than proactive, adding more services to the product, thereby decreasing margins even more, or alternatively they downsize the business, which is a move backward in a growing company. What they need to do is take the focus off price and put it on what the customer perceives as added value. They need to begin rebuilding customer relationships from the customer's point of view. Without creating new value for customers, any product is in danger of becoming a commodity over time.

GLOBAL MARKETING

Until now this chapter has focused on the role that the customer plays in a company's marketing strategy and in the tactics that it employs to implement that strategy. But other factors come into play as well. A company attempting to expand its market boundaries domestically and globally must be well grounded in the fundamental market trends that affect any marketing strategy to one degree or another. With 95 percent of the world's population and two-thirds of its purchasing power found outside the United States, it's no wonder that so many businesses are planning to market their products and services in the international arena. The U.S. Department of Commerce reports that small- and medium-sized companies (fewer than 500 employees) accounted for just less than 30 percent of the value of all U.S. exports in 2002 but represented 97 percent of all exporting companies.[12] There are many compelling reasons for a small business to consider the global market, and the following are five of them:

1. It can achieve a broader marketing base, which will minimize any adverse economic conditions that may be occurring in the home country.

2. It may be able to reduce the effects of seasonality by going into complementary countries.

3. It can more fully employ any excess capacity when dealing in the domestic market alone.

4. It may be able to increase the product's life.

5. It may be able to lower production costs by establishing foreign production facilities.

The decision to market goods and services globally can come at the start of the new venture or several years down the road after the company has established a strong domestic market. Often, small businesses choose to perfect their products, processes, and services in domestic markets before they tackle the cultural, political, legal, and general differences in doing business in other parts of the world. That is what Allegro Fine Foods of Paris, Tennessee, did with their homegrown marinades, which are now distributed in Asia, Mexico, Canada, and various European countries. "The exporting business is time-consuming and requires a lot of effort," claims International Marketing Director Rick Horiuchi, so small businesses need to be committed and focused in their efforts.[13]

Global marketing is much more than simply taking the company's domestic marketing strategies abroad. Global marketing is about finding new markets and niches, developing buying and selling opportunities, marketing goods and services, and researching international markets.

Global researcher Douglas Lamont has suggested that global market research should answer four basic questions about a particular country or a particular region of the world:

1. Who uses the product? How are these buyers similar to or different from U.S. buyers? How are U.S. products incorporated into the country's lifestyle?

2. How do the people of that country define value? Is value based on timeliness, quality, service, or price? How do products and services need to be changed to meet customer needs?

3. What signals will indicate change in the market? Does the country accept foreign ideas? Are there cross-cultural trends?

4. How can the company increase market share? Who are the local competitors? Are any of them foreign companies? How much disposable income do consumers have?[14]

How does a small business get started in the global marketplace? It is important to begin by identifying a single region that seems most compatible with the small business's products. For example, when ETI, a developer of customized software for enterprise computer systems, decided to market internationally, it chose Europe as its first target because of its technological sophistication and then assigned one person to be in charge of that effort. ETI also acquired a local manager who could maneuver the differences in each country and who could help the company with such things as where to record revenue. U.S. companies marketing in Europe typically transfer revenues to the United States where the tax rate is lower.[15]

Next, the small business must decide whether to sell directly or use a distributor. ETI's product required technical support, so it decided to sell direct, but in some countries like Japan, it is more common to use a trading company. Whichever strategy is used, it is critical to secure the first customers as quickly as possible because they become references for additional customers. Then use revenues from international sales to fund further growth in that country.

Marketing strategy is a vital part of any business that wants to grow domestically and globally. The key to a successful strategy is understanding the needs of the customer and addressing those needs in value-creating products and services.

ISSUES FOR REVIEW AND DISCUSSION

1. How does developing a marketing plan in one paragraph serve as a useful jumping-off point for a marketing strategy?

2. How can a business owner craft a strategy to develop a loyal customer base?

3. How does the promotion strategy for consumer-oriented businesses differ from that of industrial businesses?

4. Discuss the importance of national culture to the diffusion of products into another country.

5. If the product or service that your company provides is becoming or already is a commodity, what steps should you take to remain competitive?

EXPERIENCING ENTREPRENEURSHIP

1. Interview a businessperson from China and compare and contrast the way that business is conducted in China with how it is conducted in the United States.

2. Pick a business idea that interests you and develop a one-paragraph marketing plan for that business.

Garden Fresh Gourmet Inc.

What makes Jack Aaronson's salsa so special? After all, salsa can be found on grocery store shelves everywhere. But in only six years Jack's Garden Fresh products became the second-largest producer of refrigerated salsa in the United States and are found in thirty-five states in more than 4,000 stores.

In 1998, Aaronson was attending a Fiery Foods trade show in New Mexico to consider a number of bottled sauces for his Clubhouse barbeque restaurant and his Hot Zone store located in Ferndale, Michigan. As he sampled dozens of types of sauces, it occurred to him that all the sauces contained preservatives, something that most customers, he believed, do not really want to consume. Convinced that his own natural recipes were far better tasting than anything in the market, he wondered if he could produce his fresh recipes in a refrigerated form and sell them in the commercial market. To date, his Jack's Special sauces had only been used in his restaurant and sold through his store, but when a small, upscale grocery chain approached him about the possibility of selling his sauces in their stores, he saw an opportunity. The following year when he returned to the Fiery Foods trade show, he entered Jack's Special in a competition and won all the awards.

Finding a Way to Reach the Market

The food industry is highly competitive with huge players like Kraft, not to mention all the small specialty companies. Recent years have seen a growing interest in salsas. In general, salsas are mixtures of raw and partially cooked ingredients that include onions, cilantro, garlic, tomatoes, oil, acid, and various types of chili peppers to make them hot and spicy. They are used as marinades, sauces, and toppings; some are even made from fruits and put on ice cream. Aaronson was realistic about his chances; he did not have the resources to conduct advertising and promotional campaigns like the big companies. He would have to use guerrilla-marketing tactics. One thing he knew for sure was that if he could get customers to try the sauce in a taste test, they would buy them, so he started providing free

samples to get consumers hooked on the product. To make a bigger impact more quickly, he hired his own sales reps to arrange for passive sampling at fifteen grocery and deli stores by setting up chips and salsa near the deli counter or in the produce section. Even Aaronson and his family would serve as sales reps from time to time so that they could personally track the responses of the consumers. What they found was that people would keep coming back to sample the salsa, and they raved about it.

Another tactic Aaronson employed was to leave samples of the salsa with local businesses along with a flyer that told employees where they could purchase the salsa. Still another guerrilla-advertising trick was to wrap his delivery trucks in enticing advertising showing the product in a mouth-watering way. Aaronson calculated that he could either spend $10,000 a month for a billboard that stood in one place where 50,000 people a day saw it, or he could spend $5,000 to wrap a truck that would drive around the city on its deliveries and capture the attention of 44,000 people a day. Multiply that times four trucks, and it makes financial sense.

Because fresh ingredients are the foundation of his business, he had to find a way to extend the shelf life of his products from the typical two weeks to forty-seven days so that customers would not be so concerned about the speed with which they had to use up the product. Refusing to resort to preservatives as most of his competitors had, he created a sterile production facility using ultraviolet rays and HEPA filters. Each day, production begins with the 25,000 pounds of tomatoes, pepper, onions, and chilies. All finished products are tested to ensure that they will last forty-seven days.

Aaronson is consistently developing new products, and his line now includes dips, vinaigrettes, tortilla chips, and pita chips. His own vice president produces a line of salad dressings, Mucky Duck Mustard Co., in the Garden Fresh plant. In a continual growth mode and always working to stay ahead of the growing list of competitors, Aaronson wonders in which direction to take his business next.

Advising the Entrepreneur

1. What other types of guerrilla tactics could Aaronson employ to promote the business?

2. As a food company that focuses on fresh food, how can he diversify his product line?

Sources: K. Lawson, "Fresh Salsas Spice up Cinco de Mayo," *Detroit News* (October 3, 2005), www.detnews.com; "Jack Aaronson's Key Move: Grassroots Marketing," *Startup Nation* (June 24, 2005), www.startupnation.com.

Designing and Managing the Business

CHAPTER 14

Planning the Business

It is probably not love that makes the world go around, but rather those mutually supportive alliances through which partners recognize their dependence on each other for the achievement of shared and private goals.

Fred Allen, Chairman, Pitney-Bowes Company,
Leaders (1979)

▶ LEARNING OUTCOMES

- Discuss what must be considered when planning the location of the business.
- Discuss the nature of product development for entrepreneurial companies today.
- Explain how to legally protect products and services.

ScreenShop Software: Product Development in a Niche Market

Even the smallest market niche can be a winner for an entrepreneur. David Meadows found that out when he created a niche that crossed the software and corporate gift markets. ScreenShop, based in New York City, develops computer screensavers for promotional, incentive, and training purposes. Its ScreenShop™ software raises traditional screensavers to a new level by merging entertainment, information, and technology into a customized package that lets companies reach their targets—whether customers or employees—in a unique and exciting way, right on their desktops. The screensavers incorporate text, photos, sounds, animation, and often time-released messages.

Meadows didn't start out in the computer software industry. Raised in Akron, Ohio, Meadows finished high school six months early and took off for college, first at the University of Colorado at Boulder and then at Saint Petersburg Junior College in Clearwater, Florida. Finally, he returned to his home state to attend Ohio University, where he graduated in 1991 with bachelor's degrees in both communication and business administration. Over the next year, he traveled around the United States and worked in his family's business in Florida. In August 1992, Meadows moved to New York City to become the full-time national campus development director for the Association of Collegiate Entrepreneurs (ACE), an international organization created to support and inspire entrepreneurship among college students. In August 1993, however, the entrepreneurial bug bit him. He left ACE to start his own company to market a product called Worldbits!® Country-A-Day Calendars, which was the number three seller on Rand McNally's retail bestseller list.

An overheard remark while on a European trip inspired the genesis for Worldbits. Meadows recalls hearing a European say, "You Americans are so '#*@$'; you know nothing about the rest of the world!" This brash statement moved Meadows to create a product to help promote international awareness. With personal savings, loans, and credit cards, Meadows bootstrapped Worldbits into existence. The product was a printed daily calendar that presented maps and information about countries of the world.

He sold the product as a customized promotional gift to AT&T for its clients but soon found it was too costly to produce and customize. Although the product was successful and sold out on retail shelves of small bookstores, in the Rand McNally outlet, and at the United Nations, Meadows took a loss on the company and closed it in December 1995.

Armed with this experience, Meadows began to look at computer screensavers and discovered that they could act like a daily calendar but at a fraction of the cost. The Worldbits concept evolved into a screensaver, and a new company was born. On November 29, 1995, Meadows applied for a trademark on the name SmartScreen for his new software company. Six months later, however, he discovered that Pointcast, a "push" screensaver technology company, had applied for the same trademarked name on November 19, 1995. Meadows was therefore forced to change the name of the company to ScreenShop.

ScreenShop Software was profitable from the start. "The software industry has a certain magic to it," says Meadows. To help finance its growth, ScreenShop required deposits up front for customized work. There were many industry competitors because the entry barriers were low and the technology was not highly advanced. The trick to survival, according to Meadows, was to find a niche market. ScreenShop found its niche in the personalized corporate screensaver market. In July 1997, ScreenShop Software introduced its newest product, IncentiveScreen®, which was inspired by research indicating that a screensaver is used 38 percent of the time a computer is on and that having a goal enhances employee performance. For example, Xerox might sponsor a competition among its sales representatives—the top performer wins a trip to Hawaii. ScreenShop would customize a screensaver with photos of Hawaii and motivational quotes. The screensaver would then be distributed to all sales representatives to promote the program and to motivate them with a visual reminder on a daily basis.

Meadows provided another example. "Imagine the concept of going into a Mercedes dealership and having your picture taken with a digital camera, and then you're handed a normal floppy disk. Once you get home, you place the disk in your computer and install the new Mercedes screensaver. You then see all of the Mercedes cars drive across the screen with your picture in the driver's seat."

The biggest challenge facing ScreenShop is growth capital. "I have wanted to maintain a wholly owned company financed through growth, and therefore, it's a slower process," Meadows says. Meadows learned that growth from internal cash flow requires patience, which is not always easy in the volatile software industry. Being first in the market with a new niche product required large amounts of capital, but it is an exciting place to be because, as Meadows claims, "First to the market usually wins, but now the race is on."

Advising the Entrepreneur

1. What is a compatible, customized product that Meadows could create to diversify his product offering?

2. What should Meadows be thinking about as he looks to the future?

Every business produces some type of product, and every business has a service component. The "service" business's product may be a solution to a customer's problem that involves consulting, training, a manual, or new equipment—in short, a process. The "product" business works with customers to provide solutions in the form of new products and then bundles services with those products to offer a complete package. The whole arena of product or service development has undergone profound change over the past two decades, and the customer is at the root of the change. The time from concept to product launch has decreased dramatically. As a result, companies such as Intel work on multiple generations of a product simultaneously. Nevertheless, while production times have decreased, the demand for quality, reliability, and variety has increased substantially. What used to be considered inconceivable levels of quality are now looked upon as standards and are expected, regardless of the cost of the product. Manufacturers and producers are no longer in a position to dictate to the customer. Quite the contrary, they are under pressure to make the customer part of the team from the very conception of the product. It is within this dynamic context that we consider a company's operations.

Planning a business's operations involves looking at five broad areas of concern: the company culture; the business location; the development and protection of products and services; human resources; and operations. (Culture is discussed in Chapter 2, human resources is discussed in Chapter 10, and operations is discussed in Chapter 15.) In this chapter, we begin with the location for the business and then consider the development and protection of products and services.

PLANNING THE LOCATION OF THE BUSINESS

Business location plays a vital role in the success of any business. Retail businesses that depend on foot traffic and high-profile locations flounder if access is difficult. By contrast, wholesale-type businesses are usually one step removed from the end user, but today more and more wholesalers, such as PriceCostco, are selling direct "to the public." Besides selling products in bulk for less, these wholesale businesses don't have the expensive storefront demands of a typical retail outlet. Customers have been "trained" to expect an out-of-the-way location, a huge warehouse, and no frills in exchange for lower prices.

Once a site is located, the existing building must be evaluated for a lease/buy decision. If the site is bare land, building a facility is the only choice. Because a significant portion of assets can be tied up in a facility, each of these scenarios should be looked at in greater detail.

The Existing Building

Any existing building on a potential site must be examined carefully with the following questions considered:

- Is the building of sufficient size to meet current and reasonable future needs?
- Do the building and site allow for future expansion?
- Is there sufficient parking?
- Is there space for customers, storage, inventory, office space, and restrooms?

Certainly, allowing for future growth is essential. The initial higher cost of a larger building is often offset by avoiding the extraordinarily high costs of moving and the potential for lost sales and time away from the fundamental work of the business while the business is in transition. An examination of an existing building should begin with the exterior and answer the following questions:

1. Does the building have curbside appeal, assuming that customers will come to the site?
2. Is the building compatible with its surroundings?
3. Does it have enough windows of sufficient size?
4. Is the entrance inviting?
5. Is the signage attractive, and does it satisfy the local regulations?
6. Is the parking adequate to meet customer and employee demand and satisfy local building codes?
7. Does the interior of the building meet the company's needs in terms of walls, floors, and ceilings?
8. Are there sufficient lighting fixtures, outlets, and enough power to run equipment?

These are just a few questions to be asked before finalizing a decision on a building. Most companies can answer these questions to their satisfaction, but to be certain the building is not hiding anything that could be costly for the business, it is wise to hire a licensed contractor or inspector to examine it for structural soundness.

Leasing a Building

The speed of change, innovation, and technological advancement has shortened and will continue to shorten product and service life cycles, and this has an impact on the facilities in which businesses operate. Buildings have long physical lives and typically are very expensive to refurbish and remodel.

One suggested solution to the problem is for companies to hold short leases of five years or less. In this way, the company does not tie up precious capital that it may not be able to recover, and it is able to move on when a product or service is deemed technologically antiquated and no longer in demand. There are, however, some serious disadvantages to short-term leasing, described in the following list.

1. *Rents are escalated more frequently due to short-term renewal.* Many companies have been in the position of having to remain in their current locations beyond the term of the lease. When the entrepreneur renegotiates the lease terms, he or she often finds that the landlord intends to raise the rent for a new lease. This is usually justified by increasing market rents, but usually the landlord is aware that it would be costly for the tenant to relocate. Moreover, the business would have little time to do so and still maintain its current production rate. Furthermore, the potential to have to replace employees and create new logistics for suppliers and buyers is daunting. All these factors put the entrepreneur in a very weak position to negotiate a new lease. For these reasons, when the lease is first negotiated, a clause should be included that permits the option to renew at a specified rate and an escape clause in case the business must be closed. These two clauses, however, may cost a bit more initially.

2. *It is more difficult to remodel midterm.* If the company has a short-term lease, the landlord is less likely to approve any substantial tenant improvements if they do not increase the value of the building to future tenants. Therefore, when the lease is first negotiated, the entrepreneur should come prepared with a five-year plan for the facility and be able to demonstrate the benefits to the landlord of allowing the remodeling of the building.

3. *The company cannot show a substantial asset on the balance sheet.* Therefore, a leased facility is not a good vehicle for raising capital.

The cost of leasing a building is a function of the demand in the marketplace for rentals as well as a number of other factors. For example, buildings that are newer, suitable for a variety of uses, and well located generally enjoy higher lease rates, as do buildings that are in short supply. Retail and service business sites are generally more expensive than industrial sites, and a retail site in a regional mall will likely be the most expensive. It is important to consider all the costs related to leasing a facility. For example, although manufacturing sites enjoy lower rental rates than commercial sites, they usually pay higher rates for water, power, and sewage. Failure to include the cost of expensive utilities or a common-use area fee could spell disaster to the company's cash flow. A good lease agreement should also designate who is responsible for repairs to the structure and infrastructure of the building.

There are basically three types of leases in common use:

- *Gross Lease* This lease allows the company to pay a fixed rate per month, with the landlord covering the cost (and getting the benefit) of insurance, taxes, and building operating expenses such as outdoor lighting, security, and so forth.

- *Net Lease* Also known as *triple net,* with this lease the company pays a fixed monthly rate plus taxes, operating expenses, and essentially everything but the mortgage and the building insurance, which the landlord pays. In essence, the company rents a shell with stipulated improvements.

- *Percentage Lease* This is the most complicated of all the lease types because it has several variations. It can be written as a percentage of the tenant's net income or as a flat rate plus a percentage of the gross revenues. The latter is very common in retail operations.

First and foremost, leases are written from the landlord's point of view and therefore are negotiable. The fact that something appears in printed form does not mean that it is true or that it has to be agreed to. A lease represents a significant portion of a company's overhead, so it's important that it provide what the company needs to do its business. Seek the assistance of an attorney who can represent the company's interests.

Buying a Building

If a company has the resources, buying a building has some advantages. A valuable asset is immediately created on the balance sheet, which can be leveraged later on when growth capital is needed. For example, the building could be sold and leased back (called a *sale-leaseback*), withdrawing equity for other uses and negotiating favorable long-term lease terms. Sale-leasebacks are attractive options for investors, so these buildings generally sell quickly. Of course, when the building is sold, the entrepreneur effectively loses control of it. Therefore, it is vital to negotiate terms that allow the tenant to remodel and extend the lease should that be desired.

One advantage of owning a building is that it can be traded in a tax-deferred exchange for other property that the company may need. For example, if the company owns an office building but needs a distribution warehouse to support a new direction that it was taking, it might take advantage of a tax-deferred exchange by trading the office building for the warehouse. The exchange would defer capital gains tax on the sale of the office, and the company would have the warehouse it needed.

Another option is a joint venture between the company and a real estate developer on a building in which the company will be one of the tenants and co-owner. A joint venture is a partnership created to undertake a specific project. If the company is able to occupy a substantial portion of the building, it will be easier for the developer to acquire a mortgage and additional tenants. Of course, this type of arrangement has the inherent problems of any partnership and should be considered carefully with the advice of an attorney before any agreement is executed.

Buying a building requires the signing of a contract, much as a lease agreement does. The contract will spell out the terms of the purchase and the items included in and excluded from the purchase agreement. As always, it should be read carefully to make sure that what was agreed to verbally has been translated correctly on paper. It would be wise to hire a due diligence team (inspector, contractor, CPA, attorney) to inspect the building and the agreement to protect the company's interests.

Building a Facility

When a suitable facility in the desired location cannot be found, building the facility from the ground up becomes the only option. This will entail an architect, permits, possibly zoning variances, a construction bidding process, off-site improvements (curbs, gutters, water and power lines, roads), and a lengthy building and inspection process. Constructing a building is no doubt the most complex option; however, the result will be a building that completely meets the company's needs. This option is most suitable when the needs for the building and/or the location are unique, when the company has time to wait, and when it intends to remain in the facility for the long term.

The Interior of the Facility

As important as the location and type of facility are, the layout of the interior of the facility can mean the difference between an operation that moves efficiently and effectively and one that is slowed and interrupted by an ineffective physical flow. A good interior design is the province of professionals who are available to the small-business owner to provide guidance in determining the best design for a particular type of business. Here we will briefly consider some of the key elements of business design.

Retail Layout and Design Retail layouts must take into consideration the buying habits of customers. With that in mind, impulse items should be placed near the entrance, in the center aisle in a large store, or by the cashier. By contrast, necessities, staples, and major-expense items are normally located at the back of the store.

It's a good idea to use an expert when designing the layout because the most efficient and effective design can mean the difference between lackluster sales and superior sales. The following are some items that should be considered when designing the layout:

- Determine the purpose and objectives of the facility.
- Identify the activities that will take place in the facility.
- Determine how these activities will interrelate in terms of access, arrangement, and workflow.
- Calculate the space requirements for all activities.
- Evaluate alternative layouts.
- Choose the most effective and efficient layout to meet the goals of the business.

Office Layout Most businesses have office space. In fact, some service businesses are entirely composed of office space. The layout of this space will determine how efficiently and effectively work flows through the organization. The goal of any layout plan should be to minimize movement and noise and maximize communication. Therefore, people who regularly work together should be located physically near one another. Computer workstations should generally be placed away from distractions such as conversations, and common-use items such as copy machines and water coolers should be easily accessible. A design consultant can help a company determine the optimal office layout.

Wholesale/Warehouse Layout In a warehouse business, it is important to create a layout that lets employees fill orders quickly. Thus, goods that sell more rapidly are placed in one area of the warehouse, and slower-selling items are placed in another. The receiving dock is located closest to the most frequently sold items. Automated warehouse operations often use a series of conveyer belts to select items from various parts of the warehouse and send them to the receiving dock. The diversity of goods being warehoused will probably determine the methods by which items are pulled from the shelves.

An Outdoors Location for a High-Flying Business

For some businesses, nothing but the outdoors will do. Jonathon Conant started Trapeze School in New York City in 1999 with $30,000 in savings, $60,000 in credit card debt, and a passion for the flying trapeze that he acquired at a class while on a vacation at ClubMed in Mexico. Conant immediately made the connection between flying through the air and helping people build self-esteem and enjoy a happy experience. To be successful with this most unusual business, Conant knew that he had to locate the business in a high-profile spot, and that spot was New York City. But before Conant could get his business off the ground, September 11, 2001, happened, and the launch was delayed. Conant persevered in the belief that a Trapeze School on an outdoor site in the

shadow of Ground Zero would be the perfect antidote for the city. "The city needed something to believe in, especially in that area. People were looking for acknowledgment that it was OK to be alive again," Conant says. So, in July 2002, Trapeze School opened for business. By 2004, it had a net profit of $600,000 and was in the process of constructing a year-round $1 million, three-story tent on Pier 40. By 2005 Trapeze School had additional locations in Boston and Baltimore and was poised to fly even higher.

Sources: Trapeze School, http://newyork.trapezeschool.com/index.php; "Jonathon's Key Move: Location, Location, Location," *Startup Nation*, www.startupnation.com (accessed June 24, 2005).

Alternatives to Conventional Sites

Any company seeking a site for either start-up or expansion should also consider alternatives to more conventional-type locations. These nonconventional sites can be far less costly than conventional facilities, especially in the earliest stages of the business when the entrepreneur is still testing the concept in the market.

Incubators A number of communities have business incubators where a young company can locate and receive support services such as receptionist, copy service, or conference room; discounted fees with professional advisers such as attorneys and accountants; the ability to network with other companies in the incubator; and possibly financial aid. Generally, the company remains in the incubator for two to three years before moving to more traditional facilities.

Sharing Space Another choice is to locate the company within the facilities of a larger company. As the largest of the chain stores continue to downsize, opportunities to take excess space arise. A variation on this theme is to lease a location that has enough space to sublease to a complementary business. For example, a copy service might lease excess space to a computer graphics company.

Mobile Locations One of the more interesting ways to introduce new businesses and new products or services to the marketplace is through the use of pushcarts and kiosks. This was the strategy of Bill Sanderson, president of CalCorn, Inc., which owned Popcorn Palace, a chain of boutique, gourmet popcorn stores that was eventually sold to Orville Redenbacher. Its typical location is a high-traffic site in an upscale regional mall. This space is one of the more expensive in the mall; therefore, to test the potential viability of a new site, Sanderson started with a pushcart location

A Product Development Strategy Even a Pig Can Like

Some entrepreneurial companies make creativity and innovation central to everything they do. In such an environment, both employees and customers thrive. New Pig Corporation, a Pennsylvania-based company, is a manufacturer and direct marketer of industrial cleaning products. The company was founded in 1985 with only one product: the Pig, an absorbent sock that soaked up industrial leaks and spills. Today, it solves over 170,000 industrial problems with its unique products, but what is more astounding is that New Pig introduces hundreds of new products every year. How can this tremendous rate of new-product development be explained? There are four reasons why New Pig excels in the area of new products and innovation:

1. *Its focus is on innovation.* New Pig's philosophy requires that everyone, from top management to janitors, focus on a constant stream of innovation; in other words, new-product ideas come from everyone in the company.

2. *Its environment stimulates new ideas.* To encourage and keep track of new ideas from employees, vendors, and customers, New Pig uses a database called the PIT. As ideas are gathered, they are fed into the PIT. Most of these ideas relate to customers' workplace problems. When a customer calls in to New Pig with a problem, the customer-service representative dials a voice mailbox into which he or she relates the content of the conversation with the customer. That content is then coded and keyed into the PIT, which is a ready source of product ideas to test. New Pig also uses its four-color catalogs, called Pigalogs, and its website to solicit new ideas. In appreciation for their effort, customers receive a promotional reward such as a baseball hat emblazoned with the hindquarters of a pig protruding from its bill.

3. *It believes that humor helps.* New Pig has found that humor makes a potentially dull, industrial business lively and more interesting.

4. *Its product development toolkit is cutting-edge.* New Pig believes in using a full complement of the latest product development tools, and it prototypes the entire range of product activities, including the product, manufacturing, marketing, sales, and service, and it practices early testing of its products with the customers who suggested them.

New Pig Corporation is an excellent example of a scrappy entrepreneurial firm that defined a niche in the market, exploited it, and grew to own it through new-product development.

Lesson Learned: *Encourage your customers to design your products and services.*

Source: www.newpig.com (accessed August 25, 2005).

on that site before committing to a long-term lease. Pushcarts and their more fixed alternative, the kiosk—a small booth—also allow a company to expand to many new locations without the high overhead of a conventional retail storefront.

TRADE AREA

The *trade area* is the region from which the company expects to draw customers. Retail or service businesses deal directly with the customer, so naturally it is important to locate the business where there are suitable concentrations of customers. To a considerable degree, the type of business determines the size of the trade area. For example, if a company sells general merchandise that can be found almost anywhere, the trade area is much smaller because customers do not want to travel great distances

| FIGURE 14.1 | Census Tract Map, Schenectady, New York

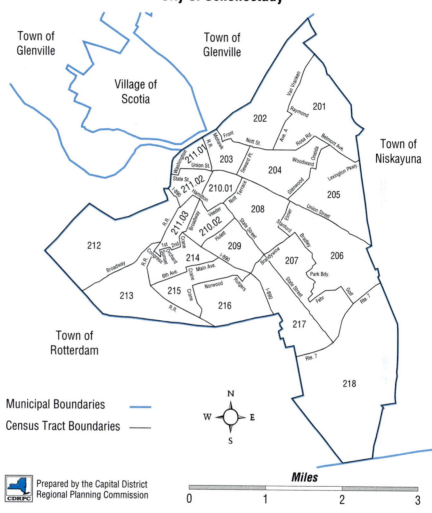

Schenectady County 1990 Census Tracts
Inset A
City of Schenectady

to purchase common goods. However a specialty outlet, such as a boutique clothing store or a well-known graphics designer, may draw people from other communities as well as the one in which it is located.

A map of the community on which the site of the business is designated is used to calculate the trade area. Placing a compass on the epicenter of the proposed site, a circle that represents the distance (the radius) that people are expected to drive to reach the site is drawn. Within the circle is the trade area, which can now be studied in more detail. Employing demographics and a census tract map, census tracts within the trade area can be identified. Census data for those tracts help determine how many people reside within the boundaries of the trade area as well as their education level, income level, average number of children, and so forth. See Figure 14.1 for an example of a census tract map.

It is important to identify the routes that customers might take to reach the proposed site. If the site is difficult to locate and hard to access, it is logical to conclude that potential customers will not exert the effort to find it. Availability of parking is also critical; consequently, most communities require a sufficient amount of parking space for new construction, through either lots or garages. In some older areas, however, street parking is the only available option, which may cause customers to seek an alternative.

A foot- and car-traffic count for the proposed site should be conducted to determine how busy the area is. Whether a high volume of foot traffic is required is a function of the type of business. A coffeehouse such as Starbucks, for example, benefits immensely from a high volume of foot traffic, whereas a hardware store such as Home Depot does not depend on foot traffic for its existence. Positioning someone near the targeted site and tallying the customers going by and into the business easily accomplish a traffic count. City planning departments and transportation departments maintain vehicle-traffic counts for major arterials in the city.

DEVELOPING PRODUCTS AND SERVICES

The dynamic environment in which new products come to life has forced a new-product development paradigm with two fundamental characteristics: (1) the importance of effective product design and (2) the importance of reducing time to market.

Effective Product Design

The effective design of new products takes on significantly more importance in dynamic environments for several reasons:

- Product design accounts for only about 8 percent of the product budget but determines fully 80 percent of the cost of the product.
- Product design determines the marketability of the product by establishing the feature set and how it will work.
- Product design determines quality, reliability, and serviceability.
- Product design determines the length of time to launch and the cost to produce.
- Good product design can reduce the need for global manufacturing through significant cost savings.
- Good design gives the company the potential to set industry standards, which can be effective barriers to entry for competitors or even open up a new market, as the Sony Walkman did.
- Good design results in lower costs, and cost savings go directly to the bottom line.

Good product definition with significant input from the customer is the first requirement for designing right the first time. In entrepreneurial firms, cross-functional communication in the early stages of design comes more naturally than it does in large, traditionally organized corporations where departments are accustomed to a more linear, functional approach to product development. But even in small businesses, structured methods for problem solving help ensure that the design is right the first time. Two examples of these methods are **quality function deployment** **(QFD)** and **design for manufacturability** (DFM). QFD enables the customer to effectively design the product by identifying critical customer preferences and requirements. These inputs are then incorporated into the design engineering. In this way, the design focuses on those things that have perceived value to the customer and the market.

DFM can significantly reduce manufacturing costs and increase productivity by producing the product concurrently with the design of the product so that the transition into production will be smoother and absent the costly delays of engineering change orders because the process doesn't match the product. (This book cannot go into sufficient detail on these two product design methods, but plenty of information about them is available on the Internet.)

Time to Market

Time to market is the other critical component of effective product development. In a volatile marketplace, if a new product is not designed right and introduced quickly, the market may change just enough to force redesign, which lengthens the development process significantly and starts a pattern of lost opportunities and higher costs. An example of failure to properly design is the classic case of the aerospace firm whose manufacturing division designed and built a new plant that could not encompass the wingspan of the new aircraft that it was about to produce. All the efforts to fast-cycle the product development were lost because of the need to redesign the production facility.

The biggest gains in shortening the time to market, or fast-cycle product development, come from (1) reducing wait time between development and production tasks, (2) shortening the time to complete activities, (3) overlapping tasks where possible, and (4) most important, designing right the first time to avoid costly redesign at the end. Achieving effective, fast-cycle product development will result in momentous gains for a company (see Table 14.1). The closer the design of the product is to market introduction, the more likely it will meet customers' needs at that moment. Moreover, bringing out the next generation of product ahead of industry standard practice can mean substantial gains at the bottom line. It is estimated that a six-month jump on competitors in a market accustomed to eighteen- to twenty-four-month design lives can translate into as much as three times the profit over the market life of the design.[1] By contrast, slow-cycle product developers typically introduce a new product every two years. Better design and performance also permits the company to charge premium prices or keep prices stable and thereby create superior value for its customers. Moreover, effective, fast-cycle product development creates a sense of excitement about the company and within the company, which attracts favorable publicity and the best people to work there.

Product Development Strategy

Small businesses face an entirely different set of constraints than do large corporations with research and development (R&D) departments and ample budgets. They work

TABLE 14.1   The Benefits of Fast-Cycle Product Development

The benefits of fast-cycle product development can be organized into four broad categories: marketing, technology, costs, and management.

Marketing	Technology	Costs	Management
Better able to exploit windows of opportunity	New technology is applied more quickly, which translates into recovering R&D costs sooner.	New generations with reduced costs can replace older, more costly generations more quickly.	Development team experiences shorter time to see the results of their work.
Design a niche and enter as the perceived and/or actual market leader	Easier to take advantage of previous R&D; better resource utilization	Reduced interest expense	Enhances the spirit of creativity and innovation in the organization.
Potential for publicity		Better utilization of plant and equipment	Attracts the best people to work in the company.
Sets standards for the industry		Potential for premium prices or superior value	
Potential for longer product life because the company is in the market first		Revenue returns earlier to recoup R&D expenses.	
Can delay product development to further refine customer needs and come out at the same time as competitor with a better product			
Better able to develop derivative products			
Can start product development at the same time as competitor and bring the product out sooner			

with very limited resources and typically rely on outsourcing certain functions or partnering with a more established company to achieve their objectives. But the lack of resources and established in-house departments has not hindered entrepreneurial companies' ability to compete effectively in terms of product development. Instead, it is precisely the need to bootstrap and use resources wisely that has compelled them to seek not only innovative product solutions but also process solutions.

Entrepreneurial product development tends to cost more and takes longer because a small business is asking the independent contractors to whom it is outsourcing many of its product development tasks to do one or two prototype units instead of the much larger quantities these contractors are used to dealing in. It costs more to do one of something than to do many.

Several solutions are available to overcome resource problems and should be considered by any entrepreneurial company undertaking product design and development:

- Prioritize development projects, focusing on those that have the highest return on investment.

- Focus on core competencies and design rather than on producing parts that other companies are already manufacturing.

- Purchase off-the-shelf parts and components whenever possible.

- Consider outsourcing component design, materials specifications, machinery to produce, ergonomic design, packaging design, assembly drawings, and specifications to firms for which these tasks are core competencies.

- Build a physical prototype earlier to more quickly converge on the optimal design and prevent later redesign, which is very costly.

- Check out job shops to make certain that they can work as quickly as needed and that they are accustomed to working with entrepreneurs.

It is important that a company develop a product development strategy that will give focus, direction, and integration to the various tactics it will employ. The strategy should arise from several critical questions:

1. What are the number, breadth, and depth of the products to be offered: platform (core products), derivative (enhanced products), number of different products?
2. Who will be the customers for these products?
3. How will customers purchase the products?
4. Why will customers choose these products over those of the competition?
5. How often will the company introduce new products?
6. How will these products fit into the overall strategy for the company?

The product development process is typically portrayed as a linear process with independent steps or stages. In reality, however, the product development process tends to have starts and stops and movement forward and backward, until the production-quality prototype is completed (the prototype that is equivalent to the final commercial product) and decisions are made about how to produce and commercialize the product. The product development process can be summarized as follows:

1. Identify the opportunity.
2. Define the requirements to develop the product and produce it.
3. Gather industry and customer data (feasibility analysis).
4. Design the product and production process.
5. Prototype the product.
6. Test the product.
7. Launch the product.

LEARNING FROM MISTAKES

A Jewel of an Opportunity

Mike Clarke, a Dallas-based jeweler, was known far and wide for his ability to get jewelry sparkling clean. His secret was a $1,500 machine that used a burst of steam to clean the jewelry. He was inspired to create a less expensive machine for the home that would accomplish the same thing. Clarke decided to name his invention Jewel Jet. Once he had the prototype completed, he applied for a patent because he knew that eventually there would be a number of copycat companies competing with him. Unfortunately, the Patent and Trademark Office responded to his application by rejecting several of his claims of novelty. He had to go back and rewrite those claims to prove that his invention was different from others already patented, which took more time and money.

Patenting is an expensive process and does not guarantee that another company won't infringe on the patent, so the inventor must decide if it is worth it to seek a patent or simply get the product out in the market as quickly as possible to establish a brand. Clarke would also have to spend money to defend his patent once he had it. Not wanting to lose a market opportunity with a narrow window, Clarke found a manufacturer in China and in 2004 proceeded to sell 35,000 units through independent jewelry stores. "We're going full steam ahead," he asserts, with or without the patent.

Lesson Learned: *Use an intellectual property attorney to write a patent, and if the window of opportunity is small, go to market quickly without a patent.*

Sources: Jewel Jet, http://www.jeweljet.com/; R. Flandez, "A Step-by-Step Guide to Getting a Patent," *Wall Street Journal Startup Journal*, www.startupjournal.com (accessed June 24, 2005).

PROTECTING PRODUCTS AND SERVICES

Given the time and costs associated with developing an innovative product, it is important for the entrepreneur to investigate the potential to acquire intellectual property rights; that is, determine if there are legal ways to protect the product idea from competitor duplication until and after it goes to market. Intellectual property rights are intangible ownership rights that include patents, trademarks, copyrights, and trade secrets. From a strategic standpoint, intellectual property gives the entrepreneur the opportunity to exploit a first-mover and potential leader position in the market by introducing something that has not previously existed in its current form. It also enables the entrepreneur to license the intellectual property rights to another company to exploit, thereby expanding market presence much more rapidly.

The issue of who owns an invention is a crucial one that could mean the difference between launching a successful product and a flop. The primary legal means to protect an original invention is through a patent.

Patents

A *patent* is a grant to an inventor that gives him or her the exclusive right to an invention for a period of years, depending on the type of patent. It also prevents others from manufacturing and selling the invention during the period of the patent. At the end of this time, the patent is placed in the public domain. Two types of patents concern most inventors: utility and design patents. Utility patents are the more common type. They protect the functional aspect of machines or processes, as well as computer programs associated with hardware. Some examples are toys, film processing, protective coatings, tools, and cleaning implements. A utility patent is valid for a period of twenty years from the first effective filing date. Design patents, by contrast, protect new, original ornamental designs for manufactured articles. The design must be nonfunctional and part of the tangible item for which it is designed. Some examples are a decoration, an item of apparel, or jewelry. These patents are easy to design around because they do not cover any functionality.

Computer programs present some special issues. They may be protected by a trade secret if the developer/owner merely licenses the program for distribution by someone else to a narrow market. If wide dissemination is the goal, a patent offers more protection and is available if the program contains at least one unique algorithm that is part of the machine or physical process. Copyrights are commonly used for programs that don't qualify for a patent. In addition, the name of the program can be trademarked and the instructions copyrighted.

Rules for Patents Before deciding to file for a patent, it is important to first determine the patentability of the invention. There are four basic rules:

1. The invention must fit into one of the five classes established by Congress for utility patents:
   a. Machine (fax, rocket, electronic circuits)
   b. Process (chemical reactions, methods for producing products)
   c. Articles of manufacture (furniture, diskettes)
   d. Composition (gasoline, food additives)
   e. A new use for one of the above

2. It must have utility—in other words, be useful. This usually is not a problem unless the invention is something like an unsafe drug or something purely "whimsical."

3. It must not contain prior art. Prior art is the state of knowledge that is publicly available or published prior to the date of the invention, which usually occurs sometime before the filing of the patent application. In addition, the invention must not become public or available for sale more than one year prior to filing the patent application. This is so that the invention is still novel at the time of application. Novelty consists of physical differences, new combinations of components, or new uses.

4. It must be unobvious. The invention must not be obvious to someone with ordinary skills in the field. In other words, the invention must contain "new and unexpected results."

The Patent Process

The process for obtaining a patent is well defined; however, it is advisable to use the services of a patent attorney. The process consists of three steps.

Step 1: File a Disclosure Document The inventor will normally file a disclosure statement that documents the date of conception of the invention. This statement is critical in the event that two inventors are working on the same idea at the same time. The one who files the disclosure document first has the right to file for a patent. The disclosure document is a detailed description of the invention and its uses and may include photos; however, it is not a patent application. The inventor has a two-year grace period in which to file a nonprovisional patent application but must demonstrate diligence in completing the invention and filing the application. If the inventor publicly uses or sells the invention more than a year prior to filing the patent application, he or she will be prohibited from applying for a patent. It is important that the inventor *not* use the tactic of mailing a dated description of the invention to himself or herself by certified mail. It has no value to the Patent and Trademark Office (PTO).

Step 2: File a Provisional Patent Application A provisional patent application is an inexpensive way for inventors to protect their inventions while talking with manufacturers and potential funders. It is legally more powerful than a disclosure document and permits the applicant to use the term *patent pending* on the invention. The term of the provisional patent is twelve months from the date of filing, and it cannot be extended. Consequently, the inventor must apply for a nonprovisional patent within that twelve-month period. If the inventor does not do so, the provisional application is considered abandoned, and the inventor loses the ability to claim the nonprovisional date of application as the date of invention. One advantage of the provisional patent is that is effectively adds one year to the length of the patent.

Step 3: File a Nonprovisional Patent Application The nonprovisional patent application is required for any patent, whether or not the inventor previously filed a provisional patent application. The patent application contains a complete description of the invention, what it does, and how it is uniquely different from anything currently existing (prior art). It also includes detailed drawings, explanations, and engineering specifications. The claims section of the application specifies the parts of the invention on which the inventor wants patents. The description of these claims must be specific enough to demonstrate the invention's uniqueness but broad enough to make it difficult for others to circumvent the patent—that is, by modifying it slightly and duplicating the product without violating the patent. The patent application should be filed within one year of offering the product for sale or using it commercially. It is infinitely preferable to file before making any public disclosures.

Once the application is received, the PTO will conduct a search of its patent records. During this period, the invention is said to be *patent applied for,* which establishes the inventor's claim and dates relative to prior art. An invention can stay in the patent-applied-for stage up to two years. The primary advantage of this is that the public does not have access to the patent application and drawings, which might allow someone else the chance to design around the patent.

The PTO contacts the inventor and states that it either accepts the claims in the application or denies the application and gives the inventor a period of time to appeal and/or modify the claims. It is not uncommon for the PTO to reject the original claims in their entirety, usually because of prior art. If and when the PTO accepts the modified claims, the invention is in the *patent-pending stage,* which means it is awaiting the issuance of the patent. The inventor may market and sell the product during this period, but should clearly label it "patent pending." Once the patent is issued, however, it becomes public record. If the patent examiner rejects the modified claims, on the other hand, the inventor has the right to appeal to a board of patent appeals within the PTO. If agreement is not reached at this point, the inventor may appeal to the U.S. Court of Appeals for the federal circuit. An inventor should realize that this process may take years.

Trademarks

A *trademark* is a symbol, word, or design that is used to identify a business or a product. For example, Apple Computer uses a picture of an apple with a bite out of it followed by the symbol ®, which means "registered trademark." A trademark has a longer life than a patent, with certain conditions, because it can be renewed every seventeen years. A business has the exclusive right to a trademark for as long as it is actively using it. However, if the trademarked term becomes part of the generic language, such as aspirin and thermos, it can no longer be trademarked. Furthermore, a trademark cannot be registered until it is actually in use. Before that time, the company should file an intent-to-use application with the PTO and use TM after the name until the trademark is registered or use SM for "service."

Copyrights

Copyrights protect original works of authors, composers, screenwriters, and computer programmers. Though not required by the PTO, it is recommended that to protect such a work, a notice of copyright be placed in a prominent location on the work using either the word Copyright or the symbol ©, the year of first publication, and the name of the copyright holder.

A copyright protects not the idea itself but only the form in which it appears. For example, a computer programmer can copyright the written program for a particular type of word processing software but cannot copyright the idea of word processing. This is why several companies can produce word processing software without violating a copyright. They are really protecting the unique programming code of their software. A copyright lasts for the life of the holder plus seventy years, after which it goes into the public domain.

Trade Secrets

Trade secrets are those aspects of the business that need to be protected from disclosure by employees or others involved with the business. This form of protection generally is achieved through a written agreement. Aspects of the business that may be considered trade secrets are recipes or ingredients (for example, Mrs. Fields cookies), source codes for computer chips, customer discounts, manufacturer costs, and so forth. The only way to protect these items from disclosure is through an employment contract.

Intellectual property rights are valuable protections for innovative new products, but they merely give the holder the right to defend their patent, trademark, or copyright against those who would infringe on those rights. Therefore, intellectual property rights should never be considered the sole competitive advantage that a company has.

ISSUES FOR REVIEW AND DISCUSSION

1. What is the role of company culture in planning the business?

2. Discuss three benefits of fast-cycle product development.

3. How is product development different for small businesses?

4. Compare and contrast finding an appropriate site for a retail store with a site for a wholesale or warehouse business.

5. What are the intellectual property protections that every company will enjoy whether or not that company produces a product?

EXPERIENCING ENTREPRENEURSHIP

1. Visit a product development and manufacturing company. Look for ways it may incorporate the customer into product design. Does it employ fast-cycle product development? What specific things is it doing to improve its product development process?

2. Create an idea for a new product and make a list of where you would go to get such tasks as design, prototyping, and manufacturing accomplished.

Finding the PerfectCurve®

Sometimes the only way to solve a problem is to invent a solution. Gregg Myles Levin had always struggled to create the "perfect curve" in the brim of his favorite baseball cap. While a student at Syracuse University in New York, he experimented incessantly—using rubber bands—to create just the right bend in his cap.

Upon graduation in 1990, Levin took a job in New York as an account executive to begin what he thought was a career in marketing. Two years later, he moved back home to Boston to work for a direct marketing firm. It was then that he came up with an idea to solve the problem of achieving a perfect curve for his baseball cap. He developed a prototype of the device out of a $1.49 can of green Play Doh® and took it to an engineer to discuss how to design and build it. He also took pictures of fans at Fenway Park to convince potential investors of the need for what he planned to call PerfectCurve. Fourteen months later, having spent $20,000 of his and his family's funds, he finished a final prototype and a business plan.

Initially, his family humored him. His father, an attorney, lamented, "This is why I spent $100,000 sending you to college?" To convince him, Levin dragged his father to several sporting goods stores touting the popularity of caps. It worked. In 1994 Levin and his father founded PerfectCurve, Inc., and incorporated as a Delaware company. In addition to the initial investment of $5,000 from Levin and $12,000 from his father and countless hours of "sweat equity," Levin convinced landscape architect Roy S. MacDowell Jr. to invest $200,000. This allowed Levin to leave his job and devote full-time effort to the fledgling venture. It also permitted the company to produce an initial production run of PerfectCurves for the Lids chain of baseball cap stores and about a dozen other stores throughout New England in time for the Christmas season. That first batch sold out in less than two weeks. This was a good sign of potential demand. According to MacDowell, 500 million caps/hats are sold in America every year.

The Growth of PerfectCurve

PerfectCurve was able to create a curved cap brim in minutes and actually provided three settings for three different looks: "Pro" was named for the slight curve preferred by professional ballplayers, "Varsity" was the setting for the most popular curve, and "Extreme" was an extremely tight curve popular with teenagers. What started as a basic solution to a simple problem evolved into a company on its way to becoming the leader and innovator of what was now called the "cap/hat maintenance market." New products in the line included the Gzonta!™, a cap retention cord; The Perfect-Curve Cap Cleaner & Deodorizer™; The PerfectCurve Cap & Hat Water Repellant™; and the PerfectCurve Cap Rack System™, a cap display and storage system. By 1999 PerfectCurve was available in more than 350 retail outlets and catalogs around the country.

Levin built the mold for the PerfectCurve and then hired a manufacturer with injection-molding technology to produce it. The finished product was then sent to a Boston area rehabilitation program site where people with disabilities assembled and packaged it. Levin then took the finished packages to his office/warehouse, where they were stored and shipped. By 2000, the company was shipping 10,000 units per month to retail locations. It also had a deal with Sony of Japan to distribute thousands of PerfectCurves throughout Japan. This was a real coup for the company because it normally takes three to five years to break into the Japanese market. Levin and his father did it in seven months by building strong relationships with their customers and capitalizing on Japan's love for baseball. They also shipped products to Israel, South Africa, and Australia.

Although Levin and his father had patents issued on the PerfectCurve, competitors came out with "knock-off" products. One competitor literally copied everything PerfectCurve, Inc. did, but it didn't have the distribution channels that Levin had or the good customer relationships that he had built. Levin was confident that the company would continue to grow and would double its revenues every year for at least the next two years.

Levin's father had always wanted to go into business with one of his children. Now that he was partnering with Levin, he dreamed of giving up law altogether because he was having so much fun. It is not often easy for a son to partner with his father because frequently neither is able to forget his or her traditional role and just become equal partners. What made it even more awkward for Levin and his father was the fact that they had what Levin calls "a family business in reverse": Levin brought his dad into the business and was the principal decision maker. However, as it turned out, this arrangement really enhanced their relationship and worked very well. Still, Levin candidly advises that this may not be a good strategy for most young entrepreneurs. "You need to have a strong relationship with your parent, bury your ego, be open to ideas, and have a good understanding of your role."

The Crisis Years

In January 2001, Levin had just shipped the largest volume of product in their private label line to its largest customer, Lids. The company paid PerfectCurve $150,000 of the $250,000 it owed and then declared bankruptcy, the result of growing too fast for its capabilities. "I was six days away from the bank calling our line of credit," Levin recalls. Levin had to save his company. He cut wages by more than half and eliminated benefits for his employees, and then he called bankers and angel investors in hopes of finding someone to get Lids out of bankruptcy. Then, in February, Levin found out that his warehouse manager was stealing from him. In April the bank told him that he couldn't survive and they were about to call his line of credit. In June Lids got an infusion of cash, and in July Hat World announced that it was going to acquire Lids. Not knowing what else to do, Levin decided to visit Hat World. The CEO of Hat World had taken a liking to Levin, and he wanted PerfectCurve to succeed, so he lent Levin $160,000 and placed some orders for PerfectCurve products. In December 2001, Levin introduced the PerfectCurve CapRadio: a 1-ounce FM radio designed specifically to attach to a baseball cap. It had a built-in contoured metal clip attached to a cap that ensured comfort.

By early 2002, Levin's company was back on track, and he had repaid the loan from Hat World. By the end of 2002, Levin had secured a new bank loan and completed the buyout of his angel investor. He had also bought out his remaining shareholder, the engineer who had helped him design the first PerfectCurve.

Now Levin and his father owned 100 percent of the company. Sadly, in December 2002, Levin lost his father to cancer.

PerfectCurve Takes on the Big Box Stores

Between 2002 and 2005, the business nearly tripled in size. PerfectCurve now manufactured more than fifteen different stock-keeping units in various retailers throughout the United States. They had become the private label for Hat World and Lids with over 600 stores. Their most successful product was the cap rack for which they won a design award.

In 2005, PerfectCurve moved from its Sudbury, Massachusetts headquarters to the top floor of a building in downtown Boston. When the company secured Lowe's (the home improvement store) as a customer, Levin decided to outsource distribution to a company in Dallas and he began manufacturing in China. In this way, the company could grow more rapidly and handle larger customers. Soon, his products were carried by Bed, Bath and Beyond and Linens `n Things. Levin was now sure that his future lay in being a product idea generator and manufacturer; he would leave the distribution to the experts.

Back in 2001, Levin's father had been working to secure a deal with Wal-Mart. At the time, PerfectCurve did not have the right product. But the cap rack changed everything. To meet Wal-Mart's stiff cost requirements, Levin redesigned the cap rack so that it could sell for $10; Wal-Mart gave him a purchase order, and Levin started shipping in April 2005. Levin expects that by the end of 2006, PerfectCurve will be shipping 300,000 to 500,000 units to Wal-Mart at a wholesale price of $5 a unit. Now Levin wonders what his next move should be.

Advising the Entrepreneur

1. If Levin's goal is to be a product development and manufacturing company, how can he expand what he is now doing to grow the company to the next level?

2. What are the critical product development issues that a small company like PerfectCurve needs to keep in mind as it thinks about new products and services?

CHAPTER 15

Managing Operations

A process cannot be understood by stopping it. Understanding must move with the flow of the process, must join it and flow with it.

Frank Herbert, U.S. science fiction novelist (1920–1986), *Dune: First Law of Mentat*

▶ LEARNING OUTCOMES

- Discuss the role of total quality management in the competitive advantage of a business.
- Explain how outsourcing can help a small business operate more efficiently.
- Identify the key issues related to purchasing.
- Discuss how to effectively manage inventory.
- Describe methods for dealing with warranties.

Outsourcing for Success

Sisters Cheryl Tallman and Joan Ahlers were determined not to feed their babies food laced with preservatives. Although they lived thousands of miles apart in rural communities, they wanted to launch a company that produced healthy baby food. Beechnut and Gerber, which had been selling a "healthy" line of foods for some time, dominated the industry. Knowing that, the sisters did not want to actually produce food and compete with these giants, but rather they wanted to find a way to take advantage of a growing interest in "make-your-own" baby food. They named the company "Fresh Baby" and developed a kit that showed new mothers how to create baby food in a blender and then freeze the servings in ice cube trays. They also targeted pediatricians in hopes of getting them to tout their products to new mothers as an antidote to childhood obesity, a topic frequently in the news. "The number of obese preschoolers has doubled in the last three decades and 30–40% of these children are now at risk of developing Type 2 Diabetes. More alarming still, a staggering 80% of overweight children grows up to be obese adults," reported Tallman.

In 2002, determined to help solve theses problems, the sisters founded the company with $100,000 that they had raised from personal savings and from friends and family. From the beginning, Tallman and Ahlers were focused on tasks within their area of expertise, which was sales and marketing. They would outsource manufacturing, warehousing, distribution, accounting, and even a good deal of their customer relations. They used a call center to field customer phone calls, but the two sisters answered all the e-mails that the company received in an effort to "establish

ourselves as experts in the industry," explained Tallman. Tallman closely managed the subcontractors to ensure quality control. She also developed a quality-control manual that specified Fresh Baby's quality requirements, and each contractor received one.

Fresh Baby's product line included the baby food kit, baby food cookbooks, baby food and breast milk storage trays, breastfeeding reminders, and child development diaries. In 2003, sales were $100,000, but that number grew to $300,000 the very next year. The year 2004 was a banner year, not only because the company was selected by *Entrepreneur* magazine as a "Hot Company to watch in 2004," but also because it secured distribution through Whole Foods, which caused its revenues to soar.

With the Whole Foods contract, the sisters found that they had to let go of more of the functions of the business. Whole Foods was perhaps the most important chain in the industry, so they had to make sure that they pushed their products "region by region, and store by store." To do this, they outsourced sales to a broker network to speed up growth. Tallman and Ahlers were sold on outsourcing. "We never have to turn down an opportunity because of manufacturing capacity, fulfillment, logistics, or manpower." The two are cautious about expanding into new-product offerings. For now, they have chosen to expand the markets into which they sell their current line. Nevertheless, at some point they need to consider how to further diversify their product line; the question is, When?

Sources: "Cheryl Tallman's Key Move: Outsourcing," *Startup Nation,* www.startupnation.com (accessed June 24, 2005); Fresh Baby, www.myfreshbaby.com.

More than 200 years ago, manufacturing was a craft industry—a process customized to meet the needs of the customer. But as customers began to value standardized goods, mass production became the new paradigm. Manufacturing became a separate function that received information through the filters of marketing, management, and finance. It was not until the 1950s and 1960s when the Japanese introduced total quality control, just-in-time production and inventory, and quality function deployment that manufacturing became part of a continual process of upstream and downstream activities and was recognized as a significant contributor to the overall performance of the firm. Productivity in U.S. manufacturing has risen dramatically over the past decade, and the ability of small business to enter the manufacturing arena has increased tremendously. The gains can be attributed to three factors: (1) the downsizing and outsourcing of anything that is not a core competency for the company; (2) the commitment to total quality product or process management; and, most recently, (3) the trend toward agile manufacturing (also called virtual manufacturing or networked manufacturing).

New companies often fall into the trap of focusing solely on the product or service in the start-up stage and then on marketing as the company grows, without ever recognizing that superior process management is also a significant contributor to competitive advantage and certainly essential to cultivating an expanding bottom line. Integrating process design into all the activities of a business saves time and money, and puts a company miles ahead of product-focused companies. Every business is a process-driven system in need of continual improvement. This chapter looks at the processes involved in running a company that produces products as the primary source of its revenues. These processes include quality management, outsourcing, and purchasing and inventory management.

LEARNING FROM SUCCESS

Suppliers Are Partners

Mercedes LaPorta learned an important lesson from her businessman father: Your suppliers are not simply vendors; they are your partners in the business. When LaPorta started her own company, Mercedes Electric Supply in Miami, she remembered that lesson. She knew she had to select only the best suppliers, those who were reliable and focused on quality. While many people suggested using multiple suppliers for a particular product to protect her company against supplier abuse, LaPorta boldly decided to use only one supplier for lamps, one supplier for wire, and so forth for every product she carried. She reasoned that as her company grew, she would have more clout with each supplier if she purchased in large volume.

"I've got relationships that I've developed not just with the sales guy who calls weekly but also with higher-up people. And that's what has kept them from taking us for granted," claims LaPorta. In this way, the daughter of a wise businessman can successfully compete with national distributor chains in a very competitive industry.

Lesson Learned: *Make your suppliers your partners.*

Sources: "Mercedes Key Move: Making Suppliers Feel like Partners," *Startup Nation,* www.startupnation.com (accessed June 24, 2005); Mercedes Electric Supply, http://www.mercedeselectric.com/.

TOTAL QUALITY MANAGEMENT

In the simplest terms, **total quality management** (TQM) is the application of the highest levels of quality in every aspect of the business. Quality is about meeting customer requirements, and to achieve the highest levels requires a process that can be managed.

The traditional Japanese models of TQM incorporated five themes: (1) management commitment, (2) leadership, (3) customer focus, (4) total participation, and (5) process analysis and improvement.[1] Within these themes are other principles important to process design: continuous improvement, total quality control, self-directed teams, automation, computer-integrated manufacturing, and just-in-time production and inventory. Many large companies have adopted TQM with varying degrees of success. Federal Express (FedEx), for example, successfully employed TQM to achieve its goal of "100 percent service performance on every package delivered." Not only did it concern itself with on-time delivery, but it also instituted a service quality indicator to measure various types of delivery problems, such as damage to packages and incorrect delivery time. FedEx has continually been named number one in its industry for quality.

TQM is not just for large companies. Whether the small business is involved in business-to-business selling or business-to-consumer, the expectations for quality today are much higher than in years past.[2] Quality includes both product quality and management quality. Product quality is determined by the customer, the user, the manufacturer, and by standards in the industry.[3] The process by which the product is produced generally reflects the management capability of the company.[4] Small businesses that decide to implement TQM from the beginning have the highest probability of success because they can develop systems and hire people at the outset who understand what they are trying to accomplish. Customer satisfaction and quality must be the highest priority for all employees, and they must be committed to it. In small companies, the CEO typically assumes the role of quality manager because of limited resources and personnel, but he or she needs to empower everyone in the organization to solve problems and implement new methods that lead to improvements in quality and customer satisfaction. Each employee needs to understand his or her role in TQM. The principles of TQM are the following:

- Quality must be managed.
- Every business has a customer and is a supplier.
- Processes must be improved.
- Every employee is responsible for quality.
- Problems must be prevented, not just fixed.
- Quality must be measured.
- Quality improvements must be continuous.
- The quality standard is defect free.
- Goals are based on customer requirements.
- Costs must be calculated over the life cycle of the product.
- Management must be involved and lead the quality process.

Continual Improvement

If TQM is the vehicle to achieve world-class manufacturing processes, *kaizen* is the engine that drives it. Kaizen, which in Japanese means "gradual, unending improvement," is a principle that focuses on improving every aspect of the business. Under this philosophy, everything a company does (and this includes service companies) is a process, and every element of that process is held under a microscope to see if it can be improved on. The *kaizen* philosophy can be applied equally to service, marketing, finance, and many other aspects of business. There are several versions of *kaizen,* but the one we discuss here is the USA-PDCA method, which is used by many companies worldwide. PDCA stands for plan, do, check, act, and it embodies the essence of *kaizen*. Assuming that employees are organized into self-directed teams for better productivity, the first step in PDCA is to understand the nature of the customer, the relevant needs and issues, and how a company may be failing to meet them. Once the nature of the customer is understood, the team can focus on the issue that needs improving and begin to analyze the process involved. As pictured in Table 15.1, the PDCA then proceeds as follows:

- *Plan.* With the process identified and analyzed, the team now plans for the change that takes place to improve the process.
- *Do.* The team implements the plan, assuming that it has been determined that doing so does not pose unnecessary risk to other parts of the system.
- *Check.* The team proceeds to analyze the results of the change to verify that it actually improved the process. If not, the team reexamines the plan to locate any errors in its reasoning.
- *Act.* Once the change has been verified, accepted, and documented, the team puts in place the changes, equipment, or whatever is required to make the change in the process routine and move on to define and research the next issue.

The three underlying principles of the TQM process are total quality control, just-in-time production and inventory, and total employee involvement.

Total Quality Control

The term **total quality control** (TQC) derives from the work of W. Edwards Deming, J. M. Juran, and Armand V. Feigenbaum following World War II. The goal of TQC is to eliminate all defects at all stages of the process—in other words, to achieve perfection. The Japanese were quick to adopt this principle to overcome the perception at that time that their products were of low quality. TQC has been practiced in the United States only for the past two decades, so U.S. firms have been playing catch-up to the experienced Japanese companies. TQM is really a spinoff of the TQC philosophy.

In the past, quality was the sole province of preproduction design and testing and postproduction inspection. Juran, however, suggested that quality encompasses product performance and satisfaction as well as freedom from deficiencies and dissatisfaction.[5] If a company waits until the manufacturing process to evaluate quality and then does it through a series of inspections by various workers along the way, it can raise production costs as much as 50 percent. On the other hand, inspecting a product before it is made, during the design stage, allows the design team to engineer a manufacturing process that is stable and reliable. In other words, quality is designed into

TABLE 15.1 The TQM Process

Plan			Do	Check	Act
Define the problem.	Identify possible causes.	Decide on a course of action.	Implement the change.	Assess the outcome and refine.	Incorporate the change into the company.
Talk to customers. Assess current processes.	Brainstorm. Review historical data.	Identify cause-and-effect relationships.	What change will correct the situation? How will the change be implemented?	Execute the strategy.	Measure the outcome. Make changes as necessary.	Ensure that the change is hardwired into the company processes.

both the product and the process, and the goal is zero defects and zero engineering changes. This preventive approach is far more efficient and less costly than resorting to design reviews, numerous versions of prototypes, and beta tests to find problems. Even after the product is launched, the product team should be in a continual improvement mode, constantly seeking ways to incrementally improve and enhance the product.

The importance of quality when designing products with many parts cannot be overstated. An example makes this clear. If the quality level is a function of the probability that any part is defect free, then

$$Q^p = (Q_a)^n$$

where Q^p is the quality of the product, $(Q_a)^n$ is the average quality level of the parts in the product, and n is the number of parts. Suppose that a product has thirty distinct parts and all are 98 percent defect free. Then,

$$Q^p = (Q_a)^n = (.98)^{30} = .54 \text{ defect free}$$

This means that only 54 percent of the products are defect free, assuming manufacturing quality is defect free. Choosing parts with a higher reliability rating can significantly improve the overall defect rate for the product. Suppose that parts with a 99.5 percent reliability rate are substituted. Then,

$$Q^p = (Q_a)^n = (.995)^{30} = .86 \text{ defect free}$$

The bottom line is this: Designing for quality in both the product and the process substantially reduces costs and increases the odds that the final product is defect free.

The basic principles of TQC are as follows:

1. **Customer Satisfaction** To achieve customer satisfaction requires going beyond customer expectations and providing products that never disappoint the customer. Continuous improvement—*kaizen*—is one route to the achievement of this goal. Customer input at every stage of product development is another.

2. **Quality Circles** The process of quality circles involves bringing employees together at the start of every day (or every shift) to discuss issues and daily plans. Quality circles have been poorly received in the United States because many firms find this approach rigid in a culture that seems to thrive on sound bites and flexibility. Nevertheless, the underlying notion of keeping everyone informed and on track, no matter how it is done, has merit and is essential to achieving total quality. Every business owner needs to develop a form of quality circles that is appropriate to his or her type of business if total quality is to be achieved.

3. ***Hoshin*** In Japanese, *hoshin* means "policy deployment," in essence a planning and review tool that consists of annual objectives and strategies. It is very similar to the U.S. "management by objectives" popular in the 1980s. It is a formalized process that requires a statement of objectives, how those objectives are achieved, and how the company knows when it has achieved them. *Hoshin* is very compatible with PDCA and is an excellent tool for company annual reviews.

4. ***Poka Yoke*** This is a Japanese term that means solutions to problems should be foolproof; that is, any process to correct a problem should be so foolproof that the problem does not occur again. Again, a sound PDCA plan helps ensure that improvements in quality remain in place.

A Home-Based Business Can Mean Less Free Time—Not More!

In her mid-thirties, Wendy Almquist left her corporate job with Minneapolis-based Carlson Marketing group to find something that would allow her to have more control of her life and to spend more time with her children. She decided to start a home-based business, reasoning that it would meet her goals.

At several craft shows that she had attended, Almquist noted that soy-based candles were very popular. She decided to become a wholesaler of soy candles and started a company called BeansWax. She and her husband experimented in their garage with various formulas. When they found the right one, Almquist conducted "informational interviews" with potential buyers, showing them samples of her work. Early demand was strong, but Almquist soon realized that this business would not give her more time with her children. She was working harder than ever, and

the home-based business had literally taken over her home. Finally, after a year of trying to make it work at home and city officials complaining about the huge trucks coming into her residential neighborhood, she leased space in a factory that produced her candles one week a month. She also leased another location where she and her family handled sales and distribution. "People think you have flexibility, but you become more of a slave to your business," Almquist says. She quit a job where she worked eight hours a day to take on one where she now works sixteen hours a day, seven days a week. Prior to starting the business, she never took the time to plan anything about the business beyond the product itself, so now she is working hard to learn as she goes.

Lesson Learned: *Due diligence enables a more informed decision about starting a business.*

Just-in-Time Production and Inventory

One tool that is finally being recognized for its ability to improve the materials management aspect of manufacturing is **just-in-time** (JIT) production. A JIT system helps companies improve cycle and delivery times, use material only when it is needed, reduce inventory and its attendant space requirements, and improve quality. Developed in the United States by Toyota, JIT production has two fundamental approaches: the continuous-flow system and the *kanban* system. In manufacturing situations where a single product is being produced in high volume, the continuous-flow system is appropriate. Under this system, the correct amount of materials inventory is placed at the start of the production line and then moved from one station to the next, with the speed determined by the slowest link in the process.

Kanban, the second approach, is a system used when production is more flexible and contains more variety. Taiichi Ohno, the creator of the Toyota production system, developed *kanban*. The idea was based on the U.S. supermarket:

A supermarket is where a customer can get (1) what is needed, (2) at the time needed, (3) in the amount needed. . . . From the supermarket we got the idea of viewing the earlier processes in the production line as a kind of store. The later process (customer) goes to the earlier process (supermarket) to acquire the required parts (commodities) at the time and in the quantity needed. The earlier process immediately produces the quantity just taken (restocking the shelves).[6]

Work at a station starts when a *kanban* signal card (*kanban* in Japanese actually means "visible record") is received from a previous station. Alternatively, assembly starts with bins full of parts. When the part bin nearest the work is empty, it moves to the source of supply, and the next full bin moves forward. This reduces cycle time, the time to take a part through the process from start to finish, because inventory queues are eliminated.

A singular advantage of the JIT system is that defects are not passed along but discovered and corrected where they occur. In terms of productivity, the benefits include less scrap and rework, less inventory, fewer work orders, less capital investment, fewer materials handling costs, and less space. For JIT to be successfully implemented, three major components must be in place: customer, production, and suppliers. All must subscribe to and be a part of the JIT system. The process begins with the customer, whose requirements establish the time to delivery and the type of manufacturing process required. Production is then set up so that at each point on the production line a task is completed, with each task designed to take about the same length of time as the previous or succeeding task so that there is no wait time. Under the continuous-flow

LEARNING FROM SUCCESS

Baldrige Quality for Small Businesses

The Malcolm Baldrige award is the United States' highest honor for quality. The competition for it is tough and the selection process daunting, but it creates a standard against which growing companies can compare themselves. The Malcolm Baldrige Criteria for Performance Excellence (CPE) is a framework for identifying and assessing organizational strengths and opportunities for improvement. Small businesses that have gone through the Baldrige assessment have seen positive results in performance and market competitiveness. Many small businesses take advantage of the CPE by working to develop the benchmark practices in their businesses without actually applying for the award.

The Malcolm Baldrige CPE sets best practices within seven categories:

1. *Leadership* Does senior management promote quality values, and do those values influence day-to-day management?

2. *Information and Analysis* Does the company effectively use competitive comparisons, and does it support quality objectives through data analysis?

3. *Strategic Quality Planning* How thoroughly does the company incorporate quality requirements?

4. *Human Resource Development and Management* What are the systems and practices that involve employees in education, training, assessment, and recognition?

5. *Management of Process Quality* Does the company exhibit quality in product and service design and in process control? Does it undertake quality assessment and documentation, and how does it ensure the quality of supplies?

6. *Quality and Operational Results* What are the company's trends in levels of improvement of products and services, business services, and suppliers' quality?

7. *Customer Focus and Satisfaction* What are the company's customer-service standards and customer satisfaction ratings, and how does it make use of customer complaints and suggestions?

Sources: P. R. Stephens, J. R. Evans, and C. H. Matthews, "Importance and Implementation of Baldrige Practices for Small Businesses," *Quality Management Journal* 12(3) (2005): 21; D. A. Garvin, "How the Baldrige Award Really Works," *Harvard Business Review* 6 (1991): 80–93.

process, raw materials inventory arrives before the previous inventory is consumed, whereas in the *kanban* process, a card goes to the supply station to secure more materials when the *kanban* queue declines to a designated level. The role of the supplier becomes critical to the whole process, because if the supplier can be an integral part of the *kanban* chain through electronic data transfer or even fax transfer, the process is made more efficient. In this way, the manufacturer does not need to store supplies. This is a critical feature for small business owners with limited resources. The ability to keep the inventory of raw materials to a minimum is important for managing cash flow and limited resources.

While it is beyond the scope of this book to discuss the JIT system in depth, it is important that the concept is considered for the improvement of the manufacturing process in a small business.

Total Employee Involvement

Successful TQM does not happen without total employee involvement in the process.[7] Unfortunately, in small businesses quality control is often handed off to one individual to manage and is therefore not considered within other employees' scope of duties. Furthermore, many small businesses, particularly manufacturers, are finding that potential customers may demand evidence of a TQM process, and that process cannot be implemented effectively through a single person. In fact some research has found that small businesses place greater importance on leadership and people than on TQM.[8] They understand the importance of a quality product or service but they tend to reject formal programs to achieve it, generally due to time, cost, resources, relevance to goals, and required bureaucracy. Nevertheless, even for a small business, TQM is important to the creation of a sustainable competitive advantage, so it is vital that all employees be focused on quality.

OUTSOURCING

Outsourcing noncore functions can often help a company get products to market faster and in greater quantities while spreading risk and delivering the capabilities of a much larger company without the expense. In fact, a Coopers & Lybrand survey of 400 fast-growing small companies found that two-thirds used outsourcing, and their revenues, sales prospects, and growth rates far exceeded those of companies that did not use outsourcing. Outsourcing permits small, growing companies to have noncore functions completed more efficiently at a lower cost and at a higher level of quality than they could achieve themselves. Innovative Medical Systems Inc., a New Hampshire–based manufacturer, outsources the manufacture of subassemblies, product design, computer networking, payroll administration, and direct mailing and advertising placement and does only final assembly, quality assurance, strategic marketing, and customer service in-house. Many retail businesses outsource fulfillment, the shipping and handling of goods, because doing it themselves costs too much money, money that the business cannot afford if it is operating on thin margins. An individual retailer cannot purchase packing materials at the same rate as a fulfillment outsourcer that buys in volume. In addition, most fulfillment companies are automated, so their processing time is faster. Some of the factors to consider when selecting a fulfillment outsourcer are the following:

- Select a fulfillment outsourcer that understands the entrepreneur's business.
- Require periodic reports on products that go in and out of the fulfillment center.
- The fulfillment company should be able to handle multiple channels.
- Find out if the fulfillment company can handle returns.
- Find a fulfillment company that can also take orders.[9]

MANAGING PURCHASING

Any business that purchases raw materials or parts for production of goods for resale must carefully consider the quality, quantity, and timing of those purchases. Quality goods are those that meet specific needs, whereas the quantity purchased is a function of demand, manufacturing capability, and storage capability. Because materials account for approximately 50 percent of total manufacturing cost, it is important to balance these three factors carefully.

Effective purchasing begins with a strategy that takes into consideration quality, service, and price. In this sense, *quality* means the product is suitable for the purpose for which it was intended. *Service* means it is delivered when needed and corrected if defective. *Price* means a competitive price, but not necessarily the lowest price. In other words, all three factors must be considered before selecting a product and a supplier (vendor). A good purchasing policy also establishes a clear line of authority for purchasing decisions and controls over ordering decisions. This means using requisitions and placing someone in charge of them. An effective purchasing policy addresses the following issues:

- Identify someone to handle the purchasing for the company and specify the spending limitations.
- Specify the procedure that the purchasing agent follows to order, receive, and pay for goods.
- Identify appropriate vendors (vendors are discussed in the next section).
- Determine a policy on the acceptance of gifts from suppliers.
- Identify the types of legal contracts in which the purchasing agent can enter.
- State the company's conflict-of-interest policy.
- Determine which purchasing information is confidential.
- Determine how legal questions are handled.

Choosing Vendors

Small business owners typically deal with a number of different types of suppliers including manufacturers, distributors or wholesalers, independent craftspeople, and importers. There are several ways to select vendors: by talking to salespeople, requesting samples, finding out who supplies the competition, and by attending trade shows. Once a list of vendors is compiled, it is time to evaluate them. Some of the criteria that should be considered for an initial screen of vendors are the vendor's reputation, its credit rating, and its ability to provide technical assistance.

The first decision to make is whether to buy from one vendor or more than one vendor. One advantage to relying on a single vendor is that it can generally provide more individual attention and better service and is able to consolidate the company's orders, which may result in a discount based on quantity purchased. The principal disadvantage of using only one vendor is that if the vendor suffers a catastrophe, it may be difficult or impossible to find an alternative source in a short period of time. To ensure against this type of disaster, a small business may want to follow the general rule of using one supplier for about 70 to 80 percent of its needs and one or more additional vendors to supply the rest. Many manufacturers are now reducing the number of suppliers that they deal with to enhance relationships and quality.

Information systems can now provide purchasing managers with detailed feedback on supplier performance, delivery reliability, and quality control results. Comparing results across suppliers gives the purchasing manager more leverage when it's time to renegotiate the annual contracts with suppliers.

MANAGING INVENTORY

Inventory is basically assets purchased and held for sale. With the possible exception of some service companies, all businesses have some type of inventory. There are three basic types of inventory: finished goods, raw materials, and work in process. The last two relate to manufacturing operations. Finished-goods inventory is items ready for sale, and this is the type of inventory that retailers hold to ensure that they have enough on hand to meet their customers' needs. Because customer demand fluctuates, retailers must have a keen sense of when to carry above-average levels of inventory. Too much inventory means high carrying costs; too little inventory results in lost sales. It is estimated that the average retailer spends from 20 to 30 percent of the original inventory investment to maintain it, and that doesn't include the cash that was used to purchase the excess inventory in the first place.[10] For all types of businesses, the goal is to minimize stockouts and eliminate excess inventory. Instead of purchasing large quantities and receiving them on a monthly basis, companies are purchasing daily or weekly in a JIT fashion to avoid costly inventory holding costs. Of course, some inventory of finished goods must be maintained to meet delivery deadlines; therefore, a delicate balance needs to be achieved among goods coming into the company, work in progress, and goods leaving the company to be sold.

One primary reason to minimize inventory on hand is that inventories carry inherent costs, ordering costs, insurance, storage, and shrinkage (theft and loss), so it is vital that a growing company have a system in place to manage its inventory. Many extraneous costs are associated with inventories that can add as much as 25 percent to the base cost of the inventory. They include

- Financing costs—the interest paid on the money borrowed to purchase the inventory.
- Opportunity cost—the loss of use of the money that is tied up in inventory.
- Storage costs—the amount spent on warehouse space to store the inventory.
- Insurance costs—the cost of insuring the inventory.
- Shrinkage costs—the money lost from inventory that is broken, stolen, or damaged.
- Obsolescence—the cost associated with inventory that has become obsolete.

The optimal quantity of inventory to purchase and have on hand is called the **economic order quantity** (EOQ), and it is composed of the total carrying costs plus the

FIGURE 15.1 The Economic Order Quantity

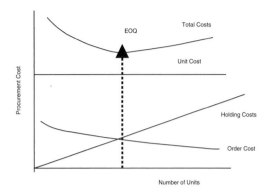

total procurement, or ordering, costs. The EOQ is the lowest point on the total costs curve that coincides with the carry costs and the ordering costs (Figure 15.1). The object of the EOQ is to find the quantity to buy with the minimum total cost EOQ where

$$\text{Total cost} = \text{Purchase cost} + \text{Procurement costs} + \text{Holding cost}$$

Given that procurement costs are fixed, total costs increase when a small business purchases small quantities more frequently. Where discounts are available, they tend to favor volume purchases, and small businesses should endeavor to take advantage of them. As the quantity purchased increases, the unit cost remains fixed, the procurement costs decline because there are fewer orders, and the holding costs increase due to larger volume of purchases. Figure 15.2 depicts some of the early warning signs of inventory problems.

To reduce some of the costs of inventory, many firms are moving toward a JIT system that links them electronically with their suppliers, who then know when the company reaches a trigger point at which it must replenish its inventory of a particular product. In a start-up venture, keeping track of inventory may simply be a matter of visually inspecting and counting because the business is growing in a fairly controlled manner in the beginning. However, once the business is growing rapidly, these simple techniques no longer suffice, and it is best to be prepared for this eventuality early on with a system for keeping track of inventory. Entrepreneurs should consider both informal and formal inventory-tracking methods.

Informal Inventory-Tracking Methods

When a company is small and its suppliers are located in close proximity to the business, it can reorder inventory on an as-needed basis. One method that smaller companies use is to divide the inventory into expensive and inexpensive items and then track more frequently the status of the expensive items because they account for a larger portion of the value of the inventory as a whole. Larger retailers, in contrast, typically use a bar-code system to track inventory and establish trigger points with their suppliers to find out when to reorder. With this system, when a sale occurs, it is recorded electronically and the inventory is updated simultaneously.

FIGURE 15.2   Warning Signs of Inventory Problems

Hardware stores and wholesale businesses typically use a two-bin system for small items whereby two containers of the item are carried at all times. The open container/display is placed on top of the closed container. When the open container is empty, it's time to reorder and open the bottom container. Bookstores that shelve books cover forward use a variation of this method by placing a reorder card in the last book at the back of the stack. Yet another method involves dividing inventory into three groups based on price. Each group is then analyzed to determine the best tracking method for that group. Usually one group requires more frequent reordering than another.

Formal Computerized Inventory-Tracking Systems

Although the smallest of companies still use manual tracking methods, most small-business owners have moved to computerized systems because they provide more information with less effort. These programs enable the company to track usage, monitor changes in costs per unit, forecast when a reorder is required, and analyze inventory levels.

Perpetual Inventory Systems

Perpetual inventory systems keep a running count of items in inventory. As items are sold, they are subtracted; as they are purchased, they are added. An electronic point-of-sale (POS) system (such as those now used in most grocery and retail stores) allows a business instant access to the status of its inventory. Bar-coding inventory with electronic tags makes it easier to achieve error-free tracking. Manufacturers today are bar-coding inventories of raw materials and components to facilitate tracking and reorders. Even if they have an electronic system, most businesses still do some form of physical tracking to detect errors in the system and account for items that may have been stolen or lost and would not show up as a sale. To make the counting process more efficient, inventories should be as low as possible before the count takes place.

Point-of-Purchase Systems Point-of-purchase (POP) systems exist for virtually every type of retail or wholesale business and ensure more accurate tracking of inventory in "real time." When an item is purchased, its code is entered into the terminal, and the inventory is immediately reduced by that item. This makes it very easy to know when to reorder.

Bar Coding Bar coding actually facilitates POP systems by relieving the salesperson from having to enter code. Consequently, one potential point of data-entry error is eliminated, which can be a significant savings to the company. In addition, the POS system enables the business to analyze sales data so that purchasing levels can be adjusted, keep a sales history, and even integrate bar-code scanners with credit card authorization ability to enhance pricing accuracy.[11] The bar code is a label containing black-and-white parallel bars encoded with information. To use a bar-code system requires a computer, a laser scanner, a decoder, and the bar-code symbols.

RFID Tracking RFID stands for radio frequency identification tracking. It is the latest technology being used to wirelessly track the location of inventory and materials and supplies. In 2003, Wal-Mart lost $8 billion in products that were stolen or that they lost track of. For companies that deal in enormous volumes of inventory, RFID has reduced the cost of tracking substantially, from about 75 cents per tag for bar coding to less than 12 cents a tag, and it has made it more feasible to tag every item.

Electronic Data Interchange Electronic data interchange takes electronic data entry one step further by linking the retailer with the supplier so that reordering essentially becomes automatic. By linking directly or through the Internet, inventory is shipped when needed, resulting in higher inventory turnover and the elimination of the need for demand forecasting or other traditional inventory-tracking devices. Small businesses that sell to large discount operators like Wal-Mart are required to link into Wal-Mart's inventory system.

Inventory Turnover

Inventory turnover is an important indicator of the effectiveness with which the company is managing its inventory. *Inventory turnover* is the average number of times an inventory is sold out during the year for a particular product line. The rate of turnover differs for each industry (for example, men's clothing is 3; restaurants, 22; and some chemical manufacturers, 100), but knowing the average rate for the industry in which the company competes is an important benchmark against which to measure the company's effectiveness. For example, if it is known that a particular industry has an inventory turnover rate of 5, the following formula represents how much inventory must be kept on hand:

$$\frac{12 \text{ months}}{5 \text{ turnover rate}} = 2.4 \text{ months' supply}$$

On average, then, a 2.4-month supply of inventory must be on hand. Once the quantity required to be on hand is known, the cost of the inventory can be calculated by using the company's forecasted sales for the upcoming year and the cost of goods sold (COGS) (inventory) percentage. For example, if the company is forecasting $200,000 in sales and the COGS is 50 percent of sales, then

$$\frac{\$\,200,000 \times 0.50}{5 \text{ turnover rate}} = \$\,20,000$$

It costs $20,000 to maintain a 2.4 months' supply in inventory, not including carrying costs. Naturally, if the company deals in several product lines, calculations for each line must be done because they may have varying turnover rates.

Using a variation of the previous formula, a company can calculate its inventory turnover rate to compare itself against the industry average. This is done by dividing the cost of sales by the average inventory:

$$\$100,000/ \$20,000 = 5$$

This means the company turned over its inventory an average of five times during the year, or every seventy-three days (365/5).

It's important to look not only at total inventory turnover but also at turnover of individual items to find the slow-moving ones. A simple analysis of the number of any item on hand against the number sold in, say, the past sixty days points up which products need to have their inventory on hand decreased and which need their inventory increased.

Shrinkage

Shrinkage is loss by theft and shoplifting from both customers and employees. It is by all accounts a significant problem in the retail industry because so many people pass through its doors. To illustrate the impact of theft on a company's profitability, consider a case in which a software retailer loses a software program valued at $39.95 every day for a year. If the store operates at a 10 percent profit margin, it has to sell an additional $145,817.50 of merchandise to compensate for the loss.

Shoplifting, the most common crime in the retail business, accounts for about 3 percent of the selling price of an item. Some tactics to help deter shoplifting include

- Keeping the store well lit and display cases low to maintain a clear view.
- Using two-way mirrors or closed-circuit TV.
- Using electronic, tamper-proof tags on articles of clothing.
- Hiring a uniformed security guard.

Though shoplifting is a frustrating problem for retailers, about 75 to 80 percent of all retail crime is actually committed by employees, who add 15 percent to the cost of consumer goods. Employees have an advantage over shoplifters; they normally have access to the business in a way no shoplifter does. A company can do several things to minimize the opportunity for employee theft:

1. Keep all nonentry or exit doors locked when not in use.
2. Control who has access to keys to the business and change the locks if theft is suspected.

3. Periodically check the trash bins because they are a typical hiding place for stolen items.

4. Watch for a large number of voided or no-sale transactions.

5. Don't let one person control a transaction from beginning to end.

6. Be careful about hiring and check references.

A few precautions taken consistently go a long way toward protecting the business and its customers.

WARRANTIES

The company that subscribes to TQM typically provides warranties with products to protect against potential liability and demonstrate that the company stands behind its products. Today, product warranties are also a marketing tool to sell a product.

Some of the decisions regarding warranties include the following:

- What is the length of the warranty?

- Which components are covered? (Some components may come from other manufacturers that have their own warranties. In this case, it's important to have that component certified by the original equipment manufacturer so that the warranty is not invalidated in the new use.)

- What is the product scope? Does the warranty cover one or all products in a line, or does each have a separate warranty?

- What is the market scope? Does the same warranty apply in all markets? This is a function of state and foreign laws.

- What conditions of the warranty must the customer fulfill? Today a product is covered by warranty from the moment it's purchased.

- Who executes the warranty? The company must decide who handles warranty claims (manufacturer, dealer, distributor), recognizing that customers do not like to mail products back to the manufacturer.

- What are the policies for refunds/returns and shipping/handling costs? Customer-oriented companies offer a generous return policy and pay for the cost of returns.

Providing a warranty involves a cost to the manufacturer; however, that cost must be weighed against the potential loss of business if no warranty is provided. In the case of a new business with a new product, it's difficult to anticipate the number of problems that might occur as the product gets into the marketplace. Careful and adequate field testing of the product prior to market entry goes a long way toward eliminating many potential problems and the possibility of a recall, which is very costly for any firm, let alone a new, growing business.

Retail/wholesale/service businesses, like manufacturing businesses, are becoming solutions oriented. An effective, total quality process strategy should include the customer, state-of-the-art technology, superior resources and processes, and continuous improvement. Entrepreneurial companies that integrate these components into their process strategies gain a significant competitive advantage in a dynamic marketplace.

ISSUES FOR REVIEW AND DISCUSSION

1. How can small businesses employ TQM to their advantage?
2. What elements do effective purchasing policies include?
3. Discuss two effective methods for tracking inventory in a small business.
4. What are some ways that a retail business can reduce shrinkage?

EXPERIENCING ENTREPRENEURSHIP

1. Identify a product line that you might want to sell through your retail business. Seek out three distributors or vendors of these products and evaluate them based on reliability, distance, and service.
2. Interview a small manufacturer about TQM. What is this business doing to implement quality initiatives?

Corporate United

Group buying has always been a way for small businesses to secure better prices from suppliers, but in the case of Corporate United, it was a small start-up that helped the Fortune 1000 save millions of dollars through their combined buying power. Founded in 1997, Corporate United today provides an end-to-end solution for sourcing and managing contracts to a wide range of companies with combined revenues of more than $200 billion. Founder Greg Mylett has accomplished all this with only three employees—Mylett himself and two sales representatives with experience in procurement. According to Mylett, "By leveraging our members' individual needs for purchased materials, services, and capital goods, Corporate United secures greater service levels and value-added pricing from suppliers and effectively assists companies in lowering their total cost of ownership across a wide range of spend categories."

Background

Mylett had been working in office products at Boise-Cascade since he graduated from college in 1986. His clients were large companies, in particular healthcare organizations, hospitals, and schools, which purchased their office products through group purchasing organizations (GPOs) such as Premier and Novation. Because the office supply industry uses a contract-bid system where price is driven by quantity, a GPO is able to leverage many small orders from its members to bid very large contracts. With this large buying power, prices for GPO members are significantly lower.

In his years with Boise-Cascade, Greg noticed that the bulk of corporations in America did not take advantage of this GPO model, and he was certain that it would work with mid-sized companies. In addition, he became aware of the enormous disparity in individual contracts with suppliers, which often resulted in the supplier taking advantage of those companies that had weaker contracts. Realizing that buying power, combined with ironclad contract management, would offer enough savings to convince companies to join him, Mylett decided that there was an opportunity there to start a business.

Not quite ready to leave Boise-Cascade, Mylett continued to work for Boise while he designed the business. His wife came up with the name of the business, and his brother designed a logo for this company that would be called Corporate United (CU). Then he hired an advertising agent who sent a live Christmas tree to mid- to large-sized companies with an attached note: "Come grow with us." This was followed a week later by an invitation to a half day meeting highlighting the following topics:

- CU's Purchasing Alliance for Corporate Transactions (PACT): A Unique Approach to Corporate Purchasing
- Leveraging Your Purchasing Power
- Bringing Corporations Together to Share Ideas
- Savings That Affect Your Bottom Line

In the invitation to prospective customers, Mylett was not specific about any areas of purchasing in particular; he simply stated that "Corporate United can show you how building strength in unity saves you time and money. And because you won't have to do as much paperwork, you'll save a few trees along the way." Despite his enthusiasm for the business concept, he was nervous about a number of challenges that he faced. Many of the companies had long-term relationships with specific suppliers, and Corporate United wasn't selling a specific supplier but rather a bid process that he was certain would show significant savings. Thus, he reasoned, a company would be unwise not to switch from a current supplier. Moreover, this was a concept that nobody was familiar with unless they had worked in healthcare. To overcome this challenge, Mylett secured a speaker from the National Association of Purchasing Managers who spoke for no fee because he was a proponent of group purchasing. He was also a teacher and had taught many of the audience members as students. The feedback from the event was very positive. Out of nineteen companies attending, six said that they wanted to move forward as "founding members" of the organization. With this group of founding members, Mylett formed a board of advisors for CU, which consisted mostly of vice presidents of procurement from each member company. The group had a few meetings and then decided to move ahead on a bid for office products.

The next step was to laboriously compare and contrast each member's needs and purchasing habits in order to come up with a strong contract that would be used to place bids with office product suppliers. After countless conference calls with attorneys and lots of paperwork, Mylett finally succeeded in landing signatories.

The risks for CU were many, not the least of which was that Mylett might get sued because of a possible conflict of interest because he still worked for Boise-Cascade, which was one of the companies from which CU was seeking a bid. There was also a risk that no one would bid for CU's contract because only four companies in the United States could handle such a contract. In the end, however, all four suppliers bid, and the result was that CU showed a 25 percent savings for member American Greetings, which subsequently enticed the company away from Staples, and an 18 percent savings for member Progressive, which then left CU's competitor Corporate Express.

CU's contract stated that 3 percent of any bid would go back to CU. As the contracts got larger, a couple of the members wanted to limit CU's profits, but Progressive stood up and said "no way" on the grounds that CU had just saved them an enormous amount of money and desired its share of the contract.

CU decided to try a similar process on a purchasing bid for copy paper, which was a serious test of the buying power of the new alliance because copy paper is a true commodity. The bid resulted in a 15 percent savings for Progressive and for Sherwin Williams.

Different Interests at Stake

CU now had a tried-and-true method of reducing costs. It was also getting a reputation for producing contracts that were much stronger than the industry standard, with very favorable terms and conditions, including several levels of guaranteed service from suppliers that did not exist in previous individual contracts. As a result, Mylett wanted to grow the partner base, but when he announced his decision to the alliance, the founding members said no. They wanted CU to go after other areas where CU could reduce costs for them rather than seek new partners. Mylett was concerned that this would limit CU's growth, but instead of limiting it, this decision on the part of the alliance turned out to be extremely advantageous for CU: The more areas that CU handled for its clients,

the more difficult it would be for a partner/client to leave if a competitor would show up.

In 1998, CU moved into purchasing copiers to leverage the digital revolution that was merging printers and copiers. Using CU's core competency of "getting people in different departments and companies to start talking," Mylett discovered that, in his partner companies, information technology departments purchased printers and procurement purchased copiers. Although his effort to merge the purchasing in these departments slowed the process down by nine months, CU posted a 24 percent savings for most of its partner/clients. Xerox had bowed out of the bidding, so CU made a dual award to two other suppliers. Progressive stopped using Xerox, but Sherwin Williams decided not to leave Xerox. This was CU's first taste of dissent by its members.

In the office supplies market, CU was able to save its alliance as much as 40 percent. This was remarkable given that this area was plagued by significant contract management problems. For example, companies would be the victims of "bait and switch" where they purchased a higher-quality product, but a cheaper one was delivered. CU made sure that didn't happen for its clients.

A New Idea

By 2001, Mylett was getting very good at dealing with corporate stickiness, contract management, and getting groups of people who traditionally didn't communicate to talk to one another. Mylett knew that most companies had a division of procurement that was interested in how other divisions like human resources could save money. But the two divisions rarely talked. Therefore, he decided to leverage CU's competencies and hold discussions between the two groups. The request for proposal that resulted was electronic, with reverse bidding online, and it produced a savings of $20 million for the group. By now it was very difficult for companies to leave CU because they were buying on three or four levels and saving so much money. Also, CU was now one of the top five customers of supplier Boise-Cascade with CEO level communication.

CU has competition but at ten times the cost and with inferior coverage. CU's ability to reduce costs has become legendary in the industry, and chief financial officers are starting to aggressively force alternatives like CU within their companies. Procurement is a cutthroat business, and Mylett must stay on top of his game to continue to grow.

Advising the Entrepreneur

1. What are the critical success factors for this business?

2. With more companies aggressively seeking ways to reduce costs and more competitors entering the market to serve that need, how can Mylett effectively grow the business and compete?

Source: This case was contributed by Edward Caner, Physics Entrepreneurship Program, Case Western University.

Financial Planning

CHAPTER 16

Cash Planning and Start-Up Financing

The wise man understands equity; the small man understands only profits.

Confucius (circa 551–circa 479 B.C.)

LEARNING OUTCOMES

- Describe the process for calculating how much capital is needed to start the business.
- Explain how to forecast sales and capital expenditures using triangulation.
- Discuss the major sources of capital for a start-up venture.
- Compare and contrast financing with equity and with debt.

Back on the Internet

In 1998, when the dot-com explosion was in its early stages, it was relatively easy to start a business and raise a lot of capital; Michael Yang and Yeogirl Yun did exactly that when they raised $30 million and launched a price comparison website called mySimon, one of the first and most successful online shopping aids.

Yang immigrated to the United States from Korea with his family at the age of 14. He went on to graduate from the University of California at Berkeley with degrees in electrical engineering and computer science, worked as a chip designer at Xerox and a marketer at Samsung, earned his MBA at Berkeley, and then managed video-card maker Jazz Multimedia. Yun graduated from Seoul National University with a degree in computer engineering and earned a master's degree at Stanford and then went on to found an Internet software company called One-Oh. The two met when Yang's company acquired One-Oh.

When Jazz Multimedia folded in 1998, a victim of more advanced storage methods like CD-ROM coming into the market, the two began to explore the possibility of starting an Internet business together. Because both had learned the fine art of comparison shopping while living on tight budgets during school, they decided on a comparison-shopping concept. At the time, no company was doing it very well. Yun designed an algorithm that would extract prices, product details, and other data from merchants' sites—no easy task because in those days every site had a different structure. By December 1999, the fast-growing company expanded from two to sixty employees, and its user base stood at 10 million; but by 2000, their investors were ready to cash out. Fortuitously, CNET acquired mySimon in early 2000—just before the dot-com implosion—for $700 million, giving its founders substantial nest eggs on which to consider their next opportunity.

The two went their separate ways for a time, but in 2005 Yang sought out Yun with an idea for another business in the online shopping arena. This time they would start with their own capital and have more control over the business and its rate of growth. The concept was designed to address the first step of the purchasing decision: deciding what to buy. Most sites focused on helping the customer decide how much to pay and completely skipped the first step. Their company, Become.com, would use a team of researchers to locate authoritative product review sites like ConsumerReports.org and ConsumerSearch.com and place them into Become.com's index. Then the company's machine-language software would rank-search pages by their relationship to these product review sites. Their core technology, called AIR for affinity index ranking, differed from competitor Google's page-ranking algorithm in that it considered the topics of the pages that it retrieved and rewarded pages that had on-topic incoming links while penalizing pages that had outgoing links that were off topic. In other words, their Web crawler, a form of search engine, focused on the relevancy of the topic over the number of incoming links.

With one of their mySimon investors, Yang and Yun invested $4.5 million in Become.com and sought advertising revenues to support the early stages of growth. The plan was to eventually charge merchants to list their products on price-comparison pages and to earn a fee on every click-through to a merchant's site and commissions on actual sales. Whereas their goal with mySimon was to get big fast, the goal with Become.com was to "get profitable fast." They wondered if this new strategy was the right one for the times.

Advising the Entrepreneur

1. With the second venture, Become.com, what assets did the team bring to the table that would be attractive to investors?

2. Under what circumstances will they need investment capital? How long can they continue to grow organically?

Source: W. Roush, "Starting Up, Post-Bubble," *Technology Review* 108(5) (2005): 36–37.

here to find start-up funding is the most commonly asked question by entrepreneurs. The answer is both simple and complex. It is simple because at start-up there are few choices for entrepreneurs, and all those choices point back to the entrepreneur: his or her resources and whom he or she knows. The answer is complex from the standpoint that putting together sufficient resources to start a business requires enormous creativity and persistence, with the ultimate reward being a company that is able to reach critical mass and take advantage of significantly more choices for growth capital.

Determining what resources are needed, when they are needed, and how to acquire them is a critical piece of the financial planning process. Start-up resources come in many forms including (1) people such as the founding team, advisors, and independent contractors; (2) physical assets such as equipment, inventory, and office or plant space; (3) and financial resources such as cash, equity, and debt. The entrepreneur's goal is to create a mix of resources that will enable the new venture to start and operate the business until it generates a positive cash flow from sales. One of the secrets to success in constructing this resource mix is to maintain flexibility by owning only those resources that cannot be obtained by any other means such as outsourcing, borrowing, or sharing.

Start-up companies are inherently risky investments, in part because of information asymmetry; that is, entrepreneurs have more information about themselves and their ventures than do the people from whom they seek funding.[1] Because of this and many other factors, the number of sources of financing for entrepreneurs is somewhat limited; however, once they achieve a successful track record, many new sources of financing become available. These sources are discussed in Chapter 18. This chapter looks at how entrepreneurs calculate the financial resources that they need and prepare to seek funding for the venture, and it considers the resources available to start-ups.

CASH-NEEDS ASSESSMENT

Estimating how much capital it will take to start a new venture and operate it until the business generates a positive cash flow from the revenues of the business is not easy. One thing entrepreneurs can be sure of is that their estimates will often be quite different from what actually happens when the business is in operation. There are many reasons why these estimates change. With product companies, it is nearly impossible to estimate parts and manufacturing costs accurately until the product is in production. With service companies, the estimates are generally based on information gathered from similar companies in the industry, but this is a difficult process without access to inside information. Fortunately, information improves as entrepreneurs become more experienced in their industries; that is why many entrepreneurs choose to start ventures in industries with which they are familiar.

Given the inherent difficulties in forecasting numbers for a new business, entrepreneurs often use a process called *triangulation* in which the problem is attacked from three angles: the entrepreneur's own knowledge, the industry, and the market or customer. Using triangulation, a cash-needs assessment involves a six-step process.

FIGURE 16.1 New Venture Process Flowchart

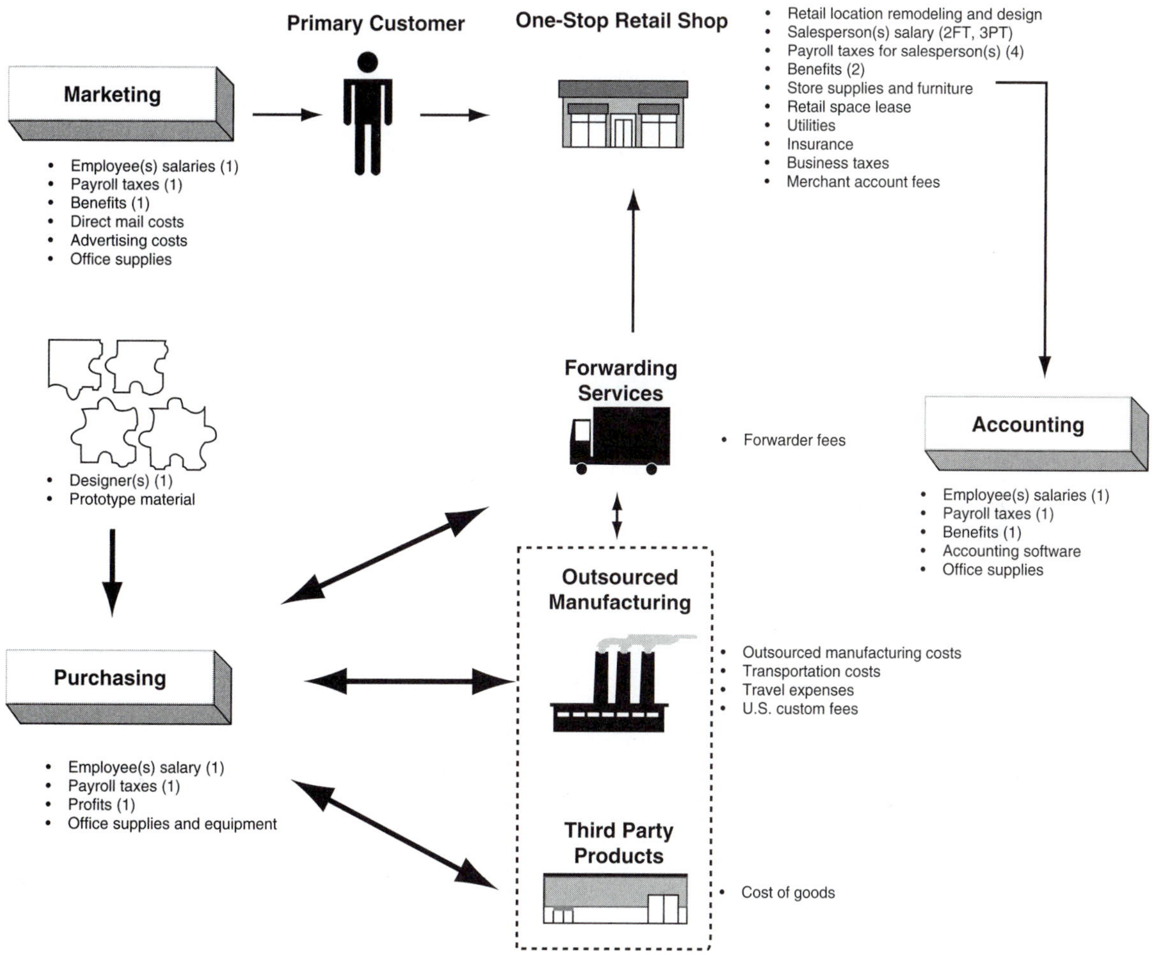

Marketing
- Employee(s) salaries (1)
- Payroll taxes (1)
- Benefits (1)
- Direct mail costs
- Advertising costs
- Office supplies

Primary Customer

One-Stop Retail Shop
- Retail location remodeling and design
- Salesperson(s) salary (2FT, 3PT)
- Payroll taxes for salesperson(s) (4)
- Benefits (2)
- Store supplies and furniture
- Retail space lease
- Utilities
- Insurance
- Business taxes
- Merchant account fees

- Designer(s) (1)
- Prototype material

Forwarding Services
- Forwarder fees

Accounting
- Employee(s) salaries (1)
- Payroll taxes (1)
- Benefits (1)
- Accounting software
- Office supplies

Outsourced Manufacturing
- Outsourced manufacturing costs
- Transportation costs
- Travel expenses
- U.S. custom fees

Purchasing
- Employee(s) salary (1)
- Payroll taxes (1)
- Profits (1)
- Office supplies and equipment

Third Party Products
- Cost of goods

Source: The process flow chart was contributed by Vivian Chang, Steve Fang, Monica Hyon, Jennifer Luo, MBAs, Marshall School of Business, University of Southern California, 2004

Step 1: Prepare a Process Flowchart

It is important to first understand how the business works. Creating a flowchart that depicts all the activities of the business and follows a customer order from marketing through delivery to the customer helps the entrepreneur look at personnel needs and equipment required to carry out the activities of the business. Figure 16.1 depicts an example of a process flowchart.

Step 2: Identify the Business's Position in the Value Chain

A new venture's position in the value chain dictates the relationship that it has with other channel members and will determine how much the company can charge for its product or service and how much it costs to acquire inventory or raw material.

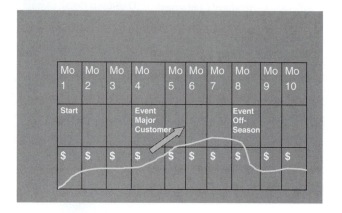

FIGURE 16.2 Step 3 in the Cash-Needs Assessment: Create a New Venture Timeline

Step 3: Develop a Business Timeline

Any forecast should begin with a timeline that depicts the seasonal patterns in the industry as well as the key events that might cause a change in the level of sales. Figure 16.2 depicts a timeline for the first ten months of a new venture with two key events that change the direction of sales: the acquisition of a lead customer and the beginning of an off-season. New customer sales do not occur immediately upon starting the business. Instead, it may take several months before a sale actually closes, so cash from sales will not come into the business at the exact point of sale. The chart also shows that in the eighth month of the new venture the industry's off-season begins with a downward trend in demand that bottoms out in months nine and ten. Identifying the key events that might trigger a change in sales level is the first step in forecasting. Next, the entrepreneur will need to calculate the impact of the change on the sales estimate. For example, will the sales go up, down, or remain stable? And what is the probability that this trigger event will occur?

Step 4: Develop Financial Premises

The **financial assumptions** are arguably the most important part of financial feasibility because they provide the explanation and justification for the numbers in the financial forecast. Each line item in the cash-flow statement should be explained and tied to the timeline and trigger. For example, the entrepreneur will explain how the sales forecast was derived and justify why the numbers are credible. Demand is another figure that must be forecast in order to determine the pattern of sales. It can be estimated by triangulating through primary research with customers and industry players. For example, suppose that six out of ten potential customers would purchase the product that the entrepreneur is offering. Because it is likely that the entrepreneur's estimates might be optimistic, the ratio should probably be reduced based on how confident the entrepreneur is in the responses received from customers and industry members. That figure can also be compared to estimates from value chain partners and adoption patterns for similar products or services to determine the best estimate.

Step 5: Forecast Sales and Capital Expenditures

Sales are often calculated first because they affect the other expenditures of the business. The method for forecasting sales for pro forma statements will vary depending on the general product or service category. For example, with a new product that is a line extension or the next generation of an established product, the business owner will be able to rely on historical data that will help ensure a more accurate estimate. With a brand new or breakthrough product, however, he or she is left to rely on market data, comparison of similar products, and the opinions of market experts. Therefore, to improve the estimate, it is useful to calculate best-case, worst-case, and most-likely-case scenarios that will cover about 90 percent of all the possible sales results.

Three sources of information will enable a good estimate of sales:

- Industry sources such as distributors, vendors, and industry experts
- Customers
- Like or substitute products

By using at least three sources of information, an entrepreneur can feel more confident that the estimate will be as accurate as possible. Remember, though, these are estimates only; any change in circumstances will affect estimates positively or negatively. Furthermore, because forecasted sales are estimates only, it is vital that they be based on a thorough understanding of the industry and market.

Forecasting Sales with Consumer Products and Services If the product or service being offered does not exist in the market in the form in which it will be introduced, a competing product or service that is similar or is a substitute product must be found to be studied. The information needed includes the volume of sell-in to the retailer and the volume of sell-through to the customer—that is, the amount of product that is sold by the manufacturer or distributor to the retailer and the amount of that product that is ultimately sold to the customer or end user. Naturally, a service business will concern itself only with the sell-through volume because service businesses generally operate with direct channels of distribution. In addition, determining if any seasonal factors in the market could affect the volume of sales during any particular period of time is important. The mistake made by many companies that sell to distributors or retailers is focusing only on how much product they are selling to their customers and structuring their production and/or inventory accordingly without carefully monitoring retail sales to the end user. Consequently, when consumer buying slows and the retailer cannot move sufficient product, the manufacturer or producer is left with excess inventory. The entrepreneur with a new product or service, therefore, should monitor retail sales of competing products to consumers in the same category to arrive at an estimate of sales demand as one component of the triangulation process. Best-case and worst-case scenarios should also be calculated.

One word of caution is in order when choosing competing companies for comparison purposes. If the rival company is a publicly held or a well-established company, a young, growing small business will most probably not be able to achieve the competitor's level of sales for some time. Therefore, the sales figures gathered will serve as an upper-limit benchmark; how much below that figure the sales level will actually lay will need to be determined. The percentage increase in sales over a three-to-five-year period will depend on

- Growth rates in the market segment in which the product or service is positioned.
- The innovations offered that will make the product or service more attractive to the customer or consumer, even at a higher price.
- The technological innovations employed that permit the company to produce the product or service at a lower cost than its competitors, thus making it more accessible and enticing to the customer or consumer.
- The effectiveness of the market penetration strategies employed.

Forecasting Sales with Industrial Products With industrial products, which are generally sold business to business, it is important to understand the needs of the customer and the buying cycles of the industry. Talking to experts (for example, distributors) in the field, getting sales figures from noncompeting product manufacturers in the same industry, and generally determining the size of the market niches that the company intends to enter will all help in arriving at an estimate of sales demand. In the industrial market, as in the consumer market, it is vital to bracket the estimate with best-case/worst-case benchmark figures to cover the most likely contingencies. The rate at which sales increase will be a function of the same three factors listed under consumer products.

Forecasting Expenditures In wholesale businesses, once the sales forecast has been determined, the figures for inventory purchases can be applied as a percentage of sales and forecast from that. So if inventory cost is 25 percent of sales, that percentage can

LEARNING FROM SUCCESS

Persistence Results in Flying High

The Klapmeier brothers are not the Wright brothers, but like those historic figures, they faced an aeronautical challenge. Their goal was to create a small plane that ensured a safe flight for its crew and passengers, something no one had been able to do. Born and raised in rural Wisconsin, Dale and Alan Klapmeier completed a prototype in 1987 for a plane that was outfitted with a parachute that attached to the top of the fuselage. It took another nine years to acquire sufficient financing, secure federal regulatory clearance, and generate market interest. First, they accessed their personal savings and that of friends and family, but they quickly realized that to manufacture an aircraft, they would need substantial outside capital. By the late 1990s, after a full-time effort by Alan, they had secured $70 million from about 240 investors. This helped but it was not

nearly enough to go into production. Finally, the team linked up with Crescent Capital, an Atlanta-based venture capital firm that invested $100 million into their company Cirrus Design, which was now based in Duluth, Minnesota. The brothers had to give up a huge amount of equity in their company to the venture capital firm, but Cirrus was able to deliver its first plane in 1999. Today, the Cirrus Design Corp. plant produces more than 550 planes a year, and their single-prop airplane is the best selling plane in the world. Its 2004 revenues were $190 million.

Lesson Learned: *Persistence pays off.*

Source: "The Klapmeier Brothers' Key Move: Finding the Right Funding," from *Startup Nation*, www.startupnation.com (accessed June 24, 2005). Reprinted by permission.

be applied to sales across the period because inventory generally increases linearly in response to an increase in sales. Some businesses will require the forecasting of cost of goods sold, discussed next.

Forecasting Cost of Goods Sold In manufacturing businesses, forecasting is a bit more complex because the **cost of goods sold** (COGS) must be derived first. This figure usually consists of direct labor, cost of materials, and factory overhead. Looking at the sales forecast in terms of units produced to arrive at a dollar figure for COGS and then applying COGS as a percentage of sales will probably suffice for purposes of pro forma statements when the business is starting. Month-by-month analysis of outcomes and use of a cost-accounting model that considers raw materials inventory, work-in-process inventory, finished goods inventory, total inventory, factory overhead, work-in-process flow-in units, and weighted-average cost per unit will give a more accurate estimate as the business grows.

In service businesses, the COGS is equivalent to the time expended for the service. The rate at which the company bills the service—say, $100 an hour—is composed of the actual expenses incurred in providing the service, a contribution to overhead, and a reasonable profit. The actual expenses incurred are the COGS equivalent.

Forecasting General and Administrative Expenses **General and administrative expenses** (G&A), the expenses of running the business, are considered fixed but must be forecast separately in a detailed breakout statement. This is because some of these items may vary over a twelve-month period, whereas others remain stable. Therefore, using percentage of sales figures for G&A expenses is not recommended. Only the totals of G&A expenses for each month are normally used in the financial statements, with a footnote directing the reader to the G&A breakout statement. Selling expenses, which include advertising, travel, sales salaries, commissions, and promotional supplies, should be handled in the same manner with only totals in the financial statements. Table 16.1 presents some of the categories of items that may appear on the breakout statements.

Forecasting Taxes The last item to forecast under expenditures is taxes. Although many businesses may be able to take advantage of a tax loss carry-forward for losses during research and development (R&D), ultimately the company will have to account for state, federal, and possibly local taxes that are paid at varying times of the year. Check with federal, state, and local agencies to get current rates. Apply these rates to net profit, which will be derived in the income statement; this will give a reasonable estimate of tax liability and the amount of cash that must be on hand to pay the taxes. If the business is formed as a pass-through entity (S-corporation, partnership, sole proprietorship, or limited liability company), taxes are paid at the owner's personal tax rate.

Step 6: Calculate Start-Up Capital Requirements

One of the most important pieces of information that entrepreneurs need to calculate is their start-up capital requirements. The total requirements will consist of several different types of money. Start-up expenses are all those expenses incurred prior to the launch of the business, such as furniture, equipment, training of employees, and deposits for leases and utilities. These start-up expenses can be categorized into capital expenses, or hard costs, such as furniture, facilities, and equipment, and soft costs,

TABLE 16.1 Categories for Breakout Statements

Sample Manufacturing or Construction Expenses List

Manager's salary paid	Employees' salaries
Payroll taxes	Vehicle lease and maintenance
Related travel	Packaging costs
Supplies	Depreciation on owned equipment

Sample Distribution and Warehouse Expenses List

Manager's salary	Employees' salaries
Drivers' salaries	Payroll taxes
Vehicle lease and maintenance	Warehouse loading vehicles Lease/maintenance
Freight expenses	Supplies

Sample list of selling expenses

▪ Sales manager's salary	▪ Inside sales salaries
▪ Inside sales commissions	▪ Telephone sales salaries
▪ Telephone sales commissions	▪ Field sales salaries
▪ Field sales commissions	▪ Payroll taxes for sales employees
▪ Sales staff vehicle lease and maintenance	▪ Sales-related travel
▪ Advertising and promotion	▪ Depreciation on owned equipment

Sample List of General and Administrative Expenses

Advertising	Rent
Salaries and wages	Utilities
Office supplies	Insurance
Office equipment	Business taxes
Payroll taxes	

such as deposits and training expenses. It is important to break out the costs because some of them, especially the hard costs for equipment, can be manipulated to reduce start-up capital requirements. For example, a piece of equipment can be leased rather than purchased, substantially reducing cash outlay. Working capital is the difference between assets and liabilities and is used to pay the expenses of the business until revenues are collected. Capital expenditures are equipment and facilities.

A **cash-flow statement** is needed to figure start-up capital requirements. Figure 16.3 displays a cash-flow statement for a retail company, New Products Retail. Notice that this statement is a simple expression of cash inflows and cash outflows to the business. The first section of the cash-flow statement records all the inflows of cash to the business when they are received. Therefore, if the business makes a sale in August, for example, but payment is not received until October, then the payment is recorded in October. The next section records the cash outflows or disbursements from the business. Start-up costs, which occur before the business is in operation, can be reflected in a month 0 or start-up column at the front end of the cash-flow statement. The final

TABLE 16.2	New-Products Retail: Cash-Needs Assessment		
Start-up hard costs in 1000's			
▪ Equipment	13.7		
▪ Remodeling	30.0		
Total hard costs		43.7	
Start-up soft costs			
▪ One month's rent	7.4		
▪ Lease deposit	14.7		
▪ Utilities deposit	2.0		
▪ Advertising	0.7		
▪ Legal	1.8		
▪ Training	3.2	29.8	
Total soft costs			
Working capital	28.9	28.9	
Minimum start-up		102.4	
Contingency factor		118.6	
Total start-up capital		217.8	

section shows the net change in cash flow for each month and the cumulative cash flow for the year. One way to figure the amount of capital required to start the business and operate to a positive cash flow with no investment capital is to take the highest negative cumulative cash balance and add to that a safety or contingency factor. In this case, the highest negative in the cash-flow statement is $102,400, and it occurs in month 9. Table 16.2 depicts an example of a breakout of the types of money that will be required for start-up. As discussed previously, the reason for breaking out these expenses is that the entrepreneur can more effectively analyze how the start-up requirements might be reduced. For example, instead of purchasing equipment at a cost of $13,700, the entrepreneur may choose to lease and pay a comparatively smaller monthly rate.

A **contingency factor,** or safety cushion, is calculated based on the volatility in the business and in the industry in which the business operates. For instance, if the entrepreneur knows that customers pay in 120 days, it would be important to be able to cover fixed costs for that period in the event that customers did not pay on time. In the example of New Products Retail, the rather large contingency factor is due to the seasonality of the business and represents the largest gap between a high-sales month and a low-sales month. There is no right or wrong way to figure a contingency factor, but the rationale behind the formula should justify the amount.

Step 7: Conduct a Sensitivity Analysis

It is important to identify the critical numbers for the business (for example, for a hotel, its occupancy rate). Because these three or four numbers will make or break the business, it is necessary to determine what might cause them to change for better or worse. Some examples of critical numbers are (1) the time to develop sales (it takes longer or shorter than planned), (2) the volume of sales (higher or lower than expected), (3) the price maintenance (initial price is not supported), and (4) costs

FIGURE 16.3 New-Products Retail Cash-Flow Statement

(in thousands)

Premise	Start-up	Month	Month	Month	Month	Month	Month	Month	Month	Month	Month	Month	Month	Total
	0 Aug	1 Sep	2 Oct	3 Nov	4 Dec	5 Jan	6 Feb	7 March	8 April	9 May	10 June	11 July	12 Aug	
Cash Inflows (1)		16.9	17.5	34.9	52.4	15.4	30.8	46.1	18.3	36.6	54.9	33.8	50.7	$408.2
Total Cash Inflows		16.9	17.5	34.9	52.4	15.4	30.8	46.1	18.3	36.6	54.9	33.8	50.7	$408.2
Cash Outflows														
Upfront Cash														
Deposits – Utilities	2													$2.0
Advertising	0.7													$0.7
Legal	1.8													$1.8
Lease Deposits (3)	14.7													$14.7
Lease (3)	7.4													$7.4
Equipment Purchase (4)	13.7													$13.7
Remodeling	30													$30.0
Training	3.2													3.2
Total Upfront Cash	73.5													73.5
Variable Cost														
Cost of Goods Sold (2)		8.6	0.0	8.9	17.8	0.0	0.0	50.2	0.0	32.9	0.0	40.7	0.0	159.1
Total Variable Cost		8.6	0.0	8.9	17.8	0.0	0.0	50.2	0.0	32.9	0.0	40.7	0.0	159.1
Fixed Expenses														
Salaries – Principal (Including taxes) (5)	0	0	0	0	0	0	0	0	0	0	0	0	0	0.0

		Start-Up	1	2	3	4	5	6	7	8	9	10	11	12	Total
Salaries – Full-time (Including taxes)	(5)		1.8	1.8	1.8	1.8	1.8	1.8	1.8	1.8	1.8	1.8	1.8	1.8	21.6
Salaries – Part-time (Including taxes)	(5)		3.2	3.2	3.2	3.2	3.2	3.2	3.2	3.2	3.2	3.2	3.2	3.2	38.4
Salary – Designer (Including taxes)	(5)		2.9	2.9	2.9	2.9	2.9	2.9	2.9	2.9	2.9	2.9	2.9	2.9	34.8
Building Rent	(3)		7.4	7.4	7.4	7.4	7.4	7.4	7.4	7.4	7.4	7.4	7.4	7.4	88.8
Insurance	(6)		2.4	2.4	2.4	2.4	2.4	2.4	2.4	2.4	2.4	2.4	2.4	2.4	28.8
Advertising			0	0	0.7	0	0	0	0	0	0	0	0.7	0	1.4
General and Administrative	(7)		0.3	0.3	0.3	0.3	0.3	0.3	0.3	0.3	0.3	0.3	0.3	0.3	3.6
Selling Expense	(8)		0.3	0.3	0.6	0.9	0.3	0.6	0.8	0.3	0.7	1.0	0.6	0.9	7.3
Travel Expense	(9)		1.1	0.0	1.1	0.0	1.1	0.0	1.1	0.0	1.1	0.0	1.1	0.0	6.6
Utilities	(10)		0.4	0.4	0.4	0.4	0.4	0.4	0.4	0.4	0.4	0.4	0.4	0.4	4.8
License, Permits, and Taxes			0.1	0.1	0.1	0.1	0.1	0.1	0.1	0.1	0.1	0.1	0.1	0.1	1.2
Misc.			0.1	0.1	0.1	0.1	0.1	0.1	0.1	0.1	0.1	0.1	0.1	0.1	1.2
Total Fixed Expenses		0.0	20.0	18.9	21.0	19.5	20.0	19.2	20.5	18.9	20.4	19.6	21.0	19.5	238.5
Taxes	(12)				0.8										0.8
Total Cash Expenditures		73.5	28.6	18.9	30.7	37.3	20.0	19.2	70.8	18.9	53.2	19.6	61.7	19.5	472.0
Net Cash In/Out per Month		-73.5	-11.7	-1.5	4.2	15.0	-4.6	11.6	-24.6	-0.6	-16.6	35.3	-27.9	31.2	-63.7
Cash Balance: Beg. of Month		0.0	-73.5	-85.2	-86.7	-82.5	-67.5	-72.1	-60.5	-85.1	-85.7	-102.4	-67.1	-95.0	-63.7
Net Cash In/Out per Month		-73.5	-11.7	-1.5	4.2	15.0	-4.6	11.6	-24.6	-0.6	-16.6	35.3	-27.9	31.2	31.2
Cash Balance		-73.5	-85.2	-86.7	-82.5	-67.5	-72.1	-60.5	-85.1	-85.7	-102.4	-67.1	-95.0	-63.7	-63.7

Based on concept developed by Vivian Chang, Steve Fang, Monica Hyon, and Jennifer Luo, Marshall School of Business, University of Southern California.

LEARNING FROM MISTAKES

Maybe the Most Important Number in Your Business Isn't Profit or Cash

If you ask business owners to tell you what the most vital aspect of their business is, most will probably claim profit or cash. But the most savvy business owners will give you a different answer—the critical factor to the success of the business. Consider this: A hotel chain in Indiana was losing money even though its manager focused on controlling expenses to increase profit levels. When asked how his hotels make money, the manager responded that the key was filling rooms, and to break even, he needed to have 71 percent of his rooms occupied; he was currently running at 67 percent. So the "critical factor" for this hotel chain was not profit but occupancy rate. Once the manager realized this, he changed his business strategy entirely and focused not so much on controlling expenses but on ways to increase the occupancy rate. He even set up an incentive program that provided bonuses to employees as the occupancy rate increased. Ultimately, his hotel became one of the very best in the chain.

Lesson Learned: *Know the critical success factor for the business.*

Source: J. Stack, "The Logic of Profit," *Inc.* (March 1996): 17.

more than anticipated. After the critical numbers are determined, it is important to establish the numbers and events that will have the most impact on the business, calculate the probability of a deviation from the expected value of the number or event, and ascertain the impact of that deviation on cash flow and start-up costs. The process of conducting a cash-needs assessment will prepare the entrepreneur to seek the right amount of money from the right source.

FINANCING WITH EQUITY SOURCES

One way to raise capital for the new venture is to have people invest their money for an ownership stake in the business. This ownership share is termed *equity,* and it means that the investor puts his or her capital at risk; there is usually no guaranteed return and no protection against loss. Equity investors inherently differ from lenders; they are looking not for "repayment" but for an exit strategy with which they can cash out of the business with their investment having appreciated by a reasonable amount. Consequently, equity investors look first at growth in earnings and second at growth in assets. When they study the company's balance sheet, they look at inventory relative to sales. If inventory is growing, it may signal poor management practices. They also examine the current liabilities of the company and in particular look for loans to founders, which may be a sign that the company funds are being used to "bail out" the founder. The income statement tells them how profitable the company is in comparison to other companies in the same competitive market. It also indicates how capital intensive the company is. If the company has more than one product line, the investor will be interested to see if revenues are moving toward higher-margin products in the line. The most important statement to the investor will be the cash-flow statement because more businesses fail for lack of cash than for lack of profits.

Because of the inherent risks in start-up ventures, most entrepreneurs seek investment capital from people whom they know and who believe in them. Naturally, in the earliest stages of a new venture, the only people willing to risk their capital to fund a start-up are those who know the entrepreneur well. As the company gets off the ground and begins to show definite indications of market interest, others will be more willing to consider the risk.

FINANCING WITH DEBT

Many entrepreneurs try to avoid debt, thinking that equity investments are always the better way to go; but debt may actually be the preferred choice. When entrepreneurs choose a debt instrument to finance a portion of the start-up costs, they are seeking a loan on which they will pay a market rate of interest. They may also be required to put up a personal or company asset as collateral, a guarantee they will repay the loan. The asset could be equipment, inventory, real estate, or the entrepreneur's house or car. The advantage of debt is that the business has more control of the timing. With investor equity, the investor pushes the entrepreneur to achieve the investor's required timing. Xytrans, a manufacturer of transceivers based in Orlando, Florida, secured a $1 million line of credit with Silicon Valley Bank of Santa Clara, California, in 2002, which gave it the capital it needed to fund its first factory. Although it had previously raised $4.5 million in equity capital, CEO Rob Strandberg decided that rather than spending his time chasing another round of capital from investors, he would take bank debt and focus on generating revenue from the transceivers that they were able to produce in the new factory.[2]

Using Convertible Debt

When KnowledgePoint, a California software company, was founded in 1987, the entrepreneur, Michael Troy, calculated that the company needed approximately $250,000 in start-up capital. Using his own resources, Troy came up with the following:

$80,000 from salaries not paid for the first year
$24,000 from Troy
$20,000 from credit cards
$50,000 home equity loan
$174,000

The company still needed another $80,000, which would come from friends, family, and business associates. Troy took an exit-strategy approach to looking at the potential investment from friends and family and chose convertible debentures as the investment vehicle. For investors it meant receiving an attractive rate of return (Troy decided on an interest rate of 5 points above prime with a cap at 15 percent) from day 1 and an opportunity to convert to equity at a specified future date. At the end of five years, the investors would receive their principal back, unless they had elected to convert the debt to common stock during the period.

When constructing a convertible debt deal, it is important to carefully spell out the conversion process in terms of when and how investors can convert to stock. Also, it often is more difficult to secure bank financing when using a convertible debenture offering because for a time the company appears to have too much debt. This is not an issue if investors elect to convert the debt to equity during the prescribed term.

Commercial Banks

Banks are not a reliable source of either working capital or seed capital to fund a start-up venture. Banks are highly regulated, and their loan portfolios are carefully scrutinized for risk, which they take great pains to avoid, and they do not make loans that have any significant degree of risk. However, with the availability of business credit cards, mutual funds, brokerage houses, leasing companies, and commercial finance and asset-based lending firms, even small companies have alternatives to commercial banks. In fact, the number of traditional banking customers declined several percentage points between 1989 and 1994 while the use of investment banks more than doubled during the same period.[3]

Generally, banks make loans based on what is termed "the five Cs": character, capacity, capital, collateral, and conditions. In the case of the entrepreneur, the first two—character and capacity—become the leading consideration because the new business's performance is based purely on forecasts. Therefore, the bank probably will consider the entrepreneur's personal history carefully. It is important, however difficult, for the new venture to establish a lending relationship with a bank. This may mean starting with a very small amount of money and demonstrating the ability to repay in a timely fashion. Bankers will also look more favorably on ventures that have hard assets that are readily convertible to cash.

How Bankers Look at a Company's Financials Bankers look at a company's financials from a totally different point of view than do investors or management. Here are some of the things they look for:

1. The primary source of repayment of a loan, or the net flow of funds (net income plus depreciation, amortization, and extraordinary items). If the company is just breaking even each month, no cash is available for repayment of the loan.

2. The secondary source of repayment—that is, if the company defaults, what can the bank take to sell and get its money back? Accounts receivable are probably worth 60 percent of their balance sheet value if liquidated. Inventory is worth even less, anywhere from zero to about 50 percent of its value.

3. The character of the parties involved.

4. Profitability ratios, which lenders compare with those of other companies in the same industry.

5. Operating margin (revenues less cost of goods, less selling, general, and administrative expenses), which signals the health of the basic operation.

A good bank will make suggestions, anticipate the company's needs, introduce the management team to people who can help the business, show the company how to save money, and generally treat the company with respect. In return, the entrepreneur should keep the banker apprised of important new developments with the business and avoid dealing with the banker only when the company needs money.

Commercial Finance Companies As banks have tightened their lending requirements, commercial finance companies have stepped in to fill the gap. They can do this because they are less heavily regulated and they base their decisions on the quality of the assets of the business. Thus, they are often termed *asset-based lenders*. They do, however, charge more than banks by as much as 5 percent over prime. Therefore, the entrepreneur must weigh the costs and benefits of taking on such an expensive loan. Of course, if it means the difference between starting the business or not or surviving in the short term, the cost may be justified.

GOVERNMENT SOURCES OF FUNDING

A variety of sources of both debt and equity financing are available through government agencies, and these funds have been the source of research, development, and operational capital. A few of these sources follow.

Small Business Investment Company

Small business investment companies are actually a type of venture capital firm licensed by the Small Business Administration (SBA) under the Small Business Investment Act of 1958 to provide long-term loans and equity capital to small businesses. They get financing through the government to invest in small and growing businesses. Because their repayment terms with the government are generous, they are able to invest over longer periods of time. They can be found by contacting the SBA or visiting www.sba.gov.

Venture Capital Institutes and Networks

Many areas of the country offer access to venture capital networks through institutes established on the campuses of major universities. The university acts as a conduit through which the entrepreneurs and investors are matched. It assumes no liability for or has no ownership interest in either the new venture or the investor's company. The entrepreneur typically pays a fee, in the $200 to $500 range, and submits a business plan to the institute. The plan is then matched to the needs of private investors listed in the database who subscribe to the service. If an investor is interested in the business concept, he or she will contact the entrepreneur. For example, the Oklahoma Investment Forum is a matchmaking program that was started by the Tulsa Chamber of Commerce to help small and mid-sized companies find investment funding.

In general, venture capital networks are a way for entrepreneurs to gain access to investors who they may not be able to find through other channels. Furthermore, the investors in the database are there voluntarily, so they are actually looking for potential investments.

Small Business Administration Loans

The small business owner may also want to consider an SBA-guaranteed loan. The SBA was established in 1953 to provide aid, counsel, and protection to small businesses. Working with intermediaries, banks, and other lending institutions, the SBA has been able to provide loans and venture capital financing to small businesses that cannot obtain such financing through traditional business channels. The SBA guarantees to repay up to $1 million on loans of up to $2 million to the commercial lender should the business default. A further incentive to banks is that SBA-funded ventures tend to be growth oriented and have a higher survival rate than other start-ups. Of course, because the government backs these loans, the documentation and paperwork are extensive, and interest rates usually are no different than with a conventional loan.

The SBA also has a number of smaller-loan programs, such as the microloan program, which makes it easier for entrepreneurs with limited access to capital to borrow small amounts (up to $35,000). Instead of using banks as in its guarantee program, the SBA uses nonprofit community-based lenders. The SBA LowDoc Loans offer amounts up to $150,000, with decisions within thirty-six hours of receiving the application. Finally, SBA*Express* loans can be made by lenders on their own forms to approve loans guaranteed up to $350,000. Entrepreneurs should check the SBA website to ensure that their business qualifies as a small business according to the small business–size standards.

State-Funded Venture Capital

Many states now provide a range of services to help new and growing ventures. From venture capital funds to tax incentives, states such as Massachusetts, New York, and Oregon are seeing the value of establishing business development programs. Texas, one of the most prolific states in terms of investment funds, has forty-four state-based venture capital funds. They usually receive their funding from the state government, which enables them to seek larger investment amounts from private sources. States that do not have equity funding typically offer loan programs aimed at new ventures. For example, in Massachusetts, favorable debt financing is often exchanged for warrants to purchase stock in the new company. Pennsylvania was the first state to create a funding program aimed at minority-owned businesses.

Small Business Innovative Research

The Small Business Innovation Development Act of 1982 requires that all federal agencies with R&D budgets in excess of $100 million give a portion of their budgets to technology-based small businesses in the form of grants to develop products in which the agencies are interested. Small businesses find out about these grants by checking the published solicitations of the Departments of Defense, Transportation, Agriculture, Energy, Education, Health and Human Services, and Interior, as well as NASA, the Nuclear Regulatory Commission, the Environmental Protection Agency, and the National Science Foundation.

These small business innovative research (SBIR) grants have three levels:

1. Phase I is the project feasibility stage, providing up to $100,000 for initial feasibility to be completed in six months.

2. Phase II provides up to an additional $750,000 for projects that have the most potential after completing phase I. This funding lasts for two years.

3. Phase III brings in private sector funds to commercialize the new technology.

To qualify for an SBIR grant, the company must employ fewer than 500 people, be independently owned, and be technology based.

CUSTOMERS AND SUPPLIERS

Many entrepreneurs neglect to consider one of the largest and most accessible sources of funding—their customers and suppliers. Customers and suppliers understand the entrepreneur's business better than anyone, and they also have a vested interest in seeing the business succeed. They are in a position to grant extended payment terms or offer special terms favorable to the business. In return, the entrepreneur's business can provide such things as faster delivery, price breaks, and other benefits.

There are as many roads to start-up as there are entrepreneurs who travel them. No one path works for everyone, so it is important to learn about all the paths to becoming an entrepreneur and all the resources available to ensure the best chance to create a business that has value for the customer and the entrepreneur.

ISSUES FOR REVIEW AND DISCUSSION

1. How do entrepreneurs calculate the capital required to start a business?
2. What role does a timeline plan in the development of a cash-needs assessment?
3. Compare and contrast financing with equity and with debt.
4. What is the gap between bankers' needs and entrepreneurs' needs?
5. How does the government get involved in funding new ventures?

EXPERIENCING ENTREPRENEURSHIP

1. Interview an entrepreneur about his or her start-up funding strategy. What resources were used?
2. Talk to a banker about what an entrepreneur should do to prepare a new company to secure a credit line or loan from the bank.

Glove Box Guides: Bootstrapping in the Publishing Industry

Mari Florence was proud as she surveyed the three new books to come out of Glove Box Guides, her Los Angeles-based company that published small format guides to the best and least expensive places to dine and drink. This time the focus had been on the Windy City where fans of her Los Angeles guide eagerly awaited *Hungry? Chicago*. This latest series served as a milestone because in it Florence introduced her newest guidebook, *Hungry? Family*. Florence describes these books as "the lowdown on where the real people eat and drink . . . the inside scoop on where to go, what to eat, where not to park, and what menu items to choose (or steer clear of)." The books, colored in shades of hot pink, lime green, and yellow, are organized by neighborhood with the listings written by the people who frequent the establishments that they write about.

Really Good Books

As an editor, a ghost writer, and an author, Florence was comfortable in the publishing industry, so in 1999 she launched Really Great Books (RGB), a boutique publishing house that would target the interests of the Los Angeles market. With about 10 million people in Los Angeles County alone, she figured she would be busy. Her first book showcased the genius of Gary Leonard, a southern California photojournalist for over thirty years and very much a cult figure in the community. The book was called *Take My Picture Gary Leonard* after his renowned weekly photo-column that appeared in *Los Angeles CityBeat*. Initially, the book flew off the shelves as fans bought it to support their hero; but, within nine to ten months, sales tapered off dramatically, a common pattern in the industry. RGB made about $5,000 after paying expenses.

Florence's next book also involved a person of some renown. Florence had just hired an assistant who had previously worked at Buzz Books on a manuscript developed by Millard Kaufman, a screenwriter best known for the Spencer Tracy film *Bad Day at Black Rock* and *Raintree County* with Elizabeth Taylor. He was also credited with introducing the nearsighted Mr. Magoo in 1949. This manuscript was a treatise on

screenwriting and titled *Plots and Characters*. Marketing drives the publishing industry, so Florence took advantage of her author's celebrity. She rented the Egyptian Theater in Hollywood and hosted a screening of *Bad Day at Black Rock* and a book signing with Kaufman. More than 600 people attended. This event and several others in the same vein landed the book a spot on the *Los Angeles Times* "Bestseller List." RGB now had a higher profile, but the company netted only about $12,000 on the deal. One of the problems that the company faced was that, because it focused on niche markets, it had to relearn the market with each new book. "We reinvented the wheel each time," said Florence. To support the business, Florence moonlighted by taking editing jobs and ghostwriting books for high-profile people.

The Publishing Industry

In 2005, book publishing was a $30.1 billion industry, up 5.3 percent from 2004. Industry watchers expect the industry to grow at a compounded annual growth rate of 3.4 percent until 2009, due predominantly to the strong sales of religious books, standardized tests, and grade school texts. Within the trade sector, *Harry Potter and the Half-Blood Prince,* the sixth book in the highly popular series, sold 6.9 million copies in its first twenty-four hours on sale, a record for publisher Scholastic Inc.

Book publishing is characterized by labor intensity as publishers employ editors, copyeditors, researchers, copyreaders, proofreaders, photographers, graphic artists, and illustrators as full-time and part-time employees or freelancers. Printing and distribution are typically outsourced, but book publishers often maintain advertising sales staffs and production personnel. Consumer books—all noneducational books—generally account for about 70 percent of publishers' net sales.[4] Several elements play a critical role in book publishing. Per-unit costs vary by the print run size and the type of book. Art books and textbooks have a much higher per-unit cost than typical consumer books. The first print run of a hardcover book is typically between 5,000 and 75,000 copies, unless a best-selling author with a track record of sales writes the book. Publishers also incur the costs of paying author advances and rights acquisition. On successful hardcover titles, these costs can run into the millions of dollars. Another significant cost for publishers is returned books, which also include handling, freight, processing, and disposal. When one considers that, on average, retailers return about one-third of all book shipments in any year, it is easy to see that returned books are a costly aspect of publishing.

With the advent of the Internet and the proliferation of used-book sellers, publishers have had to figure out how to make money and protect their copyrights in a digital world. In October 2005, the Association of American Publishers announced the filing of a lawsuit against Google over that company's plans for the Google Print Library Project, which would digitally copy and distribute copyrighted works with permission of their owners. "The lawsuit . . . reflects the deep division between publishers and Google over the meaning of fair use."[5] Google was attempting to make all books available online for downloading through its database; the publishers viewed this as scanning copyrighted material without permission. What will come of this debate remains to be seen, but it has already succeeded in uniting publishers, authors, and agents—groups that don't always see eye to eye.

For independent publishers, the industry is tough. The margins are low, and they are constantly in danger of being squeezed out by the big chains. But some independent booksellers have found ways to compete and sustain their businesses. They locate where their customers go on a regular basis, like a subway station, or they focus on their Internet capability. They provide special services that the big chains can't afford such as delivering books and stocking their stores based on the specific needs of their customers.

The Hungry Opportunity

Florence was a big believer in keeping overhead costs low. With her designer partner, Amy Inouye, she acquired the rights to books for next to nothing, so her only costs were printing and distribution. But RGB was not generating any repeat business, and this was a problem.

One evening in the summer of 1999, Florence was having dinner with some of her friends when one said, "You know, the only way you can have a great dinner at a restaurant is if someone recommends the restaurant—if they give you the inside scoop." One thing led

to another, and the group figured out that doing a guide to dining in Los Angeles based on the recommendations of people they knew who could write about the places they frequented made sense, especially if you added anecdotal information like where to park or the best place to sit. Florence decided to run with it. The cost would be low because she planned to use a smaller format with a colorful cover but black-and-white text on the inside. And thus, Glove Box Guides was born. Because of her other company, Really Good Books, Florence had found a distributor who served the bookstores. At the time, the industry was becoming more chain-store oriented so Florence, by now a veteran at developing relationships with buyers, began working with the regional buyer for Barnes & Noble. Meanwhile, the first stores to agree to carry *Hungry? Los Angeles* were the independents because they were familiar with her other company. They took the book sight unseen. Finally, however, Florence was able to get Barnes & Noble in southern California to carry her books. Borders and Amazon.com soon followed.

One issue with chain stores was to get the books positioned so that people would see them, generally at the front of the store. What Florence learned was that publishers actually pay for book positioning in the store, as much as $1,500 per store. Florence couldn't afford to do that, but fortunately, fate was on her side. Workers at the Barnes & Nobles stores liked her books so much that they began placing them at the front of the store in premium places. The books flew off the shelves, and Florence decided that it was time to consider expanding to other cities.

About the time that the first *Hungry* went to press, Inouye left the company, and Florence began to search for someone else to help her. While working on a book of her own, *Enterprising Women,* she had met Deidre Leonard (not her real name), who was the CEO of a natural foods company in northern California. During a visit there, Florence arranged to meet Leonard in person and told her about the plans for the Glove Box Guides. Leonard volunteered to help and a couple weeks later, she contacted Florence to offer herself as a partner. Florence was flattered because Leonard's pedigree seemed stellar, and Florence definitely needed the financial backing that Leonard agreed to secure for the company. The two crafted a legal agreement that would officially separate Glove Box Guides from Really Great Books and gave Leonard 50 percent of the company upon raising an agreed-upon amount of money.

Florence wanted to move into ten cities quickly and also shop the company to food companies as sponsors or investors. Over the next year, Leonard was available for planning sessions and phone calls, but she never raised any money. Whenever Glove Box was short on cash, Leonard contributed cash to cover the shortage. It turned out, however, that she did not have the financial contacts that she claimed to have, and as president of the food company, she had no power and no decision-making authority—she was merely the face for the company. Florence finally went to her and asked to terminate the contract. Leonard, who took the decision personally, sued Florence but eventually settled when she saw that she did not have a strong case. "Trust, but verify" was the lesson that Florence learned from the experience.

Glove Box Guides quickly grew to Boston, New York, Las Vegas, New Orleans, and Seattle, and Florence diversified her products by introducing the *Thirsty?* line, which was geared toward younger readers and featured the best bars and places to enjoy a drink. In Boston and New York, about 50 to 60 percent of sales came from specialty shops and the rest from bookstores. Boston was particularly successful because of all the colleges. The first edition of *Hungry? Los Angeles* sold 3000 units, but the second edition quickly sold 11,000 units at $5.50 a book. The average return rate from retailers on books like these was 44 percent, but Glove Box Guides' return rate was only 14 percent, partly because it was a smaller publishing house and the retailers did not stock as many units, but also because the books tended to move quickly. Florence benefited from a practice in the industry called *modeling*. When a retailer purchased 25 copies of a book, it entered into its system that the store should carry 25 books at all times. That way, every time someone bought a book, the stock got replenished automatically. This meant more sales.

To develop and manage content, Florence hired a freelance city editor in each city that carried the books. Typically, this person had worked on a college newspaper for little money but knew how to assemble a manuscript and meet deadlines. This person then amassed a list of about forty-five contributors who wrote the recommendations. In 2006, Florence expected to earn about $300,000 in gross sales with high gross margins. In addition, she had generated additional revenue by licensing content to the *Chicago Tribune* and the *Los Angeles Times* in the form of listings to run on their websites.

The Future

Florence needed to find a way to generate lucrative advertising revenue. Because she did not want to jeopardize the credibility of her Glove Box Guides by taking money from restaurants, she had to find another way to let these restaurants owners who appreciated what the guides had done for their businesses to support her company. Her idea was to create a free magazine (*Hungry Student?*) geared toward college students that not only focused on eating and drinking establishments that catered to that demographic but also served as a central point for anything that a college student might need. "Students are always looking for experiences; they are curious, looking for something off the beaten path." Florence wondered if this idea might be the perfect follow-up to the Glove Box Guides.

Advising the Entrepreneur

1. Assuming that Florence needs outside capital to grow, what are her best options?

2. What is your assessment of her new idea for *Hungry Student?*

CHAPTER 17

Managing and Evaluating Financial Performance

Money is of no value; it cannot spend itself. All depends on the skill of the spender.

Ralph Waldo Emerson, American essayist and poet (1803–1882)

LEARNING OUTCOMES

- Describe the accounting and record-keeping options available to a business.
- List and explain the purpose of the three main financial statements.
- Discuss the purpose of financial ratios and how they can be used to describe the health of the business.
- Describe how to use cost–volume-profit analysis to answer key questions about the financial health of the business.
- Explain key methods for accounts receivable planning and financing.

A Match Made in Heaven

Founder and CEO of New Jersey–based AnswerNet Network Gary A. Pudles learned the hard way how important choosing the right investor can be. Pudles, whose company is a leading supplier of outsourced contact center services, tapped the Small Business Administration's (SBA) small business investment company (SBIC) program for funding. SBICs are privately funded and managed firms that are licensed by the SBA from which they receive up to about two-thirds of their funding in the form of below-market-rate loans. That money is then invested in or lent to small businesses. The SBIC program has been a successful one, but like anything else, its effectiveness depends mostly on the people involved.

Pudles approached his first SBIC expecting that it would be ready and willing to help his growing company. He was looking forward to the firm's advice and the contacts it might be able to provide, in addition to the funds he was seeking. Instead, the investors attempted to find ways to extract exorbitant fees from AnswerNet Network. Pudles also ran into problems with the SBIC's requirement for two seats on his board of directors. The investors wanted to be paid for attending meetings despite the fact that they were employees of the SBIC, and, because they lived in a small city at some distance, they expected Pudles to hire a private jet to bring them to those meetings. At the meetings, the investors focused only on the financials, which were positive, and on the possibility for a liquidity event, something Pudles was not interested in. They never provided the management advice that he had been hoping for; on the contrary, SBIC managers consistently attacked AnswerNet Network's

management team on issues that were not even relevant to the company. For example, they insisted that the board institute processes to protect the company from abuses in the payment of expenses from management shareholders. However, Pudles and his management team never submitted any expenses or got reimbursed for any expenditures. After a difficult six years in which the SBIC investors cost AnswerNet Network a lucrative acquisition opportunity, Pudles was able to buy them out and seek another investor.

The next SBIC that Pudles approached turned out to be a match made in heaven. The managing investors did not require a seat on the board, extracted no fees except those directly related to the goals of the company, gave Pudles excellent advice, and led him to contacts that could help the company. What Pudles learned from these two experiences is that it is very important to conduct due diligence on any investor, even an investment group sanctioned by the SBA, because every one is different. AnswerNet Network now serves over 35,000 customers from fifty-three contact centers.

Advising the Entrepreneur

1. How would you advise Pudles to conduct due diligence on an investor partner?

2. Given the situation with the first SBIC, how would you have avoided spending six years with a bad investor?

Sources: G. A. Pudles, "A Tale of Two SBICs," *Inc.* (June 16, 2005), www.inc.com; AnswerNet Network, www.answernet.com.

Because a business is a living organism, it is in a constant state of change and evolution: No business ever reaches the point where the owner can stop thinking about cash flow. Monitoring cash flow and cash needs is a vital and ongoing activity. At start-up, the goal is to break even on cash or reach a positive cash flow from the revenues of the business. It is at that point the business has reached critical mass. By studying cash flow, sales, gross margins, and expenses, any company can calculate what it takes to reach critical mass, whether it is ten strong customers or 1,000 units a month sold. Once critical mass is achieved, a whole new set of challenges confronts the entrepreneur, including: Do we want the company to grow? How fast? Should we broaden our product base? This chapter looks at cash management and how to monitor and evaluate the performance of a business as it grows. It provides an overview of financial statement creation and analysis and then considers cash planning and working capital management.

ACCOUNTING AND RECORD-KEEPING SYSTEMS

Entrepreneurs are not expected to be accountants; in fact, most would probably abhor the tedious nature of accounting and record keeping. Still, entrepreneurs need to understand the accounting system and the ways it is integral to all aspects of the company. Furthermore, to be able to produce the financial statements so essential to raising capital, leasing major equipment, or securing a line of credit, effective accounting and record-keeping systems must be established from start-up. Any accounting system must accomplish several things:

1. Produce an accurate picture of the company's financial health.
2. Allow for comparisons of current financials with previous periods.
3. Yield accepted financial statements consistent with generally accepted accounting principles (GAAP).
4. Facilitate the filing of financial and tax reports.
5. Expose fraud, theft, waste, and errors.

A company must keep a variety of records. These records include all the functional areas of the business, from purchasing to employees to inventory. In record keeping, it is vital that there are checks and balances against fraud and theft in the system. For example, the person doing purchasing should not be managing the purchases journal; likewise, the bookkeeper should not be authorizing purchases. It is also important that the business owner stay in touch with the financial aspects of the business. A regular simple cash-flow report from the bookkeeper keeps the owner on top of what's going on with the business.

Records should be kept for the legal period required, which depends on the type of record. Tax records, for example, must be kept for three years. Today, with virtually all growing companies using computers for accounting and record keeping, the storage problem is minimized; older files can be copied to archival disks or tape and stored easily in that form.

Accounting Options

A variety of accounting systems are available to business owners to manage record keeping and help owners make decisions. This section briefly considers two systems: cash versus accrual accounting and single-entry versus double-entry systems.

The difference between the **cash** and **accrual accounting methods** lies in the way revenue and expenses are recognized. Under the cash method, the easier of the two, revenue and expenses are recognized and recorded when they are realized—in other words, when the revenue has been received and the expenses have been paid. By contrast, under the accrual method, used most often by growing companies, revenue is recognized and reported when, for example, a sale has taken place (the cash has not necessarily been received), and expenses are reported when they are incurred (not necessarily paid). This system is the better one for accounting purposes because it matches revenues with expenses in the same time period.

Many very small businesses and home-based businesses use a **single-entry system,** which is basically a checkbook system in which income and expenses are recorded in one record. A **double-entry system** uses journals and ledgers, thereby requiring that each entry be posted twice, once in the journal and once in the general ledger. The result is a built-in balancing system to check for errors and a natural basis for the financial statements. For this reason, it is highly recommended that all businesses use this system from the very beginning.

Sarbanes–Oxley Rules

The **Sarbanes–Oxley Act** was created to improve the accuracy and reliability of corporate disclosures. The act covers issues such as establishing a public company

LEARNING FROM SUCCESS

Some Advice from the Big Guys

Small businesses have a lot to learn from their much larger counterparts. Because they are faster and more flexible than the big guys, small businesses are in a better position to take advantage of big company success strategies. Here is some advice from the CEOs of two very successful companies.

Lillian Vernon started the company that bears her name in 1951 with $2,000 that she received as a wedding gift. Today, her business is a more than $240 million specialty catalog and online retailer. Her advice is not to be afraid to take on debt when the money will provide the momentum that the business needs to survive. Vernon took out a loan to avoid bankruptcy and with that money was able to grow the business enough to pay off the loan before it was due.

Walter Wriston, former CEO of Citicorp/Citibank and chairman of President Reagan's Economic Policy Advisory Board, believes that business leaders must constantly scan the horizon for change. Understanding a company's business cycle is critical to avoiding catastrophes. "In economic hard times, you have to shift your attention from the top line to the bottom line. Start thinking about profit, rather than revenue." It's important to focus on generating cash.

Source: L. McCauley and C. Canabou, "The Voice of Experience," *Fast Company* (May 2001), www.fastcompany.com.

accounting oversight board, auditor independence, corporate responsibility, and enhanced financial disclosure. U.S. Senator Paul S. Sarbanes (D) of Baltimore and Representative Michael Oxley (R) of Ohio wrote the law in response to accounting scandals at Enron Corporation and several other companies.

Although private companies are not yet required to abide by the rules of Sarbanes–Oxley, smaller public companies will soon be obliged to issue reports on internal controls.[1] And private companies that are anticipating an initial public offering, merger, or acquisition should institute a plan for implementing the new rules. A survey by Robert Half Management Resources found that almost half of 1,359 chief financial officers of private companies who responded to their survey had made changes to their accounting and reporting practices. Most of the changes were made in the area of compensation and expenditure and purchasing reporting.[2] The cost of compliance is steep. For very large companies, the average cost is $5.1 million, and the annual cost of compliance is about $3.7 million.[3] Some of the requirements are not costly, and it would be important for a small company to at least follow those. Examples might be adding an independent board member or requiring executive management to certify financial statements.

FINANCIAL STATEMENT CREATION AND ANALYSIS

Financial statements should follow the GAAP so that the reader, whether a banker, investor, or other interested party, recognizes standard terms and sees items in their normal order of presentation. This section looks at the income statement, balance sheet, and operating cash-flow statement. (Chapter 16 focused on perhaps the most important tool for entrepreneurs: the cash-flow statement.)

Pro forma financial statements are merely forecasts of the company's operations and financial position at some point in the future. Start-up ventures create pro forma statements because they have no history on which to create anything else. Growing companies create pro formas to project their position into the future based on estimated growth. If circumstances change, those projections and pro formas change as well, but decisions about cash-flow management can be made based on them. For example, if projections based on current data show that a company will become very liquid in the coming year, the owner might decide to begin paying the company's credit line down in larger payments than it had been making. In layout, pro forma statements look like any other financial statements. Again, they are a tool that entrepreneurs can use to help make the future a little less unpredictable.

Income Statement

The **income statement,** often called the **profit and loss statement,** provides information regarding the profit or loss status of the company for a specified period of time, which could be a month, a quarter, or a year. It is normally calculated first—that is, before the cash-flow statement and balance sheet—so that tax liability can be determined and reported in the cash-flow statement when the taxes are paid. Figure 17.1 displays two end-of-year income statements for a corporation. Because it is a simple statement, it does not contain breakout statements. Note that if the business were structured as a sole proprietorship, a partnership, an S-corporation, or a limited liabil-

FIGURE 17.1 Sample Income Statement

BRE Products
Income Statement
For Year Ended December 31, 2004

	2003	2004	Difference
Net Sales[1]	485,000	580,000	95,000
Cost of Sales[2]	244,200	320,925	76,725
Gross Profit	240,800	259,075	18,275
Operating Expenses:			
Wages and Salaries[3]	53,625	57,225	3,630
Rent and Lease Payments	8,910	5,940	(2,970)
Utilities	8,415	8,403	(12)
Insurance	20,955	20,955	0
Advertising	9,900	8,415	(1,485)
Vehicle Operation Maintenance	33,712	32,861	(851)
Accounting and Legal	3,960	3,960	0
Payroll Taxes	7,507	14,615	7,108
Depreciation	2,970	3,300	330
Total Operating Expenses	149,954	155,704	5,750
Net Operating Income	90,846	103,371	12,525
Less: Interest Expense	(4,620)	(5,445)	(825)
Net Taxable Income	86,226	97,926	11,700
Less: Income Taxes	(31,925)	(34,209)	(2,284)
Net Income	**54,301**	**63,717**	**9,416**

1. Based on a 19% increase over previous year, a pattern established in this industry.
2. Cost of sales was 50% in 1996; 55% in 2004 due to increasing prices from vendors.
3. Based on two employees: one full time at $40,000; one part time at $13,625

ity company, the reference to taxes would be omitted because in these forms taxes are passed through to the owners and paid by them at their personal tax rates.

Like all financial statements, the income statement should contain footnotes referencing a page of assumptions or "notes to financial statements," which give supporting evidence and explain calculations that may not be obvious. Figure 17.1 shows assumptions for the first three line items. Revenue is the inflow of value from the sale of products or services. Value should not be equated with cash because sales may have occurred using credit and the value received is a claim on the customer for the amount of the sale, which is known as an account receivable. Accountants see revenues and expenses on income statements as inflows and outflows of value, which may or may not equate to the revenues and expenses reflected on the cash-flow statement. This is because the income statement uses the accrual method of accounting, whereas the cash-flow statement uses the cash method. This is an important distinction because in the preceding example the company will pay taxes for 2004 based on profit accrued in 2004 even if no cash was received. Therefore, the income statement shows that BRE Products is profitable, but we don't know if it's healthy in terms of working capital and cash flow. This is determined from an examination of the cash flow from operations statement.

Indicating the difference between the two years offers a way to more easily spot problems. For example, BRE saw sales increase by $95,000 from 2003 to 2004; yet advertising decreased by $1,485. Why did this happen? Is it the result of being farther along on the learning curve so that its advertising expenses are more targeted and effective? This would be something to examine more carefully.

Balance Sheet

The **balance sheet** provides information about the value of the business at a specific time. It does this by looking at the company's assets (such as equipment, inventory, cash, and facilities), liabilities (such as notes payable and installment loans), and owners' equity (such as stock and retained earnings) in the case of a corporation. Figure 17.2 shows an example of a balance sheet.

The first section of the balance sheet is the assets, which are valued in terms of actual cost for the item. Current assets are assumed to be in a cash state and are those items that are consumed in the operation of the business during the year, whereas fixed assets are essentially resources with long lives. They may be tangible assets that are used over the long term or intangible assets, items such as patents and license agreements. Accounts receivable must be forecast, and how this is accomplished is based on the seasonality that the business experiences. If the business experiences no pronounced seasonality, it may be assumed that a certain percentage of sales are not paid in cash each month based on industry averages or on the accounts receivable turnover rate. Once the business is established, however, it develops its own pattern of receivables, and a more accurate turnover rate can be calculated. To account for the fact that some accounts receivable are not collected, some entrepreneurs choose to subtract from receivables an allowance for bad debt, a small percentage (2 to 5 percent) based on typical bad-debt figures for the industry. Again, as the business develops its own unique pattern over time, it is easier to predict more accurately the bad-debt rate.

Notice that depreciation is accounted for on the balance sheet and reflects asset values. Fixed assets are presented less depreciation to show their book value, with the exception of land, which cannot be depreciated and is shown at its original cost. Thus, it is clear that the worth of the business as reflected on the balance sheet may not be (and most probably is not) the actual value of the business in the marketplace. In fact, shareholders' (or owners') equity is merely a statement of the claims of the owners on the business after all other claims have been paid.

A balance sheet does, however, generally reflect the financial condition of the business based on decisions made by the entrepreneur. For example, the decision to retain earnings in the company to invest in future growth increases the equity side of the balance sheet. A predicted increase in sales typically increases the asset side of the balance sheet to account for an increase in inventory or equipment to meet the rise in demand.

For each year, the sum of the assets equals the combined value of the owners' equity and total liabilities, so the balance sheet must balance. Comparing balance sheets from different periods can answer a lot of questions about the business:

1. Did the amounts of accounts receivable and inventory increase or decrease relative to sales in the same period?

2. Did the amount of debt financing increase or decrease during the period?

3. Are accounts payable at a healthy level relative to sales?

4. Have sales increased to a level that warrants further investment in capital equipment?

5. Are the operations of the business producing sufficient cash flow?

FIGURE 17.2	Sample Balance Sheet

BRE Products
Balance Sheet
For Years Ending December 31, 2003 and 2004

	2003	2004
Assets		
Current Assets:		
Cash	21,450	4,950
Accounts Receivable	42,533	90,090
Inventory	39,875	92,606
Prepaid Excises	0	8,250
Total Current Assets	103,858	195,896
Fixed Assets:		
Land	49,500	49,500
Building	247,500	247,500
Vehicles	52,800	57,750
Equipment	33,000	37,950
Less: Accumulated Depreciation	(34,650)	(37,950)
Total Net Fixed Assets	348,150	354,750
Total Assets	**452,008**	**550,646**
Liabilities and Owners' Equity		
Current Liabilities		
Notes Payable	34,831	62,700
Accounts Payable	20,130	27,904
Accruals Payable	3,762	6,088
Total Current Liabilities	58,723	96,692
Long-Term Liabilities		
Installment Loan Payable	0	42,354
Mortgage Payable	181,500	174,900
Total Long-Term Liabilities	181,500	217,254
Total Liabilities	**240,223**	**313,546**
Owners' Equity:		
Capital Stock	49,500	49,500
Retained Earnings	162,285	187,200
Total Owners' Equity	**211,785**	**236,700**
Total Liabilities and Owners' Equity	**452,008**	**550,646**

Statement of Cash Flow from Operations

The **statement of cash flow from operations** reports on changes in the company's cash account through inflows and outflows of cash and cash equivalents. These activities are associated with the normal operations of the company, such as purchasing, that are required to produce or sell its products and services. Thus, cash inflows include cash sales and collected accounts receivable, and cash outflows involve payment for inventory, payment of accounts payable, and payments associated with such activities as payroll taxes, rent, utilities, and so forth. Nonoperating cash inflows can come from

FIGURE 17.3   Sample Statement of Cash Flows from Operation

BRE Products
Cash Flow from Operations
For the Period 2003–2004

Net Sales	580,000	
Less: Increase in Accounts Receivable	(47,557)	
Net Sales Adjusted to a Cash Basis		532,443
Cost of Sales	320,925	
Plus: Increase in Inventory	52,731	
Less: Increase in Accounts Payable	(7,774)	
Cost of Sales Adjusted to a Cash Basis		(365,881)
Operating Expenses	155,704	
Less: Depreciation Expense	(3,300)	
Less: Increase in Accruals	(2,326)	
Plus: Increase in Prepaids	8,250	
Less: Operating Expenses Adjusted to a Cash Basis		158,328
Taxes Paid		(34,209)
Cash Flow (Cash Drain) from Operations		(25,975)

loans, additional investment by the owner, or the sale of fixed assets, whereas outflows can come from the payment of principal or interest on debt, dividend distribution, the purchase of fixed assets, or the payment of legal claims.

In a financially healthy company, the principal source of cash inflows comes from operating sources and is sufficient to pay general expenses, replace and update assets, and return a reasonable rate on invested capital. Creditors look carefully at a company's cash flow because that is the source of their repayment.

Recall that profit, as reflected in the income statement, and cash flow, as reflected on the operating cash-flow statement, are not the same thing. One difference is due to timing. Cash statements reflect inflows and outflows (revenues and expenses) when they occur, not when they are incurred, so it is possible that the income statement reflects more revenues than are stated on the cash-flow statement. The same is true of expenses, which may appear higher on the income statement for the same period but lower on the cash-flow statement because payment has not yet been made on those items. Another difference is due to the fact that depreciation of equipment and inventory affects the income statement and balance sheet, but because it is not a cash item, it is not deducted from the cash statement.

Preparing a cash-flow statement from an operations statement requires that the income statement items be linked with changes in the balance sheet items that arise from normal operations from one period to the next: sales, cost of sales, and operating expenses. Figure 17.3 presents a cash-flow from operations statement.

A series of steps explain how the cash-flow statement was derived:

1. *Adjust sales to a cash basis.* Sales for 2004 were $580,000, but these were not all cash sales; some were credit. On the balance sheet, accounts receivable increased from $42,533 in 2003 to $90,090 in 2004, or $47,557. This means that BRE

extended more credit in 2004, resulting in a cash drain for revenues not collected. So, although sales increased, cash flow from sales did not. To recognize this on the cash-flow statement requires adjusting sales down by the amount of increase in receivables:

$$\$580,000 - \$47,557 = \$532,443$$

2. *Adjust cost of sales.* Cost of sales is cost of goods actually sold in the accounting period. It is affected by changes in the level of inventory (current assets on the balance sheet) and changes in accounts payable (current liabilities on the balance sheet). In 2004, BRE had a cost of sales of $320,925. If no changes in inventory or accounts payable had occurred, this figure would have represented both the expense and the cash outflow, but as it was, inventory increased by $52,731 and accounts payable by $7,774. Each has a different effect on cash flow. The increase in inventory is an outflow of cash that is not shown on the income statement, so it needs to be added to the cost of sales. On the other hand, the increase in accounts payable means that BRE was taking advantage of supplier credit and retaining more cash in the company, so the increase is deducted from the cost of sales.

3. *Adjusting the operating expenses.* Depreciation is a noncash expense on the income statement and reduces revenue; thus, in terms of cash flow, the operating expenses are not as large as they appear on the income statement. Accruals are unpaid obligations and as such are a current liability on the balance sheet. They represent cash retained within the company; therefore, the increase is deducted from the operating expenses. Prepaid expenses, by contrast, represent cash outflows and increase operating expenses. Therefore, the increase in prepaids should be added to the operating expense figure. With regard to taxes, they must be paid in cash; therefore, the amount representing the tax liability for 2004 ($34,209) must be deducted in full.

The resulting figure for cash flow from operations shows that BRE was not in a healthy cash position. Quite the opposite: for the period 2003–2004, it experienced a cash drain of $25,975. Studying the cash flow from operations statement yields some important answers to the question of how a company can be profitable and have no cash:

- The large growth in sales caused a cash drain in the form of working capital to support the growth.
- Accounts receivable increased, reducing the actual revenue from sales.
- Both inventory and accounts receivable grew at a much faster rate than did sales, which may suggest a management problem that should be examined further.

In summary, the logic of these adjustments is fairly simple and important to understand to interpret the information in the statement correctly; that is, an increase or a decrease in a particular account is a positive or a negative for the company. For example, an increase in accounts receivable reduces cash flow from sales because it means more customers paying on credit. Likewise, the reverse is true: A decrease in accounts receivable increases cash flow from sales.

An increase in inventory is a use of cash, whereas a decrease in inventory results in a decrease in the cost of sales. Similarly, an increase in accounts payable decreases the cost of sales because money that should be going out to pay bills is being retained in the company. A decrease in payables reflects payment of obligations and increases cost of sales.

RATIOS

Many tools are needed to completely analyze a company's financial picture. No one tool or technique can provide all the answers to a very complex situation. **Ratios** are a particularly good way to begin to interpret the information contained in the financial statements from a lender's or an investor's perspective. Ratios make comparisons of items in the financial statements and put them in relative terms so that they can be compared to ratios in other periods to look for important changes in the company's position. It is possible to compute ratios for virtually all the items on the financial statements, but this would be a daunting and ineffective approach. A better approach is to select financial relationships that yield useful information about important aspects of the company. The three most common groups of ratios are liquidity and activity ratios, profitability ratios, and leverage ratios. In discussing ratio analysis, we use the sample statements from BRE Products and consider the most important ratios in each category.

Liquidity and Activity Ratios

Liquidity and **activity ratios** provide information on the company's ability to meet short-term obligations over time as well as to maintain normal operations. The more liquid the current assets, the more easily they are converted to cash to pay off short-term obligations and maintain operations; thus, the lower the risk for creditors.

Current Ratio

$$\textbf{Current ratio} = \frac{\text{Total current assets}}{\text{Total current liabilities}}$$

BRE's current ratio is $195,896/$96,692 = 2.02. This means that BRE has $2 in current assets for every $1 in liabilities. The higher the number, the more liquid the firm is. Over time it would be important to look for increasing numbers, signaling a trend toward greater liquidity, or decreasing numbers, portending declining liquidity.

Cash Flow as a Percentage of Net Sales

$$\text{Cash flow as a percentage of net sales} = \frac{\text{Cash flow}}{\text{Net sales}}$$

This measure gives the amount of cash flow generated by operations per dollar of sales. If cash flow to net sales is $.20, this means that for every dollar generated by sales during the period under question, 20 cents went to cash flow. The higher this number, the more liquid the company is. Obviously, this ratio could not be calculated for BRE because the company had a negative cash flow.

Cash as a Percentage of Net Sales

$$\text{Cash as a percentage of total current assets} = \frac{\text{Cash figure from balance sheet}}{\text{Total balance sheet current assets}}$$

This is another measure of the liquidity level of the company; the larger the percentage, the more liquid the company is. Note that if the company is holding excessive amounts of cash in a nonearning capacity, this cash is a negative and may actually reduce profitability. For BRE this ratio is $4,950/$195,896 = .025, which suggests very little liquidity.

Acid Test

$$\text{Acid test} = \frac{\text{Current assets} - \text{Inventory}}{\text{Current liabilities}}$$

This is yet another way to measure a company's ability to meet its current liabilities with its current assets. But the acid test is tougher because it removes inventory, which may be difficult to convert to cash because it is obsolete or, in the case of fraudulent practices, doesn't actually exist. This forces the current assets to stand on their own, which is usually more difficult. For BRE this ratio is ($195,896 − $92,606)/$96,692 = 1.07 times, or 1.07:1. Traditionally, the rule of thumb is a minimum of 1:1, so this ratio appears to be in line.

All the liquidity ratios help the company find problems early so that they can be more easily corrected.

Profitability Ratios

The most commonly used profitability ratios are the profit margin, return on assets/return on investment, and return on equity.

Profit Margin

$$\text{Profit margin } (PM) = \frac{\text{Net income}}{\text{Net sales}}$$

LEARNING FROM MISTAKES

The Way Down Is Much Faster

PTP Industries Inc.'s ride to fame and fortune was a spectacular one. The Baltimore-based packaging company (PTP stands for Precision Thermoforming & Packaging) grew at a mind-boggling rate due to increased demand from such big-name customers as Eveready, Procter & Gamble, Revlon, and Seagram. In fact, so valuable was PTP's business in Baltimore that when it was planning to move to a larger facility in Norfolk, Virginia, Maryland's economic development officials invested $5 million in an abandoned Montgomery Ward building to retain the 150 jobs that PTP was supporting. The city and state also provided $5 million in loan guarantees for renovations. Then the federal government kicked in additional incentives.

Meanwhile PTP was hiring new employees at an increasingly rapid rate to keep up with the demand of one of its biggest clients, America Online, which represented 60 percent of PTP's sales. It hired more than 300 new employees in a relatively short time and saw sales skyrocket from $24 million in 1993 to $38 million in 1996. But in early 1997, AOL owed PTP $2.2 million and wasn't paying. PTP could not operate under those conditions and very quickly went out of business.

Then PTP's lender filed a lawsuit against AOL after PTP defaulted on the loan, and PTP followed with a breach-of-contract lawsuit of its own seeking $80 million from AOL. In June 1997, PTP, which never actually filed for bankruptcy, was able to raise $3 million in an auction of its equipment to partially pay off creditors.

Lessons Learned: *Diversify your customer base and don't let customers get far behind in their payments before you act.*

Source: K. L. McQuaid, "Obits: Packaging Company Dissked by AOL," *Inc.* (September 1997): 31.

This ratio uses net income from the income statement and net sales from the income statement to portray the amount of each dollar of sales remaining after all costs of normal operations are accounted for. The inverse of this percentage (100% − *PM*) equals the expense ratio or the portion of each sales dollar that is accounted for by expenses from normal operations. It is an important way to monitor costs. BRE's profit margin is $63,717/$580,000 = .10.

Return on Assets or Return on Investment

$$\text{Return on assets } (ROA) \text{ or Return on investment } (ROI) = \frac{\text{Net income}}{\text{Total assets}}$$

This measure uses net income from the income statement and total assets from the balance sheet. It gives the percentage that represents the number of dollars of income earned per dollar of invested capital. The higher the number, the greater the return is. For BRE this ratio is $63,717/$550,646 = .11, so 11 cents was earned on every dollar of invested capital.

Return on Equity

$$\text{Return on equity} = \frac{\text{Net income}}{\text{Owners' equity}}$$

Net income from the income statement and owners' equity from the balance sheet give a measure of the amount of net income earned per dollar of paid-in capital plus retained earnings. It is a way to look at the efficiency and effectiveness of the use of investor capital. For BRE this ratio is $63,717/$236,700 = .26, so 26 cents is earned per dollar of paid-in capital plus retained earnings.

Leverage Ratios

Leverage ratios measure the degree to which the company relies on debt. In most cases, a higher number signals a riskier company because although the firm's earnings change, debt payments remain fixed.

Times Interest Earned Ratio

$$\text{Times interest earned} = \frac{\text{(Earnings before interest and taxes)}}{\text{Interest expense}}$$

This ratio measures earnings from operating income generated to meet interest charges that must be paid, so the greater the earnings relative to the interest expense, the safer the firm is. For BRE the ratio is $103,371/$5,445 = 18.9, which means earnings are about 19 times interest expense. BRE's rate of 18.9 is not negative in and of itself; however, it is a decrease from the previous year's 19.7, which may signal future problems.

Debt-to-Asset Ratio

$$\text{Debt to asset} = \frac{\text{Total debt}}{\text{Total assets}}$$

This is a balance sheet ratio that measures the percentage of the firm's assets that are covered by creditors versus the percentage that is covered by the owners. It is estimated that most manufacturing firms have debt-to-asset ratios between .30 and

.70.1. BRE's ratio is $313,944/$550,646 = 57%, which is about average for manufacturing firms.

Ratios are important tools only as they are related to comparison periods of time or when used to compare one company with another. When looking at ratios calculated by others, it is always important to verify how the ratio was calculated—what was included—and to watch for ways in which some companies improve their appearance of liquidity by, for example, taking out a long-term loan just before the end of the fiscal year and repaying it at the start of the new year. The cash from the loan strengthens the current ratio, but it doesn't reflect the true liquidity of the company.

COST–VOLUME–PROFIT ANALYSIS

Analysis of financial statements gives one picture of the company: the strength of its financial position. But all the activities of the business are part of an integrated system, so it is also important to look at how changing sales levels affect operational costs, operating profits, and cash flows. This is known as **cost–volume–profit analysis,** or CVP analysis, and it is not only valuable for determining the viability of a new company but also serves as another tool to guide planning in a growing company. This section looks at several ways to use CVP analysis.

Determining the Selling Price

Suppose a company has arrived at operating costs for its product; fixed costs (costs that don't change in relation to sales) are $218,750, and the variable costs per unit (those costs tied directly to sales) are **$156.** The company believes that it can sell **5,000** units if it can come up with a market-accepted price. Furthermore, the company knows that the general price level set by competitors is $315. If the company wants to achieve a $250,000 profit level, at what price does it need to sell its product?

If total units (TU) equals fixed costs (FC) plus profit (P) divided by the contribution margin (CM), which is composed of selling price (SP) minus variable costs (VC), then

$$TU = \frac{FC + P}{SP - VC}$$

Using the preceding example, the calculations would produce

$$5,000 = \frac{\$218,750 + \$250,000}{SP - \$156} = \$249.75$$

This figure of $249.75 indicates that the company has a fairly broad range of prices in which it could work and still stay at or below the competition's $315.

Maintaining the Same Profit Level with Increased Costs

Suppose a company is growing and thus expects its fixed and variable costs to increase in the coming year. This necessitates a price increase if the company wants to retain its current profit margin. Given the following information, what price increase would be required to do this?

Fixed costs	$281,250
Variable costs per unit	$268
Selling price per unit	$415
Sales volume	3,000

The company expects fixed costs to rise by $6,875 and variable costs by $6.25 per unit. To arrive at the increased price requires calculating the contribution margin per unit, the total contribution margin, the established profit, and the new fixed and variable costs, as follows:

Contribution margin per unit:	$415 − $268 = $147
Total contribution margin:	3,000 ($147) = $441,000
Profit:	$441,000 − $281,250 = $159,750
New fixed costs:	$281,250 + $6875 = $288,125
New variable costs:	$268 + $6.25 = $274.25

Using the same formula as in the previous example,

$$TU = \frac{FC + P}{SP - VC}$$

we get

$$3,000 = \frac{\$288,125 + \$159,750}{SP - \$274.25} = \$423.54$$

which is the new price that would have to occur for the company to retain its current profit level.

Sales Required to Achieve a Specific Profit

In the final scenario, suppose a company has experienced a contribution margin of 40 percent over several years. Assuming its fixed costs are $406,250 and it wants to make a profit based on 12 percent of its sales, how much in dollars does it have to sell? In this case, total sales (*TS*) equal fixed costs plus profit (*P*) divided by the contribution margin ratio (*CMR*), as follows:

$$TS = \frac{FC + P}{CMR}$$

$$= \frac{\$406,250 + .12}{.40} = \$1,450,892 \text{ total sales}$$

We see that $1.4 million in total sales is required to achieve the desired profit. This is an important measure for entrepreneurs. The goal is to achieve a contribution margin that grows slowly over time, but monitoring the contribution margin ratio regularly can forecast potential problems in the variable costs that must be addressed.

The key weakness of CVP analysis is its assumption that variable costs vary in a linear fashion with sales. It is therefore important to calculate several scenarios to prepare for any unforeseen variances in projected numbers. Large changes in an answer to an equation when only a small change is made in one of the variables signal that the model is very sensitive to that item. By testing the model using several variations on the figures, those items that affect the results the most are found. The best solution is to arrive at a range of values into which the company's numbers most probably fall rather than considering a result to be the exact and correct answer.

Break-Even Analysis

Break-even analysis (*BE*) is really another tool in the CVP package. It is essentially the fixed cost divided by the contribution margin ratio and is used to determine at what point, in terms of units produced or units sold, the company will begin to cover its fixed costs and return a profit. At break-even sales volume, total fixed costs are covered; every sale thereafter only results in variable costs of producing the product, with the remainder going to operating profit. Using our continuing example,

$$BE = \frac{\text{Fixed costs}}{CMR}$$

$$= \frac{\$218,750}{.40} = \$546,875$$

This means that sales revenues produce $218,750 of variable costs and a $328,125 contribution to margin at a break-even sales volume of $546,875.

CVP and break-even analysis can help evaluate not only ideas in marketing, production, services, budgeting and pricing but also performance. It is an important tool that entrepreneurs should use.

CASH PLANNING AND WORKING CAPITAL MANAGEMENT

Cash planning begins with a cash budget, a detailed plan for inflows and outflows to the company during a specific period of time. Typically, it is an annual budget with overlays of quarterly or monthly budgets. The budget includes both operating and nonoperating cash flows divided into inflows and outflows. Consult the following guidelines for preparing a cash budget:

- Do not include depreciation in the cash budget. This is a noncash expense that appears on the income statement.
- Cash purchases appear in the budget; credit purchases do not. Credit purchases become a cash outflow when they are paid.
- Cash sales are found in the cash budget. Credit sales are not. Again, the credit sales appear as inflows to the cash budget when they are actually received.
- The total of principal and interest from loan payments appears in the cash budget when it is paid.
- Cash expenditures related to operations, such as payroll, appear in the cash budget when they are paid. They do not accrue as they do on the income statement.

Choosing a planning horizon for the cash budget is a function of the purpose of the budget and the company's goals. In general, start-up and growing companies may use monthly budgets that tie into the annual budget. This is valuable for a new company that doesn't yet have a grasp on the market or on how the business will respond under varying conditions; thus, the budget becomes an important tool for checking the accuracy of forecasts. Generally, a company should check its actual numbers at the end of each month against the budget forecast. Any differences signal changes the company must make in its projections.

Preparing a cash budget entails four steps.

Step 1: Estimate Cash Sales

The first step in preparing the cash budget is to estimate sales volume for the period. In a new company, this is extraordinarily difficult and requires that the owners have a firm understanding of the industry and the company's competitors so that their estimates are at least within a reasonable range. In a growing company, the job gets a little easier as the company develops a track record on which to base its projections.

Sales growth is rarely linear as so often depicted in budgets and financial statements. Most businesses experience some seasonality, or variation, throughout the fiscal year. In addition, the sales forecast should reflect any specific plans that the company has for growth into new markets and the addition of products or services to its product line. (Refer to Chapter 16 for suggestions on forecasting sales.)

The sales forecast is adjusted to account for the percentage of sales that are cash sales. This is accomplished by looking at patterns established since the company has been in business (a new company needs to use industry averages). For example, if the company has been doing business for three years, it looks at three years of sales, separates them by season, and again by whether they were cash or credit purchases. For each year and for each season, the company figures the percentage of total sales that were cash sales (cash sales/total sales) and then averages those percentages to arrive at an average percentage of cash sales for each season.

Step 2: Estimate Cash Inflow from Accounts Receivable

The cash inflow arising from the collection of accounts receivable must also be calculated. Similarly to adjusting sales in step 1, percentages are applied to dollars of accounts receivable collected during a particular season of the year over however many years the company has been in business. This analysis produces results such as: 25 percent of sales are collected in the month that they occurred, 50 percent in the next month, and 25 percent in the second month following the sale. Analyzing payment patterns of customers is very important and can often reveal future problems that could severely affect the company. For example, the analysis may show that one large customer is responsible for the greatest percentage of accounts receivable every month and the time to payment for that customer has been steadily increasing. This type of pattern can have a significant impact on the company's cash flow and ability to pay its vendors.

Step 3: Estimate Cash Outflows

The estimation of cash outflows is easier because most cash outflows, such as loan payments, leases, insurance, and salaries, are relatively fixed in nature for the short term. Those cash outflows that vary with the level of activity, such as wages and advertising, usually are easily predicted in the short term; those outflows that are not easily predicted, such as utilities and phone, can be estimated from historical data. The estimation also includes looking at the company's payment pattern so that reasonable predictions can be made as to when expenses are actually paid.

FIGURE 17.4 Sample Cash Budget for a Six-Month Period

BRE Products *Sample Cash Budget* *Six Months*						
	Month 1	**Month 2**	**Month 3**	**Month 4**	**Month 5**	**Month 6**
Cash Inflows						
Total Inflows	69,315	45,000	22,000	25,000	34,020	42,720
Cash Outflows						
Purchases	39,805	29,350	9,460	10,750	14,629	18,370
Wages and Salaries	4,399	4,399	4,399	4,399	4,399	4,399
Lease	1,000	1,000	1,000	1,000	1,000	1,000
Utilities	649	649	649	649	649	649
Insurance	1,587	1,587	1,587	1,587	1,587	1,587
Advertising	850	850	850	850	850	850
Vehicle	1,500	1,500	1,500	1,500	1,500	1,500
Accounting and Legal	300	300	300	300	300	300
Payroll Taxes	659	659	659	659	659	659
Income Taxes	0	0	6,000	0	0	9,000
Capital Expenditures	15,000	10,000	10,000	0	0	0
Total Outflows	65,749	50,294	36,404	21,694	25,573	38,314
Net Cash Flow	3,566	−5,294	(14,404)	3,306	8,447	4,406
Beginning Balance	17,000	20,566	15,272	858	4,174	12,621
Total Cash (Ending Balance)	20,566	15,272	868	4,174	12,621	17,028
Minus Minimum Balance	12,000	12,000	12,000	12,000	12,000	12,000
Required Financing	**0**	**0**	**(11,132)**	**(7,826)**	**0**	**0**
Surplus Cash	**8,566**	**3,272**	**0**	**0**	**621**	**5,028**

Step 4: Estimate the Minimum Cash Balance

It is critical to the success of cash budgeting to estimate the minimum cash balance that must be available for unforeseen events and errors in estimation. The size of the contingency balance is a function of the volatility of the industry and the business itself, as well as the stability of cash flows. Some businesses, such as restaurants, have regular inflows of cash, whereas others, such as real estate development and manufacturing, do not. For each business, the amount to keep as a contingency balance differs. As the company grows and its operations begin to develop patterns, it will become more adept at forecasting the amount. Figure 17.4 presents a sample cash budget for six months.

Examining the sample cash budget yields information about the three most important variables: net cash flow, required financing, and surplus cash. The cash budget has two primary sections: the determination of net cash flow based on projected operational and nonoperational cash flows on a monthly basis and the financing section, which includes the contingency balance and any other forms of financing the company might require.

Net cash flow in the budget is the same as net cash flow on the cash-flow statement: total cash inflows minus total cash outflows. Positive numbers reflect surplus cash from operations, and negative numbers represent a cash drain caused by any of a number of things—for example, seasonality or too many receivables. The minimum amount of cash required to be on hand, if subtracted from total cash available, gives an estimation of any financing required during troughs in the sales cycle.

From the sample, we can see that BRE experiences a surplus in four of the six months, due principally to increased sales. A cash deficit occurs in March and April due to decreased sales, accompanied by a capital expenditure in March and taxes paid. Consequently, BRE will require financing to make it through the period.

ACCOUNTS RECEIVABLE

The existence of accounts receivable in the company's financial statements means the company has chosen to extend credit to its customers, which affects its cash position. Of all the noncash assets the company has, accounts receivable are the closest to being cash because accounts receivable are paid on average within thirty to sixty days. Still, lack of good credit-management practices can adversely affect cash flow by lengthening accounts receivable turnover time and increasing bad-debt write-offs. To avoid this outcome, the company should:

- Minimize the time between shipping, invoicing, and sending billing notices.
- Continually review clients' credit history.
- Provide incentives to customers to pay early.
- Review accounts receivable on a regular basis.
- Develop a set of effective methods for collecting overdue accounts.[4]

Accounts Receivable Financing

When a company makes a credit sale, it does not generate the cash to replace its inventory associated with that sale, make payroll, or pay creditors. Still, while the receivable is outstanding, the company must continue to meet its ongoing obligations until the receivable is paid and cash is released for use. The cash cycle of a business runs from the date of purchase or production of inventory to the date the inventory paid for by credit is covered by payment of the receivable. Because during this time precious capital is tied up, many companies speed up the cash flow from their receivables by borrowing against them so that they have use of their money thirty to sixty days sooner than they would otherwise. The two primary sources of this type of financing are commercial banks and finance companies, and they offer two types of financing: collateral and factoring. In the first case, the company's accounts receivable are pledged as collateral against a loan from the bank. Customers' payments are forwarded to the bank to repay the loan. In the second case, the company sells its accounts receivable at a discount to a finance company known as a *factor*. The factor then assumes the bad-debt risk of the receivables and collects on them.

To estimate the length of the cash cycle of the business and the required financing to support that cash cycle, the following formulas can be used:

1. Cash cycle = (Inventory turnover in days + Average collection period) − Average payment period for accounts payable

2. Average expenditures per day = Cash operating expenses (Cost of sales + Expenses − Depreciation)/360

3. Required financing = Cash cycle in days × Average expenditures per day

An example: Suppose New Venture Inc. has a cash cycle of thirty-five days, cost of sales of $250,000, operating expenses of $143,780, and depreciation expense of $2,862. Then the calculation of the required financing to cover its cash cycle would look like this:

$$\text{Average expenditures per day} = \frac{(\$250,000 + \$143,780 - \$2862)}{360}$$

$$= \$1,085 \text{ (rounded) average expenditures per day}$$

$$\text{Required financing} = 35 \text{ days (cash cycle)} \times \$1,085$$

$$= \$37,975 \text{ total financing required to cover cash cycle}$$

Though the availability of immediate cash is enticing to a business, it is a costly form of financing because interest rates run several points above prime and a fee is charged by the factor for services rendered. This cost of credit must be taken into account in the cash budget. Furthermore, with this valuable asset removed from the balance sheet, a company may find it difficult to borrow money in general.

Credit also affects the gross margin. Suppose the company's gross profit margin is 40 percent on a product whose revenues are $40 a unit. If a sale is made for credit, an additional cost of financing is incurred, which, for discussion purposes, is 15 cents for every dollar borrowed for a year. Using the preceding example with a cash cycle to be financed of thirty-five days, we would find the following:

$$\text{Revenue} - \text{Cost of goods sold} - \text{Financing cost} = \text{Gross profit margin}$$

$$\frac{\$40 - \$24 - \$0.15}{\$40} = 39.6\%$$

If that credit is extended to sixty days, the finance charge increases and the gross margin decreases again:

$$\text{Gross profit margin} = \frac{\$40 - \$24 - \$0.29}{\$40} = 39.2\%$$

The unmistakable message is that using credit costs money. Unfortunately, if extending credit is the industry custom, than the business owner must follow suit, but credit doesn't need to be handed out indiscriminately. A company can put in place policies that minimize losses and costs to the company, such as arranging for a finance company to handle customers' credit.

Credit and Collection Policies

Extending credit to customers entails a cost to the business; this cost consists of the costs of credit checking, keeping records (accounts receivable), bad-debt write-offs, interest cost of financing accounts receivable, and the cost of collecting on delinquent accounts. Therefore, it is important that the company develop a credit policy that (1) governs how and when credit is extended, (2) sets credit standards or conditions customers must meet before being extended credit, (3) sets a credit period during which the company grants credit (for example, thirty, sixty, or ninety days), and (4) establishes a collection policy for those instances where customers fail to comply with the credit policy.

Handling Collections

The longer a debt is outstanding, the harder it is to collect. It is important to resolve problems associated with unpaid accounts as quickly as possible. During the process of trying to collect, it's effective to cancel credit, withhold products and services, and assess late charges. Under the Fair Debt Collection Practices Act, there are, however, several things a company cannot do. A company cannot threaten the customer in any manner that suggests force, arrest, or criminal prosecution; use abusive language; contact the customer's employer or family; falsely state or imply that a lawsuit has been filed; or discuss the case with others. Whichever standards the company sets, they should be applied equally to all customers. If credit is granted, the company should notify the customer of the dollar amount and terms of the credit.

Short-Term Financing of Working Capital

Companies use short-term financing, often called bridge financing, to overcome seasonal fluctuations in their cash flow. For example, if the company anticipates a strong selling season, it may choose to build up its inventories above the normal level, thus incurring a higher-than-normal level of accounts receivable. These accounts receivable must be financed until the cash comes in to pay them. Retailers often use short-term financing to build up inventories for the Christmas season, which accounts for about 25 percent of their total revenues.

Every company, in the normal course of operations, holds a certain amount of cash, accounts receivable, and inventory. Additional working capital to manage seasonal fluctuations is usually obtained through short-term financing. In addition, a firm needs to finance assets such as plant and equipment. This is usually done through long-term rather than short-term financing. However, when interest rates are high, companies don't like to commit to long-term financing that costs them much more over the life of the asset, so bridge financing may also be used to "bridge" the period of high interest rates. When those rates come down, the company may refinance the equipment for a longer term. There are several types of bridge financing mechanisms, including unsecured bank loans, lines of credit, revolving credit lines, inventory loans, and commercial paper.

Unsecured Bank Loan **Unsecured loans** are based on the excellent credit of the borrower and require no collateral. Usually, the bank and the borrower execute a promissory note, which specifies the terms of the loan.

Line of Credit With a **line of credit,** the bank commits to making available to the company a certain amount of funds on demand. The firm can then borrow the amount when needed. Typically, a commitment fee of 0.5 to 1.0 percent of the total committed amount is required whether or not the company actually uses the money.

Revolving Credit Lines In a revolving line of credit, the bank agrees to supply funds to the company up to a specified amount. For example, if the credit line is for $500,000 and the company uses $200,000 of that amount, it still has another $300,000 available. Furthermore, if the company pays down the credit line to zero, it will once again have $500,000 available. The system works much as credit cards do for consumers.

Inventory Loans The section on accounts receivable management discussed pledging and factoring accounts receivable to enhance cash flow. These are just two types of secured short-term financing. Companies can also use inventory as collateral for a loan. The value of that inventory to the lender is determined by how quickly it can be converted to cash in the event of default by the borrowing company. There are several types of inventory loans:

- *Floating Liens* With a floating lien, the company gives the lender a blanket claim against the inventory. This type of claim is used when inventory items are of little value and difficult to distinguish (for example, parts).

- *Trust Receipts* In the case of larger inventory items that carry serial numbers, the lien will specify which items fall under the claim, and trust receipts can be used. In this case, any proceeds from the sale are immediately forwarded to the lender.

- *Warehouse Financing* The highest form of collateral for the lender is with warehouse financing. If the firm has negotiated a field warehousing agreement, it can keep the claimed goods in its own warehouse but segregated from other goods. The lender then hires a warehouse company to check the goods and issue a receipt stating that in fact they are segregated in the warehouse. If the firm is under the control of a terminal warehousing agreement, the lender actually puts the inventory in a warehouse managed by the warehouse company that it has hired. The borrowing company can't have access to the goods without the expressed permission of the lender. Because this method provides the most security for the lender, the lender will generally lend a higher percentage of the value of the inventory.

Commercial Paper **Commercial paper** is short-term debt issued by corporations in the financial marketplace. This commercial paper is backed by other firms based on the borrowing company's promise to pay. Therefore, it doesn't have to be registered with the Securities and Exchange Commission, and it can't have a maturity date longer than 270 days. Under the terms, the borrower agrees to pay the holder a fixed amount at some specified future date, and the commercial paper sells at a discount from that amount. Only larger companies with excellent credit have been able to benefit from this form of borrowing.

Accounts Payable Management

Cash-flow management and accounts payable management are tied together; both are affected by timing and, in some cases, negotiation. Many growing companies find themselves in an "emergency" situation and need an extension on an obligation to a vendor or a lender. If the extension is granted, the payable remains an obligation of the company on the books but releases cash from obligation temporarily. This is an example of the effects of negotiation on cash flow. In other situations, entrepreneurs typically attempt to use other people's money to keep as much of their limited cash as possible for emergencies. This means that trade credit, credit extended by vendors, is a very valuable commodity to an entrepreneur.

However, most vendors offer discounts based on being paid by the tenth of the month after purchase. If the company's inflow of cash is rather irregular throughout the month, it may not generate enough cash by the tenth of the month to pay all its obligations. Ideally, the company has enough liquidity to cover the obligations until cash comes in, but most start-up and growing companies are short on cash and long on obligations, so leveraging their cash position by paying vendors at varying times is often the only solution.

The importance of managing the cash flow of the business cannot be stressed enough. Too often small business owners think they know how much money the business has because they know what is in the checking account. But that is only part of the story. Timing of accounts receivable, timing of accounts payable, and credit collection add three more dimensions to the picture and can make the difference between having enough cash on hand to operate and being cash poor.

ISSUES FOR REVIEW AND DISCUSSION

1. What information do the three key financial statements (income, balance sheet, cash flow) provide the entrepreneur?

2. How is it possible that a business can show a profit and not have enough cash to pay its obligations?

3. Which items found on the income statement are not present in the cash budget?

4. How can a company manage accounts receivable so as not to affect cash flow adversely?

5. Describe how bridge financing can be used to manage business cycles.

EXPERIENCING ENTREPRENEURSHIP

1. Interview a banker about ratios used to evaluate a business. Which ratios are most important to lenders, and what do they look to discover about a business by using them?

2. Interview a commercial banker to learn his or her institution's lending policy for small businesses and which types of financing it offers.

Launching the Microbanking Industry

In 1983 Sophia Khatoon was a 22-year-old furniture maker in the tiny village of Jobra in Bangladesh. Looking more than twice her age, she worked seven days a week and lived in absolute poverty. The bamboo stools and chairs that she painstakingly constructed had to be sold to a moneylender so that she would have credit to buy the raw materials that she needed. The amount of money that she received from the lender was so small that she hardly covered her costs. She was paying daily interest of 10 percent, which worked out to more than 3,000 percent compounded annually. But with the help of the Grameen Bank, a unique concept in banking, and a loan of 50 taka (just a few dollars), she was able to establish a small business, repay the loan, and increase her revenues seven times.

Since its founding in 1983, Grameen Bank has grown to employ 14,000 staff, provide services in 35,000 villages of Bangladesh, and lend over $500 million in 16 million microloans. With an on-time loan repayment rate exceeding 98 percent, it outperforms all other banks in Bangladesh and most banks around the world.

Professor Muhammad Yanus

Dr. Muhammad Yanus was a professor and the head of the Rural Economics Program at the University of Chittagong in the south of Bangladesh, a poor country surrounded on three sides by India and on the fourth by the Bay of Bengal. Yanus had launched a program designed to explore the possibilities of providing banking services to the poor. He reasoned that by putting in place a government-sanctioned framework he could eventually rid the country of the moneylenders who were exploiting the poor. He also thought that by creating opportunities for self-employment, he could tap the underutilized resources in the people of Bangladesh. Yanus believed that the more potential a person had to command credit, the more able that person was to secure the resources needed to become self-sufficient. According to Yanus, "Creating favorable conditions for making a living through self-employment is a much more dignified way of solving the unemployment than initiating a system of doles and welfare payments."

His first project took place from 1976 to 1979 in the village of Jobra, which lay in close proximity to the university. In Bangladesh women were second-class citizens who couldn't access the traditional banking system, but what Yanus learned in working with the people in the village was that women were far better credit risks and were better able to manage their limited resources. In addition, making women economically healthy led to stable families with improved living conditions. In those early days, Yanus would channel loans through wealthy people who could easily access the banking systems and then guarantee the loans himself. As it turned out, the risk was slight, so Yanus decided it was time to start his own bank to serve the poorest of the poor. The focus would be on women, and the loans would be given without collateral or security of any kind. The loan would be used for a business activity that was defined by the borrower, and the bank would serve as a mentor to the borrower to ensure that the business venture succeeded. Interest was determined by the amount needed to keep the bank afloat. The average loan was $75–$100, except in the case of housing loans. If a businessperson borrowed 2500 taka, she would typically repay the loan at a rate of 50 taka a week over fifty weeks. Interest was calculated weekly on the diminishing principal and repaid only after the principal was repaid. So the effective interest rate was 10 to 12 percent.

One of the unique aspects of this entrepreneurial bank was that borrowers were placed into groups of five, which served as a self-policing force to ensure that borrowers maintained the Grameen Bank value system: "Discipline, unity, courage, and hard work." In addition, they pledged to keep their families small, shun marriage by children and wedding dowries, build and use latrines, and "plant as many seedlings as possible during the plantation seasons." In fact, it was those who borrowed from the bank who determined who the loan recipients were. In each group of five, the two poorest members received loans first. Once they had proven their ability to repay over a period of about four to six weeks, two other members became eligible for loans. Four to six weeks later, the chairperson of the group could take a loan. The amount of the loan increased with each successful repayment. Each group set up a fund to which all members contributed 5 percent on loans distributed. Members could take out personal loans for family emergencies but had to repay them within one month. In addition, members contributed 1 taka per week from income generated as savings. The purpose of this process was to develop discipline and responsibility in the members who met regularly to discuss issues and help each other.

The Growth of Grameen Bank

What started as a small experiment by an entrepreneur in a tiny village in Bangladesh has blossomed into a huge economic development success story that has had a major impact on the alleviation of poverty in this third-world country. The Grameen Bank's massive credit program has given birth to a whole new economy among the rural landless. Yanus knew that simply moving small quantities of coins and bank notes rapidly among the poor would not necessarily create the opportunity for capital accumulation on a larger scale. Therefore, Yanus and the Grameen Bank created SIDE (Studies–Innovation–Development–Experimentation) whose purpose was to "integrate the Economy-of-the-Poor with the Country's mainstream economy and to mobilize the transfer of capital from the mainstream economy to the poorer rural sector." This effort moved Grameen Bank beyond the banking industry to create a number of nonprofit, nonstock corporations to attack poverty on many levels. One example was the Grameen Agricultural Foundation (GAF), which rid the country of the exploitative share-cropping system and allowed the aggregation of pieces of land into 50-acre parcels, or primary farms. With a loan from Grameen Bank, GAF sunk a tube well to irrigate the land, and GAF provided fertilizer, seed, pesticides, farm machinery, and such to participants. A share of the crop harvest was sold to recover the costs. This system removed the risk for small farmers for whom one failed crop could mean disaster. They can now, for example, store their grain until there is demand rather than dumping it into the market the minute it is harvested. A shareholder approach was also used to establish the Grameen Fisheries Foundation, which now harvests over 1000 tons of fish in a year.

The success of Grameen Bank has spread beyond the borders of Bangladesh to give rise to similar institutions in more than thirty countries. Today international institutions like the United Nations, private foundations, U.S. and European governments, and private individuals deposit money with the bank. The bank has enjoyed phenomenal success, with almost two-thirds of its borrowers crossing the poverty line. Because poor healthcare is one of the primary causes of poverty in the region, Grameen is now experimenting with a Medicare-type system in which each family pays $1.25 per year and 2 cents per clinic visit, which covers 40 percent of the cost of the program. The Bangladesh government and foreign donors cover the remainder. Grameen Bank is well on its way to changing the lives of the poorest in the world through entrepreneurship, but it still has a long ways to go because the problem of poverty challenges a significant portion of the world.

Advising the Entrepreneur

1. Are there other entrepreneurial ways that Grameen bank might alleviate poverty?

2. Would a program such as Grameen Bank work in the United States? How?

Sources: "UNESCO: Education and Poverty Eradication—Grameen Bank," www.unesco.org/education/poverty/grameen.shtml (accessed November 7, 2005); "Grameen Bank, Bangladesh," www.gdrc.org/icm (accessed November 7, 2005); "Grameen Bank, Bangladesh—The Project Dungganon and GBR Methodology," www.gdrc.org/icm (accessed November 11, 2005); "Grameen Bank: Banking on the Poor," www.rdc.com.au/grameen (accessed November 11, 2005).

CHAPTER 18

Financing Growth

If it's not growing, it's going to die.

Michael Eisner, former CEO of Walt Disney Productions,
60 Minutes (November 22, 1987)

▶ LEARNING OUTCOMES

- Explain how growth financing differs from start-up financing.
- Describe how angel investors approach the investment process.
- Explain the venture capital market and process.
- Contrast private placement and public offerings.
- Discuss ways to value a business for sale or investment.

What Happens When a Company Grows Too Fast?

In the late summer of 1993, Brian LeGette and Ron Wilson were first-year graduate students at the Wharton School. As they shared a beer, they talked about their mutual interest in athletics and entrepreneurship. Although both had undergraduate degrees in engineering, each had intentions of becoming entrepreneurs. By the end of the night, they decided to go into business together.

The idea for their first product was inspired by the harsh winters that Wilson spent as an undergraduate at Virginia Tech. What he remembered most about crossing the snowy campus in those days was how cold his ears would get. By the fall of 1994, the two had their first prototype for an ear warmer, and Wilson began selling them on campus out of his backpack. In March 1995, Wilson contacted the buyer at the new QVC shopping channel who gave Wilson and LeGette a chance. After touting their wares for four minutes, they had yet to sell a single unit. But in the second four minutes, they sold 5,000 units—and 2,000 people were on hold! Within a few months, the duo had become regulars on QVC.

In 1997 Wilson and LeGette moved the company to Baltimore and added two Wharton classmates and two toy designers. The goal was to develop "crazy cool ideas" like a radio-controlled kite-glider, a collapsible beach mat, and a children's talking lunch bag, products that would counter the cyclical nature of the ear warmers. The company would now be called "180s" to reflect their goal of looking at common products in brand new ways. It was backed by $1.5 million from the original eighteen Wharton investors. Then in late 1997, they raised another $1.97 million with help from a Baltimore accountant who would later become the company's CFO and president.

However, the new line of products all totaled did not bring in as much revenue as the ear warmers. By 2000 the company had $15.2 million in revenues and thirty-six employees, but it still wasn't making any money. Furthermore, Wilson and LeGette were no longer appreciating their differences. LeGette was a big-picture person while Wilson was a nuts-and-bolts type, and the difference between them was taking its toll on everyone. Wilson finally resigned and the company repurchased his stock based on a company valuation of $45 to $65 million. LeGette immediately set out to change the company's distribution strategy. Under the old business plan, sales went to big department stores. Under the new business plan, the company would sell to specialty shops and focus on competitive athletes, then move to discount sporting goods stores, and only much later to department stores. This was a much more expensive strategy, and because there were far fewer specialty stores than department stores, it would take longer to recoup the investment in marketing. LeGette found himself in a constant search for capital to fund new-product development and to market his diverse line.

By the fall of 2004, the company was in trouble because LeGette cobbled together round after round of debt and equity financing. Finally, he contacted Patriarch Partners, a private equity firm specializing in distressed debt. The firm funded 180s with just under $20 million but at a very steep cost. Patriarch took control of the company, buying out the debt holders and the institutional equity holders while diluting the management team's stock. Then they replaced LeGette, who left the company on July 11, 2005; he never saw the takeover coming. Today, 180s has professional management with offices in Baltimore and in Canada and is still pushing the envelope with innovative products.

Advising the Entrepreneur

1. What did LeGette and Wilson do wrong?

2. What is the key lesson to be learned from this case?

Source: J. Anderson, "The Company That Grew Too Fast," *Inc.* (November 2005), www.inc.com; 180s http://www.180s.com/home/index.asp.

The growth of entrepreneurial companies occurs in stages. The entrepreneur or founding team, who assumes the responsibilities of sales, advertising, purchasing, personnel, and other functions of the business, usually manages early growth. As growth continues, however, it soon becomes apparent that some of the core functions of the business must be delegated to others if the company is to grow effectively. It is often difficult for the entrepreneur to assign duties and responsibilities and give sufficient authority to others to carry them out. If growth continues, those to whom responsibilities have been delegated will in turn need to delegate a portion of their responsibilities to others, creating yet another level of control. If left unchecked, the company ends up displaying the stereotypical bureaucratic hierarchy that may ultimately prevent it from remaining flexible and competitive.

In general, fast-growth companies experience consistent 50 percent or greater annual growth over many years.[1] After an extended period of fast growth, the company usually slows to a rate closer to 20 to 30 percent per year. Clearly, however, there are firms such as Cogentrix, a developer and operator of cogeneration facilities, which grew by 141,681 percent in five years in the late 1980s ($133,000 to more than $200 million in revenues), but that type of growth usually is not sustained over a long period of time.[2] On the other end of the spectrum are industries such as steel, where the modest 16 percent annual growth rate of a Worthington Industries is actually five to ten times the industry average and is considered fast for that industry.[3] In general, fast-growth companies are found in the earlier stages of the business life cycle—the period between five and fifteen years into the life of the company.

LEARNING FROM SUCCESS

Tapping a New Breed of Venture Capitalists

Jim Procter's Melbourne, Florida, company, WiDeFi, was ready for another round of funding. The fabless (a company that does not manufacture its own silicon wafers but rather concentrates on the design and development of semiconductor chips) semiconductor developer had received a first round of financing of $1.6 million from a local venture capitalist (VC) fund, but now it appeared that the company might have to relocate to Silicon Valley to satisfy the desires of a new VC. Procter was resigned to moving the company until an offer came out of the blue from two large VC firms, Aurora Funds of Durham, North Carolina, and Axiom Ventures Partners of Hartford, Connecticut. The two groups committed to more than $6 million, and even more importantly, the company could stay in Florida.

Traditionally, VCs like to invest within a couple hours of their home base, and in Silicon Valley they can tap thousands of companies without having to get on a plane. However, recently new VC firms have been popping up in out-of-the-mainstream locales like Bozeman, Montana, and Fargo, North Dakota, hoping to take advantage of great new businesses that don't have access to traditional capital. And this new breed of VC is taking a more entrepreneurial approach to investing by taking advantage of government regional economic development programs to boost the size of their funds. Is this the wave of the future? Only time will tell, but for people like Procter, it allowed him to keep his business where he wanted it.

Lesson Learned: *For the right business, venture capitalists will invest outside their local area.*

Sources: M. Leder, "Main Street VCs: A New Breed of Venture Capital Coming Soon to a Town Near You," *Inc.* (December 2004): 40; WiDeFi, http://www.widefi.com/.

Inc. magazine tracks the 500 fastest-growing private companies and has learned what it takes to sustain rapid growth, which is very instructive to small-business owners contemplating the growth of their companies. The vast majority of Inc. 500 companies entered an established market with competing products or services and at a distinct disadvantage to their established counterparts, with 75 percent of them funded on $100,000 or less. But their CEOs typically had higher levels of self-confidence and drive to control the business than the general population. Their persistence paid off, especially when their companies had to dodge bullets. For example, Commercial Energy of Montana delivered electricity to its customers at $24.50 a megawatt-hour in June 2003. That month, electricity prices spiked to $123 per megawatt-hour. CEO Ron Perry was forced to purchase at the market price, and the losses to the company that month almost sent the company into bankruptcy. Perry managed to find a group of its customers who advanced the company money to cover the losses until the company could get back on its feet. Today, the company is expanding to California.[4]

The growth phase of a business is an exciting adventure but it also places a tremendous strain on the resources of the business at a time when it most needs them. Successful growth takes capital, and often the financial resources that saw the business through start-up and early growth are not sufficient to supply the demands of rapid growth. The next section discusses financing for growing companies.

GROWTH FINANCING

Growth capital consists of those funds needed to take the company out of the start-up phase and move it toward becoming a significant contender in the marketplace. The financing choices available to the business mirror the extent to which the entrepreneur has met the sales and earnings targets estimated in the start-up business plan and the degree to which the company has reached critical mass.

Seeking Investors

Raising growth capital is time-consuming and costly, so many entrepreneurs opt to grow slowly, depending exclusively on internal cash flow to fund growth. They may have a basic fear of debt and giving up any control of the company to investors. This attitude is sound if it works, but new ventures that begin with obvious high-growth potential will find themselves hamstrung by a level of growth that prohibits them from meeting demand. Consequently, it's important to plan for growth from the very beginning so that the entrepreneurial team is prepared for the expense and the demands on their time when rapid growth comes.

There are three keys to raising growth capital—or any capital, for that matter. The first is knowing that it typically takes at least twice as long as projected to actually have the money in the company's bank account. Raising a substantial amount of money takes several months to find the financing, several more months for the potential investor or lender to do due diligence and say yes, and up to six months more to receive the money. In other words, no growing company should wait to look for funding until it needs it, for it will then be too late, which could spell disaster for the business. Moreover, because this search for capital can take the founders away from the business at the time the company needs them most, it's helpful to use

FIGURE 18.1   The Costs of Raising Capital

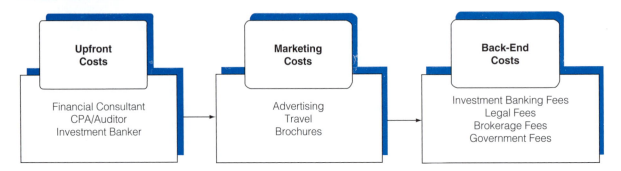

financial advisers. This allows the business to remain in good hands while the search is going on.

The second is understanding that the investors identified as a financial source may not work out, so it is vital that the entrepreneur continues to look for additional investors, if only as backups, while investigating a potential financial source. The third is knowing that second-round financiers often request a buyout of the first-round funding sources if they believe that those sources have nothing more to contribute to the business. This can be awkward, especially if the first-round financing came from friends and family.

The Cost of Raising Capital

In figuring out how much capital the venture needs to grow, many entrepreneurs concentrate on the cost of the capital in terms of interest rate or return on investment and fail to include the cost of seeking the capital, which can be substantial. The costs incurred before the money is received must be paid up front by the entrepreneur, whereas the costs of maintaining the capital can often be paid from the proceeds of the loan or, in the case of investment capital, from the proceeds of a sale or internally generated cash flow.

The costs of seeking funding for a business can be significant (Figure 18.1). Maintaining current financial statements is essential as the entrepreneur prepares to talk to a funding source. If the capital sought is in the millions of dollars, funding sources prefer that financials have the imprimatur of a financial consultant or an investment banker, someone who regularly works with investors. This person is expert in preparing loan and investment packages that are attractive to potential funding sources. The company's CPA prepares the business's financial statements and works closely with the financial consultant. In addition, if the company is seeking equity capital, it needs a prospectus or an offering document, which requires legal expertise and often has significant printing costs. Then there are the costs of marketing the offering, such as advertising, travel, and brochures. Finally, there is the cost in terms of time away from the business while the entrepreneur is out seeking capital. All these costs can amount to thousands of dollars.

In addition to the up-front costs of seeking growth capital are "back-end" costs in situations where the entrepreneur seeks capital by selling securities (shares of stock in the corporation). These can include investment banking fees, legal fees, marketing costs, brokerage fees, and various other fees charged by state and federal authorities. The total cost of raising equity capital can go as high as 25 percent of the total amount of money sought. Add that to the interest or return on investment paid to the funding source(s), and it is easy to see why it unquestionably costs money to raise money.

THE NATURE OF ANGELS

Private investors, or **angels** as they are known, are often people who the entrepreneur knows or has met through business acquaintances and networking opportunities. These angels are part of what is known as the informal risk capital market—the largest pool of risk capital in the United States, more than $50 billion. With all that power, it would seem they would be easy to find, but quite the contrary is true. Outside their own trusted circles of friends, they don't normally advertise their investment intentions. They come in all shapes and sizes, but they do have several characteristics in common:

- They typically are educated white men in their forties and fifties who have a net worth of more than $750,000 and have previously been entrepreneurs themselves.
- They normally invest between $10,000 and $500,000 in first-stage financing of start-ups or firms younger than five years.
- They tend to invest within a relatively short distance from home because they like to be involved in the investment.
- They tend to prefer manufacturing, energy and resources, and service businesses. Retail ventures are less desirable because of their inordinately high rate of failure. They are also very active in financing high-technology firms.
- They typically look to cash out of their investments within three to seven years. The risk/reward ratio they seek is a function of the age of the firm at the time of investment. If the venture is a start-up, they may want to earn as much as ten times their original investment. If the venture has been up and running for a couple years, they may want up to five times their investment.
- They find their deals principally through referrals from business associates.
- They tend to make investment decisions more quickly than professional VCs, and their requirements as to documentation, business plan, and due diligence may be lower.

Recently research has uncovered some interesting views of angels by venture capitalists. A study by the Center on Entrepreneurial Tech Transfer and Commercialization at George Washington University found that 94 percent of the VC respondents to their survey recognized the importance of angel investors in the earliest stages of a new venture, but 52 percent believed that angel involvement in the new venture "sometimes" made a company less attractive.[5] The most common reason given for this belief was "unrealistic company valuation." Another explanation was that angel investors do not understand what a company needs to achieve to attract institutional capital.

The secret to finding these elusive angels is networking. Entrepreneurs need to get involved in the business community in such a way that they come into contact with sources of private capital or people who know these sources, such as lawyers,

LEARNING FROM MISTAKES

Navigating "No Man's Land"

There is a common belief that a growing company must be doing everything right. The fact of the matter is that for some time a company may grow in spite of itself until it reaches "No Man's Land"—a point at which the company faces enormous challenges connected to further growth. This hurdle has caught many entrepreneurs by surprise.

One of the biggest problems that small companies face as they grow is managing the high costs of hiring the expensive professional management that they need to grow. Rod Hill, cofounder of Integrated Management Services in Jackson, Mississippi, found that most experienced management in his part of the country preferred to work for bigger, more stable companies. An owner of a chain of sandwich shops found that things were going fairly smoothly until he expanded from three to eight shops. It was then that he needed a bookkeeper to manage cash flow, a human resource system to track employees, and an extra manager to fill in when the regular managers were off. After analyzing the costs to hire the management that he needed, he calculated that he would not be profitable again until he had eleven stores. The dilemma was that he wasn't generating the cash to open three more stores. He was stuck in "No Man's Land."

Lesson Learned: *Plan for growth and have management and systems in place before taking on extra growth.*

bankers, accountants, and other businesspeople. Taking on an investor means giving up some ownership of the company. The process is normally completed through a private placement memorandum, which will be discussed in a later section. It is wise to include in the agreement a plan that allows the investor to exit the company should that issue arise. Including a buyout provision in the investment contract with a no-fault separation agreement ensures that the entrepreneur doesn't have to wait for a criminal act such as fraud to end the relationship. Structuring the buyout to be paid out of earnings over time avoids jeopardizing the financial health of the business. Above all, the entrepreneur should avoid using personal assets as collateral to protect an angel's investment.

The most common type of deal structure for private investors involves convertible preferred stock, which converts to common stock at an initial public offering (IPO) if the entrepreneur decides to go that route. These securities include a "put" option that lets investors sell their stock back to the company at fair market value beginning at the end of the fifth year. Most puts have a three-year payout schedule so that the investor isn't totally cashed out until the end of the eighth year. This is good for a growing company that has limited cash resources.

THE VENTURE CAPITAL MARKET

Venture capital is a professionally managed pool of funds for the purpose of investing in high-growth companies. The venture capital community in the United States has been the driving force for innovation and technology entrepreneurship as well as a model for other countries. In 2003 alone, venture capital-backed companies employed more than 10 million people and generated $1.8 trillion in sales, significantly outperforming their nonventure-backed counterparts. Venture capitalist investment in technology industries like software and communications has also increased the productivity of user industries like airlines and manufacturing. But VC funding's scope of interest is very narrow; it is generally focused and targeted toward the creation of high-growth companies. It has been estimated that less than 1 percent of all new ventures are funded with professional venture capital, a pool of managed funds. There are several reasons for this:

1. Start-up is the riskiest stage for a new company. Because there is always a steady supply of growing businesses that have a track record, the VCs generally think that their money is better placed with those companies.

2. Institutional investors—pension funds, insurance companies, and so forth—supply the bulk of venture capital today, and they tend to do larger deals than the typical start-up requires.

3. VCs normally want very high returns on their investments and a substantial stake in the company. Entrepreneurs usually don't like to give up control of the company and tend to balk at the stringent requirements of the VC.

4. The goals of the VCs often are at odds with the goals of many entrepreneurs. VCs have relatively short-term goals that revolve around getting a specific return on their investments in a specified period of time. Entrepreneurs, on the other hand, may have longer-term goals relative to building a company that endures.

Waiting until the growth stage to seek VC funding is advantageous because using venture capital in the start-up phase can mean giving up significant control of the new venture. The venture capital firm takes an equity position through the ownership of stock in the company in which it is investing. It also normally requires a seat on the board of directors and brings its professional management skills to the new venture in an advisory capacity.

The Venture Capital Process

To determine if venture capital is the right type of funding for the growing venture, it is critical to understand the goals and motivations of VCs because they dictate the potential success or failure of the attempt. The venture capital company invests in a growing business through the use of debt and equity instruments to gain long-term appreciation on the investment within a specified period of time, typically five years. The VC also seeks varying rates of return depending on the risk involved. An early-stage investment, for example, typically commands a higher rate of return, as much as 50 percent or more, whereas a later-stage investment demands a lower rate of return, perhaps 30 percent. Very simply, as the level of risk increases, so does the demand for a higher rate of return, as depicted in Figure 18.2. This relationship is certainly not surprising. Older, more established companies have a longer track record on which to make predictions about the future, so normal business cycles and sales patterns have been identified, and the company is usually in a better position to respond through experience to a dynamic environment. Consequently, investing in a mature firm through an acquisition or a leveraged buyout in which debt is used to purchase the controlling interest in the company, does not command the high rate of return realized by investing in a high-growth start-up, which may have little or no track record and no established sales patterns.

FIGURE 18.2   Risk versus Rate of Return

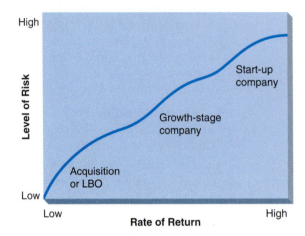

What Do Venture Capitalists Look For?

Usually (but not always) the first thing VCs look at when scrutinizing a potential investment candidate is the management team to see if experienced people with a good track record are in place and can take the company to the next level of growth. In addition to experience, they look for commitment to the company and to growth because they recognize that growing a company requires an enormous amount of time and effort on the part of the management team. Once they have determined that the management team is solid, they will look at the product and the market to see if the opportunity is substantial and if the product holds a unique or innovative position in the marketplace. Product uniqueness, especially if protected through intellectual property rights, helps erect entry barriers in the market, commands higher prices, and adds value to the business. Finally, they look for a venture that has the possibility of a liquidity event through an IPO or buyout.

Dealing with Venture Capitalists

Because the venture capital community is fairly close-knit, at least within regions of the country, it is wise not to "shop" the business around looking for the best deal. Investigating the venture capital firms in the state where the company does business helps locate VCs who specialize in the industry or type of business. Attorneys and accountants who regularly deal with business investments are excellent sources of information on VCs. In fact, the best way to approach a VC is through a referral from someone who knows the VC. Once a venture capital company has been chosen, it is preferable to stay with that company until it is clear that the deal will not work.

There is no doubt that the venture capital company will ask for a copy of the business plan with an executive summary. If the VC, cannot immediately determine that the entrepreneurial team's qualifications are outstanding, the product concept innovative, and the projections for growth and return on investment realistic, they will not bother to read the entire business plan. However, if after studying the plan the VCs like what they see, they will probably call for a meeting to determine if the entrepreneurial team can deliver what it projects. This may or may not call for a formal presentation of the business plan by the entrepreneur. During this meeting, the initial terms of an agreement may also be discussed. It is also very important that the entrepreneurial team not "hype" the business concept or make claims that they cannot substantiate. VCs readily recognize when an entrepreneur is "puffing." It's wise, however, to disclose any potential negative aspects of the business and ways to deal with them.

If the meeting goes well, the next step is for the venture capital firm to do its due diligence; that is, it will have its own team of experts check out the entrepreneurial team and the business thoroughly. If it is still sold on the business after due diligence, it draws up legal documents detailing the nature and terms of the investment. These may appear in the form of a term sheet, which is usually written to the benefit of the VC over the entrepreneur. The term sheet contains the terms and conditions of the investment.

Once the VC has declared that "the check's in the mail," receiving that check may take some time. This is because some VCs wait until they know they have a satisfactory investment before putting together a partnership to actually fund the investment. Others just have a lengthy process for releasing money from the firm. It is not uncommon for the money to be released in stages agreed on at the meeting. Moreover, the venture capital firm continues to monitor the progress of the new venture and probably wants a seat on the board of directors so that it has a say in the direction the new venture takes.

Capital Structure

It is vital to begin negotiations with VCs from a position of strength. Although VCs are presented with hundreds of deals on a regular basis, most of those deals are not big hits; they are always looking for that one business that will achieve high growth and return enough gain on their investment to make up for all the average- or mediocre-performing investments in their portfolios. If an entrepreneur approaches the negotiation with a business that has a solid record of growth and performance, he or she is in a good position to call many of the shots.

Any investment deal has four components:

- The amount of money to be invested
- The timing and use of the investment moneys
- The return on investment to investors
- The level of risk involved

How these components are defined affects the venture for a long time, not only in constructing its growth strategy but also in formulating an exit strategy.

Venture capitalists often want both equity and debt—equity because it gives them an ownership interest in the business and debt because they are paid back more quickly. Consequently, they tend to want **redeemable preferred stock** or **debentures** so that if the company does well, they can convert to common stock, and if the company does poorly or fails, they are the first to be repaid their investment. If negotiations are entered from a position of strength, it is more likely that an entrepreneur can convince the VC to take common stock, which makes things much easier. In another scenario, the VCs may want a combination of debentures (debt) and warrants, which allows them to purchase common stock at a nominal rate later on. If this strategy is carried out correctly, they can conceivably get their entire investment back when the debt portion is repaid and still enjoy the appreciation in the value of the business as a stockholder.

VCs often ask for several other provisions as well to protect their investment. One is an **antidilution provision,** which ensures that the selling of stock at a later date will not decrease the economic value of their investment. In other words, the price of stock sold at a later date will be equal to or greater than the price at which the VC could buy the common stock on a conversion. One way to ensure that dilution does not occur is to have a full ratchet clause that lets the VC buy common stock at the lowest rate at which it has been sold. For example, if the lowest price at which the stock has been sold to this point is $1, then that is the conversion rate for the VC. However, if subsequently the stock is sold at $.50, all the VC's convertible shares can be purchased at the new lowest rate. Where the VC's $1 million investment would have bought 1 million shares at $1 per share, it now can buy 2 million shares at $.50 a share, effectively reducing the equity holding of the founders. A better method from the entrepreneur's point of view is to use a weighted-ratchet approach, which uses the weighted price per share of all the stock issued after the founders' stock and before the lowest stock price that causes dilution. This is certainly fairer to the founders and prevents them from losing control of the company if the value of the stock decreases substantially.

The VC may also request a forfeiture provision, which means that if the company does not achieve its projected performance goals, the founders may be required to give up some of their stock as a penalty to the VC to guard against the VC having paid too much for his or her interest in the company. This forfeited stock increases the VC's equity in the company and may even be given to new management that the VC brings on board to steer the company in a new direction. One way to mitigate this situation is for the entrepreneur to request stock bonuses as a reward for meeting or exceeding performance projections.

Using venture capital is certainly an important source for the entrepreneur with a high-growth venture. It is, however, only one source, and, with the advice of experts, the entrepreneur should consider all possible avenues. The best choice is one that gives the new venture the chance to reach its potential and the investors or financial backers an excellent return on investment.

PRIVATE PLACEMENT

Private placement is a way of raising capital from private investors by selling securities in a private corporation or partnership. Securities are common and preferred stock, notes, bonds, debentures, voting-trust certificates, certificates of deposit, warrants, options, subscription rights, limited partnership shares, and undivided oil or gas interests. Private placement is a formal vehicle for seeking funding from private investors who are "sophisticated" in terms of the rules of private placement, which are stated in **Regulation D** of the Securities Act. Regulation D was designed to simplify the private offering process and allow the entrepreneur to seek funding from private investors as long as they met the requirements. Doing a private placement memorandum involves the completion of a business plan and a prospectus detailing the risks of the investment.

Private placement is a less costly, less time-consuming process than a public offering, and many states now offer standardized, easy-to-fill-out disclosure statements and offering documents. The advantages of a private offering are many. The growing venture does not have to have a lot of assets or credit references as it would need for bank financing, nor does it need a lengthy track record. It also does not have to file with the Securities and Exchange Commission (SEC). It must, however, qualify under the rules of federal Regulation D. Be aware that not all states recognize the exemptions under Regulation D in their **"blue sky" laws,** the securities laws designed to protect investors against fraud, so the issuer of a private placement memorandum may have to register with the state as well.

The burden is on the issuer to document that the exemption from registration requirements has been met. Therefore, the "sophistication" of all offerees should be examined closely and the reasons they qualify carefully documented. The issuer should also number each private placement memorandum and keep a record of who has looked at the memorandum or discussed the offering with the issuer.

Small-Corporate Offering: SCOR U-7

Small business owners can employ a simplified form under **Regulation A** to secure an SEC exemption when they issue securities. Regulation A lets a small business raise up to $5 million during a twelve-month period, except where a state may limit the amount to $1 million. SCOR U-7 enables the small business owner to test the waters to gauge investor interest before undertaking the more complicated and expensive Regulation D, Rule 504.

Within the structure of the corporate private placement, the entrepreneur can sell preferred and common stock, convertible debentures, and debt securities with warrants. Recall that preferred stock has dividend and liquidation preference over common stock in addition to antidilution protection and other rights as specified in a stockholder agreement. Common stock, on the other hand, carries voting rights and preserves the right of the corporation to elect Subchapter S status. Convertible debentures are secured or unsecured debt instruments that can be converted to equity at a later date as specified in the agreement. In its debenture form, however, it provides for a fixed rate of return (interest), which can be deducted by the corporation. Debt securities with warrants give the holder the right to purchase stock at a fixed price for a specified term, which can be very attractive for an investor who wants to share in the upside potential of the growing company by purchasing stock at rates that are usually below market value. Purchasing common stock under this instrument does not invalidate the preferred position of the debt holder as creditor, and if the warrants are issued as net-issuance warrants, the investor will not have to meet the SEC requirement of a two-year holding period before selling. This is because when the investor exercises the net-issuance warrant, no cash passes between the company and the investor. Instead, the company subtracts the cost of the conversion (the rate the investor pays) from the value of the stock being purchased and gives the investor the difference. This means that this type of warrant is more liquid.

As with any complex legal document, it is crucial that an attorney well versed in private placements be consulted in the preparation of the private placement memorandum and disclosure of information about the company and its principals. Problems usually don't arise if the business is successful; however, if the venture fails and the investors uncover a security violation, the entrepreneur and other principal equity holders may lose their protection under the corporate shield and become personally liable in the event of a lawsuit. The courts have dealt severely with security violations, and there is no statute of limitations on the filing of such a suit.

Direct Public Offering: Regulation A

Another type of small-corporate offering is the **direct public offering** (DPO) under Regulation A of the SEC. In contrast to SCOR U-7, it permits a maximum offering of up to $5 million over a period of twelve months. Any business owner contemplating a DPO should make sure that the business

- Can show several years of profit under the business owner's management.
- Can show three years of audited financial statements.
- Can be explained quickly, in a couple of sentences to interest a potential investor.
- Is exciting in some way, again to attract investors.
- Has a strong, loyal customer base who might invest.
- Has someone who can be assigned to manage the DPO, which takes a considerable amount of time (six months to a year).

Undertaking a DPO, SCOR U-7, or private offering is not a quick way to raise cash. It is a serious strategic decision whose pros and cons should be carefully weighed. Companies considering doing small offerings should make the decision very carefully because the costs of doing the offering, coupled with the costs of compliance with reporting requirements, are substantial when compared to the amount of the offering.

THE INITIAL PUBLIC OFFERING

An **initial public offering** (IPO) is simply a more complex version of a private offering in which the founders and equity shareholders of the company agree to sell a portion of the company (via previously unissued stocks and bonds) to the public by filing with the SEC and listing their stock on one of the stock exchanges. All the proceeds of the IPO go to the company in a primary offering. If the owners of the company subsequently sell their shares of stock, the proceeds go to the owners in what is termed a *secondary distribution*. Often a combination of the two events occurs; however, an offering may be far less attractive when a large percentage of the proceeds is destined for the owners because it clearly signals a lack of commitment on the owners' part to the future success of the business.

There is no doubt that the IPO, or "going public," has an aura of prestige and, if chosen as the method to raise growth capital, represents an exciting time in the life of a rapidly growing business. However, the decision whether or not to do a public offering is difficult at best because once the decision to go ahead with the offering has been made, a series of events is set in motion that changes the business and the entrepreneur's relationship to it forever. Moreover, returning to private status once the company has been a public company is an almost insurmountable task. It is critically important that entrepreneurs understand what it takes to prepare to go public and what life is like inside a public company.

More and more smaller corporations are using the IPO vehicle to raise growth capital; in fact, well more than half of all IPOs are companies with an asset value under $500,000. This trend has been helped by SEC Form S-18, which applies to offerings of less than $7.5 million and simplifies and reduces the disclosure and reporting requirements.

There is no "rule of thumb" for when to go public, but in general many companies consider it an option when their need for growth capital has exceeded their debt capacity. On average, a potential IPO company should have an attractive rate of annual growth, at least $10 million in annual sales, $1 million in earnings, and a history of audited returns.

Advantages and Disadvantages of Going Public

The principal advantage of a public offering is that it provides the offering company with a tremendous source of interest-free capital for growth and expansion, paying off debt, or product development. With the IPO comes the future option of additional offerings once the company is well known and has a positive track record.

A public company has more prestige and clout in the marketplace, so it becomes easier to form alliances and negotiate deals with suppliers, customers, and creditors. It is also easier for the founders to harvest the rewards of their efforts by selling off a portion of their stock or borrowing against it as needed. In addition, public stock and stock options can be used to attract new employees and reward existing employees.

However, the public offering has some serious disadvantages:

- Of the 3,186 firms that went public in the 1980s, only 58 percent are still listed on one of the three major exchanges. Moreover, the stock of only one-third of these firms was selling above its issue price.[6] Therefore, doing an IPO is no guarantee of future success.

- It is a very expensive process. Whereas a private offering can cost about $100,000, a public offering can run well over $300,000, and that figure does not include a 7 to 10 percent commission to the underwriter, which compensates the investment bank that sells the securities. One way to prevent a financial disaster should the offering fail is to ask for stop-loss statements from lawyers, accountants, consultants, and investment bankers. The stop-loss statement is essentially a promise by the investment banker not to charge the full fee if the offering fails.

- Going public is an enormously time-consuming process. Entrepreneurs report that they spend the better part of every week on issues related to the offering over a four-to-six-month period. Part of this time is devoted to educating the entrepreneur about the process, which is far beyond the scope of this chapter. One way many entrepreneurs deal with the knowledge gap is to spend the year prior to the offering preparing for it by talking to others who have gone through the process, reading, and putting together the team that sees the company through the offering. The IPO process can be speeded up by running the private corporation like a public corporation from the beginning—that is, doing audited financial statements and keeping good records. In fact, under the new Sarbanes–Oxley rules, a company must comply with the disclosure regulations prior to executing an IPO.

- A public offering means that everything the company does or has becomes public information subject to the scrutiny of anyone interested in the company.

- The CEO of a public company is now responsible to the shareholders above all and only secondarily to anyone else.

■ The entrepreneur, who before the offering probably owned the majority of the stock, may no longer have the controlling stock (only if the entrepreneur agreed to an offering that resulted in the loss of control), and the stock that he or she does own can lose value if the company's value on the stock exchange drops, which can occur through no fault of the company's performance. World events and domestic economic policy can adversely (or positively) affect a company's stock irrespective of what the company does.

■ A public company faces intense pressure to perform in the short term. Whereas an entrepreneur in a wholly owned corporation can afford the luxury of long-term goals and controlled growth, the CEO of a public company is pressured by shareholders to show almost immediate gains in revenues and earnings, which translates into higher stock prices and dividends to the shareholders.

■ Last but not least, the SEC reporting requirements for public companies are very strict, time-consuming, and therefore costly.

The Public Offering Process

The first step in the public offering process is to choose an **underwriter, or investment banker.** This is the firm that sells the securities and guides the corporation through the IPO process. Some of the most prestigious investment banking firms handles only well-established companies because they believe smaller companies do not attract sufficient attention among major institutional investors. Consequently, entrepreneurs should tap their networks for people who have either gone public or who have a connection with an investment bank to gain an entrée. The importance of investigating the reputation and track record of any underwriter cannot be stressed enough because investment banking has become a very competitive industry and the lure of large fees from IPOs is attracting some firms of questionable character. The investment mix of the bank should be carefully examined. Some underwriters focus solely on institutional investors, others on retail customers or private investors. It is often useful to have a mix of shareholders because private investors tend to be less fickle and more stable than institutional investors. The investment bank should also be able to provide the IPO with support after the offering by way of financial advice, buying and selling stock, and helping create and maintain interest in the stock over the long term.

Once chosen, the underwriter draws up a letter of intent, which outlines the terms and conditions of the agreement between the underwriter and the entrepreneur/selling stockholder. It normally specifies a price range for the stock, which is a tricky issue at best. Typically, underwriters estimate the price at which the stock is sold by using a price/earnings multiple common for companies within the same industry as the IPO. That multiple is then applied to the IPO's earnings per share. This is only a rough estimate. The actual going-out price is not determined until the night before the offering. If the entrepreneur is unhappy with the final price, the only choice is to cancel the offering, a highly unpalatable option after months of work and expense.

A **registration statement** must be filed with the SEC. This document is known as a **red herring,** or prospectus, because it discusses all the potential risks of investing in the IPO. This prospectus is also given to anyone interested in investing in the IPO. Following the registration statement, an advertisement in the financial press, called a *tombstone,* announces the offering. The prospectus is valid for a period of nine months; after that time, the information becomes outdated and cannot be used except by officially amending the registration statement.

Another major decision that must be made is on which exchange to list the offering. In the past, smaller IPOs automatically listed on the AMEX (American Stock Exchange) or NASDAQ (National Association of Securities Dealers Automated Quotation) only because they couldn't meet the qualifications of the NYSE (New York Stock Exchange). Today, however, NASDAQ, which lists companies such as Microsoft and Intel Corporation, is the fastest-growing exchange in the nation. There is a difference between the way NASDAQ and the other exchanges operate. The NYSE and AMEX are auction markets with securities traded on the floor of the exchange, enabling investors to trade directly with one another. The NASDAQ, on the other hand, is a floorless exchange that trades on the National Market System through a system of broker-dealers from respected securities firms who compete for orders. In addition to these three are regional exchanges, such as the Pacific and Boston stock exchanges, that are less costly alternatives for a small, growing company.

The high point of the IPO process is the road show, a two-week, whirlwind tour of all the major institutional investors by the entrepreneur and the IPO team to market the offering. This is done so that once the registration statement has met all the SEC requirements and the stock is priced, the offering can virtually be sold in a day. The coming-out price determines the amount of proceeds to the IPO company, but those holding stock prior to the IPO often see the value of their stock increase substantially immediately after the IPO.

ISSUES FOR REVIEW AND DISCUSSION

1. What is meant by the *cost of raising capital*?
2. Explain the four components of any investment deal.
3. Discuss the differences among the six definitions of value as they pertain to a growing business.
4. Explain the differences among an IPO, a DPO, and a SCOR offering.
5. What should entrepreneurs consider before choosing a public offering?

EXPERIENCING ENTREPRENEURSHIP

1. Secure a copy of the SCOR U-7 from your state's security agency and make a list of the information required to process a registration for a small-corporate offering. How is this different from the requirements for an IPO?
2. Interview a business owner with a growing company about his or her financial strategy for growth.

Benefield Music: When a Good Strategy Goes Bad

It was June 24, 2004, and Lindsay Benefield peered out the window of the Best Western motel in Mentor-on-the-Lake, Ohio. Tired from her long drive from Greensboro, North Carolina, she was nervous about the business deal that she was about to make. Nevertheless, she was anxious to get it done because the eighty-hour work-weeks were killing her and going with a name distributor might be just what her company needed.

Background

Benefield had built a small sheet-music publishing company that had a strong reputation for high-quality arrangements for string instruments. Although her annual revenues were just over $200,000, it was enough to provide for one full-time and one part-time employee. The problem with music publishing was that the printing fees were extraordinarily high because she couldn't take advantage of volume discounts. As a result, her margins were small. Benefield's strengths were definitely on the product development and customer side. She was effective at public relations and listening to her customers, and she was known for the quality of her product, her music editing skills, and her teaching skills. What she was not skilled at was distribution and managing a growing business. Her attempts to get distribution for her sheet-music arrangements took too much of her time and was eating into time she should have been spending on developing new products.

Benefield finally decided that it was time to send her sales sheets to three well-known distributors to see if they would take her company on. She received offers from two of them, but one, Lyria Music Publisher, also wanted to hire her as an editor in addition to distributing her catalog of arrangements, an offer that was very attractive to Benefield.

The Offer from Lyria Music Publisher

Lyria was a fifty-year-old company that had been purchased in 1999 by a fast-food franchise owner and part-time publisher who wanted to exit the fast-food business to pursue publishing full time. When he acquired the company in 1999, it was printing and distributing music from one location near Cleveland, Ohio, and was doing about $250,000 in annual sales. The new owner brought on his own board of advisors

and investors, and under his leadership the company grew at an annual rate of 25 percent per year through 2004 and enhanced its already good reputation in the industry.

On June 1, 2004, Benefield received an offer for distribution from Lyria, and on June 24, Benefield met with the Lyria management. They set a target date of October 1, 2004, for switching over the Benefield catalog to Lyria for distribution. In July the contracts were drawn up and reviewed but not signed. On October 1, Benefield began the catalog switchover. She also dismissed her staff and closed her office in North Carolina. She had approved the contract, but Lyria still had not signed it. By November, the switchover was complete, and Lyria's stamp was now on the Benefield Music. The website and other promotional materials all had the statement "Benefield Music is now distributed worldwide by Lyria Music." Still, the contract had yet to be signed by Lyria.

Between November 2004 and February 2005, Benefield began to receive complaints about Lyria's service, but she dismissed them, attributing them to growing pains. She still did not have a signed contract and had not received any editing work from Lyria. Over the next three months, some of Benefield's oldest and best customers stopped purchasing because of the service problems with Lyria. In fact, one purchaser threatened a lawsuit because a contract agreement had been violated. To date, Lyria had only paid half of the royalties that it owed Benefield and gave her no work as an editor. In July 2005, Benefield delivered legal papers to Lyria announcing a potential lawsuit if they did not pay. It also offered a timeline for pulling Benefield music from the Lyria catalog. Benefield wondered if she could ever recover her reputation in the industry.

Advising the Entrepreneur

1. What would you have advised Benefield to do about the decision to go with Lyria?

2. What should Benefield do to regain her company and its reputation?

Source: This case was contributed by Edward Caner, Project Manager, Science and Technology Entrepreneurship Program, Case Western Reserve University.

Planning for Change

CHAPTER 19

Risk Management

Take calculated risks. That is quite different from being rash.

George S. Patton, U.S. Army general (1885–1945)

LEARNING OUTCOMES

- Explain the four categories of risk that entrepreneurs face.
- Discuss how the risk management process works.
- Describe the key strategies used to respond to risk.

Removing the Risk of the CEO

When Stephen McDonnell started Applegate Farms, the Bridgewater, New Jersey, organic and natural meat company, he decided to operate it from his home, going to the office only one day a week. Why? To remove a key risk factor in the business: McDonnell is a control freak who would micromanage the business and prevent it from growing. He figured that by limiting his presence in the business to one day a week, he would minimize the potential damage that he could do. His strategy is successful: Applegate Farms' revenues have been increasing by 30 percent a year, and as of 2005 it was a $35 million company poised to move to $100 million—all without its CEO's daily presence.

In 1987, McDonnell found the opportunity of a lifetime when an investment banker friend told him about a New Jersey company called Jugtown Mountain Smokehouse. Its owner, Hiram Ely, had been experimenting with nitrate-free meat while preparing for his retirement from a company that was not performing. McDonnell saw an opportunity for a turnaround, and he planned to position the company as a supplier of natural meats. "I didn't even ask anyone's advice because I knew they'd think I was crazy," says McDonnell. His timing could not have been better because the early 1990s saw a resurgence in the desire for a healthy lifestyle.

After acquiring the company, McDonnell immediately renamed it Applegate Farms. From the very beginning, he instilled his philosophy about management. "If you want your business to run like a well-oiled machine, you need to give your employees constant access to relevant information and both the freedom and the responsibility to act upon that information. And then you need to get out of the way." The company grew to thirty employees in its headquarters and eighteen in a warehouse and a distribution center. His marketing manager and sales manager live in Massachusetts and Michigan, respectively. The company also keeps track of 300 family farms, from Uruguay to northern Quebec, that raise the meat that Applegate sells in addition to 12 slaughterhouses, 18 processing plants, and 350 wholesale customers. To keep everyone connected, McDonnell spent money on a custom database, which requires employees to score themselves and their direct reports on a scale of 1 to 5 on all the work processes of the business. The results show up in a "heat map" that color-codes the scores: Low scores show up as red blocks; 3s are yellow; and high scores are green. McDonnell reviews the scores so that he is prepared when he goes into the office every Wednesday to observe and conduct face-to-face meetings to get a better sense of what is really going on. McDonnell is concerned about the looseness of his organization and wonders if the company needs more discipline and structure. Recently, he instituted a new policy of attendance and punctuality for the customer-service team, which he felt had not been as disciplined as it should be. Most of the employees are young and have grown up in the company and don't understand what real corporate life is like. Also recently, McDonnell spent $350,000 remodeling the corporate offices to match the clean, wholesome, trustworthy, and natural image of his company's products. He is spending a lot of time figuring out what his role in the company should be as it continues to grow and wonders whether he may just have made himself obsolete.

Advising the Entrepreneur

1. As a management consultant, how would you evaluate McDonnell's style of management? Is it a source of risk for the company?

2. What sources of risk does Applegate Farms face?

Sources: R. Wright, "The Remote Control CEO," *Inc.* (October 2005), www.inc.com; A. Woodie, "Organic Food Company First in U.S. to Purchase System21 Aurora," *IT Jungle*, www.itjungle.com (accessed November 26, 2005); Applegate Farms, www.applegatefarms.com.

G iven that every business operates under some degree of risk, it is surprising that risk is one of the most overlooked factors in a small business. Perhaps this is because most people assume that entrepreneurs take risks when they start and operate businesses, so it is a natural part of the process. But recall that entrepreneurs are calculated risk takers, and a risk and its impact cannot be calculated unless it is recognized and managed. **Risk management** is simply preparing in advance to deal with the challenges that might occur in a particular type of business or the deviations from expected outcomes. Risk is any event that pushes a company's financial performance below expectations.[1] Such events range from fire and theft to loss of data files and losing a key employee. Risk, in and of itself, is not a negative because risk can have a direct relationship to reward. Taking risk creates shareholder value if balanced well in the company's portfolio of activities. So the goal is not to eliminate all risk but to manage it so that the commensurate rewards are achieved.[2] Business owners who are risk averse tend to transfer the risk of certain events to a third party such as an insurance company, which is appropriate with some kinds of risk; however, risk management is a way of thinking and a pattern of working that should become part of the organizational culture.

It is more likely that a business will be successful in its risk management process if the owner/CEO and all levels of the organization are involved, if the owner is continuously monitoring the business environment for change, and if the business model is flexible enough to allow the business to respond to change.[3]

TYPES OF RISK THAT ENTREPRENEURS FACE

Every industry has different types of risk, but in general, there are four types that businesses face:

- Strategic risk
- Financial risk
- Operational risk
- Economic circumstances risk

Strategic Risk

Strategic risk is the business's exposure to changes in market conditions. Strategic risks include such things as defining the wrong target market, pricing the product incorrectly, misestimating demand, and generally not understanding the customer. Strategic risks also involve actions of competitors that might have an impact on demand, pricing, marketing strategy, and new-product or service-development strategy in addition to sales staff hiring and budget management. A change in the level of competition in the market may make it more difficult for a small business to retain its customers. Market shifts due to new technology or changes in customer tastes and preferences are also sources of positive and negative strategic risk for the company, as are industry shifts such as those caused by the Internet as a new distribution channel in the early 1990s.

LEARNING FROM SUCCESS

Rebounding from Disaster

Sometimes success means taking a risk that doesn't work out but keeping the team together so that the company can ultimately succeed. In 1997, Ciena had achieved the best performing initial public offering of the year by more than doubling its share price. Ciena had been first to market with a critical technology in the optical networking sector: dense-wave division multiplexing that increased bandwidth-transmission capacity on fiber-optic cables. It was now in merger discussions with a telecommunications carrier, Tellabs. But when AT&T decided that it was not going to adopt Ciena's technology, Tellabs called off the merger. Ciena's stock price went from $55 a share to $8.

Instead of shrinking from further risk, Ciena decided to build a full-scale optical network, a decision that kept the company's best engineers on board. In yet another bold move, it acquired two companies that it needed to grow. Its vice president of systems and technology, Steve Chaddick, best sums up Ciena's heroic comeback: When faced with a challenge, "there are only two ways to act . . . make bold moves knowing that some will work and some won't. Or make no moves, which guarantees that you'll be an also-ran."

Lesson Learned: *Bold moves win the day.*

Source: R. Balu, "How to Bounce Back from Setbacks," *Fast Company* (April 2001): 148.

Financial Risk

Financial risk includes such things as interest rate changes, which affect the cost of capital for a growing company; foreign exchange rates when the company is doing business globally; and the availability of credit.

A business may also incur penalties if it fails to purchase insurance as required by a contract it has signed. It may be liable to customers for breach of express or implied warranty or for injury or property damage due to the company's defective product. A franchisee may lose its reputation by being associated with a franchisor that becomes insolvent or lose its right to operate as a franchisee by breaching the terms of its franchise agreement. The company may lose revenues, be required to reduce its operations, or see its costs increase from the failure of a supplier or vendor to provide goods and services that are essential to the business. If the business loses a line of credit, an important supplier, or required insurance, it may be forced to reduce or cease its operations, causing the permanent loss of customers.

Operational Risk

Operational risk is exposure to loss due to poor systems and controls. These risks affect everything from business planning to workforce management to quality assurance. For example, failure to develop a sound business plan could prevent the company from obtaining the funding that it needs to grow. Or, not putting an effective quality-assurance program in place could result in legal liability for selling defective products.

Businesses that lease property are generally responsible for any damage that they or their employees cause that results in the potential loss of the lessor's rental income.

In addition, the owner may have contractual liability to the property owner for failing to comply with lease terms. Businesses should negotiate leases in such a way as to eliminate provisions that force the business to continue paying rent when the facility is not inhabitable and assign responsibility for cost overruns.

Employees are a huge source of risk for small businesses. They can steal merchandise, file frivolous lawsuits, create bad press, and injure customers and other employees.[4] The business may also suffer due to a poor choice of independent contractors. To ensure that the company's employees are up to par,

- Develop a mission and value system that all employees buy into.
- Do background checks and reference checks on *all* potential hires.
- Treat good employees well.
- Investigate improper conduct immediately.
- Remind employees often about proper conduct.
- Use written agreements to protect the company.
- Be proactive about seeking information about problems in the workplace and make it easy for "whistle-blowers" to report improper conduct.
- Base decisions about conduct on facts to avoid lawsuits.

Economic Circumstances Risk

Economic circumstances risk comes about from changes in the economy, changes in supply and demand, and changes in the level of competition.[5] These risks are outside the control of the small business owner because they stem from changes in the environment in which the entrepreneur does business. Figure 19.1 depicts various risks found in the small business's external and internal environment. As can be seen, there are many important variables that can negatively or positively affect a small business. For example, inflation may erode the value of the business and reduce customer demand; a recession or a rise in interest rates may make access to capital difficult or interrupt the business's supply of critical materials, goods, and services if suppliers' businesses fail. In addition, the occurrence of natural disasters may require a company to lay off employees or to have to shut down operations while damage is repaired.

THE RISK MANAGEMENT PROCESS

The risk management process involves five critical steps: (1) Identify risks, (2) measure the probability of the risk occurring and its impact, (3) prepare strategies to mediate the risk, (4) prepare an action plan, and (5) monitor performance.

Identify Risks

Sources of risk are not always easy to identify, especially if they come from things with which the owner has no experience. It is impossible to anticipate everything that might go wrong in a business—machinery may be temporarily or permanently inoperable, key personnel may become ill and unable to work for some period of

FIGURE 19.1 Sources of Risk for Small Businesses

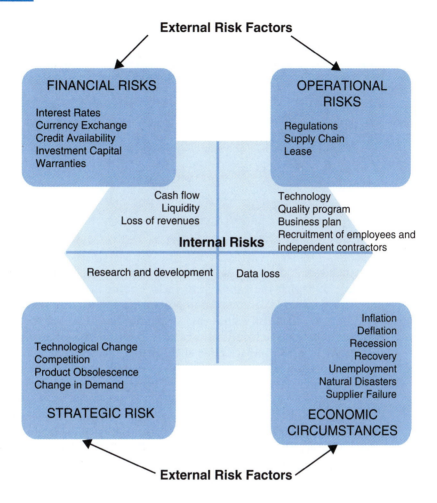

External Risk Factors

FINANCIAL RISKS

Interest Rates
Currency Exchange
Credit Availability
Investment Capital
Warranties

OPERATIONAL RISKS

Regulations
Supply Chain
Lease

Cash flow
Liquidity
Loss of revenues

Technology
Quality program
Business plan
Recruitment of employees and independent contractors

Internal Risks

Research and development

Data loss

Technological Change
Competition
Product Obsolescence
Change in Demand

STRATEGIC RISK

Inflation
Deflation
Recession
Recovery
Unemployment
Natural Disasters
Supplier Failure

ECONOMIC CIRCUMSTANCES

External Risk Factors

time—but it is important to identify the risks that might have a serious or even disastrous impact on the business. One way to do this is to list all the important assets and resources of the business that might be subject to risk and then conduct a brainstorming session to generate what-if scenarios and begin to construct a preliminary list of possible risks to those assets and resources. The initial list will probably be quite large and probably overwhelming, but the next step in the process will reduce the number of risks to a more manageable and realistic size. It is very helpful to include people who represent all the different aspects of the business in this process so that the business can be viewed from a variety of perspectives.

Measure the Probability of Occurrence and Impact

Once a company has identified the types of risk that it faces, it is important to estimate the probability that the risk will occur and the probable effect that occurrence will have on the business in financial terms. Another way to look at this task is to

| TABLE 19.1 | Risk Determination |

Risk	Probability of Occurrence in Next Three Years	Impact of Risk ($)	Probability of Impact ($)
Strategic risk: new competitor	.80	500,000	400,000
Financial risk: breach of implied warranty	.30	2,000,000	600,000
Financial risk: loss of line of credit	.10	250,000	25,000
Operational risk: loss of lease	.35	25,000	8,750
Economic circumstances risk: rise in interest rates	.90	25,000	22,500
Total Risk			$1,056,250

estimate how frequently a risk-related event might occur during a given period, such as a year, and what the expected financial cost of that event multiplied by the frequency with which it occurs. An important part of the risk management process is deciding how much risk a business is willing to take. One way to make the determination is to lay out the identified risks, their probability of occurring, and their potential impact in a risk impact table such as the one depicted in Table 19.1. In this example, the business has identified two very high risks: the strategic risk of a new competitor and the economic risk of an increase in interest rates although, because the dollar impact of an increase in interest rates is not high, the overall risk is medium. Other risks listed have a much lesser probability of occurring although the loss of a line of credit might result in a significant cost to the company in terms of money that would no longer be available to it for growth and working capital.

The numbers in a company's risk impact table are merely estimates; their accuracy depends on the experience of the owner with a particular source of risk. Furthermore, losses should not be limited to those generally covered by insurance. For example, if the business suffers a loss due to property damage, the cost of replacing or repairing the property is only one element of the total cost. Additional costs may arise from the need to find a temporary facility, increased insurance premiums, and inability to use the lost property.[6]

Catastrophic events like hurricanes and tornados, although relatively infrequent, should be considered in the analysis because when they do occur they can put an entrepreneur out of business, as we saw in New Orleans in 2005 after Hurricane Katrina devastated the Gulf Coast. However, it may be difficult or even impossible to assign a probability and dollar impact to this type of loss event. Therefore, some small business owners use a more simplified version of the risk impact table by assigning subjective values of "high impact, low impact" to specific sources of risk. In every case, the business owner must consider the potential for loss of business due not only to risks that directly impact the business but also to events that might affect suppliers, customers, or the community in which the business is located.

Some risks produce opportunities that could result in either a gain or a loss for the business, so these risk opportunities should also be part of any risk management process. Like negative risks, the potential return on the investment in an opportunity should be estimated and weighed against other uses of the company's resources.

LEARNING FROM MISTAKES

The Lessons of Hurricane Katrina

Hurricane Katrina is an excellent study in risk because it was a tragedy that was widely foreseen. Home Depot was one of the first stores to reopen in the aftermath of one of the worst hurricanes in U.S. history. In fact, two days before Katrina made landfall, Home Depot had protected its stores and moved its people to positions where they could prepare to be open for business once the hurricane had passed. Just one day after the storm, twenty-three of the company's thirty-three stores had reopened. And Home Depot was not alone. Stores that had prepared for the storm were able to respond quickly and get back in business within days.

But the vast majority of businesses did not prepare adequately. Why do so many business owners not prepare for potential catastrophes that are known to occur where they are located? Generally, it is because business owners set a target level of risk that is acceptable to them, and when something like technology reduces that risk, owners act in a way that returns them to their acceptable level of risk. For example, cars contain air bags that protect passengers from crashes, so drivers tend to drive faster under the mistaken belief that their risk of being injured in a crash is significantly reduced. The bottom line is that "ignorance and denial are not viable alternatives [to risk management]. What works in the face of risk is a combination of knowledge, humility, and willingness to change gears."

Lesson Learned: *Adopt an emergency plan and act on it.*

Source: J. Fox, "Taking Our Chances," *Fortune* (November 23, 2005), www.fortune.com.

Prepare Strategies to Mediate the Risk

An effective strategy to mediate risk results from a clear definition of the risk, its probability of occurring, and its attendant impact. In general, companies should take on only those risks that they understand and can manage, and these risks should be "stress tested" in a variety of scenarios—for example, measuring the difference in returns to investment in various situations. Businesses can use a number of strategies that will help them deal with the various risks enumerated previously. These strategies are generally grouped into three nonexclusive categories: risk control, risk sharing, and risk communication.[7] An effective risk management strategy contains elements of all three strategies. These risk management strategies then become the basis for the action plan (discussed later).

Risk Control **Risk-control strategies** are attempts to minimize the impact of a risk on the business. They are usually undertaken before an event occurs as a preventive measure. Exercising a risk-control strategy offers an opportunity to find ways to improve the operations of the business, and business owners sometimes find that these strategies produce unintended benefits. For example, if an owner believes that the company's small fleet of trucks are aging and replaces them to mitigate the risk to drivers, he may also discover that this change improves the drivers' morale and that the company's market image has been enhanced.

The types of strategies that small business owners employ to control risk include eliminating activities associated with negative risk, changing an activity to reduce risk potential, limiting the investment of resources in a new opportunity or staging the investment, developing contingency plans, and responding quickly to events that pose a risk.

First and foremost, businesses can plan in advance to deal with potential events that might disrupt their transactions with suppliers and customers. For example, businesses can invest in multiple or redundant ordering systems that allow them to continue taking orders when one system is down. Businesses can diversify their customer base to avoid too much dependence on one customer and do the same with suppliers. They can have in place backup sources of supply and essential services and prioritize critical business functions so that in an emergency they are not disrupted. Businesses should review all contracts to ensure that the party best able to assume the risk is assuming that risk.

Risk Sharing   In **risk sharing,** all or part of the risk is shifted to a third party to limit the small business's exposure and reduce its financial liability. Insurance is perhaps the most common way that businesses manage risk. The insurance company agrees to pay part of the insured's losses in exchange for the insured's premium payment. Here is a list of the most common types of insurance that small businesses may need to manage the risks in their business:

- Theft insurance
- Business interruption insurance
- Key-person insurance
- Professional liability insurance
- Commercial property insurance
- Business-vehicle insurance
- Equipment breakdown insurance
- Workers' compensation and employers' liability insurance

When examining insurance policies, it is important to consider them carefully because no two are alike. Moreover, business owners should remember that insurance

LEARNING FROM SUCCESS

When Disaster Strikes

In April 2001, *Fast Company* talked with a panel of eight turnaround artists who succeeded in helping companies avert disaster, sometimes at the last minute. Here is a compilation of some of their wisdom:

- Get everyone to calm down and think about being productive.
- Don't let emotion cloud judgment. If the dynamics of the market are good and the company has the right expertise, there is reason for hope.

- Talk to customers first, last, and always.
- Align people with a big goal and then execute it.
- Successful turnarounds have a vision from the top, time to implement the vision, talent to execute, money, and the desire to see the company succeed.
- Know where the company stands financially, especially with cash flow.

contracts are written to protect the interests of the insurance company, not necessarily the interests of the insured. It is important to get several quotes from insurance brokers and not necessarily choose the least expensive. Any insurance that the business owner acquires should be in place before the company is open for business.

Another way that small businesses share risk is to use independent contractors to perform some of the activities of the business. By definition, independent contractors assume liability for the work that they do and any losses that result. The laws regarding independent contractors are strict, so these third parties should be used carefully. (See Chapter 10 for more information on independent contractors.)

Risk Communication **Risk communication** involves informing all interested parties in order to reduce the probability of a particular risk event occurring. Interested parties include employees, customers, suppliers, community organizations, local government, and professional service providers who have a stake in risk management. For example, a small business that depends on a large customer for a significant portion of its revenues is at risk for business failure if that customer is lost suddenly. It is important that the small business owner understands the customer's business and becomes aware of any contingency plans that the customer might have to deal with its most likely risks.

Create an Action Plan

To deal with the various risks that have been defined for the business, it is important to rank the risks according to their probability of occurrence and the potential impact of that occurrence on the business. So, for example, a risk that has a huge impact on the business but that has a low probability of occurring might rank lower on a priority scale than a risk that has average impact on the business but has a much higher probability of occurring. The reason for ranking the risks is that mediating risk requires the resources of the business, and a small business will want to conserve its resources and employ them where they will have the most value—a risk that is likely to occur and has enough impact on the business to warrant preventive measures. Moreover, the business owner wants to weigh the cost of implementing a risk management measure against the cost of doing nothing. Table 19.1 presented one way to look at this decision. Table 19.2 depicts a more simplified version in the form of a "heat map" that color-codes the estimations, making it easier to see where the "hot spots" are. This method of looking at risk may be suitable for many small businesses. In this case, it is clear that the highest risk factor for this business is the entry of a new competitor into the market. This will affect customer demand, pricing, and revenues and will cost the company money to defend against a marketing offensive by the competitor.

Monitor Performance

Risk management is an ongoing process, not a one-time event, primarily because businesses and their environments change over time. Today, we are seeing increased risks in the form of terrorism, computer viruses, and piracy that were hardly discussed a decade ago. The legal environment is rapidly changing to reflect these new risks as we saw in the passage of Sarbanes–Oxley to thwart fraud in the management of public companies.

TABLE 19.2 Heat Map of Probability of Occurrence									
Risk	**Probability of Occurrence in Next Three Years**			**Impact of Risk ($)**			**Probability of Impact ($)**		
	Hi	Med	Low	Hi	Med	Low	Hi	Med	Low
Strategic risk: new competitor									
Financial risk: breach of implied warranty									
Financial risk: loss of line of credit									
Operational risk: loss of lease									
Economic circumstances risk: rise in interest rates									

Entrepreneurs must make sure that the appropriate people in their companies understand risk management by educating them and including them in the development of risk management policies. A business owner cannot eliminate all risk but assessing and managing risk will ensure that the company has fewer surprises that might damage the business significantly.

ISSUES FOR REVIEW AND DISCUSSION

1. Why is risk management a critical component of any business plan?
2. Of the four types of risk, over which type does the entrepreneur have the most control, and why?
3. Discuss some ways that entrepreneurs can identify the risks associated with their business.
4. How does one determine whether to use a risk-control, risk-sharing, or risk-communication strategy?
5. What are some critical things that must be in place for an action plan to be successful?

EXPERIENCING ENTREPRENEURSHIP

1. Interview an insurance broker to find out what types of insurance that a retail business might need to carry.
2. Interview an entrepreneur in a business of your choice about his or her risk management process. Does this entrepreneur face risks that have not been identified? What are they and how might the entrepreneur respond to them?

Flying High with a Little Black Card

Kenny Dichter, a former T-shirt entrepreneur, and Jesse Itzler, a former rapper, are known for their audacious moves. In 2001, they took the concept of prepaid calling cards to the next level with the Marquis Jet card, with which customers can buy flight time on luxury private jets. Since they began, more than 2,000 people have become regular Marquis customers, and the company produces over $300 million in revenues.

Dichter and Itzler introduced Marquis to the world in 2002 through the reality show *The Apprentice,* on which contestants are placed into two competing groups, given a business task, and by using their savvy, creativity and chutzpah, vie for the most business. In the Marquis Jet Card episode, the teams were required to create an ad campaign for the company, so the show was essentially providing free advertising for Marquis. More recently, the card was featured on the hit show *American Idol,* and it has become the latest status symbol for people who can't afford their own private jet.

The Private Jet Business

Private aviation is growing at a rate of over 15 percent a year, a number that includes charter jets, fractional jet ownership, and jet cards. The driver for the typical business or celebrity customer is convenience and saving time when traveling between second- and third-tier cities that do not have major commercial airports. The crowded major airports with their long security lines have also inspired the variety of options now available to people who have the money to pay for them.

The target market—customers who can pay from $500 to $2,000 per hour or up to millions of dollars for a quarter of a jet—is fairly small, but these customers like the idea of driving their cars out on the tarmac and putting their luggage directly on the jet. With trips that on a commercial flight would involve multiple stops, they save a tremendous amount of time. The cost is sometimes surprisingly affordable; companies that typically fly six to eight of their employees first class on a medium-length trip pay the same as for a commercial flight.

Marquis Meets NetJets

In 1986 Rich Santulli started NetJets, a company that provides access to multimillion-dollar private jets through fractional ownership. Clients sign a three- to five-year contract at a minimum of $397,000 plus management fees and hourly operating costs. This gives them partial ownership in a plane, so if they choose to end their ownership, they have to sell their share. In 1998 Warren Buffett purchased the company. Today, the company owns more than 570 planes, and in 2004 it flew 275,000 flights to more than 140 countries. The base of operations is in Columbus, Ohio, where the company has air-traffic controllers, meteorologists, and customer-service agents who manage logistics.

When Dichter and Itzler considered linking NetJets with the Marquis Jet Card, they were not new to the concept of piggybacking on successful brands. Through their first company, Alphabet City, they had created events that gave wealthy individuals access to sports and music talent for such things as a basketball clinic with Dominic Wilkins or singing backup for Christina Aguilera during one of her concerts. However, Dichter and Itzler knew that for Marquis to be a business, they needed access to the best planes in the industry, and those planes were owned by Buffett. The first time they approached NetJets Chairman Santulli, they lasted about eight minutes before he dismissed them. His biggest concern was hurting the NetJets brand that had taken so long to build. Five meetings with the persistent duo later, the two companies agreed to an exclusive alliance. Santulli saw it as a way to tap a market that they hadn't yet reached: the client who makes about $2 million a year (the average NetJets owner makes about $10 million a year). However, he took no chances on the start-up company. He made the Marquis team learn everything about aviation, including the economics and logistics of the private jet business.

The Marquis Jet card is like using a prepaid calling card. Clients purchase a yearly block of time in twenty-five-hour increments, during which they have access to the NetJet fleet. For example, for $109,900 they have access to a Citation V Ultra that seats seven in leather swivel seats and also provides catered meals. They are treated with the highest levels of customer service. "Get in their lives" is Marquis's motto, which means that the company learns the details about their clients that make a difference in customer satisfaction, such as providing flowers for a birthday flight and knowing which passengers have food allergies. Marquis also partners with upscale hotels like the Ritz-Carlton and apparel companies like Ermenegildo Zegna to provide special deals for their wealthy clients.

In 2004 Merrill Lynch reported that the number of high–net worth individuals in North America grew by 10 percent. With that kind of growth, Marquis expects to go from 2,000 owners to 5,000. At $175,000 to $200,000 a year per owner, that is a billion-dollar business. It is a big goal, and there are a lot of risks along the way. Dichter wonders if he has foreseen all of them.

Advising the Entrepreneur

1. NetJets took a big risk with their brand in partnering with a start-up. Why would Santullo not choose to do his own jet card?

2. What was the key to reducing the risk of starting a business in which the entrepreneurs had no experience? What risks does Marquis face as it grows?

Sources: T. J. Gibbons, "Your Own Private Jet," *Times-Union* (Jacksonville, FL) (December 17, 2005); "Kenny and the Jets," *New York Enterprise Report* (November–December 2005); C. Salter, "High Fliers," *Fast Company* (October 2005), www.fastcompany.com.

CHAPTER 20

Harvesting the Wealth

Success is not a place at which one arrives but rather . . . the spirit with which one undertakes and continues the journey.

Alex Noble, "In Touch with the Present," *Christian Science Monitor* (March 6, 1979)

▶ LEARNING OUTCOMES

- Explain the value of creating a harvest strategy early in the development of a business.
- Differentiate between going public, selling the business in whole or in part, merging, and selling to employees.
- Discuss how business owners should approach succession planning.
- Describe the approaches that a business owner can take when the business is failing.

The Ultimate Black Enterprise

In August 2005, *Black Enterprise* magazine turned 35 years old under the watchful eye of its founder, Earl Graves, but with the reins of the business firmly in the hands of the next generation. The successful transfer of power from the founding generation to the children is not often smooth, but over a period of five years, Graves managed to hand over management and give the company its most dynamic period of growth. Today the Graves's empire includes *Black Enterprise* magazine, with a national circulation of 425,000 and a readership of 3.8 million; an asset-management company; and a conference business. Graves is listed as number 22 on *Fortune* magazine's list of most powerful black executives in business. "I am an optimist, and I never really saw myself as not being able to make it," says Graves.

The story of the aspiring entrepreneur who struggles out of challenging economic circumstances to achieve enormous success is not a new one. Many great entrepreneurs in the news today came from deprived backgrounds. Graves was born of West Indian parents and was one of only two black graduates of Erasmus High School in the Bedford–Stuyvesant area of Brooklyn, New York. "I was not in a community where you could cut grass [to make a living]," notes Graves. However, Graves was destined for success despite, or perhaps because of, his humble beginnings. His high grades and athletic skills helped him obtain a scholarship to Morgan State University where he majored in economics and joined the ROTC. While at college he began to find his entrepreneurial roots by operating several campus businesses. Upon graduation, he was commissioned a second lieutenant in the U.S. Army and eventually became a member of the Green Beret, the elite Special Forces unit. By 1962, he had left the army to become a narcotics agent with the Treasury Department and in 1966 took a position as an administrative assistant to Robert F. Kennedy, then a U.S. senator. After Kennedy was assassinated during his bid for the presidency in 1968, Graves accepted a Ford Foundation grant to study entrepreneurship and economic development in Barbados and then formed a management-consulting firm to focus on urban affairs and economic development.

In 1969, after working to make Charles Evers the first black mayor in the United States, he saw that the time was right to produce a magazine focused on blacks and business. In 1970, after borrowing $250,000 from the Manhattan Capital Corporation of Chase Manhattan Bank, he launched *Black Enterprise.* From the beginning, the company was a collaboration of Graves and his wife, Barbara, who instilled the family's core values—God, family, education, work, leadership, community service—into the business. Their three sons were raised in an entrepreneurial environment where doing well while doing good were the watchwords. Graves believes that one needs to take an entrepreneurial approach to a career, carving out a niche and becoming the best at something. He encouraged his employees to do that, so it is no surprise that the turnover in his businesses is very low and executives generally rise from the ranks of the employees.

For years, Graves was a sole proprietor for all intents and purposes, with no one to account to but himself. In 1998, Earl Jr., also known as Butch, who had been leading the company's advertising and sales effort, took over as CEO of the core company. The other two brothers lead different divisions. As he transitions his empire to his three sons, Graves knows that they have the advantage of a team effort but that they will also face many new exciting challenges.

Sources: "Earl Graves, an Image of Black Business Success," *African American Registry* (January 9, 2005), www.aargistry.com; C. C. Graves, "Making a Success of Succession," *Inc.* (February 2000), www.inc.com; E. G. Graves, "How We Got Started," *Fortune Small Business* (September 2003), www.fortune.com/fortune/smallbusiness; "Earl Graves on the State of Black Business," *Hampton Roads* (May 13, 2003), www.hamptonroads.com.

Entrepreneurship has always been one of the great sources of wealth creation. A well-conceived business possesses value that does not depend on the founders. In other words, it continues creating value and wealth even when the original founders leave. Why would an entrepreneur ever leave a business that took so much effort and heart and soul to create? The fact is that, although many entrepreneurs remain with their businesses throughout their lives, the majority decide to reap the rewards of their hard work by passing the business to a family member, selling it, or taking it public and moving on to something else. In fact, to some entrepreneurs, starting a business is exciting and challenging, but managing a business is frustrating and mundane, so they move from venture to venture at the optimal time. In 2004 the number of people with a net worth of more than $1 million grew to 7.5 million, and more than 20 percent of that net worth was in sales of small businesses.[1] Today, entrepreneurship is the number-one way to create wealth.

Whether entrepreneurs decide to stay with their business or leave, they will probably want to enjoy some of the wealth that the business has created. Knowing how the wealth of the business might be harvested in the future will help an entrepreneur make decisions from the start. Moreover, if the business owner takes advantage of outside capital to fund the business, he or she will be asked by investors what the exit strategy is, another reason why it is important to have a well-considered harvest strategy.

HARVEST STRATEGY

In the early stages of growing a start-up, many entrepreneurs are so busy driving the business that they can't imagine ever needing a harvest plan in order to some day

LEARNING FROM SUCCESS

When Your Franchisor Files for Bankruptcy

Gail and Gordon Perry became the proud owners of a Schlotzsky's franchise in February 1999, a decision that they thought would pay for their retirement some day. But just six years later, the parent company filed for Chapter 11 bankruptcy protection. When the announcement hit the press, sales at their San Luis Obispo, California, store plummeted 25 percent. Instantly, they began having trouble getting their supplies, and their distributors, who were nervous about getting paid, put them on cash-on-delivery status. The Perrys had to find other sources to take care of their customers. Fortunately, in December 2004, the franchisor was purchased, and the Perrys were able to keep their store.

They were more successful than others in the chain who did not weather the storm as well because during the turmoil they were very open with everyone about what was going on. Also, because they always kept enough supplies for two weeks, they had enough time to figure out what they were going to do about keeping the store stocked. When they contacted the local newspaper and let people know that their store did not file bankruptcy, customers began to return and local suppliers like Smart and Final and Coca-Cola went out of their way to keep the store stocked.

Lesson Learned: *Let people who can help you know what's going on.*

Source: S. Wilson, "Surviving a System Bankruptcy," *Entepreneur.com* (October 19, 2005), www.entrepreneur.com.

leave the business. However, understanding the vision for the future of the business will help the entrepreneur make better decisions as the company grows. Entrepreneurs should take three steps as early as possible in the life of a business:

1. Create a small, informal advisory board to guide personal wealth planning. It may include an accountant, a tax attorney, and an estate-planning expert and be a subset of a more formal advisory board or board of directors.

2. Acquire a mentor to emulate. In general, successful entrepreneurs enjoy helping new entrepreneurs build their success.

3. Focus on the aspects of the company that create sustainable value, such as intellectual property, a loyal customer base, a successful network of vendors, suppliers, distributors, salespeople, manufacturers, and professional advisors, and a system of incentives and a company culture that encourages employees to remain loyal.

Small business owners have many options by which they can harvest the wealth that they have created. The choice depends on whether the entrepreneur wants to remain a part of the business: doing a public offering, selling the business, cashing out of the business but staying involved, merging with another company, and selling to employees.

Going Public

Going public is one way to harvest some of the wealth that a company has created as well as to recapture an initial investment. Many entrepreneurs, and certainly

LEARNING FROM THE GLOBAL MARKET

Selling the Business to a Foreign Buyer

In a global marketplace, it is not surprising that business owners may consider selling their business to a foreign investor as one way to harvest the wealth created. Buyers from other countries are aggressively purchasing businesses as a way to legally gain residency in the United States and have a way to support themselves. Small business owners who have active businesses with a large number of employees and an established record of profitability are eligible acquisitions by nonnationals who have the investment capital. The U.S. Immigration and Naturalization Service maintains certain investment requirements:

- A business valued at less than $100,000 requires an investment of at least 75 percent.

- A business valued at between $100,000 and $500,000 requires a minimum investment of 60 percent.

In addition, the buyer must tender a deposit before receiving an E-2 Visa, which is a nonimmigrant, long-term, temporary visa. The buyer may bring supervisory personnel to the United States from the same country, draw a salary in the United States, and bring his or her family into the country. The term of the visa is three to five years and may be renewed if the business is still operating. Permanent Residency Visas are issued to nonnationals who invest at least $1 million in a new U.S. business enterprise that creates or protects ten or more jobs.

Source: W. West, "Selling to the Foreign Investor," *Business Book Press* (November 26, 2005), www.businessbookpress.com.

investors, see the initial public offering (IPO) as the ultimate liquidity event. If the early funding of the firm was with venture capital money, then an IPO or sale may be the only options that satisfy the needs of the investors. It is, however, important to understand that going public actually limits the exit options that an entrepreneur has and definitely defines the exit strategy.[2] It may be possible to structure an IPO deal that will pay the entrepreneur a portion of the funds received when the offering is sold; however, the restricted nature of **"insider"** stock—that is, stock that does not flow through the public offering—is generally subject to a **lock-up period,** which means that for a period of time (typically 180 days) following the date of the IPO, major insiders such as founders and investors, are prohibited from selling any shares in the market. When insiders immediately sell their stock, it sends a negative signal to new shareholders who have just committed to its growth. (A more detailed discussion of IPOs can be found in Chapter 18.)

Selling the Business

Small business owners who want to leave the business behind generally sell it outright. The advantage of selling the business is that, unless the entrepreneur agrees to carry back debt for the new owner, he or she will receive his or her investment and capital gains in the sale. The entrepreneur will also be free to move on to other ventures. The ultimate goals of the sales transaction are to maximize the value of the entrepreneur's business and create a liquidity event so that the entrepreneur can exit. For most entrepreneurs, selling a business that they created from scratch is much more than a financial event; it is a very emotional event, and unless it is done very carefully with this in mind, the entrepreneur may regret the action later on. Most entrepreneurs have a difficult time making the decision to sell but soon realize that, if they want to move on, they must sell their largest asset to do so.

Deciding to sell at least three years prior to the sale makes it easier to increase the business's value prior to the sale. For example, to command a higher price, it would be important to show increasing earnings. This can be accomplished by (1) increasing advertising or adding a new salesperson to increase sales or (2) finding ways to reduce expenses. It is also a good idea to sell any unproductive assets or inventory that have lost value because the buyer does not have to purchase these in the sale and they may even discourage a higher valuation. If the business includes real estate, it might be wise to put the real estate under different ownership, such as a limited partnership or limited liability corporation (LLC), so that it does not transfer with the business. Then the company holding the real estate can lease it back to the business. The small business owner will also want to replace outdated equipment and generally spruce up the business facilities. Finally, any legal claims against the business should be cleared up because these will be sure to cause problems during the sale of the business.

To ease the difficulty that small business owners have when parting with their businesses, it is important to find a buyer who understands and wishes to maintain the culture and values of the business. Bringing aboard a new owner who has entirely different values would definitely create a culture shock for employees who were accustomed to the established culture. Besides, the entrepreneur's name will be associated with the business long after it has been sold, so holding to the values that customers expect will also be critical to a successful transition.

Selling a business is a complex process involving value appraisal, prospect acquisition, negotiation, and contracts (Figure 20.1). Some small business owners attempt

FIGURE 20.1 Using a Sale as a Harvest Strategy

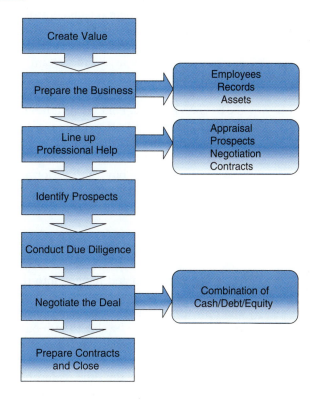

to navigate this maze themselves, which may not always be wise. The front end of the process can be doable if the seller has a realistic view of the value of the company based on market comparables, a list of likely prospects to consider, and the time to make it happen. If this is not the case, however, it is probably wiser for the seller to seek the assistance of professional business brokers, investment bankers, and appraisers. Business brokers tend to work with smaller businesses, whereas investment bankers work the larger, more complex deals.[3]

Sellers need to be aware of the tax consequences of a sale. It used to be that if a seller was paid in installments over time, he or she would be taxed only on the portion of the sale received. Under new tax laws for businesses using the accrual accounting method (which is most businesses), the full tax bill must be paid in the year the sale closes. One way to avoid this is by accepting stock rather than cash; however, there is a risk that the stock price will go down and the seller will ultimately realize less than the original price.

Cashing Out but Staying In

There are several ways to remove the entrepreneur's investment in whole or in part from the business while allowing the entrepreneur to remain involved in some way. One is by selling stock to other shareholders in the company at current market rates, assuming that the shareholders' agreement permits this.

Entrepreneurs who want to take money out of the company but leave control in the hands of the new owner often restructure the business by splitting the company in two. The entrepreneur retains control of the company that holds all the assets, such as plant and equipment, while the new owner owns and manages the operations of the business and leases the assets from the entrepreneur/parent. In this way, the entrepreneur derives an income stream off the leases as well as the appreciated value of the business.

Another possibility is a phased sale in which the small business owner decides to sell the business in stages. For example, the sale might occur in two stages. In the first stage, the entrepreneur sells off a portion of the business but retains control of operations until the company has reached an agreed-upon milestone. In the second stage, the entrepreneur sells the remaining portion to the buyer. In this way, the entrepreneur can make certain that the buyer will perform as expected.

Merging

A **merger** of one company with another is a cross between a sale and a partnership. The most common type of merger is a forward merger in which the entrepreneur's company is acquired and merged into the buyer's company so that it effectively disappears. In a **reverse merger,** by contrast, the buyer's company merges into the seller's and only the acquired company remains.[4] Depending on how the deal is structured, the entrepreneur may be able to cash out some of his or her holdings and stay on in a paid-management capacity. Or the entrepreneur may negotiate to sit on the board of directors of the other company. When considering the merger route, it is important to look very carefully at the other company to make sure that the two companies have similar goals, operations, and cultures. Trying to merge two completely different companies is a strategy bound for failure. Furthermore, it is also important that the companies be located fairly close to each other to permit effective management and that the purchasing company be part of a growth industry.

Selling to Employees

A company with more than twenty-five employees, an annual payroll of at least $500,000, and revenues of at least $5 million may be a candidate for an **employee stock ownership plan** (ESOP). This approach lets the entrepreneur cash out of the company but remain in control. Many entrepreneurs who believe that employees should become owners in the company have chosen this route. In essence, ESOPs are tax-qualified pension plans governed by the **Employee Retirement Income Security Act** and IRS regulations. Basically an ESOP works as follows:

1. An ESOP trust fund is established, and new or existing shares of stock are placed in it. A company can also elect to take out a bank loan of up to 3.5 times cash flow to buy stock and a minority interest in the company of at least 30 percent so that any cash the owners receive from the ESOP is not taxed if they reinvest it in U.S. stocks or bonds.

2. The company then makes tax-deductible contributions to the trust of up to 25 percent of the payroll to repay any bank debt. Both principal and interest used to repay the bank loan can be deducted, which makes an ESOP an attractive vehicle to fund growth.

FIGURE 20.2 Leveraged ESOP

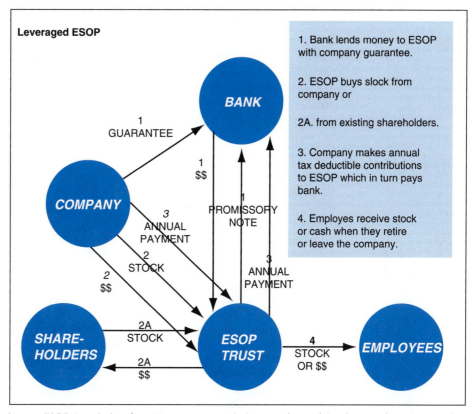

Source: ESOP Association, http://www.esopassociation.org/about/about_leveraged.asp (accessed November 19, 2005). "Leveraged ESOP" graphic copyright, the ESOP Association. Reprinted by permission.

In 1995 Jan Van Den Top formed an ESOP to sell his company, Superior Plumbing and Heating in Anchorage, Alaska, to his 100 employees. He contributed 42 percent of his shares as retirement perks and then eventually sold the remainder of his shares to the ESOP but stayed on as trustee with voting rights for all the shares.[5] The ESOP process can take several years, or at least as long as it takes to repay the bank loan if one was used. See Figure 20.2 for a diagram of a leveraged ESOP.

ESOPs have many advantages, but they are expensive to set up and maintain. A private company will have to repurchase the stock of any employees who leave the company. The biggest implication of an ESOP is that the company must now share much more information with its employees than it may have done previously.

SUCCESSION PLANNING

Succession planning is not the domain of big business exclusively. Consider the facts. As of 2000, more than 80 percent of the 25 million businesses in the United States are closely held sole proprietorships, partnerships, or LLCs,[6] and 90 percent of those are privately owned.[7] According to the Small Business Administration (SBA), only three out of ten small businesses survive through the second generation, and about a third of all businesses have no designated successor. So it would seem that planning for the successful survival of a business is a critical task that must be accomplished.

Succession is a process, not an event. Entrepreneurs don't decide to retire at 5:00 on Friday and have their partner or someone else assume the leadership on Monday. It is not that easy. Planning to have someone succeed the entrepreneur in the business is as important as any other component of business planning. Over time the business will have developed a cadre of loyal employees who have worked their way up in terms of responsibility and authority. They are the equivalent of the next generation in a family business and should be considered as candidates to succeed the owner.

Start with a Vision

Any effective succession plan begins with the owner's vision, values, goals, and an understanding of how these relate to the future of the company as well as the owner's goals for the next stage of his or her life. Does the owner want to gradually exit the business over time or perhaps sell the business outright with no continuing ties? What does the owner wants to do after exiting the business? By taking the time to identify possible exit goals, the small business owner has a better chance of aligning the harvest strategy with those goals.

Value the Business

Once the goals relative to succession and exit are established, it is time to determine the value of the business and its readiness for transfer of ownership. This is no easy task, so valuing a private enterprise usually involves bringing in a professional appraiser. (The topic of valuation is covered in more detail in Chapter 4.) Readiness refers to whether the business is in a good position to be sold or transferred or whether actions must be taken to rectify any weaknesses and increase the value.[8]

Choosing the Successor

The strategy for choosing a successor does not have to be detailed, but it should lead to some broad policies to guide the decision-making process when the time comes. These broad policies may include

- An equitable way to determine whether outside talent must be brought in to compensate for a lack of appropriate skills on the part of insiders.
- A probationary period for insiders to give them a chance to prove they are capable of doing the job.
- A set of criteria that applies to both insiders and outsiders.
- A plan for compensation at fair market value.

Internal candidates wishing to succeed the owner must be able to demonstrate their understanding of the business, its operations, and its financials; therefore, all candidates, including family members, should write a job description and match their skills and experiences with the duties of the owner. An employee who may be assuming the role of CEO should go through a period of apprenticeship before taking on the position fully. Learning the ropes from the founder/owner during an extended

Taking Success for Granted

When a company doesn't understand what makes it successful, it risks not being able to sustain that success. Rothschild, Unterberg, Towbin was a successful investment banking company that was known for the research that it conducted to solve problems. However, when the president determined that the company needed to cut costs, he unwisely decided to cut research, not understanding how much it contributed to the bottom line. Soon sales disappeared and the company eventually went out of business.

Online toy seller eToys suffered from the arrogance of the dot-com era, believing that because it was the first to sell toys online, bricks-and-mortar companies like Toys 'R Us would never be able to catch up. Unfortunately, eToys did not understand the toy industry in which it did business; neither did it understand that the Internet was really not a different way of doing business; it was simply a different distribution channel. Doing business on the Internet still required fulfillment expertise and the ability to satisfy the customer. As it headed down the road to bankruptcy, eToys completely ignored the advantages that Toys 'R Us had: its established customers, years of experience in the industry, and size that allowed it to purchase at highly competitive prices.

Lessons Learned: *Respect your competitors and know why your company is successful.*

period prior to the succession will give the new CEO a jumpstart and make the transition smoother.

Many of the most successful companies promote from within, but it is important to constantly look for fresh points of view in other important positions in the company. This will prevent the company from becoming so entrenched in tradition that it cannot change quickly to meet the demands of the marketplace.

Prepare Stakeholders for Succession

Preparing employees for succession is important, and the process should begin with regular meetings several months in advance of succession so that employees are kept abreast of what is happening in the business. Generally, a transition period in which the owner stays on and gradually phases out provides for a smoother change process.

LIQUIDATION

The business life cycle includes birth, growth, maturity, and eventually death if the business owner is unable to manage a downturn in sales, find new sources of revenue, pay its obligations, or secure sufficient capital to float the business until economic conditions improved. In general, the immediate precipitating cause of business closure is poor management, whether it is of cash flow, debt, inventory, receivables, or a myriad of other factors.

Each year, about a half a million small businesses close down, or **liquidate,** according to the SBA. When Maria Martz saw her 2004 tax return with business losses for the second year in a row, she decided it was time to close the doors on her Colorado-based gift-basket business. But she was tempted more than once to try to resurrect it. "You get phone calls afterward from people asking, 'How come you're not in business anymore?' and one side of me wanted to say, 'OK, I'll do your basket for you.'" But then her better judgment took over, and she realized it was finished.[9] Liquidation is certainly not the exit strategy that entrepreneurs would plan for or purposely choose if they could avoid it. There are two forms of liquidation: (1) when there is some marketable value in the business and (2) when the business can no longer survive.

Many businesses, particularly sole proprietorships such as services and small retail operations, cannot effectively exist without the owner. The products and services provided derive directly from the expertise of the owner and are not easily passed on to others. Generally, in these types of businesses, when an entrepreneur liquidates, a buyer will purchase only inventory and assets such as equipment and supplies or perhaps a customer list.

However, when the business can no longer generate enough cash flow to meet its obligations, the only solution may be to liquidate the assets and discharge the debts through a **Chapter 7 bankruptcy** proceeding. The goal of this type of liquidation is to reduce the assets of the business to cash and distribute that cash to the creditors. Any surplus funds remaining after claimants have been paid go to the business owner. In a Chapter 7 filing, the court appoints a trustee to manage the disposition of the business.

Bankruptcy should always be considered a last resort. If the business is showing signs of trouble that could lead to failure, the entrepreneur should immediately consult a specialist in turnarounds and have an accountant audit the books to see if the company might qualify for **Chapter 11 reorganization,** which would allow it to continue to do business while the entrepreneur works out a plan to repay creditors. For small businesses, at least one-half of the creditors affected by the plan and who represent at least two-thirds of the total dollar amount must approve the plan. Because the ramifications of bankruptcy remain on the entrepreneur's personal credit history for a long time in the case of sole proprietorships, partnerships, or instances where the owner has used personal guarantees, the decision should not be made without careful consideration of all alternative courses.

The following are some tips that will help entrepreneurs avoid a situation that could result in bankruptcy:

1. Do not rely on only one customer for the majority of revenues.
2. Keep overhead expenses to a minimum.
3. Remain as liquid as possible.
4. Keep financial advisers apprised of the current condition of the company so that there are no surprises and so that they can offer advice before it is too late.

Harvesting the wealth of a successful business venture is one of the great rewards of entrepreneurship. But it is the journey to the harvest that will determine how successful the harvest is. Planning early in the life of a business for growth and an eventual harvest will go a long way toward ensuring that the business owner reaches his or her goals.

ISSUES FOR REVIEW AND DISCUSSION

1. Why is it important for entrepreneurs to think about a harvest, or exit, strategy early in the development of their business?

2. What are the advantages and disadvantages of selling the business versus cashing out but staying in the business?

3. Under what conditions does it make sense to use a public offering as a harvest strategy?

4. What choices does an entrepreneur have when the business can no longer succeed financially?

5. Why is it important to plan for succession in a nonfamily business?

EXPERIENCING ENTREPRENEURSHIP

1. Schedule a meeting with a company that has recently gone through either a merger or a public offering. What challenges did it bring that the owner was unprepared for? What would the owner do differently?

2. Interview the owner of a business about his or her succession plan. Will he or she consider going outside the business to find a successor? Why or why not?

How Greed Can Take a Company from Success to Failure

On November 30, 2001, Gerald Stevens, the leader in the $15-billion floral industry in the United States closed its doors and left hundreds of small businesses wounded or completely destroyed. "If there was even the smallest indication that this idea would fail, I never would have done it," claims Eric Luoma, a florist who sold to Gerald Stevens and learned some hard lessons from the failure. Greg Royer, who had also been seduced into selling his floral shop to Gerald Stevens during a massive roll-up of the mom-and-pop industry, is much smarter since the bankruptcy was declared. "I learned a lot about myself," he reports. "I learned that the best people in big business aren't any smarter or more devoted than the best people in small business. It's just a different path."

The Founding of Gerald Stevens

It seemed like a slam-dunk opportunity for the founding team that had taken Blockbuster from a single store in 1985 to 3,700 stores and a sale to Viacom for $8.4 billion in 1994. Gerald R. Geddis, Blockbuster's chief operating officer, Albert J. Detz, its chief financial officer, and Adam D. Phillips, the chief administrative officer saw an opportunity to repeat their video-industry success in the floral industry, which at the time was very fragmented and ripe for a consolidation play. In September 1998, the trio invited ten florists to the Hyatt Regency in Fort Lauderdale to attend what they called a "founders' meeting." They wined and dined the business owners who had been handpicked for their performance in specific areas. John Partridge had been the president of FTD, the national floral referral network; Greg Royer's floral business was known for its productivity; and Tom Boesen of Des Moines, Iowa, was known for his customer service. Each one of the ten was good at something. During the two days in Florida, Geddis and his partners gave something akin to a timeshare pitch and created an ambiance of excitement about the wealth that would be created from these florists joining forces under the umbrella name of Gerald Stevens. What they were offering the florists was a big cash buyout and a chance at the public markets of the late 1990s. For the florists, who never thought they could realize this kind of money, it was a dream come true. For Royer, who ran a family business of sixteen flower shops in Lebanon, Pennsylvania, doing $17 million a year in sales, it was an opportunity to move to the next level. His enthusiasm for the rollup was rewarded when he was made senior vice president of operations at the Gerald Stevens corporate headquarters in Fort Lauderdale where his job was to find more independent florists for the roll-up.

In a moment of complete candor, the Blockbuster trio readily admitted that they knew nothing about the floral industry, but they did know how to relieve the florists of all the management hassles of the business and create efficiencies through volume purchasing and marketing, something they had successfully accomplished in the video industry.

The Floral Industry

At the time, the multibillion-dollar floral industry was dominated by retail florist shops; over 27,000 shops were each doing an annual average of $209,182 in sales. However, the industry was facing stiff competition from supermarkets and retail nurseries who were beefing up their floral departments. Women were the predominant purchasers of cut flowers, making up nearly 81 percent of all floral sales. Calendar events accounted for only about 15 percent of overall sales, and wire orders accounted for about 20 percent of sales. Wire services like Florist Transworld Delivery (FDT) and Teleflora provide florists with advertising and promotion materials and sent customers to florists that would not normally have access to them. Technology had made it easier for florists to communicate, but it had also increased the level of competition from traditional and nontraditional florists, including those that sold via the Internet. FTD had been the industry leader for many years with about 60 to 70 percent of the wired market. As the first floral sales organization online, its sales increased dramatically with the launch of its website.

In the early 1990s, other countries began attempting to gain more of the U.S. market by establishing retail stores, stocking them with exports, and generally driving prices down. By the mid 1990s, imports of Latin American roses accounted for 40 percent of the U.S. market.

The Beginning of the End

By April 1999, Gerald Stevens had finally acquired enough florists to realize its vision, and it went public at $15 a share through a reverse merger with a NASDAQ-listed company called Florafax. In a reverse merger, a new company merges with an existing public company and can then do business as the listed company. The market favored the deal, and Florafax's stock went from $10 a share to $20. During the months that followed, Gerald Stevens grew rapidly. It acquired National Flora and Internet Services, LP, which was the parent of the oldest e-commerce company in the floral industry. This acquisition increased Gerald Stevens's order rate by 60 percent in the first six weeks of 1999 over the same period in 1998. The florists who were part of the Gerald Stevens chain were happy; they were learning new management skills and buying at volume prices. Gerald Stevens even purchased its own floral importer, AGA Flowers, and began buying directly from growers.

In July 1999, the company had 131 stores and had purchased Calyx & Corolla, a direct-from-growers catalog company. Geddis was exuberant: "We are now building on a solid foundation in each segment of the floral industry that touches the consumer."

What Geddes did not understand but soon discovered was how difficult it was to integrate the acquired companies into the parent company, especially when each had its own culture and way of doing things. As Royer noted at the time, "I'm not sure the company ever understood that there are different niches within the industry." In other words, Geddes figured that a florist is a florist, which was far from the truth. Some florists in the chain were unhappy with the quality of the flowers that they were receiving from Gerald Stevens's wholesaler, but they were told in no uncertain terms that they must buy from that company, even if they were losing customers. The standardized floral arrangements pictured in the Gerald Stevens brochures actually served to lower the average price of a transaction because, instead of spending $75 to $100 on an arrangement as was typical for floral events like Mother's Day, cus-

tomers would choose the $45 arrangement pictured in the brochure.

The biggest blow for the member florists was when Gerald Stevens insisted that, to save money, they had to pull out of their local Chambers of Commerce and stop donating flowers for charitable events. This meant that florists were no longer supporting their communities, and the communities reacted by not buying from them. Complaints from customers came more frequently, and customer satisfaction was in a downward spiral.

Because the Gerald Stevens management team had made promises to shareholders about the level of growth it would achieve, it was compelled to continue buying any company it could until it owned more than 150 companies with 300 retail locations in addition to a cataloger, four call centers, an importer, and numerous websites. By the spring of 2000, Gerald Stevens was in a nosedive from which it would not recover. In November, its stock price was so low that it was delisted from the NASDAQ and moved to the OTC (over-the-counter) Bulletin Board. Then came the layoffs; in April 2001, the company filed for Chapter 11 protection. Its stock was now at 9 cents. On November 30, 2001, Gerald Stevens ceased operations, sending nearly half of its acquisitions into liquidation. About half of the florists were able to buy their companies back and build them up again, this time from a much wiser perspective.

Advising the Entrepreneur

1. Entrepreneurs sometimes fail after achieving a major success. What would you advise an entrepreneur to think about to avoid such a failure?

2. What were the proximate causes to the failure of Gerald Stevens? Could they have been avoided?

Sources: F. Fenn, "The Sweet Smell of Excess," *Inc.* (February 2003), www.inc.com; SIC 5992 Florists, *Industry Snapshot,* www.referenceforbusiness.com (accessed November 19, 2005); *South Florida Business Journal/American City Business Journals,* www.bizjournals.com (accessed December 5, 2005).

Notes

CHAPTER 1

1. J. Case, "The Gazelle Theory," *Inc.* (May 2001), www.inc.com.
2. W. J. Dennis Jr., "The Public Reviews Small Business," National Federation of Independent Businesses (August 2004).
3. C. Gray, "Formality, Intentionality, and Planning: Features of Successful Entrepreneurial SMEs in the Future?" Paper presented at the ICSB World Conference, Brisbane, Australia, June 2000.
4. J. Martin J. and D. Birch, "Slump, What Slump? *Fortune Small Business* (December 2002), http://www.fortune.com/fortune/smallbusiness/.
5. Ibid.
6. T. J. Stanley and W. D. Danko, *The Millionaire Next Door: The Surprising Secrets of American's Wealthy* (Athens, GA: Longstreet Press, 1996).
7. B. D. Philips, "Small Business Problems and Priorities," National Federation of Independent Businesses (June 2004).
8. W. C. Dunkelberg and H. Wade, *NFIB Small Business Economic Trends* (June 2005), www.nfib.com.
9. B. Headd, "Redefining Business Success: Distinguishing Between Closure and Failure," Small Business Administration Office of Advocacy (2003), www.sba.gov.
10. U.S. Small Business Administration, *The State of Small Business: A Report to the President,* (Washington, DC: Government Printing Office, 1997). Data for year 10 are estimated by the SBA.
11. R. H. Brockhaus, "Risk-Taking Propensity of Entrepreneurs," *Academy of Management Journal* 23 (1985): 509–520; P. F. Drucker, *Innovation and Entrepreneurship* (New York: Harper and Row, 1985).
12. X. Wu and A. M. Knott, "Entrepreneurial Risk and Market Entry," Small Business Research Summary No.249, SBA Office of Advocacy (Washington, DC: Government Printing Office, 2005).
13. D. B. Greenberger and D. L. Sexton, "An Interactive Model of New Venture Initiation," *Journal of Small Business Management* 26 (1988): 1–7.
14. E. B. Roberts, "Influences upon Performance of New Technical Enterprises," in A. Cooper and J. Komives, eds., *Technical Entrepreneurship: A Symposium* (Milwaukee: Center for Venture Management, 1972), 126–149; M. P. Rice, *Growing New Ventures, Creating New Jobs: Principles and Practices of Successful Business Incubation* (Westport, CT: Quorum, 1995).
15. G. L. S. Shackle, *Uncertainty in Economics* (Cambridge, MA: Cambridge University Press, 1955).
16. W. B. Gartner, "What Are We Talking about When We Talk about Entrepreneurship?" *Journal of Business Venturing* 5 (1990): 15–28.
17. S. Kaish and B. Gilad, "Characteristics of Opportunities Search of Entrepreneurs versus Executives: Sources, Interest, General Alertness," *Journal of Business Venturing* 6 (1991): 45–61.
18. I. M. Kirzner, *Competition and Entrepreneurship* (Chicago: University of Chicago Press, 1973).
19. Kaish and Gilad, p. 59.
20. T. Richman, "Creators of the New Economy," in "The State of Small Business," Special Edition, *Inc.,* (May 1997): 48.
21. "Capturing the Impact: Women-Owned Businesses in the United States," Center for Women's Business Research (2004), http://www.nfwbo.org/mediacenter/nationalstate trends/capturingtheimpact.htm.
22. H. E. Buttner and D. P. Moore, "Women's Organizational Exodus to Entrepreneurship: Self-Reported Motivations and Correlates with Success," *Journal of Small Business Management* 35(1) (1997): 34–36.
23. *2000 Statistical Abstract of the United States* (Washington, DC: U.S. Department of Commerce, Bureau of the Census, 2005), www.census.gov/cds/mwb.
24. Advocacy publications: "Women in Business, 2001"; "Dynamics of Women-Operated Sole Proprietorships, 1990–1998"; "Minorities in Business, 2001"; veteran self-employment data from a special tabulation of the Current Population Survey.
25. J. Pitta, "Silicon Valley South," *Forbes* (November 16, 1998): 214–216.
26. M. Henricks, "Why the Over-50 Crowd Prefers Entrepreneurship," *Wall Street Journal Startup Journal* (2005), www.startupjournal.com.
27. Ibid.; http://www.ourladyofweightloss.com/index.asp.
28. M. Henricks, "These Entrepreneurs Find Comfort at Home," *Wall Street Journal Startup Journal* (2005), www.startupjournal.com.
29. D. Jefferson, "He's the Boss," *CNN Money,* http://cnn money.

CHAPTER 2

1. J. C. Collins and W. C. Lazier, *Beyond Entrepreneurship: Turning Your Business into an Enduring Great Company.* (Englewood Cliffs, NJ: Prentice Hall, 1992).
2. J. C. Collins and J. I. Porras, *Built to Last: Successful Habits of Visionary Companies* (New York: HarperBusiness, 1994).
3. Ibid., 7.
4. A. Zaleznik, "The Leadership Gap," *Academy of Management Executive* 4(1) (1990): 7–22.
5. L. W. Fernald, G. T. Solomon, and A. Tarabishy, "A New Paradigm: Entrepreneurial Leadership," *Southern Business Review* 30(2) (2005): 1.
6. Collins and Lazier, *Beyond Entrepreneurship.*
7. Collins and Porras, *Built to Last.*

8. A portion of the full credo written by R. W. Johnson Jr. in 1943. In F. J. Aguilar and A. Bhambri, "Johnson & Johnson (A)," Harvard Business School Case No. 384–053, p. 4.

9. L. Smircich, "Concepts of Culture and Organizational Analysis," *Administrative Science Quarterly* 28 (1983): 339–358.

10. S. Davis, *Managing Corporate Culture* (Cambridge, MA: Ballinger, 1984).

11. T. Deal and A. Kennedy, *Corporate Cultures: The Rites and Rituals of Corporate Life* (Reading, MA: Addison-Wesley, 1982).

12. D. Ulrich and D. Kale, *Organizational Capability: Competing from the Inside Out* (New York: Wiley, 1990).

13. D. Snow, "Cultural Artifacts," *Leadership Excellence,* 22(5) (2005): 15.

14. M. Kaptein and J. Wempe, "Twelve Gordian Knots When Developing an Organizational Code Of Ethics," *Journal of Business Ethics* 17(8): 853–869.

15. L. D. Black and C. E. J. Hartel, "The Five Capabilities of Socially Responsible Companies," *Journal of Public Affairs* 4(2) (2004): 125–144.

16. J. G. Dees, H. J. Emerson, and P. Economy, *Enterprising Nonprofits: A Toolkit for Social Entrepreneurs* (New York: Wiley, 2001).

17. Ibid.

18. W. H. Starbuck, "Organizations and Their Environments," in M. D. Dunnette, ed., *Handbook of Industrial and Organization Psychology* (Chicago: Rand McNally, 1976). These are conceptually identical to those proposed by J. Pfeffer and G. R. Salancik "A Social Information Processing Approach to Job Attitudes and Task Design," *Administrative Science Quarterly,* 23(2) (1978): 224; H. Mintzberg, *The Structuring of Organizations* (Englewood Cliffs, NJ: Prentice-Hall, 1979).

19. J. R. Galbraith, *Designing Complex Organizations* (Reading, MA: Addison-Wesley, 1973).

20. W. M. Evan, "The Organizational Set: Toward a Theory of Interorganizational Relationships," in J. D. Thompson, ed., *Approaches to Organizational Design* (Pittsburgh: University of Pittsburgh Press, 1966).

21. J. M. Pennings, "The Relevance of the Structural-Contingency Model for Organizational Effectiveness," *Administrative Science Quarterly* 20 (1975): 393–410; J. D. Thompson, *Organizations in Action* (New York: McGraw-Hill, 1967).

22. M. Porter, *Competitive Strategy* (New York: Free Press, 1980).

23. A. P. Chandler, *Strategy and Structure* (Cambridge, MA: MIT Press, 1962); J. Bain, *Industrial Organizations* (New York: Wiley, 1959); I. Ansoff, *Corporate Strategy* (New York: McGraw-Hill, 1965).

24. K. Andrews, *The Concept of Corporate Strategy* (Homewood, IL: Irwin, 1971).

25. D. Lewin and P. D. Sherer, "Does Strategic Choice Explain Senior Executives' Preferences on Employee Voice and Representation?" in B. F. Kaufman and M. M. Kleiner, eds., *Employee Representation* (Madison, WI: Industrial Relations Research Association, 1993), 235–263.

26. P. R. Lawrence and J. W. Lorsch, *Organization and Environment: Managing Differentiation and Integration* (Boston:

Harvard University, Graduate School of Business Administration, 1967).

27. A. I. Goldberg, G. Cohen, and A. Fiegenbaum, "Reputation Building: Small Business Strategies for Successful Venture Development," *Journal of Small Business Management,* 41(2) (2003): 168–186.

28. Ibid.

29. A. Fiegenbaum, S. Hart, and D. Schendel, "Strategic Reference Point Theory," *Strategic Management Journal* 17(3) (1996): 219–235.

30. P. Holm, "The Dynamics of Institutionalization: Transformation Processes in Norwegian Fisheries," *Administrative Science Quarterly* 40(3) (1995): 342–398.

31. N. Karagozoglu and M. Lindell, "Internationalization of Small and Medium-Sized Technology-Based Firms: An Exploratory Study," *Journal of Small Business Management* 36(1) (1998): 44–59.

32. A. J. Daboub, "Strategic Alliances, Network Organizations, and Ethical Responsibility," *S.A.M. Advanced Management Journal* 67(4) (2002): 40–48.

33. A. Bhide and H. H. Stevenson, "Attracting Stakeholders," in W. A. Sahlman and H. H. Stevenson, eds., *The Entrepreneurial Venture* (Boston: Harvard Business School Publications, 1992).

34. C. Ciborra, "Alliances as Learning Experiments: Cooperation, Competition and Change in High-Tech Industries," in L. K. Mytelka, ed., *Strategic Partnerships and the World Economy* (London: Printer, 1991), 51–77.

35. M. J. Dowling, W. D. Roering, B. A. Carlin, and J. Wisnieski, "Multifaceted Relationships Under Coopetition: Description and Theory," *Journal of Management Inquiry* 5(2) (1996): 155–167.

36. O. E. Williamson, *Markets and Hierarchies* (New York: Free Press, 1975).

37. Daboub, "Strategic Alliances," 40–48.

38. A. Alchian and H. Demsetz, "Production, Information Costs, and Economic Organization," American Economic Review 62 (1972): 777–795.

39. M. Velasquez, "Why Ethics Matters: A Defense of Ethics in Business Organizations," *Business Ethics Quarterly* 6(2) (1996): 201.

CHAPTER 3

1. D. E. Terpstra and P. D. Olson, "Entrepreneurial Start-Up and Growth: A Classification of Problems," *Entrepreneurship, Theory and Practice* (Spring 1993): 5–20.

2. T. Siler, *Think like a Genius* (New York: Bantam Books, 1999).

3. D. Hall and D. Wecker, *Jumpstart Your Brain* (New York: Warner Books, 1995).

4. "PricewaterhouseCoopers Says Entertainment and Media Industry in Strongest Position since 2000, Will Grow 7.3 Percent Annually to $1.8 Trillion in 2009," *Pricewaterhouse-Coopers* (June 22, 2005), www.pwd.com.

5. M. E. Porter, *Competitive Strategy: Techniques for Analyzing Industries and Competitors* (New York: Free Press), 3.

6. W. H. Starbuck, "Organizations and Their Environments," in M. D. Dunnette, ed., *Handbook of Industrial and Organization Psychology* (Palo Alto, CA: Consulting Psychologists Press, 1992); J. Pfeffer and G. R. Salancik, *The*

External Control of Organizations (Stanford, CA: Stanford University Press, 2003).

7. G. A. Stevens and J. Burley, "Piloting the Rocket of Radical Innovation," *Research Technology Management* 46(2) (2003): 16–26.

8. W. B. Gartner, K. G. Shaver, E. Gatewood, and J. A. Katz, "Finding the Entrepreneur in Entrepreneurship," *Entrepreneurship: Theory and Practice* 18(3) (1994): 5–10.

9. M. D. Ensley, J. W. Carland, and J. C. Carland, "Investigating the Existence of the Lead Entrepreneur," *Journal of Small Business Management* 38(4) (2000): 59–88.

10. "Start-Ups from Scratch," *Inc.* (September 1994): 76.

11. J. Finegan, "A Bootstrapper's Primer," *Inc.* (August 1995): 49, http://www.encoreproductions.net/who/index.html (accessed July 17, 2005).

CHAPTER 4

1. J. Hyatt, "The Ultimate Start-Up List," *Inc.* (January 2001), www.inc.com.

2. J. Bennett, "A Business Broker Can Play Matchmaker," *Wall Street Journal Startup Journal,* www.startupjournal.com (accessed June 24, 2005).

3. E. O. Welles, "Best Practices: Acquiring New Companies," *Inc.* (February 2001), www.inc.com.

4. M. Grunhagen and R. A. Mittelstaedt, "Entrepreneurs or Investors: Do Multi-Unit Franchisees Have Different Philosophical Orientations?" *Journal of Small Business Management* 43(3) (2005): 207–225.

5. R. Gibson, "Franchise Fever: So You Want to Own a Franchise?" *Wall Street Journal* (December 15, 2003): R1.

6. I. Alon and D. McKee, "Towards a Macro Environmental Model of International Franchising," *Multinational Business Review* 7 (1999): 76–82; R. C. Hoffman and F. J. Preble, "Global Diffusion of Franchising: A Country Level Examination," *Multinational Business Review* (Spring 2001): 66–76.

7. M. Grunhagen and M. J. Dorsch, "Does the Franchisor Provide Value to the Franchisees? Past, Current, and Future Value Assessments of Two Franchisee Types," *Journal of Small Business Management* 41(4) (2003): 366–384.

8. P. J. Kaufmann and R. P. Dant, "Multi-Unit Franchising: Growth and Management Issues," *Journal of Business Venturing* 11(5) (1996): 343–358.

9. F. G. Mathewson and A. R. Winter, "The Economics of Franchise Contracts," *Journal of Law and Economics* 28 (1985): 503–526.

10. K. M. Eisenhardt, "Agency Theory: An Assessment and Review," *Academy of Management Review* 14 (1989): 57–74.

11. B. Elango and V. H. Fried, "Franchising Research: A Literature Review and Synthesis," *Journal of Small Business Management* 35(3) (1997): 68–81.

12. J. G. Combs and G. Castrogiovanni, "Franchisor Strategy: A Proposed Model and Empirical Test of Franchise versus Company Ownership," *Journal of Small Business Management* 31(2) (1994): 37–48.

13. T. Bates, Franchising Testimony of Dr. Timothy Bates to the U.S. House of Representatives Judiciary Committee's Subcommittee in Commercial and Administrative Law (Washington, DC: U.S. Government Printing Office,
1999); S. Shane, "Hybrid Organizational Arrangements and Their Implication for Firm Growth and Survival: A Study of New Franchisors," *Academy of Management Journal* (February 1996): 216–231.

14. J. I. Bradach, *Franchise Organizations* (Cambridge, MA: Harvard Business School Press, 1998).

15. P. Azoulay and S. Shane, "Entrepreneurs, Contracts, and the Failure of Young Firms," *Management Science* 47(3) (2001): 337–358.

16. D. E. Vaughn, *Financial Planning for the Entrepreneur* (Englewood Cliffs, NJ: Prentice-Hall, 1997), 68.

17. J. H. Schilt, "A Rational Approach to Capitalization Rates for Discounting the Future Income Stream of Closely Held Companies," *Financial Planner* (January 1982).

CHAPTER 5

1. "Families in Business," *NFIB National Small Business Poll* 2(6) (2002).

2. J. H. Strachan and M. C. Shanker, "Family Business' Contribution to the U.S. Economy: A Closer Look," *Family Business Review* 16(3) (2003): 211–219.

3. "Families in Business," 4.

4. Ibid., 6.

5. B. Montgomery and A. Sinclair, "All in the Family," *Business and Economic Review* 46(2) (2000): 3–7.

6. H. E. Aldrich and J. E. Cliff, "The Pervasive Effects of Family on Entrepreneurship: Toward a Family Embeddedness Perspective, " *Journal of Business Venturing* 18(5) (2003): 573–596.

7. R. Tagiuri and J. Davis, "Bivalent Attributes of the Family Firm," *Family Business Review* 9(2) (1996): 199–202.

8. B. Johannisson and M. Huse, "Recruiting Outside Board Members in the Small Family Business: An Ideological Challenge," *Entrepreneurship and Regional Development* 12 (2000): 353–378.

9. E. J. Zajac, "CEO Selection, Succession, Compensation and Firm Performance: A Theoretical Integration and Empirical Analysis," *Strategic Management Journal* 11 (1990): 217–230.

10. C. M. Daily and M. J. Dollinger, "An Empirical Examination of Ownership Structure in Family and Professionally Managed Firms," *Family Business Review* 5(2) (1992): 17.

11. L. Randoy and S. Goel, "The Impact of the Family and the Business on Family Business Sustainability," *Journal of Business Venturing* 18(5) (2003): 639–666.

12. I. Steier, "Variants of Agency Contracts in Family Financed Ventures as a Continuum of Familial Altruistic and Market Rationalities," *Journal of Business Venturing* 18(5) (2003): 597–618.

13. R. Donckels and E. Frohlich, "Are Family Businesses Really Different? European Experiences from STRATOS," *Family Business Review* 4(2) (1991): 149–160.

14. R. Goffee and R. Scase, "Proprietorial Control in Family Firms: Some Functions of 'Quasi-Organic' Management Systems," *Journal of Management Studies* 22(1) (1985): 53–68.

15. P. C. Rosenblatt, L. deMik, R. M. Anderson, and P. A. Johnson, *The Family in Business: Understanding and Dealing with the Challenges Entrepreneurial Families Face* (San Francisco: Jossey-Bass, 1985).

16. L. Moscetello, "The Pitcairns Want You," *Family Business* (February 1990).

17. J. L. Ward, "Growing the Family Business: Special Challenges and Best Practices," *Family Business Review* 10(4) (1997): 323–337.

18. J. B. Barney, "Firm Resources and Sustained Competitive Advantage," *Journal of Management* 17(1) (1991): 99–120.

19. R. M. Grant, "The Resource-Based Theory of Competitive Advantage: Implications for Strategy Formulation," *California Management Review* 17 (1991): 114–135.

20. I. Nonaka and H. Takeuchi, *The Knowledge-Creating Company* (New York: Oxford University Press, 1995).

21. T. G. Habberson and M. L. Williams, "A Resource-Based Framework for Assessing the Strategic Advantages of Family Firms," *Family Business Review* 12(1) (1999): 11.

22. T. M. Hubler, "Forgiveness as an Intervention in Family-Owned Business: A New Beginning," *Family Business Review* 18(2) June, 2005 (): 95.

23. T. S. Feltham, G. Feltham, and J. J. Barnett, "The Dependence of Family Businesses on a Single Decision-Maker," *Journal of Small Business Management* 43(1) (2005): 1.

24. E. Chittenden, L. Hall, and P. Hutchinson, "Small Firm Growth: Access to Capital Markets and Financial Structure: Review of Issues and an Empirical Investigation," *Small Business Economics* 8(39) (1996): 67.

25. L. Van der Heyden, C. Bondel, and R. S. Carlock, "Fair Process: Striving for Justice in Family Business," *Family Business Review* 18(1) (2005): 1.

26. Ibid., 16.

27. Feltham et al., "The Dependence o Family Businesses."

28. Ibid.

29. Ward, "Growing the Family Business."

30. D. C. Hambrick and S. Finkelstein, "Managerial Discretion: A Bridge between Polar Views of Organizations," in L. L. Cummings and B. M. Staw, eds., *Research in Organizational Behavior*, vol. 9 (Greenwich, CT: JAI Press, 1987).

31. Ibid., 82.

32. S. A. Zahra. "Entrepreneurial Risk Taking in Family Firms," *Family Business Review* 18(1) (2005): 23.

33. C. C. Graves, "Making a Success of Succession," *EntreWorld.org* (2000), www.inc.com.

34. "The Ponzis' Key Move: Creating a Family Business That Works," *Startup Nation*, www.startupnation.com (accessed June 24, 2005).

35. N. M. Jackson, "Sister Act," *National Federation of Independent Businesses* (2004), www.nfib.com.

36. Ibid.

37. K. Marshack, "More Than a Lemonade Stand: 5 Questions to Ask before Going into Business with Your Sibling," (2004), www.nfib.com.

38. R. Ward, "The Fundamentals of a Family-Business Advisory Board," *Inc.* (2000), www.inc.com.

39. J. L. Ward, *Keeping the Family Business Healthy: How to Plan for Continuing Growth, Profitability, and Family Leadership* (San Francisco: Jossey-Bass, 1987).

40. K. Allen, "Grooming a Successor," *The Edge* 2 (2005): 14.

41. G. W. Whitaker, "Classic Issues in Family Succession Planning," *Section of Real Property, Probate, and Trust Law,* *American Bar Association* (March–April 2003), www.abanet.org.

42. E. T. Stavrou, T. Kleanthous, and T. Anastasiou, "Leadership Personality and Firm Culture during Hereditary Transitions in Family Firms," *Journal of Small Business Management* 43(2) (2005): 189.

43. D. L. Murphy, "Understanding the Complexities of Private Family Firms: An Empirical Investigation," *Family Business Review* 18(2) (2005): 123.

44. M. Fox, V. Nilakant, and R. Hamilton, "Managing Succession in Family-Owned Business," *International Small Business Journal* 15 (1996): 15–25.

45. E. H. Schein, *Organizational Change and Leadership: A Dynamic View* (San Francisco: Jossey-Bass, 1985).

46. Stavrou et al., "Leadership Personality," 187.

47. S. M. Danes, V. Zuiker, R. Kean, and J. Arbuthnot, "Predictors of Family Business Tensions and Goal Achievement," *Family Business Review* 12(3) (1999): 241–252.

48. R. Trombly, "Passing the Torch," *Industrial Distribution* 90(4) (2001): 69.

49. D. Leonard and S. Sensiper, "The Role of Tacit Knowledge in Group Innovation," *California Management Review* 40 (1998): 112–132.

50. P. C. Haspeslagh and D. B. Jemison, *Managing Acquisitions: Creating Value through Corporate Renewal* (New York: Free Press, 1991).

CHAPTER 6

1. C. Christensen, *The Innovator's Dilemma* (Boston: Harvard Business School Press, 1997), 208–211.

2. W. L. Miller and L. Morris, *4th Generation R&D* (New York: Wiley, 1999), 1–4.

3. M. Gross, *Travels to the Nanoworld* (New York: Plenum, 1999), 3–5.

4. Barrett, "Nanotech as Disease Detector," *BusinessWeek Online* (June 21, 2005), www.businessweek.com.

5. H. Ibold, "Wireless Wearables," *Los Angeles Business Journal* (January 15, 2001), online version.

6. R. K. Chandy and G. J. Tellis, "The Incumbent's Curse? Incumbency, Size, and Radical Product Innovation," *Journal of Marketing* 64(3) (2000), online version.

7. L. M. Branscomb and P. E. Auerswald, *Taking Technical Risks: How Innovators, Executives and Investors Manage High-Tech Risks* (Cambridge, MA: MIT Press, 2001).

8. K. R. Allen, *Bringing New Technology to Market* (Upper Saddle River, NJ: Prentice Hall, 2003).

9. R. E. Lucas Jr., "On the Mechanics of Economic Development," *Journal of Monetary Economics* 22 (1988): 3–42.

10. P. E. Auerswald and L. M. Branscomb, "Valleys of Death and Darwinian Seas: Financing the Invention to Innovation Transition in the U.S.," *Journal of Technology Transfer* 28 (2003): 3–4.

11. R. Slaybaugh, "Investigation into the Effects of an Inventive Idea on the Success of a Firm," unpublished paper prepared for BAEP 551, Marshall School of Business, University of Southern California.

12. R. Kolasky, "A Clear View of Innovation: Mammography Goes Digital," *Report to the Advanced Technology Program, National Institute of Standards and Technology (NIST)*

(2003), http://www.ksg.harvard.edu/sed/docs/k4dev/kolasky_GEcase_2002.pdf.

13. A. Van de Ven and D. Polley, "Learning while Innovating," *Organization Science* 3(1) (1992): 92–116.

14. C. Robbins-Roth, *From Alchemy to IPO: The Business of Biotechnology* (Cambridge, MA: Perseus, 2000).

15. Ibid., 112.

16. T. Studt, "Drug Development Bottlenecks Not Cured by Technology Alone," *R&D Magazine* (January 1999): 40.

17. A. V. Kaplan, D. S. Baim, J. J. Smith, D. A. Feigal, M. Simons, D. Jeffreys, T. J. Fogarty, R. E. Kuntz, and M. B. Leon, "Medical Device Development: From Prototype to Regulatory Approval," *Circulation* 105 (2002): 1285–1290, http://circ.ahajournals.org.

18. G. A. Moore, *Crossing the Chasm* (New York: HarperBusiness, 1999).

19. W. Manfroy, "Licensing with Strategic Intent," *Les Nouvelles* (March 2000): 44–47.

20. S. M. Davila, "Rent-a-Brand," *The Advisor* (July–August 2001): 34–36.

21. W. J. Baumol, "Licensing Proprietary Technology Is a Profit Opportunity, Not a Threat," *Research-Technology Management* 42(6) (1999): 10–11.

CHAPTER 7

1. Statistics of Income Division, Internal Revenue Service, www.sba.gov/advo/stats/rbwosp_03.pdf (accessed August 25, 2005).

2. A. Y. Pennington, N. L. Torres, G. Williams, and S. Wilson, "The Real Deal," *Inc.* (September 2005): 74–80.

3. "Partnership Basics." NOLO Law for All, www.nolo.com/encyclopedia/articles/sb/buy_sell.html (accessed August 25, 2005).

4. K. Allen, *Launching New Ventures,* 4th ed. (Boston: Houghton Mifflin, 2006).

5. Rev.Rul 2004-77,2—4-31 IRB 119.

6. M. P. Altieri and W. J. Cenker, "Partnerships, LLCs, LLPs, and S Corporations," *CPA Journal* 71(10) (2002): 40–47.

CHAPTER 8

1. A. Bhide, *The Origin and Evolution of New Businesses* (New York: Oxford University Press, 2000); N. Carter, W. Gartner, P. Reynolds, "Exploring Startup Event Sequences," *Journal of Business Venturing* 11 (1996): 151–166.

2. P. Kelly and M. Hay, "The Private Investor–Entrepreneur Contractual Relationship: Understanding the Influence of Context," in E. Autio et al., eds., *Frontiers of Entrepreneurship Research* (Wellesley, MA: Babson College, 2000).

3. D. E. Gumpert, *Burn Your Business Plan! What Investors Really Want from Entrepreneurs* (Needham, MA: Lauson, 2002).

4. S. S. Singhvi, "Business Planning Practices in Small Size Companies: Survey Results," *Journal of Business Forecasting Methods and Systems* 19(2) (2000): 3–8.

5. Ibid.

6. G. Castrogiovanni, "Pre-Startup Planning and the Survival of New Small Businesses: Theoretical Linkages," *Journal of Management* 22(6) (1996): 801–822.

7. I. Ansoff, "Critique of Henry Mintzberg's 'The Design School: Reconsidering the Basic Premises of Strategic Management,'" *Strategic Management Journal* 12(6)

(1991): 449–461; E. Locke and G. Latham, *A Theory of Goal Setting and Task Performance* (Englewood Cliffs, NJ: Prentice-Hall, 1980).

8. A. C. Cooper et al., *New Business in America* (Washington, DC: NFIB Foundation, 1990).

9. F. Delmar and S. Shane, "Does Business Planning Facilitate the Development of New Ventures?" *Strategic Management Journal* 24(12) (2003): 1165.

10. C. Shrader, C. Mulford, and V. Blackburn, "Strategic and Operational Planning, Uncertainty, and Performance in Small Firms," *Journal of Small Business Management* (October 1989): 45–60.

11. Delmar and Shane, "Does Business Planning."

12. A. M. Hormozi, G. S. Sutton, R. D. McMin, and W. Lucio, "Business Plans for New or Small Businesses: Paving the Path to Success," *Management Decision* 40(7–8) (2002): 755.

13. S. R. Rich and D. E. Gumpert, "How to Write a Winning Business Plan," in W. A. Sahlman and H. H. Stevenson, eds., *The Entrepreneurial Venture* (Boston: Harvard Business School Press, 1992).

14. Kelly and Hay, "The Private Investor–Entrepreneur Contractual Relationship."

15. Z. Block and I. C. Macmillan, "Milestones for Successful Venture Planning," in W. A. Sahlman and H. H. Stevenson, eds., *The Entrepreneurial Venture* (Boston: Harvard Business School Press, 1992), 138–148.

16. R. N. Hankin, "Creating and Realizing the Value of a Business," *Entrepreneur's Byline,* EntreWorld.org, www.entreworld.org/Content/EntreByline.cfm?ColumnID=198 (accessed September 2, 2005).

17. C. M. Mason and R. T. Harrison, "Investing in Technology Ventures: What Do Business Angels Look For at the Initial Screening Stage?" in E. Autio et al., eds., *Frontiers of Entrepreneurship Research* (Wellesley, MA: Babson College, 2000), 293.

18. Per NFPA Fire Loss Report, 2003 statistics are compiled from data reported to NFPA by fire departments that responded to the 2003 National Fire Experience Survey. Civilian deaths are not included in this business plan. Property loss rates for the West were $60.2 per capita, compared to the $35–$37 range for the rest of the nation, due to the southern California wildfires.

CHAPTER 9

1. M. D. Ensley, W. Garland, and J. C. Garland, "The Effect of Entrepreneurial Team Skill Heterogeneity and Functional Diversity on New Venture Performance," *Journal of Business and Entrepreneurship* 10(1) (1998): 1–14.

2. B. Virany and M. L. Tushman, "Top Management Teams and Corporate Success in an Emerging Industry," *Journal of Business Venturing* 1 (1986): 261–274.

3. M. D. Ensley, J. W. Carland, and J. C. Carland, "Investigating the Existence of the Lead Entrepreneur," *Journal of Small Business Management* 38(4) (2000): 59–77.

4. D. A. Duchesneau and W. B. Gartner, "A Profile of New Venture Success and Failure in an Emerging Industry," *Journal of Business Venturing* 5(4) (1990): 297–312.

5. Ensley et al., "Investigating the Existence."

6. R. M. Monczka and R. J. Trent, *The Global Procurement and Supply Chain Benchmarking Initiative Pilot Module*

Analysis Report to Industry (East Lansing: Michigan State University, 1995).

7. R. Likert, *New Patterns of Management* (New York: McGraw-Hill, 1961), 162.

8. J. Zenger, E. Musselwhite, K. Hurson, and C. Perrin, *Leading Teams: Mastering the New Role* (Homewood, IL: Irwin, 1994), 14–15.

9. R. J. Trent, "Team Leadership at the 100-Foot Level," *Team Performance Management* 10(5) (2004): 94–103.

10. R. B. Reich, "Entrepreneurship Reconsidered: The Team as Hero," in W. A. Sahlman and H. H. Stevenson, eds., *The Entrepreneurial Venture* (Boston: Harvard Business School Publications, 1992).

11. A. H. Van de Ven, R. Hudson, and D. M. Schroeder, "Designing New Business Start-Ups," *Journal of Management* 10 (1984).

12. K. S. Buehler and G. Pritsch, "Running with Risk," *Inc.* (September 2003), www.usc.edu.

13. A. I. Murray, "Top Management Group Heterogeneity and Firm Performance," *Strategic Management Journal* 10 (1989): 125–141.

14. K. A. Bantel and S. E. Jackson, "Top Management and Innovations in Banking: Does the Composition of the Top Team Make a Difference?" *Strategic Management Journal* 10 (1989): 107–124.

15. J. B. Kamm, J. C. Shuman, J. A. Seeger, and A. J. Nurick, "Entrepreneurial Teams in New Venture Creation: A Research Agenda," *Entrepreneurship Theory and Practice* 14(4) (1990): 7–17.

16. "When Catastrophe Strikes," *Wells Fargo Small Business— Education* (October 5, 2005), www.wellsfargo.com/biz/education/general/catastrophe.jhtml.

17. B. S. Sridhar, D. Gudmundson, and D. Feninauer, "Cultural Assessment: Differences in Perceptions between Boards of Directors and Other Organizational Members," *S.A.M. Advanced Management Journal* 69(4) (2004): 31.

18. C. Brancato and C. Plath, *Corporate Governance Best Practices: A Blueprint for the Post Enron Era* (New York: Conference Board, 2003).

19. N. Gull, "How to Assemble a Board of Directors," *Inc.* (October 2004), www.inc.com (accessed August 25, 2005).

20. R. Ward, "Attracting Top Names to Your Advisory Board," *Inc.* (May 2000), www.inc.com (accessed August 25, 2005).

21. Sloane, J. "The Belt-Tightener," *Fortune Small Business* (October 1, 2004), http://money.cnn.com/magazines/fsb/fsb_archive/2004/10/01/8187276/.

22. M. Brockman, A. I. Gordon, et al., "Shareholders Agreements," *CPA Journal* 48 (1978): 12.

CHAPTER 10

1. J. Mintz, "Don't Think Big, and Other Hiring Tips," *Wall Street Journal Startup Journal,* www.startupjournal.com (accessed June 24, 2005).

2. G. F. Dreher and D. W. Kendall, "Organizational Staffing," in G. R. Ferris, S. D. Rosen, and D. T. Barnum, eds., *Handbook of Human Resource Management* (Cambridge, MA: Blackwell, 1995).

3. Ibid., 451.

4. "Total Rewards," *WorldatWork, The Professional Association for Compensation, Benefits and Total Rewards* (2005),

http://www.worldatwork.org/ (accessed September 17, 2005).

5. Ibid., S6.

6. R. A. Noe, J. R. Hollenbeck, B. Gerhart, and P. M. Wright, *Human Resource Management: Gaining a Competitive Advantage* (Burr Ridge, IL: Austin Press/Irwin, 1994).

7. R. L. Gomez-Mejia and D. B. Balkin, *Compensation, Organizational Strategy, and Firm Performance* (Cincinnati: South-Western, 1992).

8. J. L. Kerr, "Diversification Strategies and Managerial Rewards," *Academy of Management Journal* 28 (1985): 155–179.

9. M. L. Weitzman and D. L. Kruse. "Profit Sharing and Productivity," in A. S. Blinder, ed., *Paying for Productivity* (Washington, DC: Brookings Institution, 1990); D. L. Kruse, *Profit Sharing: Does It Make a Difference?* (Kalamazoo, MI: Upjohn Institute, 1993).

10. D. C. Jones and K. Takao, "The Scope, Nature, and Effects of Employee Stock Ownership Plans in Japan," *Industrial and Labor Relations Review* 46 (1993): 352–367.

11. R. Kurtz, "Firms Turn to Perks in Lieu of Bonus Checks," *Inc.* (December 2004): 26.

12. C. Coonradt, "The Game of Work," *Inc.* (May 1997): 117.

13. "U.S. Health Benefit Cost Rises 7.5% in 2004, Lowest Increase in Five Years," *Mercer Human Resource Consulting, New York* (November 22, 2004), www.mercerhr.com.

14. D. Montgomery, "Self-Funded Health Plans: The Risks and Rewards of Going It Alone," *Virginia Business* (March 1997), www.virginiabusiness.com.

15. M. H. LeRoy and J. M. Schultz, "The Legal Context of Human Resource Management: Conflict, Confusion, Cost, and Role-Conversion," in G. R. Ferris, S. D. Rosen, and D. T. Barnum, eds., *Handbook of Human Resource Management* (Cambridge, MA: Blackwell, 1995).

16. N. K. Napier, J. Tibau, M. Janssens, and R. C. Pilenzo, "Juggling on a High Wire: The Role of the International Human Resources Manager," in G. R. Ferris, S. D. Rosen, and D. T. Barnum, eds., *Handbook of Human Resource Management.* (Cambridge, MA: Blackwell, 1995).

CHAPTER 11

1. A. Seiger, "Note on Market Research," *Stanford Graduate School of Business Case E-165* (June 18, 2004).

2. F. Knight, *Risk, Uncertainty, and Profit* (Boston: Houghton Mifflin, 1921).

3. F. Hayek, *Studies in Philosophy, Politics, and Economics* (Chicago: University of Chicago Press, 1967), 25.

4. I. M. Kirzner, *Perception, Opportunity, and Profit: Studies in the Theory of Entrepreneurship* (Chicago: University of Chicago Press, 1979).

5. K. R. Popper, *The Open Universe: An Argument for Indeterminism* (London: Routledge, 1982).

6. D. N. Sull, "Disciplined Entrepreneurship," *MIT Sloan Management Review* (Fall 2004).

7. J. A. Hall, Bringing New Products to Market (New York: AMACOM, 1991).

8. Small World Kids Inc., Quotes and Information, Yahoo Finance, http://finance.yahoo.com/q/ks?s=SWKD.OB (accessed June 25, 2005).

9. M. Lee, "How Can I Find an Affordable Market Research Service?" Inc. (May 2001), www.inc.com (accessed June 25, 2005).

10. Seiger, "Note on Market Research."

11. Sieger, "Note on Market Research."

12. K. Allen, Launching New Ventures, 4th ed. (Boston: Houghton Mifflin, 2006).

13. Ibid.

14. Associated Press, "Entrepreneurs Finding Niche in Bear Market," ESPN Outdoors (February 11, 2004), http://espn.go.com (accessed June 25, 2005).

CHAPTER 12

1. A. Slywotzky and R. Wise, "Double-Digit Growth in No-Growth Times," *FastCompany* 69 (April 2003): 66.

2. C. S. Lee and W. Shu, "Four Models of Internet-Enabled Distribution Structures," *Information Systems Management* 22(3) (2005): 14.

3. P. Milgrom and J. Roberts, *Economics Organization and Management* (Englewood Cliffs, NJ: Prentice Hall, 1992).

4. G. A. Wyner, "Channel as Customer," *Marketing Management* 11(4) (2002): 6.

5. "Forrester Report," *Implementing Customer Heuristics* (April 2001).

6. M. Stone, M. Hobbs, and M. Khaleeli, "Multichannel Customer Management: The Benefits and Challenges," *Journal of Database Management* 10(1) (2002): 39.

7. Lee and Shu, "Four Models," 17.

8. S. Viswanathan, "Competition across Channels: Do Electronic Markets Complement or Cannibalize Traditional Retailers?" *Proceeding of International Conference on Information Systems* (2000): 513–519.

9. M. Kiang and R. Chi, "A Framework for Analyzing the Potential Benefits of Internet Marketing," *Journal of Electronic Commerce Research* 2(4) (2001): 157–163.

10. "How to Find and Work with Suppliers," *Inc.* (December 11, 2003), www.inc.com.

11. D. Campbell, "Making the Right Choice: Choosing Profitable Channel Partners," *Ivey Business Journal Online* (July–August 2004): 1.

12. L. F. Pitt, P. R. Berthon, and M. H. Morris, "Entrepreneurial Pricing: The Cinderella of Marketing Strategy," *Management Decision* 35(5) (1997): 344.

13. Ibid.

14. A. Diamantopoulos, "Pricing: Theory and Evidence—A Literature Review," in M. J. Baker, ed., *Perspectives on Marketing Management* (Chichester, England: Wiley, 1991).

15. B. J. Coe, "Strategy in Retreat: Pricing Drops Out," *Journal of Business and Industry Marketing* 5(1) (1990): 5–25.

16. P. M. Noble and T. S. Gruca, "Industrial Pricing: Theory and Managerial Practice," *Marketing Science* 18(3) (1999): 438.

17. J. P. Guiltinan, P. W. Gordon, and T. J. Madden, *Marketing Management: Strategies and Programs,* 6th ed. (New York: McGraw-Hill, 1997).

18. G. J. Tellis, "Beyond the Many Faces of Pricing," *Journal of Marketing* 50 (1986): 146–160.

19. Guiltinan et al., *Marketing Management.*

CHAPTER 13

1. *McWilliams Wines, Pty. Ltd. v. McDonald's System of Australia, Pty. Ltd.* (1980).

2. J. L. Zaichowsky, *Defending Your Brand Against Imitation* (Westport, CT: Quorum Books, 1994).

3. "Understanding Your Customers through Their Own Stories," *CRMToday,* www.crm2day.com (accessed October 3, 2005).

4. http://www.jimnovo.com/CRM-Lifecycles.htm.

5. D. Peppers and M. Rogers, *The One to One Future: Building Relationships One Customer at a Time* (New York: Currency/Doubleday, 1993).

6. M. Stewart, "You've Got Permission, Now Be Relevant: How to Use Segmentation, Targeting, and Personalization to Deliver Relevant Email," *CRM Today* (2005), www.crm2day.com/crm.

7. T. Hayward, "Opinion: Turning Customers Back into People," *InsightExec* (September 26, 2005), www.insightexec.com.

8. Zane's Cycles, www.zanes.com; D. Fenn, "Leader of the Pack," *Inc.* (February 1996).

9. L. Liswood, *Serving Them Right* (New York: HarperBusiness, 1990), 93.

10. S. Greco, "Selling the Superstores," *Inc.* (July 2005): 55–61.

11. J. Hyatt, "Hot Commodity," *Inc.* (February 1996): 50–61.

12. "Profits of U.S. Exporting Companies 2002–2003," www.census.gov/foreign-trade (accessed June 25, 2005).

13. D. Bruno, "Marinades Make the World Taste Better: Flavorful Rural Exports," *Export America Success Stories* (October 7, 2005), www.export.gov/exportamerica/successstories.

14. D. F. Lamont, *Global Marketing* (Cambridge, MA: Blackwell, 1996).

15. R. L. Curle, "Expanding Internationally: Grow as You Go," *Inc.* (May 1998), www.inc.com.

CHAPTER 14

1. S. C. Wheelwright and B. Clark, *Revolutionizing Product Development* (New York: Free Press, 1992).

CHAPTER 15

1. A. R. Shores, *Reengineering the Factory: A Primer for World-Class Manufacturing* (Milwaukee: ASQC Quality Press, 1994).

2. S. C. Jones, T. L. Knotts, and K. L. Brown, "Selected Quality Practices of Small Manufacturers," *Quality Management Journal* 12(1) (2005): 41.

3. J. Heizer and B. Render, *Operations Management,* 6th ed. (Upper Saddle River, NJ: Prentice Hall, 2001).

4. P. T. Ward, J. K. McCreery, P. Ritzman, and D. Sharma, "Competitive Priorities in Operations Management," *Decision Sciences* 29 (1998): 1035–1046.

5. J. M. Juran, *Juran on Planning for Quality* (New York: Free Press, 1988), 4–5.

6. T. Ohno, *Toyota Production System* (Cambridge, MA: Productivity Press, 1988), 25–26.

7. S. M. Yusof and E. M. Aspinwall, "Critical Success Factors in Small and Medium Enterprises: Survey Results," *Total Quality Management* 11 (2000): 448–459.

8. S. Rahman, "Total Quality Management Practices and Business Outcome: Evidence from Small and Medium

Enterprises in Western Australia," *Total Quality Management* 12 (2001): 201–210.

9. D. Blacharski, "Outsourcing Fulfillment," *E-Business* (July 6, 2001), www.entrepreneur.com.

10. "Inventory Control," *Management,* www.entrepreneur.com (accessed October 20, 2005).

11. "Tracking Inventory," *Management,* www.entrepreneur.com (accessed October 21, 2005).

CHAPTER 16

1. S. Venkataraman, "The Distinctive Domain of Entrepreneurship Research," *Advances in Entrepreneurship Research: Firm Emergence and Growth* 3 (1997): 119–138; P. Gompers, "An Examination of Convertible Securities in Venture Capital Investments," Working Paper, Harvard University, 1997.

2. L. Fox, "Navigating the New Funding Landscape," *Chief Executive* (March 2002), www.findarticles.com.

3. J. Freear and W. Wetzel Jr., "Who Bankrolls High-Tech Entrepreneurs?" *Journal of Business Venturing* 5(2) (1990): 77–89.

4. J. Peters and W. H. Donald, "Publishing," *Standard & Poor's Industry Surveys* (September 8, 2005), www.netad vantage.standardpoor.com.

5. J. Milliot, "A Fight for Control," *Publishers Weekly Online* (October 24, 2005), www.publishersweekly.com.

CHAPTER 17

1. A. Feldman, "Five Ways That Smart Companies Comply," *Inc.* (September 2005), www.inc.com.

2. M. Quinn, "Private Companies Make SarbOx Changes," *Inc.* (June 2004), www.inc.com.

3. "SEC Member Dismayed That SOX Costs, Burdens Still High," *Gazette.net* (November 4, 2005).

4. R. W. Kolb and R. J. Rodriguez, *Financial Management,* 2nd ed. (Cambridge, MA: Blackwell, 1996).

CHAPTER 18

1. W. K. Schilit, *Rising Stars and Fast Fades: Successes and Failures of Fast-Growth Companies* (New York: Lexington Books, 1994).

2. Ibid., 54

3. Ibid., 6

4. K. McFarland, "What Makes Them Tick," *Inc.,* www.inc.com/resources/inc500/2005/articles (accessed November 6, 2005).

5. M. Phan, "Angel Investors Overvalue Start-Ups, Say VCs," *Inc.* (June 8, 2005), www.inc.com.

6. G. D. Zeune, "Ducks in a Row: Orchestrating the Flawless Stock Offering," *Corporate Cashflow* (February 1993).

CHAPTER 19

1. K .S. Buehler and G. Pritsch, "Running with Risk," *McKinsey Quarterly* (September 2003). Reprinted in *Inc.* magazine.

2. J. Kallman, "Risk: So What?" *Risk Management* 52(11) (2005): 66.

3. C. L. Reiss, *Risk Management for Small Business* (Fairfax, VA: Public Entity Risk Institute, 2004).

4. D. Phin, "One Dozen Powerful Strategies for Avoiding Thieves, Spies, Con-Artists, and ?" *Employer Advisors Network, Inc.* (January 2004). In *Inc.* magazine, www.inc.com.

5. Buehler and Pritsch, "Running with Risk,"3.

6. Reiss, *Risk Management,* 9.

7. F. Kloman, "Four Cubed," *Risk Management Reports* 10 (2001).

CHAPTER 20

1. T. Kostigen, "Small Businesses Are Cashing out," *Wall Street Journal Startup Journal,* www.startupjournal.com (accessed June 25, 2005).

2. W. H. Payne, "Choosing Your Exit Strategy," *Kauffman Center for Entrepreneurial Leadership* (2001); 203.

3. J. A. Fraser, "Company for Sale by Owner—or Maybe Not," *Inc.* (June 2000): 129–132.

4. D. A. Prisciotta and R. M. Weber, "Raising Capital and Developing Exit Strategies for the Closely Held Business," *Journal of Financial Service Professionals* 59(3) (2005): 67.

5. A. Stone, "Selling a Family Enterprise: Tough to Decide and to Do," *New York Times* (February 19, 2004), www.nytimes.com.

6. National Business Statistics, www.bizstats.com (accessed November 25, 2005).

7. 2000 Census (Washington, DC: U.S. Census Bureau), www.census.gov.

8. Prisciotta and Weber, "Raising Capital."

9. A. Blackman, "Knowing When It's Time to Call It Quits," *Wall Street Journal Startup Journal,* www.startupjournal.com (accessed June 25, 2005).

Index

Cases Designed to Engage the Student